The
Company
of the
Creative

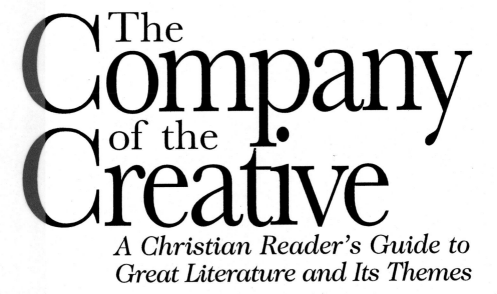

The Company of the Creative

A Christian Reader's Guide to Great Literature and Its Themes

David L. Larsen

Kregel
Academic & Professional

The Company of the Creative: A Christian Reader's Guide to Great Literature and Its Themes

Published by Kregel Publications, a division of Kregel, Inc., P.O. Box 2607, Grand Rapids, MI 49501.

Library of Congress Cataloging-in-Publication Data
Larsen, David L.
   The company of the creative: a Christian reader's guide to great literature and its themes / by David L. Larsen.
      p.   cm.
   Includes bibliographical references and indexes.
   1. Literature—History and criticism. 2. Christian literature—History and criticism. 3. Christians—Books and reading. 4. Christianity and literature. 5. Literature—Themes, motives. 6. Best books. I. Title.
PN98.R44L37   1999   809—dc21   99-36565
                                                          CIP

ISBN 0-8254-3097-6

Printed in the United States of America

For my teachers, librarians, and mother,
all of whom taught me to love books and reading—
with loving gratitude and great glory to God.

Contents

Preface

I have treasured in my bosom the words of his mouth.
—Job 23:12b (RSV)

Physically, mentally, and spiritually—we are what we consume. The Christian is called to live by the Word of God; it is a treasure more valuable than gold, a delicacy sweeter than honey (Ps. 19:10; Matt. 4:4).

But of course our minds assimilate a lot more than Bible texts. All or most of those reading this book live in an X-rated society where we need to carefully monitor what sorts of feasts we set before our inner lives. St. Paul spoke so wisely in urging us—"Whatever is true, whatever is noble, whatever is right, whatever is pure, whatever is lovely, whatever is admirable—if anything is excellent or praiseworthy—think about such things" (Phil. 4:8). Here are the recommended daily nutrients that sustain and power healthy souls.

Servants of Christ need to develop a disciplined regimen of spiritual and intellectual nourishment to supplement daily reading of the Word, lest casual television and junk reading adulterate or dilute the content of the mind. Otherwise, emotions become sickly and the interior life becomes bloated with malnourishment.

During my years of teaching at Trinity Evangelical Divinity School, I found that many of our students had little background in the liberal arts and the literature that has shaped our culture. Such an egregious gap can lead to awkward blind spots and embarrassing superficiality in cultural analysis. Hence I developed a course in "Preaching Resources in Literature." This book surveys some of the content of that course. It is intended to be a theologically nuanced look at books and plays that have made a difference. You may think of other works that should have been included. So can I. Limitations of space have forced hard choices. Inescapably my subjective tastes have led to omissions, but if I can encourage you to strike out in some of these directions, you will soon fill in the gaps.

In much of my work I have had the demands of sermon and teaching preparation uppermost in mind. I have written with the conscious desire to raise the cultural awareness of Christian communicators. If you work in such an area of ministry, I challenge you to continually fill the literary deficiencies in your own mind and to encourage those who listen to you to do the same. "Culture wars" are not won by ignorance. To know our times and surrounding worldviews, we should have an awareness of books and plays that come from the most pagan pens and word processors.

Besides, there is sheer pleasure and enjoyment in the enhanced appreciation for the good gifts God has given through the ages. Timelines can help place a literary piece into its historical and social context and its place in the development of a genre of literature. For those who are preachers and teachers, these timelines also help fit these writings into my new book on the history of preaching (*The Company of the Preachers: A History of Biblical Preaching from the Old Testament to the Modern Era,* Grand Rapids: Kregel, 1998, 894 pp.).

In the dedication of this book I acknowledge my particular debt to those who from childhood have encouraged me to be a reader. My deep appreciation to my steady and supportive publisher, Dennis Hillman, and my skilled and responsive editors, Stephen Barclift and Paul Ingram. The unfailing love and understanding of the wife of my youth, along with our entire family, represent an incalculable gift to me. To live with a bookworm can be testing, I concede readily. But at the bottom line, the vision of the irresistible rewards of reading is contagious, and I would warn anyone perusing these pages—you may develop tastes and appetites which become commanding. For those who will only taste and for those who are connoisseurs and true gourmands, I say: *"Bon Appetit."*

Ad gloriam Dei.

CHAPTER ONE

What's at Stake in Christian Exposure to Great Literature?

Of making many books there is no end.

—Ecclesiastes 12:12b

When you come, bring the cloak that I left with Carpus at Troas, and my scrolls, especially the parchments.

—2 Timothy 4:13

Reading makes the full man.

—Francis Bacon

You can learn more about a nation from reading yesterday's novel than today's newspaper.

—James H. Billington, Librarian of Congress

The Bible is our book. Though surrounded by a vast array of volumes, Sir Walter Scott on his death bed in 1832 asked for "the book." No one doubted that he wanted the Bible brought to him. The Bible is *the book* to which we are called for lifelong study and memorization. Its riches and depths are inexhaustible. But God did not intend that we study our Bibles in a mental vacuum. John Nelson Darby and G. Campbell Morgan both decided that for an extended time they would read only the Bible. They soon discovered that this plan was a mistake. The danger of reading only the Bible is that we do not then really read the Bible. The Bible comes out of an ancient cultural setting. We need the bridges to our own culture that reading more broadly can supply. We need to understand what we bring to the text.[1]

Our thesis in this study is that all Christians—especially Christian leaders and communicators—need to read broadly, deeply, and copiously. The reading enterprise is perched precariously on the edge of today's complex, stress-driven world. Christians possess the Holy Scriptures in numerous translations and paraphrases, but do today's Christians really read the Bible? Biblical illiteracy seems to be mounting. Americans are buying both secular and religious books as no other generation in history; great chains of booksellers proliferate. Do we read the books we buy? A review of one pop science best-seller, *A Brief History of Time* by physicist Stephen Hawking, was that it had been "bought by more people and read by fewer people than any book of its kind." Something similar might be said of books that are far less complex than is Hawking's.

Television has profoundly altered modern life. The average American has seen 350,000 television commercials before graduation from high school. Television has turned many Americans into shut-ins. Meaning and values develop, and are debated, via the electronic media.[2] Neil Postman has alerted us to the shift from the *Age of Exposition* to the *Age of Entertainment* courtesy the media.[3] Will this inexorably lead us further into what Andrew Delbanco calls "the decline of discourse"? Many people are reading less because of their addiction to the aural alcohol of television.

With the computerization of culture and the advent of the Internet, will books and libraries become obsolescent? Some cultural analysts warn that the information highway leads nowhere. That prophecy seems severe, though we can understand why Sven Birkerts foresees an electronic future in which there is a "vanishing assumption of coherence."[4] Still, the Net can be a virtual messiah.

Notice that the debate among "netheads" is largely carried on in printed books. Many books on the virtual world still come into existence in paper and ink.[5] More ominous to society's intellectual health, perhaps, is what Birkerts elsewhere describes as "the dethronement of the sovereignty of authorship and the revelation of the status of texts as unstable entities." Deconstructionists from Jacques Derrida on have challenged the notion that the mind of an author can be known and that any text can be authoritatively read. The implication is that given words have no meaning—or potentially have many meanings—so that one may argue that any given text says virtually anything. The same words can be interpreted in either of diametrically opposed ways.[6] Few would be as pessimistic as the Princeton scholar Alvin Kernan, who speaks of "the death of literature."

The assault on the canon of "Great Books" has left the classics gasping in the literary air of such institutions as Dartmouth and Stanford. The postmodern climate, according to Gertrude Himmelfarb, is "radical relativism and skepticism that rejects any idea of truth, knowledge or objectivity."[7] The present climate is not congenial to those who advocate absolute truth and authoritative systems of belief, yet "we do, however, speak a message of wisdom among the mature, but not the wisdom of this age, or of the rulers of this age, who are coming to nothing" (1 Cor. 2:6). Humbly, and yet most firmly, we insist that "God's secret wisdom" has been "revealed to us by his Spirit" (1 Cor. 2:7, 10).

The Christian has a high stake in the reading of classical and contemporary works of excellence. When Philip Yancey celebrates "the power of writing," he is following a concept always cherished by believers in Scripture.[8]

Study and discussion of The Harvard Classics or Britannica's Great Books of the Western World, with its invaluable "Syntopicon," are still most worthwhile. Harold Bloom's best-selling *The Western Canon: The Books and Schools of the Ages* identifies twenty-six authors whose work is indispensable.[9] David Denby, a New York magazine critic, felt depressed and lost in the media, having "information without knowledge, opinions without principles, instincts without beliefs." He turned back to study and discuss some of the great works of literature and eventually concluded that the "great books" *are* great.[10] In a "frankly oppositional work," *The Pleasures of Reading,* Robert Alter is so presumptuous as to believe reality can be represented in print persuasively.[11] How sad that such a perspective should be generally seen as outmoded and impossibly rare.

In a very thoughtful essay seeking to argue "The Reason for Reading," the author at bottom line insists that communicators must read if they are to communicate.[12] D. James Kennedy has said, "Great preachers have almost inevitably been men who were broadly read in the great books of the world."[13] The history of preaching bears this out.[14] Ravi Zacharias scores the same point in a pithy article, "Bring Me the Books," allowing that a good book "is as delectable as a slice of infinity, lasting a lifetime."[15]

In identifying what pastors need to read to become authentic pastors, Arndt Halvorson, of Luther/Northwestern Seminary in St. Paul, Minnesota, insists that pastors must read more than technical theology and exegetical works. He estimates that fewer than 10 percent of parish pastors are reading the kinds of books that will really help them in their preaching task.[16] In an issue of Fuller Seminary's *Theology News and Notes* devoted to "Literature and Ministry," Lewis Smedes, among others, makes a convincing case for reading good fiction. Smedes relates: "I like the feel of language; I like the texture of it, the flow, especially when it flows leisurely and lovingly and elaborately through the eddies of memory."[17] Eminent literary critic Alfred Kazin laments cultural trends at the turn of the twenty-first century and is particularly angered by the neglect of literature.[18]

We are pressing the irresistible rewards of reading not simply in the interests of emotional balance and personal fulfillment. There are serious faith issues that evangelicals can only address if their minds as well as their theology are engaged. Reading has a contribution to make to the advancement of God's kingdom work. This is particularly true in that reading helps us understand issues and people. It nurtures imagination and stimulates the vocabulary and stylistic skills needed to represent God effectively.

READING HELPS US UNDERSTAND ISSUES AND PEOPLE

Christians should be concerned about relating issues to people. The Bible is filled with the ways in which people relate to God in their life contexts. Compare this issues awareness with that gained by reading the novels of Charles Dickens. Dickens presented the burning social issues of his time in stories populated with unforgettable people. To be in ministry is to forever need to grow in the skills of character and personality analysis. Good biography and solid fiction can probe the human psyche in historic or modern settings.

We should be aware that many themes in literature are, at bottom, biblical:

- William Lyon Phelps of Yale contended that "The Bible has been a greater influence on the course of English literature than all other forces put together."[19]
- There is no more basic literary theme than the biblical dialectic between Eden's innocence and the post-fall need for transforming redemption. Homer's two great epic poems deal with a journey *(Odyssey)* and a battle *(Iliad)*. Here are commanding metaphors that speak to the human experience of depravity. The journey motif is picked up by Boccaccio, Chaucer, Dante, Bunyan, and James Joyce, to name but a few. It stands against the anti-novel, which demolishes rational construct and is suspicious of coherence in plot that might infuse meaning into life.[20]
- Dennis Kinlaw draws upon William Barrett's "Irrational Man" in showing how frequently modern writing flattens the climax of the plot and closes the characters off from anything that seems transcendent.[21] Much newer writing seems "market-driven" and caters (as does much late-twentieth-century preaching) to shallow culture and pop psychology. It is left to ethnic fiction, such as Maeve Binchey's stories about Ireland, to open unbelievable doors of insight. Such writing helps us to get inside the minds of people.

READING STIMULATES IMAGINATION

All studies of imagination, "the queen of the faculties" (Baudelaire), show that the fires can be fueled in one way: "Read, read, read." G. Campbell Morgan said that imagination is the supreme work in sermon preparation. How can we overcome the stereotypically dull presentation of "the glorious gospel of our blessed God"? Here is "the failure of creativity at the symbolic level." Bible-believing preachers are vulnerable to this virus. This hackneyed use of communication has been described as a *practical utilitarianism,* a subconscious bow to John Locke. Vivid communication seeks metaphors and deals with symbols. Here is where we need release from analytical "left-brain" dominance. We need the right-brain's more creatively artistic freedom.[22]

Poetry is language at its most verbal. Poet John Ciardi well observed that "reading poetry gives vicarious experience—it stretches one's capacity for life." Eugene Peterson is a contemporary writer and preacher who has partaken deeply of poetry and novels. As a result he moves away from the routine to creative centers in living. Much evangelical teaching and preaching could stand a fresh baptism of creativity. Reading is part of the strategy for growth in this freedom. David Wells of Gordon-Conwell Theological School has lectured on secular and fraudulent views of the kingdom. His launching point was the very pedestrian novel *Thornbirds,* by Kathleen McCulloch. From it he traced the worldview of a secular Christology that apes Christianity but lacks a genuine Savior. This was a powerful opening to the subject.

READING BUILDS EFFECTIVE WORD USAGE

Words are the preacher's stock-in-trade. Yet most people stop adding vocabulary by the time they reach their mid-twenties. James Cox, in his widely read study of preaching, devotes a section to words and their importance.[23] Samuel Clemens said that the difference between the right word and the "almost-right word" is the difference between lightning and a lightning bug. Let us ransack great literature for the words and phrases that grip and move and convey precise meaning. Content is primary, but form is so intertwined with content that inattention to either can be disastrous. Weary words need to be put out to pasture and their places taken by race-winning thoroughbreds. Poverty of expression can be redressed, and denatured language can be rejuvenated and enriched through reading.[24]

READING ALERTS US TO STYLISTIC MODELS

We should all identify and pursue some favorite writers, analyzing the styles that make their work so appealing. How do they introduce material? How do they conclude? What patterns in sentence structure do they utilize to effective advantage? Style is power. In today's rediscovery of narrative—so appropriate in our very visual age—we need to work on telling the story more effectively. Reading the master tellers of tales, especially the writers of short stories, can be a tonic. Reading a good short story every week can work stylistic wonders. We should not disparage the use of fictional plots when clearly designated as such. The parables Jesus told were not always factual incidents. They were hypothetical: "Let's pretend . . ." "Now picture with me . . ."

Abraham Kuyper, the great Dutch preacher, theologian, and Prime Minister, was actually converted as the consequence of reading the English novel *The Heir of Redclyffe*. During a low ebb in his own life, he was caught up in the drama of the story. Years ago Lance Morrow wrote a searching essay entitled, "Have We Abandoned Excellence?"[25] No preacher or teacher can afford to *rust* on our laurels. We need to keep working for improvement and grown-up growth to the last breath we take. Who among us ever arrives in our calling before God?

Frank Gaebelein wrote pungently about "regaining the vision of greatness" in what we do for our Lord.[26] It is time to end slackness, sloth, and lackadaisical carelessness. Let us give ourselves anew to the never-ending quest of communicating better and more effectively. The ability to paint a picture or to make it "come alive" needs cultivation.

READING YIELDS IDEAS

In a stirring appeal to read widely and without embarrassment, Fred Craddock, the distinguished homiletician, warns against "the vulgar practice of combing through literature for illustrations."[27] There is grave danger in wanting to *sound* learned by quoting literature we have not actually read. We must beware of such subtle braggadocio.

Yet there may be some material which is usable with caution. Illustrations of vicarious suffering are rare because ours is such a selfish world, but such characters as Jean Valjean in Victor-Marie Hugo's *Les Misérables* or Sydney Carton in Charles Dickens's *Tale of Two Cities* embody self-giving love. Couplets or quatrains of poetry can be of immense help in discourse or the apt quotation.

Illustrations do not always help communication. A story may have power to elicit emotion, yet not quite address the point. Theorists speak of this as a "feeling tone" that causes a desired response while raising barriers against what the communicator hoped to say. Preachers want their hearers to grasp truth in their minds, while the spiritual reality grips their hearts.

Clearly this is chiefly the province of the Holy Spirit. But discourse should be balanced. Evangelical preaching often is highly cerebral. Reading can help deepen the affective impact. This is where reading can open resources to communicators who want to refurbish and enhance the necessary balance between heart and mind. To know the truth as it is in Christ, to be persuaded of it, and to implement it in behavior and obedience involve the capture of the whole person.

READING INTRODUCES US TO BEAUTY

"A thing of beauty is a joy forever," wrote John Keats. A work of art, a musical composition, a vivid drama, a lovely poem, or an engaging story—each is a work of art. And the sermon, while being many things, can also be a presentation that is beautiful. Many evangelicals are aesthetically starved, and we of all people should worship the God of creation and redemption, who is Himself beautiful. I am not referring to nihilistic junk food fiction or the faux-arts on which many in society subsist. Henry Martyn, the missionary martyr, testified that after he was converted he came to a new appreciation of paintings, poetry, and music. Even George Fox, founder of the Quakers, exulted after he met Christ, "All things were new! Even creation gave forth another smell!" Nineteenth-century pastor-novelist Charles Kingsley told of his determination "never to lose an opportunity to see something beautiful."

Reading exposes us to new vistas, extends horizons, and opens new doors into God's plans and purposes and mighty acts. William Wordsworth had such love for the divine handiwork. He said, "We sit at His feet to emulate Him." True art can inform as well as inspire.

But where shall we find this reinvigorating art in the maze of options? About fifty thousand books are published annually in the United States alone. One of our goals here is to chart a course across the map of reading. We shall survey various types of material and recommend some of the best examples.

Concentration on certain appealing writers has merit, but it is also good to cultivate breadth. Tastes and palates differ. My biases and predilections will show in the reading lists that follow, but I shall be broad-brushed. If you feel you do not have time to read, examine the little niches and crevices of your life for moments to dedicate to reading. It can be either early or late, or in transit, or in life's waiting times. One man wrote a well-received book of poetry while traveling to and from his regular employment on public transportation. It may have been a book describing the interesting people he noticed around him.

What a privilege and pleasure to read! You may never be a bona fide book-worm or true bibliophile, but in the words of Scripture, "gird up the loins" of your mind for action.

Counsel for readers: Francis Bacon said, "Read not to contradict and confute, nor to believe and take for granted, nor to find talk and discourse, but to weigh and consider. Some books are to be tasted, others to be swallowed, and some few to be chewed and digested."

---

1. Anthony Thiselton, *The Two Horizons* (Grand Rapids: Eerdmans, 1980): "The modern interpreter, no less than the text, stands in a context and tradition" (11). Thiselton has given a strong appeal "to respect the rights of the text and let it speak." This in the context of "critical deconstructionists who have distressed, de-privileged, decentered, subverted, distanced, exposed, shadowed, binarized, forced, engaged, erased, excited, and probably sexually harassed that text," as reviewer Margot Peters has put it. The emphasis today is no longer on the correct understanding of the text but on "what's true for me is true" (436).
2. Gregor T. Goethals, *The Electronic Golden Calf: Images, Religion, and the Making of Meaning* (New York: Cowley, 1991).
3. Neil Postman, *Amusing Ourselves to Death: Public Discourse in the Age of Show Business* (New York: Penguin, 1985). Postman is a protégé of the late Marshall McLuhan who argued "the medium is the message," that is, how truth is communicated has an effect upon what is communicated. The medium can change the way we see reality.
4. Sven Birkerts, *The Gutenberg Elegies: The Fate of Reading in an Electronic Age* (New York: Faber and Faber, 1994). Birkerts argues that we are already in the post-book world.
5. Mark Kingwell, *Dreams of Millennium: Report from a Culture on the Brink* (Toronto: Viking, 1996), 138.
6. David Lehman, *Signs of the Times: Deconstruction and the Fall of Paul de Man* (New York: Poseidon, 1990).
7. Gertrude Himmelfarb, "The Christian University: A Call to Counterrevolution," *First Things,* January 1996, 18–19.
8. Philip Yancey, "The Power of Writing," *Christianity Today,* 24 October 1994, 112.
9. Kathy O'Malley, "Classics Envy," *Chicago Tribune,* 6 March 1995, 5:1f.
10. David Denby, *Great Books: My Adventures with Homer, Rousseau, Woolf and Other Indestructible Writers of the Western World* (New York: Simon and Schuster, 1996).
11. Robert Alter, *The Pleasures of Reading: In an Ideological Age* (New York: Simon and Schuster, 1996). A similar argument is advanced in a slightly different way in Alberto Manguel's very learned *A History of Reading* (New York: Viking, 1996).
12. "The Reason for Reading," *The Royal Bank Letter,* Bank of Canada, May–June 1986, 67:3.
13. Quoted in M. R. Irwin, "Effective Communicators," *The Alliance Witness,* 16 July 1986, 31.
14. See David L. Larsen, *The Company of the Preachers* (Grand Rapids: Kregel, 1998).

15. Ravi Zacharias, "Bring Me the Books," *Just Thinking,* spring 1994, 2.
16. Arndt Halvorson, in Clark Morphew, "Reading and Writing Keys to Preaching," *St. Paul Pioneer Press/Despatch,* 27 February 1982.
17. Lewis B. Smedes, "Why I Read Novels," *Theology, News and Notes,* December 1991, 4ff.
18. Alfred Kazin, *A Lifetime Burning in Every Moment: From the Journals of Alfred Kazin* (New York: Harper/Collins, 1996). It is interesting that when the Academy Award-winning movie *The English Patient* featured a character who kept and annotated a copy of Herodotus, there was a "boomlet" in the sales of *The History of Herodotus.* Of course, the classic history is more moral than is the film. Unfortunately, the trend is for universities to jettison an emphasis on reading and studying the classics.
19. William Lyon Phelps, *Autobiography with Letters* (New York: Oxford University Press, 1939). Phelps, an expert on Browning, was one of the most popular professors Yale ever had.
20. Michael Edwards, *Toward a Christian Poetics* (Grand Rapids: Eerdmans, 1984), 91–92. The nonrational anti-novel can be thought of as a Humean construct that stands against a Leibnitzian ordered and structured world that is created by God.
21. Dennis F. Kinlaw, *Preaching in the Spirit* (Grand Rapids: Zondervan, 1985), 68f.
22. David L. Larsen, "Enlarging Imagination and Creativity," in *Telling the Old, Old Story: The Art of Narrative Preaching* (Wheaton: Crossway, 1995), 248ff.
23. James W. Cox, *Preaching* (San Francisco: Harper and Row, 1985), 219ff.
24. Here is where we need to ponder Mortimer Adler's classic *How to Read a Book* (Mortimer J. Adler and Charles Van Doren, rev. [New York: Simon and Schuster, 1972]). Some materials can be speed-read, others must be slowly chewed. Taking notes on reading is almost always advisable. Certainly the alert reader keeps a word notebook at hand in which to jot down colorful and moving words and phrasing.
25. *Time,* 22 March 1982, 90.
26. Frank E. Gaebelein, *The Christian, the Arts and the Truth: Regaining the Vision of Greatness* (Portland, Ore.: Multnomah, 1985), 247ff.
27. Fred B. Craddock, *Preaching* (Nashville: Abingdon, 1985), 78f. Craddock argues that, even in seminary, students should be reading those who communicate well. "The classroom lecture, properly designed to carry a heavy freight of information, is no model for the sermon" (79). Walter Kirn celebrates "Rediscovering the Joy of Text" in a significant analysis of the fact that more people are reading. *Time,* 21 April 1997, 103ff.

CHAPTER TWO

Mining the Ore
of the Classical World

The glory that was Greece and the grandeur that was Rome.
                                        —Edgar Allan Poe
                                        "To Helen"

We are all Greeks!
                                        —Percy Bysshe Shelley

The Greco-Roman world holds special significance to Christians: This was the world into which Christ was born and in which the early church took root and grew so dynamically. An understanding of Western literature or art requires a grasp of its Greek and Roman backgrounds, for "the medieval synthesis" grew from this soil. Walk through any great art gallery and see the biblical themes and settings alongside the classical. We shall see this synthesis at work in Augustine and John Milton. Recent studies show the resulting similarities between Eastern and Western culture. In the clash of style and worldview, these cultures had much fruitful exchange.[1]

Some have argued that the rationality of the West and the "deep spiritual inheritance of the East" met in ancient Greece.[2] The tomb that loomed so large in the thinking of ancient Egypt was replaced by the theatre in Greece. Greeks were scientists, philosophers, orators, and playwrights. The Greek genius was "at once critical and constructive," observed Pericles. Greek language had a monumental weight and brevity that was ideal for the inscripturation of the New Testament.

Sweeping down on the early indigenous non-Hellenic peoples of Greece and the Minoans of Crete (possibly the progenitors of the Philistines of the Old Testament) came the Dorians in 1100 B.C.[3] A new civilization reached out through the Mediterranean world, articulate and artistically expressive.[4]

19

TABLE 1: Literature in Historical and Theological Context, 1000 B.C. to the Incarnation
A: Historical Events; B: Arts and Philosophy; C: Revelation and Preaching

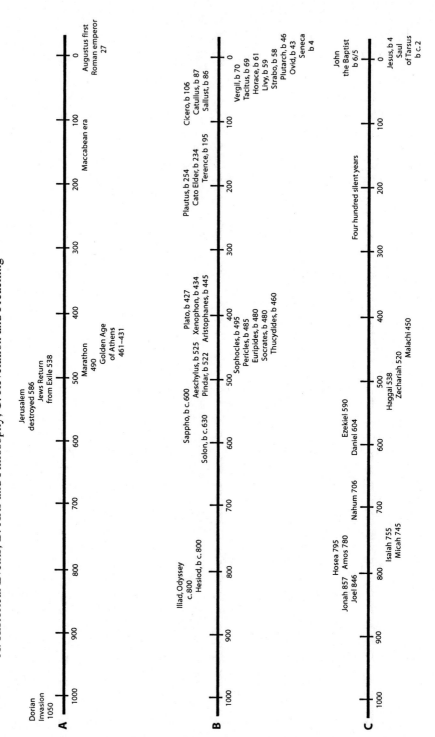

1. The scholarship of Cyrus Gordon is critical here; see also Edwin Yamauchi, *Greece and Babylon: Early Contacts Between the Aegean and the Near East* (Grand Rapids: Baker, 1967).
2. Edith Hamilton, *The Greek Way to Western Civilization* (New York: Mentor, 1948), 11.
3. J. M. Baikie, *The Sea Kings of Crete* (London: Adam and Charles Black, 1910).
4. H. D. F. Kitto, *The Greeks* (London: Penguin, 1951), 12–28.

2.1 MYTHOLOGY: WORSHIP IN THE ANCIENT WORLD

The Greek kept his formal religion in one compartment and everything that really mattered to him in another.

—Edith Hamilton

I see that in every way you are very religious. . . . Now what you worship as something unknown I am going to proclaim to you.

—Paul in Acts 17:22–23

The gods and goddesses of the Greeks, adopted and rechristened by the Romans, lent a framework of meaning to life for common people. Intellectuals would find rational and empirical conceptualization in the philosophers. Certainly the seeker might have recourse to Mount Olympus or the oracle at Delphi, but the Greeks made their deities in their own image (Ps. 115:4–8). The pantheon of divine beings was populated with dozens of gods and goddesses whose activities were immoral, unscrupulous, and pedestrian. As the Latin poet Terence intoned: If Jupiter did it, why not? A twentieth-century humanist such as Edith Hamilton (1867–1963) might revel in the mythological ethos of "a humanized world, men freed from the paralyzing fear of an omnipotent unknown."[1] Yet, in the Hellenic world, "Olympian religion faded" because it possessed an inadequate idea of God.[2] Gilbert Murray traces "the failure of nerve" in the centuries from Plato to Paul. Into the spiritual vacuum crept Stoicism, Epicureanism, and the mystery religions of the East.[3] Greek religion atrophied and the city-state collapsed.

The standard collections of the stories, gathered from many ancient sources, are still a good point of beginning.[4] The work of one late-twentieth-century Italian is recommended, for he has retold the old stories with such freshness and force that his work became a Book-of-the-Month Club selection.[5]

Christian communicators who would like to see old stories come to life should take note. Greek myths have a creation story in which Prometheus is molded from clay, the story of the fall (Pandora's box), a flood story, and a fire deluge. These seem to be pagan-world echoes of primal history.[6]

Acquaintance with classical mythology is a leg-up to an understanding of the arts and literature.[7] Some mythological situations can actually be used by communicators, just as we would use Aesop's fables or Grimm's fairy tales. Albert Camus (1913–1960) built his existential philosophy on the metaphor of Sisyphus's vain effort to roll a stone uphill. Narcissus, who fell in love with his own reflection, hence narcissism, is a commanding figure for our times.[8] King

Midas and his golden touch warn us of greed. George Bernard Shaw retold Pygmalion. Society retains the utility in stories about Hercules and Atlas, the sphinx propounding the riddle, Ariadne's thread, Achilles's heel, and the crossing of the Rubicon. A recent stamp issued by the European Parliament showed a woman riding astride a bull. Some construed this as fulfilling the picture of the harlot riding the beast in Revelation 17. Mythology shows that this actually represents the rape of Europa. Redemptive themes abound in mythology as the need for a Savior is set forth even in the shades of pagan darkness. The Titan Prometheus's theft of fire explains the human dilemma. His redemption and rescue were affected only when Chiron, an immortal, gave up immortality to save him.

For a clear, trenchant Christian analysis of classical culture and its deficient view of God and sin, read Ralph Stob's *Christianity and Classical Civilization.* Stob shows, with many examples, that Greek eschatology looked backward, not into the unknown future.[9]

1. Edith Hamilton, *Mythology* (New York: Mentor, 1953), 17. Hamilton includes Norse mythology.
2. John Ferguson, *The Heritage of Hellenism* (New York: Science History, 1973), 133.
3. Gilbert Murray, *The Five Stages of Greek Religion* (London: Watts, 1935), 123. Astrology came in at this time.
4. *Bullfinch's Mythology* (New York: Modern Library, 1863); Hamilton, *Mythology;* C. Kerenyi, *The Gods of the Greeks* (London: Thames and Hudson, 1951). It took twelve gods to get a field ploughed, planted, harvested and marketed; forty-three gods to raise a child; three gods to open a door. . . . This is polytheism with a vengeance.
5. Roberto Calasso, *The Marriage of Cadmus and Harmony* (New York: Knopf, 1993). The title refers to the Theban banquet, the last occasion when the gods sat down with humans. The gods were never intimate with humans again.
6. Hesiod, the Boeotian farmer-poet (750 B.C.), traces in his *Works and Days* the five ages of man: gold, silver, bronze, age of heroes, iron (note parallels with Daniel 2). Immanuel Velikovsky in *Worlds in Collision* (New York: Doubleday, 1950) traces the prevalence of the story of the universal flood through antiquity.
7. Herman J. Wechsler, *Gods and Goddesses in Art and Legend* (New York: Pocket Books, 1950). Sixty-four plates.
8. *Bullfinch's Mythology,* 86. Evangelist William Edward Biederwolf wrote a widely-read volume entitled *Illustrations from Mythology* (1927) in which he shares 100 key stories culled from mythology. Although classical mythology is no longer studied in public schools as in years past, an amazing amount of this material still suffuses our cultural referent. We shall see more of this in the Homeric poems and the Greek plays. Cf. C. S. Lewis, *Till We Have Faces* (New York: Harcourt Brace, 1956), a fictionalized elaboration and reinterpretation of the Cupid and Psyche myth.
9. Grand Rapids: Eerdmans, 1950, 126. See appendixes: "Greek and Roman Mythology: Three Dynasties" (p. 590) and "Greek and Roman Mythology: The Pantheon" (p. 591).

2.2 HOMERIC POEMS: WINDOWS ON THE ANCIENT WORLD

As the passing of leaves is, so is the passing of man.

—Iliad

What we call Homeric theology was a reckless interval in the lives of the gods. For a brief period the world accepted the supremacy of the visible.

—Roberto Calasso

Whether Homer is the blind, wandering bardic poet or whether "he" is a committee (the long-debated Homeric question), the two powerful works attributed to him, the *Iliad* and the *Odyssey,* stand as towering classics. Homer has been called "the first articulate European." The first work describes a few days of the Trojan War. The second work, its sequel, moves off the journey theme in the home-quest of Odysseus (or Ulysses as the Romans called him). Their literary form as we have them dates from about 500 B.C., but they reflect significant strands of prehistory and life in Greek lands more than a thousand years before Christ. For the beginner, I would recommend Books 1–4 and 12–24 of the *Odyssey*, especially in the exciting new translation of Robert Fagles of Princeton.[1] He holds to the historicity of Homer, who is claimed by seven Asian cities.

The *Iliad* is a tragedy of twenty-four books, as the *Odyssey* is a comedy of twenty-four books. In the ancient literary sense, a *tragedy* is a deep, moving narrative dealing with suffering or the human condition and ending in a dark climax. A *comedy* is a light drama that has a happy ending. The number of books in either work is intentional; there is one book for each letter in the Greek alphabet. The *Iliad* gives us a small part of the Trojan War. Troy was a great city in Ionia (Troas in Paul's time). Homer's Troy has been identified as the sixth city in the many layers excavated by Heinrich Schliemann (1822–1890) in the nineteenth century. Paris, the son of Troy's King Priam, abducted beautiful Helen and brought the wrath of all Greece upon him and his native city. One thousand Greek ships came, led by Achilles and Agamemnon, who quarreled for nine indecisive years, undercutting the Greek effort. The *Iliad* opens after nine frustrating years. We do not learn about the death of Achilles and the fall of Troy via the wooden horse until the *Odyssey*. Homer's story moves quickly, with a simple, direct style. He assumes the desire of the gods for order, but they are marginal in the *Iliad*.[2] The magnificent shield of Achilles, the aegis, made by Hephaestus, portrays in nine scenes many aspects of social and political life in thirteenth-century B.C. Greek experience (*Iliad,* 18.478–614).

In the *Odyssey* we have a greater vertical sense of the gods (Athena intervenes), as Odysseus, "the great survivor," "the model for strivers," heads home from Troy after twenty years of absence. Escaping death in the disastrous storm that killed most of the returning Greeks, Odysseus faces one obstacle after another. But he is a prudent man, of great cunning and endurance (*Odyssey,* 2.166ff.). He contends with the Cyclops; the lotus-eaters, whose fruit diminishes memories of home; the Sirens, whose songs lure to shipwreck (as in the Arabian Sinbad legend), and with Calypso, whose charms hold him for seven years. At last he breaks loose and is reunited with his wife, Penelope, and his son, who have been beset by a cadre of suitors. The *Odyssey* is a collection of entertaining melodramas. We get a sense of what life was like in this stormy period.

The quest for home is the underlying theme of much of the *Odyssey*. The home-coming of Agamemnon is stirringly depicted. The sentry waited at Argos, straining to see the tongue of flame from the distant hill, which portended the return of the king. It was a long wait. One night, he saw the beacon and shouted: "Rejoice, rejoice! Hail, thou auspicious flame, that streaming through the night proclaimest joy."[3] Such joy was short-lived, for Agamemnon was soon murdered by his wife and the lover she had taken in his absence. The return of Odysseus was happier, although Penelope could hardly recognize her husband when he returned to Ithaca after so many years. The "going home" theme is a fruitful line to ponder and probe in view of every person's longing for home.

The constant whispered exchanges between Odysseus and Athena were very critical, especially during his long voyage home. Only once did they fall out of contact.[4] Homeric prayers were plagued by the puzzling issue: To which god shall I pray? Two visits to the underworld and conversations with departed spirits are important in the *Odyssey*. These themes recur in the Roman Vergil's "book of the dead" and in the Medieval Dante.

The *Odyssey* was translated into English from Greek by George Chapman in 1598. Alfred, Lord Tennyson's (1809–1892) Ulysses, and his "The Lotus-Eaters" are obviously based on Homer's work. James Joyce in *Ulysses* (1922) traces the wanderings of one Leopold Bloom in Dublin. Nikos Kazantzakis gives us *The Odyssey: A Modern Sequel* (1938), and the Hollywood bow to Homer is *2001: A Space Odyssey*. Interestingly, Erich Auerbach's comparison of Homer and other classics has been stimulating a return to the study of biblical narratives.[5]

Michael Grant has written prolifically on related classical themes, such as *The Jews in the Roman Empire*.[6] His *The Rise of the Greeks*[7] is a lucid treatment of the years 1000–490 B.C., not only in Athens but also "in the far-flung provinces."

1. Robert Fagles, *The Odyssey of Homer* (New York: Viking, 1997). His edition of the *Iliad* was published by Viking in 1990.
2. H. D. F. Kitto in Harold Bloom, ed., *The Odyssey* (New York: Chelsea House, 1988), 22. For a provocative study of "the circumambient atmosphere," see F. M. Cornford, *From Religion to Philosophy* (New York: Harper Torchbook, 1957).
3. Agatha Thornton, "Achaean Homecomings," in *The Odyssey,* 35ff.
4. Roberto Calasso, *The Marriage of Cadmus and Harmony* (New York: Knopf, 1993), 366ff.
5. Erich Auerbach, *Mimesis: The Representation of Reality in Western Literature* (Princeton, N.J.: Princeton University Press, 1946). He observes: "The Scripture stories do not, like Homer's, court our favor; they do not flatter us that they may please us. They seek to subject us, and if we refuse to be subjected, we are rebels."
6. New York: Scribner's, 1973.
7. New York: Scribner's, 1987.

2.3 GREEK PLAYS: RECREATING COMEDY AND TRAGEDY

We are lovers of beauty with economy.

—Pericles

> But be his
> My special thanks, whose even-balanc'd soul,
> From first youth tested up to extreme old age,
> Business could not make dull, nor Passion wild:
> Who saw life steadily, and saw it whole.
> The mellow glory of the Attic stage;
> Singer of sweet Colonus, and its child.
>
> —Matthew Arnold
> of Sophocles in "To a Friend"

Dramatic representation of persons and events is as old as storytelling in the human family. Formal drama, as it developed among the Egyptians and the Greeks, had no curtain; the chorus made transitional interpretations. Richard Moulton of the University of Chicago long ago argued that the Song of Solomon was at least a lyric idyll. He identified the role of the chorus, particularly in the refrains.[1] Tragedy arose early in Greek drama. Three of the four greatest tragic playwrights are Greek (Aeschylus, Sophocles, and Euripides; the fourth is William Shakespeare). Edith Hamilton defines tragedy as "pain transmuted into exaltation by the alchemy of poetry."[2] She rightly observes that only in Periclean Athens and in Elizabethan England have tragedy flourished. Comedy looks realistically at life but does not end in disaster. High comedy is exalted, and low comedy is absurd. To these designations must be added *farce* and then *satire*, which is narrative irony. Communicators would be well-advised to become students, if not participants, in drama in the interest of more lively presentation of biblical narrative and a looser, freer style in delivery.

The search for quality translations of Greek drama, poetry, and fine literature in general can be difficult. Are we indeed reading what retains not just the general ideas, but the artistic craft of these authors? Some translators who have been at the forefront of this challenge in Greek drama include Gilbert Murray, who has made an arduous effort to present faithful English verse to capture the poetry of Euripides. See also the scholarly and interesting 1990s translation by Shirley Ann Barlow.[3] Paul Roche is a standard, worthy translator of Sophocles. See in particular Roche's *The Oedipus Plays of Sophocles*.[4] Ted Hughes has a version of Aeschylus, *The Oresteia* (London: Faber, 1999). For an enriched perspective on the history and experience of the ancient Greeks, no treatment has ever exceeded J. B. Bury's study, *A History of Greece to the Death of Alexander the Great*.[5]

---

1. Richard G. Moulton, *The Literary Study of the Bible* (London: Isbister, 1896), 194ff.
2. *Greek Way,* 127.

3. *Euripides* (Wiltshire, England: Ain and Phillips, 1996). Shirley Ann Barlow provides an extensive bibliography with her translation.
4. New York: New American Library: 1962.
5. New York: Modern Library, 1937.

2.3.1 AESCHYLUS, FATHER OF GREEK TRAGEDY

Aeschylus was born in Eleusis in about 525 B.C. Eleusis was home to the "Eleusinian mysteries," from which Eastern influence penetrated Greek thought. Aeschylus fought nobly at Marathon to defeat the Persians in 490 and possibly was at Salamis and in other battles. He competed in drama-writing contests and won in 484. We possess seven of his ninety plays. His theme is always "the grandeur and misery of man," feeling deeply human suffering and "the bewildering strangeness of life," at which he laughs and exults. He fostered dialogue in his plays and really fathered tragedy. He was said to have died when an eagle dropped a tortoise on his bald head, mistaking it for a stone on which to break the shell.

His great *Prometheus Bound* was done so vividly that women were said to miscarry and children to have seizures after watching a performance. The reading of his brilliant trilogy, *Oresteia*, is a good introduction to Greek drama. He believed in the gods, but they were distant and remote.[1] Orestes kills his mother and her lover with the connivance of his sister Electra, and the murderer is pursued by the furies. Echoes of the plot are heard in Shakespeare's *Hamlet, Mourning Becomes Electra* by Eugene O'Neill, and in Thomas Berger's *Orrie's Story.* Aeschylus believed we can choose between tragedies and that guilt adheres to families. The notion of sacrifice to placate offended deities is pervasive.[2] While there is clarification in the last play in the trilogy, *Eumenides,* hopelessness for the future of humankind persists. B. F. Westcott is right: "*Aeschylus* has not one word of true hope for a future state, not one image of another field of labor. . . . For him . . . the other world . . . exists only for the guilty."[3] As the chorus sings:

For Hades is a jealous Judge of Men, and in His Black Assize
The record writ with ghostly pen cons with remorseless eyes. [line 270]

---

1. William Kelly Prentice, *The Ancient Dramas Called Tragedies* (Princeton, N.J.: Princeton University Press, 1942).
2. Pierre Vidal-Naquet, "Hunting and Sacrifice in Aeschylus's Oresteia," in *Modern Critical Interpretations: Oresteia,* ed. Harold Bloom (New York: Chelsea House, 1988), 78ff. The classic study of Old Testament sacrifice and the meaning of blood offerings as reflected in pagan cultures is H. Clay Trumbull, *The Blood Covenant: A Primitive Rite and Its Bearings on Scripture* (Philadelphia: John Wattles, 1893; repr. ed., Minneapolis: James Family Christian Publishers, n.d.).
3. B. F. Westcott, *Religious Thought in the West* (London: Macmillan, 1891), 87. Oceanus says to Prometheus: "Thou hast not learned humility. . . . Kick not against the goads" (*Prometheus Bound,* 322).

2.3.2 SOPHOCLES, GENIUS OF GREEK TRAGEDY

A. C. Swinburne called the *Oresteia* "the greatest spiritual achievement of man," but generally *Oedipus Rex* by Sophocles is adjudged to be stylistically and substantively the true masterpiece of classical drama. Sophocles (c. 494–406) was born in Colonus in Attica and lived and wrote 122 plays, of which seven survive. At fifteen or sixteen he led the chorus that celebrated the victory at Salamis. He never traveled abroad as did Aeschylus and Euripides. He was a confidant of Pericles, Herodotus, and Thucydides.

In contrast to Aeschylus, his style is simple and direct. His cycle of Theban plays is highlighted by *Oedipus Rex,* of which Kenneth Rexroth said, "It may be the most perfect play ever written."[1] It is the story of Oedipus, King of Thebes, who comes to power by answering the riddle of the great Sphinx. He was Thebes' last hope for rescue from the grievous plague. In a dialectic like a great detective story, he seeks to learn why the plague has befallen, and learns that it is because he has in a most complex web of circumstances murdered his father and married his mother. Aristotle pays the highest tribute to *Oedipus Rex* in his *Poetics.* Despite what Sigmund Freud thought, Oedipus was not oedipal.

Doubly defiled, Oedipus blinded and banished himself in a kind of scapegoat expiation, even though the circumstances were not his fault. Sin to the Greeks was more a tragic flaw than a missing of the mark of divine expectation. The ultimate question in the play is whether prophecy can be trusted?[2] Oedipus did not fight to overcome the oracle; thus, while his experience is tragic, there is an intelligible pattern. At the end he is blind, but he now can see.[3] Herein is the essential conservatism of Sophocles, "upholder of the old order."

Euripides (c. 484–406) is such a social iconoclast and antisupernaturalist that he might be regarded as "the Walt Whitman of Athens." He best reflects the Hellenic world and its problems, and he denies the historic reality of the mythological pantheon. Read *Medea,* a difficult play but one of the most moving dramas in all literature. Euripides's *Trojan Women* and *Medea,* along with *Antigone* by Sophocles, are the Greek plays that are most frequently staged or adapted to the modern theatre. Also worthwhile is the "old comedy" of Aristophanes, such as *Frogs* and *Birds,* of which Plato was especially fond.[4] Greek drama was by this time into its decline.

---

1. Kenneth Rexroth, "Sophocles: The Theban Plays," *Saturday Review of Literature,* 13 November 1965, 40.
2. E. R. Dodds, "On Misunderstanding the Oedipus Rex," in *Modern Critical Interpretations: Oedipus Rex,* ed. Harold Bloom (New York: Chelsea House, 1988), 45. The question is: "If Athens loses faith in religion, if the views of the Enlightenment prevail, what significance is there in tragic drama, which exists to serve the gods?"
3. Charles Segal, "The Music of the Sphinx: The Problem of Language in Oedipus Rex," in *Modern Critical Interpretations,* 139, 141.
4. A recent translation of Aristophanes includes *Birds, Lysistrata, Assembly-Women,* and *Wealth.* See Stephen Halliwell, *Aristophanes* (Oxford: Clarendon, 1998).

2.4   GREEK PHILOSOPHERS: ANCIENT WISDOM

The fear of the LORD is the beginning of wisdom.

—Proverbs 9:10 (RSV)

Since the creation of the world God's invisible qualities—his eternal power and divine nature—have been clearly seen, being understood from what has been made.

—Romans 1:20

> For, from the first faint morn
> Of life, the thirst for bliss
> Deep in man's heart is born.

—Matthew Arnold
"Empedocles on Etna"

Philosophy is the love for, and striving after, wisdom. William James described it as "an unusually stubborn attempt to think clearly." Any serious communicator of biblical truth must interact with philosophical categories. In Western civilization this interaction confronts an extraordinary curiosity about ideas born in the Greek colonies of Ionia in what is now Turkey. Wilhelm Windelband attributed what happened in the sixth century B.C. to "the mighty upward movement of the national life (democracy and freedom) which unfettered the mental powers of this most gifted of all peoples."[1] What is ultimate reality, they asked. The question was more significant than their answers. Thales of Miletus (c. 625–547), "the father of philosophy," said it was water; Anaximander (610–c. 547) said it was "the boundless," and Anaximenes of Miletus (sixth century B.C.) said it was air. Heraclitus (c. 540–480) was impressed with flux and change; Parmenides (born c. 515 B.C.) was impressed with "the one." Empedocles (c. 490–430) sought a mediating position.

Some stretching is required to avoid a totally ethnocentric view. An excellent overview of non-Western philosophical systems is found in Stuart C. Hackett's *Oriental Philosophy: A Westerner's Guide to Eastern Thought*.[2] This work is written from a staunchly biblical frame of reference.

---

1. Wilhelm Windelband, *A History of Philosophy* (New York: Harper Torchbooks, 1958), 1:24. The old reliable.
2. Madison: University of Wisconsin Press, 1979.

2.4.1 SOCRATES, TEACHER

Much of what we know about Socrates we learn from Plato's *Apology* and *Crito*. Socrates was born in Athens in 470 B.C. and raised in an artisan's home. He served in the military but exerted a profound influence on a circle of young followers whom he taught through his question-and-answer method, "the Socratic dialogue." His school was called "the notion-factory" by Aristophanes (c. 450–388).[1] He saw himself as a gadfly who wanted to sting Athens awake. He sought goodness and truth, believing that to know the good was to do the good. He urged a distinction between opinion and knowledge, as well as a relentless quest for wisdom.

But military and natural reverses (three earthquakes) inclined Athenians to look for reasons for the gods' displeasure. They identified Socrates as a reason because he continually irritated authorities with his questioning and insinuations about their intelligence. He also suggested that Athens should give him free meals and other recognition for his extraordinary services. He was tried and sentenced to death by drinking the fatal hemlock. He did not seek to escape, dying in 399 B.C. I. J. Stone argues that his snobbery doomed him. He showed no compassion for Athens or for his shrewish wife, Xanthippe. He did not believe in the democratic process, and with Plato held a low view of rhetoric.[2] The contrast between the good man Socrates and the divine Son of God, Jesus Christ, stands very starkly at this point.

---

1. A. E. Taylor, *Socrates: The Man and His Thought* (New York: Doubleday Anchor, 1952), 70.
2. Isadore J. Stone, *The Trial of Socrates* (Boston: Little, Brown, 1988). A most engaging account.

2.4.2 PLATO, THINKER

Although born in Athens (c. 427–346 B.C.), Plato, "the broad-shouldered one," was so shaken by the death of Socrates, his teacher, that he left Athens and wandered for a dozen years. He established the Academy in Athens—actually the first university in Europe. His famous *The Republic* gives his political philosophy. He failed to reach his ideals in Syracuse, where he was mentor to the young prince, Dionysius II, and the reign proved to be a disaster. His "ideal state" was to be ruled by philosopher-kings. Opponents called this aristocracy "an open conspiracy of gentleman pederasts." He assumed that most people are prisoners in a dark cave. Only an educated elite know that the shadows on the wall are not true reality, but that the "real" reality consists of ideals (book 7). Plato's proposal is clearly undercut by the error of Socrates—to know the good does not mean that anyone practices it. Paul's dilemma in Romans 7 is the universal predicament.

Shaped by Socrates and by Pythagorean teaching from Italy, where he traveled widely, Plato was an idealist. As over against the materialist, the atomists, Epicureans, and stoics, Thomas Hobbes and Karl Marx millennia later, Plato's dualism made room for physical reality and beyond it "the supraphysical world of entities, eternal and immutable," called by Plato "the ideas."[1] (Note the interesting parallel in Hebrews in the New Testament, where the heavenly patterns are models for earthly artifacts.) In his *Phaedo* and *Phaedrus* he dialogues on "the ideas" and the supreme "idea of the good," which is really his god.[2] So influential have these ideas been that Ralph Waldo Emerson was not much exaggerating when he

said that "philosophy is Plato, and Plato is philosophy." Alfred North Whitehead opined that "the European philosophical tradition consists of a series of foot-
notes to Plato." Especially can we see this in his *Timaeus*, his cosmology and
creation story. In *Timaeus* the world-maker, or *demiurge*, first makes the soul and
then the body; the body becomes "the prison-house of the soul."[3] Embodiment
then becomes the real cause of sin. The early church picked up this notion and
Augustine made it an unfortunate foundation for the rule of clerical celibacy.

1. A. E. Taylor, *The Mind of Plato* (Ann Arbor: Ann Arbor Paperbacks, 1922), 39.
2. Well-critiqued by J. Oliver Buswell Jr., in *A Christian View of Being and Knowing*
   (Grand Rapids: Zondervan, 1960), 107ff. Often spurned as too topological, Will
   Durant has reservations about Plato's noninclusion of marriage in *The Republic*. See
   The Story of Philosophy (New York: Simon and Schuster, 1926), 40ff. Writers such
   as Durant and Arnold Toynbee give a sense of the forest, though they neglect a few
   trees. We need their perspective. An intriguing dual autobiography of the Durants is
   Will and Ariel Durant (New York: Simon and Schuster, 1977). Durant left Catholicism disappointed in "unanswered prayer," but called a priest before he died.
3. B. F. Westcott, "The Myths of Plato," in *Religious Thought in the West* (London:
   Macmillan, 1891), 14ff. Plato's ideas of the eternality of unformed matter and the
   preexistence of the soul have had immense ramification.

2.4.3 ARISTOTLE, TUTOR

Aristotle (384–322) can rightly be called *the philosopher*. He was born near
modern Salonika. His father served as court physician in Macedonia. At age eighteen, Aristotle became a student in Plato's Academy. He studied with Plato for
twenty years; Plato called him "the intellect" of the school. When Plato died, a
nephew took over the school. Aristotle established a colonial academy in Assus.
In 342 he became tutor to the young Alexander the Great. At Alexander's accession, Aristotle returned to Athens to found the Lyceum. Plato and Aristotle share
much in common, but Plato's surviving works flow lucidly, while Aristotle's are
tough-going, angular, and awkward. But remember that we are reading lecture notes
collected by students and followers. Clearly Aristotle's range was universal and
his knowledge encyclopedic. He classified knowledge and established the first zoo-
logical garden. When Alexander died, Aristotle was in danger in Athens, and retired to Chalcis where his mother had been born and where he died at age sixty-two.
    Although much influenced by Plato, Aristotle was plainly troubled that Plato
so loved the general and the universal that in *The Republic* he ignored and thereby
destroyed the individual, marriage, and the family in order to achieve the perfect
state. *Ideas* were reality for Plato, but these were "the forms" for Aristotle, and
he insists on the unity of form and matter, *the actual* and *the potential*. In his
effort to avoid the snares of idealism on the one hand and materialism on the
other, Aristotle sought to uphold both rational intuition and empirical experience.
This "dualistic realism" had a great influence on Western thought.[1]
    Foundational to all of his thought was logic and his identification of the syllogism

and the law of noncontradiction. Yet he sees the need for induction as well as deduction.[2] Because Aristotle is so difficult to read, the beginner should dip into his *Metaphysic, Logic, Rhetoric,* and *Nicomachean Ethics* for small doses of the highly condensed content.[3] Both his *Politics* and *Poetics* are deliciously practical, the latter being really the first book of literary criticism ever written, and in such contrast with Plato, who couldn't stand poetry, drama, or rhetoric.

God was for Aristotle the "uncaused cause," the Prime-Mover of pure form. Equivalent to Plato's "Idea of the Good," this divinity was still a step beyond Plato's conceptualization. This god was impersonal, neither caring for nor loving the world and its creatures. This would be truth unknown in natural revelation but requiring the special revelation of Holy Scripture as it climaxes in the person of Jesus Christ. Every aspect of his thought is teleological, that is, having a sense of purpose. Yet this did not ultimately lead him to peace. In a short time, Alexander, his hero, died of debauchery; Demosthenes, the great orator, drank poison; and Aristotle, depressed and disappointed, Diogenes Laertius tells us, also drank the hemlock.[4]

Yet in medieval times, such were the affinities of thinkers like St. Thomas with Aristotle that his works became almost sacred text and even today a major ethical tradition in western thought is called "modern Aristotelianism."[5] Truly an unavoidable thinker.

For a better grasp of the character and career of Alexander the Great, read Robin Lane Fox, *Alexander the Great.*[6] See also "In the Footsteps of Alexander the Great," *National Geographic* magazine.[7] This all the more because Zechariah 9:1–8 contrasts Alexander's exploits with the gracious coming of the Messiah, Zechariah 9:9. See David Baron, *The Visions and Prophecies of Zechariah;*[8] Charles Lee Feinberg, *God Remembers;*[9] and Merrill F. Unger, *Commentary on Zechariah.*[10]

1. *Christian View of Being and Knowing,* 126ff. Charles Hodge and others of the late nineteenth- and early twentieth-century Princeton Seminary held to Scottish common sense realism. This arose to counter David Hume's skepticism and is not to be seen as a streak of rationalism, but rather the insistence on rationality. Aristotle shows the same concern.

2. A. E. Taylor, *Aristotle* (New York: Dover, 1955), 29. Induction can never yield final truth.

3. Mortimer J. Adler, *Aristotle for Everybody: Difficult Thought Made Easy* (New York: Macmillan, 1978).

4. *Story of Philosophy,* 90.

5. John L. Mothershead Jr., *Ethics: Modern Conceptions of the Principles of Right* (New York: Henry Holt, 1955), 285ff.

6. New York: Dial, 1974.

7. January 1968, 1ff.

8. Fincastle, Va.: Scripture Truth, 1918.

9. Wheaton, Ill.: Van Kampen, 1950.

10. Grand Rapids: Zondervan, 1963.

2.5   GREEK HISTORIANS: WARS AND WIND SHIFTS

> We have heard with our ears, O God; our fathers have told us what you did in their days, in days long ago.
>
> —Psalm 44:1

> History is but the development and revelation of providence.
>
> —Kossuth

> What are all histories but God manifesting himself, shaking down and tramping under foot whatsoever he hath not planted.
>
> —Oliver Cromwell

Robert Walpole (1676–1745) believed that "all history is a lie," putting him in the same league with Henry Ford, who asserted that "history is bunk." Closer to the truth, George Santayana (1863–1952) contended that those who will not learn the lessons of history are doomed to repeat them. The greatest historical accounts are in the Bible. Here is the history of ancient Israel and of the church, which God inspires and interprets. It is nothing short of miraculous that Moses, "who was educated in all of the wisdom of the Egyptians" (Acts 7:22), was preserved from using Manetho's chronology or the Egyptian notion of creation, which saw the earth as a great cosmic egg from the mud of the Nile. The Genesis account was not mixed with the Hindu idea of the beginning of all things with the severed members of giants. The mistakes of the ancients are not in the Bible.[1]

Considerable profit accrues, however, in reading of the thirty-two great civilizations (Arnold Toynbee's estimate). Here we see that history is "His story." Against the Christian conviction that history is linear, with a beginning in Creation, a decisive midpoint in redemption, and a grand crescendo in the eschaton, Greeks believed history to be cyclical. They had no significant eschatology. Biblical faith is eminently historical. Careful and judicious reading of history is imperative for informed and insightful people.[2] Let us begin with the Greeks.

---

1. One has only to read *The Gilgamesh Epic* to see that it is a "fictionalized narrative" coming from the Sumerians of five thousand years ago. It contrasts with the Genesis narrative. For Greek cosmogonies, see Wilbur M. Smith, *Therefore, Stand* (Boston: W. A. Wilde, 1945), 291ff. Also, R. Laird Harris in *Modern Science and Christian Faith* (Wheaton: Van Kampen, 1948), 251; Erich Sauer, *From Eternity to Eternity* (Grand Rapids: Eerdmans, 1954), 106.
2. Perhaps the finest brief philosophy of history, Herbert Butterfield, *Christianity and History* (London: Fontana, 1949).

2.5.1 XENOPHON, ADVENTURER

Toynbee observes of the Greek historians, "In essence, the historical experiences which wrung these thoughts out of Greek souls are akin to the experiences through which we ourselves have been passing."[1] Aristocratically born in Athens, Xenophon (431–352 B.C.) was one of these. He studied under Socrates and in his *Memorabilia* pays high tribute to his pedagogue. But adventure was in his blood, and in 401 he joined a band of Greek soldiers commanded by the younger Cyrus of Persia, intent on overthrowing Artaxerxes, the reigning emperor. In his *Anabasis* he tells the story of the march of the ten thousand after the death of Cyrus at the Battle of Cunaxa. Chosen as their leader, Xenophon describes their fifteen-hundred-mile march to the Black Sea. Facing fierce and hostile natives all the way back, the Greeks cried, *"Thalassa, thalassa"* ("The sea, the sea!") when they beheld the water in one of the great scenes in all of literature.[2] It has been compared with Balboa's first view of the mighty Pacific or Moses viewing the promised land from Mount Nebo. Having obtained a large ransom from the capture of a wealthy Persian, Xenophon was well-fixed for the rest of his life. Because he had sided with the Spartans, he was banished from Athens and lived the balance of his life in Sparta and Corinth.

> **For some scintillating insights** into the educational process in such varied centers as among the Jews, Sparta, Athens, Rome, etc., cf. William Barclay, *Train Up a Child: Educational Ideals in the Ancient World*.[3] Barclay was an outstanding student of the classics, but was not reliable as a Bible scholar.

---

1. Arnold J. Toynbee, *Greek Historical Thought* (New York: Mentor, 1952), xxviii. For a thoughtful reflection, see Kenneth O. Gangel, "Arnold Toynbee: An Evangelical Evaluation," *Bibliotheca Sacra,* April 1977, 144ff.
2. Xenophon, "The March to the Sea," from *Anabasis,* Book 9. Included in Gateway to the Great Books (Chicago: Britannica, 1963), 196ff. Those who read Koine Greek and would like to try classical Greek will find the Greek text of *Anabasis* an excellent place to begin. Xenophon's style is relatively simple.
3. Philadelphia: Westminster, 1959.

2.5.2 HERODOTUS, TRAVELER

"The unexamined life is not worth living," Socrates taught, and the Greek mind was investigative and exploratory. We see this impressively in Herodotus (484–424), called the "father of history" by Cicero. Herodotus was born and raised in Halicarnassus in southern Ionia. Here one of the "Seven Wonders of the Ancient World" was located, the famous 140-foot-high Mausoleum, built in memory of King Mausolus. Persian influence was restrictive, and young Herodotus gave himself unstintingly to the mastery of Greek literature. He traveled widely and has been called "the world's first sight-seer." Similarities and contrasts with Paul's journeys are striking. In his justly famous *History,* he describes his experiences and shares his impressions in about the first two thirds of the lengthy work. Socrates had said, "Wisdom begins in wonder," and we sense that this traveler's mind was enthralled with what he saw throughout the ancient world, from Persia to Italy and possibly Libya. He had knowledge of India, although never visiting there. He reported on bribery at Delphi even though he had great love for the oracle.[1] He would include certain fanciful material, such as a mare giving birth to a rabbit. Did he really believe such? Without any authoritative standards, his exposure to many cultural customs made him a relativist, the first in a long succession. Is, then, each person on his or her own? Are genocide and incest only matters of personal preference?

The great burden of his history was the Persian Wars, toward which tensions were building. Herodotus (although a Greek) was quite dispassionate in describing the four great battles of the war. His characterization of King Xerxes is quite empathetic: on his motivation for the wars (7.18–20); his weeping as he saw his vast army crossing the Hellespont (7.45–58). Daniel the prophet's visions concerning Persia are important background for this drama (chaps. 7–8).

His description of the 490 B.C. Battle of Marathon (6.100–7), where a seemingly invincible force of Persians, led by Darius, faced only 9,000 Athenians, led by Miltiades, is a classic. The Greeks won decisively, and Athens was saved.[2] The Greeks lost 192 men and the Persians 6,400. Pheidippides, the runner who had in vain sought Spartan assistance, ran the twenty-six miles to Athens with the news of victory, gasping "Rejoice, we conquer," and then fell dead. Herodotus lived on Samos, in Athens, and probably died in Thurii in southern Italy. His history is a joy to read.

---

1. Edith Hamilton, "Herodotus," in *Greek Way,* 91.
2. H. G. Wells, *The Outline of History* (Garden City, N.J.: Garden City, 1920), 280ff. Also, Hendrik van Loon, *The Story of Mankind* (New York: Pocket Books, 1921), 68ff. Van Loon is often called "the prince of the popularizers." He had an interesting academic career at Cornell and Antioch. See G. W. van Loon, *The Story of Hendrik van Loon* (New York: Lippencott, 1972). His great gift was the knack of "taking the reader into his confidence and leading him by the hand on what was to be a personal adventure" (321). He also wrote a significant biography of Dutch master Rembrandt van Rijn.

2.5.3 THUCYDIDES, CHRONICLER

Thucydides wrote in his notable history of the war between Athens and Sparta: "The cause of all these evils was the desire for power which greed and ambition inspire" (3.83). David Hume claimed that "the first page of Thucydides is the commencement of real history." Of Thracian descent, Thucydides prospered in Athens and was admiral of seven ships in a failed action early in the Peloponnesian War in which the great sea power, Athens, and the great land power, Sparta, clashed (431–4). In his consequent exile from Athens he traveled and wrote his remarkably evenhanded account of the action in which defeated Athens was knocked out of power and victorious Sparta was exhausted to the point that Macedonia could arise to fill the vacuum. Thus, although Thucydides "never indulges in moral judgment," he shows us the futility of war.[1]

The historian sketches the ill-fated Athenian expedition against the Sicilian allies of Sparta and their total defeat (books 6, 7). These writings were described by John Stuart Mill as "the most powerful and affecting pieces of narrative perhaps in all literature." The corruption and hubris (pride) of the Athenians can be seen in his remarkable passage on the tyrannization of the little island of Melos (5.17). Noteworthy are the speeches of various dignitaries, the most striking of which is "The Funeral Oration of Pericles." For Thucydides, Pericles was the ideal statesman (2.6, 34–46). The burden of Thucydides is the cycle of hunger for more and more power, which eventuates into crass conflict and disastrous results for all (two hundred years later "condensed" and focused by the Greek historian Polybius).[2] The harvest was the collapse of Greek civilization. As Hamilton laments, "Greece's contribution to the world was checked and soon ceased."[3] The history is actually incomplete and covers the first twenty-one of the twenty-eight years of the catastrophic war. Thucydides sought to avoid embellishment and "storytelling" in order to give an honest and objective description of events to which he was eyewitness. His dedication to accuracy and a reliable account was not always found in the ancient world and is very much like Luke's, as stated in Luke 1:1–4. Tradition says that Thucydides was killed in Thrace or Athens and was buried in Athens.

---

1. William Henry Chamberlain, "Thucydides: The Historian as Prophet," *Saturday Review of Literature,* 8 May 1965, 22.
2. *Greek Way,* 104.
3. Ibid., 105. Citations from Thucydides are from the *Great Books* edition, which adds additional chapter divisions.

2.6 POETS AND PLAYWRIGHTS: WAYS OF WONDER

Poetry is music in words; and music is poetry in sound.

—Thomas Fuller

Truth shines the brighter clad in verse.

—Alexander Pope

Poetry is the intellect colored by feelings.

—Alexander Wilson

Poetry comes nearer to vital truth than history.

—Plato

The Old Testament collections of Hebrew poetry, especially in the psalter and Song of Solomon, are unique. The word *poem* is descended from the Greek word for "work or workmanship," *poiēma*. In Ephesians 2:10, Paul teaches that each Christian is God's *poiēma*. By implication, in the *poiēma* the Christian expresses God's creative thought. Poetry is compressed language and therefore of special interest to Christian communicators. In his *Poetics,* Aristotle sees human love for poetry as expressive of our desire for harmony and rhythm. He notes that in poetry we tend to focus on universals, whereas in history we focus on particulars.[1] In poetry we confront an uprush of images, symbols, and metaphors by which we can see the author's world. Twentieth-century poet John Ciardi urges that one value of reading poetry is its opportunity for vicarious experience. It stretches our capacity for life. In the poetry of the Greco-Roman synthesis, the Roman penchant for order, law, and structure was fused with the more imaginative Greek consciousness, which the Romans admired very much.[2]

> **For some informative glimpses** into the lasting and pervasive influence of Greek thought and expression on Western life, consult Michael Macrone's *It's Greek to Me!*[3] For example, the rhetorician Stentor, from whose name is derived *stentorian,* was a Greek whose voice was reportedly like bronze and as loud as fifty voices.

---

1. William Rose Benet, *Benet's Reader's Encyclopedia,* 3d ed. (New York: Harper & Row, 1987), s.v. "Poetics." A rich resource.
2. T. Walter Wallbank and Alastair M. Taylor, *Civilization Past and Present* (Chicago: Scott, Foresman, 1960), 145.
3. New York: Calder, 1991.

2.6.1 PINDAR, TRADITIONALIST

> Like to a mountain stream rushing down in fury,
> Overflowing the banks with its rain-fed current,
> Pindar's torrent of song sweeps on resistless,
> Deep-voiced, tremendous.
> Or by a mighty wind he is borne skyward,
> Where great clouds gather.
>
> —Horace, of the poetry of Pindar[1]

Inventor of the elaborate and elegant Pindaric ode and commissioned to write odes for many great athletic and patriotic occasions, Pindar (522–438) was the greatest lyric poet of Greece.

Born a Boeotian, Pindar studied music and poetry in Athens. He became the poet of all the Greeks. His choral odes were very popular with patrons. He was very traditional and conservative in politics and religion. He seemed to believe that the Greek gods really existed, and he was concerned to safeguard their reputation. He has a great passage on the afterlife, and he believed staunchly in the immortality of the soul and judgment upon evil after death.[2] He loved Delphi and was at Olympia in 476, summoned to celebrate athletic successes.[3] He had great affection for Athens, but after 460 worried about her ambition and coming collapse. His poetry was known in the great library in Alexandria, but we possess only a quarter of his work.

He has been likened to Rudyard Kipling in the forceful rush of his verse. He is not easy to read and almost impossible to translate. This "prophet of the muses—in song," tells us about the inner processes of his writing. His writing was like weaving garlands, or like the flight of an eagle or the driving force of a gale. He loved punning and used imagery powerfully. He had a great respect for truth.[4] Pindar answers the frequently-raised question about whether the ancients shared our view of truth. Pindar proves that they did.

"Forge thy tongue on an anvil of truth, And what flies up, though it be a spark, Shall have weight," he wrote.[5]

Longinus offered the memorable observation that "Pindar and Sophocles at times, as it were, burn everything before them in their onset, but are often unaccountably extinguished and fail most lamentably."[6]

Poets and preachers who soar so effusively also tend to sink ignobly. It is hard for such to be consistent and even in their output.

---

1. *Odes and Epodes*, 4.2.1, 8.
2. *Olympian Odes*, 2.56–82.
3. C. M. Bowra, *Pindar* (Oxford: Clarendon, 1964), 117.
4. Ibid., 31. See also *Greek Way*, 34.
5. *Pythian Odes*, 1.85–92.
6. *de Sub.*, 33.5.

2.6.2 PLAUTUS AND TERENCE, COMEDIANS

Plautus (254–184) and Terence (186–159) are often considered to be the founders of European drama as we know it, and they reveal Roman life after the Second Punic War. They drew heavily on Greek drama, particularly on the work of Menander (342–292), who introduced the so-called "new-comedy" to Greece. The tremendous power of Hellenizing influence, a significant factor in both Judaism and Christianity, can be measured in its formative shaping of so much that was Roman. The great tragedies of Aeschylus and Sophocles had little appeal to the Romans. "The Romans had grown too sophisticated to be interested in the presentation of moral problems by a cast of characters from a remote and alien mythology."[1] The Romans wanted entertainment and hence comedy, which says something about their approach to life. There is no Roman tragedy until Seneca.

Plautus came from Umbria near Gaul, and came to Rome as a stage hand with a traveling theatre company. When the company went broke, he returned to Rome to work in a flour mill and started writing his 130 plays. Especially tantalizing are his *The Merchant, Mother-in-Law,* and *The Ass-Comedy.* Here is banter and humor about Roman domestic life. Women appear as never seen in Greek drama, and sentimentality appears.[2] He perfected certain stock characters and had the Romans in the aisles. Mistaken identity and the recognition of lost persons are often key, and Shakespeare directly used Plautus in *The Comedy of Errors;* Ben Jonson and Jean Baptiste Molière borrowed his ideas for several of their plays.

Terence was born in North Africa and came to Rome as a slave. All of his plays have survived and have a gentler tone than the farcical Plautus. He often uses double plots and pairings of characters with little slapstick. He was a master of language. His most popular play, *Eunuchus,* is a delicate treatment of the difficult sexual self-image of the castrated slave. Hamilton contrasts the two writers and their approaches. Plautus uses the old suspense and surprise approach. This has advantages. Terence pitched to a higher audience and let them know beforehand what the actors did not know. His technique, thus, struggled with the critical issues of storytelling and how much the audience should be brought behind the scenes of the plot.[3] Before the age of twenty-six, Terence traveled to Greece to study plays and get more material, but he did not survive the journey.

---

1. Moses Hadas, *A History of Latin Literature* (New York: Columbia University Press, 1952), 32.
2. Edith Hamilton, *The Roman Way to Western Civilization* (New York: Mentor, 1957), 30.
3. Ibid., 36ff.

2.6.3 CATULLUS, FIERY POET FROM VERONA

The great lyric poet of Rome was Gaius Valerius Catullus (84 B.C.–54 B.C.). His contemporary was Lucretius (96–55), who wrote the unfinished six-book poem *De rerum natura* ("On the Nature of Things") to discredit belief in divine agency in human affairs.[1] In his poem "Lucretius" (1869), Tennyson refers to the poet's suicide. Though dependent on the Greek anticipation of evolutionary theory, Lucretius was a poet of great skill. In contrast, Catullus was born into an upper-class family in Verona, the old Celtic settlement in northern Italy. He was sent by his father to Rome when he was twenty to be polished and refined, but he was soon lost in the intrigues of "the eternal city."

Catullus fell in love with Clodia, ten years his senior. He called her Lesbia and wrote love poems of almost unequaled passion and intensity. The emotional intensity of his output reminds one of some Old Testament poetry. Only one copy of his poetry has been found in Verona. He was clearly indebted to Greek poetry and indeed translated the fragments of the great Greek poetess Sappho (c. 600 B.C.) from the Island of Lesbos. She was apparently a schoolmistress of an academy for brides.[2] Of Catullus's work, most noteworthy is a mock dirge for Lesbia's parrot. But Clodia was unfaithful to him, and he wrote an amazing elegy of grief in leaving her: "I hate and love. You ask, perhaps, how that can be? I know not, but I feel the agony."

Highet speaks of his last poems on Clodia as "beautiful and horrible," as were his unforgettable farewell verses on the death of his brother.[3] Only Solomon and Shakespeare in his sonnets have written love poetry like that of Catullus. He took a position as a minor official in distant Bithynia in northern Asia Minor, but returned home bankrupt, never really finding himself. He wrote some poetry that insulted Julius Caesar but was reconciled to him. He was apparently plagued with a terrible cough and died young. He is in his outlook what the apostle Paul described as being "without God and without hope."

1. *History of Latin Literature*, 71.
2. Kenneth Rexroth, "Sappho—Poet and Legend," *Saturday Review of Literature*, 27 November 1965, 27.
3. Gilbert Highet, *Poets in a Landscape* (New York: Knopf, 1957), 24.

2.6.4 HORACE, POET LAUREATE OF ROME

Indisputably the best loved of the Latin poets, Quintus Horatius Flaccus, or Horace (65–8 B.C.), was born in southern Italy, the son of a freed slave. His father sent him to Rome and then on to Athens for study. His mother may have been Jewish. He sided with Brutus and Cassius in the failed Republican cause, and he returned to Rome to find his assets had been confiscated. Penniless, he began to write poetry, and through the poet Vergil's good offices was introduced to a wealthy patron, Maecenas, who gave him a little farm in the Sabine Hills. This little farm has become the most famous farm in literature.

Early on he wrote poems of the city of Rome and its people, as did Juvenal later.[1] He turned down the offer to be private secretary to Augustus, fearing that he would become a slave. Perhaps he did not wish to be a sycophant of the emerging new order he had once opposed. Thus, for many years he celebrated rural life and simple things. He was a moderate in all matters.[2] He died on the farm, but his satires, letters, and odes have been read ever since. England's Prime Minister William Gladstone (1809–1898) translated some of his work. Alexander Pope described his spell over Englishmen:

> Horace still charms with graceful negligence,
> And without method talks us into sense;
> Will, like a friend, familiarly convey
> The truest notion in the easiest way.

"Carpe diem" ("seize the day") was his watchword. Bitter, purple passages of his earlier work were mellowed in the Odes of his later career. At times he is quite moralizing. Edith Hamilton alleges that no poet was ever more of a preacher.[3] Stylistically he was a master. The measure of the man is certainly the demonstrable influence he had on later poets.[4] This "genial gentleman" was truly an Epicurean. Although he assiduously sought freedom, Hamilton observes that he "was not ever able to feel he was free."[5]

The strength of the Roman genius was its penchant for law and order, for structure, for boundaries—yet this did not yield any satisfying peace within.

1. *Poets in a Landscape*, 112.
2. *Roman Way to Western Civilization*, 95ff.
3. Ibid., 98. Kipling's *Recessional* reflects not only the Bible but his immersion in the *Odes of Horace*.
4. Mary Rebecca Thayer, *The Influence of Horace on the Chief English Poets of the*

Nineteenth Century (New York: Haskell House, 1965). Thayer treats Wordsworth, Coleridge, Byron, Shelley, Keats, Tennyson, and Browning.

5. Highet, *The Roman Way,* 108.

2.6.5 OVID, FRIVOLOUS POET

"Sulmo is my birthplace," wrote Publius Ovidius Naso, "Ovid Big-Nose" (43 B.C.–A.D. 17), who left the little hamlet only ninety miles from Rome and became the most brilliant poet of his age. His well-fixed parents wanted him to be a lawyer and sent him to Athens for his education, but he wanted to be a poet. Educated in the schools of the rhetoricians, Ovid wrote poetry in many genres. He was known as "the poet of love" and was married three times himself. In the tradition of Catullus, he spoke to posterity: "That after times may know of me each thing, I was the man who tender love did sing."

He wrote *Heroides,* twenty-one fictional letters sent by mythological figures to their lovers. His three-volume *Art of Love* in A.D. 1 (written after his clever *Art of Cosmetic*) is divided into three sections: (1) how to find one's love; (2) how to win her; and (3) how to keep her. In this salacious work, Ovid shrinks from nothing. Edward Rand writes that Ovid's "audacity to the point of blasphemy leads him to disclose what in all decency should be left unsung."[1] The Emperor Augustus, who lived in serial polygamy himself, felt that Ovid was in part responsible for a scandal involving his own granddaughter Julia. Augustus banished Ovid to Constanta on the Black Sea in what is Romania today. He endlessly pled to return but died in exile in A.D. 17.

Paul's picture of Roman depravity in Romans 1:18–32 is not overdrawn, as both the bawdy artwork found in the ruins of Pompeii and the verse of Ovid and others makes plain. Ovid spoke of God stirring his heart, but there was no moral dimension in his religious aspiration.[2]

Metamorphoses, his masterpiece, begins with creation and artistically tours mythology and history through the time of Julius Caesar. We derive much of our knowledge of mythology from Ovid. In fifteen books, 250 myths, the poet coins more than 200 words.[3] He completed his *magnum opus* before being exiled at age fifty. Although the work has a flavor of disillusionment, its outlook is humanistically hopeful. Change is the stuff of life, as from chaos to order, as Io to a heifer, as Julius Caesar to a hero. In exile he left unfinished a lengthy poem intended to explain the meaning of Roman feasts and festivals. Ovid is remembered in part for his versatility. Seneca and Martial used him extensively. He was widely read in the Middle Ages and Renaissance, a favorite of Dante and Chaucer. His innate ability was, as Gilbert Highet says, "ruined by shallowness and frivolity."[4]

---

1. Edward Kennard Rand, *Ovid and His Influence* (Boston: Marshall Jones, 1925), 46.

2. Donald Grey Barnhouse, *Man's Ruin: Romans* (Wheaton: Van Kampen, 1952), 252ff.

3. *History of Latin Literature*, 217.

4. *Poets in a Landscape,* 195. This is a truly beautiful treatment.

2.7   HISTORIANS: WANDERINGS AND WRESTLINGS

But when the time had fully come, God sent his Son, born of a woman, born under law, to redeem those under law, that we might receive the full rights of sons.

—Galatians 4:4–5

The Word became flesh and made his dwelling among us.

—John 1:14

That which was from the beginning, which we have heard, which we have seen with our eyes, which we have looked at and our hands have touched—this we proclaim concerning the Word of life.

—1 John 1:1

Christianity like Judaism is anchored in time-space events, apart from which there is no Christian faith. That Christianity is intertwined and interlocked with the Greco-Roman world is vividly seen in the inscription on the cross of Christ, which was written in Hebrew, Latin, and Greek. The worlds of religion, power, and culture united in crucifying the Lord of Glory. Preparations for the coming of Messiah involved not only Hebrew messianic prophecy and a lineage, but Roman roads and law and the common language of Greek.[1] So the reports of secular historians of this era take on added significance. The histories of Polybius can be cited as an example. Polybius (202–120) was a Greek who was captured by the Romans. He tutored young Publius Scipio and his brothers and accompanied them to the battle for Carthage, in the Third Punic War. He watched Corinth fall to the Romans. Only five of his books survive, but they are sober, unadorned history. A friend of Terence, Polybius chose to visit the Alps and trace Hannibal's journey so that he could write knowledgeably about it. He was quite accurate, yet very dull.

Another early historian well worth reading is Julius Caesar himself (102–44). The *Pontifex Maximus* was a strong leader at the end of the Old Republic. Every second-year Latin student reads his *Gallic War*. His own account of his conquest of France begins with the immortal Latin words, *"Gallia est omnis divisa in partes tres"* ("All Gaul is divided into three parts").[2] His description extends to the first invasion of Britain in 55 B.C. He was assassinated while presiding over the Roman Senate, with disastrous consequences and division in the nation.

The Latin poet Juvenal (A.D. 55–130) served in the military and did not prosper when he returned to civilian life. In poetry during the reign of Nero, he critiqued Roman life and customs with bitter satire. Ultimately, the Emperor Domitian banished him to Assuan in Southern Egypt. He particularly excoriated homosexuality.[3] His motto was "a sound mind in a sound body." His sixteen satirical poems inspired such neoclassicists as John Dryden (1631–1700), Alexander Pope (1688–1744), and Jonathan Swift (1667–1745). His concern about centralized government power was ever: "Who shall guard the guardians?" The custom of indicating whether gladiators in the arena should live by a thumbs-up or thumbs-down signal also was Juvenal's innovation.

42 THE COMPANY OF THE CREATIVE

▓ **For a history of Rome** that strongly relies on actual contemporary historians, consult the work by Moses Hadas, longtime professor of classics at Columbia University, *A History of Rome*.[4] Reflect on how the gospel story is intricately placed in that history (Luke 3:1ff.).

---

1. Alfred Eidersheim, *The Life and Times of Jesus the Messiah* (Grand Rapids: Eerdmans, 1953), 3–108.
2. Arthur Tappan Walker, *Caesar's Gallic War*, Books I–IV (Chicago: Scott, Foresman, 1926). See also F. E. Adcock, *Caesar as Man of Letters* (Cambridge: Cambridge University Press, 1956). Great precision in the use of words.
3. Juvenal, *Second Satire*, 126–35.
4. Garden City, N.J.: Doubleday, 1956.

2.7.1 LIVY, MASTER OF IMAGINATION

Polybius and Cato the Elder (234–149) wrote lean, terse history. Thucydides (fifth century B.C.), following his model, Sallust (86–34), was more artistic in structuring his accounts of war. The chronicler in the Old Testament writes his record of Israel's history from the viewpoint of the House of David (he does not describe David's sin as in 2 Samuel). Each gospel writer has a point-of-view, with Luke sharing his essential process and objective in writing (Luke 1:1–4). Luke was an outstanding historian in both Luke and Acts.[1]

The Roman historian Titus Livius or Livy (59 B.C.–A.D. 17) is of special interest. He was born in Padua in northern Italy. Augustus was his patron, and he spent forty years writing a history of Rome *(Ab urbe condita libre)* in 142 books, of which thirty-six survive. He starts with the legend that Romulus and Remus were suckled by a wolf and proceeds through the death of Cicero in 43 B.C. and the Battle of Actium in 9 B.C. The scope of his undertaking is breathtaking, and few since have attempted it. He wove the people and personalities of Roman history into one continuous narrative.

Livy's narration is skilled and sensitive. He writes as a Roman patriot and a romantic. His fertile imagination carried him away occasionally, and he incorporates chunks of legend and speculation. He was brilliantly inventive.[2] Livy was retiring by nature, shows no humor, and is prudish. How fascinating to consider this gifted man writing so laboriously in Rome during the early years of the life of Jesus. Book 1 on "The Foundations of Rome" is especially rewarding.[3] His objective is to hallow Rome's glorious past and summon his contemporaries to follow in the steps of the great heroes. He was rhetorically keen but factually inconsistent and contradictory. In his mixture of fact and fable, this made no great difference. Our biblical writers would not have served us well had they written in this manner. "Born of the Virgin Mary" is every bit as historical as "suffered under Pontius Pilate."

Livy was "the perfect Roman gentleman" whose stories were retold in Macaulay's *Lays of Ancient Rome*. But many strands of his story are false and his chief representation "subtly inaccurate."[4]

1. On the accuracy and reliability of Dr. Luke as a historian, see William M. Ramsay, *St. Paul: The Traveller and the Roman Citizen* (Grand Rapids: Baker, 1960), and Doremus A. Hayes, *The Most Beautiful Book Ever Written: The Gospel According to Luke* (New York: Methodist Book Concern, 1913). Hayes argues, "It is dangerous to accuse Luke of inaccuracy in anything" (89). Colin Hemer made a similar pronouncement.
2. E. J. Kinney, ed., *The Cambridge History of Classical Literature* (Cambridge: Cambridge University Press, 1982), 466.
3. R. M. Ogilvie, *A Commentary on Livy, Books 1–5* (Oxford: Clarendon, 1965), 30ff.
4. Kenneth Rexroth, "Livy's Early Rome," *The Saturday Review of Literature,* 29 May 1965, 17.

2.7.2 PLINY THE YOUNGER, EYEWITNESS

Pliny the Younger (A.D. 61–113) was the nephew and adopted heir of the distinguished Pliny the Elder (23–79), author of *Historia naturalis,* and a scientist whose curiosity brought about his own death in the eruption of Mount Vesuvius in A.D. 79. The younger Pliny was born in the area near beautiful Lake Como in northern Italy. He was well-educated by the great orator Quintilian. At the age of eighteen he became an advocate and quickly a representative of the people in the Roman Senate. In 110 he was appointed governor of Bithynia and served until his death. His letters remain a written legacy that have substantial interest for Christians.

His letters to the historian Tacitus, about the volcanic eruption at Vesuvius, are striking. Located on a plain on the Bay of Naples, Vesuvius began to rumble ominously in 63. On his journey to Rome for trial, the apostle Paul landed at Puteoli (modern Pozzuoli) in this vicinity between 59 and 62. The volcanic ash-enriched soil from earlier eruptions made this fertile farmland, and the residents of Pompeii gave little attention to their danger. Though restored Pompeii is a display of great beauty, the visitor is quickly aware of the dominance of pornography. This aspect of his culture was not hidden from Paul (see, for example, Rom. 1:18–32). In 79, great streams of lava flowed down the slopes of Vesuvius, and Pompeii was buried under twelve to fifteen feet of ash and cinders. Many citizens were trapped and killed in Pompeii and neighboring towns. Nearby at the time, Pliny the Younger and his aunt had declined to accompany Pliny the Elder, who wanted to see the developing phenomenon more clearly, and to help friends flee. Young Pliny read Livy in the shower of ashes, but his uncle, who was Admiral of the Fleet in the area, sailed into the pumice stones and burning rocks. Pliny the Elder even took a nap in an abandoned village to show his courage and confidence, and "his breathing, which on account of his corpulence, was rather heavy and sonorous, was heard by the attendants outside."[1] Shortly thereafter, while out on the bay, he was apparently suffocated "by some gross and noxious vapour." The whole atmosphere was very apocalyptic, particularly given the Stoic and Epicurean belief that the world would end by fire.

Most significant to church history are Pliny's letters to the Roman Emperor Trajan. These contain the first direct and unmistakable references to Christians by a secular writer. As governor of Bithynia, Pliny tells Trajan what his policy has been regarding the outlawed sect, and he asks whether the emperor concurs. In his narrative he describes how he seeks to get Christians to revile Christ. There are references to their customs of worship:

> They had been wont to come together on a fixed day before dawn and sing a hymn alternately to Christ as a God, and to bind themselves by a solemn obligation not for any guilty purpose, but not to commit theft or robbery or adultery, nor to break faith or repudiate a deposit when called upon to pay it.[2]

Trajan's reply is supportive.

---

1. Pliny the Younger, *The Eruption of Vesuvius*, in Gateway to the Great Books (Chicago: Britannica, 1963), 6:264ff.
2. G. R. Haines, *Heathen Contact with Christianity During Its First Century and a Half* (Cambridge: Deighton, Bell, 1923), 43ff. The selections are given in the original Greek or Latin and then translated.

2.7.3 TACITUS, PREMIER ROMAN HISTORIAN

Early Roman references to Jesus Christ are found not only in Pliny but in Suetonius (A.D. 69–A.D. 140) who wrote *Lives of the Caesars*. He is not given to glossing their failings. One observer commented that Suetonius presents his subjects essentially as "perverts and gangsters." The preeminent Roman historian is Tacitus (55–120), who in his *Annals* refers to the death of Jesus at the behest of Pontius Pilate (15:44).[1]

We know very little of the actual life of Tacitus, and we have but two manuscripts of his epochal literary production. Like his friend Pliny, he may have been educated under Quintilian. He married the daughter of Agricola, the Roman governor of Britain, and his first work was a biography of his father-in-law. In *Life of Agricola* he lays bare his detestation for the Emperor Domitian. He accuses that Domitian, "leaving now no interval or breathing space but, as it were, with one continuous blow, drained the life-blood of the Commonwealth." He was part of what he called that "servile senate," which basically kept silent in the face of grave injustice.[2]

He also wrote *Germania* on the manners and customs of the German people. His main works, which were rediscovered half a century ago, are his *Annals*, which traces Roman history from 14–66 , and his *Histories*, which extends the narrative from 69 to 96. Of *Histories*, just short of the first five books are extant. Of interest is his focus on the Jewish Wars of Vespasian and Titus. Tacitus is unequivocally anti-Semitic. He is incensed by the separateness of the Jewish people (*Histories*, book 5) and relishes preparations for the siege of Jerusalem. The eyewitness Josephus describes this siege at length.[3]

Tacitus was a gifted orator, historian, and artist. Some of his words and phrases have entered our everyday speech. For example, he first remarked that someone was "conspicuous by his absence." He claimed to write dispassionately and without bias, but Kenneth Rexroth speaks of "the grandeur of his malice," his grimness, and "the sharpness of his bite."[4] He has a dramatic quality and takes great liberty in attributing speeches to persons who could not possibly have delivered them.[5] If such fictive speeches were credited in the book of Acts, the credibility of its narrative would be decimated. Historians have been somewhat more generous with Tacitus.

In 112 Tacitus was made proconsul of Asia. His was an extraordinary career.

---

1. Everett F. Harrison, *A Short Life of Christ* (Grand Rapids: Eerdmans, 1968), 18ff. A seasoned reflection.
2. Donald R. Dudley, *The World of Tacitus* (Boston: Little, Brown, 1968), 16.
3. Ibid., 193ff.
4. Kenneth Rexroth, "Tacitus," *Saturday Review of Literature,* 26 June 1965, 19.
5. *History of Latin Literature*, 329.

2.7.4 PLUTARCH, GREEK BIOGRAPHER OF ROMANS

By no means were all of the major contributors during the Roman period from Italy or centered there. The work of the Greek geographer Strabo (c. 64 B.C.–A.D. 24), *Geographia,* runs to seventeen books. Strabo's forty-seven-book history of Rome is lost. Apuleius came from North Africa in the mid-second century A.D., and wrote Platonic philosophical works. In his romantic novel, *The Golden Ass*, a man turned into a donkey travels the world witnessing human foibles.

Most outstanding of the non-Roman authors is Plutarch (46–120). Plutarch was born in Chaeronea in Boeotia, Greece. He studied in Athens and lectured in Rome. Many of his lectures appear in his *Moralia,* chief among which is his famous lecture "Of Bashfulness," in which he argues for the golden mean of Aristotle, "that virtues are means between extremes, between passions which are both vicious."[1]

He returned to his home town to serve in various civic capacities. He then filled the position of priest of Apollo at Delphi until the time of his death. In later years he wrote *Parallel Lives,* a compilation of the biographies of forty-six Greek and Roman notables. He makes a fascinating series of comparisons and contrasts in which the Greeks indeed appear to good advantage.

Queen Elizabeth I counted Thomas North's translation as one of her favorite books. Shakespeare drew upon Plutarch for his plays *Julius Caesar, Coriolanus,* and *Antony and Cleopatra*. In *Antony and Cleopatra,* Shakespeare imported whole sections without alteration.[2] For hundreds of years, what thoughtful people knew about many historical personages was derived from Plutarch. Tacitus and Livy tended to use one basic resource in their writing, while Plutarch sought broader testimony and more sources. Of enduring interest to us are his sketches of Romulus, founder of Rome; Solon, the reformer from Athens; Alcibiades, and his contrast between Demosthenes of Athens and Cicero of Rome, the two great orators.[3]

The inclusion of almost 900 pages of Plutarch in *Great Books of the West-ern World*, as well as volume 12 of the Harvard Classics, testifies to the substantive nature of his writings for the study of Western culture and civilization. Communicators who traffic in Bible biography can profit immensely from reading Plutarch.

---

1. Plutarch, *Of Bashfulness*, in Gateway to the Great Books (Chicago: Britannica, 1963), 7:94.
2. Ibid., 94.
3. Plutarch, *Parallel Lives*, in Great Books of the Western World (Chicago: Britannica, 1952), 14:691ff.

2.7.5 JOSEPHUS, JEWISH HISTORIAN

In the rare category "indispensable" are the works of Flavius Josephus (A.D. 37–A.D. 95), which should be on every Christian's bookshelf.[1] Joseph Ben Mathias was born in Jerusalem of royal and aristocratic lineage. His *Life of Josephus* may be the first autobiography in Western history. Trained in the Jewish schools, he was apparently governor of Galilee at the time of the Jewish revolt in 66. Rebel forces he led were defeated by the Romans, and he was a prisoner for three years. He curried favor with General Vespasian and accompanied him to Alexandria, returning with Titus to witness the fall of Jerusalem in 70. He lived the rest of his life in Rome. He became a Roman citizen, and he received a commission to write the history of the wars he had seen and concerning Jews of special interest to the Romans.

Josephus was an opportunist of the first order. Thackeray (a cousin of the great English novelist) speaks of him as an "egoist, self-interested, time-server and flatterer of his Roman patrons."[2] One must always take into account that he wants to please the Romans for whom he writes. Still, he lived during times of such great interest to us. He was himself a priest and spoke from within the system. He writes of John the Baptist, of Jesus, the "wise man," and of James the brother of Jesus (*Antiquities*, 18–20). While there are references to Jesus in the Babylonian Talmud (Sanhedrin, 43a), Josephus speaks of Jesus and his miracles and calls him the Christ, referring as well to his death and resurrection (*Antiquities*, 18.3.3). Harrison judiciously argues for the essential substance of the statement, which is remarkable indeed.[3]

Josephus writes mindfully of the great prophecies of Daniel, particularly in chapters 2, 7, 8, and 9. He tells that Alexander the Great's beneficent treatment of the Jews arose after a dream and after he had been shown Daniel's prophecies concerning his role (*Antiquities*, 11.8). The use of Daniel 9 is particularly striking in the days of Judas Maccabee (*Antiquities*, 12.7). Both Origen and Eusebius cite Josephus. Our Lord's prophecies of the fall and destruction of Jerusalem in 70 are recorded in the three Synoptic Gospels.

A. T. Pierson identifies twenty-five distinct predictions. Using the law of compound probability, the chance of all twenty-five "meeting in one event is as one in nearly twenty millions, i.e., the fraction that represents the chance of probability is one-half raised to its twenty-fourth power or about one twenty millionth chance!"[4] The eyewitness accounts of Josephus are invaluable in corroborating the literal accuracy of the predictive prophecy of Jesus (*Jewish War,* 5.11, 12; 6.1–7). The parallels between Josephus and Luke–Acts are also well worth pursuing.[5] This Roman-sponsored history remains significant.

---

1. The language of the famous William Whiston translation, *The Works of Flavius Josephus,* has been updated in *The New Complete Works of Josephus* (Grand Rapids: Kregel, 1999). For a condensed version with updated text and full-color art, cf. Paul L. Maier, *Josephus: The Essential Works* (Grand Rapids: Kregel, 1994). For exceptional background on this period, see Stewart Perowne, *The Life and Times of Herod the Great* (New York: Abingdon, 1958); and Stewart Perowne, *The Later Herods* (New York: Abingdon, 1958).
2. H. St. John Thackeray, *Josephus: The Man and the Historian* (New York: Ktav, 1967), 19.
3. Everett F. Harrison, *A Short Life of Christ* (Grand Rapids: Eerdmans, 1968), 15–18.
4. A. T. Pierson, *Many Infallible Proofs* (London: Morgan and Scott, n.d.), 55ff.
5. Steve Mason, *Josephus and the New Testament* (Peabody, Mass.: Hendrickson, 1992), 185ff.

2.7.6 EDWARD GIBBON, ROMAN EMPIRE SCHOLAR

The decline of Rome was the natural and inevitable effect of immoderate greatness. Prosperity ripened the principle of decay; the causes of destruction multiplied with the extent of conquest; and, as soon as time or accident had removed the artificial supports, the stupendous fabric yielded to the pressure of its own weight. The story of its ruin is simple and obvious; and instead of inquiring why the Roman Empire was destroyed, we should rather be surprised that it had subsisted so long.

—Edward Gibbon

At this point we jump across the centuries to consider the most significant treatment of the fall of ancient Rome ever written. The idea of a massive account of the decline and fall of Rome occurred to Gibbon in October 1764, as he sat in the ruins of the Capitol in Rome, listening to the monks singing vespers from the temple of Jupiter. Edward Gibbon (1737–1794) was born in Putney in England, the only surviving child of seven. His mother died when he was ten, and he was not close to his wealthy father. He was bored at Oxford, and when he professed conversion to Roman Catholicism he was put out.[1] His infuriated father entrusted him to the care of a Calvinistic minister in Lausanne, in Switzerland, where he sought admittance into the Protestant Church. During these years he traveled and mastered the classics. He was only five feet tall, with small feet and quick steps. He became very corpulent in his later years. He had a torrid romance with a country minister's daughter in Switzerland, but was forbidden by his father to marry her. He never did marry.

He took over twenty years to write *The Decline and Fall of the Roman Empire,* after he had served as a captain in the militia during the Seven Years' War. He spoke of François-Marie Voltaire (1694–1778) as his "old friend," and he had considerable contact with Jean-Jacques Rousseau (1712–1778). David Hume (1711–1776) influenced him to write in English rather than French. In his writing style, he attempted to imitate Charles Louis Montesquieu (1689–1755). The work (two volumes and 1,750 pages in the Great Books edition) was hailed as a masterpiece of history and literature. He suffers from the ravages of Enlightenment rationalism as in his denial of darkness at the crucifixion because of "the silence of the unbelieving world."[2] Many who took no stock in his theological perspective were yet affectionate devotees of the work.[3] Gibbon served in Parliament (where he never once raised his voice) and was part of the Literary Club where he knew well such as David Garrick the actor, Oliver Goldsmith the novelist, Joshua Reynolds the painter, Adam Smith the economist, and Edmund Burke the jurist. Samuel Johnson and James Boswell were not friendly to him, the latter dismissing him derisively as "the little infidel." Increasingly suffering with the gout and the great swellings of a "dropsical state," he died in 1794 at the age of fifty-seven.

Apart from sections where he goes too deeply into a subject, for example the Arian controversy, Gibbon is fun to read. His opening sentences in *The Decline and Fall* are majestic and compelling. Like Tacitus he was epigrammatic, as when he describes the Emperor Septimius Severus: "He promised only to betray, he flattered only to ruin."[4] Arguably his is the greatest modern historical narrative, although J. L. Motley's *Rise of the Dutch Republic* (1856) is also a contender.

Gibbon grapples with how and why the mighty Roman Empire petered out and collapsed to the Barbarians (by 476). Clearly a time of disorder followed the death of Constantine in 337 with the split of the Empire into two parts in 395. Economic, political, religious, and moral factors have been advanced in explication of the exhaustion.[5] Certainly barbarization was gradual, with the culture mainly disintegrated within. Aspects of the decay are evident in Gibbon's treatment. His analysis of the five reasons for the growth of Christianity in book 15 is classic, as is his description of persecution of Christians in book 16. Any historian whose personal hero is Julian the Apostate will be limited in his sympathy for the Christian cause, but his insights and writing style are impressive.

---

1. D. M. Low, *Edward Gibbon: 1737–1794* (London: Chatto and Windus, 1937), 44. The elder Gibbon was tutored by William Law, who influenced the Wesleys. Law's *A Serious Call to a Devout and Holy Life* has had a significant impact on pietistic Christianity.

2. Ibid., 207.

3. Shelby T. McCloy, *Gibbon's Antagonism to Christianity and the Discussions That It Has Provoked* (Chapel Hill, N.C.: University of North Carolina Press, 1933). A solid survey.

4. William Henry Chamberlain, "Decline and Fall Revisited," *Saturday Review of Literature,* 8 August 1964, 18.

5. Donald Kagan, ed., *Decline and Fall of the Roman Empire: Why Did It Collapse?* (Lexington, Ky.: Heath, 1962). A fine symposium of views on the course of dissolution, including the views of Edward Gibbon.

2.8   ORATORS AND THINKERS: WARS WITH WORDS

A group of Epicurean and Stoic philosophers began to dispute with him. Some of them asked, "What is this babbler trying to say?" Others remarked, "He seems to be advocating foreign gods." They said this because Paul was preaching the good news about Jesus and the resurrection.

—Acts 17:18

As some of your own poets have said, "We are his offspring."

—Acts 17:28b

Even one of their own prophets has said, "Cretans are always liars, evil brutes, lazy gluttons." Their testimony is true.

—Titus 1:12–13a

Greco-Roman culture and civilization have been highly formative for all of Western culture. Daniel's panoramic prophecy of the "times of the Gentiles" (Daniel 2, 7) indicates that the succession of great ancient powers would climax in a fourth empire, which in its final and inclusive form would be destroyed by the great smiting stone at Messiah's second advent (Dan. 2:44–45).

Rome is clearly the "legs of iron" (2:33) and the fourth beast (7:7), which will in some form perpetuate its influence until the end-time. Roman culture, Roman law, Roman religion (*Pontifex Maximus,* a title now applied to the Roman Catholic Pope, was given to the Roman high priest) have survived. T. S. Eliot used to say that "as we inherit the civilization of Europe, we are citizens of Rome." Goodwin Smith observed in *The Heritage of Man* that "the rule of the Caesars ended; the power of the Bishops survived." Arnold Toynbee held that "the history of Europe is the effort to reunite the Roman Empire." Even Samuel Johnson argued, "All religion, almost all our laws, almost all our art, all that sets us above the savages, has come to us from the shores of the Mediterranean."[1] Notice also "the people of the ruler who will come will destroy the city and the sanctuary" (Dan. 9:26b). Doubtless this is a reference to the destruction of Jerusalem in 70.

Points of tangency with Greco-Roman culture can be seen in the development of Roman rhetoric and Stoic philosophy.

> **Interesting thinking on the** Greco-Roman influence can be found in Duane Litfin, *St. Paul's Theology of Proclamation: 1 Corinthians 1–4 and Graeco-Roman Rhetoric*[2] and Michael A. Bullmore's *St. Paul's Theology of Rhetorical Style: An Examination of 1 Corinthians 2:1–5 in the Light of First Century Graeco-Roman Rhetorical Culture.*[3] The latter is more sharply focused on Corinth.

---

1. See David L. Larsen, *Jews, Gentiles and the Church: A New Perspective on History and Prophecy* (Grand Rapids: Discovery House, 1995), 249f. In this sense it is probably not correct to speak of the "revived Roman Empire."

2. Cambridge: Cambridge University Press, 1994.
3. San Francisco: International Scholars, 1995.

2.8.1 CICERO, KING OF ORATORS

Cicero, Marcus Tullius (106 B.C.–43 B.C.) was "the greatest Roman orator and the most important Latin writer on rhetoric."[1] Rhetoric is the art of persuasive speaking. Of course the roots were in Greece, with Demosthenes the practitioner and Aristotle the theorist, but Cicero drank deeply at these springs while studying in Athens and on Rhodes. Using this foundation, he established a Latin oratorical tradition that was equal to the Greek. He believed philosophy and rhetoric were to be closely intertwined, so that form complemented content. His early experience was as a defense lawyer. He had an up-and-down political career but came into prominence (although not always favor) by his Catiline Orations and his fourteen speeches called The Philippics. These drove Antony from Rome.[2]

His great work, *De Oratore* (55 B.C.), outlines in dialogical form the training, style, and delivery of the effective speaker. In his *Brutus,* he traces strengths and weaknesses of outstanding orators. All of this is of pivotal significance because Aristotle's rhetorical influence was largely channeled to the Western world through Cicero. Augustine was not proficient in Greek, so the Latin of Cicero was his source for baptizing Greek rhetorical form into the Christian pulpit.[3] Cicero believed that ethos (character) was even more important for the speaker than logos (content) or pathos (passion).[4] We possess nine hundred of his letters, which greatly illuminate life in his time. His dialogical essays "On Friendship" and "On Old Age" are rich indeed.[5] His prose style in writing (as his speaking style) is rhetorically ornate, and this was one of the ongoing conflicts in which he was involved. Quintilian (A.D. 35–99) published twelve volumes on the training of the speaker that are essentially Ciceronian.

Under a political cloud, Cicero retired to Tuscany to write, but was condemned and put to death by agents of Anthony while attempting flight. His head and hands were exhibited in Rome.

---

1. George Kennedy, *Classical Rhetoric and Its Christian and Secular Tradition from Ancient to Modern Times* (Chapel Hill, N.C.: University of North Carolina Press, 1980), 90.
2. Cicero, *Selected Works* (New York: Penguin, 1960), 101ff. Note *The Second Philippic Against Antony.*
3. David L. Larsen, *The Company of the Preachers* (Grand Rapids: Kregel, 1998), 3.4.3, for a discussion of Augustine's rhetorical odyssey.
4. James M. May, *Trials of Character: The Eloquence of Ciceronian Ethos* (Chapel Hill, N.C.: University of North Carolina Press, 1989). For authentic novels of ancient Rome, cf. Steven Saylor, for example *Roman Blood; The Venus Throw.*
5. Cicero, "On Friendship" and "On Old Age," in Gateway to the Great Books (Chicago: Britannica, 1963), 10:286ff.

2.8.2 SENECA, WRITER-STATESMAN

> Someone has made a joke about the baldness of my head, the weakness
> of my eyes, the thinness of my legs, the shortness of my stature; what
> insult is there in telling me what everyone sees?
>
> —Seneca

Born in Cordoba in Spain, Lucius Annaeus Seneca (4 B.C.–A.D. 65) was a philosopher, statesman, and writer. His father, Seneca the Elder, was provincial manager of finance and his mother a remarkable woman to whom he paid glowing tribute in an essay. While Cicero was influenced by Stoicism, Seneca the Younger was a full-fledged Stoic. Like Epicureanism, Stoicism brought a strong emphasis on the individual in a time of political and social breakdown. Epicureanism and Stoicism are frankly materialistic; Stoicism is pantheistic. For the followers of Epicurus the highest good is maximized pleasure, but the Stoics exulted harmony with nature. Self-sufficient detachment is virtue, duty the supreme reality. This gospel of clear-thinking patience held some natural appeal for the Romans.[1]

Touched early by Pythagorean mysticism and being a sickly asthmatic, Seneca marched along "the highway to distinction" through the usual apprenticeships. The Emperor Claudius exiled him to the island of Corsica for eight years.[2] He returned when Agrippina, the emperor's wife, brought him back to tutor her son, the future emperor Nero. Seneca became a kind of prime minister under Nero and served in Rome when Paul appeared before Nero (cf. 2 Tim. 4:16–18). Seneca's brother, Gallio, was the governor before whom Paul appeared in Acts 18:11–17.

Implicated in a plot to assassinate Nero, Seneca was ordered to kill himself and stoically opened his own veins and bled to death.

John Calvin's first writing of note was a commentary on Seneca's *De clementia* in 1532, a work in which Erasmus also was interested. Calvin's interest was largely rhetorical, but one wonders if the Stoic denial of free will was also of interest.[3] Parallels between Seneca's thought and Christian philosophy have been noted by Tertullian, Jerome, and other writers. J. B. Lightfoot, however, shows the tragic defects in Stoicism's lack of a personal Savior or redemption.[4]

Seneca was a literary innovator and a leader in the reaction against rhetorical elegance and wit. His modification of the diatribe in communication is significant because of the use of the diatribe sermon in the synagogue and by Paul. Seneca's epistles are profitably compared with Paul's letters.[5] Letter 83 against the use of alcohol is especially noteworthy.[6] He was considered by Pliny the Elder to be the leading authority on zoology of his time. His nine dramatic tragedies have been very influential, especially *Thyestes,* a play about revenge.[7] He loved games and sports and denounced "bleacherites," who were content to be only spectators. A stellar procession of writers and thinkers has acknowledged indebtedness to Seneca.

---

1. Richard Mott Gummere, *Seneca the Philosopher and His Modern Message* (Boston: Marshall Jones, 1922), 5.

2. See Robert Graves, *I, Claudius* (New York: Random House, 1934). This tingling study of the Roman Emperor was popularized by a Public Broadcasting System dramatization that aired in the U.S. through the Masterpiece Theater series. Graves, one of the English soldier poets of World War I, was cool to Christianity. His writing had an incandescent quality. He was professor in Cairo and lived on Majorca until 1936, when he fled the Spanish Civil War and became professor at Oxford. For a biography see Richard Graves, *Robert Graves* (New York: Viking, 1990).

3. Alister E. McGrath, *A Life of John Calvin* (London: Basil Blackwell, 1990), 60–62.

4. J. B. Lightfoot, *St. Paul's Epistle to the Philippians,* repr. ed. (Grand Rapids: Zondervan, 1953), 270ff.

5. *Seneca the Philosopher,* 38.

6. Ibid., 77.

7. *History of Latin Literature*, 243ff.

2.8.3 EPICTETUS, PHILOSOPHER-SLAVE

The son of a Phrygian slave woman, Epictetus (c. 55–c. 135) was a slave in Rome where he served Nero's secretary. He was converted to Stoicism while attending the lectures of a noted Stoic, Musonius Rufus. He became a street teacher after buying his freedom in 89 but was forced to leave Rome in 94 when the Emperor Domitian expelled all philosophers, accusing them of republican sympathies. Epictetus took refuge in the northern Greece city of Nicopolis. There his school drew pupils from great distances. So influential was his rhetoric that it was said that "his hearers were forced to feel just what he would have them feel."

Flavius Arrian, one of his students, collected the sayings and teachings of his master. Four books survive. We have seen that Stoicism was a system of philosophy, metaphysics, and ethics. It was born in Greece in a time of great disaffection, founded "on a therapeutic view of human potential."[1] The goal was *eudaimonia* ("the profound happiness of the virtuous and wise"), which in large part was achieved through *ataraxia* ("freedom from emotional disturbance"). Epictetus insisted that, if we seek nothing that is not within our control, we will have serenity. This presupposes considerable self-sufficiency, which Christianity would view as symptomatic of depravity. Jesus said, "Without me you can do nothing." There is no Savior in Stoicism because each person is eminently self-sufficient. Even death is to be faced without being perturbed, whereas Paul maintained that Christians do sorrow but not as those who are without hope (1 Thess. 4:13). Epictetus was more religious than some of the earlier Stoics in that he posited the guidance of an overall Providence. From his standpoint, life is like a banquet and informed by the wisdom, "in nothing too much." The guests should take a little of everything but not very much of anything. The epigrammatic maxims and sayings of Epictetus as found in *Enchiridion* are well worth browsing.[2]

For helpful insight into Roman interaction with Christians, the best novel is Lew Wallace's *Ben Hur,* very widely read and popularized by movies in the 1930s and again in the 1950s starring Charlton Heston. General Wallace was a Civil War hero who was goaded by the noted atheist Robert Ingersoll to examine the claims of Christ and become an atheist. Wallace rather became a Christian and wrote this durable novel. His conversion was very much like those of Gilbert West and Frank Morison, who examined the evidence for the resurrection of Christ from a starting point of disbelief.[3] I would select this over Henryk Sienkiewicz's *Quo Vadis?* which is a closer study of the apostles of Christ.

---

1. Martha C. Nussbaum, *The Therapy of Desire: Theory and Practice in Hellenistic Ethics* (Princeton: Princeton University Press, 1994). Nussbaum surveys Epicurean, Skeptic, and Stoic attempts to offer a cure for the ills of their times.
2. Epictetus, *The Enchiridion,* in Gateway to the Great Books (Chicago: Britannica, 1963), 10:236ff. One is impressed that some Christians seem to hold a Stoic ideal of psychological "overcontrol."
3 Gilbert West, *The Resurrection of Jesus Christ* (New York: American Tract Society, 1929); Frank Morison, *Who Moved the Stone?* (London: Faber and Faber, 1930).

2.8.4 MARCUS AURELIUS, STOIC EMPEROR

To the gods I am indebted for having good grandfathers, good parents, a good sister, good teachers, good associates, good kinsmen and friends, nearly everything good. Further, I owe to the gods that I was not hurried into any office against any of them, though I had a disposition which, if opportunity had offered might have led me to do something of this kind; but through their favor, there never was such a concurrence of circumstances as put me to the trial.

—Marcus Aurelius
Meditations 1:17

The last of the Antonine line, which gave "the five good emperors" to Rome, was Marcus Aurelius (121–180). The Antonines were of Spanish origin.

At age eight he was made part of the Salian Brotherhood by the Emperor Hadrian, who designated him as his ultimate heir. He shared power with his adopted brother until his death in 169 and then faced a series of disintegrative disasters, including floods, fires, famines, and earthquakes, to say nothing of barbarian inroads from the north. He was absent much of the time fighting wars on the frontiers in which he was largely victorious. He loved Greece and was initiated into the Eleusinian mysteries. He did not care for Christians and often persecuted them. He died while on a military campaign on the Danube and was deified by the Roman populace.[1]

Under these pressures he became more devoted to Stoic philosophy and between battles began to put his thoughts into writing. These are his famous Meditations, which have been called "the most readable exposition of Stoic philosophizing that we possess."[2] He was a true patron of the arts and highly motivated to serve and probably comes closer to Plato's ideal of the "philosopher-king" than anyone in history. He writes clearly and crisply and celebrates divine Providence as over all. He urges: "Since it is possible that thou mayest depart from life this very moment, regulate every thought and act accordingly" (2.11).

Although frequently altruistic, he does not really rise above enlightened self-interest. He truly epitomizes the cultured and sophisticated pagan of Romans 2:1–16 who "passes judgment on others" and yet will not escape God's judgment. His calm nobility, his controlled passion, his competency and remarkable insights in many fields are impressive. This later Stoicism is much more religious and has definite affinity with Eastern religion, even the later strongly egoistic Buddhism.[3]

---

1. Michael Grant, *The Army of the Caesars* (New York: Scribner's, 1974), 245ff.
2. William Rose Benet, *Benet's Reader's Encyclopedia,* 3d ed. (New York: Harper and Row, 1987), 616.
3. *History of Philosophy,* 1:213, 216, 230.

2.8.5 VERGIL, GREATEST ROMAN OF THEM ALL

We save for last the greatest Roman writer and poet, Vergil (70 B.C.–19 B.C.), who was also a philosopher and gave to Rome her national epic. He was born into a well-to-do farmer's home near Mantua, between Milan and Venice in northern Italy.[1] He was brushed by Epicurean philosophy in his legal training, but he turned away from rhetoric and began to write poetry on his father's farm in the tumultuous time of the civil war.

His earliest pastoral writings, the *Eclogues,* brought him immediate fame and on occasion when they were read, audiences would stand and acclaim him as they did the emperor. The fourth *Eclogue* is prophetic and shares a deep longing for peace. Its famous lines about the "baby-boy" to come would almost seem to echo messianic prophecies like Isaiah 11:6a:

> Only do thou, at the boy's birth in whom
> The iron shall cease, the golden race arise . . .
> This glorious age shall begin. . . .

Constantine and Augustine both proclaimed this child to be Christ, which he obviously was not, but some Jewish apocalyptic influence near Vergil may well have shaped his fervent desire for a redeemer.[2] As Hadas well observed, "The sensitive spirit of Vergil was groping out of the grim hardness of contemporary reality toward loftier aspirations for Rome and the world."[3] His famous *Georgics* were farm poems modeled after Hesiod. Dryden felt they were the best poems by the best poet. The tenth *Eclogue* unveils Arcadia, or the golden age, which threads through the poems.

The Emperor Augustus (63 B.C.–A.D. 14) ultimately became Vergil's patron and *Pax Romana* the vital expression of his dream. His masterpiece, the *Aeneid,* asserts that the Augustan family was the special instrument of the gods to further Rome's unique destiny among the nations. In the first six books, Vergil consciously simulates aspects of the Odyssey, and in the last six books, the Iliad. The epic poem is a long national poem that places events and destiny on the largest possible canvas. Later we shall look closely at epic poems by Dante, Milton, and Goethe particularly. Vergil uses many Homeric themes and weaves into them the tales of the Argonauts and their hero Jason and his quest for the golden fleece. Dante took up these motifs and enhanced them thirteen hundred years later. Cyril Bailey has argued that the Aeneid "is an epic commentary on the lyric of the fourth *Eclogue* with all of its apocalyptic overtones."[4] This great and profound work "standardized the epic form embodied in Homer."[5]

Vergil was "just about mad" to attempt his epic and essentially bases the action on Aeneas's quest after the fall of Troy to find and establish a new Troy. In legend, at least, that task would be completed by Romulus and Remus at Rome. For ten years Aeneas sought his new city. It is interesting to note that the ancient Greeks and Romans remembered and reflected on the lessons of the fall of Troy one thousand years after it took place, while such is our cultural amnesia that we have forgotten all points made by Gibbon's probing study.[6]

In the Aeneid trilogy, each of the three books ends with a great tragedy: Queen Dido of Carthage with whom Aeneas fell in love is overthrown by Venus (4); Aeneas on the site of Rome receives his divinely wrought armor and the inevitable conflict and carnage are faced (8); and Turnus, who like Dido is an obstacle on the quest, dies indeed a horrible death (12).[7] In many ways Aeneas is disappointing in his moral ambivalence. Since the poem was not in final form, Vergil sent word from Greece that he wanted the work, which took him eleven years to write, destroyed, but Augustus intervened and had it edited for publication. It has been a classic ever since. The goal and objective of the work are too mundane and earthbound. The sensitively insightful François Fénelon (1651–1715) contrasted Vergil's idea of Elysium bliss with that of Holy Scripture:

> The poet promises no other reward in the next life to the purest and most heroic virtue than the pleasure of playing on the grass, or fighting on the sand, or dancing, or singing verses, or having horses, or driving chariots and possessing arms. Such is the greatest consolation that antiquity proposed to the human race.[8]

This of course is a theme that Dante developed from within a Christian perspective in his epic poem. But picture Vergil reading the *Aeneid* to the Emperor and his wife. He had an unusually effective speaking voice and Octavia was reported to have fainted as he read from book 4.[9] With all of his symbolism and fidelity to the traditional religions of Greece and Rome, Vergil has captured what Rome was and what her highest vision could be. Yet without supernatural divine revelation, the ceiling was low and visibility greatly limited.

Vergil (often seen as *Virgil*) represents the best of an unusual genre of fiction, the Latin novel. Those who wish to explore these works can find examples of both rhetoric and fiction in the S. J. Harrison translation *Oxford Readings in the Roman Novel*.[10] See also the older work by a team of scholars, *Greek and Roman Classics in Translation*.[11]

1. *Poets in a Landscape*, 45ff. A charming description.
2. The messianic anticipation and aspirations in Vergil are similar to what Jack Finegan called "the earliest expressions of the Messianic hope in history" in the ancient Egyptian Ipuwer's words: "He brings cooling to the flame. It is said he is the shepherd of all men. There is no evil in his heart. When his herds are few, he passes the day to gather them together, their hearts being fevered." See Finegan's *Light from the Ancient Past* (Princeton: Princeton University Press, 1946), 79. Similarly, Plato sighed for "a man or a god-inspired man" who would come to guide and show the way. Plato spoke of being out at sea without rudder to steer or star to guide and hoped that "the gods will give us a strong boat to sail in." At times what Augustine called the God-shaped gap in human life becomes more specifically a Christ-shaped gap.
3. *History of Latin Literature*, 144.
4. Cyril Bailey has given us the definitive study, *Religion in Virgil* (New York: Barnes and Noble, 1935).
5. Wes Callihan, "The Greatest Roman," *Credenda/Agenda,* 7.6: 23.
6. Stephen Bertman, "Modern Values and the Challenge of Myth," *Imprimis,* March 1993, 1ff.
7. J. William Hunt, "Labyrinthine Ways," in Harold Bloom, ed., *Virgil* (New York: Chelsea House, 1986), 119.
8. Ibid., 14. Fénelon was the eminent French preacher, rhetorician, Archbishop of Cambray, and advocate of Madame Guyon. His classic work in spirituality is *Christian Perfection* (New York: Harper, 1947).
9. "Biographical Note," *Virgil,* in Great Books of the Western World (Chicago: Encyclopedia, 1952), 13:vi.
10. Oxford: Oxford University Press, 1999.
11. Charles T. Murphy, ed. (New York: Longmans and Green, 1960).

CHAPTER THREE

Identifying Our Assets from the Middle Ages

See what has befallen Rome, once mistress of the world. She is worn down by great sorrows, by the disappearance of her citizens, by the attacks of her enemies, by numerous ruins. Thus we see brought to fulfillment what the prophet [Ezekiel] long ago pronounced on the city of Samaria.

—Gregory I in 594

The Bible was the most studied book of the Middle Ages.

—Beryl Smalley

The Roman Empire disintegrated over time. In the colossal disorder that accompanied the end of stable government, considerable barbarization took place. Some blamed Christianity for the degradation.[1] Out of this shattered world something new arose, however: what Professor William Bark calls "a frontier quality" and some emergent encouragement for the Christian faith.[2] What Cicero saw as "a picture fading because of old age" and Ambrose preached as "the twilight of the world," Augustine in *De civitate Dei* visualized as the opportunity for the release of a new dynamic. Critical economic problems and the scourge of Islam dampened Christian initiative. Yet learning was kept alive in monasteries. Faith enjoyed enormous vitality in such places as Ireland.

There were many luminous pages in this generally dark and drifting time.[3] Some writings from that era and a few about it show the darkness and light of these ages.

For basic orientation on the Middle Ages from a Christian perspective see William R. Cannon, *History of Christianity in the Middle Ages: From the Fall of Rome to the Fall of Constantinople.*[4] A recently revised classic is Norman F. Kantor, *The Civilization of the*

TABLE 2: Literature in Historical and Theological Context, the Incarnation to A.D. 500
A: Historical Events; B: Arts and Philosophy; C: Revelation and Preaching

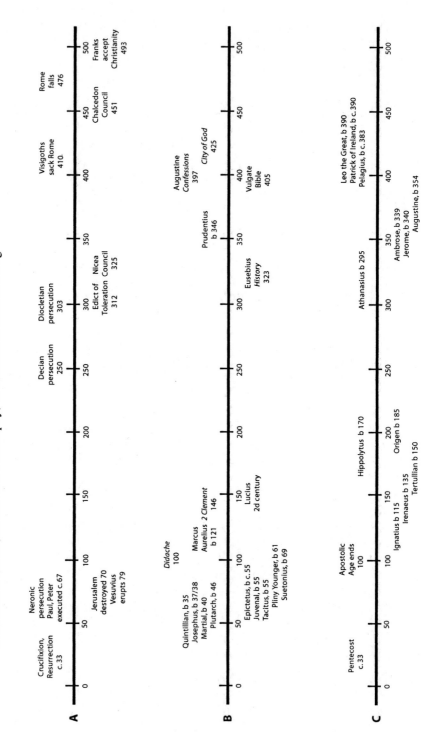

Middle Ages.[5] Michael Wood's *In Search of the Dark Ages*[6] examines archaeology related to the time. For maps and related aids, note Charles S. Anderson, *Augsburg Historical Atlas of Christianity in the Middle Ages and Reformation.*[7] For a survey emphasizing pivotal personalities, see G. S. M. Walker, *The Growing Storm: Sketches of Church History from 600 to 1350.*[8]

---

1. Robert L. Wilken, *The Christians As the Romans Saw Them* (New Haven, Conn.: Yale University Press, 1984).
2. William Carroll Bark, *Origins of the Medieval World* (Stanford, Calif.: Stanford University Press, 1958), 109.
3. Thomas Cahill, *How the Irish Saved Civilization* (New York: Doubleday, 1995). The liveliness of Patrick and Celtic Christianity, with its "migrating herds of philosophers," have not been sufficiently marked. For readers away from the wonderful museums and castles of Europe, the finest collection of Medieval artifacts and architecture in North America is at the Cloisters in Fort Tryon Park in New York City.
4. Nashville: Abingdon, 1960.
5. New York: Harper/Collins, 1993.
6. New York: Facts on File, 1987.
7. Minneapolis: Augsburg, 1967.
8. Grand Rapids: Eerdmans, 1961.

3.1 THE FATHERS

3.1.1 AUGUSTINE, FOREMOST FATHER

The greatest man who wrote in Latin.

—Alexander Souter

The incomparably greatest man between St. Paul and the reformer Martin Luther.

—Adolph von Harnack

Standing astride both the Greco-Roman and Christian worlds, Aurelius Augustine (354–430) has influenced every century since his remarkable life. His sometimes-tormented struggle was to yield himself totally to God and to the Bible. He also struggled to apply the doctrine of God to all aspects of life through a brilliant mind that was thoroughly conditioned by classic philosophy.

Augustine was born in North Africa where his pagan father and Christian mother, Monica (c. 331–387), encouraged his education. He was inflamed by reading Cicero (106 B.C.–43 B.C.) and became a teacher of rhetoric in Carthage, Rome, and Milan. He joined the Manichaean sect for awhile and lived a dissolute life. His lover and a son, Adeodatus, born out of wedlock, occasioned much guilt later in his life.[1] His mother prayed he would not go to Italy, but it was while he was there that he came under the influence of the eloquent Ambrose, bishop in Milan (339–397), and came to Christ.

His conversion is narrated in his powerful autobiographical *Confessions*. *Confessions* reads like one long prayer and paean of praise. This work explores the nature of evil, and Augustine learns the depths of his own depravity. Even the memory of a childhood theft of pears becomes a message to Augustine about the irrational impulse to sin. His radical conversion upon hearing a voice in the garden that commanded him to read the Word is one of the great conversion narratives of all time.[2] He was converted and baptized in 387.

When Augustine returned to North Africa, he established a monastic community and was ordained in 391. He was appointed bishop of Hippo in 395. Achieving considerable distinction as a preacher, Augustine wrote what must be seen as the first textbook in homiletics. In *De doctrina christiana,* he speaks of the preacher as rhetorician but insists on the priority of Scripture. Content is more important than form, but it is not all there is to the preacher's task. Book 4 is particularly valuable for its instruction on rhetoric in relation to Christian proclamation. Augustine is a superb model for the contextualization of the gospel in a cultural setting. We have 685 of Augustine's sermons, many of which he delivered in street clothes, sitting down, to a heterogeneous congregation in Hippo.

During his lifetime, the bishop of Hippo battled his former coreligionists among the Manichaeans, using as his starting point the effects of human depravity on the freedom of the will. With the super-moralistic Donatists, he debated the nature of the church, and with the self-saving Pelagians, he explained the nature of sin and salvation and the utter necessity of the redeeming grace of God.[3] *On the Trinity* remains one of the best explanations of the nature of the Godhead. Augustine saw participation in the universal church organization as indispensable to victorious Christian living and gave theological support for the centralized Episcopal structure that the medieval church was then assuming. Augustine thus is claimed by two wings of the church. He was more influential than any other past theologian in establishing the biblical theology of the sixteenth-century reformers, and he was more influential than any other churchman in establishing medieval ecclesiology.

B. B. Warfield argues that the Reformation was, in fact, "the triumph of Augustine's doctrine of grace over his doctrine of the church" in that his doctrine of the church and sacraments had not yet been thoroughly permeated by grace at the time of his passing.[4] His influence has been immense.

In *De civitate Dei (The City of God),* Augustine wrestles with the fall of Rome and argues that paganism, not Christianity, is responsible for the debacle. Rome was first sacked in 410 but then recovered. He started to write in 413 and lived to see the loss of the cornlands in North Africa to the Vandals in 428. His work is partly a magisterial philosophy of history, in which he seeks to justify the ways of God. John Burleigh shows Augustine's supreme dependence upon Scripture. Compensating for his earlier ignorance of God's Word, he now devotes himself to its exposition.[5]

In *De civitate Dei,* his master work, he shares in Books 1–10 the blasphemies and errors of pagan Rome that explain her demise. Then in Book 11 he introduces his own "tale of two cities"—Jerusalem and Babylon.[6] He starts with creation (in which his views are affected by neo-Platonism) and the fall of the angels (Books 11–12). The creation of humanity begins in 12.9 and then the fall in Book 14. The work becomes a masterful work of Christian apologetics and an exposition of scriptural *heilsgeschichte* ("salvation history").

In his interpretation of the apocalypse, he leans heavily on the lay Donatist theologian Tyconius and thereby moves away from the millennial approach to understanding end-time events.[7] In modern theological terms, Augustine developed an amillennialist interpretation of history. In Book 20 he does argue strongly for the second coming of Christ and a final judgment, but with facility he equates the visible, organized church with the kingdom of God. This means a partly realized eschatology, in which Satan is already chained by Christ's victory over sin and death.[8] He inveighs strongly for the resurrection of the body and argues that eternal punishment for the wicked is just, even it is difficult to accept.[9] Augustine stresses that God is the supreme Ruler over history. Burleigh relates:

> St. Augustine conducts a vigorous polemic against the theories of chance and fate, and vindicates at least the partial freedom of men, under the Providence of God. In making creatures rational and free, free even to disobey him, God extended the possibilities of His universe, but he did not abandon His eternal plan, or allow it to be frustrated by the rebellion of his creatures, . . . thereby giving to history a plan and a goal; not wholly disclosed it is true, but sufficiently revealed to give meaning to the course of events, and to give some kind of order to the apparently chaotic happenings of history.[10]

Augustine also wrote in *The City of God* about his belief that miracles were still taking place as evidence for the truth of the gospel (22:8–10). He includes reported resurrections from the dead.

In its totality, this towering work advances the premise of Hebrews 13:14: "Here we do not have an enduring city, but we are looking for the city that is to come."

1. The outstanding biographical study is Peter Brown, *Augustine of Hippo* (Berkeley: University of California, 1967). Augustine saw human beings as "agents of the Word of God to men" (p. 271).

2. See R. L. Ottley, *Studies in the Confessions of St. Augustine* (London: Robert Scott, 1919).

3. Augustine, *Augustine: Earlier Writings* (Philadelphia: Westminster, 1953). He argues that God's foreknowledge does not predetermine events (p. 173). Jean Bethke Elshtain's *Augustine and the Limits of Politics* (South Bend, Ind.: Notre Dame University Press, 1996) is another view of Augustine's view of sovereignty.

4. B. B. Warfield, *Calvin and Augustine* (Philadelphia: Presbyterian and Reformed, 1956), 383.

5. John H. S. Burleigh, *The City of God: A Study of Augustine's Philosophy* (London: Nisbet, 1949), 85, 90.

6. Johannes Van Oort, *Jerusalem and Babylon* (Leiden: E. J. Brill, 1991). Van Oort traces the philosophical sources of Augustine's two cities.

7. Mal Couch, gen. ed., *Dictionary of Premillennial Theology* (Grand Rapids: Kregel, 1996), 59.

8. Burleigh, *The City of God,* 142; Christopher Dawson, *St. Augustine* (New York: Meridian, 1957), 72ff.

9. Burleigh, *The City of God,* 147.

10. Ibid., 203.

3.1.2 JEROME, SCHOLAR-HERMIT

> The lamp of the world is extinguished, and it is the whole world which has perished in the ruins of this one city [on the sack of Rome in 410].

> Everyone thinks he can interpret the Bible. . . . They tear the Scriptures apart. . . . They do not even trouble to find out what the prophets and the apostles have meant, but they fit passages arbitrarily together to suit their own meaning, as if it were a splendid method of teaching, and not the worst, to corrupt the real meaning.

> —Jerome

The four "Latin fathers" of the church are considered to be Ambrose, Augustine, Gregory the Great, and Jerome. The most solitary of these leaders, Jerome (347–419) owes his place among them for his devotion to Scripture and the task of making the Bible universally available.

He was born and raised in the Julian Alps in what is now Slovenia. He mentions an earthquake, a nameless sister who was guilty of a heinous sin, and the slaves on his family estate. When the estate was overrun by Barbarian incursions, he went to Rome to study.[1] While there he was baptized. He traveled extensively doing research in Gaul (France) and then decided to live a solitary life on the coasts of Dalmatia. He copied manuscripts and wrote a commentary on Obadiah. Then he journeyed through the Middle East, spent time in Jerusalem, and lived as an austere hermit in the deserts of Chalcis near Antioch.

Eventually Jerome came again to Rome to be ecclesiastical secretary to Damasus I (305–384), the bishop of Rome and one of the first to assume the full primacy over the church that would characterize the medieval papacy. Damasus' great achievement was to encourage Jerome to replace the inferior translations of Scripture with a more precise and scholarly standard.

Jerome loathed the corruption that was infiltrating church government in Rome, but he was identified with it because of his position. When the Pope died, he was falsely accused of wrongdoing and had to flee. He went to Bethlehem, where he lived in a cave for thirty-four years. He wrote voluminously.

A contemporary of Augustine, Jerome was more the scholar. Augustine conceded to Jerome: "I have not as great a knowledge of the divine Scriptures as you have, nor could I have such knowledge as I see in you."[2] Jerome of course was a master of Latin and his Bible translation, the Vulgate, was the official Roman Catholic translation into modern times. Its stately cadences are reflected even in the King James English translation of 1611. Jerome was fluent in Greek and Hebrew and often supported his hermitic lifestyle by tutoring. We often wish the early fathers had written more on key points of theology and on customs in worship.[3]

Jerome's works on Scripture and his commentaries are of special value. His numerous letters afford rare insight into life and views at a crucial time. We sense in them something of Jonathan Swift's caustic and sharp satire. He joined Augustine in savage verbal battle against the one-eyed Welsh monk Pelagius, who denied original sin and had an unbiblical view of the human will's sovereignty. His *Concerning Famous Men* sketched the lives of various personalities. In this book he rails against Ambrose, "an upstart crow who is all bedraggled."[4]

His fine commentary on Daniel is a good place to begin reading.[5] He, as Augustine, moved from the millenarian viewpoint, but he quotes extensively from Hippolytus (170–236). Jerome does original and often unusual thinking on Daniel's "seventy weeks" (9:20–27), the Antichrist (9:26b–27), and the identification of the toes of clay and iron (2:43) with democracies.[6] Of interest are his comments on Christ's advent from Daniel 9:24–27 and his notes on the view of Hippolytus that the sixty-nine of the seventy "sevens" of Daniel 9 lead right up to Christ. The seventieth, he believed, will come at the end of history, with three and one-half years as a period for Elijah, three and one-half years for the Antichrist.[7] Despite Augustine's indifference, end-times interest did not fade.[8]

A vast literature appeared on eschatological themes during the Middle Ages. Jerome's commentary was a beginning point for that literature.

---

1. Robert Payne, *Fathers of the Western Church* (New York: Viking, 1951), 90ff. The best overall analysis of Jerome is J. N. D. Kelly, *Jerome* (New York: Harper, 1975).
2. Wilbur M. Smith, introduction to *Jerome's Commentary on Daniel,* by Jerome, trans. G. L. Archer (Grand Rapids: Baker, 1958), 7.
3. J. B. Lightfoot, gen. ed., *The Apostolic Fathers,* rev. ed. (Grand Rapids: Baker, 1980). See also Kirsopp Lake, ed., *The Apostolic Fathers,* in Loeb Classical Library (London: Heinemann, 1952). This edition provides both Greek and Latin texts.
4. *Fathers of the Western Church,* 118.
5. *Jerome's Commentary on Daniel,* Lightfoot trans., in *Apostolic Fathers.* Superb notes.
6. Ibid., 5.
7. Ibid., 103.
8. Bernard McGinn, *Visions of the End: Apocalyptic Traditions in the Middle Ages* (New York: Columbia University Press, 1979), 39. The centrality of eschatology is widely recognized but seldom addressed.

3.2 INTERPRETERS

3.2.1 DANTE, PEERLESS MEDIEVAL POET

Midway upon the journey of our life I found myself in a dark wood, where the right way was lost.

—*The Inferno,* canto 1.1

Love, who sends down your power from heaven
as the sun does its splendours
—for the greater the perfection of what its beams encounter,
the more its influence takes effect:
and just as it dispels darkness and cold, so do you, mighty Lord,
drive baseness from the heart.

—Dante Alighieri
Convivio (The Banquet)

Other than Thomas Aquinas, no one epitomizes the medieval spirit as Dante Alighieri (1265–1321). Born of an old Florentine family, he was educated by the Franciscans and began to write poetry before he was twenty years of age. As Geoffrey Chaucer (1342–1400) would shortly bring vernacular poetry into the English language, so Dante was the father of Italian literature. Some argue that he studied philosophy at Bologna and Padua and theology in Paris. He wrote *De monarchia* in Latin in which he makes a quite antipapal case for the separation of church and state. His earliest poetry praised the lovely Beatrice, who died in 1290 (his *La vita nuova* celebrates his "spiritual attachment" to her). He was then married and served in the Florentine army and achieved high office until he was exiled and lived in Verona and Ravenna.

Dante wrote movingly of his exile in *Convivio* but began planning his finest work, *Commedia* as early as 1292. Only much later did *Commedia* receive the name *Divine Comedy,* especially among Western Romantics. The actual writing was basically finished by 1315. This massive expression of medieval thought is allegorical and autobiographical, with Dante himself being his chief character. The action is set on Easter in the year 1300, when Dante is thirty-five years old. The epic poem describes Dante's journey through hell, purgatory, and paradise. The work is still widely read. In English the standard edition is by poet John Ciardi.[1] Gaining in popularity is a 1994 translation by Robert Pinsky, who was appointed poet laureate of the United States in 1997.[2]

The poet Vergil is Dante's guide through hell and purgatory, but his lost love Beatrice accompanies him through paradise.[3] The language usage of Cicero (106 B.C.–43 B.C.) and the philosophy of Anicius Manlius Severinus Boethius (c. 480–524) helped shape this precise and intricately symmetrical work.[4] Diagrams in the Great Books edition are invaluable for following the action.[5]

Many have been profoundly influenced by *Commedia*. The Baptist theologian Augustus Hopkins Strong (1836–1921) was inspired by Dante after he stumbled across the work on a summer vacation.[6]

The archetype for *Commedia* is the exodus of ancient Israel from Egyptian bondage. It begins with Dante lost in a dark wood and then finally entering the promised land, thus accounting for Dante's title, "poet of the desert."[7] The crossing of the Red Sea becomes, in the figurative language of the poem (Inf. 2.106–8), a picture of conversion and death to self.[8] Vergil personifies the wisdom that can lead the lost only so far. Dante inspects purgatory, where remaining sins are expiated, and limbo, the home for unbaptized infants. Several elements of his work owe more to medieval conceptions than to Scripture. The layout of hell and placement of its population are organized into levels and compartments around the seven deadly sins.[9] "Abandon hope, all you who enter here" says the sign above hell's gate. In fact, the entrance to the lower hell is guarded by rebellious angels so hideous that Vergil covered Dante's eyes so he would not see Medusa.

After probing into what sin is and does, the ascent to heaven begins in purgatory. Since forgiveness and pardon are offered to the penitent and believing, it is hard to understand the extrabiblical insistence on punishment. Interestingly, attention is given to the Antichrist in these regions, the lover of the whore (Revelation 17). Augustine's two cities influenced this conception, but even more obvious is the thinking of the apocalyptic Joachim of Fiore (c. 1135–1202) on the rise of the Antichrist and his defeat at the Second Coming of Christ (cantos 32 and 33).[10]

While Dante's consummate skills are in view in this third section, we regret that the final canto concludes with a prayer to the Virgin. He does liken the soul's redemption to the metamorphosis of a butterfly from the lowly worm (*Purg.* 10.121–29). Redemption is also clearly through Christ and his atoning work on the cross (Para. 8) called by some "the finest poetic expression of atonement theology ever written."[11] Here truly is the triumph of divine love. Dante sees all vice as due to some defect in love, but here God's lavish love in Christ is celebrated with such as Rahab elevated to heaven as a prime trophy of the grace of God (*Para.* 9.115–26). Canto 11, in which he meets Francis of Assisi, is exceedingly rich. Clearly unconverted Vergil could be no guide in this celebration of ultimate truth, but Dante, as a master of language and a master of the dramatic situation is God-centered.

---

1. John Ciardi prepared the Mentor Classic series (New American Library) of *The Inferno* in 1954, a small paperback by which generations of college literature students were introduced to Dante. Ciardi's translations of *The Inferno* and *The Paradiso*, returned to print in 1996 (New York: Modern Library).

2. Robert Pinsky has had the best success to date in translating the poetic feel intended by Dante, as well as the words. He published a critical parallel text (English and Italian) edition of *The Inferno* in 1994. See *The Inferno: A New Verse Translation* (London: Dent, 1994).

3. George Holmes, *Dante,* in *Pastmasters* (New York: Hill and Wang, 1980), 40.

4. Ibid., 41.

5. Dante Alighieri, *The Divine Comedy,* in Great Books (Chicago: Britannica, 1952), 159, 161, 163.

6. Augustus Hopkins Strong, *The Great Poets and Their Theology* (Philadelphia: Judson, 1897), 105–55.

7. Giuseppe Mazzotta, *Poet of the Desert* (Princeton, N.J.: Princeton University Press, 1979), 4f. A fine study.

8. John Freccero, "The River of Death, *Inferno* II, 108," in *The World of Dante* (Toronto: University of Toronto Press, 1966), 25f. Dante's Marianism is medieval, but he believes that only Christ was born without sin (34.115). He holds a very high view of scriptural inspiration, declaring that "though there are many reporters of the words of God, yet there is only One who tells them what to write, even God Himself, who has condescended to reveal His will to us through the pens of many writers." G. S. M. Walker, *The Growing Storm* (Grand Rapids: Eerdmans, 1961), 242. Alan Jones's Jungian interpretation of Dante in *The Soul's Journey* (San Francisco: Harper, 1996) is silly.

9. Henry Fairlie, *The Seven Deadly Sins Today* (Washington: New Republic, 1978). This is the best treatment I have read.

10. See Marjorie Reeves's studies, *The Influence of Prophecy in the Later Middle Ages* (Oxford: Oxford University Press, 1969); and *Joachim of Fiore and the Prophetic Future* (New York: Harper Torchbooks, 1977).

11. E. Beatrice Batson, "Dante: A Poet to Discover," *Christianity Today*, 24 September 1965, 6ff.; also John Ciardi, "700 Years After: The Relevance of Dante," *Saturday Review of Literature*, 15–22 May 1965, 16ff. Another important Dante scholar was none other than the English mystery and inspirational writer Dorothy L. Sayers (see 9.4.7). Her most popular translations were for the Penguin Classics series (1949, 1960).

3.2.2 THOMAS AQUINAS, ANGELIC DOCTOR

> You call him a Dumb Ox; I tell you that the Dumb Ox will bellow so loud that his bellowing should fill the world.
>
> —Albertus Magnus of young Thomas

> By preference you should seek knowledge in small streamlets, rather than plunging at once into the full ocean. . . . Speak sparingly. . . . Guard the integrity of your conscience. Never give up praying. . . . Be charitable to everyone, without intrusiveness or undue familiarity. . . . Avoid wandering about outside your convent. Make a mental note of everything good that you may hear. . . . Always try to store as much as you can in the chamber of memory.
>
> —Thomas to a young novice

"The metaphysical poet" and "angelic doctor of the church," Thomas Aquinas (1224–1274) was born near Naples, where he attended the University. Seventh and youngest son in an illustrious family, he resisted his family's desire that he become a soldier and entered the Dominican Order and headed for Paris. His angry family kidnapped and imprisoned him for over a year, then allowed him to return to Paris to study under German philosopher Albertus Magnus (1200–1280).[1] Teaching alternately at Paris and Italy, Thomas began to write significant works. In *Summa contra gentiles,* he defends Christian truth against arguments of pagans, Muslims, and Jews. *Summa theologica* summarizes what can be known about God. He was a gifted preacher and thorough exegete. He emphasized the primacy of the senses.[2]

Although he knew neither Hebrew nor Greek, his biblical studies were driven by a conviction that canonical Scripture is inerrant.[3]

Long in tenuous health, Thomas became ill and died on his way to the Second Council of Lyons. While he only lived to age forty-nine, he was a monumental figure.

Thomism, or the theological and philosophic synthesis of Thomas Aquinas, has long been the official position of the Roman Catholic Church and, until relatively recently, has commanded the primary loyalty of Roman Catholic thinkers.

Dante's *Commedia,* the Gothic cathedral, and Thomas's *Summa theologica* represent the best expressions of the medieval spirit.[4] Until this renaissance in the twelfth century, Plato and Augustine prevailed. Albertus Magnus spent his life seeking to make Aristotle "intelligible to the Latin West," and Thomism established Aristotelian philosophy in the church.

Fundamentally, it is Thomistic Aristotelianism and the church's interpretation of Thomist theology that now separates the Roman Catholics from the Protestant communions. Aquinas baptized Aristotle and built a system of thought expressed in the *Summa theologica.* In the Great Books edition this work consists of two massive volumes of over eighteen hundred pages. The beginner will most profit from reading the first section, "Treatise on God." While Norman Geisler has made a very spirited case that evangelicals should pay more attention to Thomistic theological formulations, he stands against the vast majority of evangelical thinkers, including E. J. Carnell, Gordon Clark, Os Guiness, Carl F. H. Henry, Arthur Holmes, Francis Schaeffer, and Cornelius Van Til. Most Protestant theologians appreciate the major thrusts in Aquinas, but feel that the less rationalistic and more biblical approach is through Augustine.[5] Thomism seems to be of a "closed (Aristotelian) system" while Augustinian theology cherishes an "open (Platonic idealist) system." William Cannon expresses the difference:

> The radical dichotomy between nature and grace established by Augustine is really set aside by Aquinas. Redemption seems more a supplementation of creation, not its transformed restoration. Reason and faith stand harmoniously together. Faith complements reason and goes far beyond it, but it never contradicts it. Thomas supplements his natural theology (philosophy) with a full-scale presentation of the body of revealed truth.[6]

For Thomas, the existence of God and the immortality of the soul are demonstrable through the laws of logic and God's revelation. Humans cannot know God directly, but they can know him by analogy and by negation. People can know what is God partly by knowing what is non-God. It is possible, he believed, for Christian apologists to make definitive *a priori* arguments to prove God's existence and many of his attributes.[7] Certainly, Aquinas concedes, some aspects of the doctrines of the Trinity and salvation are beyond unaided reason, but God has given what we need to understand these things by direct revelation in Scripture.[8] For Thomas Aquinas, the fall in Eden meant the loss of the golden bridle but did not touch the rational essence of the reasoning individual. The roots of Reformation theology's insistence on human depravity are right here.

1. G. K. Chesterton, *Saint Thomas Aquinas: "The Dumb Ox"* (Garden City, N.Y.: Doubleday Image, 1956). See also the biography by Chesterton, *Saint Francis of Assisi* (New York: Doubleday Image, 1989).

2. Thomas Aquinas, *Commentary on St. Paul's Epistle to the Ephesians* (Albany, N.Y.: Magi, 1966).

3. G. S. M. Walker, *The Growing Storm* (Grand Rapids: Eerdmans, 1961), 207.

4. Allan Temko, *Notre Dame of Paris* (New York: Viking, 1952). Umberto Eco's *Art and Beauty in the Middle Ages* (New Haven, Conn.: Yale University Press, 1986) is also helpful. Eco vividly depicts monastic life in his medieval mystery *The Name of the Rose* (San Diego, Calif.: Harcourt Brace Jovanovich, 1983).

5. Norman L. Geisler, *Thomas Aquinas: An Evangelical Appraisal* (Grand Rapids: Baker, 1991).

6. *History of Christianity in the Middle Ages*, 259. Even on such an issue as the meaning of wisdom, Augustine and Aristotle differed in approach. Compare in Kieran Conley, *A Theology of Wisdom* (Dubuque, Iowa: Priory, 1963), 13ff. See also, Etienne Gilson, *Reason and Revelation in the Middle Ages* (New York: Charles Scribner's, 1938).

7. An example of the argument from design is Michael J. Behe, *Darwin's Black Box: The Biochemical Challenge to Evolution* (New York: Free, 1996). Behe looks to biochemical complexity. James Orr and John Baillie reason that Hume and Kant have not negated the validity of theistic proofs.

8. For more secular analysis of these issues, see John Herman Randall Jr., *The Role of Knowledge in Western Religion* (Boston: Beacon, 1965); also Edwin A. Burtt, *Types of Religious Philosophy* (New York: Harper, 1951), 91ff.

3.2.3 BERNARD OF CLAIRVAUX, CHRIST-MYSTIC

Do you not understand that the Church triumphs more abundantly over the Jews in converting them than in putting them to the sword? Therefore we utter our universal prayer for the unbelieving Jews, uttered incessantly in the Church from the rising of the sun to the going down of the sun, that God shall take away the veil from their hearts and lead them out of darkness that they may be led into the glorious light of the truth. Unless, therefore, the Church believes that they will enter the fold, though now unbelieving, how vain and superfluous it were to offer prayers for them. But to kill them—this is a monstrous doctrine, a foul counciling, contrary to the prophets, hostile to the apostles, destructive of piety and grace—a damned harlot of a doctrine impregnated with the very spirit of falsehood, conceiving anguish and bringing forth iniquity!

—Bernard
Epistolae 19

Sometimes called "the last of the fathers," Bernard of Clairvaux (1090–1153) wielded amazing power as "the pope-maker" in the medieval church during his life. An aristocrat from Burgundy, he was raised under strict discipline in a castle near Dijon. He sought the monastic life and when still in his early twenties was appointed Abbot among the Cistercians (the white monks) at what would be called Clairvaux. He was a gifted preacher.[1] He would often give a public invitation after preaching in which he called for the raising of hands in response. A beautiful "Christ-mysticism" (to use Adolph Deissman's fine turn of phrase) tinctured his thinking. "To be poor with Christ" was his goal.[2]

Bernard stood in a pietistic lineage that was wary of philosophers. Anselm, Augustine, Jerome, and Tertullian stood in this van, as would Thomas à Kempis, Roger Bacon, and Ramon Llull.[3] This was the "I believe in order to understand" succession, in contrast to the "I understand in order to believe" tradition. This was one of several issues separating Bernard from the contemporary philosopher Peter Abelard (1079–1142).[4] Bernard's standing within the church and the raw political power he wielded through his itinerant preaching can be seen in how he anathematized immoral kings and popes with impunity. A darker side to his theology and authority is shown in the fact that he almost single-handedly brought about the bloody Second Crusade.[5] The view of Bernard within the church may be reflected in Dante, whose vision of the highest paradise was introduced by Bernard of Clairvaux.

Bernard was the conservative lynchpin in the twelfth century, who vigorously fought the rising worship phenomenon of adoring portraits of the saints. He opposed exaggerated papal authority (the first steps toward the doctrine of infallibility) and the notion of Mary's immaculate conception. Abelard was his antagonist, embodying the pure rationalism Bernard discerned as exceedingly dangerous. Abelard said: "A doctrine is not to be believed because God has said it, but because we are convinced by reason that it is so."[6]

Although Abelard's scandalous seduction of Heloise (and his consequent castration by a mob consisting of her relatives) was odious to Bernard, it was Abelard's *moral influence* theory of the atonement that Bernard condemned as heresy at the Council of Sens in 1141. Abelard believed the atonement provided the model and motivation to convince sinners to be holy before God. Bernard stood fast by Anselm's *satisfaction* theory. Only a God-man could make the satisfaction demanded by justice by which a person is saved.[7] Bernard's theology of love is a worthy theological and philosophical theme to follow, and James M. Houston has gathered various of his writings on this subject in a lovely edition most worthy of serious contemplation.[8]

Bernard is one thinker with whom the Reformers and their children among the Puritans felt a particularly deep affinity.

---

1. Denis Meadows, *A Saint and a Half: Abelard and St. Bernard of Clairvaux* (New York: Devin-Adair, 1963), 114. Among several collections of his sermons are Bernard of Clairvaux, *On the Song of Songs* (Spencer, Mass.: Cistercian, 1971) and *Sermons on Conversion* (Kalamazoo, Mich.: Cistercian, 1981).

2. James M. Houston, introduction to *Bernard of Clairvaux, The Love of God* (Portland, Ore.: Multnomah, 1983), xvii.

TABLE 3: Literature in Historical and Theological Context, 500 to 1500

A: Historical Events; B: Arts and Philosophy; C: Revelation and Preaching

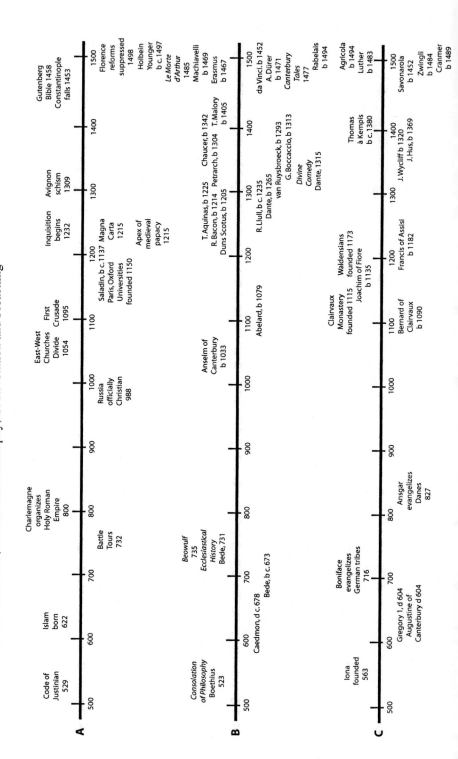

3. Etienne Gilson, *Reason and Revelation in the Middle Ages* (New York: Scribner's, 1938), 12, 88, 90. According to Gilson, Martin Luther must be seen in the succession of Tertullian, Anselm, Bernar, and Thomas à Kempis (93). On Ramon Llull, a little-known but remarkable Spanish missionary to Islam, see Mark D. Johnson, *The Evangelical Rhetoric of Ramon Llull: Lay Learning and Piety in the Christian West Around 1300* (New York: Oxford University Press, 1996).
4. For a view of the distinctions between Bernard and scholastic thought, read Bernard's "Sermon for the Feast of Pentecost," in *Reason and Revelation.*
5. Robert Payne, *The Fathers of the Western Church* (New York: Viking, 1951), 239.
6. Ibid., 253. "To know Jesus and Him crucified is the sum of my philosophy," Bernard insisted.
7. Anselm, *Proslogium; Monologium; and Cur Deus Homo?* (LaSalle, Quebec: Open Court, 1948). For analysis of Anselm, see John D. Hannah, "Anselm on the Doctrine of the Atonement," *Bibliotheca Sacra,* October–December 1978, 333.
8. Houston, introduction to *Bernard of Clairvaux.* The hymns "Jesus the Very Thought of Thee" and "O Sacred Head, Now Wounded" are attributed to Bernard.

3.3 STORYTELLERS

3.3.1 BEOWULF, OLD ENGLISH EPIC POEM

In a place far from libraries I have often read Beowulf for pleasure.
—K. Sisam

Beowulf is the picture of a whole civilization, of the Germania which Tacitus describes. The main interest which the poem has for us is thus not a purely literary interest. Beowulf is an important historical document.
—Archibald Strong

In the epoch of Beowulf a Heroic Age more wild and primitive than that of Greece is brought into touch with Christendom, with the Sermon on the Mount, with Catholic theology and ideas of Heaven and Hell. Beowulf is almost a Christian knight.
—R. W. Chambers

Standing like *The Song of Roland* in eleventh-century France or *Poema del Cid* in twelfth-century Spain, *Beowulf* is a primary myth touching Scandinavian Vikings and Great Britain from the seventh century. Roman rule effectively ended in Britain in 410, and Germanic Angles, Saxons, and Jutes filled the power vacuum. In 597 Pope Gregory the Great sent a prior named Augustine (d. 604) to be a missionary to Britain and the first archbishop of Canterbury.

At about this time a dominant Anglo-Saxon king in the south of Britain, Ethelbert, was converted after he married a Christian German princess. Christianity in Britain is early on represented in the poet Caedmon (d. c. 678). Caedmon was apparently an illiterate herdsman who entered a monastery where he was educated and wrote scriptural narratives in alliterative verse. Caedmon's "The Dream of the Rood" is a deeply moving alliterative poem on the true cross.[1]

A monk named Bede (c. 673–735) wrote the first history of the early English church. Bede's sermons made a deep impression on northern England.

Beowulf was carried by the Viking invaders from Denmark and reflects the earliest influence of Christianity upon the Vikings.[2] Viking raids began in 786 and continued for several hundred years throughout England, Scotland, and Ireland. The only original manuscript of the Beowulf stories is in the British Museum and dates from about 1000.

The Danes, as all the Vikings, were a violent people who first heard the gospel from English missionaries to Germany and other travelers.[3] The poet in *Beowulf* certainly has a Christian slant. It would seem that Beowulf is himself a Christian.[4] Beowulf is the nephew of King Hygelac in southern Sweden. He sails with comrades to challenge Grendel the monster, who is plaguing King Hrothgar of Denmark. Beowulf lives in a grim world, but his people are hardy.[5] Beowulf bests Grendel but Grendel's mother comes to avenge her son. Beowulf charges into the demon-populated pond and decapitates her. In the end Beowulf dies of his wounds. The narrative is interspersed with long speeches at feasts, including the "Sermon of Hrothgar." In what may be the moral of the story, Hrothgar warns Beowulf of pride and arrogance and undue violence (lines 1700–84).[6]

The poem has a simple static structure and consists of 3200 alliterative lines. The earliest surviving copy was written in Old English (Anglo-Saxon). The monsters are to be seen as the foes of God and are called "the offspring of Cain." The modern scholar of Middle English and fantasy writer J. R. R. Tolkien has given a spirited analysis of the monsters.[7] Christian elements are stronger in "The Dream of the Rood" or "Havelock the Dane," but those stories are from centuries later. The issue is raised as to whether Beowulf's theological accommodation to pagan culture allows it to be considered a truly Christian story. Did the poet spread a Christian veneer over the tales for his own purposes? He gives full play to the ancient ways but supplies a decisive overlay of Christian influence.[8]

---

1. A variety of translations of *Beowulf* are available in any fine bookstore, but finding interesting and well-executed translations of other pre-Chaucer medieval literature can be difficult, especially translations that capture well the feelings the author was conveying. One worth looking for, which introduces several of the authors we have looked at, from the Romans through the medieval poets, is *Latin Literature: A Book of Readings*. This anthology ranges from Cicero, Livy, and Pliny to The Vulgate, Bede, Caedmon, and others (Prospect Heights, Ill.: Waveland, 1993).

2. I think the best in its field is Gwyn Jones, *A History of the Vikings* (New York: Oxford University Press, 1968).

3. V. Raymond Edman, *The Light in Dark Ages* (Wheaton, Ill.: Van Kampen, 1949), 218ff. Of course the prime history of missions is Kenneth Scott Latourette, *History of the Expansion of Christianity*, 7 vols. (Grand Rapids: Zondervan, 1937). For some serious evangelical caveats on Latourette, see John D. Hannah, "Kenneth Scott

Latourette As Trailblazer—A Critical Evaluation," *Grace Theological Journal* 2, no. 1 (spring 1981): 3–32. Don't forget a wonderful study by the Oxford don who was most in his element in this period: C. S. Lewis, *The Discarded Image: An Introduction to Medieval and Renaissance Literature* (Cambridge: Cambridge University Press, 1964). The most recent edition of this book of which we are aware is in 1976.

4. Michael Alexander, ed. and trans., *Beowulf* (New York; Penguin, 1973), 18.

5. For some sense of the ruggedness of the Vikings, see Jane Smiley, *The Greenlanders* (New York: Knopf, 1988); also *Njal's Saga* (New York: New York University Press, 1955). These books mirror Icelandic life and struggle.

6. Fred C. Robinson, "Apposed Word Meanings and Religious Perspectives," in *Beowulf: Modern Critical Interpretations* (New York: Chelsea House, 1987), 84ff. Beowulf dies from wounds received in battle.

7. Clyde S. Kilby, *Tolkien and the Silmarillion* (Wheaton: Harold Shaw, 1976). A helpful guide to this complex alternate universe.

8. Ibid., 108–9. *Beowulf* is considered the most important extant Anglo-Saxon literature now in our possession.

3.3.2 CHAUCER, CANTERBURY TALES

Old Chaucer shall, for his facetious style,
Be read, and prais'd by warlike Britains, while
The sea enriches, and defends their Isle.
—John Evelyn, 1685

Chaucer will, no doubt, be admir'd as long as the English tongue has a being; and the changes that have happen'd in our language have not hinder'd his works, outliving their contemporary monuments of brass or marble.
—John Oldmixon, 1712

Picking up the journey-motif of the *Odyssey* and Dante's *Commedia,* Geoffrey Chaucer (1342–1400) has given us one of the truly charming legacies of the late Middle Ages in *Canterbury Tales.* He also wrote many short poems and translations, as well as the elegant poem of courtly love *Troylus and Cryseyde,* at a time when he was influenced by the Italian writer Giovanni Boccaccio (1313–1375) and the Roman philosopher Boethius. His father was a vintner and saw to it that his son was well-educated. He was fluent in Latin, French, and Italian. Chaucer served as a page in a noble family when he was young and went on to key diplomatic and economic positions in both the private and public sectors.[1] He was a justice of the peace, a member of Parliament from Kent, and held a key forestership. A lawsuit accusing him of abduction and rape *(raptus)* was settled out of court. He was buried in Westminster Abbey in what is today called "Poets' Corner."[2]

Chaucer has been called "the Father of English poetry," and stylistically the Chaucerian roundel was a major adaptation of the French poetic pattern. Chaucer's verse was immensely popular among the emerging English middle-class in the late Middle Ages. This was the exhausting time of the Hundred Years' War with the French, an era of intrigue and confusion when the manor system flourished. Bubonic plague, "the black death," decimated England in 1348–49, and the Peasant Revolt destabilized the nation in 1381. Drunkenness was a severe problem. Chaucer's miller, summoner, and cook all have a weakness for alcohol.[3] In the prologue, Chaucer describes a gathering of twenty-nine persons who embark upon a pilgrimage to Canterbury Cathedral and the shrine memorializing Thomas à Becket who was martyred there in 1170. Chaucer commenced this work in 1387, the year his wife, Philippa, died. Perhaps he made such a pilgrimage.

The work was never finished, but what we have follows the scheme of the agreement of the wayfarers to tell stories as they journey along. "The Knight's Tale" has been called "the finest metrical romance in English."[4] Chaucer regales us with comedy in the five romances of the deaf wife of Bath. All of the characters are in the emerging middle-class. Their dilemmas frequently involve money and its uses.[5] The entire work could be a sort of commentary on the "seven deadly sins."

Although ostensibly on a religious quest, these characters are not very spiritually minded. The exceptions are the poor parson and possibly the plowman. The time is permeated with religious ferment. John Wycliffe, "morning star of the Reformation" (1330–1384), and his traveling preachers, the Lollards, have upset society. Is the parson a Lollard? Chaucer seemed to sympathize with them.[6] Some light may be shed on these issues.[7] The parson is "a good shepherd and no mercenari." Different from all of the others, "The Parson's Tale" is really a treatise on doctrine. He gets under the skin of some by rebuking swearing. His "meditation" uses many quotes from Scripture and the Fathers. He is clear on the meaning of the death of Jesus for our sins and concludes his tale and Chaucer's work with "the sight of the perfect knowledge of God." What a description of a faithful servant of the Christ:

> There was a good man of religion, too,
> A country parson, poor, I warrant you;
> But rich he was in holy thought and work. . . .
> Who Christ's own gospel truly sought to preach;
> Devoutly his parishioners would he teach.
> He had no thirst for pomp or reverence,
> Nor made himself a special, spiced conscience,
> But in Christ's own lore, and His apostles twelve
> He taught, but first he followed it himself.[8]

The life of a fifteenth-century woman is traced in *Memoirs of a Medieval Woman: The Life and Times of Margery Kempe* by Louise Collis.[9] Kempe leaves her husband and fourteen children to make pilgrimage through Europe to the Holy Land to expiate a secret sin. The author's conception of people and places is well-researched, but the heroine's views are convoluted and bizarre.

---

1. Donald R. Howard, *Chaucer: His Life, His Works, His World* (New York: Dutton, 1987), 13. The standard. Another interesting work is Christopher Cannon, *The Making*

of Chaucer's Language: A Study of Words, Cambridge Studies in Medieval Literature (Cambridge: Cambridge University Press, 1998).

2. Ibid., 317ff. The Great Books volume gives both middle and modern English. For something "state of the art," see Harold Bloom's *Geoffrey Chaucer* and other works in the Bloom's Major Poets series (Philadelphia: Chelsea House, 1999).

3. Edwin J. Howard, *Geoffrey Chaucer* (New York: Twayne, 1964), 31.

4. Ibid., 130. A delightful edition with illustrations by Rockwell Kent (Garden City, N.J.: Garden City, 1934).

5. Ruth Nevo, "Motive and Mask in the General Prologue," in *The General Prologue to Canterbury Tales* (New York: Chelsea House, 1988), 11: "Money is the touchstone to which each of these characters is brought."

6. Howard, *Geoffrey Chaucer*, 37. Wycliffe, an Oxford scholar, sponsored the first English Bible translation. His Lollard Movement applied the authority of Scripture to all of life.

7. Douglas C. Wood, *The Evangelical Doctor: John Wycliffe and the Lollards* (Welwyn, England: Evangelical, 1984).

8. Geoffrey Chaucer, "Prologue," in *Canterbury Tales*, Garden City ed., 15–16.

9. New York: Harper Colophon, 1964.

3.3.3 THE ARTHURIAN LEGEND, PERENNIAL STORY OF VIRTUE

> And Arthur and his knighthood for a space
> Were all one will, and thro' that strength the King
> Drew in the petty princedoms under him,
> Fought, and in twelve battles overcame
> The heathen hoardes, and made a realm and reign'd.
>
> —Alfred Tennyson
> *Idylls of the King*

The Arthurian cycle probably dates to the twelfth century and uses Celtic, Welsh, and other sources. Arthur was a historical Celtic ruler who lived in Wales and after battle was carried to Glastonbury, Somerset in England to die and be buried.[1] Glastonbury was traditionally where Joseph of Arimathea planted a church and his blossoming staff. In legend, Arthur is married to Guinevere and proves his right to be king by drawing the magical sword Excalibur from the stone. Merlin, a magician, is his advisor. The holy grail—the cup Jesus used in the Last Supper—is the object of their quest. Galahad, son of Lancelot, finds the coveted artifact.

The first to collect this material was Sir Thomas Malory (1405–1471). His work is viewed as the first narrative romance in English. William Caxton, the first English printer, published it in 1485. Malory was a member of Parliament who fell from favor, finishing *Le Morte d'Arthur* ("The Death of Arthur") in prison, where he died. Particularly fine is Malory's treatment of Sir Galahad. Popular editions are numerous,[2] and Roger Lancelyn Green's *Sir Lancelot of the Lake* is especially apt for young people.[3] "Sir Gawain and the Green Knight" is also in this cycle. Gawain was Arthur's favorite cousin. This material is part of the identity of those who speak English, particularly those of Celt and Anglo-Saxon heritage.

Tales of Robin Hood in Sherwood Forest near Nottingham are also part of this heritage, Robin representing the disenfranchised, as Arthur and his knights recall the lives of the landed classes.[4] Many writers have used the Arthurian Legend as a base. Tennyson's *Idylls of the King* is worthy of notice. Tennyson somewhat sanitizes the stories, making Arthur an unexampled paragon.[5] Edmund Spenser (1552–1599) centered *The Faerie Queene* around Arthur. Chaucer was his inspiration, and he was thoroughly Protestant in his outlook.

T. H. White, the delightful twentieth-century American writer, produced a prose adaptation, beginning with *The Sword in the Stone*. He finds parallels between the sixth-century milieu and the twentieth-century; in both the motto seems to be "Might makes right." White revels in Arthurian valor, honesty, goodness, and loyalty. He said: "I don't much believe in the modern theory that the whole object of life is gratified desire."[6] The story of Tristan and Iseult, which Malory includes, is an enthralling romance. It is the basis of one of Wagner's great operas by that name and a lovely poem by Matthew Arnold.[7]

Some of the finest research into medieval life and experience is being done by scholarly writers of mystery novels of suspense. Peter Tremayne in his "Sister Fidelma Mysteries" sets his stories in Celtic history. The late Ellis Peters's Brother Cadfael mysteries (played by Derek Jacobi in the Public Television series) is set in western England and Wales. Also authentic are the works of P. C. Doherty, who also writes under the names Paul Harding and Edward Marston. Doherty's *Satan's Fire* is a medieval mystery featuring Hugh Corbett that touches the Norman-Anglo-Saxon tensions in the days of Edward I of England (1272–1307). Doherty's C. L. Grace series is another good series.[8]

---

1. A truly magnificent contemporary novel tracing the Christian history of England is Donna Fletcher Crow, *Glastonbury: The Novel of Christian England* (Wheaton: Crossway, 1992). Book 3 is devoted to Arthurian (pre-Anglo-Saxon) England.
2. A solid edition is Elizabeth Lodor Merchant, ed., *King Arthur and His Knights* (Philadelphia: John C. Winston, 1957).
3. London: Purcell, 1966.
4. George Cockburn Harvey, ed., *Robin Hood* (Philadelphia: John C. Winston, 1957). Subject of many movies.
5. Alfred Tennyson, *Selected Poetry,* in "Twelve Books" series (New York: Modern Library, 1951), 320ff.
6. T. H. White, *The Sword in the Stone* (New York: Putnam, 1939). This features his "The Once and Future King."
7. Matthew Arnold, *The Poems of Matthew Arnold* (Oxford: Oxford University Press, 1924), 126–47.
8. Some titles in Doherty's mystery list are *Satan's Fire* (New York: St. Martin's, 1995); C. L. Grace, *The Eye of God* (New York: St. Martin's, 1994); and Edward Marston, *The Merry Devils* (New York: St. Martin's, 1989). See also Ellis Peters, *The Confession of Brother Haluin* (New York: Mysterious, 1988); and Peter Tremayne, *Absolution by Murder* (New York: St. Martin's, 1994).

CHAPTER FOUR

Tapping the Vitality of the Renaissance and Reformation

All over the world, as if on a given signal, splendid talents are stirring and conspiring together to revive the best learning.

—Erasmus, 1517

The end of the fifteenth century is generally seen as the end of the Middle Ages, although the Italian Renaissance or awakening already was well under way. From 1270 the medieval center had been in collapse, and a new humanism was taking its place.[1] Soon would come what John Calvin called *Europae concussio,* the shattering of the Reformation. This is now a time of population surge, eschatological uneasiness, and new classical learning. Painting turned from Gothic forms, and music was written with broad appeal. Interest in drama surged. European cultures absorbed all things Italian. The long medieval winter was over. The merchant class and commercial interests burgeoned. The availability of and interest in all kinds of learning exploded, and exploration and colonization became a passion among governments.[2]

Yet as Francis Schaeffer has argued, the new humanism tended to install in the collective Western worldview an anthropocentrism—a philosophy of autonomous humankind. Thomas Aquinas opened the door for autonomous humanism upon which the Enlightenment later built its structures of unbelief and rebellion. Schaeffer argues that nothing is autonomous apart from the Lordship of Jesus Christ and the authority of Scripture.[3]

A **choice analysis** of the Renaissance has been assembled by John Hale of the University of London in *The Civilization of Europe in the Renaissance.*[4] Significant soundings from a contemporary account are in Emmanuel Le Roy Ladurie, *The Beggar and the Professor: A Sixteenth-Century Family Saga.*[5] Unusual and vivid. A newer study is William Manchester's *A World Lit Only by Fire: The Medieval Mind and the Renaissance.*[6]

77

TABLE 4: Literature in Historical and Theological Context, 1500 to 1700
A: Historical Events; B: Arts and Philosophy; C: Revelation and Preaching

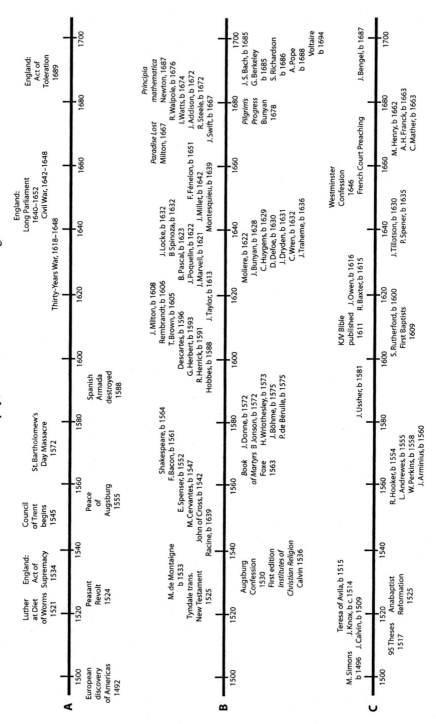

1. Norman F. Kantor, *The Civilization of the Middle Ages* (New York: Harper/Collins, 1993), 566ff.
2. John Hale, *The Civilization of Europe in the Renaissance* (New York: Athenaeum, 1994). A great survey.
3. Francis A. Schaeffer, *Escape from Reason* (Downers Grove, Ill.: InterVarsity, 1968), 29. See also Schaeffer's *How Should We Then Live? The Rise and Decline of Western Thought and Culture* (Old Tappan, N.J.: Revell, 1976), 57ff.
4. New York: Athenaeum, 1994.
5. Chicago: University of Chicago Press, 1997.
6. Boston: Little, Brown, 1992.

4.1 HUMANISM: CELEBRATING THE SELF

4.1.1 Petrarch, Humanism's Forebear

My wishes fluctuate and my desires conflict, and in their conflict they tear me apart. Thus does the outer man struggle with the inner.

Rule a child till he is fourteen; then advise him, don't force him. Let God and nature guide him. In my case, the struggle against nature was vain.

Such was my youthful ardor and earnestness to see new things that I would have gone to far China, to the Indies, to the ultimate land of Taprobane.

—Petrarch

Sometimes called "the father of humanism or the first modern man," Francesco Petrarca or "Petrarch" (1304–1374) was born in Italy but educated early on in Avignon in Southern France. He studied for the law at Bologna but became a cleric in the Roman Church even without a vocation. He was a consummate classical scholar and was crowned with the laurel for his poetry in Rome in 1340. He loved reading so much that at age fifteen his father burned his books. He was much influenced by Augustine and Cicero and wrote a series of eclogues after the style of Vergil in impeccable Latin. When in church in Avignon, he fell in love with a beautiful married woman named Laura, for whom he wrote some of the most exquisitely beautiful Italian sonnets ever written.[1] Though appointed canon of a cathedral in 1334, he fathered a child out of wedlock.[2]

In a number of respects, Petrarch epitomizes Renaissance humanism:

- He was such a lover of books and poetry.
- He was an inveterate traveler. His account, *Journey to the Tomb of Our Lord Jesus Christ* was widely read.
- He was a textual critic strongly determined to establish the correct ancient text.
- He had considerable political involvement.
- He was a master in the writing of personal letters.
- He loved solitude and climbed Mount Ventoux in 1340, just for the sake of doing it.

- Consciously leaving behind "the dark ages," he wrote epic poems like *Africa* showing "numberless originalities."

Medieval overtones are seen in Petrarch. He prays to the Virgin for forgiveness, but clearly he is fascinated with himself and holds a somewhat autonomous worldview.[3] He is frequently autobiographical. He makes self the locus and point of reference in an idolatrous narcissism. Thomas Greene speaks of Petrarch's "humanist hermeneutic" as being typical of the humanist enlightenment. "The centre is the self" for Petrarch who makes himself "the major theme of all of his work."[4] His lyric poetry was the model for Europe for centuries, and his influence marked.[5]

---

1. Morris Bishop, *Petrarch and His World* (Bloomington, Ind.: Indiana University Press, 1963), 61, 66.
2. Nicholas Mann, *Petrarch* (New York: Oxford University Press, 1984), 5.
3. *How Should We Then Live?* 16.
4. Giuseppe Mazzotta, "The Canzoniere and the Language of the Self," in *Petrarch* (New York: Chelsea House, 1989), 57, 77. This bent in literature is seen passionately in Walt Whitman's "The Song of Myself" from *Leaves of Grass*.
5. Aldo Scaglione, "Classical Heritage and Petrarchan Self-Consciousness in the Literary Emergence of the Interior 'I,'" in *Petrarch*, 126, 130. This self-absorption has been applied to our time by many. For example, see Robert W. Glasgow, "In the Twilight of Authority: The Obsessive Concern with Self—A Conversation with Robert Nisbet," *Psychology Today*, December 1973, 43ff., and "The Curse of Self-Esteem: What's Wrong with the Feel-Good Movement," *Newsweek*, 17 February 1992, 46ff. The key book is Paul C. Vitz, *Psychology as Religion: The Cult of Self-Worship* (Grand Rapids: Eerdmans, 1994).

4.1.2 BOCCACCIO, MASTER OF ITALIAN PROSE

Books are full of the voices of the wise, full of lessons from antiquity. . . . So great is the power of books . . . that without them we would all be rude and ignorant. Without books, we should have almost no memory of the past, no examples to follow.
—Cardinal Johannes Bessarion of Venice in 1648

Along with his friend Petrarch, Giovanni Boccaccio (1313–1375) was a founder of the Italian Renaissance. Born in Paris, he was educated in Naples, where he worked for the Bardi Bank. He then moved to Florence and lived most of the balance of his life there, except for forays abroad. He served for a time as Florentine ambassador to Avignon. His early works were in magnificent Latin, and he learned Greek so that he could translate Homer. He was an eager disciple of Ovid and Dante. His early life was quite loose, and he fathered five children out of wedlock. If the watchword in medieval times was authority, its Renaissance counterpart was liberty—a liberty that frequently became license.[1]

His masterpiece was *Decameron,* a series of one hundred novelle or short stories told by the characters, in the style of Chaucer's pilgrims. Seven young women and three young men meet in a Florentine church, refugees of the Black Death in 1348. They flee into the countryside.[2] On ten days they tell stories to each other. Some of the stories have become quite famous and do tend to be ribald, reflecting the moral hypocrisy of persons in religious orders. Hundreds of characters appear in the stories, which have a "rational-hedonistic, earthbound texture."[3] The descriptions are powerfully vivid, as the priest's old mother:

> He had an old mother who was a horrible creature and very avaricious. Hunch-backed she was, and black and hideous and opposed to everything that was good. Everybody loathed her. Even the priest, because of her unreasonableness, would under no conditions let her come into his house. She was too much of a gossip and too disgusting.[4]

Several of the stories help us understand attitudes toward the Jews at this time (in the very city in which the word *ghetto* was first used in Venice of the area to which Jews were consigned). In one story told on the first day, for example, a Jew named Abraham goes to the court of Rome, where he saw such corruption that he returned to Paris convinced that Christianity must be of divine origin to grow notwithstanding this and was baptized in Notre Dame.[5] The First Day, Third Story is also about a Jew named Melchizedek who escape's Saladin's trap by means of a short story about three rings.[6] The stories of seduction and infidelity are doubtless realistic reflections.

Toward the end of his life, Boccaccio had a spiritual experience, after which he apparently rejected all vernacular writing and regretted parts of *Decameron.* He lived his last years in considerable poverty. In many ways he is quintessentially a Renaissance man.

Renaissance novels of suspense by Elizabeth Eyre are set in Italy and feature the peerless Sigismondo and Benno. Well researched, they are published by Harcourt-Brace. The latest, *Dirge for the Doge,* builds on *Death of the Duchess, Curtains for the Cardinal,* and *Ax for an Abbot.*

---

1. Crane Brinton, *The Shaping of the Modern Mind, vol. 2* (New York: Mentor, 1953), 19ff.
2. Other great works on plagues: J. H. Powell, *Bring Out Your Dead: The Great Plague of Yellow Fever in Philadelphia in 1793* (Philadelphia: University of Pennsylvania Press, 1949); Albert Camus, *The Plague* (New York: Knopf, 1949).
3. Thomas C. Bergin, "Introduction to Boccaccio" in *The Decameron* (New York: W. W. Norton, 1977), 166.
4. Ibid., 287.
5. Ibid., 28–31.
6. Ibid., 31–34. This edition publishes twenty-one of the novelle.

4.2 HUMANISM: DISCOVERING THE IMPLICATIONS

4.2.1 MACHIAVELLI, POLITICAL THEORIST

> If the rulers of Christian lands had kept religion true to the principles set
> down by its founder, the states and republics of Christendom would be
> happier. . . . But there is no better evidence of its decline than to see how
> the people who are closest to the Church of Rome, the center of our re-
> ligion, have the least faith. Anyone examining the principles of our reli-
> gion and observing how far present practice has strayed from them would
> doubtless conclude that ruin or severe punishment is at hand.
>
> —Machiavelli
> *Discourses* [on Livy]

Like buds bursting in the spring after a long, cold winter, architecture, music,
art, and sculpture returned to life in the Renaissance. There was, however, a difference from even pagan arts of centuries past. Increasingly life and thought operated within a closed, self-absorbed universe. Twentieth-century attitudes abounded
in Renaissance Florence.[1] Even existential despair is found in Niccolò Machiavelli
(1469–1527), pioneer of political theory. Born and raised in Florence, Machiavelli
and his family saw firsthand the machinations of the Medici political dynasty and
likely heard in person the radical denunciations of the Florentine friar Girolamo
Savonarola (1452–1498), who went to his death at the stake. Machiavelli served
the republic in various ways during the reforms begun by Savonarola, but when
the Medicis were restored in 1512, he was imprisoned and tortured.

In *The Prince,* which deals with pragmatic issues of governing, he recommends
that the leader be cruel, even bestial, in order to cope with "his subjects' bestiality."[2] The ruler must avoid traps like a fox and intimidate like a lion. Kenneth
Rexroth observes that, although Machiavelli "is the most astute philosopher of
history after Thucydides, both believed history might be taught to behave itself,
a belief for which their narratives give little warrant."[3] Thus *Machiavellian* became synonymous with tyranny. *The Prince* would seem to be patterned after
the despicable Cesare Borgia, and Machiavelli's curious thesis was that "the virtues of Christ could only survive under the protection of Anti-Christ."[4]

His own experience perhaps made him cynical, but he was realistic about the
society in which he lived. He described the prince of the church as "often of one
mind outside the Conclave and of another within." Retirement gave him opportunity to write plays and novelle as well as serious discourses. He was truly a
Renaissance man in his broad range of interests and involvement:

> In the evening I return to my house and go into my study. At the door I take
> off the clothes I have worn all day, mud-spotted and dirty, and put on regal
> and courtly garments. Thus appropriately clothed, I enter into the ancient
> courts of ancient men, where being lovingly received, I feed on that food
> which alone is mine, and which I was born for; for I am not ashamed to ask
> the reasons for their actions, and they courteously answer me.[5]

Yet while the realities of power on occasion require a tragic moral choice, that is the least of the evils involved; Machiavelli advanced the notion that only raw ruthlessness could "improve the cycles" of history and hence supplied autocrats and dictators with a rationale for despotism.[6] Even H. G. Wells, in his well-known novel *The New Machiavelli,* seeks to use this paradigm for his own revolt against morality.[7]

---

1. *How Should We Then Live?* 78. Schaeffer notes that Michelangelo's sculpture, "The David," is uncircumcised—not the Jewish David of the Bible.
2. "Machiavelli," in *The Great Ideas Program* (Chicago: Encyclopedia Britannica, 1959), 2:11, 92. "Machiavelli regards ethical judgments as irrelevant in the scientific approach to politics."
3. Kenneth Rexroth, "Machiavelli," *Saturday Review,* 2 October 1965, 25.
4. Ralph Roeder, *The Man of the Renaissance* (New York: Viking, 1961), 272; an excellent sketch of Savonarola.
5. From a letter quoted in Great Books of the Western World (Chicago: Britannica, 1952), 23:x.
6. *How Should We Then Live?* 112. Elizabethan literature frequently links Machiavelli with Satan.
7. Lovat Dickson, *H. G. Wells: His Turbulent Life and Times* (New York: Athenaeum, 1969). H. G. Wells, *The New Machiavelli* (London: Duffield, 1910), reflects H. G. Wells's conflicts within Fabian socialism. He had rejected all religion and loosened all moral restraint; hence there was left only the raw, naked power struggle. At last showing signs of great weariness, he wrote his desultory *A Mind at the End of Its Tether* and his bizarre *All Aboard for Ararat.*

4.2.2 MONTAIGNE, INVENTOR OF THE ESSAY

> I go out of my way but by license not carelessness. . . . I want the material to make its own divisions . . . without my interlacing them with words, with links and seams put in for the benefit of inattentive readers. . . . I love a simple, natural speech, the same on paper as in the mouth . . . succulent and sinewy, brief but compressed, better difficult than boring . . . irregular, disconnected and bold.
>
> —Michel Eyquem de Montaigne

Still one of the most read French authors, Michel Eyquem de Montaigne (1533–1592) was born of merchant stock, his mother being a Sephardic Jewess. His father was a linguist and raised his son to speak Latin before his native tongue. He was awakened each morning by the playing of music. He served in the Bordeaux parliament and at the law, but he retired to the family chateau in 1571 to write. He traveled extensively to spas, seeking relief from gallstones. He served two terms as mayor of Bordeaux. Harold Bloom calls him "the greatest man of the Renaissance until Shakespeare."[1] He invented the open, rambling essay form, organized in the mode of conversation. This form was applied by Archbishop

John Tillotson (1630–1694) and his heirs as the basic model for preaching. It
still is so used by some, although it is scarcely suited for biblical exposition.[2]

Montaigne lived in France during a time of religious strife between Roman
Catholics and Huguenot Calvinists. Montaigne was a nominal Catholic, while
three of his siblings and many of his friends were Calvinists. He himself was an
advisor to the Huguenot Henry of Navarre. Not a systematic thinker, he was
plagued with doubts about miracles, divine providence, and the reality of witches.
He opposed translation of the Bible into the vernacular. He was of a skeptical
frame of mind, a moralist with keen affinity for the Stoics. He maintained that
"our religion is a matter of custom."[3] His essays are stuffed with quotations (1264
from the Latin classics). He wove in the language of religious orthodoxy, which
was to be expected in an age of persecution.

His essays are dramatic and stimulating, and one should perhaps begin with
"On Pedantry" (1.24) and "Of the Education of Children" (1.25). His famous
essay "On Cannibals" (1.30) is intriguing. Here he shows the power of language,
as he also does in "Of the Force of Imagination" (1.10). "Of Repentance" (3.2)
curiously insists that repentance, in contrast with regret, is prospective, rather
than retrospective. It looks with a view to future actions, rather than to the past.
Good and evil may for him be matters only of opinion. Philip Hallie sees
Montaigne as close to such modern analytic thinkers as Ludwig Wittgenstein
(1889–1951) in his view of the function of language. He believes that the self in
the thrall of passion is dead.[4]

Montaigne described what he called "a sick age," expressing the skepticism
of the age. His was classical skepticism. His "scar" was "the self," to which he
was totally dedicated. "I exist in myself," he contended in his extended *apologia*
for privacy. He tells his readers that "I am the subject of my book." He wrote not
to communicate but to know himself in the Socratic sense. His was a defense of
the self, an analysis of the self, and a poetics of the self. In the mainstream of
Renaissance humanism, he rejected the Reformation insistence that sin is the
assertion of self to the exclusion of God (Luther insisted that sin is *incurvatus in
se,* "turning in on oneself").[5]

No one has written more of himself and his own whims and fancies than has
Montaigne. Since self-knowledge is so important, he deeply resents religious
constraints and other interference.[6] The acceptance of self as it is must be the
summum bonum. Lost in his own subjectivity, he shakes his head at the real possibility of objective truth.[7] This self-satisfaction agitated Blaise Pascal (1623–
1662) when he studied Montaigne. One critic observed: "Montaigne doesn't teach
anything, for he never takes a stand on anything."

Toward the end of his life, Montaigne's self-centeredness brought grief to himself and to his family. At one point, the family became virtual refugees from the
plague, wandering about the countryside. This was the physical correspondent
to his moral and philosophical escapism—bitter fruit of the noninvolvement that
had followed the egoistic stance in his life. Into modern times, his *Essays* remained on *The Index,* the list of writings banned by the Vatican. While he did
not attack the church with vehemence, he never stood squarely for the validity
of divine truth, as revealed either through Scripture or the church.

1. Harold Bloom, ed., *Michel de Montaigne* (New York: Chelsea House, 1987), 1.
2. "Montaigne," in *The Great Books Program* (Chicago: Encyclopedia Britannica, 1962), 8.131.
3. Peter Burke, *Montaigne* (New York: Hill and Wang, 1981) 48. The strong biography and analysis of Montaigne remains Donald M. Frame's *Montaigne: A Biography* (New York: Harcourt Brace, 1965).
4. Philip P. Hallie, *The Scar of Montaigne: An Essay in Personal Philosophy* (Middletown, Ohio: Wesleyan University Press, 1966), 89ff. See also Ray Monk, *Wittgenstein: The Duty of Genius* (New York: Free, 1990). In his verification principle, Wittgenstein abandoned any idea of a common structure between the world and language, 274. Yet he came to believe in the resurrection of Christ. "Consciousness of sin is a real event," he argued, 376. He regretted that Bertrand Russell was not a Christian, 210.
5. Ibid., 5.
6. Donald M. Frame, "The Whole Man, 1586–1592," in Bloom, ed., *Michel de Montaigne*, 42.
7. Ibid., 45. Another arresting article in this book is Jefferson Humphries, "Montaigne's Anti-Influential Model of Identity," 219ff. Humphries deals with Montaigne's equivalency of text and the self.

4.2.3 RABELAIS, SATIRIST

"Fay ce que vouldras." ["Do what you please."]

—Rabelais

"Archdeacon Grantley" in Anthony Trollope's *The Warden* had a volume of Rabelais hidden in a secret drawer so that he could pass the morning by amusing himself "with the witty mischief of Panurge."[1] In fact this precursor of Jonathan Swift exerted a considerable influence on continental and English writers.[2] François Rabelais (c. 1483–1553) was born in France, the son of a lawyer and gentleman farmer. He was trained by the Franciscans, who ordained him as a priest, but he transferred to the Benedictines, who were more lax. Ultimately he became a secular priest and studied medicine at Montpellier. He practiced and taught medicine, twice accompanying the Bishop of Paris to Rome as his private physician. He had a loose and free spirit and loved to act. His amorous affairs, and his efforts to legitimize his children are matters of record.[3] Suffering financial extremity in Lyon in 1532, he found and embellished on some old folk tales. The resulting *Gargantua* is the story of a giant with a voracious appetite, and *Pantagruel* tells how the giant's son became "the King of Drunkards."

Rabelais's writing is coarse, grotesque, and riotous. He subscribed to all of the views of the humanistic Renaissance, including the self-sufficient perfectibility of human nature, the inevitability of progress and of natural virtue. He saw the Renaissance as the "dawn of the inevitable millennium."[4] His naughty satire and contempt for women flow from the callous narcissism of the new age.[5] His own experience is interwoven with the outrageous stories, as in his description of the Abbey of the Thelemites. Among the Thelemites there were no rules, only totally unrestrained behavior. Doubtless this reflects his own revolt against the discipline of a religious order.[6]

There are fleeting references to Christianity in his works, and he corresponded with Erasmus, the Rotterdam humanist. He takes a whack every now and then against the Protestants and consistently exposes his vague materialism and "deistic commonplaces." *Rabelaisian* came into the English language to refer to crude, loud, unrefined discourse and attitudes. His works were constantly under interdict. Calvin was severely critical of these works, yet some of Rabelais's closest friends in Lyons identified themselves as followers of Luther and Calvin. Occasional glimmers of serious and thoughtful reflection shine through his work, as when Gargantua writes to his son Pantagruel when he goes to Paris:

> "Love . . . fear God and on him cast all your thoughts. . . . Cleave to him that you may never be separated from him by your sins. Suspect the abuses of the world. Set not your heart upon vanity, for this life is transitory, but the Word of the Lord endureth forever. My son, the peace and grace of our Lord be with you. Amen."[7]

Or what shall we make of the inscription on the great Gate of Theleme:

> Here enter you, pure, honest faith, true,
> Expounders of the Scriptures old and new.
> Whose glosses do not blind our reason, but make it to see the clearer, and who shut
> Its passages from hatred, avarice, pride, factions, covenants, and all sort of vice.
> The Holy Sacred Word, May it always afford
> T's us all in common, both man and woman,
> A spiritual shield and sword, The Holy Sacred Word.[8]

Rabelais was assigned to parishes, but apparently he did not minister at them. His basic training and contacts in the ferment of Renaissance thought did not leave him ignorant of revealed truth but adamant against surrendering his will to trust or obey it.

The Christian Renaissance was unrelated to the Italian Renaissance and was generated by a return to the Bible and its proclamation in the beautiful Yssel Valley in the Netherlands. Laypeople were encouraged to read the Word, and the focus was on the saving cross of Christ. We are much indebted to the late University of Michigan historian Albert Hyma for *The Christian Renaissance*.[9] The Brethren of the Common Life Movement was essentially Augustinian and gave us such worthies as Jan van Ruysbroeck (1293–1381), Gerhard Groote (1340–1384), and Thomas à Kempis (c. 1380–1471). Both Johann Tauler (1300–1361) and Erasmus (c. 1466–1536) studied with the Brethren. *De imitatione Christi* by Thomas à Kempis is typical of this emphasis and has gone into six thousand editions. In George Eliot's *The Mill on the Floss,* Maggie Tulliver is brightened by her discovery of this book ("the corners turned down in many places") and especially the passage: "Both above and below which way soever thou dost turn thee, everywhere thou shalt find the Cross." John Wesley recommended it for every house.

1. Anthony Trollope, *The Warden* (Oxford: Oxford University Press, 1952), 105. See the entry on Anthony Trollope.
2. Huntington Brown, *Rabelais in English Literature* (New York: Octagon, 1967). Examples of writers influenced by Rabelais are Ben Jonson (1572–1637), Tobias Smollett (1721–1771), and Laurence Sterne (1713–1768).
3. D. B. Wyndham Lewis, *Doctor Rabelais* (New York: Sheed and Ward, 1957), 111.
4. Ibid., 10.
5. Ibid., 15.
6. François Rabelais, *Gargantua and Pantagruel* (Chicago: Great Books of the Western World, 1952), 24.I.53–57.
7. Ibid., 24.II.8.
8. Ibid., 24.I.54.
9. New York: Century, 1924.

4.2.4 BACON, PROPHET OF THE NEW SCIENCE

In establishing any true axiom the negative instance is the more powerful.

"What is truth?" said jesting Pilate; and would not stay for an answer.

Men fear death, as children fear to go into the dark.
—Francis Bacon

Francis Bacon (1561–1626) possessed a creative and brilliant mind. He even gave his life in the cause of science, contracting a fatal pneumonia and bronchitis while experimenting with snow as a preservative of food. He led the protest against scholastic philosophic systems and their incessant wrangling. In his strong advocacy for the inductive method, he was prophet for the new science. Bacon believed in the Bible and insisted on its proper role: "To conclude, therefore, let no man out of weak conceit of sobriety, or in ill applied moderation, think or maintain, that a man can search too far or be too well studied in the book of God's Word, or in the book of God's works."[1]

Both Alfred North Whitehead and J. Robert Oppenheimer (neither a Christian) admitted that modern science actually rose from within the matrix of Christian presuppositions of human rationality and the essential regularity of nature.[2] Andrew Dickson White's massive assault on historic Christianity in his two volume *A History of the Warfare of Science with Theology in Christendom* takes insufficient account of the evidence and the clear commitments of faith in such pioneers of modern science as Francis Bacon.[3]

Bacon was born in London in favorable circumstances, his father being keeper of the seals for Queen Elizabeth for twenty years. His Calvinist Puritan mother kept up a steady correspondence with her two sons, Francis and Anthony, while they were studying away from home. Her letters are peppered with Greek and Latin phrases and such blessings and admonitions as, "The Lord our Heavenly Father heal and bless you both as his son in Christ Jesus."[4] As early as age sixteen, Francis joined the staff of the British ambassador to France. Though always frail physically and not a systematic thinker, Bacon's genius overflowed in many directions, not least in his famous essays, in which he developed a more formal form for Montaigne's essay pattern.

He studied at Cambridge and for the law at Gray's Inn, with a particular interest in the Roman roots of the English common law. Bacon served Elizabeth and then James I as solicitor general, member of the Privy Council and of Parliament, and then lord chancellor (1607), in which capacity he was regent when the king was absent in Scotland. Although he was noted for his political acumen, he had a penchant for getting into trouble. This was apparent in his betrayal of his friend Essex, in his service on the commission that examined and condemned Walter Raleigh, and in behavior leading to his own impeachment for accepting improper gratuities. He was imprisoned and then pardoned by the king, escaping degradation and the loss of his titles by but two votes.[5]

After his release from prison, he wrote his well-known *A History of the Reign of Henry VII,* but far more significant was *The Great Instauration* (or Reconstruction), published in 1620. Here he proposes a total revamping of philosophy on a scale attempted previously only by Aristotle. While some have attributed various of the plays of Shakespeare to Bacon (in the so-called Baconian controversy that started in 1865), the truly abiding work of Bacon can be seen in his *Advancement of Learning* (1605), which he dedicated to the king; in his *Novum organum;* and his *New Atlantis,* which continues the tradition of Thomas More's *Utopia.* His sketch of the ideal society stresses the sociological dimensions with skill.

Novum organum is the piece to read. Bacon offers arresting analysis of those prejudices that block investigation of the truth.[6] These prejudices include (1) idols of the tribe, those inherent in human nature; (2) idols of the cave, those fostered by environment; (3) idols of the marketplace, those fashionable but false notions; and (4) idols of the theatre, false systems to which we adhere even after they are no longer defensible. His writing is highly aphoristic. It is interesting that Immanuel Kant, however radically his thought differed from Bacon's, dedicated his *Critique of Pure Reason* to the philosopher/scientist. Bacon's style is rich and yet his meaning plain, as in Jonathan Swift[7] or Thomas Brown's *Religio Medici,* in which Brown records the triumph of orthodoxy over nagging doubt.[8]

Bacon counted as his close friends such worthies as Lancelot Andrewes, a translator of the King James Version; George Herbert, the poet; and Ben Jonson, the playwright.

Bacon's insistence on the necessity of induction speaks to Christian communication, in which both induction and deduction are essential. It is significant that Bacon, who has been called by Jean d'Alembert "the greatest, the most universal, and the most eloquent of philosophers,"[9] was solidly orthodox in his Christian faith right down to his understanding of the fall as an underlying doctrine:

> Man by the Fall fell at the same time from his state of innocence and
> from his dominion over nature. Both of these losses, however, can even

in this life be in some part repaired; the former by religion and faith, the latter by the arts and sciences.[10]

The struggle of science against conventional Aristotelian thinking and entrenched ecclesiastical interests can be seen in Galileo Galilei (1564–1642), whose father forced him to give up any idea of the priesthood. Galileo felt that spots on the sun or moons around Jupiter brought into question the whole Christian plan of salvation.[11] The Jesuits campaigned to destroy Galileo. He broke under his inquisitors when in danger of the rack.[12] Both Thomas Hobbes and John Milton visited him.

---

1. Francis Bacon, *On the Proficience and Advancement of Learning, Divine and Human*, 1.6.16.
2. *How Should We Then Live?* 132. A classic study that offers evidence in support of this matrix, see E. A. Burtt, *The Metaphysical Foundations of Modern Science* (Garden City: Doubleday Anchor, 1954).
3. Andrew Dickson White, *A History of the Warfare of Science with Theology in Christendom*, 2 vols. (New York: D. Appleton, 1896). White was president of Cornell University.
4. Catherine Drinker Bowen, *Francis Bacon: The Temper of a Man* (New York: Atlantic Monthly/Little Brown, 1963), 59.
5. Ibid., 203.
6. Anthony Quinton, *Francis Bacon* (New York: Hill and Wang, 1980), 55.
7. Quinton, *Francis Bacon*, 74.
8. John S. Bonnell, "*Religio Medici,*" *Pastoral Psychology*, September 1955, 35ff.
9. Will Durant, *The Story of Philosophy* (New York: Simon and Schuster, 1926), 134.
10. Francis Bacon, *Novum organum* (Chicago: Great Books of the Western World, 1952), 30.2.52.
11. James Reston Jr., *Galileo: A Life* (New York: Harper/Collins, 1994), 55.
12. Giorgio de Santillana, *The Crime of Galileo* (Chicago: University of Chicago Press, 1955).

4.2.5 HOBBES, TAKING THE WRONG TURN

The Universe, that is to say, the whole masse of all things that are, is Corporeall, that is to say, body: and hath the dimensions of Magnitude, namely, Length, Breadth and Depth: also every part of Body, is likewise Body, and hath the like dimensions; and consequently every part of the Universe is Body; and that which is not Body, is no part of the Universe: And because the Universe is All, that which is no part of it, is nothing; and consequently nowhere.

—Thomas Hobbes
Leviathan

Through the Middle Ages there was no theoretical materialism, but rationalism led Thomas Hobbes (1588–1679) to embrace notions previously found in the Epicureans and Stoics. As Hobbes separated philosophy from theology, he laid a naturalistic foundation for the Enlightenment.[1] Certainly the "metaphysical barbarism" of recent centuries can be traced back in part to René Descartes and Hobbes's doubts about the validity of final causation. Reinhold Niebuhr saw behaviorist psychology as an elaboration of Hobbes's position.[2]

Thomas Hobbes was born the son of an Anglican vicar in Westport, England, on April 5, 1588. It is said his premature birth was induced when his mother heard the fearsome news of the coming of the Spanish Armada. His father subsequently fled his home after striking a worshiper. Young Hobbes was precocious, at age fourteen translating Euripides's *Medea* from Greek into Latin iambic poetry. His uncle sent him to Oxford at age fifteen, after which he served as a secretary to Francis Bacon. For most of his career, he was a tutor to the Cavendish family with whom he traveled often to the Continent. Because of his views and the English Civil War, he migrated between England and France. In France he became acquainted with Descartes.

Whereas Bacon advocated inductive study, Hobbes was a champion of deduction. He influenced British utilitarianism and the French encyclopedists. At age eighty-four, he wrote an autobiography in Latin elegiacs and thereafter translated Homer. Political theory dominates his *Leviathan or the Matter, Form and Power of a Commonwealth,* published in 1651. He earlier translated Thucydides to show the weakness of democracy.

Many see Hobbes as the first modern political theorist. He was an ultra Erastian, a supporter of the absolute power of the sovereign. While in France at one point, he tutored the future Charles II of England, who took his ideas of the powers of the sovereign very seriously. He developed an excellence in style that makes reading him a pleasure.

His severely logical theory of absolutism in government is not the most disturbing part of his legacy. He also banished spirit from the universe.[3] Man is only a mechanism of matter in motion. The soul is a superfluity.[4] Hobbes greatly resented all clergy and thought the Puritans anathema. He did not care for sermons and opposed Bible translation, seeing only some moral value in Scripture. While he seems to use the language of theism, his *Cause of the World* is incomprehensible. We know nothing of God other than that he is omnipotent.[5] His views on the Bible, as set forth in chapter 33 in *Leviathan,* are precursory to the higher critical notions of Benedict de Spinoza.[6] We can easily see that making God the deduction of natural reason leaves us without the God of supernatural revelation. Rationalism is on its rampage.[7]

Hobbes's determinist system is highly egoistic. He rejects the old doctrine of damnation. His "trinity" consists of Moses, Jesus, and the apostles. Miracles are but natural causes, and there have been no martyrs since Christ's ascension.

One of Hobbes's ablest contemporary antagonists was the Puritan preacher Richard Baxter of Kidderminster (1615–1691).

---

1. Wilhelm Windelband, *A History of Philosophy* (New York: Harper Torchbooks, 1958), 2:448f., 502, 512f.

2. Reinhold Niebuhr, *The Nature and Destiny of Man* (New York: Scribner's, 1955),

1.73. See also *Metaphysical Foundations of Modern Science*, 320. On Watsonian behaviorism, see critiques by Gordon H. Clark. In Daniel W. Bjork, *B .F. Skinner* (New York: Basic, 1993), we see Skinner's conversion to behaviorism followed by promiscuous sexuality and alienation from his colleagues at Minnesota and Harvard. He and his wife did read Trollope to each other, but he saw himself as "a teaching machine" and told *Time,* "We can't afford freedom" (see *Walden II*).

3. Samuel I. Mintz, *The Hunting of Leviathan* (Cambridge: Cambridge University Press, 1969), 10.

4. Leslie Stephen, *Hobbes* (Ann Arbor, Mich.: University of Michigan Press, 1961), 30.

5. Ibid., 169. Later materialists to emerge included Ludwig Feuerbach and Karl Marx, with Marx's dialectical materialism.

6. *Hunting of Leviathan,* 43. Hobbes wanted to outdistance others on the race track of life.

7. Rationalism overstresses the capability of human reason and intellect and understresses or fails to see at all the effects of human depravity upon intellectual function. Rationality is the insistence on the survival of essential intellectual function in humankind in relation to the *imago dei,* which makes communication possible through the abiding reality of the law of noncontradiction. Hobbes, Descartes, Spinoza, and Leibniz are considered rationalists.

4.2.6 DESCARTES, FOUNDER OF MODERN SCIENCE

Cogito ergo sum ["I think, therefore I am"]. . . . I knew that I was a substance the whole essence or nature of which is to think . . . this "me," that is to say, the soul by which I am what I am, is entirely distinct from the body, and is even more easy to know than is the latter; and even if the body were not, the soul would not cease to be what it is.

—René Descartes
Discourse of Method

A brilliant philosopher, scientist, and mathematician, René Descartes (1596–1650) set himself to reform the rather muddled state of things in philosophy. Descartes was a metaphysical dualist. He took seriously both *res extensa* (matter and force) and *res cogitans* (the mind and thinking). Indeed he argues for the existence of God from "the clear and distinct" idea of God. The dualistic realism J. Oliver Buswell advocated was indebted to Descartes.[1] As the originator of analytic geometry, he felt that mathematics was the key to unlocking the secrets of nature. The world is orderly and geometric, and the particles of matter obey set laws.[2]

On the other hand, while systematic doubt subjects just about everything to question, one cannot doubt self-existence. Doubt itself establishes the existence of the doubter.

Certain "clear and distinct" ideas are *a priori,* including the idea of God. He argues that "the idea of God has so much 'objective reality' that I know my mind is not capable of producing it." In Cartesian thought, the locus of meeting and interaction between body and soul is the pineal gland. Spinoza carried the essential

rationalism of Descartes to an insistence on "the unity of all things" and a mo-
nistic pantheism. He felt that, through thought, one could achieve oneness with
God. Spinoza was expelled from his synagogue in Portugal for his atheism.
Descartes is also the spiritual progenitor of Pascal, whom he met when Pascal
was a sixteen-year-old genius.

Descartes was born in La Haye, near Tours in France. He was a sickly child
and a melancholic, who lost his mother when he was fourteen months old and
never had much contact with his father. He attended one of the finest schools in
France, the Jesuit school at La Fleche. In 1614 he was graduated from the University of Potiers in civil and canon law. Thereafter he served in the military.
While stationed in the Netherlands, Descartes met Isaac Beekman of Dort, who
stimulated his interest in algebra and music. He conducted further study of the
scientific method while on postings in Germany and Italy. He spent much time
mastering Cicero and Quintilian in rhetoric studies.[3] The condemnation of Galileo
in 1633 troubled him.

While in Paris from 1625 to 1628, he discovered the law governing the re-
fraction of light. He was encouraged by Cardinal Pierre de Bérulle (1575–1629),
who fostered a revival of Augustinianism.[4] Certainly some interesting parallels
can be drawn between Augustine and Descartes.

In 1629 he returned to the Netherlands but was isolated in his work on hyper-
bolic lenses as Protestants in this liberal country were uneasy with him. He was
"a zealous Roman Catholic who feared the displeasure of the church above all."[5]
He tutored Christian Huygens (1629–1695), who pioneered in the study of optics and light. The last decade of Descartes's life was momentous and difficult.
In 1640 he fathered a daughter, Francine, by his Protestant maid Heline. The child
lived only a brief time.

Following his new interest in metaphysics, he wrote *Meditations*. At about the
same time, he broke with the University of Utrecht. After a dispute with Gisbertus
Voetius and attacks by other theologians, he found respite in Sweden in 1649,
enjoying the patronage of Queen Christina. He died in the severe winter of 1650.
In *Discourse of Method* or *Meditations,* the reader can journey to the vortex of
this great mind at a time of transition and change.

---

1. James Oliver Buswell Jr., *A Christian View of Being and Knowing* (Grand Rapids:
   Zondervan, 1960), 126ff. Buswell argues for epistemological dualism, not ontological
   dualism. Ontologically Christians are contingent dualists unlike the Zoroastrians or
   the Manichaeans. God and Satan are not equipowerful, for Satan is a created being.
2. *Metaphysical Foundations of Modern Science*, 105ff.
3. Stephen Gaukroger, *Descartes* (Oxford: Clarendon, 1995), 119.
4. Gordon H. Clark, "A Complete Reversal of Scholasticism," *Christianity Today,* 22
   October 1965, 6ff.
5. Gaukroger, *Descartes*, 291. Descartes was restless and lonely. In a riveting 1994 book,
   Descartes' Error, Antonio Damasio argues for the larger place of emotion in human
   behavior and urges that *cogito ergo sum* be expanded to "I think and feel, therefore
   I am."

4.3 RETURNING TO THE CREATOR

4.3.1 LUTHER, CHAMPION OF THE GOSPEL

Therefore we let bishops and church councils decide and establish what ever they desire; wherever we have on our side the Word of God, we shall decide and not they, whether it is right or wrong, and they should yield to us and obey our word.

Unless I am convinced by testimony from Scripture or evident reasons—for I believe neither the Pope nor the councils alone, since it is established that they have often erred and contradicted themselves, I am conquered by the Writings cited by me, and my conscience is captive to the Word of God.

The cross is the safest of all things. Blessed is the man who understands this.

—Martin Luther

The church had swelled in corruption and decadence. At the end of the medieval era, the institution was spiritually tired, morally bankrupt, and doctrinally confused.[1] The Protestant Reformers drastically challenged the drift of renaissance humanism and reshaped human history. Their recovery of the Scriptures as the supreme authority had seismic effects on culture and society. Francis Schaeffer shows that the Reformation dismantled the humanistic distortions in the church.[2] *Sola Scriptura* ("Scripture alone") was the motto of the Reformation.

Martin Luther (1483–1546) was an Augustinian monk who lived in great fear of the judgment of God and God's law. He had no grasp of Jesus as Savior and the gospel as good news for the sinner![3] After his encounter with grace, Luther conceded that "when I became a Doctor I did not know we cannot expiate our sin." Luther's break with medieval soteriology and his discovery of the righteousness of God (1514–1515), with full forensic justification before God by faith alone apart from law, led to the emergence of his theology of the Cross. This was all in the context of an eschatological cosmic conflict between God and Satan. "The Scriptures must be preached!" he insisted.[4] The German mysticism of Tauler and *Theologia Germanica* are also in evidence in his massive output of sermons and other writings. His commentaries include particularly significant and moving works on Romans and Galatians and such hymns as "A Mighty Fortress Is Our God" and "Fear Not, Little Flock."

Luther could be bombastic and crude, as we learn especially from his *Table Talk*.[5] Strangely neither the first-generation Reformers nor the later Puritans believed that the Great Commission applied to the contemporary church. His burden was: *solo Christo* ("Christ alone"); *sola gratia* ("grace alone"); and *sola fidei* ("faith alone"). So deep was his confidence in the noncontradictory nature of Scripture that he questioned the canonicity of James because it seemed at odds with Paul's epistolary teaching on salvation apart from good works (Eph. 2:8–10). Although not a systematic thinker, Luther was always theological as we sense in his catechism.[6]

The most beautiful of all of Luther's writings in the judgment of many is his striking *A Treatise on Christian Liberty*. This is the gentle Luther setting forth "the whole of Christian living in a brief form." Here he argues two propositions with regard to liberty and bondage: that the Christian is "perfectly free lord of all," and "perfectly dutiful servant of all."[7] Living in a world tyrannized by sin and law, we can be freed by Christ! Now the believer is free to do whatever love permits (we certainly hear the echoes of Augustine and St. Bernard here). "The Word of God cannot be received and cherished by any works whatever, but only by faith. . . . Hence true faith in Christ is a treasure beyond comparison, which brings with it all salvation and saves from every evil."[8]

In typical Lutheran fashion, the strong emphasis is on commands versus promises, law versus grace. But faith is the uniting of the soul with Christ as a bride is united to her bridegroom and hence the opportunity and the obligation of love to fulfill the commandments and expectations of our God and hence to escape the snare of antinomianism. Think how refreshing in all of the Pelagian and semi-Pelagian darkness of this time to hear such a clear resonation of gospel truth: "No good work helps an unbeliever so as to justify and save him."[9] It necessarily follows:

> Although the Christian is thus free from all works, he ought in this liberty to empty himself, to take upon himself the form of a servant, to be made in the likeness of men, to be found in fashion as a man, and to serve, help and in every way deal with his neighbor as he sees that God through Christ has dealt and still deals with himself. And this he should do freely, having regard to nothing except the divine approval.[10]

Reformers then saw humankind as totally fallen and needful of Christ's atoning satisfaction on the cross. This message was preached in the vernacular and promulgated through Bibles and literature printed in the common language. It changed the church and the history of Western civilization.

---

1. Alister E. McGrath, *Luther's Theology of the Cross* (Oxford: Basil Blackwell, 1985).
2. *How Should We Then Live?* 82.
3. McGrath, *Luther's Theology of the Cross*. A more recent significant statement is Martin Hengel, *The Cross of the Son of God* (London: SCM, 1986). Hengel shows how the forgiveness of sins is at the heart of early proclamation.
4. For a recent treatment, see Heiko A. Oberman, *Luther: Man Between God and the Devil* (New Haven, Conn.: Yale University Press, 1982). Chapter 5, "The Reformation Breakthrough" is especially good.
5. Thomas S. Kepler, ed., *The Table Talk of Martin Luther* (New York: World, 1952).
6. Martin Luther, *Luther's Large Catechism* (Minneapolis: Augsburg, 1935). See on the Ten Commandments, the Apostles' Creed, and Lord's Prayer.
7. Martin Luther, "A Treatise on Christian Liberty," in *Three Treatises* (Philadelphia: Muhlenberg, 1947), 251.
8. Ibid., 254. Mackinnon speaks of Luther as a "religious genius and intellectual giant."

9. Ibid., 272. Luther's polemical language sometimes shocks with its vituperative violence.

10. Ibid., 278. J. H. Newman says of this piece, "It is written with such masterly skill, seraphic fervor, and convincing logic, and is so free from his later extravagances as to be universally acceptable to evangelical Christians always and everywhere."

4.3.2 CALVIN, PRINCE OF BIBLE EXPOSITORS

God by a sudden conversion subdued my heart to teachableness.

Concerning my doctrine, I have taught faithfully . . . and God has given me the grace to write. I have done this as faithfully as possible and have not corrupted a single passage of Scripture or knowingly twisted it.

Hence the office of the Spirit promised to us is not to form new and unheard of revelations but to seal on our minds the very doctrine which the gospel recommends.

—John Calvin

Even the theological antagonist of Calvinism, James Arminius (1560–1609) described John Calvin (1509–1564) as "incomparable in his interpretation of Scripture." Although exceedingly frail physically, he gave himself to writing, teaching, and preaching with such abandon that the sum of his writings fills fifty-nine large Latin tomes. Fundamental to his life's ministry was the deathless conviction that "the human authors of Scripture were controlled by God in every detail of what they wrote."[1] He insisted that the church's attention move from the medieval glosses on the text to the actual text of Scripture itself. Calvin was born in Noyon in France and studied in Paris, Orlean, and Bourges. He became a master of rhetoric and, as we have seen, even wrote a book on Seneca. His radical conversion, as the result of setting himself to reading the New Testament through, greatly changed his life, and his new views necessitated flight from Paris. Ultimately he became preacher-teacher in Geneva but went into exile for a time, only to return to lead the theocratic regime.[2]

In 1536 (at the age of twenty-six), he wrote the first edition of *Institutes of the Christian Religion* in order to make the case for Protestantism to Francis I, king of France. This remarkable statement of doctrine was enlarged to its present size over several French and Latin editions by 1559. Calvin wanted his theology to be based solidly and squarely on the exegesis of Scripture, and in this he is a delight. Calvinists and Arminians alike give him accolades for the beauty and clarity of his expression. Kenneth Scott Latourette, the redoubtable historian of missionary expansion, well says that the *Institutes* are "the most influential single book of the Protestant Reformation." T. F. Torrance calls him "the father of modern theology." Stephen Zweig asserted that this is "one of the ten or twenty books in the world of which we may say that they have determined the course of history and changed the face of Europe."[3]

The themes of the work are the knowledge of God and the knowledge of man. The movement in this theology is always from God to humanity.[4] Knowledge of God is implanted in the human heart, so that each person is and moves in a theater of God's glory. But by the fall this natural knowledge has a minus sign, and people are "as blind as moles" to God's revelation. Calvin sees the heart as an idol factory, which requires supernatural interposition for any positive outcome.

So God bends down to his uncomprehending human infants and lisps baby talk to make them understand at their level. This is the special revelation of Scripture, to which he applies the words *infallible* and *unerring*. Calvin is the first Reformation theologian to emphasize the testimony of the Holy Spirit in accrediting and authenticating Holy Scripture. This dependence on the work of the Spirit is a distinctive of Reformed theology from Calvin and succeeding confessions through the Westminster Confession of Faith and Catechisms in the 1640s.[5] *Institutes* book 1, chapter 8 (1.8) discusses the evidences for inspiration and 1.13 is his classic discussion of the Trinity. These are "musts" for those who would better understand God, as is his discussion of providence, a doctrine often neglected in modern systematics.[6]

In Book 2 Calvin looks to the sinfulness and fall of man and the saving work of Christ. Book 3 stresses the work of the Holy Spirit and the Christian response in holy living. The most controversial chapter is his view of predestination (3.21). Calvin is a careful diagonal or dialectic thinker who seeks the essential unity of truth after sorting through the complexity of opposites. Except where he launches into polemical attacks on his opponents, he has a spare prose style and a concise manner.

The extraordinary influence of Calvin, not only on the Continent where he lived and ministered but in Scotland and England as well as America, is overwhelming, largely because of the theological school at Geneva where exiles from France, Britain, and Scotland particularly gathered. Many of its graduates returned as missionaries to France, knowing that they would be caught and martyred at the stake within weeks.

Many of the old stereotypes of the cold and calculatingly logical Calvin are now recognized to be inaccurate.[7] His discussion of election and reprobation actually ends with a treatment of the resurrection and the believer's hope of seeing God face-to-face. Undoubtedly Alister McGrath is right that the successors of Calvin were more Calvinistic than was Calvin and that some preoccupation with predestination has been read back into *Institutes*.[8] R. T. Kendall has made a convincing case that Calvin did not hold to a limited atonement.[9] Calvin stood in conscious succession with Augustine and Bernard of Clairvaux. In the battle for truth and the gospel of Christ, Calvin was on the firing line, and his stand for biblical supernaturalism had wide and vigorous reverberations.

---

1. Kenneth S. Kantzer, "Calvin and the Holy Scriptures," in John F. Walvoord, ed., *Inspiration and Interpretation* (Grand Rapids: Eerdmans, 1957), 140. Kantzer shows Calvin's commentaries apply the doctrine of verbal inerrancy.
2. W. Stanford Reid, *John Calvin: His Influence in the Western World* (Grand Rapids: Eerdmans, 1982). Traces the founding of the Academy of Geneva and its impact upon students from all over Europe (e.g., John Knox).
3. Alister E. McGrath, *A Life of John Calvin* (Oxford: Basil Blackwell, 1990), xiii, 209. This is a grudging tribute. Zweig is a fierce critic who considers Calvin the dictator and tyrant of Geneva.

4. John Calvin, *Institutes of the Christian Religion* (Grand Rapids: Eerdmans, 1953), 1.1.39.

5. Bernard Ramm, *The Witness of the Spirit* (Grand Rapids: Eerdmans, 1959). This is an unusual study of the *testimonium.*

6. Calvin, *Institutes,* 1.192–93.

7. Randall C. Zachman, "Theologian in the Service of Piety: A New Portrait of Calvin," *Christian Century,* 23–30 April 1997, 413ff. Not unlike the picture painted by William J. Bouwsma, *John Calvin: A Sixteenth Century Portrait* (Oxford: Oxford University Press, 1988), 7; n.b. "Calvin's Influence in Scotland and England," *Christian Century,* 27 May 1964, 699ff.; C. Gregg Singer, "John Calvin: America's First Founding Father," *Eternity,* July 1959, 5ff.

8. McGrath, *A Life of John Calvin,* 150. Peter Toon details Calvin's differences with later theologians who wrote the Westminster Confession. He also lists changes in Reformed theology from Calvin to 1648 and the end of the English Civil War, 1560–1648. *Puritans and Calvinism* (Swengel, Penn.: Bible Truth, 1973), 59ff.

9. R. T. Kendall, *Calvin and English Calvinism to 1649* (Oxford: Oxford University Press, 1979). This is Kendall's doctoral dissertation at Oxford. He has been serving as pastor of Westminster Chapel, London. That Calvin taught that Christ died for all is convincingly demonstrated also in Brian G. Armstrong, *Calvinism and the Amyraut Heresy: Protestant Scholasticism and Humanism in 17th Century France* (Madison, Wis.: University of Wisconsin Press, 1969), 160, 166.

4.3.3 CERVANTES, SPANISH STORYTELLER

Christian and lover and gentleman—his discourse is like a silver torrent; therefore do I admire and cherish him.
—Ruben Dario (a sonnet on Cervantes)

The soul of Don Quixote, light as thistledown, snatched up in the illusory vortex, goes whirling like a dry leaf; and in its pursuit everything ingenuous and sorrowing still left in the world will go forevermore.
—José Ortega y Gasset
Meditations on Quixote

"That's the kind of love," said Sancho, "I've heard sermons about. They say one should love our Lord for Himself, without any hopes of glory or fear of punishment. Me, I love and serve Him for what he can do for me."
—Miguel de Cervantes
The History of Don Quixote de la Mancha

The greatest Spanish writer of all time and one of the truly great writers in the world, Miguel de Cervantes (1547–1616) merits serious reflection.[1] He was born in the university town of Acala de Henares, the son of a poor traveling physician. He had a meager education but loved to write poetry and served in a Cardinal's household in Rome. In the army, he lost his left hand in the Battle of Lepanto against the Turks. On the way back to Spain, he was taken captive by pirates on the Barbary Coast (Algiers) and held hostage. He did military service for Portugal for awhile and then married, after fathering a daughter by a mistress. He acknowledged and cared for his natural daughter.[2]

Cervantes was enormously creative, but he had a past as a rascal and makes allusion to "youthful imprudence" without specific explanation. For a time he was employed to requisition supplies for the Spanish Armada in Andulasia and got into trouble with his accounts and his personal finances. He was thrown into jail on several occasions and there started writing his masterpiece, *Don Quixote*. He lived successively in Seville; Valladolid, where he finished his novel; and Madrid, where he died of what seem to be diabetes complications. While his poetry, plays, and other novels met with indifferent success, *The History of Don Quixote de la Mancha* was immediately popular in Spain. It was also appreciated in English and then other languages when it was translated. Twelve of his short stories have special literary interest, but it is the one book that became the model for the modern novel.[3]

Goethe loved it, Voltaire scorned it, and Migel Unamuno, another great Spanish writer (1864–1936) detested it. It is more than a farce, but rises up out of the great national epic tradition. This tradition includes ballads about the mythical hero Rodrigo Diaz de Bivar or El Cid from the days when the Christian kings were seeking to expel the Moors from Spain. At the time of this writing, Spain was the most powerful nation in the world, with her explorers and conquistadors opening up the new world. But Spain declined as she persecuted Jews and other nonconformists to the church. The nation suffered in the fiasco of the defeat of the Armada in 1588. This is Spain of the Counter-Reformation, at the peak of the Inquisition.

Now Cervantes tells his tale of the tall, emaciated knight-errant who loses his mind reading too many stories of chivalry and goes forth on his equally emaciated nag, Rocinante. The delusional knight goes out to change the world, having been knighted in jest by the innkeeper whose sleazy establishment he has mistaken for a castle. In his mind a peasant girl is transformed into Lady Dulcinea. His squire is a rotund peasant. He thinks the windmills with which he jousts are giants. The livestock are armies and the galley-slaves are oppressed gentlemen. Sancho Panza, his servant, is in touch with reality:

> "It's my opinion that those who made spirit with me were not phantoms or enchanted men, as your worship says, but men of flesh and blood like us; and they all had names as I heard when they were tossing me" (1.18).

To use the word Cervantes has given us, the world of this knight is *quixotic*. The issue Cervantes explores in the book is how to discern reality from unreality. What is reality? Few heed the voice of reason. Often the description is of what "seems" to be.[4] Don Quixote is troubled with doubts. Sometimes he is lucid and recovers sanity on his deathbed, as his friends the priest and the barber purge his bookshelves in hopes of bringing him back to reality.

Cervantes knew enough Italian to have read Petrarch and Boccaccio. More important, he knew the Spanish peasant.[5] Some have compared his style to that of English author P. G. Wodehouse (1881–1975). Still, the literary elite of his time disdained him. His first literary champion was Samuel Taylor Coleridge (1772–1834), who advised reading him regularly. Franz Kafka, the twentieth-century existentialist, identified with Sancho and entitled one of his strange parables "The Truth about Sancho Panza."[6] An undertone of sadness throughout the work appeals to existentialists such as Kafka. In the world of Quixote, as perhaps in that of Cervantes, brainsick dreams are grim—but reality is more so.

Alban Forcione of Stanford is the leading Cervantes scholar in the United States. He finds "the epiphany of evil" in one of Cervantes's short stories, "The Dialogue of the Dogs," in which a witch confesses her crass immorality. Forcione finds help in understanding this "epiphany" in the book of Job, Augustine's *Confessions,* and the raising of Lazarus from the dead in John 11. The question raised by the story is how someone can sink into death confessing "how habit has made sin second nature to her, how the pleasures of the flesh have so dulled her soul that it has lost its faith and forgotten its Christian identity and God's laws."[7]

It is interesting that a few critics have compared the variety and sophistication of Cervantes with the works of William Shakespeare. They died on the same day.

A delightful takeoff on Cervantes's masterpiece was written by Graham Greene.[8] Greene pictures a modern "Msgr. Quixote," who fears he will become a whiskey-priest. He goes off with Mayor Sancho of El Toboso, a fervent Communist. They are stopped by the Guardia. Their adventures in Salamanca, the old university town where Unamuno taught and Cervantes may have attended, and in Valladolid are hilarious. The issue is whether one can buy salvation (197). The next best thing to a visit to Spain and Portugal is James Michener's panoramic introduction to the peninsula, *Iberia: Spanish Travels and Reflections.*[9] Michener recommends reading *Don Quixote* as spiritual preparation for visiting Spain. He believes Cervantes is lampooning the Hispanic sense of honor. "Quixote country" is the desolate, sunbaked Central Plain.

1. D. B. Wyndham Lewis, *The Shadow of Cervantes* (New York: Sheed and Ward, 1962), 128. The cultural significance of Cervantes is seen in commemorations of his death and continuing popularity of the classic, which is more popular than ever in Spain. See "Dramatic readings tilt at a classic adventure," *Chicago Tribune,* 27 April 1997, 9. In English the J. M. Cohen translation (Penguin Classics) and the Walter Starkie abridged version (Signet) are excellent.
2. *Cervantes: His Life, His Times, His Works,* in Giants of World Literature Series (New York: American Heritage, 1968), 27.
3. Ibid., 161. The paintings and illustrations in this book are fantastic!
4. Richard L. Predmore, *The World of Don Quixote* (Cambridge: Harvard University Press, 1967), 63.
5. *Shadow of Cervantes,* 33. Some see Quixote as showing the spiritual world of the European man at midcareer as Homer showed him at the beginning and as *The Brothers Karamazov* in his decline (Kenneth Rexroth).
6. Harold Bloom, "Introduction," in Harold Bloom, ed., *Cervantes* (New York: Chelsea House, 1987), 4.

7. Alban Forcione, "The Descent into the Grave: Cervantes' Apocalypse," in *Cervantes and the Mystery of Lawlessness* (Princeton, N.J.: Princeton University Press, 1984). The section beginning on 169 explores this theme of profanation.

8. Graham Greene, *Monsignor Quixote* (New York: Simon and Schuster, 1982). Several visual interpretations of the knight-errant and his faithful partner have been created. The very best is by Francisco Goya (1746–1828) and hangs in the British Museum. I would choose Gustave Doré (1832–1883) as runner-up.

9. New York: Fawcett Crest, 1968, 14, 72.

4.3.4   JOHN OF THE CROSS, MYSTIC-DOCTOR

Love of God and love of created things are contrary the one to the other; two contraries cannot coexist in one and the same person.

One who does not seek the cross of Christ isn't seeking the glory of Christ.

—John of the Cross

Another influence in Spanish literature has also made an impact in Christian mysticism—John of the Cross. There is new interest in publication of the works of Juan de Yepez y Alvarez, or San Juan de la Cruz as he was known (1542–1591). He is the outstanding figure in the post-Tridentine spiritual awakening that developed in Spain. Surveys of great literature (for example "Great Books" and "Harvard Classics") tilt strongly toward natural science in their selections and ignore the vast literature of Christian spirituality. In recent years an avalanche of books and studies of classical spirituality has been eagerly consumed.[1]

The fact that some of this material may have Roman Catholic echoes should not blind us to its positive values. Writers in this category include Bernard of Clairvaux and Thomas à Kempis. While some denigrate all mysticism, a streak of what Adolph Deissmann calls "Christ-mysticism" is present in Paul (for example, Gal. 2:20). We have seen it in Luther. There is a metaphysical mysticism that is dangerous. But I must confess my own increasing appreciation for mysticism with regard to prayer. The Bible tells us much about prayer, but I do not begin to understand and comprehend its marvelous and effectual workings.[2]

John of the Cross was born in Fontiveros near Avila, in the rugged area of Spain lying some distance northwest of Madrid. His Jewish forebears were active in the silk trade, but he was raised in poverty by his widowed mother. He received schooling from the Jesuits in Medina del Campo and joined the Carmelite order, which afforded him opportunity for study at the University of Salamanca.[3] John became well-known for his love and insight into the Scripture. He always had his Bible with him: "The Scriptures became so deeply planted in John's being that his memory was easily stirred by words that echoed or alluded to scriptural phrases and passages, which in turn would suggest other passages in the sacred books."[4]

This saturation in Scripture safeguarded John's mysticism from becoming heretical; he rebuffed anyone who claimed "new" knowledge or revelation that did not agree with Scripture.

When Teresa of Avila was leading a movement for the reformation and renewal of the Carmelites, John was one of the first two to join her discalced friars (unshod). Teresa's works on prayer are rich.[5] John became a spiritual director in the movement. In 1577 he was arrested, taken to Toledo, flogged, and imprisoned for nine months for his defiance of ecclesiastical and political authority. While jailed, he began his famous lyric poem "The Spiritual Canticle," one of the greatest in Spanish literature. After release, he served in monasteries in Granada and Segovia. He proclaimed his doctrine of *nada, nada, nada* (nothing, nothing, nothing) in the spirit of John the Baptist, who vowed, "He must become greater; I must become less" (John 3:30), or Theodore Monod's "None of self but all of Thee."

John's major prose works are *The Ascent of Mount Carmel,* which begins with verse stanzas, and *The Dark Night,* for which he is best known. The "dark night of the soul" is the discipline of privation. Both Teresa and John see self-renunciation as necessary for progress toward union with God (Matt. 16:24). Two kinds of life experiences or "nights" aid in this progress: The *active night* is the Christian's voluntary work of self-discipline, and the *passive night* is the involuntary struggle "into which God himself leads the Christian, whether directly or through external circumstances."[6] John pleads for seeking more direct, experiential knowledge of God, rather than settling for understanding God "by analogy." This is knowledge by acquaintance that supplements knowledge by inference.

Although not generally a trustworthy guide, Georgia Harkness has given us a beautiful interpretation of the dark night that shows how the shadow experiences have been very heavy for such Christian philosophers as Tauler, Madame Guyon, and John Bunyan.[7] I myself visited Avila in Spain for the express purpose of feeling something of the environment in which these spiritual giants sought after and tasted of the living God. The austerity of the land reflects in their spirituality; it is not all that congenial to our self-indulgent ways. John was known as "patron of the afflicted," keeping his spiritual life in good balance.

A thoughtful and engaging historical novel of sixteenth-century times is Stephanie Cowell's *Nicholas Cooke: Actor, Soldier, Physic, Priest.*[8] "The renewed closeness to God" comes alive in this chronicle of an extraordinary pilgrim. Her research provides some interesting background on the early Reformation. For example, we learn that in the wake of the English Reformation there were 109 parish churches in London.

1. Samples could be seen in Louis Bouyer, *A History of Christian Spirituality,* 3 vols. (Minneapolis: Winston/Seabury, 1960); and his *World Spirituality: An Encyclopedic History of the Religious Quest* (New York: Crossroad, 1985), vols. 16, 17, and 18 treat Christian spirituality; Michael Cox, *Handbook of Christian Spirituality* (New York: Harper and Row, 1983); The Classics of Western Spirituality series (New York: Paulist). The granddaddy of them all is Cheslyn Jones, Geoffrey Wainwright, and Edward Yarnold, eds., *The Study of Spirituality* (New York: Oxford University Press, 1986).
2. Arthur L. Johnson, *Faith Misguided: Exposing the Dangers of Mysticism* (Chicago: Moody, 1988). A well-intentioned warning but too broad in its condemnation. The author challenges Watchman Nee for distinguishing soul and spirit. It seems to me a case can be made for Nee (see Heb. 4:12).

3. Loyola's goal was to live the mysteries of the cross.
4. Kieran Kavanaugh, ed., *St. John of the Cross: Selected Writings*, The Classics of Western Spirituality series (New York: Paulist, 1987), 28.
5. James M. Houston, ed., *St. Teresa of Avila, A Life of Prayer* (Portland, Ore.: Multnomah, 1983). This study includes her widely read *A Life of Prayer* and her remarkable *The Interior Castle*.
6. Jones, Wainwright, and Yarnold, *Study of Spirituality*, 371.
7. Georgia Harkness, *The Dark Night of the Soul* (Nashville: Abingdon-Cokesbury, 1945).
8. New York: Ballentine, 1993, 311.

CHAPTER FIVE

Revisiting Crucial Ideas, from the Enlightenment to Postmodernity

See to it that no one takes you captive through hollow and deceptive philosophy, which depends on human tradition and the basic principles of this world rather than on Christ. For in Christ all the fullness of the Deity lives in bodily form, and you have been given fullness in Christ, who is the head over every power and authority.

—Colossians 2:8–9

We know that we all possess knowledge. Knowledge puffs up, but love builds up. The man who thinks he knows something does not yet know as he ought to know. But the man who loves God is known by God.

—1 Corinthians 8:1b–2

Medieval culture was challenged by Renaissance humanism on the one hand and by the powerful tidal waves of the Protestant Reformation on the other. To the degree that human autonomy surfaced in Renaissance humanism, the stage was set for the rationalism of Thomas Hobbes, René Descartes, and Benedict de Spinoza. Crane Brinton says:

Rationalism even in these years owed much of its slowly growing prestige to the achievements of natural science. Finally, when with Newton science succeeded in attaining to a marvelously complete scheme of the universe, one that could be tested mathematically and that worked in the sense that it enabled successful prediction, the stage was set for

TABLE 5: Literature in Historical and Theological Context, 1700 to 1800

A: Historical Events; B: Arts and Philosophy; C: Revelation and Preaching

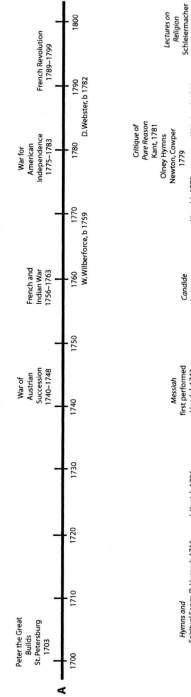

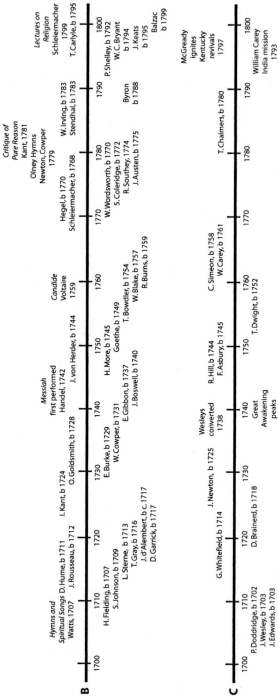

the new rationalist world-view, for a cosmology as different from that of St. Augustine or St. Thomas Aquinas as theirs was from that of a Greek of the fifth-century B.C.[1]

"The Enlightenment" (German: *Aufklarung*) was a scientific revolution or triumph of rationalism. The moderate first generation—François-Marie Voltaire (1694–1778), Charles Louis Montesquieu (1689–1755), Alexander Pope (1688–1744) and English deists—are on a slippery slope.[2] Romanticism raises an emotional protest against the denuding reduction of the human spirit. Conservative thinkers such as Edmund Burke (1729–1797) in England make a stand. Puritans also stood as relevant and vital articulations of Christian and biblical conviction, but it was divine intervention in the revivals of George Whitefield and John and Charles Wesley that saved England from a blood bath Revolution like that of France.[3]

---

1. Crane Brinton, *The Shaping of the Modern Mind* (New York: Mentor, 1953), 110ff.
2. Richard Popkin, *The History of Skepticism from Erasmus to Descartes* (Berkeley, Calif.: University of California Press, 1979).
3. Helpful discussions into the philosophical implications of the Enlightenment to the mid-twentieth century are to be found in Carl F. H. Henry's studies *Remaking the Modern Mind* (Grand Rapids: Eerdmans, 1946); *The Protestant Dilemma* (Grand Rapids: Eerdmans, 1948); and *The Drift of Western Thought* (Grand Rapids: Eerdmans, 1951). Henry shows the progression of antisupernaturalism to naturalism—the ultimacy of nature.

5.1   ENLIGHTENED MINDS

5.1.1 NEWTON, SUPER-GENIUS OF SCIENCE

If I have seen farther [than other men], it is because I have stood on the shoulders of others.

I do not know what I may appear to the world, but to myself I seem to have been only like a boy playing on the seashore, in diverting myself in now and then finding a smoother pebble or a prettier shell than ordinary, whilst the great ocean of truth lay all undiscovered before me.

—Isaac Newton

The Enlightenment stood for autonomy, nature, harmony, and progress. While it was anticlerical and opposed to organized religion generally, it still began in the confident assumption that God was keeping the universe running just fine.[1] This bipolar tendency can be seen in Isaac Newton (1642–1727), who is variously eulogized as one of history's foremost geniuses, one of the greatest names in human thought, and the greatest scientist of all time. Manifestly he was a convinced theist, but he essentially studied a mechanistic universe, disregarding the teleology of God's design.

Newton's father died soon after Isaac was born in Lincolnshire, England. His mother remarried a clergyman. The child was mostly raised by his maternal grandmother. He was not distinguished as a student until he won a fist fight with a bright student and decided that he ought to excel in intellectual as well as physical challenges. As a youth he invented a four-wheel carriage. The London plague of 1665–66 came just after his graduation from Trinity College, Cambridge. During these two years of forced retirement, he discovered the law of gravitation. Voltaire says it was Newton's niece who told him about dropping the apple. He also developed the concept of a planetary magnetic field "fluxion waves" and studied the colors of light. Of these matters he told only his friend and mentor, Isaac Barrow, Lucasian Professor of Mathematics at Cambridge and Puritan preacher.[2]

Before his twenty-seventh birthday, Newton succeeded Barrow at Cambridge. When he presented the second telescope he had invented to the Royal Society, he was elected a member. He also experimented with principles related to medieval alchemy. Not drawing many students, he was an increasingly solitary scholar.[3] He carried on several extended public controversies, including one with German philosopher Gottfried W. von Leibniz (1646–1716). In 1687 he published *Principia,* covering many of the contemporary issues in science. His basic work stood until superseded by Albert Einstein. In this work he even considers the possibility of projecting an artificial satellite into space orbit.[4]

Newton insisted on distinguishing observation from hypothesis ("I shall not mingle conjecture with certainties").[5] Newton for a time served in Parliament as a member from Cambridge. In his later years he directed the Mint for England.

He was an authority in several scientific fields. He desperately wanted to preserve the God of the Bible as the Master Mechanic of the universe, although he never understood how to do this consistently.[6] The Bible was important for Newton, but he, like some other rationalists of his day, saw Christ as a created being separate from the Father and generally was Arian in his view of Christ. He worried that Descartes had effectively banished spirit from the universe, and he gave himself to demonstrating that matter is dependent on God. He had a major health breakdown in 1693 and thereafter gave himself almost wholly to Scripture study, concentrating on Bible prophecy.[7] He was knighted by Queen Anne in 1705. He died at eighty-five years of age and was buried in Westminster Abbey.

Newton's concessions to naturalistic presuppositions over biblical truth were not as sweeping as were those of the next generation of scientists.[8] However, he gave up ground at points that would prove disastrous to faith. His biblical studies show preponderant emphasis on technical and historical matters. At first he was more involved in the book of Revelation, but Daniel's prophecies engaged him in later years.[9] He interpreted Daniel 9:24–27 as a chronological prophecy predicting the time of Christ's crucifixion,[10] and wrote a chapter on "the times of the birth and passion of Christ."[11] He concluded his observations on the Apocalypse with a description of the Day of Atonement in relation to Christ.[12] Yet Newton lacks a deep sense of personal devotion to the Lord Jesus, whom he does not see as God. So in Isaac Newton can be found cracks and fissures that would become devastating chasms to separate the Enlightenment from Christianity.

William Wordsworth (1770–1850) memorialized him in the *Prelude* and his friend Edmund Halley (1656–1742), who discovered Halley's comet, wrote a moving ode. But the words of Pope are the best remembered:

> Nature and Nature's laws lay hid in night;
> God said: "Let Newton be," and all was light.[13]

---

1. Stanley J. Grenz is one who points out the theistic worldview of the early Enlightenment. See *A Primer on Postmodernism* (Grand Rapids: Eerdmans, 1997).
2. See the biographical section on Isaac Barrow in David L. Larsen, *The Company of the Preachers* (Grand Rapids: Kregel, 1998), 7.3.3.6. Barrow is an example of an Arminian Puritan.
3. Richard S. Westfall, *Never at Rest: A Biography of Isaac Newton* (Cambridge: Cambridge University Press, 1980), 75. This massive work is stronger on scientific subjects than on the theological/spiritual aspects of Newton's thought. Westfall's field is the history of science. Reading this with parts of the *Principia* would be best.
4. The Newtonian physics that was upset by Einstein is explored in Lincoln Barnett, *The Universe and Dr. Einstein* (New York: Harper, 1948). Barnett also looks at Max Planck's quantum physics and Werner Karl Heisenberg's principle of indeterminacy. See also Thomas Powers, *Heisenberg's War* (New York: Knopf, 1993) on the secret history of German military research into fission. For a look at post-Einstein physics, see books by Stephen J. Hawking.
5. Quoted in H. W. Turnbull, ed., *The Correspondence of Isaac Newton,* 2 vols. (Cambridge: Cambridge University Press, 1965).
6. E. A. Burtt, *The Metaphysical Foundations of Modern Science* (New York: Doubleday Anchor, 1954), 284ff.
7. *Never At Rest,* 540. His successor, William Whiston, spoke out more and was tried and ousted from the post for holding Arian views.
8. Michael White and John Gribbin, *Einstein: A Life in Science* (New York: Dutton, 1993). Einstein committed immorality, was indifferent to family responsibilities, and rejected Judaism.
9. William Whitla, *Sir Isaac Newton's Daniel and the Apocalypse* (London: John Murray, 1922). Professor Whitla taught at Queen's College, Belfast. He has given us a sterling introduction to Newton's work as well as lectures on the evidential value of predictive prophecy. He himself has been influenced by the late Grattan Guiness.
10. Ibid., 128. Newton did see a future siege of Jerusalem at the time of Christ's second coming. The scintillating new study in the field is Michael White's *Isaac Newton: The Last Sorcerer* (Reading, Mass.: Addison-Wesley, 1997). This volume gives evidence for his Puritan faith (see 49).
11. Ibid., 235ff. This is high-density biblical scholarship that expresses full confidence in Scripture's record.
12. Ibid., 343, 350. Newton correlates the 144,000 of Revelation 7 with the two witnesses of Revelation 11.
13. Epitaph for Isaac Newton. Herbert Davis, ed., *Pope's Poetical Works* (London: Oxford University Press, 1966), 651.

5.1.2 PASCAL, GENIUS ON FIRE

The heart has its reasons of which reason knows nothing. *(Pensée 277)*

Jesus Christ is the object of all things. . . . Whosoever knows him knows the reason for everything. *(Pensée 556)*

God alone is man's true good, and man has rejected him. It is strange that no thing has been found in all creation to take his place. *(Pensée 131)*[1]

—Blaise Pascal

In 1647 Blaise Pascal (1623–1662) met the eminent René Descartes (1596–1650), who advised him on his frail health. Pascal was a scientific prodigy, even though his widowed father deliberately avoided scientific disciplines in the education of his children. Their learning was chiefly in languages. At age twelve, Pascal discovered Euclid's geometric axioms on his own. Before he was sixteen, he wrote a work on conic sections and was a pioneer in hydraulics. His work in integral calculus was a great contribution, and at age twenty, he invented a calculating machine. In 1652 he sent a letter and a calculating machine to Queen Christina of Sweden (1626–1689), the patroness of many scientists. A sickly child, Pascal suffered throughout his life with excruciating headaches, possibly caused by cranial abnormality. His financial prospects were always uncertain, and he died at age thirty-nine.[2]

Biographer Ernest Mortimer called Pascal's career "curiously disjointed." He was known and respected in the scientific community by leaders as diverse as the architect Christopher Wren (1632–1723) and philosopher-mathematician Leibniz. He was intrigued with the Stoic Epictetus (A.D. 50–130), although he came to believe that the "virtuous pagan" was an oxymoronic concept. He was much influenced by the essays of Michel Eyquem de Montaigne (1533–1592).

During a worldly time in about 1649, Pascal entered into the flow of ideas and lifestyle that would characterize the Enlightenment. He was uneasy with Descartes, yet he was greatly indebted to Cartesian dualism for his freedom to experiment without metaphysical intrusion. "I cannot forgive Descartes," Pascal wrote. "In his whole philosophy he would have been quite willing to dispense with God. But he had to have Him give a fillip to set the world in motion; beyond this, he had no further need of God."[3]

Pascal also answered the English deists, whose philosophical theology became a popular offspring of the Enlightenment through such thinkers as Voltaire, Pope, and Samuel Taylor Coleridge (1772–1834). Pascal's family came under the influence of Jansenists from Port Royal southwest of Paris.[4] Cornelis Jansen (1585–1638) wrote a reforming theology of Augustine, which was published after his death. From 1640 on there was a bitter controversy in France between Jansenists and the Jesuits. Traditional beliefs were shaken by the new science, the voyages of discovery, and increasing knowledge of other cultures and religions. It was stylish to doubt.

In 1646 Pascal had an evangelistic awakening, and then after a life threatening experience in 1654, he had a second conversion.[5] He now stood solidly on Scripture and gave himself almost continuously to serious Bible study. Modern analysts tend to dismiss Pascal's Scripture-founded pietism.[6] They are quick to belittle his view that biblical prophecies have found fulfillment in Jesus Christ and that they establish his messianic claims. Such biblical scholarship is now regarded as outdated.[7] However, many leading scholars join this devout Christian layman in affirming the centrality of Christ and his cross as the basis of salvation and a right relationship to God.

In 1658, when his health began to totally break down, Pascal commenced writing a defense of religion, but before his death, he had completed only fragments of this work, his thoughts or *Pensées*. In these writings, he stands with Descartes to insist on human rationality. But there is also the foundation for an existentialism. True religion is not contrary to reason (*Pensée* 187), indeed it is through reason that God puts religion into the human mind (185). However, reason is so easily distorted by custom and diverted from reality (97, 139). Reason is fragmentary and often overcome by imagination (72, 80).

Yet there is a case to be made for the reasonableness of the Christian faith. As a philosopher-mathematician who worked with probabilities, he pressed his famous "Wager" (section 3), in which he argues that humankind is doomed to be miserable without God and that the odds "are infinitely in favor of a bet that faith is right." One has everything to win and nothing to lose by playing on faith; whereas, if one does not believe, one gains nothing and loses all.

The modern apologist Os Guiness testifies:

> Pascal, then, I have found second only to Augustine as a hero-saint whose life is an inspiration and challenge as well as a drastic antidote to late twentieth-century discipleship.[8]

In his earlier *Provincial Letters,* which he wrote in defense of the Jansenists, he scores the Jesuits for mocking Christ's perfect sacrifice. He often wrote the words: *"ne crux Christi evacuetur"* ("lest the cross of Christ be made of no effect"). As Émile Calliet, a student of Pascal's thought, expressed it, "It is as fascinating as profoundly moving, to realize how Calvary marked the great Divide along the path of Pascal's quest for truth."[9] Christ on the cross is for Pascal the basis of pardon and redemption and the model for Christian life and service. Alexander Vinet observed that vocations such as Pascal's exist in such spiritual abundance that we can all be significantly nourished and fortified here.[10] We are beneficiaries of the overflow of the concentrated intensity that was the life of Pascal.

▨ **A peek at the pessimism** of the Enlightenment, what Howard Mumford Jones calls "the dark trumpets of doom," can be found in Henry Vyverberg's *Historical Pessimism in the French Enlightenment.*[11] According to Vyverberg: "The Enlightenment was characterized by a heightened sense of earthly destiny, and if it was conscious of progress so too was it conscious of decadence and historical flux. In force and attraction these pessimistic doctrines could not compete on even terms with the greater lure of historical optimism, but the notions of decadence and flux stubbornly resisted destruction by progressionist imperatives. The strength of this resistance, moreover, was not an accident. Historical pessimism was by no means an obscure and irrelevant reaction against the ideals of the Enlightenment; it was firmly rooted in the thought of the age."

1. *Pensée* 131, as quoted in Os Guiness, *The Mind on Fire: An Anthology of the Writings of Blaise Pascal* (Portland, Ore.: Multnomah, 1987), 109.
2. Ernest Mortimer, *Blaise Pascal: The Life and Work of a Realist* (New York: Harper, 1959), 31. A beautiful study.
3. *Pensée* 77. For a provocative discussion, cf. Charles Frankel, "Pascal and the Sphere of Progress," in *The Faith of Reason* (New York: Octagon, 1969), 29ff. Pascal always observed a limit for the working of the scientific method.
4. Mortimer, *Blaise Pascal* (46ff.), analyzes the Arnauld family and Cardinal Richelieu's imprisonment of Saint-Cyran. See also Marvin R. O'Connell, *Blaise Pascal: Reasons of the Heart* (Grand Rapids: Eerdmans, 1997).
5. For the best study of the spiritual development of Pascal, see Émile Calliet, *Pascal: The Emergence of Genius* (New York: Harper Torchbooks, 1961). Calliet's thesis is that "Pascal's growing concentration upon the Bible is the vital clue both to the content and method of his thinking." Calliet, long a faculty member at Princeton Theological Seminary, gives his own testimony to the power of the Word in his own conversion, *Journey into Light* (Grand Rapids: Zondervan, 1968). Also worthwhile are his *The Christian Approach to Culture* (Nashville: Abingdon, 1953) and his later *The Recovery of Purpose* (New York: Harper, 1959). He was our foremost expert on Pascal.
6. Alaban Krailsheimer, *Pascal* (New York: Hill and Wang, 1980), 61. This Oxford scholar laments Pascal's Augustinian pessimism about human nature, but does acknowledge that Christian redemption through the cross of Christ is presented in Pascal as the drastic solution to the human predicament.
7. Elfrieda Debois, "Pascal," in *The Study of Spirituality* (Oxford: Oxford University Press, 1986), 407.
8. Os Guiness, introduction to *The Mind on Fire,* 28. Guiness speaks of Pascal's "brief intense flame-burst of a life."
9. Émile Calliet, "Pascal's Illumination at the Cross," *Christianity Today,* 31 (August 1962), 23.
10. Ibid. In 1654 Pascal reportedly had a vision in which he heard the Crucified speak: "I was thinking of thee in my agony; I have shed such and such drops of blood for thee." Pascal fell on his knees before the cross and said: "Lord, I give Thee all." He had been reading John 17 where Jesus is preparing himself for the cross and praying for those who trust in him.
11. Cambridge: Harvard, 1958.

5.1.3 LOCKE, STATESMAN OF THE ENLIGHTENMENT

Faith can never convince us of anything that contradicts our knowledge.
But whether it be a divine revelation or no, reason must judge.
Reason must be our last judge and guide in everything.

—John Locke

John Locke (1632–1704) has been called "the intellectual ruler of the eighteenth century." He was the most significant English philosopher, although not the most insightful. He presided at the enthronement of the "Age of Reason" over biblical Christianity. Hobbes, the most influential rationalist, had devastated faith while supposedly magnifying the Bible (see *Leviathan,* chap. 32). Newton had made major concessions to naturalism in formulating the philosophy of science that would dominate the scientific disciplines for two hundred years.[1] Pascal had displayed a wiser balance within the Roman Church. Puritans and the Continental pietists were a counterbalance within Protestantism.

Now appeared Locke, writing as a professing Christian. By nature a cautious man, he became the progenitor of deism, which confessed belief in God but denied revealed religion.

In a study sympathetic to the French Enlightenment, Peter Gay shows how Voltaire made Locke "the hero of the Continental Enlightenment."[2] Denis Diderot (1713–1784), with his *Encyclopédia,* and Voltaire led the march to modernity. Voltaire admired Locke's naturalistic assumptions.[3] Newton and Locke were his heroes. Jean-Jacques Rousseau (1712–1778) leaned on him. Bishop George Berkeley (1685–1753), who denied that matter has existence independent of the mind, was profoundly influenced by Locke. So were David Hume (1711–1776) and Immanuel Kant (1724–1804) in their efforts to bury historic Christianity.[4]

Locke thus is a seminal thinker. His four letters on "Toleration" and his *Essay Concerning Human Understanding* were decisive for Thomas Jefferson in his writing of the Declaration of Independence and are must reading. Indeed, while he was confidential secretary of Anthony Cooper, Earl of Shaftesbury (1621–1683), he wrote the "Constitution for the Carolinas in the New World." His new philosophy of liberty, while not as strong as John Milton's (1608–1674), was often used as justification for the Glorious Revolution of 1688 in England and the later American Revolution. In his philosophy Locke proscribed the liberty of papists and atheists while Milton excluded no one. Locke was the premier influence on Blackstone's famous treatises on law.

Locke was born into a Somerset home of Puritan sympathies. He studied at Oxford at the time John Owen had a high profile. D. J. O'Connor describes his character as seen in his writings. He was "cautious, patient, and tolerant, a firm believer in the powers of the disinterested human reason and a fierce hater of authoritarianism and its associated bigotry, both in religion and politics, he embodies the virtues that most of Europe in the seventeenth century so conspicuously lacked."[5] He taught at Oxford and was a practicing physician. He fled England during the reign of James II because he was suspected of involvement in plots against the government and lived in the Netherlands from 1684 to 1689.

Locke championed the separation of church and state and the right of private property. He returned home to England to write, and although suffering from ill health, he enjoyed a relatively quiet and productive retirement. He spent much time studying the Bible and writing a commentary on the Pauline Epistles.

Some have maintained that Locke was himself a deist, but this is not really so; Locke was too conservative and cautious for the deists, who were radicals.[6] Still, Locke has an obvious affinity for deism. Many English thinkers, among them Richard Hooker (1554–1600) and the Cambridge neo-Platonists, saw the importance of rationality. William Paley defended biblical morality solely from reason.[7] There were voices of protest. Milton was wary of misused reason, and Isaac Watts (1674–1748) warned of overindulging reason.

Locke was a churchman, holding his affiliation with Benjamin Whichcote in the St. Lawrence Jewry Congregation. He writes from within the language of Christian theology. But Locke, as cogent and valuable was his thinking in many respects, essentially made the way for eighteenth-century rationalistic skepticism, from which Western Europe never recovered philosophically. Locke's damage came in the areas of:

1. *epistemology.* Denying that there are innate ideas, he held that the human mind at birth is *tabula rasa* (a blank slate). All knowledge is acquired through the five senses and reflection upon what the senses gather. The grave danger here as R. W. Harris has seen is that "Revelation could not be admitted against the clear evidence of reason."[8] If all knowledge is based on experience, is there any knowledge? Carl F. H. Henry stressed that Locke's empiricism inevitably ends at "the wailing wall of agnosticism, as Hume learned firsthand in expounding its implications."[9]
2. *authority.* The rejection of Augustine is complete, for as Augustine believed, to put reason above scriptural revelation is to make reason the highest authority. Locke sees God's own knowledge as deductive. Tilting from the "enthusiasm" of the Puritans, he believed that Jesus is the Messiah, without any ontological Sonship or Triunity. He was accused of being a Socinian or Unitarian. He did believe God's existence could be demonstrated (in a cosmological argument). God's providential care and the miracles of Jesus certified him as Messiah. His approach to Scripture was rationalistic, critical, and very selective.[10]
3. *depravity.* Locke denied the historic doctrine of human depravity and took a very much more sunny view of the human condition. Like Newton, he was strong on natural law and saw the human problem to be a lack of clear understanding. Christ's mission was essentially to clarify and renew the sanctions behind the moral law. Redemption then becomes the new moral law of Christ.[11]
4. *soteriology.* While he wrote *The Reasonableness of Christianity* in 1695 to assuage concerns about his orthodoxy, the fact is, as John Yolton observes: "his sympathies with some of the newer currents in religion placed him again on the side of those who were challenging orthodoxy: the reasonableness and simplicity of doctrine that he insisted upon were seen as threats to religious beliefs."[12]

Locke denied any priestly role by Christ. His sense of justice was offended to contemplate that Christ came to carry the sins of the world.[13] Since Christ's coming then was to complete the moral law, was he anything more than a great ethical teacher? Locke does uphold Christian morality, but the problem in his ethics is to grasp just how such actual rules derive from reason so enthroned to which all matters of revelation must be subservient. Having rejected the medieval (biblical?) notion of "universals," it does appear that for Locke, Christ came to reform but not to redeem in the biblical sense. Salvation is by works entirely, that is, by obeying the moral law.[14]

What becomes problematic is that the major American theologian, Jonathan Edwards, was so fond of Locke. In fact, Samuel Hopkins quoted Edwards as saying that he derived more pleasure from Locke's pages "than the most greedy miser finds when gathering up handfuls of silver and gold."[15] The difference was that Edwards believed the Bible to be literally true. How Lockean was Edwards's psychology in his *Treatise on Religious Affections*?[16] Was Locke blunting the older Edwards's conviction on substitutionary atonement so that it was but a short step for Jonathan Edwards Jr. to move away from satisfaction altogether in his adoption of the governmental theory of the atonement? Very clearly, Locke bears serious scrutiny.

The bottom line for us would seem to be the urgent necessity of defending a rational faith and objective truth. A superb example can be seen in D. Elton Trueblood's *A Place to Stand*[17] and in his *Philosophy of Religion*.[18] In both he laments the shift from ideas to events in contemporary theology and the surrender of any objective reference in ethics and aesthetics. The rejection of apologetics is symptomatic. True Christianity is rational and evangelical. See also Trueblood's 1974 autobiography, *While It Is Day*.[19]

1. Gordon H. Clark, *The Philosophy of Science and Belief in God* (Nutley, N.J.: Craig, 1964). Clark shows the concessions of Newtonian science and its collapse in the face of the dominance of mechanism.

2. Peter Gay, *The Party of Harmony: Essays in the French Enlightenment* (New York: Norton, 1954), 42.

3. Will Durant, "Voltaire and the French Enlightenment," in *The Story of Philosophy* (New York: Simon and Schuster, 1926), 187ff. In the wake of the great earthquake and tidal wave that killed so many in Lisbon in 1755, Voltaire's novel *Candide* dismantles Leibniz's "best of all possible worlds" notion. Here is the thinking behind the wave of skepticism that swept over Europe in the eighteenth century.

4. David Hume, the radical empiricist, loved to hear the sound preaching of John Brown of Haddington because of Brown's moral earnestness, but his vicious assault on the resurrection of Christ and the other foundations of Christian faith did incalculable harm. The core of his case is in his *Dialogues Concerning Natural Religion*. He describes positive religion as "the playful whimsies of monkeys in human shape." Hume was "a convinced follower of Locke in his radically empirical doctrine of the origin of ideas and of knowledge" (Edwin A. Burtt, *Types of Religious Philosophy* [New York: Harper, 1939], 207). We shall have more to say about Immanuel Kant's removal of religion and Christian theology from the realm of cognition, an attitude that was to affect so much of modern theology.

5. D. J. O'Connor, *John Locke* (London: Penguin, 1952), 22. He says Hume worked out what was implied in Locke.

6. S. G. Hefelbower, *The Relation of John Locke to English Deism* (Chicago: University of Chicago Press, 1918).

7. R. W. Harris, *Reason and Nature in the Eighteenth Century* (New York: Barnes and Noble, 1969), 7.

8. Ibid., 73. Harris insists that Locke writes as a Christian, not a deist. Whatever his personal faith, his enthronement of reason has consequences. Read his view in *Human Understanding*, 4.3.27.

9. Carl F. H. Henry, *God, Revelation and Authority* (Waco, Tex.: Word, 1976), 310ff.; Gordon H. Clark, *A Christian View of Men and Things* (Grand Rapids: Eerdmans, 1952), 302ff.; and Émile Calliet, *The Christian Approach to Culture* (Nashville: Abingdon, 1953), 164ff. Calliet deals with "The Aftermath of the Ontological Deviation."

10. Hefelbower, *Relation of John Locke,* 176. "The lion of rationalism is made to lie down with the lamb of traditionalism and not devour it," is the thesis propounded. But the question is, does the lamb emerge unscathed and intact?

11. Ibid., 135. "Christ's redemption is made to consist in restoring what Adam lost by setting up the new law of faith."

12. John W. Yolton, *The Locke Reader* (Cambridge: Cambridge University Press, 1977), 4.

13. Harris, *Reason and Nature,* 77. So clearly in the illumination/redemption tension, Locke is part of the former.

14. John Locke, *The Reasonableness of Christianity,* in *Works,* 7.10–15.

15. Iain H. Murray, *Jonathan Edwards: A New Biography* (Edinburgh: Banner of Truth, 1987), 67; see especially the introduction, p. xx, and the note, p. xxv.

16. One of the best defenses of Edwards is Harold Simonson, *Jonathan Edwards: Theologian of the Heart* (Grand Rapids: Eerdmans, 1974). On the influence of Locke, see pp. 12–14, 23–29, 32, 35, 37, 95–101, 107–8.

17. New York: Harper, 1969.

18. New York: Harper, 1957.

19. D. Elton Trueblood, *While It Is Day* (New York: Harper, 1974).

5.2 THE PURITAN MIND

5.2.1 Bunyan, Puritan Pilgrim

I dreamed and behold I saw a man clothed in rags, standing in a certain place, with his face from his own house, a Book in his hand, and a great burden on his back. I looked and saw him open the book and read therein; and as he read, he wept and trembled; and not being able longer to contain, he broke out with a lamentable cry, saying, "What shall I do?"
—John Bunyan
Pilgrim's Progress

That lonely figure with the Bible and the burden of sin is not only John Bunyan himself. It is the representative Puritan of the English Puritan epoch. The poor man seeking salvation with tears, with no guide save the Bible in his hands, that man multiplied, congregated, regimented, was a force by which Oliver Cromwell and George Fox and John Wesley wrought their wonders, being men of a like experience themselves.
—G. M. Trevelyan, *English Social History*[1]

A greater contrast can hardly be imagined than between John Locke, the philosopher who conformed to the intellectual fashion of his times, and John Bunyan, the preacher who at tremendous personal cost would not bend like a willow in the breeze but resolutely stood for and proclaimed the historic gospel. Bunyan (1628–1688) was born in Elstow near Bedford and followed his father's trade as a tinker, mending pots and pans. This was a time of great restiveness in England and tortuous conflict between Charles I and the royalists and what would be increasingly a Puritan Parliament.[2] This conflict culminated in the bloody English Civil War between royalists and Parliament and the execution of Charles. From 1644–46 Bunyan served in the Parliamentary Army, narrowly escaping death on several occasion. Much of the vivid imagery in *The Holy War* undoubtedly comes out of this experience.

As a young man, Bunyan was a carouser. His personal testimony is movingly told in his autobiographical *Grace Abounding to the Chief of Sinners*.[3] Puritanism became a powerful force for spiritual renewal in England and the New England colonies as was Europe's Continental pietist movement. God was at work in the lands of the Reformation and beyond. Bunyan's first wife (whose name we do not know) read to him from such books as Arthur Dent's *The Plain Man's Path to Heaven* and Luther's commentary on Galatians. He heard several women talking about the joy of the Christian life and he sought the new birth. His extended agony of conviction for sin at this time and the elusiveness of assurance are classic examples of the Puritan concept of the Holy Spirit's usually lengthy process of "legal work" in the sinner's heart.[4]

At last the chains fell off (as from Christian at Mount Calvary in *The Pilgrim's Progress*), and he joined St. John's Church, a nonconformist fellowship in Bedford. He still could neither read nor write. Many Puritans were educated at Cambridge or Oxford, so Bunyan's call to preach was questioned for his lack of academic preparation. Yet he became pastor of St. John's.[5] With the restoration of the monarchy in 1660, Bunyan was imprisoned for twelve years. He began writing in prison. After a brief time of release in 1671, he was again jailed in 1672. During his second imprisonment, he wrote *The Pilgrim's Progress*.

This elaborate allegory in two parts shows how Christian and his wife made their trek from the City of Destruction to the Celestial City. This work went through 160 editions in the eighteenth century alone. Bunyan scholar J. A. Froude does not exaggerate when he writes: "He was a man whose writings have for two centuries affected the spiritual opinions of the English race in every part of the world more powerfully than any book or books except the Bible."[6]

Beyond this classic, readers should enjoy *The Holy War,* which was published in 1682. While his best-known work uses the metaphor of journey, in *The Holy War* he uses the metaphor of warfare: King Shaddai's battle with Diabolus to regain the Metropolis of the World, or as he subtitles it, "The Losing and Taking Again of the Town of Mansoul."[7] Batson argues that Bunyan drew upon Augustine's advocacy of the use of the figurative to set forth the invisible and unseen realm with spiritual reality.[8] If Bunyan had never written his earlier masterpiece, it is widely conceded that *The Holy War* would be considered the finest allegory ever composed.[9]

The action in relation to Mansoul is at both the level of humankind's experience corporately and the experience of the individual. The narrative recounts the original fall of Diabolus and his assault on Mansoul through the five gates (the five physical senses). He shows how Lord Understanding and Mr. Conscience are incapacitated in the fall. The decision to retake Mansoul is announced and Satan takes immediate steps to prepare for the invasion. King Shaddai's siege is described, in which Lord Willbewill's commitment is crucial. Ultimately Mansoul is retaken and cleansed and the glory of Emmanuel radiates on every side. The trial of atheism is a classic, but alas, the cunning connivery of Mr. Carnal Security leaves Mansoul still vulnerable, and Emmanuel withdraws. Then Emmanuel is petitioned to return and the machinations of Diabolus are frustrated. The book climaxes with the gracious and powerful address of Emmanuel.

The skill and stylistic genius of Bunyan are in clear evidence in this unabashed and courageous explanation of the supernatural gospel. What leaders and teachers do is critical over the long haul, but we must never lose sight of the fact that the battle is waged down in the trenches among the masses, and this is where John Bunyan took his stand. Something of the breadth and genius of Bunyan are to be observed, as D. Martyn Lloyd-Jones himself called to our attention, in the fact that he was an "open baptist" with freedom in the fellowship as to the mode, although his own preference was for believers' baptism by immersion.[10] Indeed he wrote a treatise entitled *Differences in Judgment About Water Baptism No Bar to Communion.* He most earnestly wanted the unity and oneness of the people of God. Interestingly, when there was no preacher at Auguste Franck's (1663–1727) orphanage at Halle, Germany, the model for George Müller's later institution, John Bunyan would be read in translation.[11]

This phenomenon of acceptance and "networking" frequently crossed theological lines and was a strength of both Puritans and pietist movements. This was remarkable in the context of the times and a model for twenty-first-century ecumenical dialogue. The Puritan Movement in itself was an umbrella for various Church of England and Nonconformist nuances. These theologians held firmly to their faith distinctives but were able to differentiate between Christian essentials and nonessentials, make common cause, and in fact learn from one another to a degree conservative believers later seemed unable to do.

---

1. Cited in Wilbur M. Smith, "Introduction" to John Bunyan, *The Holy War* (Chicago: Moody, 1948).

2. C. V. Wedgewood, *A Coffin for King Charles: The Trial and Execution of Charles I* (New York: Macmillan, 1964). Other titles in this trilogy are *The King's Peace* and *The King's War.*

3. John Bunyan, *Grace Abounding to the Chief of Sinners* (Grand Rapids: Baker, 1978). Bunyan wrote one hundred books.

4. Ibid., 35. "I was more loathsome in mine eyes than a toad, and I thought I was so in God's eyes also." J. I. Packer writes on many aspects of Puritan life and culture, including the assurance of salvation. See, for example, Packer, *A Quest for Godliness: The Puritan Vision of the Christian Life* (Wheaton, Ill.: Crossway, 1990), 179.

Puritans tended to emphasize ultimate assurance over immediate assurance, although both seem to found in Scripture. Attention is given to both preaching and evangelism in the Puritan context.

5. E. Beatrice Batson, *John Bunyan: Allegory and Imagination* (London: Croom Helm, 1984).

6. Quoted in Wilbur M. Smith's introduction to *The Holy War* (Chicago: Moody, 1948), 33.

7. I recommend the beautiful Wycliffe Classics edition by Moody, if a copy can be located. Smith's bibliographic notes are unusually rich.

8. *Allegory and Imagination.* This advice in Augustine's *De doctrina christiana* has been taken by Bunyan, Dante, and many others.

9. Ibid., 71. Professor Batson traces the influence of Augustine upon preaching and education. Her examination of the major Puritan literary form, the sermon, focuses on such classic Bunyan messages as "The Holy City," "Sighs from Hell," "The Doctrine of Law," and "Grace Unfolded." The striking use of metaphor and allegory are to be seen in the sermons also. An example of classic preaching on the characters and truths of *The Holy War* is to be seen in Alexander Whyte's *Bunyan Characters, III* (London: Oliphant, Anderson and Ferrier, 1902). Especially good is his discourse on "Old Mrs. Prejudice, the Keeper of Ear-Gate, with the Sixty Deaf Men Under Him," 73ff.

10. D. M. Lloyd-Jones, *The Puritans: Their Origins and Successors* (Edinburgh: Banner of Truth, 1987), 399, 401. An especially fine newer study of Bunyan is Gordon Wakefield's, *Bunyan the Christian* (New York: Harper, 1992).

11. An exceedingly keen volume is W. R. Ward, *The Protestant Evangelical Awakening* (Cambridge: Cambridge University Press, 1992). The interchange between Puritans and Continental pietists is clearly documented here.

5.3 THE MODERN MIND

5.3.1 MONTESQUIEU, RELATIVIST

I write not to censure anything established in any country whatsoever. Every nation will here find the reasons on which its maxims are founded. . . . Could I but succeed so as to afford new reasons to every man to love his prince, his country, his laws, new reasons to render him more sensible in every nation and government of the blessings he enjoys, I should think myself the happiest of mortals.

—Charles Louis Montesquieu
The Spirit of Laws

Biblical authority was the foremost issue in the post-Reformation world.[1] The Enlightenment was the direct challenge to orthodox Christianity and all of its institutions. Crane Brinton defines the Enlightenment as: "the belief that all human beings can attain here on this earth a state of perfection hitherto in the West thought to be possible only for Christians in a state of grace, and for them only after death."[2] Renaissance humanism sowed the seeds, elevating reason until it became the judge of all truth—even revelation.[3] Despite the overlay of faith, we see the triumph of the immanent in Newton and Locke. Hume went on to the conclusion that religious truth was illusory. We see the "corrosiveness of the Enlightenment" in Germany where Leibniz basically abbreviated and modified Christianity so that it might be more reasonable. For Leibniz, Christ's death has no significance and the Holy Spirit seems incomprehensible.[4] Pure Enlightenment was preached from many German pulpits.

One of the most effective carriers of this virus to France was Montesquieu, Charles Louis de Secondat, Baron de la Bréde (1689–1755), one of the French *philosophes* whose writings stirred the coals that would flame as the French Revolution. His *Lettres Persanes* are fictitious letters from a Persian who has been exposed to Christian faith. He reflects on many subjects, including religion, in biting satire. Under the guise of the opinions expressed in the letters, he takes his shot at "the Christian God who can make one out of three gods, who can make flesh out of bread . . . who must be a great sorcerer."[5] Montesquieu is relatively moderate in tone, but he is a turning point, and those who followed him would be far more radical.

Montesquieu was born to wealth near Bordeaux, as was Montaigne, yet he was placed in the care of a poor man's wife so that he might know true humanity. Classically educated, he married a wealthy Huguenot woman. He trained for the law and became a distinguished jurist, serving as president of the Bordeaux Parliament. In 1729 he visited England where he spent eighteen months, with visits to Pope, Robert Walpole (1676–1745), and Jonathan Swift (1667–1745). As Locke, Montesquieu influenced American founding fathers when his insistence on the separation of powers was installed as a principle of the U.S. Constitution.

Émile Durkheim, the Jewish French scholar, hailed Montesquieu as the founder of modern social science (Durkheim's Latin dissertation was on Montesquieu). Montesquieu's key work was *De l'Espirit des Lois* (*The Spirit of Laws,* 1748). He is dependent on Locke and can be seen as the first "sociologist" (although the word was coined by Auguste Comte many years later). Montesquieu made a comparative study of social phenomena—religion, law, morality, and trade. His survey of diversity made him very tolerant. In fact, he finds fault with no custom, including polygamy and moderate slavery. Laws derive from human custom.[6] For him, there are natural laws, but there is no "Natural Law" originating in the mind of God. Norms for human behavior come from "the things themselves." Only "a certain idea of God" is mentioned in passing.[7] Durkheim correctly observes that Montesquieu has not "the slightest concern for metaphysical problems."[8] The static in human experience derives from "accidental and fortuitous deviations." Nothing is fixed or immutable. The laws he describes in fascinating fashion depend only on "the nature and condition of the society."[9] The problem for the genial latitudinarian is always how to handle monstrous evil—a Hitler and Stalin.

Montesquieu may have preferred a constitutional monarchy and the separation of church and state, but without any transcendent referent to the living God and his Word, humanity wanders over a trackless sea of subjectivity, and each person must find a personal way. Relativism has been one of the scourges of the Enlightenment, and Montesquieu was among its most successful agents.

1. Paul Johnson, *A History of Christianity* (New York: Athenaeum, 1976), 281. Johnson sees the doctrines of heaven and hell as touchstones of liberalism or orthodoxy. Harmonic and gnostic themes have great appeal (322, 340).
2. Crane Brinton, *The Shaping of the Modern Mind* (New York: Mentor, 1953), 2.113. Wilhelm Windelband also shows that the Enlightenment was essentially anthropological, *A History of Philosophy* (New York: Harper, 1901), 2.437.
3. Kurt Aland, *A History of Christianity*, II (Philadelphia: Fortress, 1986), 272. This is the natural religion of all people.
4. Ibid., 283. The Christian imprint is undeniable in Leibniz, who personifies the German Enlightenment in many ways.
5. Ibid., 275f. The Enlightenment had a certain passion that we certainly see erupting in the French Revolution.
6. Émile Durkheim, *Montesquieu and Rousseau: Forerunners of Sociology* (Ann Arbor: Michigan, 1960), 11, 42.
7. Ibid., 19. Truth or falsity of a doctrine is not really the big issue, but rather its utility, cf. 24.19. Pragmatism?
8. Ibid., 45. Another Jewish French philosopher, Henri Bergson (1859–1941) advocated an open city of total brotherhood in which religion and morality are no longer static, cf. *The Two Sources of Morality and Religion* (New York: Doubleday Anchor, 1935). Bergson loses any supernaturalistic faith in his "creative evolution."
9. Ibid., 149. Since individuals and societies have natures subject to change, all is in constant flux, as in Heraclitus.

5.3.2 ROUSSEAU, DISSOLUTE ROMANTIC

Man is born free; and everywhere he is in chains.
Man is naturally good.

—Rousseau
The Social Contract

While reason was crowned in the Enlightenment, building on Renaissance humanism, there were rebels against authority and advocates of human autonomy for whom reason by itself was arid and sterile. Protesting against the supremacy of reason, Romantics set their stress on the affections—feeling. The midwife of French Romanticism was Rousseau. Brinton argues that the Romantic Movement was a revolt against rationalism but that it was a revolt of the child against the parent—"both rejected the doctrine of original sin."[1] So Voltaire the rationalist (whose brother was a Jansenist) and Rousseau the romantic are both precursors of the French Revolution. Liberty, fraternity, and equality are in the air and, as with Locke and Montesquieu, Voltaire and Rousseau made positive and significant contributions, especially to political theory. It would be a colossal error to hold that the Enlightenment created evangelicalism.[2] Rousseau's own view was, as the Vicar expressed it in *Émile ou sur l'Education*, "This same Gospel is full of unbelievable things, of things repugnant to reason and impossible for any sensible man to conceive or to accept!" This was not the womb from which evangelicalism sprang.

Rousseau was born in Geneva to a watchmaker and his wife, Huguenots whose roots were in France. His grandfather was a Calvinist minister, and he was raised in these doctrines. His mother died while giving birth to him, so his father taught him to read, and they read history and "the romances" together. He fled his apprenticeship as an engraver and found refuge with a Madame de Warens in Turin, Italy, where he converted to Catholicism. For ten years, she was his benefactress and mistress. Then for a brief time, he was a tutor in a wealthy family and Secretary to the French Ambassador in Venice. In 1745 he returned to Paris where he developed deep ties with the *philosophes* and contributed the article on musical notation to the *Encyclopédie*. At this time he also began his relationship with Thérèse Levasseur, a half-literate servant girl who became his life companion and mother of his five children, all of whom were placed in a foundling home. He later had several torrid affairs.

He wrote much and quarreled with his friends. When Parliament condemned *Émile,* he feared imprisonment and fled to Switzerland, then followed Hume to England. They parted in a dispute. Thérèse followed. Rousseau became a Protestant again in 1754 and lived his last years around Paris.

"Back to nature!" was the cry of this proto-Romantic. Historian Will Durant says that "Europe was ready for a gospel that would exalt feeling over thought."[3] One senses here that Napoléon might not have been so wrong in attributing the French Revolution foremost to Rousseau. Though afflicted with deep pangs of conscience that caused him to write his *Confessions,* he fiercely denied original sin and proclaimed that "feeling is all." He acknowledges that "The dread of hell frequently tormented me," but "an almost passionless pantheism had replaced the God of the Bible."[4] The noble savage of nature has been infected by the disease of civilization. The natural goodness of man is the underlay of his view that dependence on one another as social beings is the root cause of all crime and vice.[5] His own presumed return to Protestantism was publicly hailed as the return of the prodigal in Geneva. He was in fact a Unitarian with respect to his basic doctrine but had his political angles in occasionally lapsing into a profession of orthodoxy. He would have no truck with any idea of redemption through the death of Christ. Our own era of "feel-good theology" should be right at home with Rousseau. *The Social Contract* is important to read for its insights into the powerful influence of Rousseau. The notion of "the pursuit of happiness" is his shadow cast upon the Declaration of Independence. Madame de Stael said of him: "Rousseau invented nothing, but he set everything on fire."[6]

In *Intellectuals,* Paul Johnson purports to examine "the moral and judgmental credentials of certain leading intellectuals to give advice to humanity on how to conduct its affairs."[7] As these self-appointed beacon lights of modern culture who have renounced revealed religion are examined, we realize they are incompetent to do so. He sees Rousseau as the archetype of them all, the modern Prometheus. Calling him "one of the greatest grumblers of history," Johnson scores Rousseau for his simplistic view of human nature and education, and his opposition to competition and private property. Rousseau made ingratitude a virtue and was the first to set down the lurid and licentious details of his exploitative sex life.

"Although they know God's righteous decree that those who do such things deserve death, they not only continue to do these very things but also approve of those who practice them," Paul wrote in Romans 1:32. There is no escaping that a person's writings and public statement must be evaluated in some measure by the life lived. Rousseau was unquestionably a genius, but he was also a lost soul, not a trustworthy guide.

---

1. *Shaping of the Modern Mind,* 2.116. Last half of *Ideas and Men.*
2. Curiously D. W. Bebbington, the Scottish historian, argues that "Evangelicalism was actually started by the Enlightenment," cf. "Evangelical Christianity and the Enlightenment," *Crux,* December 1989, XXV.4, 29ff. The fact that evangelicals stood for human rationality does not mean they were rationalists. To stress positive contributions, particularly in human liberty and tolerance, must not blind us to the deeper and more significant antipathies. With all of his fine points, Bebbington sees biblical inerrancy as an innovation and the doctrine of the second coming of Christ as "no part of accepted doctrine." See his *Evangelicalism in Modern Britain: A History from the 1730's to the 1980's* (London: Unwin Hyman, 1989), 74, 83, 87. He quotes George Bernard Shaw: "I hate the atonement!" He accurately characterizes evangelicals as conversionist, activistic, biblicistic, and crucicentrist.
3. Will Durant, *Rousseau and Revolution,* vol. 10 (New York: Simon and Schuster, 1967), 3.
4. Ibid., 13, 14. Durant shows Rousseau as a "haunted spirit," filled with jealousy and diminished by bitterness.
5. Arthur M. Melzer, *The Natural Goodness of Man: On the System of Rousseau's Thought* (Chicago: University of Chicago Press, 1990). He finds Rousseau's contrary solutions, communitarianism, and individualism to be inconsistent.
6. J. Christopher Herold, *Mistress to an Age: A Life of Madame de Stael* (New York: Bobbs-Merrill, 1958). A classic study of the life of one who took Rousseau to heart (238, 240). She was from the famous Necker family in Switzerland and an intimate of Edward Gibbon. This study affords remarkable insights into the age and its defiant mood.
7. Paul Johnson, *Intellectuals* (New York: Harper, 1988). So many of these brilliant persons were like Rousseau: They loved humanity in general, but not individuals in particular. Very telling points are scored on Marx, Ibsen, and Brecht.

5.3.3 BURKE, ELOQUENT CONSERVATIVE

Because half a dozen grasshoppers under a fern make the field ring with their importunate chink, whilst thousands of great cattle, reposed beneath the shadow of the British oak, chew the cud and are silent, pray do not imagine that those who make the noise are the only inhabitants of the field; that, of course, they are many in number or that after all, they are other than the little, shrivelled, meagre, hopping, though loud and troublesome insects of the hour.

—Edmund Burke
Reflections on the Revolution in France

A gutsy fighter against the Enlightenment, his conservatism also pled for the rights of Roman Catholics and the Irish. He opposed British colonial imperialism in India and North America and was one of the first to express alarm about the French Revolution.

Of Norman ancestry, Edmund Burke (1729–1797) was born in Dublin to a Protestant father and a Roman Catholic mother. He enjoyed a classical education at a Quaker School and at Trinity College, Dublin, where Oliver Goldsmith was a classmate. He developed a passion for the theatre, and his charming Irish brogue only enhanced the persuasive power of his rhetorical gifts. In 1750 he moved to London to study law at the Middle Temple. There he came to a deep burden for the poor. At age twenty-seven, he published two books, *A Vindication for Natural Society* and *A Philosophical Inquiry into the Origin of Our Ideas of the Sublime and Beautiful*.[1] A Grubb Street scribbler for awhile, he held an Irish post four years, then was secretary to the Marquis of Rockingham, who became Prime Minister. He served in Parliament from 1766 to 1794, where his prowess as an orator and advocate was legend. He was known for his searing maxims.

Burke championed "Permanent Things." Some have called him "the first conservative."[2] A supporter of the Church of England and all she stood for, Burke was planted deeply in medieval Christianity's natural law concept, with an admiration for the Magna Carta of 1215 and the Glorious Revolution of 1688.[3]

Burke held Rousseau's "new morality" in the highest contempt. In all of his speaking and writing, he shows his conviction that there is a standard, against the notion of such philosophers as Hume that there are "no fixed principles".[4] This standard is virtue as defined by the Bible and the Church of England catechism.[5] In his "politics of Christian humanism," Burke argued from the premise that "all power to govern was from God, and God approved the exercise of power only in conformity to His law."[6] As he put it:

> If we should uncover our nakedness (release our instincts) by throwing off that Christian religion which has been . . . one great source of civilization among us, . . . we are apprehensive (being well aware that the mind will endure a void) that some uncouth, pernicious and degrading superstition might take the place of it.[7]

Lord Acton said that "history begins with Burke." Twentieth-century German scholar Hans Barth believes Burke is "the most important political thinker of recent centuries."[8] As a witness to the relative morality of his day, he was faithful for life to one wife.[9] He was a friend of Adam Smith and founder of the Literary Club with Samuel Johnson and Joshua Reynolds. John Marshall, first Chief Justice of the United States Supreme Court, was a follower. Perhaps his greatest disciple in North America was John Randolph of Roanoke, Virginia.[10]

His first speeches in the House of Commons were against the Stamp Act. A friend of the Colonies, Burke's speech on allowing self-determination for the colonists was delivered on March 22, 1775, and lasted for three hours. He was applauded for his eloquence, but his resolutions did not carry.

Burke had a tendency to overwork, and he lacked the perspective of history in his analysis. His weakness in speaking was the temptation to dazzle.[11] This is always the effective speaker's snare. He did not himself have an outstanding speaking voice. His strength was content and the sense of appropriate and convincing structure. He was troubled by the slave trade, and the violence of the French Revolution profoundly stirred him. He prophesied that out of the flagrant excesses of the Revolution would come a dictator and a tragic war. His speeches called back some younger men who were enamored by the French call for liberty, among them Walter Scott, William Wordsworth, Samuel Taylor Coleridge, and Robert Southey. In his last years he was pensioned by his old nemesis, King George III, but was left desolate in the death of his remaining son. He dictated letters to his last day of life.

Burke was so thorough and solid in making his case. He tended to reason in metaphor and wrote "in white hot heat." Then he would deliver his soul. But his words were not simply words "with sledgehammer force." There is a rhetorical artistry in Burke—what Browne describes as "the discourse of virtue." "Virtue was for Burke a pervasive subject, warrant and reward for rhetorical action."[12]

He had a theory of virtue that was scriptural and doctrinally grounded. It is still highly profitable to read his *Reflections on the Revolution in France* or *Letter to the Sheriffs of Bristol*. Wordsworth describes Burke and recognizes his integrity in *Prelude*:

> I see him,—old, but vigorous in age,—
> Stand like an oak whose stag-horn branches start
> Out of its leafy brow, the more to awe
> The younger brethren of the grave, . . .
> While he forewarns, denounces, launches forth
> Against all systems built on abstract rights,
> Keen ridicule; the majesty proclaims
> Of Institutes and Laws, hallowed by time;
> Declares the vital power of social ties
> Endeared by Custom; and with high disdain,
> Exploding upstart Theory, insists
> Upon the allegiance to which men are born.

Burke's chief antagonist, Thomas Paine, wrote *The Rights of Man* in reply to Burke's *Reflections on the Revolution in France*. An excellent study of Paine is John Keane's *Tom Paine: A Political Life*.[13] Keane shows how Paine was influenced by his impoverished Quaker father. He heard a sermon on the cross and rebelled.[14] Still he preached as a Methodist in England and confessed belief (John Wesley mentions him in his Journal). But he soon wrote satirical deist poetry, becoming increasingly radical. In *Age of Reason,* he shows contempt for the Bible. He was in America from 1774 to 1787. He visited France and hailed the French Revolution. For this reason he took umbrage with Burke's published views. Paine helped draft the Constitution of the Revolution in France in 1793, but was imprisoned there and barely escaped execution. Bursting with bitterness against George Washington, he continued to show his "radical suspicion of dogma."[15] The Second Great Awakening angered him. The sad story of this wanderer on earth is so different from the story of Burke.

1. Edmund Burke, *A Philosophical Inquiry into the Origin of Our Ideas of the Sublime and Beautiful* (Notre Dame: University of Notre Dame Press, 1958). A pioneering work in psychological aesthetics.
2. Russell Kirk, *Edmund Burke: A Genius Reconsidered* (Peru, Ill.: Sherwood Sugen, 1967), 21.
3. C. B. Macpherson, *Burke* (New York: Hill and Wang, 1980), 49, 62. Natural law continued to be an issue. In the 1990s, Robert Bork was rejected as a U.S. Supreme Court justice because he agreed with Burke.
4. James T. Boulton, introduction to *A Philosophical Inquiry,* xxx; also Stephen H. Browne, *Edmund Burke and the Discourse of Virtue* (Tuscaloosa, Ala.: University of Alabama Press, 1993).
5. Ross J. S. Hoffman and Paul Levack, eds., *Burke's Politics* (New York: New York, 1959), xv.
6. Ibid., xv. Burke was an emotional and deeply impassioned speaker.
7. Edmund Burke, *Reflections on the Revolution in France* (New Rochelle, N.Y.: Arlington House, 1966), 87.
8. Alice P. Miller, *Edmund Burke and His World* (Old Greenwich: Devin-Adair, 1979), xiii.
9. *Genius Reconsidered,* 28, 113. Kirk speaks here as dean of the conservative movement in the United States.
10. Russell Kirk, *John Randolph of Roanoke* (Indianapolis: Liberty, 1951). Burke was the greatest influence, 34.
11. *Edmund Burke and His World,* 90.
12. *Edmund Burke and the Discourse of Virtue,* 5, 125. While Burke is not in Great Books of the Western World, he is in *Gateway to the Great Books,* vol. 7.
13. Boston: Little-Brown, 1995.
14. Ibid., 25.
15. Ibid., 429.

5.3.4 WILBERFORCE, PASSIONATE PARLIAMENTARIAN

It is all the more important to expose the false optimism concerning human nature, so that it does not take away the moral responsibility of man.

Thus mature Christians exhibit in their hearts a glowing love toward their Redeemer—not superficial and unmeaningful, but constant and rational.

Let us labor, then, to affect our hearts with a deep conviction of our need for the Redeemer, and of the value of His offer to mediate. Let us fall down humbly before the throne of God, pleading pity and pardon in the name of the Son of his love. Let us beseech Him to give us a true spirit of repentance, and of heart, undivided faith in the Lord Jesus.

—William Wilberforce
Real Christianity

Culture wars were fought in Europe in the late seventeenth and eighteenth centuries.[1] Strategically placed spokesmen took their stand for orthodoxy and made a significant difference in the church and society. One of the most effective was William Wilberforce (1759–1833). Born in Hull in Yorkshire into a well-to-do family, he was sent to live with an uncle and aunt at Wimbledon when his father, who had been Mayor of Hull, died. Up to then he had been at Hull Grammar School, where Joseph Milner was headmaster and Isaac Milner his assistant. Isaac would become Dean of Carlisle and a great influence on Wilberforce. His mother was a nonevangelical Anglican, in his description "an Archbishop Tillotson Christian."[2] She called him home when his uncle and aunt at Wimbledon exposed the young man to Methodism. His relatives were influenced by George Whitefield (1714–1770) and John Wesley (1703–1791), and he often heard John Newton preach. The Great Awakening was shaking the English-speaking world to its foundations, and young Wilberforce was converted at age twelve.

The evangelical Awakening had immense impact on the Church of England.[3] Wilberforce went to Cambridge, where his selfless aims already were becoming apparent. He spoke of slavery as "an odious traffic."[4] Possibly the former slave-trader John Newton planted these seeds in his heart. In Cambridge, he began a lifelong friendship with William Pitt (1759–1806), the son of the prime minister and a future English statesman in his own right. Wilberforce was slight of build and frail in health; James Boswell (1740–1795) first saw Wilberforce rise to speak and thought him a shrimp, but after the speech "he went away calling him a whale."[5] In 1780 he entered Parliament for Yorkshire at a time of generally low standards of morality. He traveled to France with Pitt where he met Marie-Joseph de Lafayette (1757–1834).[6] Several years later, he made a similar trip to the Continent with Isaac Milner. Together they read Philip Doddridge's (1702–1751) *The Rise and Progress of Religion in the Soul* as well as the *Greek New Testament*. Their studies led them to a profound rededication of their lives to the cause of Christ.

Wilberforce began an eighteen-year battle in the House of Commons against the slave trade. Opposed by the merchants, his struggle was often discouraging. As Wilberforce fought the importation of slaves, seventy thousand came into the country each year. He was undergirded by a life of prayer, devotion, and meditation in the Word and conscientious observance of the Lord's Day.[7] He often heard Newton preach at St. Mary Woolnoth. The other leading evangelical pulpit voice in London was William Romaine (1714–1795). He enjoyed the independent William Jay at Bath, who expounded Scripture beautifully but was sensitive to charges of disloyalty to the Church of England. Wilberforce read Walter Scott, William Cowper, and John Milton and listened to G. F. Handel's music.[8]

He also drew inspiration from Richard Baxter (1615–1691), the Quaker George Fox (1624–1691), and Wesley. Wars and politics interrupted his efforts, but every year he made the motion in the House that finally passed in 1807. Then he turned to the abolition of slavery itself and the emancipation of the slaves, but this came immediately after his death in 1833.

In 1797 he married and founded a fascinating family, including a son Samuel, who became Bishop of Oxford and then Bishop of Winchester. Several of his progeny went with John Newman (1801–1890) and others of the Tractarian Movement into the Roman Catholic Church.[9]

Associated with the antislavery crusade was the Clapham Group of like-minded evangelical Anglicans, which included the rector of Clapham, John Venn; Hannah More, the educator; Henry Thornton, the banker; Zachary Macaulay; and Granville Sharp, the Greek scholar.

Wilberforce had a warm evangelistic burden and witnessed relentlessly.[10] In his last years, he suffered great financial losses, the death of his second daughter, and the defection from biblical faith of his sons. His book *A Practical View of the Prevailing Religious System . . . Contrasted to Real Christianity* still is valuable to read. By 1826 it had gone through fifteen editions in England and twenty-five in North America. The volume deals very forthrightly with the problem of sin in human nature and the necessity of the atonement and the ministry of the Holy Spirit.[11] The dogged drive of Wilberforce with reference to societal problems and his genuine Christian faith are examples of why the gospel flourished in an age of cultural decomposition.[12]

If Johann Sebastian Bach (1685–1750) represents Protestantism on the Continent with its very rich Lutheran emphases (e.g., *St. Matthew Passion*), the German Handel (1685–1759) most firmly influenced music in England with an undiluted passion for Scripture. His operas and oratorios are rich in biblical text. The most often played example of this is *Messiah*. H. C. Robbins Landon's *Handel and His World*,[13] replete with magnificent pictures, is a marvelous study of this versatile man.

1. Joan DeJean, *Ancients Against Moderns: Culture Wars and the Making of a Fin de Siècle* (Chicago: University of Chicago Press, 1996). Professor DeJean argues that a large part of the war was a debate and argument about books.
2. See *Company of the Preachers*, 6.2.7.
3. Francis John McConnell, *Evangelicals, Revolutionists and Idealists* (Nashville: Abingdon-Cokesbury, 1942), 158ff. He cites William Makepeace Thackeray's *The Newcomes* as fiction affording insight into evangelicals in the established church.
4. Travers Buxton, *William Wilberforce: The Story of a Great Crusade* (London: Religious Tract Society, n.d.), 12.
5. *Evangelicals, Revolutionists and Idealists,* 165. On one occasion, Wilberforce was chosen to mediate between George IV and Queen Caroline. He had the respect of those who disagreed with him.
6. Ibid., 20, 22. Pitt came to the same view on slavery as had Wilberforce, although later he grew somewhat cold.
7. Ibid., 44. In 1787 he helped found the British Antislavery Society, which kept strong pressure constant.
8. Murray Pura, "The Spirituality of William Wilberforce," in *Crux,* XX, 4, 12–20; and David Lyle Jeffrey, ed., *A Burning and Shining Light: English Spirituality in the Age of Wesley* (Grand Rapids: Eerdmans, 1987), 507ff.
9. David Newsome, *The Parting of Friends: The Wilberforces and Henry Manning*

(Grand Rapids: Eerdmans, 1966). This unusual study traces the shifting tides. John Henry Newman was himself an evangelical early in his life.

10. Lord Reginald Coupland, *Wilberforce* (London: Collins, 1945), 202ff. "Wilberforce lived in two worlds," he argues.

11. Mark Hatfield, foreword to *William Wilberforce, Real Christianity* (Portland: Multnomah, 1982), xxi. Although he loved and associated with Calvinists, Wilberforce was not a Calvinist and remarked of his friend William Romaine, "Oh how unlike this is to the Scripture! He writes as if he sat at the Council Board with the Almighty!" ("The Spirituality of William Wilberforce," 17.)

12. For tributes to Wilberforce see Charles Ludwig, *He Freed Britain's Slaves* (Scottdale, Pa.: Herald, 1977); and Charles W. Colson, "Standing Tough Against All Odds," *Christianity Today,* 6 September 1985, 26ff. Perhaps the last letter that the dying John Wesley wrote was to Wilberforce, urging him not to give up in the battle.

13. Boston: Little, Brown, 1984.

5.3.5 *Smith, Classical Economist*

The clergy of an established and well-endowed religion frequently become men of learning and elegance, who possess all the virtues of gentlemen, or which can recommend them to the esteem of gentlemen: but they are apt gradually to lose the qualities both good and bad, which gave them authority and influence with the inferior ranks of people. . . . they have in general ceased to be popular preachers. The Methodists, without half the learning of the Dissenters, are much more in vogue.

—Adam Smith
The Wealth of Nations

The first classical economist in Western thought is Adam Smith (1723–1790). Smith was born in Kirkaldy, County Fife, Scotland, his father dying before his birth. In this community of 1500, nails were still used for legal tender. At age four, he was kidnapped by gypsies but given up after hot pursuit by his uncle and other men.[1] He matriculated at the University of Glasgow at age fourteen and then went on to read French and Italian literature at Oxford. At Glasgow he came under the teaching of the Scottish philosopher Francis Hutcheson (1694–1746), whose posthumously published *System of Moral Philosophy* established the "benevolent theory" of morals. As a result, Smith took on a basically optimistic bent, in contrast with the next generation's economist Thomas Malthus (1766–1834). Malthus feared that population growth would lead humankind away from Utopia to disaster as sheer numbers outstripped resources.[2]

Smith took a professorship of logic and then moral philosophy at Edinburgh, where his lectures on literature were so popular they were repeated for several years. In 1751 he transferred back to Glasgow and in 1759 issued his work *Theory of Moral Sentiments*. This work shows the strong influence of his friend David Hume and anchors ethics totally in the social life of the community, very much as in Charles Louis Montesquieu (1689–1755).[3] Self-interest is countered by sympathy spawned by awareness of the body-politic. Smith was an absorbing and engaging lecturer and exerted an expansive influence on his students, including Hugh Blair and William Robertson. They became conspicuous examples of Scottish "moderatism," whose moralistic preaching was a rhetoric of optimism.[4] He was notorious as the absentminded professor who on occasion descended into his garden in his dressing gown and continued to walk on for fifteen miles. Robert L. Heilbroner, in a captivating essay of his book *The Worldly Philosophers,* observes that Smith always was troubled by a nervous affliction. His head shook, and he stumbled in his speech.[5]

In 1763 he took a pension from the wealthy Charles Townshend family in exchange for tutoring the family's stepchildren.

Meanwhile, he was beginning to work on his magnum opus, *The Wealth of Nations.* This massive work on economic life is a system of laissez-faire economics, totally based on enlightened self-interest. One need only look at the sixty-three page index to see the amazing scope. Some earlier chapters are good to read if only to see how he recognizes the rapacious greed of human beings. Still his basic advice is always: Let the market alone! The inevitable transmutation of human selfishness is crucial for him. Never married, Smith made his home with his mother and soon followed her in death.

Book 5, Article 3, treats the church among instructional institutions. He is restive under the austere Scottish church, protesting its "excessive rigor" in religion. Yet he portrays "the vices of levity" also.[6] He is skittish about the authority of religion, but he cautions against coercion against religion by the sovereign. He is the first to call the English "a nation of shopkeepers." Church finance is within his purview.[7]

As a devotee of natural theology, he is moderate in his advocacy of a "just price" in conformity with the natural order. Crane Brinton is correct in assuring us that Smith is no anarchist, nor a believer in natural goodness. However, Enlightenment thought has tinctured him with "this-worldly" values. Brinton cites Carl Becker's *Heavenly City of the Eighteenth Century Philosophers.* Becker describes the hopeful eschatology, in which "the heavenly city of the eighteenth century is indeed to be on earth."[8] Brinton continues:

> The faith of the Enlightenment is a kind of Christianity, a development of Christianity, it is from the point of view of the Middle Ages a heresy, a distortion of Christianity; and from the point of view of Calvinism a blasphemy. The faith of the Enlightenment has no logical place for a personal God accessible to human prayer. . . . It admits no supernatural above the natural. . . . The Enlightenment promised heaven on earth soon, and by a process that meant for the individual a "natural" release of expansive, appetitive forces within himself, not self-denial and inner discipline.[9]

This is the trail upon which Adam Smith and many of his compatriots embarked.

---

1. Robert L. Heilbroner, *The Worldly Philosophers: The Lives, Times and Ideas of the Great Economic Thinkers* (New York: Simon and Schuster, 1953, 1961), 38. The chapter on Smith is called "The Wonderful World of Adam Smith."

2. Ibid., 73ff. This is a brilliant classic. Economic theory has generally been neglected by Christians.

3. Wilhelm Windelband, *A History of Philosophy,* II (New York: Harper Torchbooks, 1901, 1958), 517.

4. *Company of the Preachers,* chap. 8.

5. *Worldly Philosophers,* 37. His friendship with Hume often got him into hot water.

6. *Great Books,* 37, 346–47. Article 11 on "Educating Youth" is timely.

7. Ibid., 356. The "Introductory Note" indicates that other good friends were Edward Gibbon and Benjamin Franklin.

8. *Shaping of the Modern Mind,* 2.142. The best piece on natural law is Carl F. H. Henry, "Natural Law and a Nihilistic Culture," *First Things,* January 1995, 54ff.

9. Ibid., 143–44. Consider what ultimately happened to this ripened optimism in each century, particularly the twentieth.

5.3.6 JOHNSON, WIZARD OF WORDS

Depend upon it, when a man knows he is to be hanged in a fortnight, it concentrates his mind wonderfully.

The chief glory of every people arises from its authors; whether I shall add anything by my own writings to the reputation of England must be left to time.

To James Boswell: My dear sir, clear your mind of cant.

If I have repented as I ought, I am forgiven.

—Samuel Johnson

Thomas Carlyle wrote of Samuel Johnson: "A mass of genuine manhood, a man who would starve before he would barter away his independence, and who was loved and honored by all who knew him." Though hardly read today, Johnson (1709–1784) stands in a unique niche among England's great man of letters. He remained a man of faith during a time of turmoil. Much of what we know about him comes from *The Life of Samuel Johnson,* written by the brilliant Scottish lawyer James Boswell.[1] Novelist Tobias Smollet called him "the great Cham (Khan) of literature." Born in a bookseller's home in Lichfield in the Midlands, Johnson was a "big ungainly lad with short sight."[2] He loved to read and mastered Latin and Greek. He went up to study at Pembroke College at Oxford, where he drifted from what his mother had taught him about heaven and hell. He seemed to prefer to go into the fields rather than to church on Sunday. Then he read William Law's *A Serious Call to a Devout and Holy Life* and became a deeply convinced believer.[3]

After only thirteen months at Oxford, he was penniless because his benefactors did not keep promises to him. He turned in dejection to London, writing essays for a Birmingham journal and translating a travel narrative from French. He never blamed others for his misfortunes.[4] In 1735 he married a widow twenty years his senior. While he and his wife unsuccessfully attempted to found a school, he worked on a tragedy he entitled *Irene,* the story of a Greek slave girl that showed the misery of absolute governments. He wrote a Latin poem in the Augustan mode but made his living from articles on the debates in Parliament. He was an omnivorous reader, holding that "an accurate knowledge of any subject is based on its bibliography."[5]

Now commissioned by various responsible persons, he gave himself for nine years to the production of his masterful dictionary. While he had a proper respect for reason, he felt that the deepest realities required faith. Though very high in academic density and written in "pompous and involved language," as Virginia Woolf's father was wont to say, the dictionary was a landmark. John Ruskin's father always took "a little volume of Johnson" with him. Young Robert Browning read it from cover to cover. With his meager knowledge of Anglo-Saxon and Middle English, there are limitations to the scholarship. Its definitions of forty thousand words are sometimes quaint, but his illustrations are often priceless. At about the time of its publication, his beloved wife passed away, and he was distraught. He never remarried and was from this time in decline.

Uneasy with Leibniz, Johnson believed the Bible and eschewed speculative philosophy. He disdained both Voltaire and Rousseau. He was committed as a writer to bringing people closer to heaven.[6] To pay for his mother's funeral, he wrote his philosophical novel, *The History of Rasselas: Prince of Abyssinia*. Boswell read it every year.

Though pensioned by George III, he dressed like a beggar. Boswell pictures him walking up and down after his audience with the King "shaking his vast bulk." Book dealer Tom Davies described him as "firing verbal volleys across the Atlantic at the colonists, laughing with the good-natured growl that inspired the riposte: He laughs like a rhinoceros."[7] He still read the Bible through every year and, with his Bible open, argued with Voltaire the truth of the Christian religion.[8] It was his unfulfilled desire to teach theology in ancient St. Andrews.

In his Literary Club, he became known as a conversationalist. He engaged his friends Edmund Burke, Robert Clive, David Garrick, Oliver Goldsmith, Joshua Reynolds, Adam Smith, and Josiah Wedgewood of fine china fame. It was said that "he liked a dispute but hated a quarrel." He spoke only when spoken to. His speech was filled with "strong, vivid, concrete detail."[9] He edited an eight-volume edition of Shakespeare, wrote political pamphlets as an unmovable Tory, struggled with prayer, and wrote sermons for his friend John Taylor. He took a three-month walking trip with Boswell through the Hebrides and the following year traveled to Wales, where he sat through a Welsh sermon that was "not unpleasant."[10]

His last major work was the ten-volume *Lives of the Poets*. His treatment of Milton from a royalist perspective enraged William Cowper. He is best on John Dryden (1631–1700) and Pope (1688–1744). As he aged, friends died or moved from the literary social sphere, and he was increasingly lonely. He suffered slight paralytic strokes.[11] He was afraid of damnation but found comfort in God's forgiveness in Christ. He died in calm with his last words a blessing.

Johnson was an extremely influential man of letters, yet a true commoner. The moral issues of human sin are faced here with candor that many children of the Enlightenment avoided. We could wish he might have entered more deeply into the wonder of the forgiveness of sin, but we honor a soul committed to facing up to his moral responsibility and duty.

One of the most solid explorations of the richness and weaknesses of English is *The Story of English*, by Robert McCrum, William Cran, and Robert MacNeil.[12] This invaluable study is the companion to the PBS television series on the subject. Those who use English need background in the development of its words.

---

1. I recommend dipping into Boswell's biography, which is available in many editions. Daniel J. Boorstin pays high tribute to Boswell in his splendid *The Creators: A History of Heroes of the Imagination* (New York: Random House, 1992), 586ff. Like its antecedent, *The Discoverers,* this volume is full of scintillating insights.
2. John Wain, *Samuel Johnson* (New York: Viking, 1974), 24. One of the finest biographies of Johnson of which I have knowledge.
3. Ibid., 54. Johnson suffered throughout his life from pathological depression. He always regretted not studying William Law more closely.
4. Ibid., 60. His Latin poetry shows some dependence on Juvenal's *Third Satire*. He rigidly abstained from alcohol.
5. Ibid., 118. He also wrote a brilliant essay on Shakespeare's *Macbeth* (125).
6. Ibid., 199. The one obvious downside for Johnson was that his religion did not make him very joyful (203).
7. William Henry Chamberlain, "The Withering Wit of Samuel Johnson," *Saturday Review,* 4 September 1965, 14.
8. Wain, *Samuel Johnson,* 231. Wain argues that, compared with the flippant *Candide* (published the same year), *Rasselas* has gravity and poignancy. Johnson shows endless situations of disappointment. Every character speaks as the author speaks, highlighting the odd and curious.
9. Ibid., 247. Joshua Reynolds pays highest praise to his closest friend in *Discourses on Painting*.
10. Ibid., 339. He lived with the wealthy Thrale family for seventeen years. The children called him "Elephant."
11. Ibid., 371. His book on the poets was "a book of remarkable ripeness," 352, his most "companionable work."
12. New York: Penguin, 1986.

5.3.7 KANT, KING OF PHILOSOPHERS

I had to abolish knowledge in order to make room for faith.

—Immanuel Kant
Critique of Pure Reason, 19

A diminutive figure of five feet in height but shorter because of curvature of the spine, he took his long lonely walks through Königsberg in East Prussia, where he lived his long life with such precise regularity that the townspeople could set their clocks by his rounds. He did not own his living quarters until he was fifty-nine years old, and he never married out of fear of poverty. He never traveled beyond the narrow bounds of the territory surrounding Königsberg and after some years of declining prowess, died and was buried there at age eighty.

Immanuel Kant (1724–1804) was raised in a devoutly pietistic home—his father being Scottish and his mother German.[1] He studied for eight years, until he was sixteen, in *The Collegium Fredericianum,* a pietist school, where the day began at 5:30 with a half hour of prayer. Immanuel, the fourth of eleven children, reacted against the teaching and strictness.[2]

At the University in Königsberg in 1740, his interest shifted from theology to science under a pietistic professor who introduced him to rationalism. Kant had been studying for the ministry and had preached several sermons. He lived in poverty, tutoring as a *Privatdozent,* earning his doctorate and finally, in 1770, achieving a professorship in philosophy and mathematics. He advanced "a nebular hypothesis" in 1755 and reacted, as did Voltaire, in anger and rejection of God after the devastation of the Lisbon earthquake and tidal wave of 1755. His religious faith already had been tottering.

An interesting lecturer, Kant was remembered fondly by his students, such as rationalistic Bible critic Johann von Herder (1744–1803). Herder wrote that "he encouraged and gently compelled his hearers to think for themselves; despotism was foreign to his disposition. This man whom I name with the greatest gratitude and reverence, is Immanuel Kant; his image stands before me, and is dear to me."[3]

Notwithstanding his unimpressive physical attributes, Kant was able to advance a philosophical answer to what he believed was the critical issue of the Enlightenment. Regarding the *metaphysical problem,* the problem of whether anyone can know about God, death, immortality, moral freedom, and other things in the spiritual sphere, Kant felt the pervasive skepticism of Hume's empiricism. He said that Hume awakened him from "dogmatic slumber." He sensed the appeal of Rousseau's flight from reason to feeling. Hidden in Rousseau's *Émile,* he believed, was the way to salvage faith in a mechanistic world.[4]

For fifteen years he toiled on his masterpiece, *The Critique of Pure Reason.* Despite his heavy style, abstruse argument, and endless redefinition, the book immediately revolutionized philosophy by destroying knowledge to save faith. The scope of the paradigm shift is vast, both for those who agreed with him and those who sought alternative directions. Here are just a few observations:

- Antoine Suarez: "Kant authored a methodological skepticism about knowing the truth."
- Henrich Heine: "Kant beheaded belief in God, and God therefore is nothing but fiction."
- Will Durant: "One of the most destructive analyses Christian theology ever received!"
- S. Korner: Metaphysics is totally an illusion. We do not know, we cannot know.
- Francis Schaeffer: "The shift from the older optimistic view to the modern loss of hope."
- Carl F. H. Henry: "Kant excludes conceptual knowledge of God for ontological nihilism."
- Émile Calliet: "Real reality remains unknown; no transcendental metaphysic."[5]

We came to the great turning point in the history of philosophy because Kant divided knowledge into two categories: (1) the *phenomenal* realm we experience through the physical senses and (2) the metaphysical *noumenal* realm, of which we can have no knowledge. We cannot know the thing in itself. He severely restricted the range of reason by injecting a sweeping agnosticism into all of human experience. Thus Gustave Weigel, a prominent Roman Catholic theologian, can speak of "Protestant intellectualism as empirical, skeptical, relativistic, qualitatively derived from Kantian philosophy," and he calls Immanuel Kant a Protestant Thomas Aquinas.[6]

Neoorthodoxy is Kantian as R. Birch Hoyle insightfully observes: "The philosophies of Barth and Brunner are based chiefly on Kant. . . . Brunner says frankly that he regards the critique of Kant as standing nearest in their basal tendency to the Christian faith."[7]

The story is told that when Kant finished *The Critique of Pure Reason,* he heard sobbing behind him and turned to find his faithful valet Lampe crying, "You have taken my God away!"[8] So Kant might write sentimentally to the Abbe Sieyes in 1796 about his love for the Bible, but what was left of the supernatural after Kant's bifurcation of knowledge and resulting anti-intellectual agnosticism? Kant recognizes that human freedom and immortality are important for human behavior. He posits the existence of "as if" knowledge, actually using some of the ideas of pure reason as a practical necessity.[9] "The starry skies above and the moral law within" are inescapable.

Here is where Kant defers to Rousseau and his servant Lampe. All religion must believe in an afterlife. Even though we have no real knowledge, we must project a "supreme principle of the moral life" in order to make life a practical possibility. He calls his universal law "the categorical imperative," which he construes to be: "Act only on the maxim through which you can at the same time will that it should become a universal law."[10]

Thus Kant sought to salvage something from the ruins of his slash-and-burn assault on revealed truth and metaphysics (read his *Religion Within the Limits of Pure Reason* for the sum of it). Durant sagely observes that "Kant was never content with his hesitant 'as if' theology."[11] In daily life he never prayed, nor did he attend church. He did not believe it necessary for "a Christian to affirm faith in miracles, or the divinity of Christ, or the atonement by Christ's crucifixion for the sins of mankind, or the predestination of souls to heaven or hell."[12]

Ultimately Kant's skepticism about truth left the human ego as the center. He radically reduced the epistemology for finding meaning in human existence. Immanuel Kant installed a religion of subjective relativist truth in the place of objective truth about God and His will through the propositions of Holy Scripture.

---

1. Pietism, frequently used pejoratively in today's discussions, protested the tendency toward scholastic aridity in post-Reformation Protestantism. Yet the emphasis on experience left pietism vulnerable to doctrinal erosion. See *Company of the Preachers,* 6.4.2. F. Ernest Stoeffler is the scholar to read on pietism.
2. *Rousseau and Revolution,* 531.

3. Ibid., 532. The Pietism of Kant's background emphasized "faith, repentance and immediate access to God."
4. *Story of Philosophy*, 244.
5. Richard McKeon, *Philosophy*, in The Great Ideas Program (Chicago: Britannica, 1963), 251.
6. Quoted in *Time*, 26 September 1966.
7. R. Birch Hoyle, *The Teaching of Karl Barth* (New York: Charles Scribner's, 1930), 71.
8. Émile Calliet, *The Christian Approach to Culture* (Nashville: Abingdon-Cokesbury, 1953), 167.
9. S. Korner, *Kant* (New York: Penguin, 1955), 124. Korner provides one of the better introductions and guides to Kant's thought.
10. See John L. Mothershead Jr., *Ethics: Modern Conceptions of the Principles of Right* (New York: Henry Holt, 1955), 275. His critique is not Christian but it is exceedingly lucid.
11. *Rousseau and Revolution*, 544.
12. Ibid., 546. In Kant's ethics, "there are no objects of knowledge but objects of will" (Windelband).

5.3.8 HEGEL, SYNTHESIZER

The Christian doctrine that man is by nature evil is loftier than the other which takes him to be by nature good. This doctrine is to be understood as follows in accordance with the philosophical exegesis of it: As mind, man is a free substance which is in the position of not allowing itself to be determined by natural impulse. When man's condition is immediate and mentally undeveloped, he is in a situation in which he ought not to be and from which he must free himself. This is the meaning of the doctrine of original sin without which Christianity would not be the religion of freedom.

—G. W. F. Hegel
Additions, number 18

G. W. F. Hegel recast classic Christian doctrine into something that is unrecognizable. Hegel (1770–1831) was born in Stuttgart in Germany, the eldest child of a minor government official. An avid student from his earliest days, he had the habit of making copious notes on all of his reading and arranging the notes systematically.

While a young man, he wrote a life of Jesus and studied at Tübingen and then taught privately in Berne and Frankfurt. He was a professor at Jena in October of 1806 when Napoléon crushed a Prussian army there. Later he was a professor at the universities of Heidelberg and Berlin. His books and lectures rallied a significant following. His seminary classmate, the poet Friedrich Hölderlin cried: "Kant is our Moses who has led us away from God." Kant had indeed, by his exclusion of the cognitive knowledge of God, moved God into the hinterland, far from the life of realities. The question was whether Hegel would take philosophy the rest of the way into atheism, like Joshua leading into the land of promise.

Initially Hegel was enamored with everything Greek and classical. He aspired to a system of reason more comprehensive and satisfying than Kant's. He wanted to counter the tendency to abstract the self and thus developed what he felt would be the grand integration of all philosophy. He projected a series of integrated stages in terms of which God the Absolute Spirit would achieve the ultimate synthesis. There are three stages to the influential dialectic, a Hegelian Trinity:

1. position
2 negation
3. reconciliation

Hegel was the first scholar to stake out the philosophy of history. He surveyed all religions and anticipated evolutionary theory and the whole developmental schema that enveloped later Enlightenment thought.[1] Søren Kierkegaard was typical of those who reacted strongly against this massive system, which totally submerged the individual. He felt Hegel's both/and was heretical and pushed for an either/or approach.[2]

Hegel was prolific, but his style was ponderous. Samuel Clemens is alleged to have said that Hegel was the closest thing we have to chloroform on paper. Hegel sensed that the Enlightenment was failing and that God as understood classically was no longer a key figure. Therefore he keeps referring to "the death of God," the motto of postmodernity. He is a key figure in preparing the way for postmodernity, the post-Enlightenment denial of truth.[3] He says: "Good Friday must be speculatively reestablished in the whole truth and harshness of its Godforsakeness."

Nature is a "slumbering spirit." Hegel reworks theology with the panpsychism of his old friend Friedrich Wilhelm von Schelling (1775–1854). He banishes as irrelevant the transcendent God. The Genesis creation story is myth. He repudiates the belief that God could create by the power of his word from nothing. Instead, a weak and dependent God needs the world for his own self-realization. A similar theology developed into panentheism, or process theology, in the twentieth century. God needs the world for his own self-realization. This approaches Spinozan pantheism.[4] The "fall" was actually upwards. Fallen humanity has an indomitable spirit, which continually becomes stronger.[5] He rejects God's wrath and the idea of human guilt and need for salvation. No pantheistic system can handle sin or failure (for example, Christian Science doctrines). His fertile imagination scorned religion for effacing human imaginative capacities.[6]

Hegel's thinking along these lines is to be found in *The Phenomenology of the Spirit*. His *Philosophy of Right* gives his political application of his thoughts. He was very favorably disposed toward Napoléon and did speak of the state as "divine" in its power and centrality. Hegel has been seen as friendly to dictators and autocrats.

Hegel's ferment of ideas gave rise to left-wing Hegelians such as Ludwig Feuerbach (1804–1872) who became a blatant atheist. Miceli says: "All modern atheism will thus be seen to be rooted in Hegel's rejection of the God of the master-slave relationship, the God who begets an 'unhappy conscience' in man, the God who reduces man from being a hero to being a 'beautiful soul.'"[7]

Hegel also spawned Karl Marx and the dialectical materialists of modernity.[8] Sussman traces the marked influence of Hegel on such thinkers and writers as Sigmund Freud, Henry James, William Butler Yeats, Marcel Proust, James Joyce, and Franz Kafka.[9] Friedrich Engels himself wrote (in a scene set in hell where Hegel explains what his battle strategy in point-of-fact is):

> And Hegel, whose mouth until this moment grimness locked,
> Suddenly rose up giant high and spoke:
> "I consecrated all my life to Science,
> Preached atheism with my whole strength:
> I placed Self-Consciousness upon her throne,
> Convinced I had already conquered God."[10]

1. Clark Butler, *G. W. F. Hegel* (Boston: Twayne, 1977), 38. While we shall deal more extensively with post-Darwinian thought, I do recommend Robert E. D. Clark, *Darwin: Before and After: An Examination and Assessment* (London: Paternoster, 1958); Philip E. Johnson, *Darwin on Trial* (Downers Grove, Ill.: InterVarsity, 1991); and a popular-level biography, Irving Stone, *The Origin* (New York: Signet, 1980).

2. It is interesting to read Karl Barth on Kant, whom he largely praises, and Hegel, whom he despises to the extent of using a rather crude *argumentum ad hominem,* Karl Barth, *Protestant Thought from Rousseau to Ritschl* (New York: Harper, 1959), 150ff., 268ff. Of course Barth is engaging to read on other thinkers, for example, Rousseau's Pelagianism.

3. Deland S. Anderson, *Hegel's Speculative Good Friday: The Death of God in Philosophical Perspective* (Atlanta: Scholars, 1996). Hegel holds that the world is under a "speculative Good Friday!" (192).

4. Butler, *G. W. F. Hegel,* 146. Higher criticism is an accommodation to cultural and evolutionary developmentalism.

5. Ibid., 131. Hegel argues that if good is to be done, evil must be done. Thus evil is necessary and hence good.

6. *Hegel's Speculative Good Friday,* 21. Hegel tries to do away with the middle-term between God and man, so that there is no need for a mediator.

7. Vincent P. Miceli, *The Gods of Atheism* (Harrison, N.Y.: Roman Catholic, 1971), 24.

8. Isaiah Berlin, *Karl Marx* (Oxford: Oxford University Press, 1963). Hegel supplied the process of change for Marx. Berlin makes the observation that "Hegelianism became the official creed of almost every man with intellectual pretensions" (47).

9. See Henry Sussman, *The Hegelian Aftermath* (Baltimore: Johns Hopkins, 1982), esp. 90. Sussman is especially cogent in analyzing Kierkegaard's problems with the futility of dialectic logic in his great *Either/Or.* For Hegel, truth lies in synthesis, which became a theme of twentieth-century literature. Writers with a philosophical bent seem irresistibly attracted by the Hegelian dialectic and his other ideas.

10. Quoted in *Gods of Atheism,* introduction to part 1. Miceli's argument in this passionate volume is that the crime of atheism is its "sustained act of Supreme Self-Will in a total preoccupation with the human" (xvi).

5.3.9 NIETZSCHE, PROPHET OF ANTICHRIST

I am not a man, I am dynamite.

I condemn Christianity. I raise against the Christian church the most terrible of all accusations ever uttered. It is to me the highest of all conceivable corruptions.

Regarding David Strauss' denial of Christ's historicity: "If you give up Jesus, you must also give up God. . . ."

I hunger from wickedness. Oh the lonesomeness. There is ice around me, thirst within. It is night.

I hate unspeakably everyone I have ever met, especially myself.

I live without an answer to the question—"Whither?"

A man of spiritual depth needs friends, unless he still has God as a friend. But I have neither God nor friends.

—Friedrich Nietzsche

"O thou proud European of the nineteenth century!" So came the challenge from Friedrich Wilhelm Nietzsche (1844–1900), one of the most influential philosophers of modern times and the greatest German philosopher since Kant and Hegel. Nietzsche was born into a family of Lutheran pastors. Called "Fritz" at home, he was dubbed "the little minister" and expected to join the clergy. At age nineteen, he still showed outward evidence of a vital faith in Christ.[1] His father had died and his mother relocated to Naumberg, where he was raised in an environment of five strong women.[2] At age twenty, he enrolled at the University of Bonn. It was there he abandoned his faith. At Bonn he also apparently contracted syphilis in a brothel, which led to the general paresis that pushed him eventually into a fatal dementia. Nietzsche gave himself to classical philology. He loved Arthur Schopenhauer (1788–1860), whose pessimism he imbibed and whose notion that there can be salvation without a savior he liked very much.[3] His other loves were Robert Schumann's music and solitary walks.[4] In 1868 he took the chair in philology at Basel, where he was disinclined to social life except for an occasion visit with the old Renaissance historian, Jacob Burkhardt, who did not seem part of the herd he despised so much.

He had few students but did become close to the German composer Richard Wagner and to Wagner's mistress, Cosima, the daughter of composer Franz Liszt. Endowed with genuine literary skill, Nietzsche wrote his first significant book, *The Birth of Tragedy*, to celebrate Wagner and the Dionysian spirit's intoxicating ecstasy, a triumph over against the rational Socratic spirit.[5] He broke with Wagner and in a collapse of health left Basel for France, where he read avidly in Montaigne, Pascal, and Stendhal. "Stendhal" was the pen name for French writer Henri Beyle (1783–1842). In 1878 his *Human All Too Human* was added to his work *Thoughts out of Season*. The former was dedicated to Voltaire. Back in Switzerland now for a decade of wandering, he published his best work, *Thus Spake Zarathustra*. "I was born as an old man," he lamented.

Zarathustra speaks of the death of God and the superman. Nietzsche hated rationalism of all kinds, especially science and the search for any absolute. But his special animosity was directed against Christianity. His attack was bitter. His ideal was the warrior whose will to power embodied the Dionysian ideal of defending one's high rank and achievement.[6] Jesus is the embodiment of weakness. Nietzsche regards him as "a mob orator, arrogant, advocate of petty folk."[7] He detests prayer and the doctrine of immortality. He believed Jesus had no sense of humor. It has been theorized that Nietzsche projected onto Christ his own bitter personality.[8] As Wagner, Nietzsche was a virulent anti-Semite, and he hated the Jewish origin of Christianity.[9] In *The Antichrist* he sets up Buddhism as "one hundred times more realistic."[10]

A coming new race of supermen would renounce the herd mentality and all compassion and gentleness. Espousing the "great man" who would be master of his own right and wrong, Nietzsche's model was the infamous Cesare Borgia. "I teach you the Superman," Nietzsche boasted: "The Superman is the meaning of the earth. Let your will say: The Superman shall be the meaning of the earth!" He argued to justify the deeds of Napoléon that without the strong man there would be collapse.[11]

As venereal-disease-induced psychosis claimed his mind, he slipped in and out of lucidity during his last tormented years. By then he was alienated from almost everyone he had known. His sister Elizabeth, who had always expressed jealous dislike for him, took over his affairs and edited his manuscripts. She allowed their publication only after his death. His final publications, *The Antichrist, The Will to Power,* and *Ecce Homo* have her hand upon them.[12]

Nietzsche died at fifty-six and was buried with full Lutheran rites.

It is not difficult to see Nietzsche's appeal to the Nazis and why fascist Benito Mussolini relished reading him and corresponded with his sister.[13] Nietzsche was a spiritual child of Charles Darwin (1809–1882) and was carried along in an optimistic social Darwinism. He escaped Schopenhauer's pessimism at this point.

Nietzsche was a "physician of culture" in the sense that he correctly diagnosed the approaching crisis of Europe. With the death of God in the Enlightenment, there was a moral and spiritual vacuum. Here was nihilism—motion but no goal, "passions whirling about without value. The means are still here but there are no ends." He is eminently quotable about the blight on Western culture and its demise, but his engine for change is the emergence of an elite aristocracy reminiscent of Plato's philosopher kings. The supermen would inaugurate a transvaluation of all values. But having rejected Christ and Christianity, can his Superman be other than Satan and his Beast, the Man of Sin? At one point he cries, "I call Christianity the one great curse, the immortal mark of shame on the human race." Yet elsewhere he writes in desperation, "Come back to me, my unknown God!" Ego has taken the place of God in his life, and there is total emptiness. Did this destructive person speak somewhat wistfully when he challenged a Christian: "If you want me to believe in your Redeemer, show me that you have been redeemed."

Nietzsche's significance, Karl Schlecta has maintained, is that

> Nietzsche is the seer whose volcanic revulsion against what James Gibbons Huneker once called the Seven Deadly Virtues furnished existentialists of modern France and Germany with much of their original

inspiration, and whose evocations of the darker side of human consciousness lighted the way to some of the first insights of Freud and psychoanalysis.[14]

The naive and foolish optimism of the nineteenth century was in for some rough going, and Freud, who traced some of the sludge and slime in the human psyche, was a true soul brother of Nietzsche. But Nietzsche's god and intellect

represent the final phase of a historical evolution which took its start from the declaration of absolute human autonomy in the age of the Renaissance, an evolution which is carried to its logical conclusion in the self-deification of the Superman, the Man-God, who in his attempt to dethrone God strikes at the very roots of his own self.[15]

And that establishes the principles of postmodernism, with its total relativism and pluralism.

---

1. *God's of Atheism,* 45–46. Miceli shares an early poem by Nietzsche which contains intense spiritual devotion. One might recall that the young Karl Marx's graduation paper expounded "The Relation of Christ and the Believer as Set Forth in John 15:1ff. on the Vine and the Branches."
2. Curtis Cate, "With the Nietzscheans of Naumburg," *Chronicles of Culture,* April 1996, 12ff. Cate argues that the "soft, flabby and corrupting" world that Nietzsche excoriated is much like today's "mushy, pulpous world."
3. Kurt F. Reinhardt, *The Existentialist Revolt* (Milwaukee: Bruce, 1952), 65. Professor Reinhardt's scintillating lectures on Nietzsche in my undergraduate years left an indelible impression.
4. Crane Brinton, *Nietzsche* (New York: Harper Torchbooks, 1941, 1965), 18. One of the finest biographies.
5. Carl Pletsch, *The Young Nietzsche: Becoming a Genius* (New York: Free, 1991). Documents the angry anti-Semitism of Wagner and his circle. Describes the impact of Professors Ritschl and Tischendorf at Leipzig.
6. Brinton, *Nietzsche,* 134. Brinton shows the "gentler Nietzscheans" who were drawn to aspects of his thinking, yet we must face the fact that he became a cult figure to degenerates and a hero to H. L. Mencken, André Gide, Havelock Ellis, Martin Heidegger, Thomas Mann, and many others who influenced twentieth–century culture in profoundly negative ways.
7. Harold Bloom, "Introduction," in Harold Bloom, ed., *Friedrich Nietzsche* (New York: Chelsea House, 1987) 25, 33. The fact so many deconstructionist thinkers write for the "Modern Critical Views" series does in some measure limit its value.
8. For a contrarian view, see D. Elton Trueblood, *The Humor of Christ* (New York: Harper, 1964).
9. Brinton, *Nietzsche,* 105. "The Jews are the strangest people in world history. . . . They chose to be at any price."
10. Walter Kaufmann, ed., *The Portable Nietzsche* (New York: Viking, 1954), 586, 592.

He banished "the crippling notion of sin." This is the best collection of Nietzsche in my judgment. Kaufmann adds meaningful introductory material. The principle works are here.

11. Crane Brinton, "Nietzsche and the Nazis," in Brinton, *Nietzsche,* 200–31.

12. Ben Macintyre, *Forgotten Fatherland: The Search for Elizabeth Nietzsche* (New York: Strauss Giroux, 1992). Macintyre tells of an 1886 venture of Bernhard Forster and his wife Elizabeth Forster-Nietzsche to transport a boatload of German peasants to Paraguay to escape Jewish-dominated Germany. The remnants of *Nueva Germania* remain. Elizabeth went back to Germany after her husband's suicide and launched the Nietzsche cult. She praised *Mein Kampf.* When she died in 1935 at ninety, Josef Mengele attended her funeral, as did Willie Brandt.

13. Ibid., 176. She had contacts with Hitler himself. Hans Frank observed: "Nietzsche has become the mentor of Nazi Jurisprudence," 186.

14. "Of Karl Schlecta of Darmstedt," *Time,* 17 March 1958, 34. Schlecta charged that Elizabeth was guilty of serious fraud.

15. *Existentialist Revolt,* 118. Reinhardt, a devout Roman Catholic, argues against Luther and Calvin's conviction that sin has completely corrupted human nature (120). See in this volume, 3.4, where this issue is discussed regarding Thomas Aquinas.

5.3.10 KIERKEGAARD, DOLEFUL DANE

The whole of existence frightens me, from the tiniest fly to the mystery of the Incarnation. Existence is inexplicable to me in its totality, and the most inexplicable thing of all is my own existence. . . . My suffering is great, boundless. No one knows it but God in heaven, and He does not want to have mercy on me.

Christianity without the following of Christ is merely mythology, poesy. . . . The enlightened nineteenth century treats Christianity as a myth, but it lacks the courage to give it up.

The birds on the branches, the lilies in the field, the deer in the forest, the fishes in the sea, countless hosts of happy men exultantly proclaim: God is love. But underneath all these sopranos, supporting them as it were, as the bass part does, is audible the *De profundis* which issues from the sacrificed one: God is love.

Out of love of mankind, and out of despair at my embarrassing situation, . . . I came to regard it as my task to create difficulties everywhere.
—Søren Kierkegaard

Though very different from each other, Friedrich Nietzsche and Søren Kierkegaard (1813–1855) are the cofounders of modern existentialism. They did share a disdain for Hegel and they both experienced deep and pervasive despair *(angst).* Perhaps this is one of the reasons many in the disillusionment and cultural decomposition of the twentieth century have identified with both an atheist and a convinced theist. Kierkegaard was born in Copenhagen during a time of great disruption and modernization for the Danes. He was youngest of seven children.[1] His father, Michael Pedersen Kierkegaard, who had fled poverty in flat, windswept Jutland, profoundly influenced Søren.[2] Michael prospered in Copenhagen and retired at age forty to pursue theological and philosophical studies. Raised in very pietistic circumstances, he carried with him the oppressive guilt of having once cursed God. With all of his biblical insight, Michael Kierkegaard was never able to claim the peace of forgiveness.

He also felt he was under a curse from God because a few months after the death of his first wife, his servant-girl gave birth to a stillborn child. He was its father.[3] He married the girl, and she became mother to his seven children. Søren was Michael's favorite and was like him in a tendency to melancholia.

Very able at his studies, at age seventeen Søren began preparation for the ministry at the University of Copenhagen. He broke with his father and left home to pursue another course of study. His father endowed him with a substantial sum, but he went through it quickly. He partied and drank but did not find inner peace. He did pass his theological examination in 1840. That year he almost married Regina Olsen, who was already engaged to Fritz Schlegel, the future governor of the Danish West Indies. After finally winning Regina's heart, he broke the relationship because he felt he was not worthy of her, despite the protestations of her family. She finally married Schlegel.

Out of this crushing experience, he began to travel to Berlin to attend philosophical lectures (particularly those of Schelling) and to do some writing, which was published anonymously. He wrote his M.A. thesis on the concept of irony. He had certain physical limitations, perhaps tracing to a childhood fall from a tree.[4] Tall, angular, and awkward, he drew teasing of children and youths as he ambled through central Copenhagen. Hans Christian Andersen caricatured him as "the conceited parrot with its harsh voice, its sharp beak, and its delights in flattery."[5] He was mercilessly ridiculed by one of the Copenhagen papers.

However, as a young adult he made a commitment to Christ. In *Either/Or* he sets forth the stark alternative: "Either wholehearted obedience to God's law or open rebellion against it; either for or against Christ, for or against truth; either hot or cold, but never lukewarm or halfhearted."[6] There must be "a razor-edge decision made by man's free will."[7] In 1846 he wondered if he should seek a parish for ministry but did not. His significant literary production came from 1848–1851. Over these four years, he wrote a small library of volumes, none of which received much notice. *Concluding Unscientific Postscript* did not sell sixty copies. After suffering a stroke and fall, Kierkegaard quickly declined and died at age forty-two.

For Kierkegaard, Christianity had ceased to exist in Denmark. People were spectators but not participants. He identified Hegel and Hegelian identification of the world with God as the enemies. He despised the systematic and opted for inquiries that were individualistic and subjective.[8] He never balanced his emphasis on individual pietism and the support of the community of believers. Although there was a "parsimony" or thinness in his theology, he was very Christ-centered. He dreaded objectivity, making impossible any kind of apologetic. Kierkegaard's truth is subjectivity. He launched a massive assault on religious liberalism. In *Sickness Unto Death,* which he felt was his most significant work, we have a reflection of his argument against the institutional bishops and churchmen whose Christianity had become "a diluted, enervated sentimentality and a refined Epicureanism." Kierkegaard accepted natural theology, unlike his fond disciple Karl Barth, but he saw three stages or phases in human life with the great either/or beyond them:

1. the aesthetic, as in enjoyment of great music
2. the ethical, as in Abraham's willingness to offer Isaac[9]
3. the religious leap of faith, as made by Abraham and Job

   This is not a palliative theology, but clear focus on "the God-man as the sign of contradiction."[10] The effort of the established order to take the offense out of Christianity is a travesty. We must break with the universal and "give all."[11] Professor David Swenson of the University of Minnesota, one of the discoverers of Kierkegaard in the English-speaking world, described the result as "the restoration of the personal consciousness to its normal integrity." We become what God intended that we be.[12] There is something refreshing and renewing in Kierkegaard, and we see it nowhere more poignantly than in *Purity of Heart Is to Will One Thing,* arguably his devotional masterpiece.[13]

   Still as the forebear of Barth and Emil Brunner, Rudolf Bultmann, H. Richard and Reinhold Niebuhr, the Roman Catholic Marcel, and so many in the firmament of religious thinkers in our century, Kierkegaard has some fatal or near-fatal flaws. His faith without reason is an epistemological disaster. Faith is a leap but we can hardly agree that it is a leap into the absurd. Reason is the launching pad for the rocket of faith. There are evidences and reasons for believing. Edward John Carnell commends many aspects of Kierkegaard's thought, particularly his "rare grasp of self-love," but decries his denial of the relevance of evidence.[14]

   We may indeed see the incarnation of our Lord as what seems to be an absolute paradox from our viewpoint, but a theology of paradox, which claims Christ's life is not just a seeming paradox but an actual one, is extreme and dangerous. The irony is that existentialism has created new systems of worldview-shaping thought while persuading us that thought cannot shape a worldview. Carnell also sees a grave deficiency in that Kierkegaard missed entirely the glory of imputed righteousness.[15] Neither Michael or Søren Kierkegaard seemed to grasp the wonder of the forgiveness of sin. Lacking a theology of forgiveness, Søren missed the meaning of the substitutionary atonement.

   At bottom line, Kierkegaard's subjective faith is the harvest of an unreconstructed Kantian denial of propositional revelation. Kierkegaard is free to deny the existence of an historical Adam or Eve in the interest of our history and our own sin. He rejects original sin in any traditional or Augustinian sense, and this undercuts the atonement. God as "totally other" is the motif of modern neoorthodoxy or dialetical theology, but is it the God of the Bible? In his *Philosophical Fragments,* Kierkegaard opens the door to a wide variety of curious interpretive schemes by Barth, Brunner, Bultmann, Paul Holmer, Paul Tillich, and many other radical theologians, all of whom minimize or reject entirely saving history and divinely revealed interpretation of that history. Bernard Ramm concludes that the "existentialists' platform is too subjective to supply us with a true *principium* for theological construction."

Without the entirely reliable and trustworthy propositions of revealed Scripture, how can we be sure that the Christ we meet in the divine-human encounter is, in fact, the Christ of God and not Satan incognito? P. T. Forsyth spoke realistically when he called Kierkegaard "the Pascal of the North," and Ramm accurately described him as "the Danish time-bomb." There is so much benefit in Kierkegaard, but in his baggage are the seeds of twentieth-century ecclesiastical apostasy.

----

1. John W. Elrod, *Kierkegaard and Christendom* (Princeton, N.J.: Princeton University Press, 1982). This book offers helpful background on Kierkegaard and existentialism. Another helpful overview, using Kierkegaard's own words, is Thomas Oden, ed., *Parables of Kierkegaard* (Princeton: Princeton University Press, 1978).

2. Isak Dinesen's book and film, *Babette's Feast,* are set in the crassness of small-town Jutland.

3. Robert L. Perkins, *Søren Kierkegaard* (London: Lutterworth, 1969), 1–2. Perkins is informative regarding Michael Kierkegaard.

4. Edward John Carnell, *The Burden of Søren Kierkegaard* (Grand Rapids: Eerdmans, 1965), 20. Carnell's doctoral dissertation at Boston University was on Kierkegaard. Something of Carnell's genius is laid bare in Kenneth W. M. Wozniak's *Ethics in the Thought of Edward John Carnell* (Lanham, Md.: University Press of America, 1983).

5. *Existentialist Revolt,* 26.

6. Ibid., 24. "Existence for Kierkegaard is attaining self-possession in the spiritually directed and determined life" (16).

7. Benet, William Rose Benet, *Benet's Reader's Encyclopedia,* 3d ed. (New York: Harper & Row, 1987), s.v., "Soren Kierkegaard."

8. J. M. Spier, *Christianity and Existentialism* (Philadelphia: Presbyterian and Reformed, 1953). Spier gives a sound critique.

9. H. V. Martin, *Kierkegaard: The Melancholy Dane* (New York: Philosophical Library, 1950), 54. Martin explores the debt of Kierkegaard to the still-much-neglected J. G. Hamann. See Isaiah Berlin, *J. G. Hamann and the Origins of Modern Irrationalism* (New York: Farrar, Strauss and Giroux, 1994). Hamann (1730–1788) converted to pietistic Christianity.

10. Søren Kierkegaard, *Fear and Trembling* (on Abraham and Isaac) and *The Sickness Unto Death* (Garden City, N.Y.: Doubleday Anchor, 1954). Cf. Edmund Perry, "Was Kierkegaard a Biblical Existentialist?" *The Journal of Religion,* January 1956. Perry shows that Kierkegaard misunderstands the biblical narrative. "The knight of faith described in *Fear and Trembling* is not the knight of biblical faith, the father of the faithful."

11. David F. Swenson, as quoted in *Kierkegaard: The Melancholy Dane,* 63. Swenson was a devout evangelical Christian.

12. Søren Kierkegaard, *Purity of Heart Is to Will One Thing* (New York: Harper Torchbooks, 1938). This classic is a spiritual preparation for confession. As a corrective to what many feel is hyperindividualism in Kierkegaard, see Robert N. Bellah, et al., *Habits of the Heart: Individualism and Commitment in American Life* (New York: Perennial Library, 1985). New information in the tenth-anniversary edition of

Bellah's study indicates that the dilemma has intensified. Voluntary associations are in serious decline in North America. See Robert Bellah, et al., "Individualism and the Crisis of Civic Membership," in *Christian Century,* 8 May 1996, 510ff.

13. *The Burden of Søren Kierkegaard,* 70, 105, 169. Reinhold Niebuhr demonstrates "The Relevance of an Impossible Ethical Ideal" in his *Interpretation of Christian Ethics* (New York: Living Age, 1956), 97ff. John Stott points out that Jesus gave two commandments, not three, when he commanded love for God and for neighbor, but not for self. Pelagians, semi-Pelagians and all Christianity-related cults argue that if God tells us to do it we can do it by strength of will.

14. Ibid., 170. Carnell maintains that "Unless the Christian religion is responsibly related to evidences that are both public and sufficient, it is simply not worth talking about." Part of this book is movingly autobiographical.

15. Bernard Ramm, "The Existential Interpretation of Doctrine," *Bibliotheca Sacra,* 112:154–63, 256–64. It is interesting that over time Ramm himself became more enveloped in this approach.

CHAPTER SIX

Weighing the Christian Heritage of William Shakespeare

The play's the thing.

—William Shakespeare

We have touched on the significance of Greek and Roman drama as expressions of those ancient cultures (2.3, 2.6). Drama (enacting a story) and its twin, storytelling, are ancient human art forms. During the Middle Ages, miracle and mystery plays were important and consciously designed vehicles for teaching Christian truth to audiences in and out of the church. A segment of the Puritan, old Calvinist, and Victorian communities opposed all drama (except in preaching) because they thought the medium unbiblical and salacious and characterized all who went on stage as loose in morals. The notion that George Whitefield could have loved the stage and used dramatic technique can seem almost unimaginable, given the reputation of the art in his time.[1]

By the middle of the fifteenth century, "royal players of interludes" provided court entertainment alongside court jesters and troops of actors who wandered across Europe. In 1576 "The Theatre" was established by the Burbages in London as a settled venue for public plays.[2] During the reign of Elizabeth I, particularly through the genius of Shakespeare, the drama as a medium of education and entertainment exploded in popularity.

Plays belong in this pilgrimage through literature because the enacted story both mirrors and shapes the age.[3] The communicator is drawn to drama because of its peculiar intensity of image and emotion, and because its environment—the physical boundaries of a stage—is so defined that it thoroughly challenges the imagination and verbal skills of the one who wants to tell a story. Experience in dramatic reading, acting, and other forms of oral interpretation are generally recommended in the training of preachers and other Christian communicators.

Before coming to Shakespeare himself, we shall examine French and British playwrights who established his context.

---

1. Harry S. Stout, *The Divine Dramatist: George Whitefield and the Rise of Modern Evangelicalism* (Grand Rapids: Eerdmans, 1991). George Whitefield as a youth studied theatre and performed on stage.

2. Allardyce Nicoll, *English Drama: A Modern Viewpoint* (New York: Barnes and Noble, 1968), 31. A fine study.

3. Francis Schaeffer and his colleague H. R. Rookmaaker (*Modern Art and the Death of a Culture*) pioneered in Christian thought on the worldview connection between the arts and culture. While studies have abounded in this area of social commentary during the 1990s, of particular interest is Jane Dillenberger, *Style and Content in Christian Art* (New York: Crossroad, 1986).

6.1 CONTEMPORARIES AND COLLEAGUES

6.1.1 MOLIÈRE, FATHER OF FRENCH COMEDY

> I stop at nothing, you shall see; I mean
> To prove it myth that humankind is wise—
> And every heart will do what in it lies.
>
> —Molière
> *Le Misanthrope*

Molière and Racine forged the French and Continental European theatre. Molière was the pen name of Jean Baptiste Poquelin (1622–1673), who was born in Paris to an upholsterer who did work for the king. In a family line of court violinists, young Jean Baptiste was educated by the Jesuits at Clermont, and his interest in acting was encouraged by his father. He sometimes traveled with troops of budding actors to fairs in France while continuing his studies in the law. He was a serious student of the classics, with a particular addiction to Lucretius (98–55 B.C.). In 1643 he cofounded *L'Illustre Théâtre* in Paris, but the pioneering venture was swamped by financial collapse, and Poquelin actually spent time in debtor's prison.[1] He formed an alliance with the actress Madeline Bejart and barnstormed for several years until, as the "mouthpiece of comedy," he was invited with Madeline and the troop to settle in Lyons from 1652 to 1655. He wrote and performed before growing audiences, and Louis XIV found his farces especially appealing.

While bringing joy and laughter to others, the playwright was chronically depressed and faced serious professional challenges: "His physical endowments, his gestures, and his presence hardly tallied with people's implicit image of the tragic actor. He was not forgetting the Demosthenean struggles he must have undertaken to improve the distinctness of his voice and to slow down his delivery—struggles that had left a trace in the unfortunate hiccup he studied to obscure."[2]

In 1658, under the patronage of the king's brother, Philippe d'Orleans, Molière returned to Paris as director of a company that performed next to the Louvre and later in the Palais-Royal. The companies produced tragedies by Pierre Corneille and one that he himself wrote, but afterward his output was largely in comedies. In 1662 he married Armande Bejart, Madeline's daughter born out of wedlock. She was half his age, which fueled a scandal as to the paternity of Armande that smoldered throughout their stormy marriage.[3]

Molière's play *Tartuffe,* or as it was sometimes called *The Impostor,* was a biting comment on religious hypocrisy. Indeed the title *Tartuffe* has come to mean "hypocrite" in France. The play brought down the wrath of the church on Molière and was repeatedly banned. The Jansenists were zealous crusaders against Molière's work (see p. 108). Skeptical by nature, he valued reason above emotion. He generally had a low view of humanity.[4] He died while performing and was refused church burial.

His 1664 play, *Le Misanthrope,* is generally considered his finest work. It reflects something of the bitter cynicism to which his own troubled marriage gave rise. Of this play and the circumstances of its origin, Fernandez observes: "It is the work of a man who, for the time being at least, no longer knows where he stands in relation to goodness and truth, justice and reason—a man floundering in one of those spiritual fogs that all of us, in some chapter of our lives, have to work our way through."[5]

His characters are more types than real persons, but he is brilliant in his "comic exposition of human character." Alceste, first played by Molière himself, cries out in the beginning of the play, "I want to be angry! I don't want to listen!" Alceste (meaning "man of strength") is a strong and steady but also rigid, intractable, and unbending man. The object of his love, Celimene, originally played by his own young wife, has fine qualities and does seem to love Alceste, but she also loves the world and so continually temporizes and compromises that Alceste is driven to distraction. He piously and obdurately says:

> I want straightforwardness and upright dealing
> And no word said except from honest feeling.

Finally Alceste erupts. He will not negotiate the smallest matter. His friend Philintes stands with him and steadfastly purposes to help him. The tragic overtones almost overcome us in the final scene, in which Alceste reminds us of Psalm 55:6–8 in his desire for escape. He laments:

> Betrayed on all sides, oppressed with injustice,
> I am going to escape a gulf where vice reigns triumphant;
> and to search out some retired corner of the world,
> where one may have the liberty to be a man of honor. [Act 4]

Like Jeremiah, Alceste, and possibly Molière, longs to cease and desist, to check out, but Philintes pledges to seek "to break this savage purpose of his heart."

How much did the audience laugh in all of this? The play has never been very popular.

1. Ramon Fernandez, *Molière: The Man Seen Through the Plays* (New York: Hill and Wang, 1958), 9.
2. Ibid., 48. Many speakers know these struggles. Even such a remarkable communicator as Phillips Brooks struggled with speech defects. Of value is E. Winston Jones, *Preaching and the Dramatic Arts* (New York: Macmillan, 1948).
3. Ibid., 80ff. Madeline and her daughter remained in Molière's life in this bizarre triangle until Madeline died in 1671.
4. Introductory essay, *Gateway to the Great Books* (Chicago: Britannica, 1963), 4.2.
5. *Molière: The Man Seen Through the Plays,* 144. "This extremely moody and restive man never put up with self-deception."

6.1.2 RACINE, TRAGEDIAN

Theseus: "Oh, may the Gods shed their light on my troubled mind,
And reveal the truth which I came seeking here."

—Jean Racine

Phaedra is at the apex of classical French drama. Its plot was drawn from the Greek culture like many formal plays of its time. Plutarch told the original story. With Pierre Corneille, its author stands in the tragic tradition and experimented with limiting time and space for dramatic effect. His female characters are particularly well done, and he is considered one of the French masters of all time.

The author of this auspicious play was Jean Racine (1639–1699), born near Soisson to a minor public official. When his parents died, he was raised by a grandmother with strong Jansenist convictions. He was educated in the classics at Port-Royal, the Jansenist center. Jansenists were Augustinian in cast and strongly emphasized sin and redemption, seeking to reform Roman Catholic theology from within. In Paris, Racine joined an acting colony that did not always encourage his spirituality. He wrote eight masterpieces and received a small pension for an ode he wrought on the occasion of the marriage of Louis XIV.

His family was long burdened for his spiritual welfare, and he was encouraged to live for awhile with an uncle who sought his reformation. In the end, Racine was drawn back to Paris and a friendship with Molière, who produced several of his plays. *Phaedra,* his best known, tells the story of Phaedra, wife of the King of Athens, who falls in love with her stepson and causes his death. Such subject matter was shocking, an open description of incest and adulterous desire. Blood is mentioned twenty-nine times, guilt twelve times, and crime twenty-four times. "The atmosphere of the play is one of perversity, unnaturalness and scandal."[1] Phaedra speaks candidly of her passions and allows her servant to tell a lie for her. While none of this was exactly new in the extravagance of the French court, Racine seemed to subtly criticize French life.[2]

In 1677, the year he was married, Racine retired from the theatre and took a small position as historiographer for the French king. He also reconciled with his Port-Royal ties. Twelve years of silence followed. Both plays he wrote thereafter had religious themes, the powerful *Esther* (1689) and *Athalie* (1691), which were done for Madame de Maintenon, Louis XIV's mistress. They were performed in her school. Powerful court preachers spoke out about this loose and licentious time.[3] Of *Esther,* Pucciani says, "the presence of Christianity permeates every scene."[4] He spoke of "the terrible depravity" of the court and was buried as a true son of Port-Royal.

Very evidently in Sophocles and Euripides we have the pagan view in tragedy; in Corneille and Racine we have the Christian view in tragedy. Some have argued that Racine was among the first to write about "the passions of the heart." In Shakespeare, we sense cosmic forces working destructively; in Racine, the inner depraved passions of the human heart are in their destructive fury.[5] Jansenistic Puritanism was not popular in France but made a deep mark, and we see it in Racine. As Pucciani says: "Phaedra was a valid portrayal of human corruption, the corruption of consciousness which reason could not explain."[6]

The play action is inexplicable apart from the doctrine of original sin. It ends with "the triumph of the moral order," with Theseus's repentance and reconciliation with Aricie.[7] Phaedra has "a strong moral awareness of her guilt."[8]

This play should be read. Racine is a master of emotional intensity—Phaedra's fate seems to be cast in a moment, although it has been years in forming. Racine crafts transitions brilliantly. His characters are realistic, and his dialogue and direction splendidly simple. A study of his endings helps us understand the storyteller's sense of the climacteric.

---

1. Oreste F. Pucciani, *Racine: Phaedra* (Northbrook, Ill.: AHM, 1959), vi, vii.
2. Ibid., viii.
3. See David L. Larsen, *The Company of the Preachers* (Grand Rapids: Kregel, 1998), 6.3.2.3. Did Racine hear the great preachers Jacques-Bénigne Bossuet (1627–1704), or Louis Bourdaloue (1632–1704), or François Fénelon (1651–1715), or Jean Baptiste Massilon (1663–1742)? This was great preaching.
4. *Racine: Phaedra,* 131.
5. Odette de Mourgues, *Racine, or the Triumph of Relevance* (Cambridge: Cambridge University Press, 1967), 4–5.
6. *Racine: Phaedra,* xiii.
7. *Triumph of Relevance,* 129.
8. Ibid., 130.

6.1.3 MARLOWE, RECKLESS GENIUS

> I count religion but a childish toy
> And hold there is no sin but ignorance.
>
> O, I'll leap up to my God!—Who pulls me down?
> See, see where Christ's blood streams i' the firmament!
> One drop would save my soul, half a drop: Ah, my Christ!"
> —Christopher Marlowe
> *The Tragical History of Doctor Faustus*

Christopher Marlowe (1564–1593) presents two very different sides. The brilliant playwright was also a brash young poet and dramatist. He is certainly the first great writer of English tragedy and lifted the use of blank verse to unparalleled heights. He exerted immense influence on William Shakespeare, who doubtless attended his plays in London.

Marlowe's life was brief and controversial. He was a university man who studied and loved the classics and yet a religious freethinker who died in a brawl in a tavern, accused by the Privy Council of atheism and treason.

Marlowe was born in Canterbury, the son of a tanner and shoemaker. There he attended the King's School where he learned Latin by acting in plays. In 1580 he began study at Corpus Christi College in Cambridge on an Archbishop Matthew Parker scholarship. Cambridge at this time was polarized sharply over Ramian logic, but there young Marlowe learned to love the Greek and Latin classics.[1] Here it was reported that he had some leaning toward Roman Catholicism, which in the Elizabethan era was politically incorrect to say the least. At this time, he abandoned any inclination for the pulpit to follow his love for the stage.

Christopher Marlowe shrank from expressions of religious or political stricture in his work. Marchette Chute observes: "Marlowe was a true son of the Renaissance in his intense ambition and love for beauty, and when he wrote a play about a great tyrant king he did it as much to please himself as to please the London public."[2] Actually nothing he wrote was published during his life. One early work was a translation of Ovid's (43 B.C.–c. A.D. 17) elegies, the *Amores,* as well as Marcus Lucan's (A.D. 39–65) *First Book.* His able mind could have rivaled Shakespeare had he lived beyond age thirty. His writing was beginning to thunder and blaze with lightning.

When Marlowe arrived in London in 1589, three theatre companies were active. He began to write plays and always showed a remarkable faithfulness to his sources. In his earliest play, *Dido, Queen of Carthage,* Marlowe seemed to find his own voice.

To Vergil's (70–19 B.C.) *Aeneid,* he adds lavish gore of the carnage in Troy and his "sugared speech changes to acid tone."[3] His powerful play on the Sycthian conqueror Tamburlaine (Tamerlane) the Great was done in two parts. Biographer Frederick Boas speaks of the "sonorous roll of Eastern place-names" reminiscent of Milton.[4] He observes that "the warrior-king of superhuman mould took Elizabethan theatre-goers by storm." His representation of this challenge to the corrupt royal house of Persia was not lost on Elizabeth's hypersensitive advisors. What was the bold young playwright saying? The triumphant hero's wedding that closes the story is stunning.

Interspersed with his writing (moving on now to a sequel to *Tamburlaine* and *The Jew of Malta*) were frays in taverns and public houses. Once he was arrested on suspicion of murder and held in Newgate for two weeks. Then he was charged with atheism by Thomas Kyd, his chief tragedian rival. Kyd himself had been charged and arrested; for evidence Kyd produced a paper from his effects, which he claimed were Marlowe's profane and blasphemous sentiments.

The primary charge was more serious, since it connected Marlowe with

Walter Raleigh (1554–1618) in the actions for which Raleigh was executed. Marlowe was apparently a member of "the school of night," which was interested in Pythagorean ideas and the teachings of Niccolò Machiavelli. The accusation was:

> Of Sir Walter Raleigh's school of Atheism by the way, and of the conjurer that is master thereof, and of the diligence used to get young gentlemen of this school, wherein both Moses and our Savior are jested at, and the scholars taught among other things to spell God backward.[5]

Both Raleigh and Marlowe certainly believed in God, as can be seen of Raleigh in his *History of the World* and Marlowe in *The Tragical History of Doctor Faustus*. However, both were feared nonconformists. "Marlowe hated conformity with all the passion of his free-ranging intellect and he felt an actual sense of suffocation under the series of tight religious rules the average Englishman took for granted."[6]

Scholars wonder if the struggle over the dagger in Eleanor Bull's Tavern in Deptford Strand and the "sudden blow from behind" were not a government assassin's assignment.[7] The ambiguities and intrigues of Marlowe, and the rumor that his politics tilted toward the Scottish royal Stuarts, only a few years after Mary of Scotland was beheaded, make political murder a reasonable possibility. Marlowe and his work quickly passed from view and has only slowly come back, but there can be no question that, as Charles Lamb put it, this gifted man was "the true father of our tragedy."

Marlowe's premier play, *The Tragical History of Doctor Faustus*, uses sources as skillfully as he did in such historical plays as *The Massacre at Paris* and *Edward II, King of England. The Massacre at Paris* dealt with the St. Bartholomew's Day slaughter of the Huguenots and was repressed by the Queen's agents out of deference to France. For *Edward II*, Marlowe referred to the same Holinshed's Chronicles used by William Shakespeare in his historical plays.

The Faust stories are originally from Germany but were gathered in *The English Faust Book*, which Marlowe used. The Devil's ploy of offering sex, riches, and power in exchange for souls was a motif enshrined in the Faustus stories. Marlowe shows how a scholar's love for knowledge could be contaminated by lust for occult power.[8]

Faustus had been a divinity student at Wittenberg, but he was dissatisfied after a subject-by-subject examination of the various disciplines. He is thus open to Satan's offer. Some rather silly interludes of humor with the servant Wagner don't really work, but Marlowe's vivid writing on hell has been seen by some critics "as more spiritual than Milton's."[9] Faustus repents and desperately calls to the Savior, but inevitably the awful end comes. Act 5 movingly shows Doctor Faustus's anguished anticipation of the coming of the fiend.[10] One cannot escape a sense that in the horror of the closing scene there was something painfully autobiographical.

Marlowe's classical diction and his obviously brilliant lyrics are seen again and again, as when Doctor Faustus beholds Helen of Troy:

> Was this the face that launch'd a thousand ships
> And burnt the topless towers of Illium?
> Sweet Helen, make me immortal with a kiss!

The truly dominant figure during her forty-five-year reign was Elizabeth I (r. 1558–1603). The Virgin Queen (after whom Sir Walter Raleigh named Virginia) is a baffling and complex character. My recommendation for the best overall biography, Elizabeth Jenkins's *Elizabeth the Great*,[11] shows her skill in politics and broad understanding as a complete Renaissance woman. This research helps in our understanding of religious changes and literature during this pivotal era.

---

1. Frederick S. Boas, *Christopher Marlowe: A Biographical and Critical Study* (Oxford: Clarendon, 1940, 1953), 16.
2. Marchette Chute, *Shakespeare of London* (New York: E. P. Dutton, 1949), 74.
3. Boas, *Christopher Marlowe*, 56, 59. The version of *Doctor Faustus* edited by Boas is superior (1932; repr. ed., New York: Gordion, 1966).
4. Boas, *Christopher Marlowe*, 77, 79. An interesting allusion to the Spanish Armada is 3.3.60–163.
5. Peter Milward, *Shakespeare's Religious Background* (Chicago: Loyola University Press, 1973), 203.
6. *Shakespeare of London*, 77.
7. A fascinating fictional study on who killed Marlowe by Judith Cook is *The Slicing Edge of Death* (New York: St. Martin's, 1996).
8. John Hale, *The Civilization of Europe in the Renaissance* (New York: Athenaeum, 1994), 581.
9. Boas, *Christopher Marlowe*, 210, 262.
10. Ibid., 216. Two centuries later, Goethe shows us Faustus "in his sinful pleasures," as Marlowe does not.
11. New York: Howard-McCann, 1958.

6.1.4 JONSON, CLASSICAL CRAFTSMAN

> It is not growing like a tree
> In bulk, doth make men better be,
> Or standing long an oak, three hundred years,
> To fall at last, dry, bald and sere:
> A lily of a day
> Is fairer far in May
> Although it fall and die that night
> It was the plant and flower of light.
> In small proportion we just beauty see;
> And in short measure, life may perfect be.
>
> —Ben Jonson

"O rare Ben Jonson!" is the epitaph on the burial stone in Westminster Abbey for this poet and crafter of plays. Jonson (1573–1637) was the child of a minister, who died a month before he was born. His mother remarried a bricklayer who raised him. Though he would be the most classical of the English playwrights with his Roman models always before him, Jonson had little educational opportunity beyond Westminster School—which he attended through the courtesy of its master. He served in the military in the campaigns against the Spanish in the Low Countries.[1] He was married in 1592 and worked as an actor and writer.

After he killed Gilbert Spencer in a duel, he was remanded to prison and was in some danger of being executed. During this stressful time, he converted to Catholicism, a faith he followed for twelve years. Expecting the worst, his old mother brought poison so he would not suffer the disgrace of execution as a criminal. He was released but forfeited his property and was branded on his thumb. James I (r. 1603–1625) liked Jonson's work, so he wrote many skits, songs, and pantomimes for the royal court.

Sometimes his lyrical poetry was set to music, as in "Celia" with its well-known opening line: "Drink to Me Only with Thine Eyes." A club patron, he ate and drank heavily and gathered around him a circle called the "Tribe of Ben." He was friends with John Donne (1573–1631), Francis Bacon (1561–1626), and Robert Herrick (1591–1674). In social deportment, quaint Thomas Fuller (1608–1661) said Shakespeare was like an English "man o' war" (less in bulk and lighter in sailing) while Jonson was like a Spanish galleon (higher in learning, solid, but slow). Theatre historian Robert Knoll likens Jonson to J. S. Bach and Shakespeare to Ludwig van Beethoven. Jonson was a commanding personality. He often harped on "the humours" as he analyzed character.[2]

Critics agree that Ben Jonson was a Christian humanist. His plays are "elaborations of the Tudor morality plays" with a Christian message. Knoll sees Christian sermons in them.[3] After all of Jonson's escapades, he was in the end "basically a humble Christian."[4] His faith is most clear in the five comedies that together became his climactic work. Most worthwhile of the five to read are *Volpone, or the Fox* (1606) and *The Alchemist* (1610).

Volpone is "a sombre and savage comedy."[5] It is derived from the universally known old beast fable about "The Fox Who Feigned Death." *Volpone or the Fox* is much like *Doctor Faustus* and displays the "unnaturalness" and "bestiality" of human sin.[6] The play begins with Volpone slavering over his hoard of gold. He is a humanist who is undirected and untrammeled by religion. Mosca is the arch-parasite who helps him deceive the crow (who offers his wife to the fox to further his own aspiration), the vulture, and the raven. In the final restoration, the rascals are all banished.

The Alchemist also is a play of Christian import. Coleridge cited the plot along with *Oedipus Rex* and *Tom Jones* as the three most perfect plots in all of literature. This play of great fervor and frenzy grew out of a night vision. Knoll is right that it is more a collection than a development. It is "a satire of the gulls and the sharks," and begins with Subtle, the alchemist "drunk with his own pretensions," and his coconspirator bickering. Five groups of characters come into the action, and the idols and perversions of the human heart are clearly seen.[7]

Jonson uses alchemy and witchcraft and the occult with subtlety for his ulterior purposes. He also gets a good whack in on the pesky Puritans (who of course shut him down) and the Anabaptists are tricked too. Each of the dupes has an action of his own. This play recasts Jesus' parable of the talents from Matthew 25.[8] It is fascinating to picture Ben Jonson and all of his involvements on the stage of English history from Elizabethan days up through the days of rising Puritan ascendancy.

---

1. The American diplomat John L. Motley's three volume *The Rise of the Dutch Republic* (New York: Harper, 1880) depicts the conflict of William of Orange and the Protestants versus Philip II of Spain and Catholicism.
2. Robert E. Knoll, *Ben Jonson's Plays: An Introduction* (Lincoln, Neb.: University of Nebraska Press, 1964), 2ff.
3. Ibid., vii. In Jonson's later play, *The Devil Is an Ass,* the author shows that Satan himself is a piker.
4. Ibid., 132. Knoll is insistent that Jonson came through the vicissitudes on course as a believer.
5. Ibid., xxvi. These comedies are heavy as compared to Shakespeare.
6. Ibid., 96, 104. In the original story, the fox pretends he is dying and lures his victims close and then pounces.
7. Ibid., 118. Ben Jonson had a settled aversion to any kind of romanticism.
8. F. H. Mares, introduction to *The Alchemist* (Cambridge: Harvard University Press, 1967), xlii.

6.1.5 SHERIDAN, COMEDIAN POLITICIAN

Snake: Everyone allows that Lady Sneerwell can do more with a word
or a look than many can do with the most laboured detail, even
when they happen to have a little truth on their side to support it.
You can, indeed each anxious fear remove,
For even Scandal dies, if you approve.
                                                                —Richard Brinsley Sheridan

Puritans shut the theatres down in 1642, and after the Restoration, with dramatist William Congreve (1670–1729) and others, the "Restoration comedies" flourished—the comedies of manners. After awhile, they degenerated into sentimental twaddle, "a mixture of strained loftiness and easy tears."[1]

These plays were founded on the Enlightenment conviction that the human being is innately good, "and he can be softened into virtue through tears which are made to flow from contemplation of undeserved suffering."[2] Oliver Goldsmith crusaded against this sentimentality, but Richard Sheridan (1751–1816), in his two marvelous comedies *The Rivals* (1775) and *The School for Scandal* (1777), probably wrote the best plays in England between Shakespeare and Shaw.

Richard Sheridan was the son of an actor, born in Dublin but educated for six years at Harrow. His mother also wrote plays. His family by this time was living in beautiful Bath, England, where William Jay preached for sixty-two years at Argyle Chapel.[3] Here he courted and fought two duels for his young bride, whom he triumphantly escorted to London. He wrote plays to keep bread on the table but lived his whole life heavily in debt. His first major play, *The Rivals,* set in Bath, met with very positive response, with its polished prose, stock characters, and hilarious plot. When he was twenty-three years old, he succeeded David Garrick as manager of the Drury Lane Theatre. One of the unforgettable characters in this play is Mrs. Malaprop, who has given the word *malapropism* to our language to refer to the outrageous and pretentious misuse of a word. (A modern example of a malapropism would be: "Hospital insurance covers *impatient* care.")

The School for Scandal, with its "sharper satiric tone," is one of the most popular comedies ever performed. The play shows scandal-mongering at its worst. Lady Sneerwell and her compatriot, Snake, become embroiled with the Surface brothers, both of whom want to claim lovely Maria, the ward of Sir Peter Teazel. The play is a riot of mirth and joy, but it shows us "theatrical climax of the first order."[4] The outstanding scenes are the auction of family portraits and the scandal-hiding screen, which inopportunely falls over.

The play castigates upper-class hypocrisy. In reading plays, one should imagine a live performance. Charles Surface, the prodigal, is clearly shown to be a person of loyalty and integrity, and his more priggish brother, Joseph, the sentimental favorite, is a pretender and a rake. His rank duplicity only brings him grief. This play stands with *As You Like It* and *Much Ado About Nothing* among the finest examples of period drama.[5]

From this point Sheridan wrote very little for the stage. He entered Parliament where he served with distinction for more than thirty years and was known as an outstanding orator, a contemporary of Edmund Burke (1729–1797) and William Wilberforce (1759–1833). He was dedicated to parliamentary reform and freedom of the press. Sheridan was buried in Westminster Abbey near David Garrick.

As early as 1777, Sheridan became part of Samuel Johnson's "Literary Club" and must be considered by any standard one of the all-time movers and shakers in the business of entertainment.[6]

---

1. Oscar James Campbell, *Chief Plays of Goldsmith and Sheridan* (New York: Harcourt Brace, 1926), v.
2. Ibid., v–vi. Laughter is aroused "by the penetrating comment on the follies which still stalk among us."
3. *Company of the Preachers,* 8.5.2. See also *The Autobiography of William Jay* (1854; repr. ed., Edinburgh: Banner of Truth, 1974).
4. Frederick A. Boas, *An Introduction to Eighteenth-Century Drama* (Oxford: Clarendon, 1953), 356.
5. Ibid., 357. Sheridan grafts novel elements onto the conventional frameworks.
6. A strong entry in Sheridan biography is Fintan O'Toole, *A Traitor's Kiss: The Life of Richard Brinsley Sheridan* (New York: Garrar, Strauss and Giroux, 1998).

6.1.6 GOLDSMITH, CREATIVE VAGABOND

Imagine to yourself a pale melancholy visage with two great wrinkles
between the eyebrows, with an eye disgustingly severe and a big wig,
and you have a perfect picture of my present appearance.

I can neither laugh nor drink, have contracted an hesitating disagreeable manner of speaking, and a visage that looks ill nature itself.

—Oliver Goldsmith

One of the most accomplished craftsmen of English literature in his time was
born Oliver Goldsmith (1728–1774) in Pallas, Ireland. Oliver was the son of
Charles and Ann Oliver Goldsmith, both children of Anglican rectors. Goldsmith
was encouraged by his first teacher to versify in Latin. He early learned profi-
ciency in French. He went on to Trinity College, Dublin, where he read the classics, but he was not a good student nor regular in attending lectures. He presented
himself for ordination but was turned down because he was too young and because he wore red breeches. His extravagant dress during his whole life probably was an effort to turn attention from his physical appearance, scars of smallpox
he contracted at age nine.

From 1752 to 1754, Goldsmith lived in Edinburgh, studying medicine. Then
he went to Leyden, Holland, to study before dropping out to spend a year wandering Europe with his flute and tall tales. He never returned to Ireland, settling
in England in 1756. While he loved the countryside more, (see his poem "The
Deserted Village"), he lived in London for the next eighteen years, until his death
at age forty-six. It was a hard life. The writer fought great bouts of depression
and physical weakness and probably had Bright's Disease, with chronic problems in his kidneys. He died in violent convulsions.[1]

Goldsmith dabbled in many enterprises: translating, teaching at Milner's
school, writing book notices, compiling anthologies, and writing for magazines.
Once he started out for America. He considered going to India to practice medicine in the military. Joshua Reynolds saw his genius and encouraged him, and
he met Samuel Johnson (1709–1784) as early as 1761 and became part of the
Literary Club. He dipped into music, drama, and politics. In 1764 he wrote *The
Captivity,* a musical oratorio based on Psalm 137 and the deportation of the Jews
to Babylon.[2] He was appointed professor of ancient history in the Royal Academy and wrote two biographies, several volumes of history, and his acclaimed
novel *Vicar of Wakefield.* He always regarded himself as a believer in Christ,
though he gambled himself into heavy debt and could be irascible.

He wrote well in several literary genres, but his plays are seen as his best work,
especially *She Stoops to Conquer,* which was immediately successful in 1772 and
was still being produced over two centuries later. It is most tightly constructed plot
and narrative. Oscar James Campbell, who compiled the playwright's work, describes
She Stoops to Conquer as "an uninterrupted flow of good spirits."[3] There are no sentimental interludes and all of the complications are plausible. Like Sheridan, he de-
plored the sentimental comedy and crusaded for genuine comedy with real humor.
He sought to develop plays in which the comic rose from faults in character.[4]

Goldsmith derived the essential plot of *She Stoops to Conquer* from an incident in which he had mistakenly wandered into someone's home, thinking it was an inn, and behaved accordingly. This was Marlow's blunder in the play. Quickly, however, the traveler is smitten with a lovely young lady he mistakenly thinks is the barmaid. The characters are rare. Miss Hardwicke, the high-spirited heroine, is the one who "stoops to conquer."

Samuel Johnson wrote a Latin epitaph for Goldsmith, which is inscribed in Westminster Abbey, although the writer was buried in Temple Church Cemetery. After some false starts, Oliver Goldsmith has left a vibrant look at eighteenth-century English life and outlook.

In a day of spiritual torpor in the Church of England, William Law (1686–1761) wrote books that influenced the course of Britain's Great Awakening. Notable is *A Serious Call to Devout and Holy Life,* in which Law argues that "every state of life is to be made a state of piety and holiness in all its parts." Samuel Johnson called it "the finest piece of hortatory theology in any language." Historian William Edward Lecky observed it as "one of the most solemn and powerful works of its kind in any literature, and is well fitted to exercise a deep and lasting influence upon the character." Law, a graduate of Cambridge, would not vow fidelity to the House of Hanover and so could not be ordained in the Church of England. He lived and taught in the household of the Gibbons, from whence Edward Gibbon came (2.7.6). John and Charles Wesley were friends until Law plunged into a sort of religious mysticism. Law's theology uses delightful characters to illustrate his points.

---

1. A. Lytton Sells, *Oliver Goldsmith: His Life and Works* (New York: Barnes and Noble, 1974), 328. Goldsmith covered his depression with buffoonery.
2. Ibid., 106.
3. *Chief Plays of Goldsmith and Sheridan,* xi.
4. Clara M. Kirk, *Oliver Goldsmith* (New York: Twayne, 1967), 118. "Humor had been driven off the stage."

6.2   SHAKESPEARE: CHARACTER AND CAREER

> Speak the speech, I pray you, trippingly on the tongue:
>> but if you mouth it, as many of your players do,
>> I had a lief the town-crier spoke my lines.
> Nor do not saw the air too much with your hand, thus, but use all gently;
>> for . . . you just acquire and beget a temperance
>> that may give it smoothness.
> O, it offends me to the soul to hear a fellow tear a passion to tatters,
>> to very rags, to split the ears.
>> Be not too tame neither . . .
>> suit the action to the word, the word to the action.
>> —Hamlet to the players (3.2.1)

William Shakespeare (1564–1616) is offered many superlatives, among them the title "the world's greatest dramatist" and "the best poet who ever wrote in English." But with Shakespeare, it is difficult to overstate his influence. Next to the Bible, his works are the most translated of any in the English language.

- Johann Wolfgang von Goethe (1749–1832) said, "I do not remember that any book or person or event in my life ever made so great an impression on me than the plays of Shakespeare."
- Thomas Carlyle (1795–1881) called him "the greatest intellect who has left record of himself in the way of literature."
- In euphoric hyperbole, Ralph Waldo Emerson (1803–1882) asserted: "In climes beyond the solar road, this planet is probably not called earth, but Shakespeare."
- Wrote John Keats (1795–1821): "Shakespeare led a life of allegory; his works are the comments on it."

In innumerable respects, the literary heritage of the bard from Stratford-on-Avon is an indescribable treasure and of immense benefit to Christians who want to be effective and literate communicators. Shakespeare's work personifies Aristotle's definition of poetry as "an expression of the universal."

6.2.1 HIS PEDIGREE

> Some men are born great,
> some achieve greatness,
> and some have greatness thrust upon them.
> —*Twelfth Night* (2.5.157–59)

Shakespeare was born in beautiful Stratford-on-Avon some eight miles southwest of Warwick, the son of John Shakespeare, a prominent glover, and his wife, Mary Arden, from a prominent Roman Catholic family. Shakespeare set *As You Like It* in the Forest of Arden.[1] William was the third child and oldest son. Parish records show that he was baptized in Holy Trinity Church on April 26, 1564.

He probably attended King Edward School in Stratford, where he studied Latin and became especially fond of the dramatists. Ovid and the Geneva Bible influenced his fertile mind. Perhaps he went "unwillingly to school," loving even more the picturesque countryside and lovely river.[2]

Beyond the fact that he arose from the shopkeeping English middle-class, few specifics are known about the eighteen and one-half years before he married Anne Hathaway, a woman who was eight years his senior. Their marriage may not always have been happy, but it was not scandalous, as some have imagined. The Bishop of Worcester at the time, Whitgift, was quite a stickler, and that very year moved on to become Archbishop of Canterbury.[3] The curious feature of the union was that Anne and the children always lived in Stratford, even during the extended periods that Shakespeare lived in London. He seems to have left Stratford in some controversy, perhaps because he was caught poaching on a nearby estate. These are the "lost years" about which nothing is known. Perhaps he taught school.

By 1592 he was in London, writing and acting in plays (although the theatres were shut down between 1592 and 1594 because of the plague). This was the rough-and-tumble London of Marlowe and Jonson. While the theatres were closed, William wrote his 154 sonnets. He was in several theatre companies, chiefly the Lord Chamberlain's Company, some of whose leading actors, including Shakespeare, formed a syndicate to build the Globe Theatre. As a result of his writing (two plays a year in his prime) and his acting and his part ownership of the Globe, he was quite successful and bought a large home in Stratford.

Wealth did not bring happiness at home, though. In 1596 his eleven-year-old son, Hamnet, died. Their older daughter was Susanna, a name Puritans tended to favor. With some other evidence, this seems to indicate the Puritan inclination of Anne and her family and may explain her estrangement with William.[4] Acting was forbidden, or at best avoided, among the Puritans.

A professional blow came with the sudden imprisonment and near-execution for treason of his patron, Henry Wriothesley, earl of Southampton (1573–1624), who was charged with aiding Robert Devereux, earl of Essex (1566–1601), in a plot to remove Queen Elizabeth's advisors. Shakespeare himself was appreciated by Elizabeth, and it was rumored that he wrote *The Merry Wives of Windsor* because the queen wanted to see Falstaff in love.[5] James I actually became Shakespeare's patron upon his accession, and the company was known as the "King's Men."

In 1608 the playwright seems to have had a physical or emotional breakdown. His entire regimen changed, and he wrote only five plays in the last seven years of his life. Some of those were actually coauthored.

Shakespeare died at fifty-two of unknown causes, although one chronicler reported that "Shakespeare, [poet Michael] Drayton and Ben Jonson had a merry meeting, and it seems drank too much hard for Shakespeare died of a fever there contracted."[6]

In his will, he stated: "I commend my soul into the hands of God my Creator, hoping and assuredly believing through the merits of Jesus Christ, my Savior, to be made partaker of life everlasting." He was buried in Holy Trinity Church.

---

1. Libraries have been written on Shakespeare, but the idea that he was a closet Catholic has been best argued (but with futility) by John Henry de Groot, *The Shakespeares and "The Old Faith"* (1946; repr. ed., Fraser, Mich.: American Council on Economics and Society, 1995). The idea that Shakespeare was a strongly orthodox Christian is best put forth in Roy W. Battenhouse, *Shakespeare's Christian Dimension* (Bloomington, Ind.: Indiana University Press, 1993).

2. Ivor Brown, *Shakespeare* (1949; repr. ed., New York: Time Reading Program, 1962). A solid and colorful overview.

3. *Shakespeare of London.*

4. Ibid., 53. Anne's father and her brother requested "Puritan burial."

5. William George Clarke and William Aldis Wright, "Introduction," in *Great Books* (Chicago: Britannica, 1952), v.

6. Brown, *Shakespeare,* 326.

6.2.2 HIS PRODUCTIVITY

> All the world's a stage,
> And all the men and women merely players.
> They have their exits and their entrances;
> And one man in his time plays many parts.
>   —*As You Like It* (2.7.139–42)

Shakespeare was not an innovator, introducing new forms as did Marlowe or Jonson, nor was he an originator, since he used sources from Holinshed to Plutarch, as was the custom of the time. His output was so voluminous and brilliant that some have looked for the hand of one or more other authors. Francis Bacon has frequently been nominated as a collaborator. But such theories are speculative and unsupported by evidence.[1] Whoever the writer, the literary body of work has so influenced the English language that Shakespeare is assured a place of honor as long as the English arts are celebrated. Countless terms and expressions are Shakespearean coinage, including *assassination, barefaced, dwindle, bumps, catching a cold, disgraceful conduct, foregone conclusion, elbowroom, countless, baseless, courtship, denote, fitful, mortal coil, primrose path, flaming youth, pomp and circumstance, gloomy,* and *exposure.*

Shakespeare is still read everywhere, although, incomprehensibly, English majors in fewer universities are required to read him or any of the classics. Deconstructionists condemn the writing as "the instrument of pedagogical oppression." More than fourteen annual Shakespearean festivals thrive, not only in Stratford-on-Avon itself, where the reconstructed Globe is in almost constant use, but in such towns and cities as Stratford, Ontario, and Stratford, Connecticut. The popularity of late-twentieth-century film and stage adaptations attests to the perennial viability and vitality of the bard.[2]

His first published works were two long narrative poems, *Venus and Adonis* and *The Rape of Lucrece.* These poems alone would have carved Shakespeare's niche in literature. His sonnets are quite instructive. A sonnet is a fourteen-line poem, usually in iambic pentameter. The Shakespearean poetry is unusual among sonnets in that he seldom varies from the organization of three quatrains and a couplet. For those interested in Shakespeare's spiritual life and comments, Sonnet 129 reflects some sort of disillusionment over a moral debacle. At its center is "the dark lady." Was this a real or imagined lover? The poem proceeds from anticipation of sin to realization and finally retrospection. The sin is not excused. It is seen as blameworthy, shameful, and destructive. A Christian view prevails:

> All this the world knows well; yet none knows well
> To shun the heaven that leads men to this hell.

Sonnet 146 is also of special interest with its focus on the interior life.

Of course the vast Shakespearean trove is found in his thirty-seven plays. He would always begin with the old plot and then write in faithfulness to his sources, in relation to the times in which he lived and his own personal life.[3]

In his first phase, he wrote *Henry VI, Part 1, Part 2,* and *Part 3; Titus Andronicus; The Comedy of Errors; Richard III;* and *The Two Gentlemen of Verona.* Here we see the playwright increasing his "mastery of rhetorical force" with "decreasing crudity."[4]

In the next time of high productivity, he wrote the narrative poems and sonnets, and then *Love's Labour's Lost, Romeo and Juliet, A Midsummer Night's Dream,* and *The Merchant of Venice.* Critics see a waning influence of Marlowe here and "a new pursuit of beauty in words." Although the ending in *Romeo and Juliet* is contrived, I would agree with Brown that it "contains as much of sheer verbal beauty as anything he wrote."[5]

Between 1596 and 1599, he wrote his heaviest historical plays, *King John; Richard II; Henry IV; Part 1* and *Part 2;* and *Henry V.*

Age four is "high-fantastical," consisting of *Much Ado About Nothing, The Merry Wives of Windsor, As You Like It,* and *Twelfth Night.* Ivor Brown reminds us that Shakespeare is only thirty-six years old when all of this had been accomplished.

With the turning of the century, there are the three bitter comedies: *All's Well That Ends Well, Troilus and Cressida,* and *Measure for Measure.*

The sixth period has been called the "Age of the Dark Vision." From this time are the brooding masterpieces *Julius Caesar, Hamlet, Othello, Macbeth, King Lear, Timon of Athens, Coriolanus,* and *Antony and Cleopatra.*

The last spurt of productivity has been called "Fancy Free" and features *Pericles, Cymbeline, The Winter's Tale, The Tempest,* and *Henry VIII,* as well as the little known *The Two Noble Kinsmen.*

---

1. Brown, *Shakespeare,* 326. Jonson said of him: "I lov'd the man and do honour his memory as much as any."
2. Stephen Goode, "Literary Class Struggle: The Bard's Identity Crisis," *Insight,* 31 October 1994, 9ff.
3. "To Man from Mankind's Heart," *Time,* 4 July 1960, 60ff.
4. A truly magnificent presentation, "The World of Elizabeth I," *Journal of the National Geographic Society,* November 1968, 668ff.
5. Brown, *Shakespeare,* 170.
6. Ibid., 172. This is a fine summarization of the development of Shakespeare and his plays.

6.2.3 HIS THEOLOGY

> There's a divinity that shapes our ends,
> Rough-hew them how we will.
>
> —*Hamlet* (V.2.10–17)

Shakespeare sees all of humankind as interrelated and considers that we must seek to live in harmony with the nature of which we are a part.[1] But many miss the hierarchical universe at the core of Shakespeare's perspective: The God of the Bible is the Judge and Savior through his Son Jesus Christ.

A. H. Strong built a strong argument at the end of the nineteenth century that

Shakespeare was an ethical and moral teacher who saw humankind as responsible to a just and holy God.[2] He was a Christian humanist in the Erasmian mold, who studied and knew the Bible. More than twelve hundred allusions to Scripture suffuse his corpus. He quotes from fifty-four of the sixty-six books of the Bible in thirty-seven plays. He uses the word *God* more than seven hundred times. Peter Milward in his classic study concludes that Shakespeare's is Christian drama in every sense of the word.[3] He used the Bible and *The Book of Common Prayer* as his base.

The outlook on salvation is Protestant and Reformed in orientation. He sees our sins as damning us justly, but God's mercy in Christ interposes a solution. Consider:

> That, in the course of justice, none of us
> Should see salvation. We do pray for mercy.
> —*The Merchant of Venice* (4.1.199–200)

Salvation is clearly a free gift to those who believe.[4] The mirror he held up was the moral law revealed by God. So Coleridge observes that Shakespeare "has no innocent adulteries, no interesting incests, no virtuous vice."[5] Strong considers: "In his ethical judgments he never makes a slip; he is as sure-footed as a Swiss mountaineer; he depicts vice, but he does not make it alluring or successful."[6] Rich lines bear on redemption:

> As surely as my soul intends to live
> With that dread King that took our state upon him
> To free us from his Father's wrathful curse.
> —*Henry IV* (3.2.153–56)

> I charge you as you hope to have redemption
> By Christ's dear blood, shed for our grievous sins.
> That you depart and lay no hands on me.
> —*Richard III* (1.4.195)

> And water cannot wash away your sin.
> —*Richard II* (4.1.242)

Even Emerson conceded that Shakespeare had leaned on the Bible. He makes six references to Judas Iscariot, eight to Cain and Abel, and many to speeches and miracles of Jesus.

He certainly influenced the work of his contemporary English translators who were, from the accession of James I, working on the King James Version, which was issued in 1611.

Historical novelist George Garrett has given us three dynamic studies, published by Harcourt-Brace-Jovanovich: *Death of the Fox: A Novel of Elizabeth and Raleigh; The Succession: A Novel of Elizabeth and James;* and *Entered from the Sun: The Murder of Marlowe.*

1. Virgil K. Whitaker, *Stanford Today,* spring 1964.
2. Augustus Hopkins Strong, *The Great Poets and Their Theology* (Philadelphia: Judson, 1897), 193.
3. *Shakespeare's Religious Background.*
4. Robert E. Fitch, "Shakespeare and Man's Salvation," *Christian Century,* 15 April 1964, 488.
5. John Lewis Gilmore, "What Shakespeare Thought of the Bible," *Eternity,* September 1964, 31ff.; Steve J. Van Der Weele, "Shakespeare and Christianity," *Christianity Today,* 21 September 1961, 9ff.; and Roland Mushat Frye, "Shakespeare and Christianity," *Christianity Today,* 17 July 1964, 3ff.
6. *The Great Poets,* 209–10. Do not overlook the eminently useful *Tales from Shakespeare* (1924, repr. ed., Philadelphia: John C. Winston, 1958). These are well-crafted synopses of the plays.

6.3 SHAKESPEARE: CRAFTSMANSHIP AND CREATIVITY

> This royal throne of kings, this scep'red isle,
> This earth of majesty, this seat of Mars,
> This other Eden, demi-paradise,
> This fortress built by Nature for herself
> Against infection and the hand of war,
> This happy breed of men, this little world,
> This precious stone set in the silver sea,
> Which serves it in the office of a wall,
> Or as a moat defensive to a house,
> Against the envy of less happier lands;
> This blessed plot, this earth, this realm, this England.
> —*Richard II* (2.1.40–50)

Ben Jonson said of Shakespeare, "He is not of an age, he is for all time." Few have more successfully or spectacularly probed the human predicament. No wonder the greatest actors aspire to these characters. The plays are of three sorts: histories, tragedies, and comedies. We shall select representative examples of each.

6.3.1 HENRY IV, PART 1: STRUGGLE FOR POWER

> Uneasy lies the head that wears a crown.
> —*Henry IV, Part 1* (2.1.31)

Shakespeare was a clever and insightful politician as well as a gifted playwright. His historical plays are half of his total output, and his cycle of ten plays about the succession of English kings shows discerning use of historical sources to make a statement that extends from the past to the contemporary scene. Machiavellian figures abounded in the Elizabethan hierarchy and, in excavating into England's War of the Roses, Shakespeare tread on raw nerves.

Henry IV (1367–1413), often called Henry of Bolingbroke, was the son of John of Gaunt (1340–1399), the Duke of Lancaster. He was the first king of the House of Lancaster. His cousin, Richard II (1367–1400), ruled before him. As always, the times "are out of joint" and rife with conspiracies and revolts. To consolidate his power, Richard banishes Bolingbroke and Thomas Mowbray (1366–1399). The tyranny of Richard II paved the way for a challenge, and while he was fighting the Irish, Henry invaded England and defeated Richard handily. In 1399 Parliament elected Henry as king. This was an important extension of parliamentary power that made clear that Parliament was more powerful than the king.

Richard died shortly thereafter (perhaps assassinated), and other descendants of Edward III, who were closer in bloodline to the throne than was Henry IV, were restive. The Mortimers rebelled and joined hands with the Percies. *Henry IV, Part 1,* ends with the Battle of Shrewsbury where Henry Percy (Hotspur) is killed and the Percy Rebellion quashed.

Henry IV was capable in many ways, encouraging the development of towns and fostering growing trade and commerce. He was very intolerant of religious differences, regarding them as threats to undermine political stability, and is of special interest to us because of his dogged persecution of the Lollards, the Bible preaching believers of that time. A major issue throughout his reign was whether he was a legitimate ruler or a usurper. His speeches genuinely impress us with the fact that he was desirous of being a man of peace and fairness (1.1.1–34, 5.1.101–14). Worn out by his troubles, Henry IV dies in 1413.

His son, "Prince Hal," is contrasted by Shakespeare to Hotspur of the rebellious Percies. Each has been in pursuit of honor in his own way. Hotspur is hasty and impulsive but still has a princely sense of honor. He disdains both music and poetry, which is a grievous fault line for Shakespeare. Hal is a wastrel, a heavy drinker, and a carouser. Sir John Falstaff has not been a good influence.[1] Still it is Prince Hal who kills Hotspur in battle and who turns out to be a very fine king as Henry V, banishing Falstaff and the old connections. He is, in Shakespeare's view, "the mirror of all Christian kings."[2]

Sir John Falstaff, originally Sir John Oldcastle in the early versions, must be seen as the tutor to Prince Hal. This very generously proportioned knave became Shakespeare's greatest comic character and one of his most popular creations. He is a scoundrel as he holds forth in the Boar's Head Tavern with his bragging and boasting buddies. J. Dover Wilson has argued masterfully that this play is a kind of morality play in which Falstaff fills "the devil part," in which he ceaselessly seeks to divert Prince Hal from royal responsibility.[3] Hal's growing estrangement from Falstaff would then represent steps on the prodigal's way back to his father. The disgraceful old gentleman, whom we first meet in this play as he sleeps like a sow, brought "howls of unregenerate joy" from Shakespeare's audiences.

Shakespeare reminds us that tragedy and comedy are inseparable in human experience, unlike the view in ancient Pompeii where tragedies and comedies were presented in separate theatres. Shakespeare has the knack of showing how persons who are totally absorbed in their own quest for power or aggrandizement, like Macbeth, Iago, or Richard III, do achieve some heroic stature. Even Falstaff does.

1. Mortimer J. Adler and Peter Wolff, introduction to *Henry IV,* in The Great Books Program (Chicago: Britannica, 1959), 127. This is in volume 2, *The Development of Political Theory.* Falstaff, "at once a comic and dark character," steals candy from children and can charm himself out of almost any scrape. He hates himself and hates being fat.
2. Peter J. Leithart, *Brightest Heaven of Invention: A Christian Guide to Six Shakespearean Plays* (Moscow, Idaho: Canon, 1996), 33.
3. John Dover Wilson, *The Fortunes of Falstaff* (Cambridge: Cambridge University Press, 1944). It is well in studying the histories to make constant reference to a carefully researched historical survey, such as David Greenwood, *History of England* (Ames, Iowa: Littlefield, Adams, 1958), 62.

6.3.2 *Julius Caesar: Struggle of Ambition*

> Men at some times are masters of their fate:
> The fault, dear Brutus, is not in our stars,
> But in ourselves, that we are underlings.
> —*Julius Caesar* (1.2.139–41)

> There is a tide in the affairs of men
> Which, taken at the flood, leads on to fortune;
> Omitted, all the voyage of their life
> Is bound in shallows and in miseries.
> —(4.3.218–22)

In several of his great plays, Shakespeare turns to the classical world, as in *Troilus and Cressida,* where we are back in Homer's Greece at Troy. *Timon of Athens, Pericles: Prince of Tyre, Antony and Cleopatra, Titus Andronicus,* and *Measure for Measure* all draw on ancient stories. Critics generally agree that the best of this crop is *Julius Caesar,* which has always found a ready audience in theatres and has been made into memorable cinematic presentations. That with John Gielgud as Caesar and Charlton Heston as Mark Antony is especially good.

This gripping drama is set in the declining days of the Roman Republic, when Julius Caesar, Pompey, and Crassus form a triumvirate to rule Rome. When Crassus is killed, civil war ensues and in 46–45 B.C. Caesar emerges as sole ruler and is proclaimed dictator for life. Some of Rome's citizens are deeply perturbed over this concentration of power, notwithstanding Caesar's many admirable personal traits. Cassius is one such, a man of piercing discernment. Caesar says of him:

> Let me have men about me that are fat,
> Sleek-headed men, and such as sleep a-nights.
> Yon Cassius has a lean and hungry look.
> He thinks too much. Such men are dangerous.
> —(1.2.192–95)

Cassius hatches an assassination plot and recruits Brutus, who truly loves Caesar yet suffers over developments. He has immense respect and is essential for the success of the plot. Though variously motivated, the conspirators and Caesar act out their destinies with greater or lesser altruism but all with considerable ambition. Where is the ethical line? Are all assassinations wrong? What about the Hitler bomb-plot in which Bonhoeffer was implicated? Even Antony pays tribute to Brutus:

> This was the noblest Roman of them all,
> All the conspirators, save only he,
> Did that they did in envy of great Caesar;
> He only, in a general honest thought
> And common good to all, made one of them.
> His life was gentle, and the elements
> So mix'd in him that Nature might stand up
> And say to all the world, "This was a man!"
>
> —(5.5.6)

Peter J. Leithart discerns that Brutus represents the "Old Republican Roman."[1] Brutus has a wrenching discussion with his wife Portia, who senses that he is embroiled in something serious. Caesar's wife Calpurnia has a dream and warns him.

The soothsayer sees portents. Immediately upon entering the conspiracy, Brutus becomes *de facto* leader and really becomes everything he detests in Caesar.[2] Even though Caesar has three times rejected Mark Antony's proffer of a crown, the conspirators yield to no logic or reason. In act 3, the plot is carried out. Caesar is slain in front of Pompey's column. *"Et tu, Brute?"* ("You too, Brutus?") Caesar says, as he dies. The executioners exult in high-blown rhetoric such as "liberty, freedom and enfranchisement" and "peace, freedom and liberty" (3.1.81, 110).[3]

Brutus seems to persuade the crowd that the murder was necessary, but commits a grave mistake in allowing Mark Antony to give the funeral oration. The shrewd and savvy Antony, speaking over the body of Caesar, in fact turns the crowd against the conspirators and forms a triumvirate with Caesar's grandnephew Octavius and Lepidus and joins in battle against the conspirators and their forces on the plain of Philippi. Brutus sees the ghost of Caesar on the night before battle and learns of his own doom. He and the others are defeated and die, realizing that the new rulers will be worse than Caesar had ever been.

From within the Christian doctrine of sin and the fall, we hear in *Julius Caesar* a basic pessimism about what all efforts in governance can accomplish. Such realism shields us from unwise expectations.

---

1. *Brightest Heaven*, 85. This is an insightful study guide to six plays for academic or small group study.
2. Ibid., 87. How quickly the persecuted become persecutors, victims the new tyrants.
3. Ibid., 93. The French and Russian Revolutionists shouted slogans; calling killing, as in abortion, "liberation" does not make it so. It would seem that revolution and rebellion are justified only as the last resort under great provocation.

6.3.3 KING LEAR: STRUGGLE OVER PRIDE

> How sharper than a serpent's tooth it is
> To have a thankless child!
> —*King Lear* (1.4.310–11)

Essential elements of a tragedy, according to Robert Foulke and Paul Smith, come together in a situation in which there is an encroachment, then a complication, a possible reversal, and finally catastrophe.[1] The Bible recounts a true-life situation in which these elements can easily be seen in Samson (Judges 13–16). In Greek drama, the tale of Oedipus presents these classic elements. Tragedies probe the question of suffering. A society's tragedies, then, reveal the culture's worldview. Either the theistic view of original sin and the effects of a fall are in view or the Greek idea of fate. The difference is great. What happens in time and space may be unmitigated loss from the Greek view, yet a painful means to a positive eternal outcome in theism.[2]

Many see *King Lear* as the definitive achievement of Shakespearean tragedy. This is a play of great intensity, and it begins with an emotional explosion. Actors have found the role immensely difficult. How does one sustain that intensity? Laurence Olivier is noted most for his magnificent depiction of the king.

Lear, King of Britain, is over eighty years old when we meet him in act 1, but he is still vigorous. The decay of old age is just beginning to set in. We are quickly aware of the presence of fatal pride. Lear is not thoughtful or reflective but impatient and peevish. In his heady power, he has become isolated and idiosyncratic. He demands overt expressions of love from his three daughters and completely misunderstands "the glib and oily art" (1.1.227) of Goneril and Regan. Only Cordelia escapes maudlin sentimentalism, and her father completely misunderstands. The characters seem very real as Lear banishes his beloved Cordelia and Kent, who speaks up for her. She finds refuge in France, where she marries the king, but Lear's life disintegrates.

This is an eminently biblical play. George Morrison, one of the great Scottish preachers of the early twentieth century, lectured on Shakespeare and pointed out "the selfish stupidity" of Lear.[3] Power blinded the king, making him rash and headstrong[4] against Cordelia's pure, true spirit. Aaron Hill in 1735 observed that Lear "catches fire at first impressions and inflames himself into a frenzy by the rage of his imagination. He dotes on Cordelia yet disinherits her and leaves her to misery."[5] There also is contrast between Lear and his daughters and Gloucester and his sons. Gloucester despairs after initial arrogance when he realizes that his son seeks his life. Old Lear is made of stouter courage. To be sure, he is drifting toward madness. His is "the domination of a fixed idea," what Harold Goddard calls "the extreme form of absolute power."[6]

Some have likened the play to the book of Ecclesiastes, with its taste of disillusionment and disappointment before the discovery of God. Others hear echoes of Michel Eyquem de Montaigne (1533–1592). Beyond question, what is at issue are Elizabethan notions of divine providence and order. How does one live in the face of death?[7]

For a century, playgoers were given Nahum Tate's "happy ending" to King Lear. But this is not what was written. The last scene is almost unbearable. Samuel Johnson said he could not read about King Lear carrying the corpse of dead Cordelia. Bradley speaks of "The Redemption of King Lear." That is, in his anguish and suffering, Lear revives somewhat in greatness and sweetness.[8] He begins to feel and be sensitive again. Christian principles resonate around Cordelia. While Lear is still greatly enfeebled, we have references to heaven and the last judgment and to his praying. He is confined to a hovel because his daughters order that no haven be afforded him. Yet their doom is sure, and they murder each other. On the other hand, a bad king becomes a new man. Like most old men in Shakespeare's stories, he possesses considerable wisdom and insight at last. He thought he had awakened in hell. He can only turn to God, and in the last scenes he does so in three outpourings of mad rage. Remember that all of this action was presented without scenery or lights. Much resting upon the actor's skill.

When the British and French clash, Cordelia is captured and then hanged by the victorious Edmund, and Lear carries her body in lament—"Howl, howl, howl, howl!" (Sir John Gielgud really howled in playing this role.) Then Lear thinks for a moment that she is indeed yet alive and falls dead of joy. This is a profound wrestling with vast issues.

---

1. Robert Foulke and Paul Smith, "Narrative Tragedy," in *The Anatomy of Literature* (New York: Harcourt Brace, 1972), 338ff.
2. A. C. Bradley, *"King Lear,"* in Harold Bloom, ed., *King Lear* (New York: Chelsea House, 1992), 89.
3. George H. Morrison, *Christ in Shakespeare* (London: James Clarke, 1928), 22.
4. Ibid., 30.
5. Aaron Hill, *"King Lear,"* in Bloom, ed., *King Lear*. Hill's essay was written in 1735.
6. Harold C. Goddard, *"King Lear,"* in *King Lear,* 101. Goddard feels that *King Lear* is Shakespeare's greatest play.
7. Arthur Kirsch, "The Emotional Landscape of *King Lear,*" shows Freud's view.
8. Bradley, *"King Lear,"* 91. Bradley from Glasgow, Liverpool and Oxford Universities was "the preeminent Shakespeare scholar of the early twentieth century." His masterpiece on Shakespearean tragedy is a classic.

6.3.4 THE MERCHANT OF VENICE: STRUGGLE OF GREED

The devil can cite Scripture for his own purpose.
—*The Merchant of Venice* (1.3.99)

This epic study of the human penchant for greed and bigotry is generally labeled a comedy, but with the vanquishing of its principal character, Shylock, and the underlying triumph of anti-Semitism, it must be seen as a tragedy. Although probably the most popular of his plays and the one that is read by many beginners, this is not Shakespeare at his best. Here is Shakespeare as a child of his times unable to extricate himself from a straitjacket of bigotry.

The story is of the Jewish moneylender, Shylock, who advances funds to Antonio. Shylock's estrangement from Antonio is deepened when Antonio's friend, Lorenzo, elopes with Shylock's daughter, Jessica, who absconds with a considerable fortune. In a disaster at sea, Antonio loses his ships and Shylock is determined to collect his bond, a pound of flesh. The lovely Portia comes to court disguised as a lawyer and successfully outmaneuvers Shylock. The merchant is humiliated, forced to become a Christian and to give a further half of his possessions to Jessica. Shylock is vilified and made the butt of vicious anti-Semitism.

Harold Bloom calls *The Merchant of Venice* the problem play of the Shakespearean corpus. He much prefers Marlowe's *The Jew of Malta*. Marlowe mocks Judaism, but Shakespeare is plainly Jew-baiting.[1] Elizabethans did not see Jews speak except on stage. Jews came to England after William the Conqueror in 1066.[2] The Magna Carta of 1215 legalized injustice against the Jews, and Edward I expelled them, though British monarchs had used Jews as moneylenders because of the very unrealistic Christian view of usury. After their expulsion in 1290, their place was taken by Italian bankers.[3] Many in England were uneasy with this bigotry. Finally in 1656, Oliver Cromwell readmitted Jews into England, although no Jew was permitted to serve in Parliament until 1858.

In Antonio, the most admirable and humblest of the main characters, we have nonetheless a man who kicks and spits at the Jew. Moaning, "O my daughter! O my ducats!" Shylock is, to be sure, as greedy as is anyone else, but he is made a scapegoat in the crudest way.[4] Here Shakespeare is the father of centuries of "pound of flesh" stories.

Shakespeare is usually neutral with his characters, but he takes an "unambiguous stand for Antonio against Shylock."[5] In this sordid anti-Semitism, he is one with the Grimm brothers of Germany, with Martin Luther, Fëdor Dostoevsky, and Anton Chekhov, Chaucer, Charles Dickens, and T. S. Eliot. This shameful tradition in Western literature has few exceptions. Fagin in *Oliver Twist* was such a malignant figure that Dickens tried to balance him with Mr. Riah in *Our Mutual Friend,* a more exemplary Jewish personality. But the damage had been done.

Portia does make a great speech that touches theological chords, but Portia herself forgets about mercy. Goddard puts it well when he says that Portia is not true to her inner self here, but reverts to her "worldly self."[6]

This is an awkward play to read or watch when one realizes that it articulates the hatred that led to the ovens of the Holocaust.

---

1. Harold Bloom, ed., *William Shakespeare's The Merchant of Venice* (New York: Chelsea House, 1986).

2. For a history of anti-Semitism, see David L. Larsen, *Jews, Gentiles and the Church* (Grand Rapids: Discovery House, 1995), 71, 124. This work argues that the New Testament documents are decidedly not anti-Semitic, 84ff. See also H. Wayne House, gen. ed., "The Appropriation by the Church of Israel's Blessings," in H. Wayne House, *Israel—The Land and the People: An Evangelical Affirmation of God's Promises* (Grand Rapids: Kregel, 1998).

3. Greenwood, *History of England*. A shameful chronicle.

4. Bloom, *Merchant of Venice*, 41. Lorenzo's enterprise in stealing Jessica shows that all are sinners (39).

5. Leslie A. Fiedler, "These Be the Christian Husbands," in *Merchant of Venice*, 64. A "lovely but perverse text."

6. Harold C. Goddard, "Portia's Failure," in *Merchant of Venice*, 34–35. Portia is worried that the duke will be too merciful to Shylock.

6.3.5 *MACBETH: STRUGGLE OF GUILT*

> To-morrow, and to-morrow, and to-morrow,
> Creeps in this petty pace from day to day,
> To the last syllable of recorded time;
> And all our yesterdays have lighted fools
> The way to dusty death. Out, out, brief candle!
> Life's but a walking shadow, a poor player
> That struts and frets his hour upon the stage
> And then is heard no more: it is a tale
> Told by an idiot, full of sound and fury,
> Signifying nothing.
>
> —*Macbeth* (5.5.19–28)

"We mustn't deify Shakespeare!" ranted the chairman of the Dartmouth University English Department in the late 1990s, trying to justify the politically correct aversion to the bard in some higher educational circles.[1] But the same year the opening of the New Globe Theatre in London was an international news event. Seating fifteen hundred people, the theatre was made to approximate the specifications of the original Globe.[2] The enduring popularity of Shakespeare is no doubt due in part to the relevance and pertinence of themes with which Shakespeare wrestles. *Macbeth*, Shakespeare's shortest drama, and one of his most popular plays, probes the depths of human guilt and consequent fear and anguish. *Macbeth* reminds us that the greatest source of suffering is our own wrongdoing and its consequences.

Set in eleventh-century Scotland at the roots of the House of Stuart, and clearly appealing to James I's interest in occult spirituality, the play begins as Macbeth and Banquo return victorious from battle. They encounter three witches who speak prophetically of their destiny and sow overreaching ambition in Macbeth. The witches forebode what temptation and tragedy will befall Macbeth. They twist and turn word meaning so that "fair is foul and foul is fair" and values are overturned.[3] The atmosphere on the heath is "foul, heavy, dark and thick."

Lady Macbeth shares her husband's ambition and becomes his accomplice, pressing him to throw over all of his inhibitions. Like Jezebel goading her husband King Ahab to murder in 1 Kings 21, MacBeth's wife urges him to "ignore all moral restraints" (1.7.41–44). His murder of King Duncan unfolds to become the collapse of Macbeth's soul, damnation for him and the end of Lady Macbeth. Macbeth becomes increasingly isolated, even from his wife, who slides toward insanity and suicide. The violation of the moral law of God and the negation of

His order translates into chaos. As Duncan observes: "Boundless intemperance is a tyranny (4.3.67–68).[4]

Though now king as he wanted, the cycle of violence becomes endless as Macbeth seeks the death of Banquo and Banquo's son. The play is a commentary on the scriptural verse, "'There is no peace for the wicked,' says the LORD" (Isa. 48:22; 57:21 NASB). Banquo's ghost plagues Macbeth at the feast in a foreshadowing of his descendant's ultimate victory over the murderer. King Macbeth is haunted and distraught. He immediately seeks the counsel of the witches (3.5, 4.1), very much as King Saul in the Old Testament sought the Witch of Endor (1 Samuel 28). Consequently, he orders the murder of Macduff's wife and children when he learns of Macduff's flight to England. Macbeth is caught in the whirling vortex of evil.

The famous sleepwalking scene in 5.1, when Lady Macbeth is utterly unhinged by her wrongdoing, is important to Shakespeare's point. The doctor concludes:

> She is troubled with thick-coming fancies,
> That keep her from her rest.
>
> —(5.3.37–38)

Macbeth is desperate for a cure to be administered to his frenzied spouse:

> Canst thou not minister to a mind diseased,
> Plauck from the memory a rooted sorrow,
> Raze out the written troubles of the brain,
> And with some sweet oblivious antidote
> Cleanse the stuff'd bosom of that perilous stuff
> Which weighs upon the heart?
>
> —(5.3.40–45)

Lady Macbeth is unable to wash away the "damned spot" on her hands.[5] The defiled conscience, bitter remorse, and guilt are portrayed in epic scale. Here is the guilt without grace or forgiveness found in Fëdor Dostoevsky's *Crime and Punishment* and Nathaniel Hawthorne's *The Scarlet Letter*.[6] The point is driven home by Macbeth's wrenching speech in response to her suicide (5.5.17–28).

Yet as the play ends, Malcolm predicts the triumph of grace and Scotland's national salvation. No comic scene like that of the porter in 2.3 (one of the best comic relief scenes in all of Shakespeare) can address this need. Malcolm looks with poised perspective to the future:

> This, and what needful else
> That calls upon us, by the grace of Grace,
> We will perform in measure, time and place.
> So, thanks to all at once and to each one,
> Whom we invite to see us crown'd at Scone.
>
> —(5.8,72–75)

In the hour of success, Macbeth met temptation and was overcome. The result was pure tragedy, no sentimental, fairy tale life of happily forever after. There is spiritual calamity for the king and queen who refused "the grace of Grace."

---

1. *World* Magazine, 11 January 1997, 10.
2. *Chicago Tribune,* 9 June 1997, 1.
3. *Brightest Heaven,* 167.
4. Ibid., 164. As Duncan makes his piercing statement, Macbeth and Banquo are caught up in outward pleasures. They find nothing more profound to say than that the air smells sweet.
5. In quoting these lines of Lady Macbeth, one is perhaps advised to "bowdlerize" them into "Out cursed spot!" Thomas Bowdler (1754–1825), an English physician, went through Shakespeare and Gibbon, excising or replacing whatever might not be proper to read in a family circle. He rendered demented Macbeth's "The devil damn thee black, thou cream-faced loon! Where gotest thou that goose-look?" to "Friend, what meanest thy change of countenance?"
6. For a classic evangelical study of guilt, see Paul Tournier, *Guilt and Grace* (New York: Harper, 1962).

6.3.6 HAMLET: PRINCE OF DENMARK: STRUGGLE FOR IDENTITY

> The time is out of joint; O cursed spite
> That ever I was born to set it right!
>
> *—Hamlet* (1.5.166–67)

> This above all: to thine own self be true,
> And it must follow, as the night the day,
> Thou canst not then be false to any man.
>
> —(1.3.78–80)

Hamlet is Shakespeare's most famous, and possibly his most complex, piece. Interpreters differ as to who Hamlet really is, and he has been portrayed in a variety of ways. This is Shakespeare's longest play. One 1990s uncut film lasted four hours. When Hamlet is not sifted through Freudian analysis, he comes off as an intelligent man caught between his sin-prone will and his Christian conscience. Hamlet rejects suicide when he comes to trust in God's providence.[1]

Some of the play's gloom and indecision may reflect what all of England felt as the reign of Elizabeth approached its end. "Even at its lowest level, Hamlet is a magnificently constructed piece of melodrama, with enough blood and pageantry and swordplay to please the sleepiest ten-year-old. It travels into the secret countries of the heart that even the wisest should be able to see a new landscape."[2] This play also has the largest vocabulary of new words among Shakespeare's plays. The more we excavate the sublayers of personality and action, the more we see.

Hamlet is a thirty-year-old heir to the Danish throne who has studied at Wittenberg

University in Germany. He becomes depressed when his father dies and his mother Gertrude quickly marries his father's brother Claudius. It is all part of Claudius's plot to take the throne, and he succeeds. And there is evidence that his fiancée, Ophelia, daughter of Polonius, lord chamberlain in the court, has been unfaithful.

Hamlet's father's ghost informs him that Claudius is his murderer. Belief in ghosts or spirits was nearly universal. The reality of the unseen spiritual world as a backdrop for the external world was part of a biblical worldview.[3]

The play is essentially about revenge. Students of Shakespeare disagree about whether the bard intended that Hamlet becomes insane, or whether he feigns madness. He certainly is a melancholic, but I agree with Branagh that Hamlet is "excitable, volatile, impassioned, even severely distressed, without anything clinical being implied."[4] Hamlet is torn—should he seek revenge on Claudius and his mother? But his Christianity forbids revenge (Rom. 12:19, 13:4). On an even more basic level, Hamlet wrestles with his self-identity. Don Quixote could say: "I know who I am," but not Hamlet.[5] Curiously, Morrison, in commenting on the Christian ethical dimensions of Hamlet's conundrum, argues that it was Hamlet's duty to take revenge.[6] Hamlet is like Gideon—the hesitant hero.

Hamlet seems unglued. Convinced that address must be given to the times, which are "out-of-joint," he uses a visiting troop of actors to trick Claudius into incriminating himself. Claudius orders Hamlet's execution, but he escapes and returns to Elsinore just in time for Ophelia's funeral. Act 5 begins with the dialogue of the two grave-diggers. Death is the theme of this final act, and by its end eight characters will be corpses, including Hamlet.[7]

The cryptogram in the play is the character of Hamlet. Robert Maynard Hutchins used to say that one of the chief criteria of a "great book" is that there are many possible interpretations. *Hamlet* qualifies. Horatio in his eulogy calls him noble; T. S. Eliot and W. H. Auden are dismissive; Harold Goddard says that "Hamlet is his own Falstaff." We hear high praise and sense serious doubt. And is this not Hamlet?

> To be, or not to be: that is the question.
> Whether 'tis nobler in the mind to suffer
> The slings and arrows of outrageous fortune,
> Or to take arms against a sea of troubles,
> And by opposing end them? To die, to sleep;
> No more; and by a sleep to say we end
> The heartache and the thousand natural shocks
> That flesh is heir to, 'tis a consummation
> Devoutly to be wish'd. To die, to sleep;
> To sleep? perchance to dream. Ay, there's the rub;
> For in that sleep of death, what dreams may come
> When we have shuffled off this mortal coil,
> Must give us pause. There's the respect
> That makes calamity of so long life. . . .
> Thus conscience makes cowards of us all.
>
> —(3.1.55ff)

▓ **A piece of fiction** many notches above average is Stephanie Cowell's *Nicholas Cooke: Actor, Soldier, Physician, Priest.*[34] This historical novel is set in the Elizabethan world in which our hero is drawn to Marlowe, has a friendship with Shakespeare, and becomes a successful actor. Very well done.

---

1. Pamela C. Johnson, "Shakespeare Uncut," *World,* 1 March 1997, 23f.; and Gary Arnold, "To Film or Not to Film, That's the Question," *Insight,* 17 February 1997, 40f.
2. *Shakespeare of London,* 228-29.
3. Harold Goddard, "Hamlet: His Own Falstaff" in Harold Bloom, ed., *Hamlet* (New York: Chelsea, 1986), 24.
4. Arnold, "To Film or Not to Film," 40.
5. Miguel de Cervantes, *The History of Don Quixote de la Mancha* (Chicago: Great Books of the Western World, 1952), 29:112. While his presuppositions are not Christian, psychologist Erik Erikson made helpful insights on the process of identity formation.
6. *Christ in Shakespeare,* 80ff. Morrison laments Hamlet's delay.
7. *Brightest Heaven,* 153f.

6.3.7 OTHELLO: STRUGGLE OF JEALOUSY

> [Of Cassio's liquor] O God, that men should
>   put an enemy in their mouths
> to steal away their brains.
>
> —*Othello* (2.3.291–92)

> But he that filches from me my good name
> Robs me of that which not enriches him
> And makes me poor indeed.
>
> —(3.3.155–61)

> Then must you speak
> Of one that lov'd not wisely, but too well;
> Of one not easily jealousy, but, being wrought,
> Perplex'd in the extreme; of one whose hand,
> Like the base Indian, threw a pearl away
> Richer than all his tribe.
>
> —*Othello* (5.2.343–48)

Samuel Johnson was persuaded that "Shakespeare is above all writers, at least above all modern writers, the poet of nature; the poet that holds up to his readers a faithful mirror of manners and life."[1] His great tragedies in particular explore the devious vices that wreak havoc on humankind.[2] In *Othello*, Shakespeare exalts a "cheap melodrama" with some of his highest poetry.[3] It is one of his Italianate tragedies about love; in *Romeo and Juliet,* love is threatened from without; in

Othello, it is threatened from within. In the former, a bitter family feud turns fatal because the governor fails to administer justice, while Friar Lawrence fails to preach God's Word. Either of them does what the other should be doing. In *Othello,* malignant jealousy festers and kills. So poignant is the action that Morrison wrote that he could never read the play with dry eyes.[4]

Othello has been called "the most Christian of Shakespeare's tragic heroes."[5] He is a middle-aged Moor and Roman general in the service of the Venetian state. Though of royal blood, he had been sold as a slave. His race is a factor in what transpires. His marriage to lovely Desdemona was without her senator father's approval and in spite of her husband's "blackness." "O heaven," her father Brabantio cries, "how got she out?" (1.1.169).

The drama reflects the highest Christian view of marriage. Jealous Iago cannot abide the promotion of the heavy drinking Cassio to be Othello's lieutenant. Perhaps Iago's "primal jealousy" of Othello is the root difficulty. Iago is called by Goddard "a moral pyromaniac." He feigns love for Othello but is consumed by envy. Step by step, Iago capitulates to the tyranny of passion. Iago sees to the fall of Cassio and plants the seeds of suspicion about Desdemona's fidelity. He is master of fabrication and revisionism.

Why did Othello believe Iago? Patricia Parker uncovers the dynamics of Othello's jealousy. She points out how jealousy enlarges and dilates, as shown in the discovery of the incriminating handkerchief. Othello says:[6]

> Trifles light as air
> Are to the jealous confirmation strong
> As proofs of holy writ.
>
> —(3.3.322–24)

Othello collapses in fury and cannot accept Desdemona's protestations of innocence. He strangles her, only too late hearing the truth from her maid, Emilia, the wife of Iago (5.2.26–28, 54–57). Iago then kills his wife. Iago is led away to torture and death. Interestingly, the word *devil* is used more in this play than in any other, and the word *faith* is prominent. How strong is love's commitment? Shakespeare probes this in Sonnet 35. In Sonnet 116 he advances the thesis:

> Love is not love
> Which alters when it alteration finds,
> Or bends with the remover to remove.
> O, no! it is an ever-fixed mark
> That looks on tempests and is never shaken. . . .
> Love alters not with his brief hours and weeks,
> But bears it out even to the edge of doom.

Solomon speaks of this love:

> Place me like a seal over your heart,
> like a seal on your arm;

for love is as strong as death,
its jealousy unyielding as the grave.
It burns like blazing fire, like a mighty flame.
Many waters cannot quench love;
rivers cannot wash it away.
If one were to give all the wealth of his house for love,
it would be utterly scorned.

—Song of Solomon 8:6–7

Othello is properly a tragedy because jealousy inflamed has the last word, not love.

---

1. New York: Ballentine, 1993.
2. Preface, *The Plays of William Shakespeare,* 1765.
3. Brown, *Shakespeare,* 181.
4. *Shakespeare of London,* 266.
5. *Christ in Shakespeare,* 107. Morrison presents Iago as "the most masterly presentation of incarnate evil in the whole of Shakespeare, if not in all literature."
6. Stanley Cavell, "Epistemology and Tragedy: A Reading of *Othello,*" in Harold Bloom, ed., *Othello* (New York: Chelsea House, 1987), 11. Othello's "perfect soul" (I.2.31) was matched by Desdemona's beauty and largess of spirit.
7. Patricia Parker, "Shakespeare and Rhetoric," in Bloom, ed., *Othello,* 116.

6.3.8 THE TAMING OF THE SHREW: STRUGGLE OF DOMESTICITY

'Tis the mind that makes the body rich;
And as the sun breaks through the darkest clouds,
So honour peereth in the meanest habit.
What, is the jay more precious than the lark
Because his feathers are more beautiful?
Or is the adder better than the eel
Because his painted skin contents the eye?
O no, good Kate; neither art thou the worse
For this poor furniture and mean array.

—*The Taming of the Shrew* (4.3.169–77)

Western civilization has been Bible-drenched, as can be shown in an inspection of such cultural icons as William Shakespeare's plays. The larger frame-of-reference within which the action moves is governed and guided by a sovereign God. Motifs of human sin and guilt and the need for intervening redemption and providence surface repeatedly. In *The Taming of the Shrew,* we come to grips with how human nature is molded. A drunken old tinsmith named Christopher Sly is picked up out of the gutter and put in a lovely bed in a luxurious mansion as a matter of sport. But putting fancy clothes on Sly does not affect any change in his dissolute and debauched character.

The plot focuses on Katherina, the ill-tempered older daughter of the wealthy Baptista of Padua. The younger, more comely daughter, Bianca, would like to marry the student Lucentio, but her father insists the older daughter must be married first.

Now enters Petruchio, the gentleman from Verona, who will marry Katherina, "a fiend of hell" (1.1.88) and a "devil's dam" (1.1.104). Petruchio likens Katherina to a falcon that must be tamed (4.1.175–83).[1] Katherina is genuinely changed by Petruchio's tough love and insistence on submission. Her father says, "She is changed, as she had never been" (5.2.115). Authority is the critical issue in our time, and Shakespeare shows that Katherina must decide whether she will submit "to the way Petruchio names the world, whether she will submit to his words, whether she will submit to becoming 'Kate' (her new name)." Leithart points out that "Luther's sermons and tracts changed the face of Europe because thousands of spiritually starved people believed the biblical gospel of justification by grace through faith, rejected the myriad idolatries of late medieval Christianity, and began to live according to the truth."[2]

Much changing of names and costumes creates confusion and deception, but does not really change anyone. Interestingly, Petruchio and Katherina are the two principals who do not engage in the disguise and deception game. Petruchio surely puts Katherina on notice as he is late to their wedding, comes wearing bizarre clothes, and refuses to stay for the wedding feast. At home he behaves outrageously. Through it all, he and Kate are learning to love, and her shrewish disposition is being replaced by wifely piety.

The change is pervasive. Katherina is not a person in whom the positive "Kate" qualities lie dormant. She is a repulsive soul, but she is invited by her husband into a new reality of positive and acceptable behavior.[3]

This is not simply auto-salvation as promulgated by the human potentials movement. Initially Katherina resists and rebuffs Petruchio at every turn, but increasingly she is attracted to his qualities. Bianca also is liberated in the process. In scene 2 of act 5, the transformation is evident. Leithart quotes J. Dennis Huston:

> Kate is actively included in the feasting which celebrates social harmony, and here, too, her husband . . . turns all attention temporarily away from himself and toward her, revealing her as the true bride not as a suffering victim. For in speaking of the duty that a wife owes her husband, Kate also speaks of the duty a husband owes a wife; she describes the mutual responsibility and trust necessary in any successful marriage.[4]

A comedy in the classic sense has shadows and hard realities, but it ends with a good outcome. This is why the Christian is a realistic optimist. We know God's good will win.[5]

---

1. *Brightest Heaven,* 210.
2. Ibid., 209. The analogy is drawn between Christ's training of his unruly church and the training of Katherina.

3. Ibid., 222. Petruchio keeps everyone off balance. He is a master of the unexpected.
4. Ibid., 242. Kate is not allowed to come to the table until she is submissive. Sounds strange to modern ears.
5. E. Beatrice Batson, ed., *Shakespeare and the Christian Tradition* (Lewiston, N.Y.: Edwin Mellen, 1994). The proceedings of the 1992 Shakespeare Institute at Wheaton College. The degree and depth of Christian influence on Shakespeare's thinking and writing are debated.

CHAPTER SEVEN

Appreciating the Treasures of British Poetry

Even the least knowledge of things superior is of greater value than the most extensive knowledge of things inferior.

—Thomas Aquinas

Poetry has special appeal and utility to the Christian communicator, not only because there is so much poetry in Scripture, but also because this compact, emotive writing is "language of the soul."[1] The principles of parallelism in Hebrew poetry have been studied since the eighteenth century, but as more has been discovered about biblical poetry, the strict canons about how it worked have been relaxed. On the other hand, the late twentieth century saw a new interest in crafting poetry by structure and meter after the shapeless existential blank verse that characterized much modern poetry.[2]

Poetry as a vehicle of the heart's expression is particularly needed in an age in which materialistic and secularist categories have become so evidently bankrupt. Plato's "garden of the muses" and (with caution) Carl G. Jung's "heavenly land of the psyche" are inviting. Overly cerebral preachers can revolutionize their organization and delivery if they but read poetry aloud. William Blake prescribed the antidote for materialism long ago when he argued that the beautiful and holy "poetic intoxication and love reveal what the five senses cannot—REALITY ITSELF!"[3] C. S. Lewis made the case for the great power of poetic language, that words can generate and transform experience.[4]

I rise a flag of caution in the quotation of poetry in preaching. Too much poetry can seem affected and overly ornate in discourse. W. E. Sangster urged caution in such quotation in his classic work on illustration.[5] I will only quote what I have memorized, occasionally something extended as from Thompson's "The Hound of Heaven" but more frequently just a quatrain or a choice couplet.

TABLE 6: Literature in Historical and Theological Context, 1800 to 1900

Page 180 A: Historical Events; B: Arts and Philosophy; Page 181 C: Revelation and Preaching

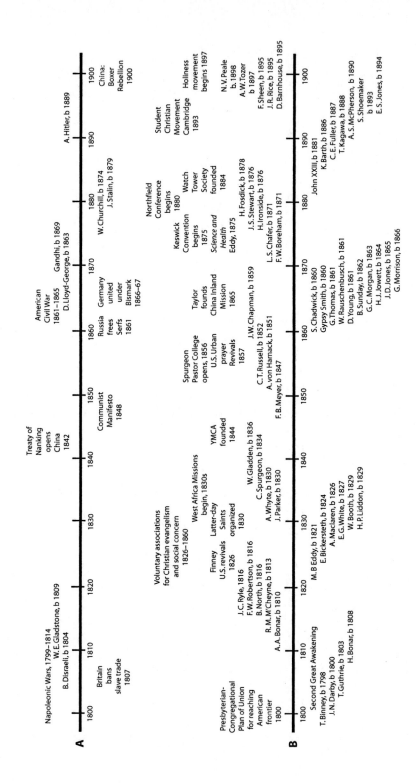

A timeline chart marked with decade gridlines: 1800, 1810, 1820, 1830, 1840, 1850, 1860, 1870, 1880, 1890, 1900. Marked "C" at the lower left.

Works (italic):
- *Philosophical Fragments* Kierkegaard 1844
- *Moby Dick* Melville 1851
- *Uncle Tom's Cabin* Stowe 1851
- *Les Misérables* Hugo, 1862
- *Crime and Punishment* Dostoevsky 1866

Entries:

J.S.Mill b 1806

C.Darwin b 1809

S.Kierkegaard, b 1813
A.Trollope, b 1815
H.D.Thoreau, b 1817
I.Turgenev, b 1818
W.E.Channing, b 1818
K.Marx, b 1818
G.Eliot, b 1819
C.Kingsley, b 1819
J.R.Lowell, b 1819
H.Melville, b 1819
J.Ruskin, b 1819
W.Whitman, b 1819
F.Engels, b 1820

T.B Macaulay, b 1800
V.-M.Hugo, b 1802
A.Dumas, b 1802
E.Bulwer-Lytton, b 1803
R.W.Emerson, b 1803
N.Hawthorne, b 1804
H.C.Andersen, b 1805
F.D.Maurice, b 1805
J.G.Whittier, b 1807
H.W.Longfellow, b 1807
A.Tennyson, b 1809
E.A.Poe, b 1809
O.W.Holmes, Sr., b 1809
H.B Stowe, b 1811
W.M.Thackary, b 1811
R.Browning, b 1812
C.Dickens, b 1812

C.Baudelaire, b 1821
F.Dostoevsky, b 1821
G.Flaubert, b 1821
M.Arnold, b 1822
H.Schliemann, b 1822
J.E.Renan, b 1823
G.MacDonald, b 1824
H.Ibsen, b 1828
L.Tolstoy, b 1828
J.Verne, b 1828

E.Dickinson, b 1830
C.Rossetti, b 1830
G.Dore, b 1832
S.Clemens, b 1835
B Harte, b 1836
J.Miller, b 1839

E.Zola, b 1840
T.Hardy, b 1840
W.James, b 1842
G.M.Hopkins, b 1844
F.W.Nietzsche, b 1844
J.W.Riley, b 1846
E.Husserl, b 1849

S.Aleichem, b 1859
A.E. Housman, b 1859
F.Thompson, b 1859
B Potter, b 1858
J.Conrad, b 1857
S.Freud, b 1856
G.B Shaw, b 1856
O.Wilde, b 1854
R.L.Stevenson, b 1850
G. de Maupassant, b 1850

E.Wharton, b 1862
G.Santayana, b 1863
M.Unamuno, b 1864
W.B.Yeats, b 1865
R.Kipling, b 1865
A.Deissman, b 1866
H.G.Wells, b 1866
J.Galsworthy, b 1867

S.Crane, b 1871
T.Dreiser, b 1871
B.Russell, b 1872
G.K.Chesterton, b 1874
R.Frost, b 1874
A.Lowell, b 1874
W.S.Maugham, b 1874
C.Jung, b 1875
T.Mann, b 1875
R.Rilke, b 1875
W.Cather, b 1876
J.London, b 1876
C.Sandburg, b 1878
E.M.Forster, b 1879
H.James, b 1879
V.Lindsay, b 1879
W.Rogers, b 1879

S.Asch, b 1880
H.L.Mencken, b 1880
A.Noyes, b 1880
J.Joyce, b 1882
A.A.Milne b 1882
K.Jaspers, b 1883
F.Kafka, b 1883
R.Bultmann, b 1884
W.Durant, b 1885
S.Lewis, b 1885
F.Mauriac, b 1885
P.Tillich, b 1886
J.Huxley, b 1887
T.S.Elliot, b 1888
E.O'Neill, b 1888
R.Benchley, b 1889
M.Heidegger, b 1889
L.Wittgenstein, b 1889

B Pasternak, b 1890
P.Buck, b 1892
St.Vincent Millay b 1892
D.Sayers b 1893
e.e. cummings b 1894
J.Thurber b 1894
Lin Yutang b 1895

W.Faulkner b 1897
C.S.Lewis b 1898
J.L.Burges b 1899
Hemingway b 1899
E.B White b 1899

1. Kathleen Raine, *The Inner Journey of the Poet* (New York: George Braziller, 1982), 88.
2. For a brief introduction to Hebrew poetry, see Gleason L. Archer Jr., *Old Testament Introduction* (Chicago: Moody, 1964), 418ff. Another descriptive explanation is a lesser-known work of C. S. Lewis, *Reflections on the Psalms* (New York: Harcourt Brace, 1958).
3. *Inner Journey of the Poet,* 187; emphasis Blake's. Pascal speaks to this in part in his oft-quoted line, "The heart has its reasons that reason knows not of."
4. Alister McGrath, *A Passion for Truth: The Intellectual Coherence of Evangelicalism* (Downers Grove, Ill.: InterVarsity, 1996), 86, 139, 144. While making good points, McGrath is needlessly hard on fundamentalists who fought a battle in the 1920s and evangelicals who countered neoorthodoxy. He seems to confuse their defense of rationality with aberrant rationalism. Much of the book seems to be an apology for Karl Barth.
5. W. E. Sangster, *The Craft of Sermon Illustration* (1950; repr. ed., Grand Rapids: Baker, 1981), 95ff.

7.1 CADENCES OF THE METAPHYSICAL POETS

7.1.1 DONNE, DEAN AMONG METAPHYSICALS

> Death, be not proud, though some have called thee
> Mighty and dreadful, for thou art not so;
> For those whom thou think'st thou dost overthrow
> Die not, poor Death, nor yet canst thou kill me.
>
> —John Donne
> "Death Be Not Proud"

Samuel Johnson first called them the "metaphysical poets." They wearied of the shallow ditties then prevalent and seized the spiritual with highly compact and overdrawn comparisons and paradoxes, overlaid generously with philosophy and theology. The metaphysical poets were contemporaries of Shakespeare and the King James Bible. They were children of the Renaissance and Reformation.[1] Almost all of them were Church of England clergy who held significant pulpits and a reputation for powerful preaching.[2] Their poetry was little noticed and read in their time, but T. S. Eliot and others in the twentieth century took them up and used them for models. Eliot acknowledged a great spiritual debt to Lancelot Andrewes (1555–1626), court preacher for James I, and especially to John Donne (1572–1631).

Ten volumes of Donne's sermons have been published by the University of California at Berkeley. He was an unusually gifted speaker and writer. Donne came from an old Roman Catholic family, which traced its genealogy to Thomas More. John was privately tutored at Oxford, where Roman Catholics were barred from official degree programs. He was much shaped by an interest in St. Teresa of Avila and St. John of the Cross. He witnessed the martyrdom of the young Roman Catholic Edmund Campion, who was memorialized by Evelyn Waugh's famous biography in 1935. Donne studied further at Cambridge and prepared for the law, but he was restless and wrote highly erotic love poetry. He accompanied

Robert Devereux, earl of Essex (1566–1601), and Walter Raleigh (1554–1618) on their ill-fated expedition to Spain in 1596. He clearly felt the disintegration of the medieval synthesis during his lifetime. As he put it, "'Tis all in peeces, all cohaerence gone."[3]

He became a Protestant but still could not get the blessing of his superior, Thomas Edgerton, keeper of the seal, to marry Edgerton's niece. Donne was left unemployed and desolate. In the midst of suicidal depression, he had a true conversion and was ordained to the ministry in 1615. His rich biblical preaching drew large audiences at Paul's Cross. In 1621 he was made dean of St. Paul's in London. He ministered there until his death ten years later.[4] Donne seems quite fixated on death in his sermons and poems but this is quite understandable. His wife died young, and six of their twelve children died during childhood. The death of his mate led to a noticeable deepening in his poetry. While at St. Paul's, he saw three waves of the Black Death sweep over London with forty thousand mortalities. Thirty-two of his fifty-four songs and sonnets are funerary.

His religious poems have been fertile ground for authors and composers seeking titles for their work. Much of confession of sin and the redemptive cross surface in Donne. As one critic observes of his style: "What is most striking here is the continuously shifting nature of the argument, the way in which the speaker's mind seems to be racing ahead of itself, answering questions implicitly even while they are being asked. It is this constantly shifting nature of the speaker's stance that makes Donne's poems basically inimitable."[5]

Donne poised his readers on the edge of quicksand, yet held up by a strongly Augustinian substratum.[6] He was a dramatic preacher and a master of metaphor and imagery. Such epigrams as "For whom the bell tolls," "Go catch a falling star," and "No man is an island" abound. Particularly commendable are such poems as "Knowing Christ's Bride," "Saved by Grace," "Mourning for Sin," "Resigning to God," "Imputed Righteousness," "Ravished by God," and "A Hymn to God the Father."[7]

Eliot saw Donne's contribution in his "power of figurative language and in the tonality of his rhythms through which he relates his own private meditation dramatically to the persisting themes of Christianity."[8] Donne as both preacher and poet has much to say to us today. Who can match Donne's description of Mary's conception of the Christ as "immensity cloistered in thy dear womb" in *La Corona*?

---

1. Isabel Rivers, *Classical and Christian Ideas in English Renaissance Poetry* (London: Allen and Unwin, 1979). Rivers shows how both streams of thought influenced these poet-preachers.

2. David L. Larsen, *The Company of the Preachers* (Grand Rapids: Kregel, 1998), 6.2.

3. John Carey, *John Donne: His Life, Mind and Art* (New York: Oxford University Press, 1981), 95, 123.

4. For the best collection, see C. M. Coffin, ed., *The Complete Poetry and Selected Prose of John Donne* (New York: Modern Library, 1952).

5. Louis L. Martz, "The Action of the Self: Devotional Poetry in the Seventeenth Century," in Malcolm Bradbury and David Palmer, eds., *Metaphysical Poetry* (Bloomington, Ind.: Indiana University Press, 1970), 106.

6. *Classical and Christian Ideas,* 127. Rivers quotes Augustine's *Grace and Free Will:*

> Now wherever there is the express statement not to do this or that, and when-
> ever the performance of the will is required to do or refrain from some ac-
> tion, in keeping with God's commandments, that is sufficient proof of the
> free choice of the will. Let no man, therefore, blame God in his heart when-
> ever he sins, but let him impute the sin to himself. Nor does the fact that
> something is done in accordance with God's will transfer such an act from
> one's own will.

7. E. P. Rudolph, ed., *The John Donne Treasury* (Wheaton, Ill.: Victor, 1978).
8. Charles M. Coffin, introduction to *Complete Poetry and Selected Prose,* xxxv.

7.1.2 HERBERT, SOFT VOICE

> Sorrie I am, my God, sorrie I am,
> That my offenses course it in a ring.
> My thoughts are working like a busie flame,
> Untill their cockatrice they hatch and bring:
> And when they once have perfected their draughts,
> My words take fire from my inflamed thoughts.
>
> —George Herbert
> "Sinnes Round"

While he lacks the fire and vehemence of John Donne, George Herbert (1593–1633) attracts us with his winsome gentility.

George Herbert was born into a titled family and studied at Cambridge where he was made orator of the university in 1619. Drawn to government service in the tradition of his old Welsh family and to the court of James I, he was broken up by the king's death and sensed the call of God to preach.[1] He took a small living in a congregation at Bemerton near Salisbury and there spent the remainder of his short life preaching and writing his heart out. Described as "not witty or learned or eloquent but holy," Herbert wrote many poems, chiefly in Greek and Latin.

His one volume of 169 poems entitled *The Temple* uses many verse forms and ranges over numerous aspects of pastoral ministry and such doctrinal areas as election and eschatology. Richard Baxter said of Herbert: "I confess that next to the Scripture poems, there are none so savory to me as Mr. George Herbert's, because he speaks of God, like a man that really believeth in God, and whose business in the world is most with God."[2]

Herbert was quite "High Church," and late-twentieth-century scholarship has noticed his verbal skill and hidden wordplays.[3] Among his best works are his magnificent poems on "The Events of the Passion" *(Passio Discerpta)*. These brief, almost terse, lines about the Savior's sufferings are some of the most moving verses on the atoning death of Jesus.[4] These twenty-one pieces include such unspeakably precious meditations as "On the bloody sweat," "On the spitting and mocking,"

"On the slaps," and "On the ripped veil." At the heart of it is "Christ on the Cross":

> Here, where the healed world's
> Smooth balm distilled,
> I, joyous, and my mouth wide open,
> Am driven to the drenched cross:
> By the falling of that distillation,
> Sins depart; dead things, they cannot bear
> That blood's rigorous assaults.
> Christ, keep welling up, for if your flooding stops,
> Revived guilt will say you're not eternal God.[5]

---

1. Robert B. Shaw, *The Call of God: The Theme of Vocation in the Poetry of Donne and Herbert* (Athens, Ohio: Ohio University Press, 1965). Herbert's mother was a woman of great culture and beauty. Through his upbringing and education, he developed high tastes. His struggle was with "the pride of life."
2. Quoted in M. C. Allen, "George Herbert—Poet to the Clergy," *The Pulpit,* September 1964, 7.
3. M. M. Mahood, "Something Understood: The Nature of Herbert's Wit," in *Metaphysical Poetry,* 123ff.
4. Herbert insisted on his deathbed that all "must be sprinkled with the blood of Christ."
5. Mark McCloskey and Paul R. Murphey, trans., *The Latin Poetry of George Herbert,* bilingual ed. (Athens, Ohio: University of Ohio Press, 1965), 62ff. Another extraordinary collection is by the Icelandic pastor, Hallgrimur Petursson, *Hymns of the Passion,* A. C. Gook, trans. (Reykjavik: Hallgrims Church, 1966). Petursson (1614–1674) is the leading religious poet of Iceland.

7.1.3 CRASHAW, STYLIST

> Yet may these unfledg'd griefes give fate some guesse,
> These cradle-torments have their towardnesse.
> These purple buds of blooming death may bee,
> Erst the full stature of a fatall tree.
> And till my riper woes to ages are come.
> This knife may be the speares Praeludium.
>
> —Richard Crashaw
> "Our Lord in His Circumcision to His Father"

The conclusion to "Our Lord in his Circumcision to his Father" is typical of Richard Crashaw's (1612–1649) quite untypical work. He sees the drops of blood at the circumcision of Jesus as adumbratory of Calvary and the knife as foreshadowing the spear. The poets of this time reflect the massive theological and ecclesiastical shifts that swirled around them: Donne became a Protestant; Robert Southwell (1561–1595) served as a Jesuit spy, was caught and executed;[1] Richard Crashaw converted to Roman Catholicism. Crashaw's father was a Puritan preacher who inveighed strongly against "popish corruption." Yet after his son took degrees at Cambridge he fled as a Roman Catholic convert and lived thereafter successively in Leyden, Paris, Rome, and at the Shrine of Loreto. There Crashaw remained for the rest of his life as chaplain to Cardinal Palotto.

Crashaw has been called the most "unenglish" of English poets. His early poetry shows ecstatic mysticism and this developed as he endeavored to express his ideas in "the continental mode of the baroque."[2] He was influenced early on by Herbert but had swings between brilliance and overwrought insipidity. He seemed on an emotional roller-coaster in his spiritual pilgrimage from Puritanism through Laudism to Romanism.

Some of his sacred poems are outstanding, such as "Hymn to the Name of Jesus" (which shows the influence of godly Joseph Hall, bishop of Norwich in the Church of England), and "On Hope."[3] His meditations on various Psalms are engaging. Of special interest are his poems "Upon Bishop Andrewes His Picture Before His Sermons," about Lancelot Andrewes, his master at Pembroke in Cambridge, and his lovely poems to Teresa of Avila (1515–1582).[4] The latter are especially significant beneficiaries of Teresa's classic work on prayer. In Crashaw's brilliance we perceive both depth and danger.

---

1. Robert Southwell's "Mary Magdalene's Funeral Tears" was circulated before his incarceration. I have a special fondness for his "Upon the Image of Death" and "A Child My Choice." But his best are the Christmas-related "The Burning Babe" and his scintillating "Joseph's Amazement," which treats the faith of Joseph.
2. "The Action of the Self."
3. George Walton Williams, ed., *The Complete Poetry of Richard Crashaw* (New York: New York University Press, 1972). This volume runs to 707 pages.
4. Ibid., 52ff. For a superb introduction to Teresa's exposition, see Clayton L. Berg, ed., *Teresa of Avila: A Life of Prayer* (Portland, Ore.: Multnomah, 1983). Her *Garden of Prayer* and *The Interior Castle* are devotional classics.

7.1.4 HERRICK, WORLDLY VICAR

> Gather ye Rose-buds while ye may,
> Old time is still a flying:
> And this same flower that smiles today,
> Tomorrow will be dying.
>
> —Robert Herrick
> "To the Virgins to Make Much of Time"

Like Obadiah, who was a devout believer while in charge of the king's palace (1 Kings 18:3ff.), many Stuart loyalists walked a razor's edge. Was compromise necessary for preferment? Puritans were temperamentally unsuited to sustain such ambiguity. All of the metaphysical poets struggled, but Robert Herrick (1591–1674) seems to have crossed the line. One critic said: "Herrick has been called pagan, but the label is misleading; for his poems constantly echo Scripture, and what at first seems heathenish proves to be not so much Roman and classical as a universalized religious sentiment expressive of Latitudinarian Anglicanism."[1]

In many ways, he was more a "son of Ben" (Jonson) than a clergyman serving Christ and his church. His goldsmith father apparently committed suicide, and he was apprenticed to his prosperous goldsmith uncle for ten years. He aspired to court life without success, putting off his M.A. at Cambridge until he was twenty-nine and not seeking ordination until he was thirty-eight (as a last resort). In 1630 he was installed as vicar at Dean Prior in Devonshire, a kind of exile in his bitter opinion. Yet here the never-married pastor wrote poetry. He did lose his benefice in the Civil War in 1647 and fled to London, where he published *Hesperides* in 1648. Perhaps relatives supported him until he went back to Dean Prior in the Restoration of 1660. There he died and was buried in 1674.

Asks M. C. Allen: "Is it any wonder that the Puritans ejected this pleasure-loving priest who preferred sack to tea and wrote in praise of the drink like a wine-bibber?"[2] "Pray and prosper" seems to have been his motto. Of a curious bent, he wrote "A Hymn to Bacchus" and poems about Julia and other women unknown to us. We sense an exhilaration and wistfulness in Herrick, a reaching for the higher, but his aspirations are largely secular. He worries about his gray hair.[3] He anticipates William Wordsworth and the Romantics in his absorption with robin redbreast, the daffodil, the lark, the death of his sparrow, and such. These poems are in his *Hesperides,* the voluminous book that has much to say about milkmaids and marigolds.

Herrick was a skilled metrist and did address spiritual concerns in his books *Noble Numbers* or *Pious Pieces* (1647). His "An Ode of the Birth of Our Saviour" is meager and measly compared with Milton's (see 7.2.1). One arresting piece is his "The Dirge of Jepthah's Daughter: Sung by the Virgins," inspired by Judges 11.[5] He wrote several poems on hell and another he calls "The Widdowes Teares: or, Dirge of Dorcas."[5] Very little of gospel truth shines through the massive verbiage, but he does have several short pieces on the Cross including a very unique "Crosse-Tree," in which the poem is in the shape of a cross.[6]

Herrick epitomizes the dilemma of the latitudinarian, the person who adopts the "Christ of culture" position, who espouses and absorbs the culture in order to reach the culture.[7] The gospel may be swallowed up. A subtle Epicureanism quickly becomes restless narcissism, as when Herrick sings in "Of Himselfe":

> I feare no Earthly Powers'
> But care for crowns of flowers:
> And love to have my Beard
> With Wine and Oile besmear'd.
> That day Ille drowne all sorrow;
> Who knows to live to morrow?[8]

1. J. Max Patrick, ed., *The Complete Poetry of Robert Herrick* (New York: New York University Press, 1963), x. A very fine historical novel about Herrick is Rose Macaulay, *The Shadow Flies* (London: Harper, 1932).
2. Marion C. Allen, "The Sensuous Delight of Robert Herrick," *The Pulpit,* June 1965, 7ff.
3. *Complete Poetry of Robert Herrick,* 91, 259.
4. Ibid., 476ff.
5. Ibid., 493ff.
6. Ibid., 532.
7. See H. Richard Niebuhr, *Christ and Culture* (New York: Harper Torchbooks, 1951), 83ff. We must be against culture if we are to change and transform culture.
8. *Complete Poetry of Robert Herrick,* 95.

7.1.5 TRAHERNE, ALPINIST

Come, Holy Ghost, Eternal God
Our Hearts with Life Inspire
Inkindle Zeal in all our Souls
And fill us with thy Heavenly Fire.

—Thomas Traherne
The Book of Private Devotions, 2.1–2

Such a biblical invocation explains the peculiar fascination with these preacher-poets who proliferated in the sixteenth century. Thomas Traherne (1636–1674) was distinctive. He was from an old Welsh family that had settled in humble circumstances in Hereford. His father was a shoemaker. In circumstances we do not know, he received three degrees from Oxford and took a living in Credinhill near the city of Hereford.[1] He was well-read in all of the classics as well as in Hobbes and the Cambridge neo-Platonists. After almost ten years there, he was made chaplain to Orlando Bridgman, who was made keeper of the seals in 1667. So valued was he that he continued as private chaplain after Sir Orlando retired.

Herrick was largely discovered after his death and not popularized until early in the twentieth century. He authored prose sketches entitled *A Century of Meditations* as well as his *Christian Ethicks,* in which he analyzes virtue and valor. Each of his poems comes across as a gift of the author to the reader. One reason for this is his idiosyncratic use of capital letters to control flow.[2] His love for Scripture comes across more clearly than in Herrick. He is truly mystical and metaphysical and in passages reminds us of William Blake, or Wordsworth's "Intimations of Immortality," or Thomas Gray's "Elegy." I think his unusual "Meditations on the Six Days of Creation" present him at his best.[3] He is enthralled with "the glory of the universe and its Creator." He writes "catalogues of wonder" as he contemplates nature like a primitive. He has a new way of seeing as he describes "Walking" and "One Leaping over the Moon." In his poetry on creation, he seeks the heights of praise, climbing ever toward the secret councils that framed the cosmos and the Incarnation.

His exquisite poem on "Wonder" reminds us that general revelation as well as special revelation should stir and grip the believer (Psalm 19). He writes movingly of "Eden" and "Innocence," but does not skip over "Adam's Fall" or "Sin." His "Love" is like molten lava, and his metaphors powerful even though he never married.[4] I wish all of this were more balanced with clearer christological affirmation, although his "On Christmas Day" clearly presents justification ("Clad in my Savior's Righteousness") but does not bridge to the atonement with clarity.[5] In *Christian Ethicks,* he does articulate the substitutionary death of Jesus for us sinners in a supernal burst of soundness:

> O holy JESUS who didst for us die,
> And on the Altar bleeding lie,
> Bearing all Torment, pain, reproach, and shame,
> That we by vertue of the same,
> Though enemies to GOD, might be
> Redeem'd, and set at liberty.
> As thou didst us forgive,
> So meekly let us Love to others shew,
> And live in Heaven on Earth below.[6]

---

1. Gladys I. Wade, ed., *The Poetical Works of Thomas Traherne* (New York: Cooper Square, 1965), xxxviii. Anthologies usually do not contain lesser known poets' work; browse through used book sales.
2. Ibid., vi.
3. Ibid., 237ff.
4. Traherne has an almost Rousseau-like doctrine of the innocence of children.
5. Ibid., 136.
6. Ibid., 231.

7.1.6 MARVELL, POLITICIAN

> That Majesty which through thy Work doth Reign
> Draws the Devout, deterring the Profane.
> And things divine thou treatest of in such state
> As them preserves, and Thee, inviolate. . . .
> Where couldst thou Words of such a compass find?
> Whence furnish such a vast expense of Mind?
> Just Heav'n Thee, like Tiresias, to requite,
> Rewards with Prophesie thy loss of Sight.
> —Andrew Marvell
> "On Mr. Milton's *Paradise Lost*"

Almost alone among the metaphysical poets as a layman, not a clergyman, Andrew Marvell (1621–1678) wrote with compelling strength and verse. He was born in Yorkshire, the son of a devout Puritan pastor. His father was described by Thomas Fuller as "an excellent preacher"; another spoke of him as "facetious and yet Calvinistic." His son called him "a conformist to the established rites of the Church of England, though I confess none of the most over-running or eager in them."[1] Young Marvell matriculated at Cambridge in a time when the nation groaned with deep fissures, spiritual, political, and ideological. He was seduced by the Jesuits to London where he had a brief conversion, but his father came after him and found him in a bookstore. They returned to Cambridge and the faith.

From 1642 to 1647, he traveled in Europe and polished his Latin and French. T. S. Eliot much admired Marvell's command of these languages. During the English Civil War, he was tutor for the children of Lord General Thomas Fairfax (1612–1671), commander in chief of the Parliamentary Army. Then he was assistant to John Milton, who was Latin secretary in the Commonwealth. During the Commonwealth, he was elected to Parliament from Hull and served as a member of Parliament until his death.

In 1656 he visited the famous Protestant Academy at Saumar on the Loire, France. But he also maintained close ties to Royalists and made the transition in the Restoration. His intervention probably saved Milton's life when Charles II took power. He made trips abroad for the new government to Russia, Denmark, Sweden, and Germany.

Long a prolific writer of lyric poems, he was especially fond of the eight-line stanza. Most of these were "private poems" not intended for publication.[2] His biblical substructure can be seen in his "The Coronet" on the death of Jesus and his reference to the future "conversion of the Jews."[3] His was a "sentimental Royalism." He severely disapproved of Charles I, but he opposed the king's execution in 1649. He wrote two long poems in tribute to Oliver Cromwell, "the Lord Protector." Was this political schizophrenia? Is he a ventriloquist? Is he a voice or an echo?

Eliot found in Marvell "a tough reasonableness beneath the slight lyric grace." He had a fidelity to the Stuarts and yet couldn't avoid recognizing in Cromwell "the leader capable of achieving 'The Great Designes Kept for the Latter Dayes.'"[4] In other words, the issues were not simply black or white. So complex were the decisions and dilemmas that in integrity he had to make "a tragic moral choice," attempting to find the least of the evils in a murky situation. He never denigrated the king, nor did he hail the return of Charles II.[5] Nor did he ever slander Cromwell, "whom he had so much praised." Summers well says that "his principles and practices remained remarkably consistent."[6]

As the Restoration proceeded, he became more and more disappointed and disillusioned with the Stuarts and began to write satirical poetry, which was admired by the master of satire Jonathan Swift (1667–1745). He was deeply motivated to write on behalf of personal liberty and freedom and against strict Calvinistic determinism. Even his earlier and better poetry, like his "An Horatian Ode on Cromwell's Return from Ireland," shows a mature and exemplary balance, a deliberate and determined purpose to maintain proper tension and eschew simple, popular, premature conclusions. The fact that we don't know everything doesn't mean that we don't know anything.

Samuel Pepys (1633–1703), secretary of the Admiralty and member of Parliament, kept a *Diary* from 1660 to 1669, a look at life through the eyes of the time. Committed to advance the king, he nonetheless lined his own pockets. Cecil S. Emden's *Pepys Himself*[7] reveals this character, who loved money and drinking above all else. Ill-tempered and a capricious husband, he witnessed the plague of 1665 and the Great Fire of 1666. He prayed much, used pious language—but confessed he went to church "to gaze at women."[8] Impaired sight eventually limited this activity.

---

1. Andrew Marvell, *The Complete Poems,* ed. George deF. Lord (New York: Knopf Everyman's Library, 1984), xxxiv.
2. *Metaphysical Poetry,* 182.
3. *Complete Poems,* 23.
4. *Metaphysical Poetry,* 199.
5. Ibid., 205.
6. Ibid., 206.
7. London: Oxford University Press, 1963.
8. Ibid., 84–85.

7.2 CONTOURS OF THE PURITAN/RESTORATION POETS

From Elizabethan days, the Puritans were dedicated to reforming the Church of England. Some remained in the Church; others separated; most were Calvinists, although a substantial minority were Arminian. Some Puritans in England and in the American Colonies were even pietists. Anne Hutchinson was tried for heresy for teaching mystical pietism. Some stressed discipline; others experience. Their chief literary genre was the sermon.[1] Milton was an atypical Puritan poet, particularly in his early phase, but a biblicality solidifies in his epic poems. John Bunyan is more typical (see 5.4) in that he wrote verse to accompany prose allegories. *The Bay Psalm Book* from New England versifies Scripture. This was about as far as many Puritans would go. With John Dryden in the Restoration, we pick up the more direct thread of the metaphysical weaving.

---

1. *Company of the Preachers* treats British and American examples of "The Genius of Puritanism" (7.2) and "The Glories of the Puritan Pulpit" (7.3).

7.2.1 MILTON, ORGAN VOICE OF ENGLAND

> Let us then discard reason in sacred matters, and follow
> the doctrine of Holy Scripture exclusively. . . .
> The hungry sheep look, and are not fed
> But swollen with wind, and the rank mist they draw,
> Rot inwardly.
>
> —John Milton
> "Lycidas"

> I may assert Eternal Providence
> And justify the ways of God to men.
>
> —John Milton
> *Paradise Lost*

Standing in any top list of English poets and very influential through his prose pieces as well, John Milton (1608–1674) is not always easy to understand, but he is important to read. Joseph Addison, who first resurrected Milton, gave him "first place among our English poets." Eliot disliked his rhetorical style and didn't much like his doctrine (preferring the somewhat inchoate Donne to Milton's clarity and certainty). Since Milton accepted Christianity as the final truth, many in the last century have regarded his work *Paradise Lost* as "a monument to dead ideas." But C. S. Lewis and Charles Williams argue that the poem "is overwhelmingly Christian."[1] John Ottenhoff points out that even detractors acknowledge that *Paradise Lost* is "the canonical text par excellence of English literature" and that our difficulty in reading it reflects our distance from both its classical and Christian context.[2] Stanley Fish says that the hardest thing to get across in teaching *Paradise Lost* is that God is God.[3]

John Milton was born on Bread Street in London, the son of a London notary who converted from Roman Catholicism to the Church of England. He studied at St. Paul's and Christ's College, Cambridge, where he didn't always get along with others, although he studied very hard, and was called "the lady of Christ's" by his classmates. He turned from ambition to enter holy orders because of Archbishop William Laud's (1573–1645) stringencies and became a Puritan. In 1629 he wrote the delightful "Ode on the Morning of Christ's Nativity," which shows his Christian bent. Paganism is routed not so much by the birth as by Messiah's death. A more Italian style is seen in "L'Allegro" and "Il Penseroso," as well in *"Comus"* (written during five years of study at his father's estate at Horton) and the beautiful pastoral "Lycidas." From 1640 to 1660, he left poetry and wrote political and theological prose. He served as Latin secretary to the Council of State until 1660. His unhappy first marriage gave rise to *On the Doctrine and Discipline of Divorce*. His works *On Education* and *Aereopagitica* on freedom of the press would by themselves secure his niche in English literature.

In the restoration of the monarchy, Milton escaped execution, at least in part because of his friend Marvell. But there was another challenge in his life. Since 1652 he had been totally blind. One striking sonnet from this time comments on his blindness and concludes epigrammatically with the line: "They also serve who only stand and wait."

Paradise Lost, Milton's masterpiece, is from the Restoration. The heroic epic traces the fall of Satan, the fall of humanity, and divine redemption. This is Milton being "doctrinal to the nation." As early as 1629, he expressed the desire to write an epic in which the stage is the universe. An epic poem is on a grand scale and seeks meaning and value for all of life. His work was a theodicy, justifying God.

In twelve sections or "books" he tells the story. Written in blank verse style, the phrasing has the flow and texture of a complex piece of organ music. The whole was dictated to Milton's three daughters—all of whom resented him and neglected his care. The story begins with the fall of Satan, and so vivid are his descriptions that

Percy Bysshe Shelley (1792–1822) suggested "nothing can exceed the energy and splendor of Satan" and that possibly Satan is the hero. But Satan is a fool and in his impenitent "sense of injured merit," his is a "study of revenge, immortal hate, and courage never to submit or yield" (1.98, 109). Milton was a firm believer in free will and genuine responsibility and portrays the angel Raphael warning our first parents.

Totally orthodox early on, the case can be made that like William Law (1686–1761) later, Milton was influenced by the mysticism of Jakob Böhme (1575–1624) and his conviction that imagination must have precedence over reason.[4] Notions of the inner light and "the all-inclusive harmony" increasingly surface. There are even suggestions of subordinationism, if not outright Arianism.[5] These troubling shadows most darken the posthumously published *De doctrina christiana,* a kind of early biblical theology. Milton's *Paradise Regained,* in which the focus is on Christ's victory over temptation in the wilderness rather than on his passion at Calvary follow an emphasis that is very clear in Böhme.[6]

Milton's last major work was the tragedy of Samson's life, *Samson Agonistes,* in which the blind Samson brings down the temple upon himself and others. Milton adds repentance and confession of sin to Samson's story. One has no difficulty sensing autobiographical elements.

In some respects, Milton was the forerunner of Romanticism. He was an enormously gifted and exceedingly versatile craftsman of Christian ideas.

For a rich, full picture of the Puritan Commonwealth, note Antonia Fraser's *Cromwell: The Lord Protector.* Fraser tells of Milton's appreciation for Cromwell and "the native vastness of his intellect." The poet supported Cromwell's protest against the persecution of the Protestant Waldensians in the Piedmont and wrote a magnificent sonnet on the Waldensians' behalf.

---

1. C. S. Lewis, *A Preface to "Paradise Lost"* (Oxford: Oxford University Press, 1942). Helen Gardner, *A Reading of Paradise Lost* (Oxford: Clarendon, 1965), 9, 11. The Alexander Lectures in Toronto.

2. John Ottenhoff, "God, the Flesh, the Devil: Why *Paradise Lost* Matters," *Christian Century,* 16 June 1993, 638ff.

3. Stanley Fish, "Why Can't All Just Get Along," *First Things,* February 1996, 18. Fish has a fascinating book on Milton, *Surprised by Sin: The Reader in* Paradise Lost (London: Macmillan, 1967). See also the important study by J. M. Evans, *Paradise Lost and the Genesis Tradition* (Oxford: Clarendon, 1968).

4. Margaret Lewis Bailey, *Milton and Jakob Böhme: A Study of German Mysticism in Seventeenth-Century England* (New York: Haskell House, 1964). See also Gertrude Huehns, *Antinomianism in English History: With Special Reference to the Period 1640–1660* (London: Cresset, 1951). It is interesting that Roger Williams was a close friend of Milton.

5. Michael Bauman, *Milton's Arianism* (Frankfurt am Main: Peter Lang, 1987).

6. Bailey, *Milton and Jakob Böhme,* 158. George F. Sensabaugh, *That Grand Whig Milton,* traces the cultural and political overtones that influenced the life and career of this great writer.

7.2.2 DRYDEN, MASTER OF THE RESTORATION

As from the pow'r of sacred lays
The spheres began to move,
And sung the great Creator's praise
To all the blest above;
So when the last and dreadful hour
This crumbling pageant shall devour,
The Trumpet shall be heard on high,
The dead shall live, the living die,
And Music shall untune the sky.

—John Dryden
"A Song for Saint Cecilia's Day"

In this grand ode by John Dryden (1631–1700) in honor of St. Cecielia, patron saint of music, we learn two lessons about the poet and his times. First, though Dryden is not known for religious perception, the worldview of the later 1600s was very much shaped by the expectation of final judgment and accountability to God. This supposition will soon go by the boards in the Enlightenment. Second, we see that Dryden could demonstrate stylistic maturity and even poetic genius. He was, in fact, an influential master of language, who pioneered and popularized such artistic conventions as the "heroic couplet."[1]

John Dryden was the son of a Northamptonshire clergyman with pronounced Puritan and pro-Parliament leanings. While Charles I was being decapitated, young Dryden was praying for the monarch in Westminster School nearby, where he was on scholarship. There his allegiance was totally captured by staunchly royalist instruction.[2] With Marvell, he praised Cromwell, but his "Coronation Ode" for the accession of Charles II in 1660 features a clear assumption of the divine right of kings. With virtually all of his peers in the day's literary community, he shows great confidence in the Bible. The fall in the garden was one of his favorite images.[3]

Thus consumed with Tory zeal, he soon became the first public man of letters in England. In 1663 he married Elizabeth Howard, the wealthy sister of dramatist Robert Howard (1626–1698). Howard was Dryden's patron until they had a serious break.[4] Dryden became the first public critic, and Samuel Johnson described him as one who "thought naturally and expressed himself forcibly."

He had a strong social conscious, as was shown in his 1664 play *The Indian Emperor*. The play tells of the destruction of Montezuma by Pizarro and reflects a fear that barbarism might return. Dryden was known as a "cheerful and hard-working" writer who used several media and became in time the Poet Laureate of England, with the title *Royal Historiographer*.

In the history of ideas, Dryden linked the later Renaissance and the Enlightenment. He was by nature "skeptical and diffident." He loved to question. Thomas Hobbes (1588–1679) was Dryden's friend, yet the crisis of Hobbes's philosophy in the New Science made Dryden wary after 1650. He was more negative about William Chillingworth (1602–1644) and John Owen (1616–1683), who ardently argued for the ability of human rationality enlightened by the Holy Spirit to under-stand and interpret Scripture (see 1 John 2:26–27).[5] He was enamored with the Roman Catholic Richard Simon (1638–1712), who argued from the difficulty and obscurity of Scripture not only for the need of infallible interpretation by the church but for "higher critical" scholarship (in his *Critical History of the Old Testament*).[6] In 1685, John Dryden converted to Roman Catholicism.

Everything that Dryden wrote is worth savoring. Unusually significant is his *Religio laici* (*Layman's Religion*), which commences in a cloak of mystery.

> Dim as the borrowed beams of moon and stars
> To lonely, weary, wandering travelers,
> Is Reason to the soul; and, as on high
> Those rolling fires discover but the sky,
> Not light us here, so Reason's glimmering ray
> Was lent, not to assure our doubtful way,
> But guide us upward to a better day.
> And as those nightly tapers disappear
> When day's bright lord ascends our hemisphere;
> So pale grows Reason at Religion's sight;
> So dies, and so dissolves in supernatural light.

We sense longing for special revelation. Yet as Harold Bloom points out, his *Layman's Religion* concludes with "dangerously bland assurances." What begins with clear dependence on Milton's invocation to "Celestial Light" in book 3 of *Paradise Lost* ends with little more than amiability and a whine and whimper.[7]

Of interest is Dryden's biting satire and irony as he becomes increasingly disil-lusioned with Charles II. What he hailed in *Astraea redox* (1660), as the fleet of ships from Holland bringing Charles II to England, he now views with apprehen-sion. In 1680 his great *Absalom and Ahithophel* depicts David's estrangement from Absalom and the rebellion of Absalom (2 Samuel 13–18). Dryden takes the king's case to the nation and to the king as well.[8] The opening lines, it has been pointed out, are exceedingly witty and risky because of the political situation.[9] The king's penchant for heavy-handedness (such as The Act of Uniformity of 1662) unnerved Dryden, but he remained loyal to the House of Stuart in the face of the derelictions of Charles II and the cruelty of James II. He lost all preferment in the Glorious Revolution of 1688 and the establishment of the House of Orange with William and Mary. Unwisely, he had considered David's restoration to be the paradigm for England. Old Testament students should see what Dryden makes of the counsel of Ahithophel (2 Samuel 17). But turning historical narratives of Scripture horizon-tally in another context abuses revelation. This is why *Religio laici* fell flat.[10]

---

1. Despite its name, the heroic couplet is simply a rhyming couplet in iambic pentam-eter. In iambic verse, each foot or beat is an unstressed followed by a stressed syl-lable. Pentameter means each line contains five poetic feet. Heroic couplets have been so trite since the Romantic Period, but once they were a fresh idea.

2. George McFadden, *Dryden: The Public Writer* (Princeton, N.J.: Princeton University Press, 1978), 23.

3. Ibid., 27.

4. Ibid., 65. Louis I. Bredvold, *The Intellectual Milieu of John Dryden* (Ann Arbor: University of Michigan Press, 1966), 14.

5. McFadden, *Dryden,* 86. Chillingworth's *Religion of Protestants* (1638) argued that Christianity must be reasonable.

6. Ibid., 98. Cf. Stephen N. Zwicker, "Religion and Politics in *Religio Laici,*" in Harold Bloom, ed., *John Dryden* (New York: Chelsea, 1987), 180. Simon attacked the integrity of the Old Testament. Those who argue that the high view of the inspiration of Scripture was invented in the Enlightenment need to see the evidence that inerrancy was assumed throughout church's history. See also John D. Woodbridge, "Some Misconceptions of the Impact of the 'Enlightenment' on the Doctrine of Scripture," in D. A. Carson and John D. Woodbridge, eds., *Hermeneutics, Authority and Canon* (Grand Rapids: Zondervan, 1986), 241ff., and John D. Woodbridge, *Biblical Authority: A Critique of the Rogers/McKim Proposal* (Grand Rapids: Zondervan, 1982). Alister McGrath seems oblivious to this evidence; cf. 7.0.

7. Harold Bloom, "Introduction," to Bloom, ed., *John Dryden,* 5.

8. McFadden, *Dryden,* 243. A plot to put James, Duke of Monmouth, a Protestant sympathizer, on the throne after the death of Charles II is the background of this poem.

9. Ibid., 239. The famous line in this work is, "Beware the fury of a patient man" with reference to David.

10 Sidney Greidanus warns of this peril in preaching in *The Modern Preacher and the Biblical Text: Interpreting and Preaching Biblical Literature* (Grand Rapids: Eerdmans, 1988). Greidanus makes too strenuous a rule. Scripture itself uses Job as an example of patience. See my review of Greidanus in *Trinity Journal,* fall 1990, 237–39.

7.2.3 POPE, GIANT OF THE AUGUSTANS

> Vice is a monster of so frightful mien,
> As to be hated, needs but to be seen;
> Yet seen too oft, familiar with her face,
> We first endure, then pity, then embrace.
>
> —Alexander Pope
> *Essay on Man,* 1.217

Few poets are so quotable as Alexander Pope (1688–1744). His familiar lines include:

- "Fools rush in where angels fear to tread."
- "A little learning is a dangerous thing."
- "To err is human, to forgive divine."
- "Hope springs eternal in the human breast."
- "An honest man's the noblest work of God."

Pope was a consummate craftsman of the *Augustan Age* in English Literature. The era is called "Augustan" because, like Rome's Augustan Period, it was a high point of national literature.[1] The first half of the eighteenth century was also "the Age of Reason," when reason and "common sense" governed the intellectuals' search for truth. Samuel Johnson said that Alexander Pope learned his poetry from Dryden, and certainly Pope perfected Dryden's heroic couplet and other artifices. He was a great wit, with an acid pen. He was known as the "wicked wasp of Twickenham" (the name of his villa) and has been called "the most European of English poets." Pope withdrew from the kinds of public controversy that constantly embroiled John Dryden.

He spoke to his society through a literary burlesque that tended toward the satirical or ironic mode. It was pervaded with classical allusions. He translated many classics, including Homer.

Alexander Pope was born a Roman Catholic in London, the son of a linen merchant and his second wife. He studied in Winchester and London, where he learned French and Italian. In 1705 he had his first attack of the tubercular infection that resulted in severe curvature of the spine. He never grew beyond four and a half feet tall and was constantly plagued with headaches and ill health.[2]

Not a devout Catholic, he leaned toward the deism popular at this time. Deism believed in a Creator God who had essentially evacuated from his universe. Deism was the religion of reason without recourse to revelation. No wonder that where deism flourished, society tended to be marked by great corruption and immorality generally. Pope demonstrates the intellectual and spiritual drift of this time. When Pope advised that "the proper study of mankind is man," he was in fact declaring that man has no need for God.[3] This worldview inevitably shows through in his writing. For skill and style, Pope has no peer; but there is a ubiquitous spiritual sterility to his writing. Several of his pieces have significance in this regard:

The *Pastorals,* which he claimed to have written at age sixteen, brilliantly depict the rural scene, but they lack substance when compared to Milton's "Lycidas" (7.1.1). Pope is too studied in his imitation of others.

Messiah merges the child-king of Isaiah's great prophecies (Isaiah 7–11) with Vergil's fourth *Eclogue* (2.8.5). The ideal of the golden age is projected with dual sources: the Isaianic expectation of the divine child with Vergil's tradition of the golden age. Reuben Arthur Brower well points out that the difference between Isaiah and Vergil makes them incompatible: A substitute for God and supernatural power is presented by Vergil and Pope. "The secular is being worked up as a substitute for the religious."[4]

With rich Ovidian tones and style, Pope writes "Epistle from Eloise to Abelard," building on the illicit romance between Eloise and the theologian and author of the exemplarist view of the atonement. Interestingly, there is neither praise nor blame assigned in the poem. Eloise's love is seen as her fall from grace, but a vagueness triumphs.[5] While we get the feel of Pope's Roman Catholic background, there is no reference to Christ, and God is reduced to the level of humanity.[6]

In "The Rape of the Lock" we have an example of the "mock-heroic." Pope turns his fangs on epic poetry and the manners of snobbish society, borrowing heavily from Rosicrucianism.[7] He writes in this instance with Horace looking over his shoulder. The tightly-knit imagery is impressive. He leans to the Homeric and disdains Milton's representation of the powerful adversary of our souls. Basic to the poem is the empirical philosophy of Thomas Hobbes and John Locke, which Pope has lapped up.

In his "Dunciad," we catch considerable allusion to the Old Testament but virtually nothing from the New Testament. This work is bitingly satirical. Harold Bloom characterizes the work as a reversal of the gospel of John and Milton's variations upon it. Pope focuses on "the uncreating Logos," the descent of the anti-Messiah and the "restoration of chaos."[8] The consequence then must be "the twilight of the moral will."

In *Essay on Man,* Pope does not resort to his customary satire. He represents human life as "a mighty maze! but not without a plan." The order of nature stands and his counsel continues to be: "Follow nature."[9] The peril is in projecting an Absolute God. "One truth is clear, Whatever is, is right."[10] Thus at bottom line, "And all our Knowledge is, ourselves to know."[11] Bloom is right that Christian doctrine is excluded.[12]

Pope is not above taking a swipe at George Whitefield in his "Dunciad." He fiercely denounced Joseph Addison, then an upcoming poet and essayist. To what degree does his bitterness and sharp edge reflect Pope's physical handicap and resentment toward God? His genius was never directed toward the amelioration of humankind's woes. Rather, he accentuated them. The Great Evangelical Awakening in Britain and America provided God's answer in the gospel of Christ.

1. On the Augustan age, see William Rose Benet, *Benet's Reader's Encyclopedia,* 3d ed. (New York: Harper and Row, 1987), 61.
2. "Chronology," in Harold Bloom, ed., *Alexander Pope* (New York: Chelsea House, 1986), 171.
3. Earle E. Cairns, *An Endless Line of Splendors: Revivals and Their Leaders from the Great Awakening to the Present* (Wheaton, Ill.: Tyndale, 1986), 154. See also Larsen, "The Malaise of Apathy and the Preaching of Revival," in *Company of the Preachers,* chap. 8, in which the cultural background and the revival preaching are sketched.
4. Reuben Arthur Brower, *Alexander Pope: The Poetry of Allusion* (Oxford: Clarendon Press, 1959), 39, 40. Brower observes the absence of any tenderness in Pope.
5. Ibid., 78. Eloise slips into "a deep tangle of feeling" in which "bright purity is dim and remote." How sad; cf. John 8:12.
6. For a fine introduction and collection, see Peter Quennell, *The Pleasures of Pope* (New York: Pantheon, 1950).
7. K. M. Quinsey, "From Moving Toyshop to Cave of Spleen: The Depth of Satire in 'The Rape of the Lock,'" in Harold Bloom, ed., *Alexander Pope's The Rape of the Lock* (New York: Chelsea House, 1988), 81.
8. Bloom, ed., *Alexander Pope,* 4; see also in this volume, Robert Griffin, "Pope, the Prophets and the 'Dunciad,'" 142.
9. *Pleasures of Pope,* 17. Pope sees nature as "unerring," and "still divinely bright." This sentiment was written when he was twenty, but he did not back away from it with maturity.

10. Ibid., 86. The human predicament arises when humankind defies nature. But can nature show us God's love?

11. Ibid., 117. But nature is "red in tooth and claw" and Leibniz's rationalistic "best of all possible worlds" can be a nightmare, as even François Voltaire (1694–1778) shows in *Candide* after the great Lisbon tidal wave.

12. Bloom, ed., *Alexander Pope*, 44. Bloom candidly contrasts Milton's reliance on the sacrifice of Christ and the hope of redemption with Pope's earthbound, cheerless perspective.

7.2.4 GRAY, LONELY MEDITATOR

> The boast of heraldry, the pomp of pow'r,
> And all that beauty, all that wealth e'er gave,
> Await alike th' inevitable hour:—
> The paths of glory lead but to the grave.
>
> —Thomas Gray
> "Elegy Written in a Country Churchyard"

One of the best known poems in the English language and the most famous poem of the eighteenth century is certainly "Elegy Written in a Country Churchyard" by Thomas Gray (1716–1771). Samuel Johnson paid it high tribute, declaring that it "abounds with images which find a mirrour in every mind, and with sentiments to which every bosom returns an echo."

Northwest of London, not far from Windsor Castle and Eton, stands charming Stoke Poges Church, which dates to Norman times. St. Giles Church is adjacent to the Manor House, where the ancestors of William Penn lived. Here are buried Gray with his mother and her sister. A walk about this idyllic site moved the poet to write the immortal lines so many have loved.

Gray was born in London, but his parental home was unhappy because of the insane jealousy of his father. Only Thomas survived of twelve, and his mother gave the money that enabled him to attend Eton and Cambridge. He spent most of his life at Cambridge and died there. "Melancholy marked him for her own," to use his own words. He wrote volumes of poetry and was known for his correspondence. One of his most famous compositions was "Ode on a Distant Prospect of Eton College," which contains the famous lines, "Where ignorance is bliss, 'tis folly to be wise." He enjoyed a long friendship with Horace Walpole, son of the prime minister. They traveled Europe together from 1739 to 1741, became estranged, and finally reconciled many years later.

He consciously simulates the styles of Vergil and Horace. His use of the Pindaric ode also is a link with the past. Yet he seems to anticipate the Romantics, particularly Wordsworth. "Elegy" is a very personal poem. It echoes the melancholy of Milton's "Il Penseroso." Scholars have debated the interpretation of the poem, which was completed in 1750, when Gray was thirty-four years old.[1] His friend Richard West had died, and the poet feels lonely and fatalistic. He seeks, as Carper suggests, "escape from solitary existence in a pastoral setting."[2] He wonders if his own life is a failure. Interpersonal relationships have always been difficult for him. The "forefathers" whom he describes as "rude" have not supplied him with a comforting context for discovering the meaning of life. He wonders if his own death will be mourned. He posits the adversarial relationship between the humble and the proud. The myth of fame is in ashes.

Yet *Epitaph,* which I take to be a projection of the kind of earthly memorial he would like, does suggest an acceptance of God's will.[3]

> No farther seek his merits to disclose,
> Or draw his frailties from their dread abode
> (There they alike in trembling hope repose),
> The bosom of his Father and his God.

Many modern critics mock and scorn Gray's refuge in what they term "a medieval" hope. From the standpoint of Christian theology, we would wish it were even stronger for Gray. Harold Bloom no less speaks of the "moderately Christian conclusion—the minimal and figurative immortality" to which the poet turns for solace.[4] The emphasis on the immortality of the soul (as in Wordsworth and so many others) is more reflective of Plato and the Greeks. Oscar Cullmann's 1954–55 Ingersoll Lectures entitled "Immortality of the Soul or Resurrection of the Body" properly points to the biblical emphasis on resurrection.

Still, the eternality of the human soul is an essential implication of Scripture.[5] Gray reminds us that the inevitability of our death makes even the brightest and sturdiest among us apprehensive on occasion. Only the Bible and its Christ can bring "life and immortality to light" (cf. 2 Tim. 1:10). Gray stands against annihilationism and for eternal punishment as set forth in Scripture.

------

1. Herbert W. Starr, ed., *Twentieth-Century Interpretations of Gray's Elegy* (Englewood Cliffs, N.J.: Prentice-Hall, 1968).

2. Thomas R. Carper, "Gray's Personal Elegy," in Harold Bloom, ed., *Thomas Gray's "Elegy Written in a Country Churchyard"* (New York: Chelsea House, 1987), 45. Gray was offered the poet laureateship of England but turned it down; he did accept the post as professor of modern history at Cambridge. He wanted to leave some "trace" behind.

3. Howard D. Weinbrot, "Gray's Elegy: A Poem of Moral Choice and Resolution," in *Thomas Gray's "Elegy Written in a Country Churchyard,"* 80.

4. Harold Bloom, introduction to Bloom, ed., *Thomas Gray's "Elegy Written in a Country Churchyard,"* 1, 4. Bloom has edited the wide-ranging collections of studies in the "Modern Critical Interpretations" series. Bloom, in his *Book of J* and other works, is a strong advocate of "the American religion"—his beloved gnosticism. He deifies humankind and denies the supernatural.

5. Stewart D. F. Salmond, *The Christian Doctrine of Immortality* (Edinburgh: T & T Clark, 1895). An extensive treatment.

7.2.5 ADDISON, "REASONABLE" RELIGIONIST

> When all Thy mercies, O my God,
> My rising soul surveys,
> Transported with the view,
> I'm lost in wonder, love and praise.

The author of these artfully fashioned words was unquestionably one of the models of English prose for generations. Joseph Addison (1672–1719), with his colleague, Richard Steele (1672–1729), edited and wrote the famous *The Tatler* and *The Spectator,* using invented characters to give their commentary on contemporary manners and customs. His librettos for opera, essays, and poems were widely circulated.

Addison was born in his father's rectory in Wiltshire. He studied at Lichfield, where his father became dean, and went on to a distinguished academic career at Queen's and Magdalene at Oxford, where he achieved the rank of Don. Here he knew Dryden and became known for his Latin verse. Preparing for a career in diplomacy, he studied abroad extensively on scholarship.

On returning home at the death of his father, he wrote the famous "The Campaign," on Winston Churchill's relative's Marlborough's victory at Blenheim. As undersecretary of State, he fulfilled assignments overseas, and he was Irish secretary. In Parliament from 1708, he was successively commissioner of Trade and then secretary of State. He overtaxed himself with work and collapsed and died in 1719, just months after the birth of his only child, Charlotte.[1]

Through this frenzied career, Addison's work in the arts was stormy. His long friendship with Jonathan Swift (1667–1745) was not always amiable. Pope denounced him with vitriol. He was a paragon of civility and shrank from the boisterous controversy that delighted Dryden and Pope. He refused to answer back in kind. Addison embodied the ideal of a tolerant, balanced, religious, world citizen. As R. W. Harris observes, "He taught his age the art of conversation, how to judge drama or poetry, how to dress and how to conduct themselves as civilized members of a society in the New Age of Reason."[2] What could be more congenial than such a dedication to the Golden Mean? What was more important than reasoning carefully in an "atmosphere of free discussion?"

The follies of excess must be faced and overcome, Addison argued. Restoration laxity is irrational and overdone. "Nothing too much" is the watchword. "Happiness to Addison was a quiet contentment equally removed from the strife of desires and the ecstasy of 'enthusiasm.'"[3] Prosperity and English preeminence in the Age of Queen Anne became the sum of it. On religion, he stated the orthodox themes "tempered by the new attitude of reasonableness and even complacency."[4] Harris explains:

> "Enthusiasm" implied some special divine intervention, some personal communication between God and his chosen vehicle. But this was quite contrary to the new view of the universe, governed as it was by the immutable laws of nature. God's plans for the universe were revealed in

the Scriptures, or in the principles inherent in the nature of things, and it was a mere illusion to suppose that he interrupted the divine plan to make special revelations to particular people. The seventeenth century had seen too many false prophets and crazy enthusiasts (the Puritans?) and Addison and his age saw only dangers in religious fanaticism.[5]

It is most profitable to leaf through an anthology of Addison's work because his argument for spiritual detachment has been influential in the history of philosophy. In *Spectator* 465, he argues for "the great excellency of the Faith." This faith is "the sweet reasonableness" of Matthew Arnold. Any good Unitarian could subscribe to such a faith. Nowhere is there room for Christology; certainly there is no cross.

Most traditional hymnals include hymns that Addison wrote extolling the greatness of God in nature. How unfortunate that his supernaturalism never moves from the stars and planets into human hearts and crises.

> The Spacious Firmament on high,
> With all the blue Ethereal Sky,
> And spangled Heav'ns, a Shining Frame,
> Their great Original proclaim:
> Th' wearied Sun, from Day to Day,
> Does his Creator's Power display,
> And publishes to every Land
> The Work of an Almighty Hand.

---

1. Robert J. Allen, ed., *Addison and Steele: Selections from* The Tatler *and* The Spectator (New York: Holt, Rinehart and Winston, 1957), xvii.
2. R. W. Harris, *Reason and Nature in the Eighteenth Century* (New York: Barnes and Noble, 1969), 95.
3. Ibid., 103.
4. Ibid., 109. To be dispassionate about the gospel and heaven and hell is not virtuous. We sense no call to Christian arms or spiritual warfare anywhere in this sweet talk.
5. Ibid., 110. Charles Sheldon's *In His Steps* is the same saccharine overindulgence in the miasma of our time.

7.2.6 SWIFT, SUPREME SATIRIST

> For once there was a time, God wot,
> Before our friends were gone to pot,
> When Jonathan was great at court,
> The ruin'd part made his sport,
> Despis'd the beast with many heads,
> And damn'd the mob, whom now he leads.
> But things are strangely chang'd since then,
> And kings are now no more than men;
> From whence 'tis plain, they quite have lost

God's image, which was once their boast.
For Gulliver divinely shows
That humankind are all Yahoos.

—Jonathan Swift
Gulliver's Travels

Satire and irony are so close to sarcasm that the Christian communicator is right to be wary. Swift, the greatest satirist among the early English writers, illustrates this difficulty. Swift was born in Dublin to English parents. His father and uncles were seeking their fortune in Ireland after their royalist clergyman father had been ruined in the cause of the Cavaliers. Jonathan's father actually died before he was born, and as an adult he blamed his parents' "imprudent marriage" for his woes.[1] Kidnapped as a child by his nurse, his early years were spent on the brink of homelessness. He suffered from vertigo all his life as a consequence of Meniere's Disease. Yet he was still a prodigy, who could read any chapter in the Bible when he was three. He studied at Kilkenny until he was fourteen and then went to Trinity College, Dublin, where he received his B.A. and M.A.

He was always in trouble. Despite his uncle's patronage, he smarted under what he saw as the humiliation of his poverty and complained that he was given "the education of a dog." He did take an M.A. at Oxford and found employment as secretary to Sir William Temple at Moor Park, Surrey.

Here he met Esther Johnson (or Stella as she was known in his poetry and letters), who was eight years old when he was twenty-two. The evidence is not conclusive as to whether they were ever actually married, but their lives intertwined until her death in 1728. With Temple's encouragement, he begins to write longish poetry out of a "struggling and baffled energy of mind."[2] His propensity for satire began to take over in his frustration. More and more isolated, he was ordained in 1695 and took a parish near Belfast at Kilroot. He detested the Ulster Presbyterian atmosphere. For one year he served as secretary and chaplain to Lord Berkeley. He also was vicar in Laracor, where he had fifteen members, and a prebendary at St. Patrick's in Dublin. In 1714 he was named Dean of St. Patrick's Cathedral in Dublin.

Inexplicably he courted another woman—Vanessa—while continuing his relationship with Stella. In the end he decided he could not marry Vanessa because of his duty to Stella. Both women died in sadness, and Swift's animus against women became increasingly shrill.[3]

He hoped for a diplomatic appointment, but while waiting for direction, he became a popular and powerful political pamphleteer. His friendship with Addison led to publication of his "Vindication of Isaac Bickerstaff," which became immensely popular. While he preferred England, he had lampooned Queen Anne and was none too popular at court. On the other hand, the Irish increasingly regarded him as a hero for his constant needling of the English.[4]

He wrote with "withering invective," and his poetry became more and more of the unprintable type, often called his excremental verses. His last years were in the shadows with the "clouding of his faculties" and endless "bits of violent irritability." The dean seldom, if ever, smiled or laughed. He gave himself to fierce exercise, running up and down the deanery stairs.

His great prose masterpiece was of course *Gulliver's Travels*. Gulliver went on a series of voyages, perhaps inspired by Daniel Defoe's *Robinson Crusoe*. His adventures among the little people of Lilliput or the giants of Brobdingnag are hilarious but sharply pointed. Clearly Swift sees himself as "the giant among pygmies" in his "irksome Dublin exile."[5] He is the captive giant.

Swift is especially effective in recreating dialogue, although some of his poetry is simply doggerel. He spoke of himself as "the left-handed poet." We have only twelve of his sermons, which are of questionable authenticity. Obviously Swift had little interest in preaching or in doctrine. One of his sermons was entitled "Upon Sleeping in Church," and he began it: "I have chosen these Words with Design, if possible, to disturb some Part in this Audience of half an Hour's sleep, for the Convenience and Exercise whereof this Place, at this Season of the Day, is very much celebrated."[6]

Swift's narrative line is better in Gulliver's Travels than in anything else he wrote, but *A Tale of a Tub* has the most theological significance. In Gulliver, we do have his searing indictment of humankind as Yahoo. As Gulliver says: "I began to view the actions and passions of man in a very different light, and to think the honour of my own kind not worthy managing."[7] Though Wesley did not care for much in Swift, he agreed that the doctrine of man as sinner was supported in *Gulliver*.

Yet in his comic masterpiece, *A Tale of a Tub,* Swift indicates that he would not be so foolish as to try to defend "real Christianity," but will make an effort to advance "nominal Religion."[8] With John Locke, he saw a place for "the simple gospel" as a means of establishing more decorum in society.[9] He worries that Roman Catholics will botch it by adding tradition to the minimal Jesus of his improvising. Puritans and other sectarians will run mad in zeal, for the latter are irrational.[10] His satire runs amuck. In their preaching and praying, these Aeolians, as he calls them, are Bedlamites. In "Digression on Madness" and "The Mechanical Operation of Spirit," he blasts all dissenters and any who alter the traditional worship patterns. Swift advances the ribald thesis that such enthusiasm is little more than "the sublimation of physical desire."[11]

Middleton Murray charges that Swift's vision lacks integrity. There is no antidote to his own "egoistic power."[12] As one of his contemporaries observed: "Dean Swift has had a statute of lunacy taken out against him. His madness appears chiefly in most incessant strains of obscenity and swearing—habits to which the more sober parts of his life were not absolutely strangers."[13]

Thus the flawed autonomous man of the Enlightenment founders.

---

1. John Middleton Murray, *Jonathan Swift: A Critical Biography* (New York: Farrar, Straus and Giroux, 1955), 13.
2. Ibid., 31. Of several excellent studies, I think Murray presents us with the most helpful analysis.
3. Ibid., 484. Swift was really a misanthrope. Stella was buried in the great aisle of St. Patrick's.

4. Ibid., 459. His feelings for the Irish may have reached hatred, but he opposed British misrule publicly and so became a folk hero to the people.

5. Patrick Reilly, "The Displaced Person" in *Gulliver's Travels,* ed. Harold Bloom (New York: Chelsea, 1986), 165f.

6. Robert Hunting, *Jonathan Swift* (New York: Twayne, 1967), 83. A conscientious administrator but no preacher.

7. Ibid., 112. The diagnosis is simple, but what is the remedy?

8. Murray, *Jonathan Swift,* 142.

9. See section 5.3 in this volume on John Locke. See also *Reason and Nature in 18th Century Thought,* 147ff.

10. The best analysis here is by Phillip Harth, *Swift and Anglican Rationalism* (Chicago: University of Chicago Press, 1961). Richard Hooker's rationalistic *Ecclesiastical Polity* is Swift's model.

11. Murray, *Jonathan Swift,* 79. What he calls "worship of the wind" is simply vapor and flatulence.

12. Ibid., 354. His resource is but his own genius, which translates out to be his undiminished desire to control.

13. Ibid., 442. The irony is that Swift's own rationality collapsed, and he is counting heavily on man as rational animal.

7.2.7 COWPER, BROKEN MAN WHO FOUND GRACE

> I was a stricken deer, that left the herd
> Long since; with many an arrow deep infixed
> My panting side was charged, when I withdrew
> To seek a tranquil death in distant shades.
> There was I found by one who had himself
> Been hurt by the archers. In his side he bore,
> And in his hands and feet, the cruel scars
> With gentle force soliciting the darts,
> He drew them forth, and healed, and bade me live.
>
> —William Cowper
> "The Task"

These haunting, healing lines are from William Cowper's (1731–1800) foremost work, a long piece in blank verse that earned acclaim in 1785. Cowper (pronounced *Cooper*) has substantive theological significance. While Swift remained angry and bitter, unsupported by his Enlightenment rationalism, Cowper was depressed and sometimes psychotic; but he remained a victorious Christian because his dependent faith affords a foundation for life. Bishop Joseph Butler (1692–1752) inveighed against Enlightenment deism with rational apologetic arguments. John (1703–1791) and Charles (1707–1788) Wesley and George Whitefield (1714–1770) proclaimed the life-giving gospel. Cowper was probably the best poet in his time, and he ministered to his and succeeding generations through his poetic pen and letters.

Cowper was born in Berkhamsted in Hertfordshire, where his father was rector and sometime writer of ballads. His mother had known many crushing sorrows and died when William was age six. She was a descendent of John Donne. His father struggled with episodes of melancholy and temptations to suicide.[1] While some critics blame Cowper's evangelical theology for his bouts with despair, and others accuse his companion John Newton for being too fastidious with him, the fact is that this tendency to depression was common to both sides of his family. What William called "gloomy thoughts, led on by spleen" afflicted his brother John as well. He had a disappointing romance with a cousin, which left him dejected and suicidal. While he professed conversion in 1764, he had a lifelong battle for assurance, fearing at times that he had committed the unpardonable sin.[2]

William was well-grounded in Scripture and was educated at "the Old Vicarage" and Westminster School and in preparation for the law in London. He disliked the practice of law, and while preparing to assume a clerk's position in the House of Lords, he went into depression. He convalesced in Olney with an Anglican clergyman William Unwin and his family.

After William Unwin died in an accidental fall from a horse, Cowper stirred gossip when he remained with Mrs. Unwin and the children. He had a troubling relationship with his first cousin Martin Madan, who helped him come to Christ but turned to the view that the Bible encourages bigamy.[3] But Cowper also came into association with John Newton, who would be his friend and collaborator in *Olney Hymns*. Cowper was often laid low by worry that he was not one of the elect, while Newton was close to the Wesleys and the Clapham Sect. Newton dominated their relationship, and Cowper served as unpaid curate for Newton's parish. But he had time to write poems and hymns.

Romans 3:24–25 became the bedrock of hope during Cowper's despair.[4] He found poetry an antidote to depression, especially Milton and Herbert. He translated Homer and was writing a commentary on *Paradise Lost* and *Paradise Regained* at the time of his death.[5] He felt increasingly clear of his call to be a teacher and spiritual mentor, especially through his poems. He had great love for the Jews and a confidence that many would come to accept Jesus as Messiah.

Cowper may be seen as a pre-Romantic, anticipating Wordsworth and others in verses about nature, such as "On the Death of Mrs. Throckmorton's Bullfinch," "The Dog and the Water-Lily," "Epitaph on a Hare," or "The Retired Cat."

In contrast to Pope, Cowper did not concentrate on perfecting his style. He sought simple and direct expression. Out of his painful searchings and groanings came such beautiful treasures as "God Moves in a Mysterious Way," "There Is a Fountain Filled with Blood," "The Spirit Breathes upon the Word," "Jesus, Where'er Thy People Meet," "O for a Closer Walk with God" and many others. His final poem, "Castaway," is almost despairing.

Yet God's servant, despite these furious fluctuations, was mightily used. A nonevangelical historian John H. Overton made the observation:

> Poems do not make converts in the sense that sermons do; nevertheless, it is doing no injustice to the preaching power of the Evangelical school to assert that Cowper's poetry left a deeper mark upon the Church than any sermons did. Through this means Evangelical theology in its most

attractive form gained access into quarters into which no Evangelical preachers could have ever penetrated. The bitterest enemy of Evangelicalism who read Cowper's poems could not deny that here was at least one man, a scholar and a gentleman, with a refined and cultured mind and a brilliant wit, who was not only favorably disposed to the obnoxious doctrines, but held them to be the very life and soul of Christianity.[6]

Who can gainsay the winsome truth and ever relevant redemption of which he speaks in "Praise for the Fountain Opened," inspired by Zechariah 13:1:

> E'er since by faith, I saw the stream
> Thy flowing wounds supply,
> Redeeming love has been my theme,
> And shall be till I die.
> Lord, I believe Thou hast prepared
> (Unworthy though I be)
> For me a blood-bought free reward,
> A golden harp for me![7]

----

1. George Melvyn Ella, *William Cowper: Poet of Paradise* (Durham: Evangelical, 1993), 38.
2. Hugh l'Anson Fausset, *William Cowper* (New York: Harcourt Brace, n.d.). Fausset launches devastating criticism. He fiercely dislikes Cowper's faith and hymns. He does picture the frightened little boy, alone and bullied (15). See also Peter Steese, "The Religious Faith of William Cowper," in *Christianity Today*, 3 July 1964, 22f.; Virginia Stem Owens, "The Dark Side of Grace: How Could William Cowper write Hymns Extolling the Goodness of God While on the Verge of Suicide?" *Christianity Today*, 19 July 1993, 32ff.
3. *Poet of Paradise*, 250ff. Madan was also at the vortex of the controversies over the use of hymns and other kinds of music. We must remember also that the Puritans were against organs, choirs, and stained glass.
4. Frank W. Boreham, "William Cowper's Text," in *A Bunch of Everlastings* (New York: Abingdon, 1920), 120ff.
5. Ibid., 581ff. Through his work with Milton's story of damnation and salvation, Cowper did battle with those who denied the eternality of hell and those who argued that even Satan would be saved.
6. Ibid., 593ff. Cowper participated in the antislavery crusades despite his frail health.
7. William Cowper, *William Cowper* (London: Thomas Nelson, n.d.), 151.

7.3   THE GRIPPING CRESCENDO OF THE ROMANTICS

Romanticism, as we have seen in our consideration of Jean-Jacques Rousseau (1712–1778), reacted against the sterility of Enlightenment rationalism, although Romanticism and rationalism share a common parentage in skepticism and later rejoined hands in the philosophy of existentialism (5.6).

Romanticism affirmed feeling, imagination, and emotion over intellect and reason. Romantics revolted against classicism's form and propriety, advocating freedom, passion, and liberty. Its hero is the rebel. The idealism of Immanuel Kant (1724–1804) and G. W. F. Hegel (1770–1831) fed the movement, as did the American and French revolutions. The movement proclaimed human goodness and autonomy. Such revelation existed as private, without mediating authority or institution. Pantheistic regard for nature, a mystical primitivism, pervaded the work. Transcendentalism was a vigorous expression by American Romantics.

7.3.1 SOUTHEY, FASTIDIOUS ROMANTIC

Go thou and seek the house of prayer!
I to the woodlands bend my way,
And meet religion there.
She needs not haunt the high-arched dome to pray
Where storied windows dim the doubtful day:
With liberty she loves to rove,
Wide o'er the healthy hill or cowslipt grove,
Or with the streamlet wind along the vale.
Sweet are these scenes to her; and when the night
Pours in the north her silver streams of light,
She woos reflection in the silent gloom,
And ponders on the world to come.

—Robert Southey
"Written on Sunday Morning"

"Written on Sunday Morning" by Robert Southey (1774–1843) expresses typical Romantic themes. Southey was born in Bristol in beautiful Somerset, where his father was a linen-draper. He was actually raised by an unmarried aunt, who greatly loved drama and the stage but had a compulsive need for cleanliness. As a very young boy, he often patronized the theatre with his aunt. He attended Westminster School, from which he was expelled for writing a satirical article on corporal punishment. With his father's death, his clergyman uncle arranged that he could go up to Oxford. It had been hoped he might go into the church, "but he had no religious opinions to justify this."[1]

At Oxford, Southey met Samuel Taylor Coleridge, who had left Cambridge. The two shared radical notions of reforming society. In 1795 Southey published some poetry. His elongated *Joan of Arc* came out in 1796, breathing, as Hazlitt said, "the love of liberty" as if it were the highest value to be sought.[2] The story of the young French visionary from Orleans reflects the French tilt of the Romantics. In "Romance," he acknowledges his debt to Rousseau, the "Guide of my life."[3]

When his uncle, a chaplain in Portugal, returned home and found his nephew "without belief in revealed religion," he dispatched him to Portugal, but Southey married Edith Fricker, Coleridge's sister-in-law before he left. After six months, he returned and tried to take up law but gave it up to concentrate on writing. His relationship with Coleridge was stormy, particularly when Southey had to step in and support the abandoned Mrs. Coleridge and children on more than one occasion. He was poet laureate of England (1813–43) and worked incessantly. His output was prolific but not brilliant. In his later years, he became more conservative and in his last year stopped writing altogether.

Among his notable poems are "The Death of Moses," a theme also addressed in an even more striking way in Helen Alexander's "The Burial of Moses,"[4] "The Death of Mathias,"[5] and a number of sonnets against the slave-trade. His lyrical poems on "The Destruction of Jerusalem" are the only extrabiblical verse on the city's fall in 586 B.C. Other historical poems include "The Spanish Armada" and "King Charlemagne." His poem on "The Battle of Blenheim" is often anthologized. This battle in 1704 was the turning point in the War of the Spanish Succession and rid Germany of French troops.[6]

His poem on "The Battle of Pultowa" celebrates the defeat of "that bloody Swede" King Charles XII. His pieces on "God's Judgment of a Bishop" and "Bishop Bruno" reflected his anticlericalism. He could be humorous as in "Elegy on a Quid of Tobacco."

Southey was not at the forefront of England's Romantic Movement, but his life was intertwined with the Romantics. He plays on Romanticism's theological motifs.

French historian Fernand Braudel (1902–1985) approaches history through the everyday details of life. In *The Structures of Everyday Life: Civilization and Capitalism 15th–18th Century*,[7] Braudel gathers a mass of data on what people wore, what they ate, how they handled their money, etc. The strength of the Romantics is a sensitivity to common aspects of life among all classes and types of people.

---

1. Robert Southey, *Joan of Arc: Ballads, Lyrics and Minor Poems* (London: George Routledge, n.d.), xi.
2. Ibid., xii.
3. Ibid., 149. We shall see in Wordsworth how the French movement toward "liberty, equality and fraternity" was so appealing before the blood started flowing.
4. Mrs. Charles A. Alexander (who in widowhood became A. C. Dixon's second wife) has a much better piece that begins:

> By Nebo's lonely mountain,   And no man dug that sepulchre,
> On this side Jordan's wave,   And no man saw it o'er,
> In a vale in the land of Moab,   For 'the sons of God' upturned the sod,
> There lies a lonely grave;   And laid the dead man there.

The poems are based on Deuteronomy 34, describing the strange funeral of Moses.
5. Ibid., 185. Southey also has a poem based on chapters 3–4 in Esdras in the Apocrypha. Quite a rare source. Of course G. F. Handel's oratorio *Judas Maccabaeus* (1747) was the most popular during his life.
6. The Duke of Marlborough defeated Talleyrand on the upper Danube and saved Vienna from the French.
7. New York: Harper, 1978.

7.3.2 WORDSWORTH, "KING-POET" OF THE ROMANTICS

My heart leaps up when I behold
A rainbow in the sky;
So was it when my life began;
So is it now I am a man;
So be it when I shall grow old,
Or let me die!
The child is father of the man;
And I could wish my days to be
Bound each to each by natural piety.

—William Wordsworth
"My Heart Leaps up When I Behold"

Elizabeth Barrett Browning gave the epithet "King Poet" to William Wordsworth (1770–1850). In his early output, he embodies the Romantics' love of nature, which gave birth to a love for humankind and a sense of "the still sad music of humanity." He was born in Cockermouth in Cumbria, the son of a solicitor. His mother died when he was three and his father five years later. He lived much of his childhood with his grandparents in Penrith and studied at Hawkshead Grammar School, where he was grounded in the classics and in natural science. Two of his uncles helped pay for his studies at Cambridge (1787–92).

Visits to the Continent enmeshed Wordsworth in radical politics and encouraged in him a profound sympathy for the French revolutionaries. He believed the French Revolution was the paradigm for what must take place in Britain. We hear echoes of Rousseau in the early Wordsworth. In 1792 he fathered a daughter by Annette Vallon, a French woman four years older than he. In 1796 he met Coleridge. He and his sister Dorothy lived with, and then nearby, Samuel and Sara Coleridge. Both poets were fired up with "Miltonic ardour" until reports of the Reign of Terror in France cooled their empathy. Already in his brilliant "Tinturn Abbey," some revolutionary fire was burning down.[1]

The search for religion by Coleridge was chaotic, but Wordsworth was like the peddler of whom he wrote, "Nor did he believe, he saw."[2] The two share powerful expressions of "radical humanism" in their collaborated piece, *Lyrical Ballads* (1798).

After traveling to Germany with Coleridge (while Coleridge imbibed of German higher criticism), William and Dorothy settled in their native Lake District at Grasmere in Dove Cottage in 1799.[3] He commenced his greatest work, the autobiographical *Prelude* and started *The Recluse,* in which he described city life as essentially barbaric. Stephen Gill concedes that William had a "profoundly sexual" relationship with his sister, but he believes William also felt genuine love for his bride, Mary Hutchinson, whom he married in 1802. His sister Dorothy did not attend the wedding and wore the wedding ring herself the night before.[4]

Wordsworth believed himself to be Milton's heir, yet his healthy self-image did not keep him from reading deeply in Jonson, Spenser, and Abraham Cowley.[5] His nature poems are numerous and all beautiful; "She Was a Phantom of Delight," and "I Wandered Lonely as a Cloud" are among favorites.[6] The danger in the religion of nature is, of course, that nature becomes God (see Rom. 1:18–25). Even Coleridge warned Wordsworth to stay away from pantheism. Generally indifferent to history, the Romantics picked up the first part of Psalm 19 about nature but neglected the last half of the psalm, extolling God's revealed word.

While always respectful for the institutional church, Wordsworth felt little need for it until his life came under heavy stress. That siege came with the disintegration of his long friendship with Coleridge and the death of two of his five children. Dorothy expressed faith in Christ, and Wordsworth began to explore Christianity.[7] In 1816 he published *The Statesman's Manual: The Bible the Best Guide to Political Skill and Foresight, an Essay or Lay Sermon.*[8] In *The River Duddon,* he describes Seathwaite Chapel and the gospel teacher who ministers there:

> Whose good works formed an endless retinue:
> Such Priest as Chaucer sang in fervent lays;
> Such as the heaven-taught skill of Herbert drew;
> And tender Goldsmith crown'd with deathless praise!

This man who had earlier said, "I have no need for a Redeemer," is speaking from within a more Christian frame-of-reference.[9]

His last years should have called him toward dependence. Once his eyesight dimmed there were many visitors but few visits from the Muse. Dorothy lapsed into dementia; his brothers and then his daughter died. He revised some earlier works because he wanted to be known as a Christian poet. He wrote his *Ecclesiastical Sonnets.* His son John became a clergyman.

Yet Wordsworth remained liberal, "loose and vague."[10] Was his a genuine return to Christian faith or the religious spasms and melancholy of an aging poet?[11] He companioned with Tractarians, including Frederick Faber, John Henry Newman (who converted to Roman Catholicism), and Keble. He was worried about "popery," but when Faber asked him to alter his description of Milton as "the holiest of men," he did so.[12]

The Romantics speak to something in our hearts; yet authentic Christianity is not to be found here. The Wordsworths and his sister are buried at Grasmere.

The Link between the Romantics and the French Revolution is complex. For reflection, R. R. Palmer's *The World of the French Revolution*[13] is especially good. Emil Ludwig's *Napoléon*[14] describes what transpired after the Revolution. See also Count Philippe-Paul de Segur's compelling war history, *Napoléon's Russian Campaign.*[15]

---

1. Stephen Gill, *William Wordsworth: A Life* (Oxford: Clarendon, 1989), 130. The best biography.
2. Ibid., 137. Keats spoke of Wordsworth's poetry as "the egotistical sublime." He was "the celebrant of man" at this stage.
3. Penelope Hughes-Hallett, *Home at Grasmere: The Wordsworths and the Lakes* (London: Collins and Brown, 1994).

4. Gill, *William Wordsworth: A Life,* 203, 211. Wordsworth gave his blessing to, but did not attend, his daughter's wedding. As he faced the exigencies of life, Wordsworth began to speak about trusting God (241). At this writing, recent Wordsworthian scholarship has shown that William Wilberforce, who almost married Dorothy, had at one time a close relationship with Wordsworth. Later the men were estranged and Wilberforce ridiculed Wordsworth. See Kenneth R. Johnson, *The Hidden Wordsworth: Poet, Lover, Rebel, Spy* (New York: W. W. Norton, 1998), 181, 363.

5. Abraham Cowley (1618–1667) was an earlier poet; see his *Poems* (London: Astolat, 1932). "The Grasshopper" and "The Swallow" are readily seen as precursors of the nature poetry of the Romantics.

6. John Morley, introduction to *The Complete Poetical Works of William Wordsworth* (New York: A. L. Burt, 1888).

7. Gill, *William Wordsworth: A Life,* 294f. Gill is former librarian of the Wordsworth papers at Grasmere and knows this field.

8. Ibid., 321. Politically, Wordsworth became more conservative—standing with the Tories and taking a patronage job.

9. Ibid., 343f. He was very spasmodic in writing in later years. He felt his earlier work had too much "swagger."

10. Geoffrey H. Hartman, "The Romance of Nature and the Negative Way," in *William Wordsworth,* ed. Harold Bloom (New York: Chelsea House, 1985), 50. Wordsworth's poetry was commentary on nature, while Blake's was commentary on God.

11. Ibid., 51. He gives himself to welding some transcendent dimension to the naturalistic world.

12. Gill, *William Wordsworth: A Life,* 418.

13. New York: Harper, 1971.

14. Garden City, N.J.: Garden City, 1926.

15. Boston: Houghton-Mifflin, 1958.

7.3.3 COLERIDGE, INTELLECTUAL ROMANTIC

> The Saviour comes! While as the Thousand Years
> Lead up their mystic dance, the Desert shouts!
> Old Ocean claps his hands! The mighty Dead
> Rise to new life, who'er from earliest time
> With conscious zeal had urged Love's wondrous plan,
> Coadjutors of God.
>
> —Samuel Taylor Coleridge
> "Religious Musings"[1]

> Friend pure of heart and fervent! We have learnt
> A different lore! We may not thus profane
> The Idea and Name of Him whose Absolute Will
> Is Reason—Truth Supreme! Essential Order!
>
> —Samuel Taylor Coleridge
> "To Edward Irving"[2]

Samuel Taylor Coleridge (1772–1834) was probably the most philosophical and intellectual of the English Romantics. He was a brilliant literary critic with widespread influence and an engaging conversationalist. Coleridge was the tenth son of a poor clergyman, born in Ottery St. Mary, Devonshire. He was a charity student at age ten at Christ Hospital School in London, where he met Charles Lamb, who was to be a steadfast friend. Later he would form a life patronage in the dissenting Wedgewood brothers, Josiah and C. V., manufacturers of Wedgewood china. They supported him with an annual annuity.

He went on to Cambridge but left for a brief stint of service in the army. He never returned to finish his degree. While at Cambridge, he did meet Robert Southey at Oxford who shared with him great sympathy for the French Revolution. Together they hatched an aborted scheme for starting a utopian community on the Susquehanna River in Pennsylvania. "The Rime of the Ancient Mariner" was originally written for a jointly-published work that he and Southey called *Lyrical Ballads*.

Coleridge married Southey's sister-in-law, discovering too late that Mary Evans did not reciprocate his love. Domestic tensions plagued him—he was not home when his son Hartley was born—and his closest friends regularly had to try to pick up the family pieces. He was frequently ill, probably with rheumatic fever. He also developed addictions to alcohol and opium. Although sharing children, the Coleridges were not happy, and after seven years they separated. Coleridge had various affairs, including an intense relationship with Sara Hutchinson, sister to Wordsworth's wife.

Coleridge had a brilliant mind, an effective "plain style" in writing, and a prolific output. One biographer speaks of his "pathological dependence on stolen materials." Plagiarism was always a serious problem for him, as was "punomania," as he called it.[3] He had a deeply religious bent, going through a Unitarian phase when he seriously considered serving a Unitarian church. He did much preaching in dissenting chapels. Frequently his sermons had millennial overtones.

Wordsworth and his sister Dorothy accompanied Coleridge to Germany where Coleridge immersed himself in the German language and Kant's philosophy. Thereafter he was receptive to the negative higher critical biblical theories of Johann Gottfried Eichorn (1752–1827) at Göttingen. He dabbled much in the higher criticism ideas of Eichorn and Gotthold Ephraim Lessing (1729–1781). His low views of Bible authenticity and authority influenced many, including such thinkers as Thomas Arnold (father of Matthew Arnold) and F. D. Maurice. Matthew Arnold later wrote:

In papa's time the exploding of the old notions of literal inspiration in Scripture, and the introducing of a truer method of interpretation, were the changes for which, here in England, the moment had come. Stiff people could not receive this change, and my dear old Methodist friend, Mr. Scott, used to say to the day of his death that papa and Coleridge might be excellent men, but that they had found and shown the rat-hole in the temple.[4]

Yet even in his earlier "Rime," Coleridge cannot escape basic Christian truth. Coleridge produces what is truly one of the great ballads, epic in its scope. The old mariner of his story is held back from the joys of life (the wedding) because he needs to tell his story. He had been trapped in an Antarctic ice floe. Unconscionably, he killed an albatross and endangered the crew. Only when he blessed the water snakes was the ship released, but he alone had survived the voyage.

Inclining toward Robert Penn Warren's moral interpretation, I would see this poem as a wrestling with "the mark of Cain," "the wandering Jew motif," the problem of Judas Iscariot.[5] The mariner commits a real crime and experiences true guilt and proper remorse. The bird is a kind of Christ-figure. A deliverance from outside does come (the breeze).[6]

Coleridge, as Wordsworth, does surrender something to Christianity. Religion did preoccupy him. Through the swirling circumstances of his life, he could not escape Christ and his cross. In "Kubla Khan," he unbears a quest for the celestial city and supernal power. Marshall Suther uses the poem "Dejection: An Ode" (1802) to show that, notwithstanding his considerable theological sophistication, Coleridge feels a tremendous sense of loss because he is disillusioned with the French Revolution and has failed in love. Neither could he come to rest in the skeptical philosophies of his generation. His subjectivity cannot furnish "passion and life."[7] He finally comes to realize that nature is not God. As Suther puts it, "Coleridge was led from poetry to love to abstruse researches in his quest for salvation."[8]

He finally drifts closer now to Thomas Aquinas than to Kant. Suther goes so far as to assert that Luther was becoming his model.[9] We do know he warned Wordsworth of Spinoza's pantheism.[10] Coleridge is the ancient mariner, a lost soul who misses the wedding feast, yet cannot escape an innate regard for, and exposure to, biblical truth.

Toward the end of his life his productivity dropped drastically, and he experienced the total loss of joy. He fled from his work of composing poetry. How do we explain this if it was not a corollary to his quest for God? The question is whether he ever fulfilled that quest. A few days before his death, he wrote to his godson indicating he might well have:

> And I thus, on the brink of the grave, solemnly bear witness to you, that the almighty Redeemer, most gracious in his promises to them that truly seek him, is faithful to perform what He has promised; and has reserved, under all pains and infirmities, the peace that passeth all understanding, with the supporting assurance of a reconciled God, who will not withdraw His spirit from me in the conflict, and in His own time will deliver me from the evil one. Oh, my dear godchild! Eminently blessed are they who begin early to seek, to fear, and love their God, trusting wholly in the righteousness and mediation of their Lord, Saviour, and everlasting High Priest, Jesus Christ.[11]

Nothing in "Rime of the Ancient Mariner" foreshadowed anything that might pass for a remedy to the underlying difficulty—neither his most famous lines:

"Water, water everywhere and not a drop to drink,"[12] nor his humanistic moral near the poem's end:[13]

> He prayeth best, who loveth best
> All things both great and small;
> For the dear God who loveth us,
> He made and loveth all.

1. Ernest Hartley Coleridge, ed., *The Poems of Samuel Taylor Coleridge* (London: Oxford University Press, 1931), 358ff. Coleridge's sidebar observations are significant. Here he speculates on conditions that will obtain during the thousand-year reign.
2. Ibid., 505. Edward Irving (1792–1834) was a widely-heard Scottish preacher in London, once assistant to Thomas Chalmers (1780–1847). This was written after Coleridge and Irving had come to agreement on a matter relating to infant baptism. See Larsen, *Company of the Preachers*, 9.1.7.
3. Richard Holmes, *Coleridge* (New York: Viking, 1989). Holmes describes the preaching of Coleridge in the Unitarian Church in Shrewsbury. Holmes said his voice "rose like a stream of rich, distilled perfume." Coleridge expressed deep convictions about the prejudice faced by Jews in Germany. "The Jews are horribly, unnaturally oppressed and persecuted all through Germany," he wrote in 1799 (219).
4. Daniel Hoffman, "S. T. Coleridge and the Attack on Inerrancy," *Trinity Journal*, 7 NS (1986), 55–68. A study that is to the point.
5. Harold Bloom, ed., *Samuel Taylor Coleridge's "The Rime of the Ancient Mariner"* (New York: Chelsea House, 1986), 1.
6. Geoffrey H. Hartman, "Representation in The Ancient Mariner" in *Samuel Taylor Coleridge's*, 47; Camille Paglia, "Sexual Personae" in *Samuel Taylor Coleridge's*, 105. Indeed Charles Lamb wonders if Coleridge is lurching toward Trinitarianism, away from Unitarianism, 38.
7. Marshall Suther, *The Dark Night of Samuel Taylor Coleridge* (New York: Columbia University Press, 1960), 158. He had written six poems by age twenty-five including "Rime"; from sixteen to thirty years of age, he was exceedingly productive.
8. Ibid., 175. He could no longer go out to nature alone. Nature remains a corpse.
9. Ibid., 202. He felt Luther throwing the ink pot at the Devil was the apogee: "He did not write; he acted poems."
10. Thomas McFarland, "The Wordsworthian Rigidity," in *William Wordsworth*, ed. Harold Bloom (New York: Chelsea House, 1985), 151. For some years, he lived near the home of Wordsworth at Keswick. During his last eighteen years, he was a resident patient in London at the home of a doctor friend. It was his hope that he might be cured of his life-controlling addiction to opium. Both Wordsworth and Coleridge were close to Thomas de Quincey, who wrote *Confessions of an English Opium Eater*.
11. *Dark Night of Samuel Taylor Coleridge*, 212. Suther argues Coleridge finally called his desire for salvation "by its right name."
12. 2.121–22.
13. 2.614–17.

7.3.4 BLAKE, MYSTICAL ROMANTIC

> To see a World in a grain of sand,
> And a Heaven in a wild flower;
> Hold infinity in the palm of your hand,
> And eternity in an hour.

> —William Blake,
> "To See a World in a Grain of Sand"

The delightful *Eerdmans Book of Christian Poetry* includes four poems by William Blake (1757–1827). This strange poet, painter, and engraver deserves inclusion in a general anthology, but he is not truly among the ranks of "Christian poets." While his ideas were steeped in biblicism, he was a mystic cultist.[1] Hess well cautions us that Blake "did not sing the Christian song, however unconditionally he employed Christian terms."[2] The neo-Platonic undercurrents threaten to inundate anything Christian.

Blake was born in London the third son of James Blake, a hosier and a Baptist, and his wife, Catherine. He saw visions from the age of eight or ten years and it was not uncommon that King Arthur would come to visit.[3] Self-educated, he loved to read John Bunyan (1628–1688) along with Francis Bacon (1561–1626), Edmund Burke (1729–1797), and John Locke (1632–1704). He saw no use in formal education, arguing that "it is the great sin. It is eating of the tree of Knowledge of good and evil."[4]

At age fourteen, he was apprenticed as an engraver, having always loved the visual. He was a convinced republican and an incessant worker. A muscular five foot five and with gleaming eyes, he married Catherine Butcher. They had a long and happy marriage, although she said of him: "I have very little of Mr. Blake's company; he is always in paradise."[5] In the making of their books, he would develop copper engravings by hand and color them himself, and she would bind them. The beginner in Blake should read his *Songs of Innocence* and *Songs of Experience,* which includes his famous "Tyger, tyger, burning bright."[6]

After the death of his brother, Blake became profoundly religious. He and his wife became followers of Emanuel Swedenborg (1688–1772), the curious Swedish scientist-mystic who founded the Church of the New Jerusalem, which still exists today. They believed that Christ's body was "tainted with hereditary evil" and that on the cross he expunged the evil he had obtained through his mother. This cult was anti-Trinitarian and believed in explicit sexuality among all the creatures of heaven. Friends would find the Blakes in their yard unclothed, maintaining that they were in the Garden of Eden. With such eccentricities, Blake had a difficult time getting along with any prospective patrons or friends, and ultimately he broke even with the Swedenborgians.[7]

Blake and his wife were always near destitution. Miraculously acquitted of criminal sedition, William lived with Catherine in Felpham on the coast in Sussex for three years. Then he returned to subsistence living and the publication of his books. His tempura illustrations of the Bible are outstanding, especially his water colors of Job. His work is very sensuous and his ideas often opaque.

Blake became paranoid and surly, and Mrs. Blake began to have visions as well. Then, as he reached sixty, he began to mellow somewhat.

The big question about Blake has always been the specific nature of his religion. At this time, such movements as Freemasonry, the Druids, the Rosicrucians, Philadelphians, Boehemists (devotees of Jakob Böhme), and the Hutchensonians (students of an eccentric scholar whose reading of the Hebrew led him to oppose Newtonian science) were proliferating. There were antinomians on every side. Everyone agrees that Blake was antinomian and wanted to protest the rhetoric of the Enlightenment.

E. P. Thompson summed up his opinion: "The strongest influence upon Blake comes from one major source—the Bible—but the Bible read in a particular way, influenced by Milton and by radical dissent."[8]

Thompson argues convincingly that the Blakes became Muggletonians and that his mother had been in fact such. This cult was a strongly predestinarian group that followed seventeenth-century mystic Ludowicke Muggleton (1606–1698). They were intensely anticlerical and had no meeting place as such. They would gather in pubs and order a pot of beer and then sing songs written to popular tunes. They raised money only to keep their founder's ideas in print. Muggleton wrote two commentaries on the book of Revelation. Muggletonians were pacifistic and did not practice evangelism. They opposed capital punishment. The last known Muggletonian, Philip Noakes, died in 1978.[9]

In several cults, the proto-New Age idea prevailed that "Christ is God and so am I and so are you." These groups became "an extreme recourse open to the excluded."[10] The question we always face in Blake: Was he odd, or was he mad?

---

1. Pat Alexander, ed., *Eerdmans Book of Christian Poetry* (Grand Rapids: Eerdmans, 1981).
2. M. Whitcomb Hess, "A Key to William Blake," *Christian Century*, 21 August 1963, 1027f. Important caution.
3. James King, *William Blake: His Life* (New York: St. Martin's, 1991).
4. Peter Ackroyd, *Blake: A Biography* (New York: Knopf, 1996), 23.
5. King, *William Blake: His Life*, 192. King shows "the lavish extent to which Blake could distort reality."
6. David V. Erdman, ed., *The Complete Poetry and Prose of William Blake* (New York: Doubleday, 1988).
7. Ackroyd, *Blake: A Biography*, 154. "The Ranters 'preached stark naked many blasphemies.'" See p. 104 in Ackroyd's biography, which points out an inconsistency concerning Blake. He was an angry loner, yet he cared much for the down-and-out.
8. E. P. Thompson, *Witness Against the Beast: William Blake and the Moral Law* (New York: New, 1993), 33.
9. Ibid., 104.
10. Ibid., 110, 159. Theosophical and Philadelphian ideas like these reached Swedenborg through pietism. As with most groups that have gnostic tendencies, there was little agreement on doctrine within these sects.

7.3.5 BURNS, COLLOQUIAL ROMANTIC

The priest-like father reads the sacred page,
How Abram was the friend of God on high;
Or, Moses bade eternal warfare wage
With Amalek's ungracious progeny;
Or, how the royal Bard did groaning lie
Beneath the stroke of Heaven's avenging ire;
Or Job's pathetic plaint, and wailing cry;
Or, rapt Isaiah's wild seraphic fire;
Or other holy Seers that tune the sacred lyre.

Perhaps the Christian volume is the theme:
How guiltless blood for guilty man was shed;
How He, who bore in Heaven the second name,
Had not on earth whereon to lay His head;
How his first followers and servants sped;
The precepts sage they wrote to many a land:
How he, who lone in Patmos banished,
Saw in the sun a mighty angel stand,
And heard great Bab'lon's doom pronoun'd by Heaven's
command.

—Robert Burns
"The Cotter's Saturday Night"

Some years ago, I was asked to address the Scot's community's annual Burns Supper. What possibly could I share that would be appropriate? It was then that I hit upon the topic, "The Cotter's Saturday Night: A Window on Scottish National Life." I used the Scottish national poet's most famous poem, which depicts the lowly cotter reading Holy Scripture and kneeling to pray for his family. This is truly a beautiful poem that goes to the heart of the great spiritual renewal and the renascence of preaching. Its author, Robert Burns (1759–1796), knew about the renewal, but he never had the personal experience of the Savior who was at the heart of it all.

Burns was born in Alloway in Ayrshire in western Scotland, the oldest of seven children, to a father in advancing years who failed in his farming, and to a mother who was scarcely literate but who sang the Scottish songs to him. The latter, along with the tales that the serving girl told, were what Burns called "the latent seeds of poesy."[1] He was schooled in the village with Mr. Murdoch, who taught him classical English and even some French. He developed the young student's great love of reading. Burns actually had less of a Scottish brogue than did David Hume. Young Burns already had bouts with a deep melancholy and with the rheumatic fever that ultimately would kill him at age thirty-seven. He worked hard but had a breach with his father over the issue of his dancing in the village. His father was very devout, and later Robert remembered his father with great appreciation.[2]

From dancing, he moved to more blatant kinds of depravity. A sailor influenced this breaking down of his inhibitions against fornication until, throughout his life, Burns was a notorious womanizer, with a number of illegitimate children. He and his brother rented a farm at Mosgiel with indifferent success.[3] Loyalty to freemasonry surpassed any tie to the church, especially since three times he was ordered to come as a penitent to the church for fathering Jean Armour's twins. He mocked the church and the clergy in his satirical "Holy Willie's Prayer,"[4] and then slammed the great open air communion services in "The Holy Fair." After the stillborn birth of another child by Mary Campbell, he determined to emigrate to Jamaica.

Before he left, he set himself to publish his poems, especially his love-poems. These achieved immediate notice. The literati in Edinburgh were much taken with his Scottish dialect poetry. They loved his "To a Mouse," the best of his animal poetry, and "Scotch Drink" in praise of whiskey. "The Cotter's Saturday Night" was included (written after the pattern of Gray's "Elegy") and became popular. His "Address to a Haggis," celebrating the unspeakable dish served at Burns' family suppers, and his "Kirk's Alarm" on a complaint against a Scottish minister were widely appreciated. Seen as a primitivist, he was wined and dined and traveled through Scotland.

He continued to have scandals and disasters in his personal life, but finally married Jean Armour. At this time, he wrote his narrative masterpiece, "Tam O'Shanter." He hobnobbed with the elite, such as Hugh Blair, the Edinburgh scholar who led the charge against orthodoxy in Scotland.[5] He ventured into politics, to everyone's regret, but kept up his hard-drinking and dissipated ways. Truly he is a poet of the people in so many ways, and his poetry was "wrung from real life," but it was, at the same time, "celebratory of life."[6] At last he procured a home for Jean and their children in Dumfires but died soon afterward.

Burns was the least transcendent of the poets we look at here. His work, from "Auld Lang Syne" to "Coming thro' the Rye" have given great pleasure. How unspeakably sad that this poet passed through the great spiritual revival in Scotland, with its powerful biblical preaching, and yet never learned about the peace of "The Cotter's Saturday Night."

---

1. David Daiches, *Robert Burns and His World* (New York: Viking, 1971), 10. His father died in bankruptcy.
2. Ibid., 16.
3. Students of preaching may recall that Frank Boreham, after emigrating, pastored in the Scottish settlement Mosgiel in southern New Zealand. See Frank Boreham, *My Pilgrimage* (London: Epworth, 1954).
4. James Barke, ed., *Poems and Songs of Robert Burns* (London: Collins, 1955), 61, 222.
5. Blair did him no good. See Larsen, *Company of the Preachers,* 8.
6. *Robert Burns and His World,* 50. One of my favorite couplets is from "To a Louse" about the creature he watched march up the back of a staid matron: "O wad some Pow'r the giftie gie us/To see oursels as others see us!" Also often quoted, "The best laid schemes o' mice an' men gang aft agley."

7.3.6 BYRON, RENEGADE ROMANTIC

> My days are in the yellow leaf;
> The flowers and fruits of Love are gone;
> The worm, the canker, and the grief
> Are mine alone!
>
> —George Gordon, Lord Byron
> "On This Day I Complete My Thirty-Sixth"

These sad lines were written on George Gordon's ("Lord Byron's") thirty-sixth birthday. It would be his last birthday, for he died of fever in Greece shortly thereafter. Lord Byron, or George Gordon as he was born (1788–1824), was, according to one of his many lovers, "Mad, bad and dangerous to know." He was born with a deformed club foot, which only gave his striking physical appearance a kind of mesmerizing appeal. He was a true manic-depressive.[1] His life was a shipwreck and his poetry not as brilliant as others of the Romantics (for example, Shelley). Yet there is a vigor and thrust to his words. A saying within the literary community is that "Walter Scott describes; Byron creates."

He was born in London, heir to a baronage, but his wayward father died when he was three, and he was raised in Scotland by his mother. Scot Presbyterianism left an indelible mark upon his life. By age nineteen, he had read deeply in Blair (see 7.3.5 n. 5), Richard Hooker (1554–1600), and John Tillotson (1630–1694).[2] Early on he was ready to deny the atonement of Christ.[3]

When he assumed his peerage to become Sixth Lord Byron, he and his mother moved to Newstead Abbey near Nottingham in England, the ancestral estate. He was graduated from Harrow and Trinity College, Cambridge, although he was not a good student. His first poems were so roundly panned by the critics that he decided to get away from England and traveled abroad for two years. His account of the journey inspired his long poem entitled *Childe Harold's Pilgrimage*. It was an immediate success.

He took his place in the House of Lords and attempted to settle down by marrying Annabelle Milbanke. After a year and the birth of their daughter, the marriage broke up. His daughter later died in the convent where he had placed her. Such were the rumors and blight on his reputation that he left England for good. He lived in Italy for some years (often with the Shelleys, his best friends[4]) and in Vienna. In 1823 he went to Greece to foment and finance a rebellion against Turkey. There he died.

Byron was a sensualist, yet he could never escape his stern religious upbringing. He was hard-bitten by doubt after a heavy diet of Spinoza, Lucretius, Pope, and Rousseau.[5] Yet Edward Marjarum makes a good case for a deep vacillation in Byron. In his wildly fluctuating moods, he denies everlasting punishment and later swings toward faith, asserting in a letter, "I assure you that I am a very good Christian."[6] He used the argument from design in creation and then lurched toward pantheism. His "swift alternations of temper" led him from evolutionary thought to a quest for the clarification of the meaning of the soul and death.[7] He could be crassly anti-Semitic and hostile to the House of Rothschild,[8] yet he had a special brooding love for the Old Testament and wrote proto-Zionist poems in *Hebrew Melodies*.[9]

His mind could be anarchic and his style verbally careless, but there is an energy and brightness in Byron that deserve attention. Just a few of his works include:

- *Childe Harold's Pilgrimage* is "the greatest confessional poem" of the Romantic Period. Byron is haunted by a sense of original sin. Melancholy moralizing.
- "The Prisoner of Chillon" describes the sufferings of a prisoner in a beautiful little castle on Lake Geneva. A tightly and neatly constructed poem.[10]
- *Hebrew Melodies* gives his magnificent "The Destruction of Sennacherib," about the plague that wiped out the Assyrians as described in 2 Kings 19:35–36.[11]
- His poetic drama *Manfred* wrestles with a keenly oppressive sense of guilt.
- *Cain,* another speculative play, uses the biblical story to attack orthodox Christianity. It was a bombshell when it debuted in 1821.[12]
- *Heaven and Earth* grapples with Genesis 6:2 from the days of Noah.
- "Beppo" is a satirical poem, which illustrates Byron's tendency for digression.
- *The Vision of Judgment* ridicules George III on his entry into heaven as Lucifer contests for the soul of the king. This is a riot.
- His vast, unfinished *Don Juan* (pronounced for his purposes as "Joo-ahn," with a hard "J"). The successive rambling cantos of this memorable poem trace "the Byronic hero" in his fall from sexual innocence, his travels, shipwreck, and romances.

Don Juan describes Byron's own life.[13] There is no escaping God—although Byron makes every effort.

---

1. Phyllis Grosskurth, *Byron: The Flawed Angel* (Boston: Houghton Mifflin, 1996). This study tends to be psycho-biography at its best and worst. The author does give a thoughtful study of Byron's mental instability.
2. Edward Wayne Marjarum, *Byron as Skeptic and Believer* (New York: Russell and Russell, 1938), 2.
3. Ibid., 11. In his passionate curiosity, the young Byron abandoned Pope for Rousseau.
4. John Buxton, *Byron and Shelley: The History of a Friendship* (New York: Harcourt Brace, 1968).
5. *Byron as Skeptic and Believer,* 47–48. Byron is the quintessential "double-minded man" of James 1:6–8.
6. Ibid., 75, 85. His earlier hostility to Roman Catholicism softened as he lived in Italy.
7. Ibid., 61–62. Byron had a fascinating discussion about faith with Walter Scott (76).
8. Byron was a contemporary of Mayer Amschel Rothschild (1743–1812), founder of

the House of Rothschild. See Amos Elon, *Founder: A Portrait of the First Rothschild and His Time* (New York: Viking, 1996). In *Age of Bronze,* Byron satirizes the Rothschild family (11.699–703).

9. Leslie A. Marchand, *Byron's Poetry: A Critical Introduction* (Boston: Houghton, Mifflin, 1968), 133.
10. Ibid., 67–70. The prisoner Bonnivard, the persecuted prelate, said when he was released: "My very chains and I grew friends" ("The Assyrian Came Down").
11. Mark Twain, *The Adventures of Tom Sawyer* (Philadelphia: John C. Winston, 1957).
12. Marchand, *Byron's Poetry,* 85. Byron could not shake his childhood awe of the Old Testament.
13. Harold Bloom, ed., *Lord Byron's Don Juan* (New York: Chelsea House, 1987), 107ff.

7.3.7 SHELLEY, RECONDITE ROMANTIC

> Congenial minds will seek their kindred soul,
> E'en though the tide of time has rolled between;
> They mock weak matter's impotent control,
> And seek of endless life the eternal scene.
>
> —Percy Bysshe Shelley
> "Fragment: Epithaliun"

Even these very early lines from Percy Bysshe Shelley (1792–1822) show something of the brilliance and stylistic virtuosity of the embryonic poet. He is a classicist in form (even more than Dryden, C. S. Lewis argued) and unquestionably, as Wordsworth admitted, he was "one of the best artists." He was born into a wealthy Sussex family, the son in a family of girls (until finally a baby brother came along). His father was a member of Parliament who, in many years there, made only one speech. From the beginning, Percy set himself against all conventions. He attended Eton where he resisted tradition, and he lasted at Oxford only five months because he published *The Necessity of Atheism.* His early "Melody to a Scene of Former Times" signals his break with all orthodoxies.[1] His several fragments on "the wandering Jew" do pick up an old recurrent theme.[2]

If his expulsion from Oxford did not strain his parental ties to the breaking point, then his elopement with sixteen-year-old Harriet Westbrook surely did. They lived for awhile at Keswick, where they made the acquaintance of Robert Southey. They traveled widely and got close to William Godwin, absorbing many of his radical ideas. Shelley declared his love to Mary, the sixteen-year-old daughter of Godwin. During this erratic behavior, he and his circle subscribed to free love, regarding marriage as a tyranny. Shelley tried to commit suicide, and Harriet succeeded in taking her own life.[3]

From 1816 Shelley lived in Switzerland and Italy.[4] While living at Leghorn, Italy, only twenty-nine years of age, he and Edward Williams drowned when a squall suddenly arose while they were out in a small boat.

Shelley rejected everything British, and Britain rejected Shelley. Imbued with Enlightenment thinking to the core of his being, Shelley was eclectic, adding the thinking of other freethinking philosophers and poets. Writes one scholar, "Shelley was at one with the thought of his time."[5] As a Romantic, he revolted against what he saw as vapid intellectualism. In this, his thinking was like that of Byron and Keats.

Any tour of Shelley's poetry should include several of his best works:

"Queen Mab" (1812–13) is his most radical poem, a totally subjective rejection of thought. He draws on Isaiah's prophecy of the Kingdom (Cantos VIII, IX), but sees God as the "arch-superstition."[6]

"Alastor, or the Spirit of Solitude" is the work of a man who is groping for truth. He had rejected God, and he wrote a pamphlet in 1814 to refute the middle ground of deism. In the symbolic mode, a youth seeks a secular Garden of Eden. It is not only subjective, but also destructive.

"Hymn to Intellectual Beauty," one of his finest poems, shows Wordsworth's influence.

"The Cenci" (1819) is a blank-verse drama in which Count Cenci determines to violate his daughter. She adopts evil ways to thwart him, but in vain. Bloom sees the tragedy as a "demonic parody of Jehovah-God."[7]

"The Sensitive Plant" (1820) is dark melancholy and deeply skeptical. Shelley is most Humean of these poets (and George Bernard Shaw is most Shelleyan).

The drama *Prometheus Unbound* draws by far the most discussion among scholars. Harold Bloom sees this work as a "dark parody of the Christian salvation myth."[8] It is written in the classical mode. In Act IV there are intriguing allusions to Ezekiel and Revelation. C. S. Lewis observes that its grand conclusion seems Dantean.

"The Epipsychidion" is Shelley's appeal for free love. Its emotionalism is pitiable.

"Adonais" is his great elegy on the death of Keats. Bloom points out that for Milton, as in Scripture, death is unnatural and intrusive; for Shelley death is natural. "He can no longer sustain ironic hope."[9] This is a materialistic philosophy, so it is bound by skepticism.

"In the Triumph of Life," unfinished at his death, is full of bitter eloquence. T. S. Eliot saw this exploration of the power of evil as the apex of Shelley's work. There is something Dantean here, but Rousseau's is the presence felt. The only answer to be found is within humankind. When Shelley can lift himself smiling from the heap of misery, it is to celebrate humanity as redeemer of the universe. This is not to escape the vicious cycle of our depravity.

"To a Skylark" is my own favorite. "Ozymandias" and "Ode to the West Wind" also are striking in artistry. Not worth reading is "The Revolt of Islam," a long, tedious poetic argument that love conquers all. This was written before his rift with Mary, when he abandoned the notion.

---

1. Thomas Hutchinson, ed., *The Complete Poetical Works of Percy Bysshe Shelley* (London: Oxford, 1919), 857.
2. Ibid., 872. For the rootage here, see Eugene Sue, *The Wandering Jew* (New York: Modern Library, n.d.).

3. Donald H. Reiman, *Percy Bysshe Shelley* (Boston: Twayne, 1969), 34.
4. With the death of his grandfather, Shelley had a modicum of financial security.
5. Ibid., 29.
6. James Reiger, "Orpheus and the West Wind," in *Percy Bysshe Shelley,* ed. Harold
   Bloom (New York: Chelsea House, 1985), 17, 69. We sense again the Spinozan pantheism in this poet (201). Shelley uses the classical myth as his background for contemporary application, cf. 2.3.1.
7. *Percy Bysshe Shelley,* 85. Shelley inveighs against the French Revolution and Christianity. The death of a child, "Elena Shelley" was at this time. Whose child she was
   is not known.
8. Ibid.
9. *Percy Bysshe Shelley,* 24. For a good analysis of the theological matrix of such an approach, see Hugh Ross Mackintosh, *Types of Modern Theology* (New York: Scribner's,
   1937). Notice the excess of Friedrich Schleiermacher's theology of feeling, 60ff. For
   comment on the philosophy inherent in Shelley's memorable phrase, "We must learn
   to imagine what we know," see Roger Rosenblatt, *Time,* 9 June 1997, 90.

7.3.8 KEATS, RADICAL ROMANTIC

> O for a life of sensations, rather than of thoughts.—
> A thing of beauty is a joy forever.
>
> —John Keats
> "Endymion"

Considered by many students of poetry to be the most stylistically skillful of
the Romantics, John Keats (1795–1821) was probably "the most Shakespearean
[writer] since Shakespeare." While Wordsworth carried "the burden of the mystery," and "knowledge is sorrow" to Byron, in the thinking of Keats "sorrow is
wisdom." In contradiction to Shelley's inward search for beauty, Keats looked
outward to a beauty external to self. Like all of the Romantics, Keats "lovingly
struggles with his ghostly father, Milton."[1]

An unlikely poet, Keats was the oldest of five children born to a livery service
operator who died in an accident while riding his horse drunk. His wife did not
long survive him. Young Keats read novels to his dying mother. The surviving
daughter and her three brothers were made wards of a crooked businessman
named Richard Abbey, who was described as "a priggish evangelical." Abbey
did not make the spiritual journey easier.[2]

Though Keats was not very bookish as a young person, he became "the most
literary of nineteenth century poets."[3] He took an apprenticeship in surgery and
was licensed in both surgery and apothecary before he was twenty. But gradually his love for writing poetry overcame his need for a more steady source of
income. His very early "On First Looking into Chapman's Homer" exposes the
latent genius of the man, as he speaks of "stout Cortez" who "with eagle eyes
star'd at the Pacific." His "Ode to a Grecian Urn" was called "the most sculptur-
esque of English poems, of power kept in reserve."[4] Going to the seaside at

Margate or the Island of Wight, he would prime himself with massive ingestion of Shakespeare before writing such as his large *Endymion,* based on the Greek myth of the shepherd on Mount Latmos.

In three years, he developed into a well-rounded poet whose output began to flow with brilliance. His premise was "What the imagination seizes as beauty must be truth."[5] When his brother became ill and then died from consumption (tuberculosis), he overwhelmed his grief with work and wrote four of the greatest lyric poems in English literature within three weeks: "Ode to Psyche," "Ode to a Nightingale," "Ode to a Grecian Urn," and "Ode to Melancholy."[6]

Reviewers were hard on Keats; Shelley argued that their criticisms were responsible for his death. This is manifestly not the case, but he flailed about in every direction, seeking for financial and inner peace. He at one point was engaged to be married. Nothing, however, gave him the solace he sought. He turned to alcohol and opium as escapes and felt increasingly frustrated.[7] In his new narrative poem, "Lamia," he experimented with Dryden's iambic pentameter versification. In one final year, his output of top-quality poetry was astounding.

Pressured by concerned friends to get away from the English winter by going to Rome, he died near the Spanish Steps in November of 1821.

Wordsworth himself described some of Keats's work as "little more than pagan," but we do sense something of the inner turmoil. Keats was not drawn to the church, and, as far as he could see, "the great object of modern sermons is to hazard nothing: their characteristic is decent debility."[8] Between his fifteenth and twentieth year, he broke off his identification with Christ and the church. He had little connection to break; J. A. Froude said that Keats never heard a word of doctrine in his life.[9]

Keats had heard the Bible read in his grandmother's home, but his teacher at Enfield was Unitarian. By the time of his apprenticeship at Guy's Hospital, skepticism had given way to a radical empiricism and overt unbelief. The universalism of Leigh Hunt, his editor and a close friend, reinforced this anti-Christian feeling. Hunt opposed the "gloomy repentance" of the evangelicals.[10]

As a result, church bells were only a melancholy dirge to Keats, calling folk

> to the sermon's horrid sound.
> Surely the mind of man is closely bound
> In some black spell; seeing that each one tears
> Himself from fireside joys, and Lydian airs.
> And converse high of those with glory crown'd.[11]

The abandonment of whatever childhood faith he may have felt was aimed most directly at Christianity's central article of faith—redemption through the death of Jesus.

One friend who was a Christian, the Rev. Benjamin Bailey, made a defense for the atonement and influenced Keats to read the Bible. Keats had no trouble accepting a totally benevolent deity, but he hated the atonement.[12] He wanted a scripture of the heart, not the Bible. He came to learn some Christian doctrine, but he believed the study of comparative religion undermined the claim of Christ's uniqueness.

The reality of moral evil and his own suffering from tuberculosis troubled him. He said to his friend Severn: "I now understand how you can bear all this—it is your Christian faith." But he had chosen his own "vale of soul-making." He said to Severn: "I can't believe in your book—the Bible—but I feel the horrible want of some faith."[13] At the end, he wanted Jeremy Taylor's *Holy Living and Dying*. He was given ecclesiastical burial, and those present heard intoned: "Man that is born of woman hath but a short time to live, and is full of misery. He cometh up and is cut down, like a flower."[14] He was twenty-six.

---

1. Harold Bloom, ed., *John Keats* (New York: Chelsea House, 1985), 1. Keats fed on Milton, Spenser, Wordsworth. There are as many as ninety-two allusions to the Bible, particularly the Old Testament.
2. Robert M. Ryan, *Keats: The Religious Sense* (Princeton, N.J.: Princeton University Press, 1976), 46.
3. W. Jackson Bate, *John Keats* (Cambridge: Belknap, 1963), 28.
4. Ibid., 128.
5. Ibid., 265. Keats argues in "Ode to a Grecian Urn" that "beauty is truth, truth beauty." At this early stage his subjectivity already is total.
6. His brother Tom's hemorrhaging and death devastated him. "All is not well" he conceded.
7 Morris Dickstein, "The World of the Early Poems," in *John Keats*, 49ff.
8 Ryan, *Keats: The Religious Sense*, 18. We must remember that clergy were not trained much in either theology or homiletics.
9. Ibid., 29. A letter written to help his sister pass her confirmation examination shows that Keats knew some Bible doctrine.
10. Ibid., 90. Did Keats later reject terming Christianity a "vulgar superstition" when he indicates he would rather be "a clapping bell" in some Kamchatkan missionary church "than with these horrid moods be left in lurch" (165).
11. *John Keats*, 136. This is from his sonnet, "Written in Disgust of Vulgar Superstition."
12. Ryan, *Keats: The Religious Sense*, 112, 199. Benjamin Bailey had considerable doubt about the reliability of imagination.
13. Ibid., 214. At one point, he read deeply in Joseph Milner's conservative *A History of the Christian Church*.
14. Ibid., 217. "I cannot understand this," he said as he died. His doctor wrote, "He has no religion." Here we see the tragic shipwreck of a very gifted man who followed Enlightenment rationalism and Romanticism to the bitter end.

7.4   THE BRACING CHARACTER OF THE VICTORIANS

We may not need to be informed, but we do need to be reminded.
                                                                —Samuel Johnson

The Victorian age—so called because it corresponds roughly to the sixty-three years of Victoria's reign in England (1837–1901)—is caricatured.[1] Vitality surged through evangelical wings of the national churches in England, Protestant Ireland,

and Scotland. Charles Spurgeon (1834–1892), Alexander Maclaren (1826–1910), and Joseph Parker (1830–1902) drew world attention.

Yet storms of unbelief swirled, starting with René Descartes (1596–1650), John Locke, and Michel Eyquem de Montaigne (1533–1592). "The inner experience of the isolated self" loomed.[2] Social critic Matthew Arnold (1822–1888) in "Dover Beach" heard "the melancholy, long, withdrawing roar" of the recession of faith. Historian philosopher Joseph Renan (1823–1892) perceived "God dwindling into the distance."[3] Idealism, rationalism, Romanticism, and early existentialism inflicted casualties. But Bible-believing Christian faith flourished. Author Thomas De Quincey (1785–1859) may have lamented that man is "the eternal prisoner of his own past acts" and felt profoundly "the fathomless solitude of death,"[4] but Robert Browning saw God at the center of human existence.[5]

---

1. For a survey of the Victorian pulpit, see Larsen, *The Company of the Preachers,* chap. 9.
2. J. Hillis Miller, *The Disappearance of God: Five Nineteenth Century Writers* (Cambridge: Belknap, 1963), 8.
3. Ibid., 7. "Resolve to be yourself" is Arnold's final platform in delineating the "absence of God."
4. Ibid., 61. In his "artificial paradise of opium," poor DeQuincey could only bemoan: "Man, alas, cannot see" (31).
5. Ibid., 155. Browning wrote: "A poet's affair is with God, to whom he is accountable and of whom is his reward."

7.4.1 Browning, Greatest Victorian

> I say the acknowledgment of God in Christ
> Accepted by reason, solves for thee
> All questions in the world and out of it,
> And hath so far advanced thee to be wise.
>
> —Robert Browning
> "Death in the Desert"

It could be argued that Robert Browning (1812–1889) was the most significant Victorian poet. William Lyon Phelps (1865–1943), the brilliant Browning scholar from Yale, said that Browning was the most definitely Christian of all the English poets, the most sure of his ground. He called him "the happiest man in the nineteenth century."[1] Josiah Royce, addressing the Boston Browning Society, paid tribute to the poet for his contribution to "the Christian concept of God."[2] Samuel Clemens loved Browning, and Scottish preacher A. J. Gossip acknowledged his indebtedness.[3] The influential English preacher John A. Hutton wrote a book on Browning's Christian impact.[4] Through much of his life, he was not appreciated, but finally recognition came.

He is not as perfect a craftsman as Tennyson, but his verse is rugged, original and pulsating. He is exceedingly robust in tempo. Sense the galloping of the horses in his magnificent "How They Brought the Good News from Ghent to Aix."[5]

Born in London, his father was a bank clerk who had a personal library of six thousand books and knew *The Iliad,* the *Odes* of Horace, and much of the Bible by heart. His mother was called by Thomas Carlyle "a fine type of Scottish gentlewoman," although she was as much German as Scottish by heritage. She was a strict nonconformist and raised Browning in a Congregationalist chapel. Browning got his great love for animals from his mother, who was able to tame butterflies. (In the 295 lines of "Caliban," he makes sixty-three references to animals.)

Paul Johnson contends that Browning was the most learned of the English poets, though he did not attend Oxbridge because nonconformists were not admitted. Johnson quotes Chesterton that Browning obtained his learning "in the same casual manner in which a boy learns to play cricket or walk."[6] He started writing verse very early, and his mother brushed his hair to the strains of Isaac Watts's hymns. He was ready to meet "the disruptive influence" of Shelley when he read him, although "Queen Mab" made him a vegetarian for two years.[7] Oscar Wilde thought Browning second only to Shakespeare in his ability to create exciting characterizations.[8] Whether this hyperbole is justified, his characters do come alive—the Greek Cleon, the Arab physician Karshish, Reformer Johannes Agricola, Rabbi Ben Ezra, and Bishop Blougram.[8]

Browning skirted atheism after reading Voltaire during a brief matriculation at the University of London. This time of uncertainty is reflected in his beautiful "Pauline." He led his friend Sarah Flower astray doctrinally before he was sent packing. She recovered quickly and wrote the verses for the hymn "Nearer, My God, to Thee." Before he was thirty, Browning knew the languages and literature of Greece, Rome, Italy, France, and Germany and had traveled to Russia.

He lived at home until middle age and his family paid for the publication of all of his early poetry. He spent much time devouring and digesting Samuel Johnson's dictionary. By age twenty, he had thirsted and hungered for God and overcome his doubts. He reflected an awed trust in such lines as:

> Shall man refuse to be aught less than God?
> Man's weakness is his glory—for the strength
> Which raises him to heaven and near God's self.
> Came spite of it—God's strength his glory is,
> For thence came with our weakness sympathy
> Which brought God down to earth a man like us.[9]

In 1845 he met Elizabeth Barrett the poetess and eloped with her, living in Italy until her death.[10] She was even more vigorously a nonconformist than he and truly loved the Bible. As her health deteriorated, Elizabeth sought clues to spiritual realities through "spiritism," which was extremely popular at the time. Browning opposed her efforts and shares his conviction in "Mr. Sludge the Medium" that cheating was going on during the seances.

Browning's meaning is at times obscure. This is a large reason why his attempts to write plays were unsuccessful. Sometimes his "bursts of half-coagulated syntax"[11] are trying. Those lapses are made up for by the charm of "Pippa's Song," in which he expresses his deeply-felt optimism that "God's in his heaven and all's right with the world." That optimism was shattered by the tragic death of his wife from tuberculosis. Browning was the master of the dramatic monologue, and "The Spanish Cloister" and "The Last Duchess" are worth perusing. His "Death in the Desert" goes to the heart of the incarnation and is written to counteract the German critic David Strauss's attempts to deny the historicity of Jesus in *Life of Christ*.[12]

Christmas Eve and Easter Day is among his strongest compositions. It contains a study of the differences among three places for living Christian faith in the light of the resurrection—St. Peter's in Rome, the musty critical lecture hall in Göttingen, or the little nonconformist chapel with "Mr. Irons bawling out his sermons."[13] He grapples with how hard it is to be a Christian and the difficulty of believing, yet his heart is with the chapel, with the Word of God and the gospel.

Browning did not surrender either transcendence or immanence but held them in proper creative tension. He saw the ruin of "Romantic Prometheanism" and picked up the pieces for the believing of his generation. His majestic "Saul," on the Old Testament king, is a case in point. He speaks of God more than does any other major poet of the time, and his conviction that Christ is God and Savior is the foundation of all for time and eternity.[14] He was determined to defend the essential reasonableness of Christianity against all comers. This did not ingratiate him with many in the culturally elite. He took on the Darwinians and the German critics when it was not fashionable to do so.

In *Christmas Eve and Easter Day,* Browning reminds us of the Second Advent, a rare theme among the poets:

> Earth breaks up, time drops away,
> In flows heaven, with its new day
> Of endless life, when he who trod,
> Very man and very God,
> This earth in weakness, shame and pain,
> Dying the death whose signs remain
> Up yonder on the accursed tree—
> Shall come again, no more to be
> Of captivity the thrall,
> But the one God, all in all,
> King of Kings, Lord of Lords,
> As his servant John received the words
> "I died, and live forevermore."[15]

---

1. William Lyon Phelps, *Autobiography with Letters* (New York: Oxford University Press, 1939), 207ff. Phelps was one of Yale's most popular professors and a Browning scholar. This is an outstanding autobiography. Phelps heard D. L. Moody and Ira Sankey and shares reasoned impressions that illuminate many people of letters.
2. M. Whitcomb Hess, "Browning: An English Kierkegaard," *The Christian Century,* 2 May 1962, 569.

3. Phelps, *Autobiography with Letters,* 65.

4. John A. Hutton, *Further Guidance from Robert Browning in Matters of Faith* (London: Hodder and Stoughton, 1929).

5. W. E. Williams, *Browning: A Selection* (New York: Penguin Books, 1954).

6. Paul Johnson, *The Birth of the Modern: World Society 1815–1830* (New York: Harper/Collins, 1991), 727.

7. Maisie Ward, *Robert Browning and His World: The Private Face 1812–1861* (New York: Holt, Rinehart, 1967), 30.

8. Donald Thomas, *Robert Browning: A Life Within Life* (New York: Viking, 1982).

9. Ward, *Robert Browning and His World,* 59. These six lines were in the original "Paracelsus" but dropped by Browning at Pisa.

10. Elizabeth Barrett Browning was an outstanding poetess in her own right: See "Aurora Leigh" and "Sonnets from the Portuguese." An excellent recent study is Margaret Forster's *Elizabeth Barrett Browning* (New York: Doubleday, 1986). Her most famous lines are: "Earth's crammed with heaven and every common bush aglow with God; but only he who sees, takes off his shoes." The romance of this couple is dramatized on stage and in the film *The Barretts of Wimpole Street.*

11. J. Hillis Miller, *The Disappearance of God: Five Nineteenth Century Writers* (Cambridge: Belknap, 1963), 88.

12. M. Whitcomb Hess, "Browning and Kierkegaard as Heirs of Luther," *Christian Century,* 19 June 1963, 799ff.

13. Ward, *Robert Browning and His World,* 26. See also James Wesley Ingles, "Browning's 'Christmas-Eve,'" *Christianity Today,* 7 December 1959, 6; "Browning's 'Easter-Day,'" *Christianity Today,* 11 April 1960, 5. Ugly little Zion Chapel in great Dickensian realism is home. The sermon as described had ten headings and a quaint hermeneutic.

14. Augustus Hopkins Strong, *The Great Poets and Their Theology* (Philadelphia: American Baptist, 1897), 430.

15. Ibid., 238. From 1871 to 1877, when he was sixty-five, he wrote twenty-five thousand lines of poetry, "very little of which is weak."

7.4.2 TENNYSON, GALLANT VICTORIAN

> Strong Son of God, immortal Love,   "That God, which ever lives and loves,
> Whom we, that have not seen thy face,   One God, one law, one element. . . .
>
> By faith, and faith alone, embrace,   And one far-off divine event,
> Believing where we cannot prove";   To which the whole creation moves.
>   —Alfred, Lord Tennyson
>   Opening and closing couplets, *In Memoriam*

When Wordsworth died in 1850, Alfred Tennyson (1809–1892) became the poet laureate of England. A young man of such promise, he bore all the marks of success, in contrast to Browning, who seemed the perennial loser. Tennyson better fit the role of the Victorian. Coupled with undercurrents of self-doubt and a kind of obsession with death, he was euphoric about what poetry can do:

> Methinks I see the world's renewed youth
> A long day's dawn, when Poesy shall bind
> Falsehood beneath the altar of great Truth.
> —from a sonnet in 1828 when Tennyson was nineteen

He gives us better music than Browning and is crystalline in clarity but lacks something of the verve and willingness to risk and venture that we sense in his contemporary.

Tennyson was born in the tiny village of Somersby near Lincoln. Here his father preached in a church so small it was crowded when thirty-seven people were present. The rectory was directly across the road and well-remembered by the poet ("Ode to Memory"). His father had been disinherited and "was increasingly depressed, alcoholic and epileptic."[1] He had been forced into the ministry against his will, and while his marriage was not harmonious, he was the father of twelve children. Something of "the black blood" seemed to infect all of the Tennyson males, and Alfred suffered frequent bouts with melancholy. "Temperamentally the nonconformist,"[2] the Rev. George Tennyson loved the classics and forced Alfred, his favorite son, to recite by rote the *Odes* of Horace when he was six years old. His Aunt Mary's hyper-Calvinism seemed to consign all her relatives to hell, though she was "fervidly confident of her own election to eternal bliss."[3] Nothing in the Christian faith had thus far been very attractive. He began writing early, often in the manner of Pope.

At eighteen, he went up to Trinity College at Cambridge, where from 1827 to 1831 he was contemporary to Charles Darwin (1808–1882). His "lonely sensibilities" and "morbid shyness" made him feel awkward, and he left without taking a degree. Quite the eccentric, he became a convinced rationalist and high-and-dry in theology and churchmanship. He seemed always in the throes of doubt. Charles Simeon (1759–1836), the great evangelical preacher at Holy Trinity, was exerting a powerful influence on many at this time, but young Tennyson was more drawn to the German idealists and critics of Scripture.[4] He had affinity for F. D. Maurice (1805–1872) and Charles Kingsley (1819–1875) and the other Christian Socialists. He and Arthur Hallam (1811–1833) were leaders of a group called "the Apostles." Hallam had come up from Eton, where his best friend had been the future prime minister of England, William E. Gladstone (1809–1898).[5] Hallam was engaged to Tennyson's sister, Emily, but died tragically while visiting Vienna with his father. After the tragedy, Tennyson began to write "In Memoriam," on which he worked for seventeen years. This remarkable piece has 131 sections and "the directness of the dramatic spoken word."[6] Frances Patton, president of old Princeton Seminary, was so taken with the poem that he was said to have quoted at least one line from it in every sermon he preached.

What especially endeared Tennyson to the Apostles was his receipt of the Chancellor's Prize for a long poem, "Armageddon," he had written when he was fourteen under the prescribed title, "Timbuctoo."[7] Among members of the group critical of Tennyson the aesthete were Richard Trench, later archbishop of Dublin, author of works on the miracles and parables of Christ and the first to propose the Oxford English Dictionary; as well as Henry Alford, who became Dean of Canterbury and translator of the Greek New Testament.

Tennyson was tall and athletic, "a great-boned, loose-limbed, gigantesque man, with domed head, soft dark hair, gentle eyes."[8] Yet he was psychologically frail, and when his father died in 1831, he had a total nervous collapse. He was under pressure to take holy orders. Hallam's death in 1833 led to years of poetic silence from 1833 to 1842 that were interrupted only by entries in his diary. He married Emily Sellwood in 1850 and issued *In Memoriam* at last. This publication made his professional reputation and assured his selection as poet laureate. He continued to write notable poetry even after his last serious illness began in 1888.

Tennyson is part of "the art school of poets," in which form seems frequently emphasized over substance (Keats is a salient example of this set of priorities). Perhaps his most moving defense of his idea of poetry is to be found in "The Hesperides." Other earlier works that should not be ignored are such poems as "The Lotus-Eaters," "Lady of Shalott," "The Palace of Art," and "A Dream of Fair Women." As already noted (3.8), Tennyson returned several times to the Arthurian legend and Christianized it, as in his twelve books of poetry called *Idylls of the King*. "Break, break, break" allows the reader to hear the waves pounding on the shore. "Locksley Hall" has a Victorian vision of peace and a misogynistic treatment of women. President Kennedy's favorite poetic lines are from "Ulysses":

> We are not now that strength which in old days
> Moved earth and heaven; that which we are, we are;
> One equal temper of heroic hearts,
> Made weak by time and fate, but strong in will
> To strive, to seek, to find, and not to yield.

Maud is a lengthy monodrama of great lyric beauty and force, which greatly affected the future literary critic and educator Phelps (see p. 227).[9]

Ever so slowly, Tennyson moved from orthodox Christian faith. Some proto-Darwinian notes are sounded early in Tennyson, and he essentially accepted the hypothesis. He assailed the literal-mindedness of evangelical piety as self-righteous and intolerant.[10] His compatriots were the broad churchman A. P. Stanley; Maurice, who was suspended from King's College for his higher critical views; and Benjamin Jowett from Oxford, who wrote some of his controversial work under the poet's roof. In "Sea Dreams," he undoubtedly is thinking of the well-know evangelical preacher John Cummings when he parodies "this Boanerges with his threats of doom and loud-lung'd Antibabylonianisms."[11]

Tennyson satisfies deeply with "Charge of the Light Brigade,"[12] and with the haunting "Rizpah," from the obscure biblical text about the tragedy of the concubine of King Saul (2 Sam. 3:7–12; 21:1–14). William Cullen Bryant (1794–1878) also picked up this story. The sermon in "Aylmer's Field" is of interest. More telling is the tribute to Tennyson by the notoriously heretical Bishop of Natal in Africa, John William Colenso (1813–1883). By the time

The Origin of Species was published in 1859, Tennyson had moved far afield. Darwin's theories worried him because of the implications regarding human animality. While he believed in human sinfulness (see his "The Vision of Sin"), he espoused what he liked to call "The Higher Pantheism," which is rife with his evolutionary vision. His affinity for James Frazer's *The Golden Bough* (1890) and his short piece "By an Evolutionist," or his disillusionment in "Despair" show how thin had become the veneer of orthodox faith as Tennyson neared the end of his life.

Still he charms us with "Flower in the Crannied Wall." His "Crossing the Bar" (1889) has often been spoken or sung at Christian funerals. However, the intellectual elitism he championed jeopardized the gospel. Tennyson stands as an example of the less-than-persuaded.

Contrasting Victorian biographies are to be seen in Cecil Woodham-Smith's *Florence Nightingale*[13] and Irving Stone, *The Origin: A Biographical Novel of Charles Darwin*.[14] Lytton Strachey's *Eminent Victorians*[15] treats such personalities as Cardinal Henry Manning (1808–1892), Florence Nightingale (1820–1910), and General Charles George Gordon of Khartoum (1833–1885). Strachey shows General Gordon's eccentric evangelicalism and indefatigable distribution of Samuel Clarke's *Scripture Promises*. Such works give us the Victorian "feel."

---

1. *The Birth of the Modern,* 730.
2. Jerome Hamilton Buckley, *Tennyson: The Growth of a Poet* (Cambridge, Mass.: Harvard University Press, 1973), 3. Probably the best two biographies of Tennyson are *Tennyson: The Unquiet Mind* by Robert Bernard Martin (London: Faber, 1983) and *Tennyson* by Peter Levi (New York: Macmillan, 1994).
3. Buckley, *Tennyson: The Growth of a Poet,* 5. George Tennyson had been forced into the ministry against his will and deeply resented his father.
4. Ibid., 25. Charles Simeon had as great an influence at Cambridge as Newman had at Oxford. He was rector at Holy Trinity Church for fifty-three years. Cambridge still has evangelical strength. See "Cambridge Evangelicals," *Christian Century,* 27 October 1993, 1036ff. A dozen churches are identified that stressed expository preaching.
5. Thomas R. Lounsbury, *The Life and Times of Tennyson* (New York: Russell and Russell, 1962), 599–615.
6. Buckley, *Tennyson: The Growth of a Poet,* 115. A lack of cohesion is reflected in its first title, *Fragments of an Elegy.*
7. Douglas Bush, ed., *Alfred Tennyson: Selected Poetry* (New York: Modern Library, 1951).
8. *The Great Poets and Their Theology,* 463.
9. William Lyon Phelps, *Autobiography with Letters* (New York: Oxford University, 1939), 463. First reading of Maud.
10. *Tennyson: The Growth of a Poet,* 137. He also attacked Richard Cobden and John Bright.
11. Ibid., 139. Cumming was a Scottish Presbyterian who pastored the National Scots Church of Crown Court in London, 1832–1879. He was polemically anti-Roman Catholic and a premillennarian. An article on his ministry is found in Nigel M.

de S. Cameron, ed., *Dictionary of Scottish Church History and Theology* (Downers Grove, Ill.: InterVarsity, 1993), 227. He predicted the last vial of the apocalypse would be poured out in 1867. When that did not happened, his popularity declined.

12. Cecil Woodham-Smith, *The Reason Why* (New York: McGraw-Hill, 1953). This study explains—"Theirs not to reason why, theirs but to do and die." The reason is the ridiculously antiquated and inefficient system then used.

13. New York: McGraw-Hill, 1951.

14. New York: New American Library, 1981.

15. Garden City, N.J.: Garden City, n.d.

7.4.3 THOMPSON, GRIM VICTORIAN

> I fled Him, down the nights and down the days;
> I fled Him, down the arches of the years;
> I fled Him, down the labyrinthine ways
> Of my own mind; and in the midst of tears
> I hid from Him, and under running laughter.
> Up vistaed hopes, I sped;
> And shot, precipitated,
> Adown Titanic glooms of chasmed fears,
> From those strong Feet that followed, followed after.
>
> —Francis Thompson
> "The Hound of Heaven"

"The Hound of Heaven" is quoted more often than any other single poem from Western pulpits. Its author, Francis Thompson (1859–1907), was as pitiable an individual as any introduced in this volume. He was born in Preston, Lancashire. His father, Charles, a medical doctor, was the brother of Edward Healy Thompson, professor of English literature in the university at Dublin. The brothers were deeply devout converts to Roman Catholicism. Francis likewise was fervent and sought to enter the priesthood, but he was rejected because of signs of emotional instability. His father sent him to Manchester to study medicine. After failing his examinations three times in six years, he left for London in 1885.

His health began to fail, and he became an opium addict. He subsisted by selling matches and newspapers and working in a shoemaker's shop. He would sleep near Covent Garden where street people still gather. After a suicide attempt, he began to write verse. A publisher, Wilfrid Meynell, saw his potential and encouraged him.[1]

His poems show the influence of metaphysical poet Richard Crashaw (1612–1649), another convert to Catholicism (7.1.3), and of Shelley, whom he greatly admired. "The Hound of Heaven" has a kind of seventeenth-century framework. Other unusual Thompson poems include "The Mistress of Vision," "Ode After Easter," "In No Strange Land: The Kingdom of God Is Within You," and "To a Snowflake."[2] More well known are the charming child's lines:

> Little Jesus, wast Thou shy
> Once, and just as small as I?

One of his poems seems to have the idea of radiation in it.[3] In 1892 he moved into a Sussex monastery where he did some of his best writing as he struggled with tuberculosis.[4] There he died in 1907. Biographer Brigid Boardman maintained that the tendency to excess marred his poetry and his whole life.

In "The Hound of Heaven," the shepherd God relentlessly pursues the straying, lost sheep. R. H. Ives Gammell, the well-known painter, began in 1930 a cycle of paintings based on "The Hound of Heaven," in which he portrays "the stripped soul of Everyman who seeks and finds a home in heaven."[5] C. S. Lewis expresses a very similar metaphor to Thompson's as he speaks of "God closing in" on him.[6] No one has expressed this better than has "The Hound of Heaven":

> But with unhurrying chase,
> And unperturbèd pace,
> Deliberate speed, majestic instancy,
> They beat—and a Voice beat
> More instant than the Feet.

---

1. Gilbert Thomas, "Francis Thompson After Fifty Years," *Christian Century,* 13 August 1958, 925–26.
2. Pat Alexander, ed., *Eerdmans Book of Christian Poetry* (Grand Rapids: Eerdmans, 1981), 77.
3. "Francis Thompson After Fifty Years," 926. A strange anticipation of electrical energy is seen in his "Orient Ode."
4. Everard Meynell, *The Life of Francis Thompson* (London: Burns and Oates, 1920). A disorderly life is traced.
5. Rachel Heise and Daniel James Sundahl, "R. H. Ives Gammell and Francis Thompson," *Chronicles of Culture,* January 1994, 47. Gammell's work was in stark contrast to the "modern art establishment."
6. C. S. Lewis, *Surprised by Joy* (London: Fontana, 1955), 179: "The hounds barely a field behind." For an exploration of the seeking God, see excellent case studies in Hugh T. Kerr and John M. Mulder, eds., *Conversions* (Grand Rapids: Eerdmans, 1983). Another vantage point is by Jewish scholar Alan F. Segal, who argues that conversion is the Pauline paradigm in *Paul the Convert* (New Haven, Conn.: Yale University Press, 1990). See also David L. Larsen, *The Evangelism Mandate* (Wheaton, Ill.: Crossway, 1992), 13–42.

7.4.4 SWINBURNE, GROTESQUE VICTORIAN

I could worship the dying lamb were it not for his leprous bride.
—A. C. Swinburne

The full and tragic harvest of Enlightenment and Romantic defection from historic Christianity is seen in "the utterly perverted moral sense" and violent paganism of the brilliant poet, Algernon Charles Swinburne (1837–1909). He was born to wealth in London. Both parents were ardent Anglo-Catholics caught up in the Oxford Movement.[1] Swinburne was at Eton from 1849 to 1853. There he began his life practice of self-flagellation. His biographer Henderson makes the case for his unusual brilliance—perhaps almost as learned as Milton or Browning.[2] Swinburne was at Oxford from 1856 to 1860 but did not take his degree. One of his best friends was Edwin Hatch of *Hatch and Redpath Septuagint Concordance* fame. Hatch was a poet in his own right, as in his exquisite hymn, "Breathe on Me, Breath of God." The friends took different courses.

Residing in Chelsea, London, from 1860 to 1863, Swinburne absorbed the work of the Marquis de Sade (1740–1814) and Charles Baudelaire's (1821–1867) "feline style of beauty." He wrote plays after the Greek classical model. He was under the spell of Shelley and Victor-Marie Hugo (1802–1885). He wrote on Blake. Excitable, even bizarre as an individual, Swinburne's poetic style is lilting and elegant. Such poems as "When the Hounds of Spring" and "An Interlude" are vivid.

His life was a wreck of intemperance. He was an alcoholic, and his defiance of convention led to homosexuality. Ralph Waldo Emerson (1803–1882) described him as a sodomite. He studied Walt Whitman's *Leaves of Grass* (incongruously alongside Dickens, whose works he read through every three years). He plummeted in depression and loneliness until the well-known critic and man of letters Theodore Watts-Dunton sheltered him in 1879. He spent the last thirty years of his life at the Pines in Putney.

Sick of "Victorian pieties," he spoke against an age "that has room only for those who write for children and girls." Most fascinating is Swinburne's evident fascination with the Christian doctrines he detested. Behind what can be shocking vulgarity, "Before a Crucifix" is significant as the author finds he cannot dodge the impact of Calvary. He confronts "this piteous God" with "lean limbs that shew the labouring bones, and ghastly mouth that gapes and groans."[3] He puzzles over the necessity of the cross and its impact. He addresses Christ, "if indeed thou be not dead." He marvels at the attachment to the cross after nineteen centuries.

> So still, for all man's tears and creeds,
> The sacred body hangs and bleeds.

He inquires: "Is there a gospel in the red old witness of thy wide-mouthed wounds?"[4] He sees the haunting "phantom of a Christless cross," sneering at the idea that this cross can remedy the human plight—but in the last stanza he calls for the inescapable cross to be hidden and to "be no more."

For a neglected view of the Victorians, read the works of Gertrude Himmelfarb, such as *The Demoralization of Society: From Victorian Virtues to Modern Values*.[5] She shows that the Victorians took sin seriously. Her quarrel is with the liberalism of John Stuart Mill who divorced law and morality. The Victorian rate of illegitimacy rose from 5 percent to 7 percent in 1845 and fell back to 4 percent in 1900. Whatever the faults of the Victorians, they elevated the family.

---

1. David Newsome, *The Parting of Friends: The Wilburforces and Henry Manning* (Grand Rapids: Eerdmans, 1966). This is a deeply moving study of the tensions created by the conversion of Manning and Newman to Roman Catholicism.
2. Philip Henderson, *Swinburne: Portrait of a Poet* (New York: Macmillan, 1974). Fascinated by all deviation.
3. A. C. Swinburne, *Collected Poetical Works,* I (New York: Harper, 1927), 741. He was "an inimitable parodist."
4. Ibid., 744. Extremely deaf and very depressed in old age, his final works were examples of a shrill jingoism.
5. New York: Knopf, 1995.

7.4.5 ROSSETTI, GENTLE VICTORIAN

> What can I give Him, poor as I am?
> If I were a shepherd, I would bring a lamb;
> If I were a wise man, I would do my part;
> Yet what can I give Him—Give my heart.
> —Christina Rosetti
> "In the Bleak Midwinter"

One of four children born to a noted Dante scholar who abandoned his wife, Christina Rossetti (1830–1894) was educated at home in London. She wrote some of the finest lyric poetry of her time. Her two brothers followed their father into agnosticism, but Christina and her sister Maria were staunch Anglicans with their mother. The mother, Frances Rossetti was an evangelical who believed in "the absolute and divine truth of everything to be found in the Old and New Testament."[1] While they were High Church Anglicans, they opposed all "romanizing" tendencies. Christina shared her mother's "warlike spirit." Their home was a rich and stimulating environment—brother Gabriel was a painter and poet, and William was a writer.[2]

Christina made her debut writing poetry in 1847. Her verse often has a "broken-hearted motif."[3] She turned down one suitor when he became a Roman Catholic. At the age of seventeen, she was moved by the attention of a well-known poet then thirty-six years old, but he was married. She believed that sin "like the upas tree emits a poisonous influence."[4] Divorce was not an option. Much of her poetry reflects Scripture, as her beautiful "A Bruised Reed Shall He Not Break" or the funeral anthem for her father, which she wrote based on Hebrews 12:5. She and Gerard Manley Hopkins (7.4.6) corresponded appreciatively about their poetry. She worked at Highgate, the institution for unwed mothers. After turning down another avid suitor on religious grounds, she plunged into depression and wrote such classics as "By the Waters of Babylon" and "Despised and Rejected." When her irreligious brothers and close friends dabbled in spiritism (popular among such Victorians as Elizabeth Barrett Browning, Arthur Conan Doyle, and Oliver Lodge), Christina rebuked them.[5]

She knew Swinburne but pasted strips of paper over certain of his "irreligious" lines. She zealously sought to win various of the "Pre-Raphaelite Brotherhood," to which her brothers belonged.

She was a lover of assonance in form (believing that rhyme may be for the eye rather than the ear). Perhaps she wrote too much, but everything I have read of Rossetti is gripping—see especially "A Better Resurrection" and "O Lord, Seek Us."

With the death of her family, she became a recluse after 1890 and struggled with pulmonary problems and Grave's Disease. In her last years, she became more mystical and read Emily Dickinson. She believed Dickinson had "a Blakean gift."[6] She wrote until her death. Now hunched as "a mysterious black-robed figure" and crushed by cancer in her chest and shoulders, she died on December 29, 1894. Here is another leading Victorian poet whose life was suffused with biblical faith. When everything collapsed around her at the end, she bore stalwart witness to the sustaining grace and goodness of God in "None Other Lamb":

> None other Lamb, none other Name,
> None other hope in heaven, or earth or sea,
> None other hiding place from guilt and shame,
> None beside Thee.
>
> My faith burns low, my hope burns low;
> Only my heart's desire cries out in me,
> By the deep thunder of its want and woe
> Cries out to Thee.
>
> Lord, Thou art life though I be dead;
> Love's Fire art Thou, however cold I be;
> Nor heaven have I, nor place to lay my head
> Nor home, but Thee.

---

1. Lona Mosk Packer, *Christina Rossetti* (Berkeley: University of California, 1963), 5. This work is much to be preferred to the more recent piece by Jan Marsh, *Christina Rossetti: A Writer's Life* (New York: Viking, 1995), which, like so much psychobiography, advances without evidence the notion of parental sexual abuse. This trend is ridiculous.
2. See Dante Gabriel Rossetti, *Ballads and Sonnets* (London: Ellis and White, 1881). There is no soaring or lilt in this poetry.
3. Packer, *Christina Rossetti,* 24. Christina was a great reader and a lover of the hymns of Reginald Heber.
4. Ibid., 61. Her "Letter and Spirit" is a devotional commentary on the Ten Commandments.
5. Ibid., 212. When Tennyson died, some proposed Christina for poet laureate, but not Queen Victoria.
6. Ibid., 383. One has spoken of her elegance as a kind of "chastity of speech." Quite

Victorian indeed. The Pre-Raphaelite Brotherhood included such artists as Christina's brother Gabriel, Holman Hunt (1827–1910), and John Millais (1829–1896). They inclined toward detailed representation of nature in its simplicity and power.

7.4.6 HOPKINS, RESTLESS VICTORIAN

> And for all this, nature is never spent;
> There lives the dearest freshness, deep down things;
> And though the last lights off the black West went
> Oh, morning, at the brown brink eastward, springs—
> Because the Holy Ghost over the bent
> World broods with warm breast and with ah! bright wings.
> —Gerard Manley Hopkins
> "God's Grandeur"

Gerard Manley Hopkins (1844–1889) met and corresponded with Christina Rossetti. His extraordinary poems are not numerous, certainly not in comparison with her production, and they were not published until his friend Robert Bridges brought them to the public thirty years after his death. Still they demand attention.

Hopkins was the oldest of eleven children born in a middle-class Essex family of strong Anglican convictions. As early as grammar school at Highgate, he won prizes for poetry. He went up to Balliol College, Oxford University, where he soon accompanied the Oxford Movement in its lurch toward Roman Catholicism. In these years, he experimented with word rhythms in poems.[1]

Benjamin Jowett (1817–1893), the great classicist, was his first tutor, and H. P. Liddon (1829–1890), who became dean of St. Paul's in London, was his close friend.[2] In his years at Oxford (1863–67), he was influenced by Walter Pater (1839–1894), an essayist who carried the torch for the "art for art's sake" point-of-view, and art critic John Ruskin (1819–1900). His poetry strikes us at times as Parnassian in style in the mode of Pope, Milton, and Spenser. Yet there is the surge of Keats and the Pre-Raphaelite artists as well. Reformer Girolamo Savonarola of Florence (1452–1498) was one of his heroes. He cherished the poetry of Frederick Faber (1814–1863), who converted to Roman Catholicism, became a priest, and wrote such hymns as "Faith of Our Fathers."

In 1865 Hopkins entered a time of spiritual crisis, and in 1866 he was received into the Roman Catholic Church by John Henry Newman.[3] No one else in his family followed him, and in his loneliness he identified with Duns Scotus, the Franciscan professor at Oxford. He treasured the medieval theologian's "validation of the individual."[4]

In 1868 he became a Jesuit, receiving theological training in Northern Wales. He burned much of his earlier poetry. He was not successful in pursuing theology as a career, nor as a parish priest in four parishes in England and Wales. Recorded sermons preached in Liverpool gyrate between rationalism and sentimentality. He concluded that "written sermons do no good." Overweening sentimentality extended to his poetry, which was self-indulgent and had a low emotional flashpoint in the estimation of biographer Robert Bernard Martin.[5]

In 1875 his rector urged him to give up an extreme asceticism and to write poetry. He immediately wrote a masterpiece, "The Wreck of the Deutschland," in memory of five Franciscan nuns who had drowned that year. This is really the poem of his conversion to Rome. An even more satisfying piece is "Windhover," in which we sense his ties with Marvell and Milton. Here is the "Christ-assaulted heart."[6] When these poems were turned down for publication, he totally gave up the idea of seeing them in print.

Hopkins was an intensely original poet. His introductions are almost abrupt—his work has a Wordsworthian "naked straight-forwardness." His use of what he called "sprung rhythm" (intricate wordplays, puns, internal rhymes, as William Rose Benet defines it),[7] and his "bizarre compound words" achieve "verbal freshness."[8] In an "age of dilution," here is something full and lush. In 1884 he became professor of Greek in Dublin and began to write his "Sonnets of Desolation," which were almost inchoate because of their deep emotion. "To seem a stranger lies my lot," he said. "I wake and feel the fell of dark, not day." "To Seem the Stranger" is his most autobiographical work. There is a sensuous quality in Hopkins, which helps us understand the appeal of the Roman liturgy. In "The Wreck," he contemplates the names of the suffering Savior.

Hopkins's behavior became increasingly eccentric before he contracted typhoid and died at age forty-four. He was almost always in depression or on the edge of despair, particularly after his friend Digby Dolben drowned in 1865. He also was obsessed with fears of illness and obsessed with thoughts of his death. And yet there came to him the hope of resurrection in his "That Nature Is a Heraclitean Fire":

> But vastness blurs and time beats level. Enough! the Resurrection,
> A heart's-clarion! Away grief's gasping, joyless days, dejection.
> Across my foundering deck shone
> A beacon, an eternal beam. Flesh fade and mortal trash
> Fall to a residuary worm; world's wildfire, leave but ash:
> In a flash, at a trumpet crash
> I am all at once what Christ is, since he was what I am, and
> This Jack, joke, poor potsherd, patch, matchwood, immortal diamond,
> Is immortal Diamond.

1. W. H. Gardner, ed., *Poems of Gerard Manley Hopkins* (New York: Oxford University Press, 1948), xviii.

2. For more on H. P. Liddon, see *The Company of the Preachers,* 10.6.6.

3. On John Henry Newman, see ibid., 9.3.3. Newman went over to Roman Catholicism in 1845, but Liddon remained an Anglican.

4. Harold Bloom, ed., *Gerard Manley Hopkins* (New York: Chelsea House, 1986), 7.

5. Robert Bernard Martin, *Gerard Manley Hopkins: A Very Private Life* (New York: G. P. Putnam, 1991), 322.

6. Geoffrey G. Hartman, "The Dialectic of Sense-Perception" in *Gerard Manley Hopkins,* 25. Note also the poem "Peace."

7. Benet, *Benet's Reader's Encyclopedia*, 459. In this collection find the Hopkins poems "Pied Beauty" and "Spring."

8. Anthony Burgess, "The Ecstasy of Gerard Manley Hopkins," *New York Times Book Review*, 17 August 1989, 15.

7.4.7 ARNOLD, AGNOSTIC VICTORIAN

> The Sea of Faith
> Was once, too, at the full, and toward earth's shore
> Lay like the folds of a bright girdle furled.
> But now I only hear
> Its melancholy, long, withdrawing tear,
> Retreating to the breath
> Of the night wind, down the vast edges drear
> And naked shingles of the world.
>
> —Matthew Arnold
> "Dover Beach"

Even while Spurgeon, Maclaren, Liddon, and Parker were preaching powerfully to the masses in Britain, the recession of faith was taking place rather widely. Matthew Arnold (1822–1888) was the son of the distinguished broad churchman and educator, Thomas Arnold, most famous for his tenure at Rugby. So commanding a presence was the elder Arnold that when his son saw the Himalayan Mountains, he was reminded of his father. He attended Winchester and Rugby and then Balliol College. His anticlerical inclinations turned him to law, but he also taught briefly at Rugby and became inspector of schools for the government. His rather uneventful life was interrupted by the two terms as professor of poetry at Oxford.

Early in his education, he began to write prize-winning poetry and became a master "of both blank verse and statelier stanzas."[1] His wide contacts included Emerson in the United States. Some of his especially good poems include "To the Duke of Wellington" ("whose track across the fretful foam" was laudatory); "To an Independent Preacher" (his prejudice against the "heat" of his preaching ruined any listening to the message); "The Buried Life"; and "Monica's Last Prayer" (on Augustine's mother). His "Haworth Churchyard" resonates with associations to the Brontë sisters, whose father served this parish.

Eventually his poetic mine began to play out. He gave himself increasingly to essays and books on substantive issues. He has been called "the apostle of culture" and "the prophet of sweetness and light." Religion is at the heart of Victorian life, and it is the subject for Arnold. He was a liberal in politics to the point that even the Liberal Party was uneasy with his support.[2] His delight was, as Morris Dickstein puts it, "to direct a free play of thought onto subjects that had become petrified by received opinion."

The Bible was the great challenge. He felt his Anglican Church had failed, but he detested Puritans and other dissenters. When Oxford admitted the children of dissenting families, Arnold felt snobbish disgust.[3] He most appreciated the radical French critic Renan and adopted Renan's "dilettante attitude toward religion as a whole."[4] Spurgeon and other evangelicals particularly galled him.

He loved Hellenism's philosophy of truth at any price over Judeo-Christian goodness at any price. He dedicated himself to skepticism and empiricism and saw "the receding tide of the Sea of Faith" as he denied the supernatural.[5] He dismissed the cross—almost. On the very Sunday of his fatal heart attack in 1888, he heard Ian Maclaren speak on "The Shade of the Cross" and the congregation close with Isaac Watts's "When I Survey the Wondrous Cross." He walked home humming the tune and remarked: "Ah yes, the cross still stands, and in the straits of the soul makes its ancient appeal."[6]

Arnold saw the Bible as human literature and accepted higher criticism against the champions of "literalism."[7] He believed miracles to be impossible. T. S. Eliot diagnosed his substitution of culture for religion as ultimately most dissatisfying. All religions are on a continuum. Of Arnold's work *St. Paul and Protestantism,* Ruth apRoberts well observes: "Paul was more of a fundamentalist than Matthew Arnold would have him."[8] In his *Literature and Dogma,* he dismisses both prophecy and miracles as in any way evidential.[9] Natural and revealed religion are the same. Education is salvation, and "metaphor can ravish and remake the world!"[10] There can be no personal God.

Even Newman recoiled from Arnold's radical thinking.[11] He detested the Salvation Army. Still he could not just lay the Bible down. He interacted with Isaiah in his last book and cherished some of the great directors of the spiritual life like Tauler and Amiel. His hope was that poetry might prevail! He had but a few hollow husks to hold. Melancholy.

For a stethoscopic reading of negative attitudes toward evangelicals inside the Church of England and dissenters without, read Samuel Butler's *The Way of All Flesh.*[12] Butler was the son of a clergyman and grandson of a bishop, and he wrote this work from 1872 to 1884. This sharp parody of and protest against Victorianism traces the career of Theobald Pontifex, who professed evangelical conversion and was ordained. He was inundated by Darwin and Colenso and took up the cudgel against the Simeonites, as they were called (282). As Pontifex, Butler scuttled all supernaturalism. This account is fascinating in showing how evangelicals were perceived.

---

1. George Saintsbury, *Matthew Arnold* (New York: Russell and Russell, 1899), 17. The standard biography.

2. Political liberalism is a theme in one of the most recent biographies, Nicholas Murray, *A Life of Matthew Arnold* (New York: St. Martin's, 1996).

3. Saintsbury, *Matthew Arnold,* 52. Arnold projected a relaxed intensity (112).

4. Ibid., 102. "The traditional history of the Bible is not even to be considered" (141).

5. Ruth apRoberts, *Arnold and God* (Los Angeles: University of California, 1983), 3. Arnold scathingly criticized Bishop Butler because he sought absolutes.

6. E. M. Blaiklock, "Dover Beach," *His,* May 1957, 25; Roger Scruton, *The Philosopher on Dover Beach* (New York: St. Martin's, 1957). Scruton, as Arnold, preaches redemption through art and culture.

7. *Arnold and God,* 30. John W. Burgon's statement was the kind that infuriated Arnold: "The Bible is none other than The Voice of Him that sitteth upon the Throne. Every book of it—every chapter of it—every verse of it—every word of it—every syllable of it (where are we to stop?)—every letter of it—is the direct utterance of the Most High! The Bible is none other than the Word of God—not some part of it more, some part of it less, but all alike the utterance of Him who sitteth upon the Throne—absolute—faultless—unerring—supreme."

8. Ibid., 183. He saw Christianity as the "annulment of our ordinary self through the mildness of Jesus Christ" 187.

9. Matthew Arnold, *Literature and Dogma: An Essay Toward a Better Apprehension of the Bible* (Boston: James R. Osgood, 1873), 109–39. Newman said of Arnold: "But is he a Christian?"

10. *Arnold and God,* 216. In his "sweet reasonableness," Arnold is a faithful adherent of the Enlightenment.

11. Ibid., 260. Similarities to Leo Tolstoy can be seen, though Tolstoy and Arnold did not read each other's work. Two of Arnold's most important essays, "The Study of Poetry" and "Sweetness and Light" are in *Gateway to the Great Books* (Chicago: Britannica, 1963), V, 19–61.

12. New York: Modern Library, 1950.

7.4.8 KIPLING, JINGOISTIC VICTORIAN

> God of our fathers, known of old—Lord of our far-flung
> battle line—
> Beneath whose awful hand we hold Dominion over
> palm and pine—
> Lord God of Hosts, be with us yet,
> Lest we forget—lest we forget.
>
> —Rudyard Kipling
> "Recessional"

The first writer in English to win the Nobel Prize for Literature, Rudyard Kipling (1865–1936) was an immensely popular poet and writer of fiction.[1] When he wrote "The Recessional" to mark Queen Victoria's Diamond Jubilee, she was enraged because the poem clearly warned Britain that she faced the fate of Nineveh and Tyre unless she turned to God. Henry James spoke of Kipling as "the most complete man of genius I have ever known," and T. S. Eliot spoke of Kipling's "immortal genius." A writer of such gross inconsistency, he elicited intense feelings both of admiration and disdain. C. S. Lewis never "understood how any man of taste could doubt that Kipling was a great artist." While valuing the great old standard treatment by Charles Carrington and the work of J. M. S. Thompkins, I have found Philip Mason's more recent study to be of inestimable insight into Kipling and his writing.[2]

Kipling was born in Bombay. His father directed an art school. Rudyard learned Hindustani from his nurse, who also taught him stories of the jungles, which are reflected in *Jungle Book* and *Kim*. His mother was a sister of the wife of Prime Minister Stanley Baldwin (1867–1947). Raised an Anglican and conversant with the Bible and its symbols, he early rejected evangelical religion. His poem "Baa Baa Black Sheep" derides "a narrow evangelical with a strong sense of hell-fire."[3] Biographer Edmund Wilson divided Kipling's career into three phases:

1. Lively, inquiring, cocky, cosmopolitan, lapsing into vulgar showmanship.
2. Closed-minded—cautious of the sentimental.
3. Compassionate, following the death of his only son in World War I.

A private person, he loved children, as his Mowgli and Puck stories demonstrate. Swashbuckling Cecil Rhodes of South Africa was one of his heroes. His voluminous correspondence disclose an inner warmth.[4] Kipling was a lonely man and finally married an American and lived in Vermont, where he feuded with relatives and grew to hate Americans as shrill and brash. After the death of his daughter, he never returned to the United States. He settled in Sussex and continued to write.

Kipling always wrestled with fears and nightmares. He tended to be eclectic in his religious perspective, thinking that people make God in their own image. Revenge loomed large in his writing after 1915. He thinks much about death, but has no creed. The gods are blind and life is mere chance.[5] Several of his last stories have visions of heaven and hell in them. His very last story is a dialogue with angels.[6]

He died in 1936 at the age of sixty-one. He was awarded but refused to accept knighthood and the poet laureateship in 1896. The only honor he would allow to be bestowed on him was the position of rector at St. Andrews University (an honorific position *in absentia*). Still, he was the poet of the British Empire—at the very moment it was collapsing.

He always regretted not having a university education, but he learned his writing skills as a newspaper writer in India. By the time he left India, he had written many stories and poems. His *Plain Tales from the Hills* reflects the competition among the great powers for control in Central Asia.[7] *The Light That Failed* is about a newsman who lost his sight. This story sprawls into a novel and probably is somewhat autobiographical. *Captains Courageous* is a good sea story.

Browning was the greatest influence on his poetry. We sense his personal warmth and playful humor in "Fuzzy-Wuzzy," a tribute to Indian fights. His *Barrack-Room Ballads* defined the British military overseas for generations. "The Ballad of East and West" and "The White Man's Burden" are colonial jingoism in its quintessential essence.

In both his stories and poems, the language of the King James translation of the Bible echoes. His "The Road to Endor" is based on King Saul's resort to the witch of Endor from 1 Samuel 28:3–25. In it he rejects conventional spiritualism:

> Oh, the road to Endor is the oldest road,
> And the craziest road of all.
> Straight it runs to the witch's abode

As it did in the days of Saul,
And nothing much has changed of the sorrow in store
For such as go down on the road to Endor.[8]

1. Alfred Nobel (1833–1896), who established the prize, made his fortune as a Swedish inventor and sometime poet. See Kenne Fant, *Alfred Nobel* (New York: Arcade, 1991).
2. Philip Mason, *Kipling: The Glass, the Shadow and the Fire* (New York: Harper, 1975). Martin Seymour-Smith, in *Rudyard Kipling* (New York: St. Martin's, 1990), traces Kipling's nonconformist Anglo-Scottish roots, but its psycho-biography is hopelessly speculative.
3. Ibid., 32. There is defensive anger in his early work. His parents were absent, and he was raised by servants.
4. At this writing, the University of Iowa is publishing his letters, which will run to four volumes of 380 pages each, edited and annotated by Thomas Pinney. They bespeak an often generous and warm spirit and are of immense value in revealing the man.
5. *The Glass, the Shadow and the Fire,* 248. His novels resemble the plotless meandering of *Pickwick Papers, Huckleberry Finn,* and *Don Quixote.*
6. Loraine Boettner quotes this key stanza in his helpful study, *Immortality* (Philadelphia: Presbyterian and Reformed, 1956), 149.
7. Rudyard Kipling, *The Works of Rudyard Kipling* (Roslyn, N.Y.: Black's Readers Service, n.d.), 269ff.
8. Ibid., 270. He was very lonely toward the end and suffered much from a duodenal ulcer. In the vacuum, he turned to healing and astrology for solace, but found none.

7.5   *THE CACOPHONY OF THE MODERNS*

Confidence was the keynote of the Victorian Age, but hesitancy is the character of the Twentieth Century.

—Ernest Payne
Free Church Tradition in the Life of England[1]

Coming down the stretch of the nineteenth century, Christianity was tinctured with a euphoric optimism generated by the Industrial Revolution, the Enlightenment, and a social vision extrapolated from Darwinian evolution. Many in the church syncretized biblical teaching with rationalistic and hedonistic philosophies. The evidence of growth and strength at home and abroad must be seen in the context of wholesale compromise. Of course the twentieth century, with its brutal world wars; economic depression; and genocidal movements, such as the Jewish Holocaust, shattered the flimsy expectation of a technological golden age. The poets reflect and represent deeper feelings and responses during this time.

1. London: SCM, 1944.

7.5.1 YEATS, SOARING EAGLE

> Things fall apart; the centre cannot hold;
> Anarchy is loosed upon the world,
> The blood-dimmed tide is loosed, and everywhere
> The ceremy of innocence is drowned;
> The best lack all conviction, while the worst
> Are full of passionate intensity.
> Surely some revelation is at hand;
> Surely the Second Coming is at hand.
>
> —William Butler Yeats
> "The Second Coming"

Evangelical Christians are hasty to quote William Butler Yeats (1865–1939) as a coreligionist. After all, he was an Irish Protestant. Unquestionably he is in the first tier of English poets of the twentieth century. He won the Nobel Prize for Literature in 1923. Unfortunately his beliefs are not so easily characterized, so we must read and cite Yeats with caution. His thinking was riddled with a hodgepodge of Rosicrucian ideas, theosophy, and spiritualism. He chose to follow one of his mother's sisters "down the muddy road of 'magic' studies."[1] Despite the unfortunate paganism into which he wandered, he is well worth reading as a great poet and intellect.

William Butler Yeats was born into a somewhat middle-class Irish family in Dublin, but a family that led a spartan, almost impoverished lifestyle. His father was from a family of clergy but was himself a celebrated portrait artist who often forgot to charge his customers.

Yeats was raised in Sligo on the west Irish coast, where his mother's family were mill owners and shippers. After attending art school, he began to write poems and plays. Considered by some to be "the last of the Romantics," he was part of the "Celtic twilight," the waning of the oldest nationalism. He was of the old Irish Protestant ascendancy, and he could speak soundly. He observed that "Our doctrine is that by faith the Saviour enters into us and lives His life through our bodies."[2] He tried to rally the Irish to a love for eighteenth-century Protestantism, the "one Irish Century that escaped from darkness and confusion." Of course he failed. He became a spokesman for the new Irish Renaissance.

He delved into Blake and sampled the occult. With the Irish dramatist and promoter of Celtic heritage John Synge (1871–1909), he founded Dublin's Abbey Theater. He served in the Irish Free Senate and was seen as a leading Symbolist. As he got older, his political views became increasingly conservative.

All of his work shows his knack for compressing ideas into tight and powerful packages. "The Second Coming," for example, rose out of his mounting concern "about socialist revolutions." He spoke of the Holy Spirit as "the intellectual fountain."[3] His plays *Calvary* and *The Resurrection* are most striking.

His collected works run to fourteen volumes and are published by Macmillan. His "Easter, 1916" deals with the Republican Revolt and is a powerful instance of his use of analogy and moving imagery.

I write it out in a verse—
MacDonagh and MacBride
And Connolly and Pearse
Now and in time to be,
Wherever green is worn,
Are changed, changed utterly:
A terrible beauty is born.

Gems such as "The Folly of Being Comforted," "Adam's Curse," "To a Friend Whose Work Has Come to Nothing," "Solomon to Sheba," "The Hawk," and "Sailing to Byzantium" are outstanding. After his death, T. S. Eliot eulogized him "as the greatest poet of our time." W. H. Auden memorialized Yeats. When Yeats married an English woman at age fifty-two, poet Ezra Pound (1885–1972) was his best man. M. L. Rosenthal calls him "the boldest, most vigorous voice of this century."[4]

His wife was a spiritist medium, and one picks up whiffs of curious side-lines in his writings (as is also the case of Oswald Chambers and Arthur Pink, who also have some occult in their backgrounds). He was "a haughty public man" but tender and generous to his troubled relatives.[5] Yeats had a good theo-logical foundation, but his dabbling in the occult foreshadows later New Age philosophy. This occult revival also had Celtic dimensions and was a pas-sionate protest against the sterility of rationalism and the Enlightenment. For both New Age philosophy and its early proponent, Yeats looked in the wrong place.

------

1. Yeats studied with Madame Helena Petrovna Blavatsky (1831–1891), the Russian "Mother of the New Age," whose escapades into Hinduism and Buddhism and or-ganization of the theosophical movement are chronicled in Sylvia Cranstrom's *H.P.B.: The Extraordinary Life and Influence of Helena Petrovna Blavatsky* (New York: G. P. Putnam, 1993). Her cherished conviction was "the omnipotence of man's own immortal self." She influenced not only Yeats, but also Thomas Edison; writers L. Frank Baum, E. M. Forster, William James, James Joyce, Jack London, and Thornton Wilder; and composers Gustav Mahler and Jean Sibelius.

2. Donald T. Torchiana, *W. B. Yeats and Georgian Ireland* (Evanston, Ill.: Northwest-ern University Press, 1966), 48.

3. Ibid., 214, 251. Yeats appreciated Burke more and more. Both despised Revolution-ary France. He said: "I cannot discover truth by logic unless that logic serve pas-sion." Chafing at the Enlightenment.

4. M. L. Rosenthal, ed., *William Butler Yeats: Selected Poems and Three Plays* (New York: Collier, 1962), xv.

5. William M. Murphy, *Family Secrets: William Butler Yeats and His Relatives* (Syra-cuse, N.Y.: Syracuse University, 1991). The standard authority on Yeats is what will eventually be a two-volume work by R. F. Foster. Volume 1 is in publication: R. F. Foster, *W. B. Yeats: A Life* (Oxford: Oxford University Press, 1996).

7.5.2 ELIOT, "OLD 'POSSUM"

I will show you fear in a handful of dust.

Human kind cannot bear much reality.

I doubt whether what I am saying can convey very much to anyone for whom the doctrine of original sin is not a very real and tremendous thing.

The humanist has suppressed the divine and is left with a human element which may quickly descend again to the animal from which he has sought to raise it.

—T. S. Eliot

Arguably T. S. Eliot (1888–1965) gave this century its poetic voice. Though an American by birth and education, he joined and became very much a part of the English literary scene. He was awarded the Nobel Prize for Literature in 1948, not only for his poetry but also for his plays and literary criticism. Thousands would gather to hear him read and speak. While his popularity has ebbed and flowed, both during his lifetime and since his death, he certainly fits into the ranks of great poets of this century—with qualifications. The actual quantity of his poetry is very small but has recently been augmented by some unpublished early work and the embryonic forms of several of his best-known poems. There are no masterpieces in these new pieces, and some are bawdy.[1] His obvious anti-Semitism is troubling.[2]

Yet *Time* magazine speaks of him as "the only major poet of this century who was intensely and essentially Christian" and called him "the model Christian gentleman."[3] Eliot argued in life and word that "what the world really needs is something in which to believe." Such sentiments endeared him to evangelical intellectuals. So we are left wondering whether he was truly "a poet of faith." Did he have a conversion experience?[4]

Thomas Stearns Eliot was born in St. Louis, Missouri, the youngest child of a wholesale grocer. His grandfather, William Greenleaf Eliot, a Unitarian minister and founder of Washington University, ruled his son and his son's son "from the grave," Eliot was to write later. He was raised in a Midwestern "brownstone" but went to Harvard at eighteen where his grandfather's cousin, Charles W. Eliot, was the retired president. There he finished his B.A. in three years and his M.A. in his fourth year.

At Harvard, Eliot came under the spell of Irving Babbitt (1865–1933), a leading intellectual voice in the movement away from Romanticism and toward humanism. He also dabbled in Sanskrit and Oriental religions. He wrote his Ph.D. dissertation on the idealist and anti-utilitarian philosophy of F. H. Bradley, though he never defended it. However, Bradley's prose was ever after his model.

After he finished his master's degree, his personal life became more complicated. He broke with his family in America and, after study abroad, settled on a goal to conquer London. He was acutely pained by what he called "the barbarism of America." He impulsively married the chronically-ill Vivienne Haigh-Wood in 1915, which further estranged him from his family.[6] He suffered a total nervous collapse in 1922, out of which came *The Waste Land*. His wife's marriage counselor was his former tutor at Harvard, Bertrand Russell (1872–1970). Slowly Vivienne slipped into mental illness. His published letters on these matters are very reserved.[7] After 1933 his wife was always in an asylum, where he visited her weekly. After her death in 1947, he married his secretary, Valerie Fletcher, who was many years his junior.

In 1927 he became a British subject and professed conversion to Christianity, seeking baptism at Finstock Church in the Cotswolds. He announced in a preface to *For Lancelot Andrewes* that he would henceforth be known as "a classicist in literature, a royalist in politics and an anglo-catholic in religion."[8] He was always preoccupied with life's ultimate issues.

For years, Eliot edited his own magazine, *The Criterion*. He taught briefly at a boy's school, then worked for Lloyd's Bank. Late in his life, he was involved with the publishing firm of Faber and Faber.

It has been argued that what James Joyce did for the contemporary novel, T. S. Eliot did for poetry. He left the oratory of the Romantics and opted for conversational speech, natural rhythms, and sense experience. His originality seemed appropriate to the postwar mood. And while there is a kind of "top-heaviness" in his work and a regrettable move from the Anglo-Saxon to the more Latin hyphenated words and the German, we sense a "radioactive emotion" in what he has to say.

Three discernible phases developed in his thought and writing:

First, his preconversion work demonstrates his weariness with the arid, decadent culture about him. In "The Love Song of J. Alfred Prufrock," he acknowledges the human fall and its abiding consequences. Prufrock was a "futile, indecisive" Boston bachelor who lived in fear and futility. "I have measured out my life with coffee spoons," he admits. In his "Gerontion" comes "Christ the tiger," but only by way of introduction, not solution.[9] One senses imminent judgment—people are dead while they live—"etherized upon a table." In "The Waste Land" of 1922, his disillusioned disgust is complete.[10]

Second are works associated with his movement into Anglican Christianity. All of Eliot's poetry to some extent either anticipates or affirms conversion. But the influences of Lancelot Andrewes, Dante, and Donne are strong in such works as "Journey of the Magi," "A Song for Simeon," and "Ash Wednesday." In the more discursive *Four Quartets,* Eliot meditates on the reality of time and the meaning of life.[11] Roger Lundin writes that Eliot always struggled to reconcile his "theological and aesthetic convictions" in a somewhat unsettling sense that baffles critics.[12]

Third, Eliot moved toward dramatic verse for the theatre in his five verse plays. In *The Cocktail Party* (in which "happy hour" becomes the secular substitute for Holy Communion), Celia concedes of her love for a married man: "It sounds ridiculous—but the only word for it that I can find, is a sense of sin." Her concern becomes, "I must atone!"[13] Eliot's change in direction and devotion was all the more noticeable because it occurred at the very time in which modern literature was being sanitized of morality and totally secularized in philosophy. Eliot observes this himself in his 1935 essay "Religion and Literature." Elsewhere he assists students of Daniel 2 with his observation that "as we inherit the civilization of Europe, we are citizens of Rome."

This versatile and gifted man demonstrated a firm commitment to Jesus Christ, all the while dialoguing personally with culture. He corresponded with Groucho Marx. His *Old Possum's Book of Practical Cats* was made into a Broadway musical.

Yet in all this, as Nicholas Jenkins observed, "He exercised an almost unrivaled poetic authority." A case in point is his outstanding play *Murder in the Cathedral,* which would in itself guarantee his reputation. He leaves us with the classic picture of "the hollow men" of modernity and such unforgettable pictures as "sweet and cloying through the dark air, falls the stifling scent of despair."

He was a character and a snob and so British. Just as North American evangelicals wondered about some ideas they read from the pens of C. S. Lewis and J. B. Phillips, they wondered even more about T. S. Eliot.

A woman sitting next to him at a table said, "Isn't the party wonderful?"

He replied: "Yes, if you see the essential horror of it all."[14]

---

1. T. S. Eliot, *Inventions of the March Hare: Poems 1909–1917* (New York: Harcourt Brace, 1997).
2. Wendy Lesser, "The T. S. Eliot Problem," *The New York Times Book Review,* 19 June 1996, 31.
3. "T. S. Eliot: He knew the anguish of the marrow, the ague of the skeleton," *Time,* 15 January 1965, 86.
4. J. Bottum, "What T. S. Eliot Almost Believed," *First Things,* August/September 1995, 25ff. In total this critique seems a bit too fussy in its estimation of what an authentically Christian poet would have to be and do.
5. Peter Laurie, "Mr. Eliot's Dreams," *Chronicles of Culture,* September 1988, 15ff.
6. James W. Tuttleton, "The Scandal in T. S. Eliot's Life," *Chronicles of Culture,* April 1988, 14ff.
7. Valerie Eliot, ed., *The Letters of T. S. Eliot: I, 1898–1922* (New York: Harcourt Brace, Jovanovich, 1988).
8. Tuttleton, "The Scandal in T. S. Eliot's Life," 15. This article shows how Eliot moved "toward the Christian conception of God and the necessity of conversion."
9. T. S. Eliot, *The Complete Poems and Plays 1909–1950* (New York: Harcourt Brace, 1971). The best compendium currently available.
10. James Wesley Inglis, "Christian Elements in the Poetry of T. S. Eliot," *Christianity Today,* 13 October 1961, 3ff.
11. Calvin D. Linton, "T. S. Eliot: Prophet with Honor," *Christianity Today,* 26 March 1965, 10ff.
12. Roger Lundin, "The Rest is Prayer: T. S. Eliot at 100," *Christian Century,* 28 September 1988, 831.
13. Eliot, *The Complete Poems and Plays,* 359. Another instance of efforts at self-atonement is Ian Bedloe in Anne Tyler's *Saint Maybe* (New York: Random House, 1991).

He is abetted by the Church of the Second Chance, which taught that "we must earn forgiveness." Ian's efforts were, needless to say, utterly in vain.

14. Martin P. Marty, *Context,* 1 April 1991, 3. Some other treatments of Eliot's faith include Alzina Stone Dale, *T. S. Eliot: The Philosopher Poet* (Wheaton, Ill.: Harold Shaw, 1988), and the massive critical biography by Peter Ackroyd, *T. S. Eliot: A Life* (New York: Simon and Schuster, 1984).

7.5.3 AUDEN, DARTING HAWK

> All proofs or disproofs that we tender
> Of His existence are returned
> Unopened to the sender.
>
> Now, did He really break the seal
> And rise again? We dare not say;
> But conscious unbelievers feel
> Quite sure of Judgment Day.
>
> —W. H. Auden
> *The Age of Anxiety*

As brilliant as any poet who ever wrote, Wystan Hugh Auden's (1907–1973) checkered career and character both please and perplex conservative Christians. In an early poem, he describes his desire to have the elevated perspective of a hawk. Surely his huge quantity of work, his diverse interests, and his fascination with words give him elevation. He won the Pulitzer Prize in 1947 for *The Age of Anxiety* but missed the Nobel Prize because the Swedes thought him abrasive. Scholar Edward Callan says that he has "greater variety of poetic forms than any other poet in England."[1] He was offered a niche in Westminster Abbey, but before his death at age sixty-six, he decided to be buried in Austria where he spent his last years.

W. H. Auden was born in York. Both grandfathers and four uncles were Church of England clergy. His father was a doctor and his mother university-educated. Callan cites three factors that predisposed the young man to letters and study:

1. His father's library in "a home full of books. . . . In my father's library, scientific books stood side by side with works of poetry and fiction, and it never occurred to me to think of one as more 'humane' than the other."[2]
2. His rural childhood fostered "early imaginative experience."[3]
3. He found tutors at Oxford University in whom he could confide, one of them the associate of C. S. Lewis and Christian fantasy writer J. R. R. Tolkien.

The left-wing atmosphere at Oxford and the moral climate of Britain drew him to Marxism and into gender confusion. After Oxford, he was a schoolmaster in England from 1930 to 1935, and in 1939, he went to America to teach poetry at the University of Michigan and Smith College. He lived half of his life in the U.S. and in 1946 became a citizen. He married Erika Mann, daughter of Thomas Mann (1875–1955) in 1935. As many leftists, he visited the Spanish Civil War and Sino-Japanese War zones. But in the 1940s, he moved to more conservative political and religious convictions. He remained in Anglo-Catholicism. Toward the end of his life he speaks of his conversion, but it is hard to define that change as spiritual or merely intellectual:

> Finally, hair-raising things
> That Hitler and Stalin were doing
> Forced me to think about God.
> Why was I sure they were wrong?
> Wild Kierkegaard, Williams and Lewis
> Guided me back to belief.
>
> —"A Thanksgiving"

In 1947 Auden produced *The Age of Anxiety,* a poetic formulation of Carl Jung's *Modern Man in Search of a Soul,* heavily influenced by Søren Kierkegaard. Auden concluded that Sigmund Freud was wrong—pleasure would not lead to rest.[4] While Jung saw religion as positive, he and Freud were on the same epistemological page as Kant, who destroyed reason for the sake of faith.

In quest of spiritual healing, Auden followed the lead of Karl Barth (1886–1968) and took refuge in paradox. The Niebuhr brothers, H. Richard, 1894–1962, and Reinhold, 1892–1971, were friends who influenced him, as was Paul Tillich (1886–1965). In his essay "Balaam and His Ass: The Master-Servant Relationship in Literature," Auden argues for the necessity of absolutes. He wrote the introduction to Charles Williams's *The Descent of the Dove,* an exploration of the work of the Holy Spirit.[5]

The definitive reflection of his return to religion is *For the Time Being: A Christmas Oratio* (1944). Dedicated to his hyper-possessive mother, this focuses on the principle of the Incarnation as it works out in the nativity of Christ. On the heels of his conversion, he refers to "the Logos-Child, the Divine Word made flesh in history."[6] In the treatment of the characters, especially King Herod, one cannot escape the robustly materialistic aspect of Christian faith in this piece. In *Homage to Clio,* he is the diagnostician, as always, but with recourse to God.[6] His great nature poems, including "In Praise of Limestone,"[7] and his gripping commentary on "The Tempest" show us that he is "the poet's poet."[8]

For some years, Auden lived on the Bay of Naples and in 1956 went back to England as professor of poetry. "Re/the Cross" becomes a point of reference for him.[10] There is much that continues to puzzle us in Auden, yet through all of his struggles there does come a clear, convincing call for commitment to Christ:

> Dream. In human dreams earth ascends to heaven
> Where no one need pray nor ever feel alone.
> In your first hours of life here, O have you
> Chosen already what death must be your own?
> How soon will you start on the Sorrowful Way?
> Dream while you may.
>
> —"At the Manger Mary Sings"

Another great poem is Auden's "Luther" (1940), in which he describes how "the fuse of Judgment spluttered" in Luther's head: "The Just shall live by Faith . . . he cried in dread." He closes with "And men and women of the world were glad,/Who'd never cared or trembled in their lives." This is a powerful insight.

One of the impressive works on the twentieth century was Paul Johnson's *Modern Times: The World from the Twenties to the Eighties*.[11] This survey and analysis contains profitable facts and perspectives. For example, we learn that in the 1920s Charles Dickens's (1812–1870) *David Copperfield* was the favorite American novel. Adolf Hitler (1889–1945) and Joseph Goebbels (1897–1945) both devoured the Scottish philosopher and Germanophile, Thomas Carlyle (1795–1881).

1. Edward Callan, *Auden: A Carnival of Intellect* (New York: Oxford University Press, 1983), 10. Great elegies.
2. Ibid., 25. Although he paid high tribute to Yeats, Auden said he believed that Yeats was trying to recreate the bygone epoch.
3. Ibid., 30. Versatility in form is found in the three books of *The Orators* (1930–31).
4. Ibid., 53. As so many young persons who were disappointed, he turned in vain to Marx and Freud.
5. Charles Williams, *The Descent of the Dove: The History of the Holy Spirit in the Church* (New York: Living Age, 1956).
6. William French, "Auden's Moral Comedy: A Late-Winter Reading," *Christian Century*, 24 February 1982, 205ff.
7. Review of Auden's *Homage to Clio*, *Time*, 30 May 1960, 76. Many "preachments" observed.
8. *The Norton Anthology of Poetry* (New York: W. W. Norton, 1983), 670f.
9. *Auden: A Carnival of Intellect*, 247. Other heroes were soldier-writer T. E. Lawrence, diplomat Dag Hammarskjold, philosopher Edmund Husserl, and Roman Catholic theologian Friedrich von Hügel.
10. Richard Davenport-Hines, *Auden* (New York: Pantheon, 1995). The author conclusively shows from various sources that, along with being "correct in religious orthodoxy," Auden regarded himself as a sinner who battled evil.
11. Rev. ed., New York: Harper Colophon, 1983.

7.5.4 MASEFIELD, LUMBERING WHALE

You think the church an outworn fetter;
Kane, keep it till you've built a better . . .
Then, as to whether true or sham
That book of Christ, whose priest I am;
The Bible is a lie, say you,
Where do you stand, suppose it is true?
Goodbye. But if you've more to say
My doors are open, night and day.

Meanwhile, my friend, 'twould be no sin
To mix more water in your gin.

—John Masefield
"The Everlasting Mercy"

Poet laureate of England from 1930 to 1967, John Masefield (1878–1967) was a plodding writer of verse, novels, and plays. He was born in Herefordshire and there staked out his "own world," where his maternal grandfather was minister at Great Cumberton for fifty-seven years. He gained from his mother a biblical frame-of-reference. He wrote his first poem—about a pony—when he was ten. Long before that he memorized Tennyson's "The Dying Swan" and Thomas Hood's

I remember, I remember,
The house where I was born. . . .
But now 'tis little joy
To know I'm farther off from heav'n
Than when I was a boy.

Dramatic reversals changed life for John. His mother died, his nurse left, and his solicitor father's finances were wiped out through the speculation of his grandfather. Even before his father died in 1890, Masefield was carted off by his Uncle William and Aunt Kate. Kate was an avid follower of Charles Kingsley and his social-issues-oriented "muscular Christianity." Masefield had little spiritual guidance.[1]

At thirteen, he was sent to sea. Growing up fast, he was enthralled by a ship-mate, Wally Blair, who was a natural storyteller. Otherwise, sea life was not good; he never felt warm, dry, full, or rested. He became sick with malaria and tuberculosis. So Masefield deserted in New York City and found a factory job in Yonkers. In 1897 he returned to England and took a bank clerking job in London where his godmother, a Miss Flood, introduced him into the high lit-erary circle in which she moved. Masefield dined with Yeats and was invited to his Monday evening soirees, where poetry was read and discussed.

Soon young Masefield published his *Salt Water Ballads,* which did very well.[2] In 1903 he married Constance Crommelin, who was nearly a dozen years older than he. She had studied at Cambridge and taught Bible classes. He tried freelancing and moved briefly to Manchester where he could not get ahead. This was a long winter in his spirit. Part of his pessimism came as the result of a long infatuation he would have with Elizabeth Robins.[3]

His breakthrough came in 1911. He was bitter that April, but while looking at bursting primroses, he heard a voice: "The Springtime is beginning." Soon came publication of the long narrative poem, *The Everlasting Mercy*—arguably the most beautiful poetic conversion narrative in English. The poem is about a carousing Saul Kane who tells the parson what he thinks of the church. The cleric's reply touches him (see the opening quote), but it is saintly Miss Bourne of the Society of Friends who reaches him as she confronts him in the pub and challenges him to open his heart to Christ. The miracle takes place.[4]

> I did not think, I did not strive,
> The deep peace burnt me alive;
> The station brook, to my new eyes,
> Was babbling out of Paradise.
> The waters rushing from the rain
> Were singing Christ has risen again.
>
> O glory of the lighted mind.
> How dead I've been, how dumb, how blind.
> The bolted door had broken in,
> I knew that I had done with sin.
> I knew that Christ had given me birth
> To brother all the souls on earth.

Masefield hesitated to follow up this statement with a personal Christian affirmation. The onset of war deeply shocked him, and he wrote "England at War" in 1914. He went to France and even to Gallipoli with the Red Cross. He was contacted by commander of the army General Douglas Haig to write a poem on "The Battle of the Somme," as he had written the best-selling "Gallipoli."[5] He made a number of successful American tours and read his poetry.

He wrote drama on various biblical themes, including "A King's Daughter" on Jezebel, "The Trial of Jesus," "Easter," and "The Coming of Christ." All were performed in Canterbury Cathedral. His work was seen all around as "moving toward Christian belief."[6] He was made poet laureate in 1930. John Masefield wrote much and achieved stature among the English poets. At times he is robust and daring. Yet questions about his own spirituality linger.

---

1. Constance Babington Smith, *John Masefield: A Life* (New York: Macmillan, 1978), 6. Another distinguished man of English letters from Cornwall, A. L. Rowse, was quite hostile to things Christian. In his memoirs, he chronicles how their local rector had preached a particularly moralizing sermon one Sunday and the next day decamped with the church organist. His successor was intolerably tedious and had a penchant for the pyramids, British Israelitism, and Christadelphianism (*A Cornish Childhood* [Clarkson L. Potter, 1942], 136).

2. Ibid., 42. His poems of the sea are outstanding. "Dauber" is considered by Constant Smith to be "the best English poem on sailing ships ever written."

3. Ibid., 101. She ended the affair, leaving him devastated.

4. Ibid., 113. His work has, according to Smith, "realistic dialogue, graphic description, swift and tense action." See also John Wesley Ingles, "Masefield's Poem of Conversion," *Christianity Today,* 12 April 1963, 9ff.

5. General Haig was known for odd obsessions. He was devoted to spiritism and put great stock militarily in messages conveyed in seances. Leon Wolff (*In Flanders Fields: The 1917 Campaign* [New York: Viking, 1958], 52, 302, 304) shows that Haig would not change tactics despite losses of two hundred thousand. He was relieved.

6. Smith, *John Masefield: A Life,* 192.

7.5.5 HOUSMAN, FEISTY FERRET

> That is the land of lost content,
> I see it shining plain,
> The happy highways where I went
> And cannot come again.
>
> —A. E. Housman
> *A Shropshire Lad*

Alfred Edward Housman (1859–1936) was a true Wordsworthian Romantic in the sense that Romanticism was a corrective to rationalism. Born in Fockbury in England and educated at Oxford, he taught classics at the University of London and at Cambridge University.

In his highly controverted Leslie Stephen Lecture at Cambridge University in 1933 on "The Name and Nature of Poetry," he attacked the lack of feeling in eighteenth-century poetry. Pound was outraged at this revisionism, but Eliot was unperturbed. Auden paid him tribute by writing a sonnet depicting him as a literary curiosity.[1]

It is difficult to detect a cohesion to his work. B. J. Leggett argues for a thematic unity in his collection of sixty-three poems, *A Shropshire Lad* (1896). Leggett said he portrays "the dilemma posed by an awareness of the mutable nature of man's existence."[2] In "The Carpenter's Son," he presents a humanistic Christ in the mode of the British Roman Catholic modernist George Tyrell, who saw in Christ a mirror image of the time.[3]

Writing for Queen Victoria's golden jubilee in 1887, Housman does not share the general spirit of optimism.[4] He speaks more of death and has a progressively tragic view of love. This deep-dyed pessimism has been attributed to disappointments in his education or love.[5] His pessimism anticipates Bertrand Russell's "courageous despair" and "Invictus" by William Ernest Henley (1849–1903).[6] In one of his last poems, "Hell-Gate," there is "much less good than ill" in the world. Hope is a liar, and death is better than life. Malt does more than can Milton to justify the ways of God. As is sadly argued in "Invictus":

> It matters not how straight the gate,
> How charged with punishment the scroll,
> I am the master of my fate,
> I am the captain of my soul.

---

1. B. J. Leggett, *The Poetic Art of A. E. Housman: Theory and Practice* (Lincoln, Neb.: University of Nebraska Press, 1978), 30, 87.

2. B. J. Leggett, *Housman's Land of Lost Content: A Critical Study of* A Shropshire Lad (Knoxville, Tenn.: University of Tennessee Press, 1970), 67. The poet laments his growing loss of harmony with nature itself.

3. A. E. Housman, "The Carpenter's Son," in *Seashell Anthology of Great Poetry*, ed. Christopher Burn (New York: Park Lane, 1996), 74. Also in this anthology is Housman's poem on death, "With Rue My Heart Is Laden" (299).

4. Leggett, *Housman's Land of Lost Content,* 79.
5. Benet, *Benet's Reader's Encyclopedia,* 463.
6. Henley knew great physical adversity and is remembered for this defiant poem.

7.5.6 NOYES, PEPPERY PARROT

The wind was a torrent of darkness among the gusty trees,
The moon was a ghostly galleon tossed upon cloudy seas,
The road was a ribbon of moonlight over the purple moor,
And the highwayman came riding—
Riding—riding—
The highwayman came riding, up to the old inn-door.

—Alfred Noyes
"The Highwayman"

Some English poets wrote only nonsense rhymes, like Edward Lear and his "Owl and the Pussycat." Others, like poet laureate John Betjeman, produced nostalgic Victorian bypaths. G. A. Studdert-Kennedy was an Anglo-Irish army chaplain whose "Rough Rhymes of a Padre" spoke deeply of the ravages of war, an area of English society for which nonconformists took a disproportionate hit because they furnished so few officers. Alfred Noyes (1880–1958) reacted to the growing secularization of the Church of England and British society generally and became a passionate convert to Roman Catholicism.

He was born in Staffordshire and educated at Oxford. His family was religious. His father and three of his brothers were clergymen. His first wife was an American.

Noyes became known for ballads and historical pieces, especially his serial, *Drake.* Each installment was awaited eagerly by the reading public.[1]

It was after Noyes's first wife died that he was converted to Rome in 1925. In 1927 he remarried. The following year he reentered the spotlight with a defense of historic Christianity against Anglican Bishop Ernest W. Barnes (1874–1953) of Birmingham. Barnes derogated the Virgin Birth and denied the divinity of Jesus. Noyes argued that Christianity is distinct from Unitarianism and in this was supported by E. G. Selwyn, dean of Winchester, and other Anglican worthies.[2] Noyes also had considerable contact with another expert on mysticism, Evelyn Underhill, whom he described as "a lean, brown, ascetic wisp of a woman with an astringent face."[3]

In his book *To the Unknown God* (1934), he expresses Mephistophelian gloom over the future and reflects on life among the agnostics.[4] He leans heavily on William Paley's (1743–1805) watchmaker analogy to argue that a "god" exists.[5]

His most famous individual poem, "The Highwayman," is gripping.[6] His poem "From England to Italy" reflects his continuous travel. He lived and traveled for periods in the United States. His lectures in 1940 were entitled "The Edge of the Abyss" and are prophetic. Gradually losing his sight to glaucoma, he would sit at the seashore and stare blindly upwards and cry: "Is anybody there?" Yet his faith gyroscopically shepherded him. His autobiography concludes with a ringing reaffirmation of Christ as "the Resurrection and the Life!"

1. *Benet's Reader's Encyclopedia,* 702.
2. Alfred Noyes, *Two Worlds for Memory* (Philadelphia: J. B. Lippincott, 1953), 241ff. A refreshing autobiography.
3. William Ralph Inge, *Christian Mysticism* (London: Methuen, 1899). These are the Bampton Lectures for 1899. Another invaluable older study is Evelyn Underhill, *The Mystics of the Church* (New York: George H. Doran, n.d.).
4. *Two Worlds for Memory,* 248. "Christ-mysticism," as Deismann described it, is New Testament mysticism.
5. Ibid., 276. He quotes a close friend to the effect that *Tristam Shandy* is the greatest English novel (see 9.1).
6. *Seashell Anthology of Great Poetry,* 68.

7.5.7 THOMAS, TERRIFIED DEER

> And death shall have no dominion.
> Dead men naked they shall be one
> With the man in the wind and the west moon;
> When their bones are picked clean and the clean bones gone,
> They shall have stars at elbow and foot;
> Though they go mad they shall be sane,
> Though they sink through the sea they shall rise again;
> Though lovers be lost love shall not;
> And death shall have no more dominion.
> And death shall have no more dominion.
>
> —Dylan Thomas
> "And Death Shall Have No Dominion"

This first stanza of a 1933 poem supplies a significant clue to the character of the great Welsh poet Dylan Thomas (1914–1953). The Wales of Christmas Evans and D. Martyn Lloyd-Jones has a rugged beauty with a glorious spiritual heritage. Thomas was born among uplanders in Swansea in a tradition whose literature was the Bible, collected sermons, and Welsh classics; whose entertainment was chapel on Sunday. They respected preachers and poets.[1] Although his father—bitter about a Welsh religiosity that was harder on sins of the flesh than on sins of the spirit—claimed to be an atheist. His mother faithfully brought her children to chapel and read only the Bible. The poem quoted is built around Romans 6:9 and corroborates what one biographer observes:

> When Sunday came it was to the pulpit that they turned, Bible in hand, forefingers quivering toward Heaven, threatening damnation to those who flirted with temptations of the flesh, or the perils of Demon Drink. Of his use of Biblical phrases, Thomas testified: "The things that first made me love language and want to work in it and for it were nursery rhymes and folk tales, the Scottish ballads, a few lines of hymns, the most famous Bible stories and the rhythms of the Bible. . . . the great rhythms

that rolled over me from the Welsh pulpits; and I had read for myself from Job to Ecclesiastes, and the story of the New Testament is part of my life."[2]

Always frail and a chain-smoker from fifteen years of age, Thomas was spoiled by his mother and distant from his schoolmaster father. Although he was raised on Shakespeare and influenced by Poe, Charlotte and Emily Brontë, and Hopkins, he was an academic failure at Swansea Grammar School. In 1931 he went to London but soon returned to Swansea to write for the local paper. He wrote poems and stories but found no publisher. Mysterious illnesses and a nervous breakdown plagued him, and an unsuccessful romance with Pamela Hansford Johnson wiped him out. She made every effort to get him to stop his smoking and heavy drinking.[3] A religious friend remarked: "I never met anyone with comparable gifts who possessed comparable charm."[4] Yet he suffered great guilt but had no Savior. He agreed with the Buddha that life is evil and with Schopenhauer that life has no purpose. "I have seen the gates of hell," he claimed.[5] "I am the drunkest man in the world," he admitted. His writing abounds with both Christian and Freudian imagery.

In 1936 he met Caitlin Macnamara, an Irish dancer. They were married the next year. Rev. Leon Atkin, a Swansea nonconformist minister whom Thomas admired, advanced the opinion that Thomas's religion was "pessimistic pantheism."[6] He was a very selfish, childlike man.

His finances were a disaster. For three years, he wrote no poetry but gave himself to the British Broadcasting Company (BBC) and film work. He made four trips to the U.S. He owed large amounts for taxes. His endless affairs and alcoholism had soured his marriage, although he greatly loved his wife and children. His work tended to be inconsistent, but he wrote twenty great poems with heavily marbled phrases. He had a great bass voice that was deeply moving.

In his last poetry, he spoke of his work as "poems in praise of God's world by a man who doesn't believe in God."[7] He had long since abandoned Christianity, but he couldn't totally leave it. In one of his last poems, occasioned by the final illness of his father, he wrote movingly "Do Not Go Gentle into That Good Night."[8] The death of his father and sister, his mother's fall, his penniless condition, and a final estrangement from his wife were too much. He died in New York City, tragically and alone. Blackouts had made his work erratic and unreliable.[9] Igor Stravinsky (1882–1971) had wanted him to write the libretto for an upcoming opera. But like Brendan Behan, the gifted Irish playwright, Thomas was too early a victim of an outrageous lifestyle. He died at age thirty-nine.

The subsequent popularity of his limited writing output made his wife and family wealthy. He wrote movingly of childhood, growth, and death. Yet such a drastic ceiling limited his insight and output. We can lament the terrible waste.

---

1. Constantine FitzGibbon, *The Life of Dylan Thomas* (Boston: Little, Brown, 1965), 7. The child never grew up.

2. George Tremlett, *Dylan Thomas* (New York: St. Martin's, 1991), 15, 19.

3. FitzGibbon, *The Life of Dylan Thomas,* 118. Thomas accepted morality but hated it. In this he was typically Welsh.

4. Ibid., 121. Augustus John said: "A typical Welsh Puritan and Nonconformist."

5. Ibid., 126. Pamela's worry about his drinking doomed their relationship.

6. Ibid., 229. FitzGibbon writes: "His was a religion that excludes dogma, morality and even sureness of belief" (230). Yet his "There Is a Savior" is heart-rending.

7. Ibid., 287. These words are a "personal valediction" and a *nunc dimittis.*

8. *The Norton Anthology of Poetry* (New York: W. W. Norton, 1983), 718. Note also "After the Funeral," 714.

9. FitzGibbon, *The Life of Dylan Thomas,* 342. This author sees Thomas "losing touch with the young." Alec Guiness played a powerful Thomas in "Dylan" on Broadway in 1964. See his memoir of that experience in Alec Guiness, *My Name Escapes Me: The Diary of a Retiring Actor* (New York: Viking, 1997).

CHAPTER EIGHT

Inquiring into the Values of American Poetry

The colonization of the U.S. and Canada and the founding of the federal republic of the United States of America had spiritual and secular aspects. One can overstate or understate the quality of faith among framers of the U.S. Constitution in 1789. Biblical and Enlightenment influences mixed in their worldviews. But C. Gregg Singer's premise is essentially sound: "Only in the light of the Christian revelation can American history be brought into a proper perspective, that the intellectual, political, social and economic trends of the past and present can be rightly interpreted only in the light of the Scriptural norm."[1]

North American experience was shaped by New England preaching, the awakenings and revivals, development of denominations, theology generally, and European Christian philosophy in particular.[2] The loyalist migration after the American Revolution transported Christian ideals into Canada. Garry Wills asserts that "the Bible is not going to stop being the central book in our intellectual heritage."[3] This premise will be constantly reinforced in the sections to follow. From *The Bay Psalter* and the mass of Puritan sermons and other writings, the Bible was the touchstone of national interaction.

Ernest R. Sandeen shows that the nineteenth century was "drunk on the millennium." Religious metaphor dominated the Jacksonian campaign. Lincoln used theological categories. Whatever the state of faith in urban centers, on plantations, and on the frontier, the consensus was largely Christian.[4] American poetry reflects this.

---

1. C. Gregg Singer, *A Theological Interpretation of American History* (1964; repr. ed., Greenville, S.C.: A Press, 1995).

2. Ellis Sandoz, *A Government of Laws: Political Theory, Religion and the American*

TABLE 7: Literature in Historical and Theological Context, 1900 to 2000

A: Historical Events; B: Arts and Philosophy; C: Revelation and Preaching

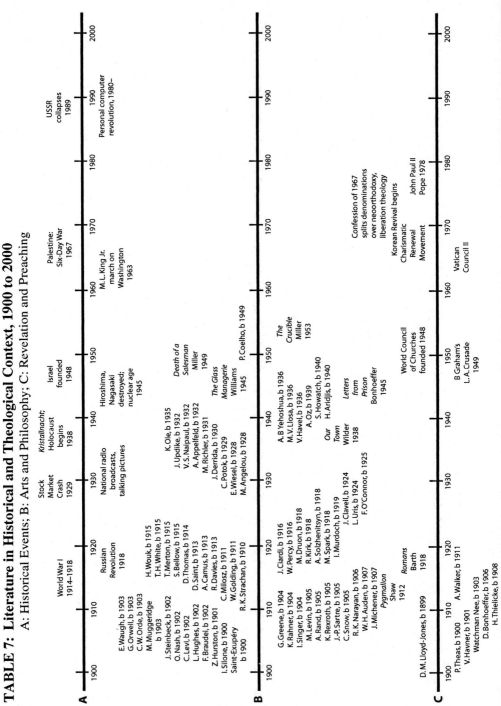

Founding (Baton Rouge: Louisiana State University Press, 1991). Sandoz has also collected sermons from the founding era.
3. Garry Wills, *Under God: Religion and American Politics* (New York: Simon and Schuster, 1990), 124.
4. Ernest R. Sandeen, *The Roots of Fundamentalism: British and American Millenarianism, 1800–1930* (Grand Rapids: Baker, 1978).

8.1   POETIC PATHFINDERS

American poets have often written in a conscious effort to create an original American poetry free from slavish imitation to English writers. This was not easy to achieve. One who helped was William Cullen Bryant (1794–1878), whose work was influential on all who followed him, especially Ralph Waldo Emerson (1803–1882) and Henry Wadsworth Longfellow (1807–1882).

8.1.1 BRYANT, BUILDER

> He who, from zone to zone,
> Guides through the boundless sky thy certain flight,
> In the long way that I must tread alone
> Will lead my steps aright.
>
> —William Cullen Bryant
> "To a Waterfowl"

The last lines from William Cullen Bryant's "To a Waterfowl," with which this section opens, were written in 1815 when he was twenty-one years of age. Yet Matthew Arnold considered "To a Waterfowl" to be "the best short poem in the English language." The young man was feeling a bit forlorn and uncertain when he caught a glimpse of a solitary bird in flight. He is sustained through his depression by the realization of God's support and gracious providence to the bird and to him.

Often called "the Father of American poetry," William Cullen Bryant was born in Cummington, Massachusetts. He and Henry Wadsworth Longfellow both were descended from John Alden of the Mayflower. Bryant's father and grandfather were successful physicians, active in politics, and lovers of letters. His father's library of more than seven hundred volumes was rich in the English poets. Bryant was a prodigy. He knew the alphabet at age sixteen months and read the Scriptures at age five. His mother was a devout believer, and his life and work reflected his Puritan upbringing:

> In a community so religious, I naturally acquired habits of devotion. My mother and grandmother had taught me, as soon as I could speak, the Lord's Prayer and other little petitions suited to childhood, and I may be said to have been nurtured on Watt's devout poems composed for children. The prayer of the publican in the New Testament (Luke 18:9–14) was often in my mouth and I heard every variety of prayer at the Sunday evening services conducted by laymen in private houses. But I varied

in my private devotions from those models in one respect: namely, in supplicating as I often did, that I might receive the gift of poetic genius and write verses that might endure.[1]

At age eight, he wrote devotional poetry influenced by John Dryden and Alexander Pope. His early blank verse can be seen in his version of David's grief over the death of King Saul.[2] He studied classical languages with one of his many clergy relatives and mastered the Greek New Testament. He spent a year at Williams College. At the time, this college was a hotbed of missionary zeal. He was then licensed to practice law in 1815.[3] He wrote his immortal "Thanatopsis" ("On Looking at Death") when he was only eighteen. In this poem, the influence of William Wordsworth can clearly be traced.

> So live, that when thy summons comes to join
> The innumerable caravan, which moves
> To that mysterious realm where each shall take
> His chamber in the silent halls of death,
> Thou go not, like the quarry-slave at night.

In 1824 he moved his law practice to New York City, where he also began to edit two magazines and later became chief editor and owner of the New York *Post*. As an influential journalist, he was really the man behind the founding of Central Park, the New York Public Library (outside of which his statue stands), and the Metropolitan Museum of Art.[4] His translations from Greek, Latin, Spanish, Italian, and French by themselves would have secured him a niche of note in American literature. Though he was always active in church, Bryant did not make a strong public profession of faith until later in his long life.[5]

He clearly follows the Puritan doctrine of the fall of man. He believes in God's great superintending providence and the ultimate triumph of truth, as in his lines:

> Truth, crushed to earth, shall rise again;
> Th' eternal years of God are hers;
> But Error, wounded, writhes in pain,
> And dies among his worshippers.
>
> —"The Battle-Field"

He introduced Abraham Lincoln to the East and was a strong supporter of the Lincoln administration through the agony of war. He issued a masterful translation of Homer and continued to write poetry, including some choice pieces on "Mary Magdalene." Like Alfred Tennyson (1809–1892), Bryant wrote a strong version of "Rizpah" (see 7.4.2). His hymns are outstanding, including the striking "Hymn of the Waldenses" honoring the beleaguered followers of Peter Waldo, the twelfth-century Reformer, who were persecuted in the Italian mountain valleys.

One beautiful hymn celebrates Christ's birth, and the hymn "Send Forth Thy Heralds, Lord, to Call" communicates the need to share the gospel around the world:

Send forth thy heralds, Lord, to call
The thoughtless young, the hardened old,
A wandering flock, and bring them all
To the Good Shepherd's peaceful fold.

He wrote lines that still are used for the dedication of church buildings. In "Waiting by the Gate," he celebrates the saving death of Jesus.[6] Bryant does not soar, but his extraordinarily broad sphere of service and expression make his poetic productivity all the more remarkable. Somewhat doleful at times, he is well worth picking up.

---

1. Nathan Haskell Dole, ed., *Poems of William Cullen Bryant* (New York: Thomas Y. Crowell, 1893), xii. I recommend this collection; look for it in used book stores specializing in older books.
2. Ibid., vii.
3. Kenneth Scott Latourette, *The Great Century: Europe and the United States,* vol. 4, in *History of the Expansion of Christianity* (1941 repr. ed., Grand Rapids: Zondervan, 1969), 80.
4. Russell Lynes, "Countryman-poet lets some fresh air into old New York," *Smithsonian*, September 1975, 81ff. He did not drink spirits and abhorred tobacco. James Fenimore Cooper and Samuel F. B. Morse were best friends.
5. Augustus Hopkins Strong, *American Poets and Their Theology* (Philadelphia: Griffith and Rowland, 1916), 20.
6. Ibid., 36. Sadly, toward the end of his life, he was leaning toward Unitarianism.

8.1.2 EMERSON, DOUBTER

By the rude bridge that arched the flood,
Their flag to April's breeze unfurled,
Here once the embattled farmers stood
And fired the shot heard round the world.
—Ralph Waldo Emerson,
"The Concord Hymn," first sung at the
completion of the battle monument, 4 July 1837

The stirring vitality of New England Puritanism had long since given way to dull habit and a crusty externalism. Unitarian reactionism had made strong inroads. Coming at the end of eight successive generations of divines, Ralph Waldo Emerson (1803–1882) struggled all his life with the truth of what he preached. His own father was a bookish Unitarian minister who died when "Waldo" was only eight.[1] His mother read François Fénelon (1651–1715) and John Flavel (d. 1691) and emphasized "keeping of the heart." Strapped as she was financially, she put four of her sons through Harvard. After Harvard, Waldo taught young women in a school in the family's home. Schooled in Scottish Common Sense Realism, he had come to prefer a rationalistic form of Puritan thought to Unitarianism, but he had doubts.

266 THE COMPANY OF THE CREATIVE

One influence on the young Emerson was his father's sister, Mary Moody Emerson. A staunch Puritan, she inspired him to seek excellence and spirituality.

Never robust, young Emerson had problems with his eyes and his lungs. But his increasing struggle was with the Bible and historic Christianity. At Harvard, the seeds of the destructive higher criticism of Johann Gottfried Eichorn (1752–1827) were sown. Emerson came to see the Bible as just another book; he gave up its study. In 1829 he married Ellen and took the prestigious pastorate of Second Church in Boston. By now he was imbibing all of Friedrich Schleiermacher (1768–1834), though Schleiermacher's opponent Immanuel Kant (1724–1804) was his starting point. His reconstituted theology began with the goodness and sufficiency of human nature. He put this theology to work when his wife died seventeen months after their marriage. He determined to use his own resources and to endure his grief alone.[2] He abandoned any notion of redemption. He resigned his pastorate and sailed for Europe, where he came under the influence of Samuel Taylor Coleridge (1772-1834) and Thomas Carlyle (1795–1881). He had concluded that "Christianity is wrongly received by all such as take it for a system of doctrines."[3] Therefore, "the highest revelation is that God is in every man." Generous admixtures of Eastern mysticism and Swedenborgianism cast Emerson loose from any vestige of historic Christianity.

Upon his return to the U.S., he married Lydia Jackson, a descendent of John Cotton. He was studying Johann Wolfgang von Goethe (1749–1832) and the idea that "the highest reverence is reverence for the self." Under Emerson's leadership, the transcendentalists provided "the soul for modern liberalism."[4] He was the poet of transcendentalism. His cult of the self became a recurrent theme in American religious thought, down to Norman Vincent Peale and Robert Schuller in the twentieth century. His essays on "Self-Reliance" and "Compensation" are brilliant and frame his amazing gift for aphorism and the epigram. His poetry is stiff and brittle, but beyond his famous "Concord Hymn," one should look at his "Boston Hymn," "Good-bye," and "Blight." In "Blight," he so characteristically begins: "Give me truths; For I am weary of the surfaces."[5]

Emerson's famous address at Harvard Divinity School, in which he advocated the divinity of man and the humanity of Christ, stunned the clergy to the point that he was not invited back for thirty years. He lectured widely in the U.S. and abroad, and his ideas became popular in certain philosophical circles. He had a mixed relationship among the intelligentsia personally. There were serious tensions with Carlyle and a complete break with Henry David Thoreau (1817–1862). He respected Daniel Webster (1782–1852), whose words were "like blows of an axe" or "a great cannon loaded to the lips," "as real as a blast furnace."

Caught up in German idealism, Emerson became increasingly radical in all aspects of life. He advocated, and may have practiced, open marriage. He absolutely dismissed any idea of human sinfulness.[6] The center of his message was self-deification. Father Taylor the Seaman's Preacher was quoted as saying, "Emerson knows no more of the religion of the New Testament than Balaam's ass did of the principles of human grammar."[7] Emerson gave up public prayer and any conventional idea of the afterlife. He asserted the transmigration of the soul and other Eastern notions. He was a monist if not a pantheist.

He scoffed at George Müller's (1805–1898) message and mission to orphans. Rationalistic revivalist Charles Finney was Emerson's idea of a preacher. After hearing Finney, he marveled that "I did not suppose such a style of preaching still survived."[8] He put Jesus side-by-side with Plato, Philo, and Shakespeare. His sermons were eloquent, but devoid of anything from Scripture.[9]

Gradually Emerson lost his powers, energy, and memory before his death at almost eighty years of age. "Nothing can bring you peace but yourself," was his view. His theology might be described as a self-saving Pelagianism, only without the desire for holiness in the original Pelagius (c. 383–410). The humanistic Emersonian gospel has been trumpeted from American pulpits both long before the poet and to the current time.

---

1. Robert D. Richardson Jr., *Emerson: The Mind on Fire* (Berkeley: University of California Press, 1995), 21.
2. Ibid., 98, 102, 113. "I am the universe" was his perspective. Everything is in the state of mind. Christianity is "a rule of life, not a rule of faith." In more modern times, theologians have tried to reverse the false dichotomy. Christianity is a rule of faith that is divorced from life experience.
3. Ibid., 151. "Every man's reason is sufficient for his guidance," he maintained.
4. Ibid., 171, 251. "God can only be found in the depths of one's own heart" is the keynote of New Thought. Margaret Fuller, a close friend of Emerson, counseled each person to make a personal "Bible."
5. Eduard C. Lindeman, ed., *Basic Selections from Emerson: Essays, Poems and Apothegms* (New York: Mentor, 1954), 140. An excellent collection of such gems as "A foolish consistency is the hob-goblin of little minds," and other quotables.
6. *American Poets and Their Theology*, 66. A probing article on the development of Emerson's "autonomous self" is Wilfred M. McClay, "Mr. Emerson's Tombstone," *First Things*, May 1998, 16.
7. Ibid., 72. Emerson had his eccentricities; for one he ate pie at breakfast every day.
8. Richardson, *Emerson: The Mind on Fire*, 527. Richardson observes that Henry Ward Beecher had the energy of ten men.
9. Wesley T. Mott, *The Strains of Eloquence: Emerson and His Sermons* (State College, Penn.: Pennsylvania State University Press, 1990); Susan L. Roberson, *Emerson in His Sermons: A Man-Made Self* (Columbia, Mo.: University of Missouri Press, 1996).

8.1.3 HOLMES, BACKSLIDER

I do not give a fig for the simplicity that is prior to complexity; but I would give my right arm for the simplicity that is beyond complexity.
—Oliver Wendell Holmes

An astounding versatility of accomplishments make Oliver Wendell Holmes Sr. (1809–1894) a true Renaissance man. He was born in Cambridge, Massachusetts, where his father was pastor of First Church while it was still orthodox (before it became Unitarian).[1] Oliver was a true Boston Brahmin in every sense of the word. From early on, he was grounded in the Westminster Confession of Faith and Shorter and Larger catechisms, as well as the lessons of *The Pilgrim's Progress*. He attended Philips Academy and Harvard.

Along the way, he rebelled against some of the hyper-Calvinist preachers who came into his father's pulpit. He later said: "I might have been a minister if a certain clergyman had not looked and talked so much like an undertaker."[2] His love for poetry and writing verse was early manifest. He wrote his popular "Old Ironsides" while at Harvard, where he was class poet for the Class of 1829. He wrote poems for forty-four consecutive class reunions until 1889, when only three members survived. His protest against the dismantling of the old ship begins with the incendiary lines:

> Ay, tear her tattered ensign down!
> Long has it waved on high,
> And many an eye has danced to see
> That banner in the sky;
> Beneath it rung the battle shout,
> And burst the cannon's roar; —
> The meteor of the ocean air
> Shall sweep the clouds no more.

Only five foot three inches tall, Holmes was a sprightly and peppery soul. He turned to law and then to medicine, which he practiced for some years, before teaching anatomy at Dartmouth College. He was Park Professor of Anatomy and Physiology at Harvard Medical School and Dean of the Medical School (1847–53). He made several significant contributions to the medical arts. His brilliant son, Oliver Wendell Holmes Jr., became one of the most influential associate justices ever to sit on the United States Supreme Court. He more than any other individual in judicial history began turning the courts toward dynamic interpretation of the Constitution and judicial activism.[3]

Still with immense systemic energy, the elder Oliver wrote prose and poetry for magazines, including *The Autocrat of the Breakfast Table* for *Atlantic Monthly*, which was edited by James Russell Lowell. These far-ranging essays were flavored with poetry strong enough that it was collected and published years later on its own. His novels tended to be theological, with large doses of vituperative aimed at religious orthodoxy.

He was a scintillating classroom lecturer, and his poetry showed wit, erudition, and poetic fancy. He was popular on the Lyceum circuit and gave a significant series of lectures on the English Poets at the Lowell Institute.

Holmes was a rationalist. Strong shows how Unitarianism's dethroning of Christ left those who attended many Eastern churches with Jesus as model but not Savior. This serious disease ravaged early American poetry. Both Longfellow and Lowell succumbed in their later years.[4] Holmes ignored the doctrine of regeneration. He was a poet of this life, ignoring entirely the life to come. His hymns are widely sung and found in many collections; "Lord of All Being, Throned Afar," "O Love Divine, That Stooped to Share," and "Thou Gracious God Whose

Mercy Lends" do not contain a syllable of gospel or redemption. They celebrate the God of creation, implying that favor with God can be found apart from the mediating work of Jesus Christ. Holmes advocated a kind of worship, as when he observed that "There is a little plant called Reverence in the corner of my Soul's garden, which I love to have watered about once a week."

Holmes was an inveterate conversationalist of immense gifts. He had no interest in the cause of abolition of slavery, to the great disappointment of his friend John Greenleaf Whittier (1807–1892). Rather, he was selfish and somewhat pessimistic: "Life is a fatal complaint and an eminently contagious one," he observed.

He satirized the orthodoxy of Jonathan Edwards in "The Deacon's Masterpiece or, the Wonderful One-Hoss Shay." Occasionally he dipped into Scripture for a poem such as "Choose You This Day Whom Ye Will Serve."[5] Yet the agile sculpting of words is striking. He aspires to enlarge the soul:

> Build thee more stately mansions, O my soul,
> As the swift seasons roll!
> Leave thy low-vaulted past!
> Let each new temple, nobler than the last,
> Shut thee from heaven with a dome more vast,
> Till thou at length art free,
> Leaving thine outgrown shell by life's unresting sea!

This stanza of "The Chambered Nautilus"[6] shows both the heart and need of the artist.

"The unhesitating rotundity of Yankee speech" bears analysis. A superlative treatment of reasonable length is found in chapter 7 of Robert McCrum, William Cran, and Robert MacNeil, *The Story of English.*[7] Regional variations are explored. Noah Webster's contribution in the publication of his first dictionary in 1806 is evaluated.

---

1. New England Unitarianism featured the high Arianism of William Ellery Channing and the quasi-pantheism of Theodore Parker, which became the total pantheism of Emerson. Parker repudiates distinctive Christian doctrine, especially inerrancy. See John Fea, "Theodore Parker and the Nineteenth-Century Assault on Biblical Authority," *Michigan Theological Journal* 3 (1992), 65ff.
2. *Dictionary of American Biography,* IX (New York: Scribner's, 1932), 169ff. It has been said humorously that "hyper-Calvinism" is actually "six-point Calvinism," the sixth point being "total inflexibility."
3. A recent very rewarding study of Oliver Wendell Holmes Jr., is Liva Baker's *The Justice from Beacon Hill* (New York: Harper/Collins, 1991). Justice Holmes was a strong advocate of "judicial restraint" and served thirty years on the High Court.
4. *American Poets and Their Theology,* 343.
5. Oliver Wendell Holmes Jr., *The Poetical Works of Oliver Wendell Holmes* (Boston: Houghton, Mifflin, 1882), 217.
6. Ibid., 161.
7. New York: Penguin, 1986.

8.1.4 WHITTIER, BELIEVER

We may not climb the heavenly steeps
To bring the Lord Christ down:
In vain we search the lowest deeps,
For Him no depths can drown.

But warm, sweet, tender, even yet
A present help is He;
And faith still has its Olivet,
And love its Galilee.

Our Lord and Master of us all!
Whate'r our name or sign,
We own Thy sway, we hear Thy call,
We test our lives by Thine.

—John Greenleaf Whittier
"Immortal Love, Forever Full"

"There is something in the doctrine of total depravity and regeneration," John Greenleaf Whittier (1807–1892) insisted, and in this he stood almost alone among early American poets. Whittier is sometimes called "the American poet" because his identification with the common man was much like that of Robert Burns in Scotland. He has been called "the country poet" because he was country born and bred. Some of his poetry is not linguistically beautiful, and his rhyming schemes can be unrefined. However, what he wrote made up in substance of thought for what it lacked in sophistication of form.

He was born in East Haverhill, Massachusetts, and raised on the farm of his devout Quaker parents. He was a tall, slender, quiet boy who "seemed alone when he was with people." Although the Bible was the book on which he was raised, his imagination was kindled by a wandering Yankee troubadour and by *The Pilgrim's Progress,* which was the literary staple in most literate families.[1] His family was among evangelical Quakers, who insisted that the Scriptures interpret experience against the followers of Elias Hicks. In the 1820s, the Hicksites developed an early form of what 150 years later would be called "liberation theology." They made experience and social justice the authorities that interpreted Scripture.[2]

Perhaps because he came from the Quaker context, Whittier did not live in reaction against the Puritan moral and spiritual ideals. He wrote:

Praise and thanks for an honest man!
Glory to God for the Puritan!

Whittier always remained avowedly and unashamedly a Christian. He cherished and knew the Bible; he was solidly and soundly Trinitarian; he saw Jesus as the divine Son of God. He protested against the trend toward "Puseyism" or the Tractarian Movement. E. B. Pusey (1800–1882) was an extreme leader of the Oxford Movement, who fought to see Protestants reunited with the Roman church. Whittier remarked: "Has thee noticed the general tendency toward the old trust in man—in priests and sacrifices, in ghostly mummery and machinery?"[3] Most rare among the poets of his generation, he recognized the centrality of the perfect atoning sacrifice of the Christ. In "The Crucifixion" he confessed:

> The Sacrifice! The death of Him,
> The Christ of God, the Holy One!
> Well may the conscious Heaven grow dim,
> And blacken the beholding Sun!

Studying briefly at Haverhill Academy, Whittier could not afford to go to college. His early writings were not very good, but the abolitionist editor William Lloyd Garrison (1805–1879) submitted some of his pieces for publication. Then began the cyclical pattern that would mark Whittier's life. He incessantly suffered fierce migraine headaches and also had heart problems. So he would build up his health and stamina on the family farm, then plunge with all his energy into the editing of reform and temperance journals. When he overtaxed his strength, he would collapse, turn his editing duties over to others, and go back to the farm.

Dedicated like his model Milton to "the reforming spirit," he took up the cudgel for such causes as the welfare of Native Indians, prohibition of liquor, and the rights of women and blacks.[4] Whether serving in the Legislature or editing in Philadelphia, his abolitionist conviction was straightforward: Slavery was contrary to the will of God! Though he was the object of violence, he remained a Quaker pacifist and broke with Garrison and other radicals who advocated violent opposition to slavery. He fought his cousin Daniel Webster when Webster supported the Fugitive Slave Act. Whittier averred that Webster had been drinking too much to be clear-minded enough to grasp the issue.[5]

Whittier never married and cared for his mother and infirm sister until their deaths. He was in vital contact with such national leaders as John Quincy Adams and Charles Sumner. He was toasted and honored in his old age. Even Helen Keller came to visit. He had a stroke and died in his eighty-fifth year.

Whittier was a gifted balladist. His "Maud Muller" and "Barbara Frietchie" are lilting. His "Snow-Bound: An American Idyll" confirmed him in the hearts of Americans as their village poet. Seventy of his poems have been sung as hymns, including "Dear Lord and Father of Mankind, Forgive Our Feverish Ways."

The poet had a nostalgic spirit and admitted that "I love the vanished past." Yet many of his lines are classic, such as "Blessings on thee, little man, Barefoot boy with cheek of tan," and "Of all sad words of tongue or pen, The saddest are, 'It might have been.'" He wrote protests against slavery, with such lines as:

> Our fellow-countrymen in chains!
> Slaves in a land of light and law!
> Slaves, crouching on the very plains
> Where rolled the storm of Freedom's war!

He couldn't understand why his friends Holmes and Longfellow were reticent to enter the lists against this wicked business. He was so upset with Whitman's sentiments on many issues that he threw his writings into the fire.

He acknowledged his own limits as a literary craftsman, admitting that his work lacked "rounded art." Obviously for many, he was too Puritan and too much a Quaker, as well, but it was this faith that gave him his appreciation of the beauty of nature and of holiness. His "Eternal Goodness" reflects this light as a gem:

> Yet, in the maddening maze of things,
> And tossed by storm and flood,
> To one fixed trust my spirit clings;
> I know that God is good!

He writes movingly about the camp-meeting revivals and "The Christian Slave." Cotton Mather is one of his subjects. While his narrative gift was not the best, we sense the surge of "Skipper Ireson's Ride" and "The Prophecy of Samuel Sewall." More than five hundred pieces are in the standard collection of his work.

For this humble man of God, we must ever be grateful that an evangelical Christian stood in the nineteenth-century literary world.

---

1. Lewis Leary, *John Greenleaf Whittier* (New York: Twayne, 1961), 21.
2. A superb study is D. Elton Trueblood's *Robert Barclay* (New York: Harper, 1968). Barclay, who was the strong theologian in Quaker theology, maintained that anything contrary to Scripture was of the Devil.
3. Strong, *American Poets and Their Theology,* 113.
4. Leary, *John Greenleaf Whittier,* 37. Whittier was dedicated to "the cause."
5. Ibid., 105–8. In "Ichabod," the clear background is Genesis 9 and 1 Samuel 4:21.

8.1.5 LONGFELLOW, PROFESSOR

> Life is real! Life is earnest!
> And the grave is not its goal;
> Dust thou art, to dust returnest,
> Was not spoken of the soul.
> Lives of great men all remind us
> We can make our lives sublime,
> And, departing, leave behind us
> Footprints on the sands of time.
>
> Let us, then, be up and doing,
> With a heart for any fate;
> Still achieving, still pursuing,
> Learn to labor and to wait.
>   —Henry Wadsworth Longfellow
>   "Psalm of Life"

These stanzas forever etched on the national consciousness show why Henry Wadsworth Longfellow (1807–1882) inhabits a special niche among American poets. A bust of Longfellow is to be seen in Poets' Corner in Westminster Abbey in London—the only American so honored. While his poetic stock has risen or fallen with literary critical fashion, Longfellow always stands tall as a North American man of letters and educator.

Longfellow was born in Portland, Maine, the son of a prominent lawyer and politician; his mother was a woman of religious devotion and a love for music and literature. He matriculated at Bowdoin College in Brunswick, Maine, and was offered, upon graduation, a professorship in modern languages, in preparation for which he spent three years in Europe.

No early American poet was so well experienced and appreciated in Europe as was Longfellow. In 1834 he was offered the chair of modern languages at Harvard and again went to Europe, where both his wife and baby died tragically. He later met and, for agonizing years, courted Fanny Appleton, whom he married. They lived for eighteen years in Craigie House, Cambridge, Massachusetts, until she died in a fire. His face was so severely burned in his effort to save her that he wore a full beard thereafter to conceal the scars.

Longfellow's early works include such classics as "The Wreck of the Hesperus" and "The Village Blacksmith." "Evangeline" was written in 1847, honoring the struggles of the Nova Scotia Acadians. From "the forest primeval" in Acadia, Evangeline and her beloved were exiled and then separated from each other.[1]

Strong influences on these early years were Vergil (70 B.C. to 19 B.C.), Washington Irving (1783–1859), and Bryant. In his most productive time, he wrote "Song of Hiawatha" and "The Courtship of Miles Standish." Something of a dandy, he had a musically powerful organ-like voice. Plagued with insomnia, neuralgia, dyspepsia, and poor eyes, Longfellow was even-dispositioned and generous to a fault. His son-in-law Richard Henry Dana (1815–1882), author of *Two Years Before the Mast,* described him as somewhat aloof. Charles Kingsley (1819–1875) felt, "I never saw a finer human face."

Fastidious in his own habits, he was shocked by the smoking, drinking, and card-playing among Swedish clergy he encountered on a trip to Scandinavia.[2] His *Poems on Slavery* satisfied John Greenleaf Whittier on the burning issue. He was a consistent backer of Lincoln, and Sumner was one of his best friends.

Longfellow was a lover of opera, and the musical star of the mid-1800s, Jenny Lind, captivated him.[3] He loved Shakespearean readings along with Walter Scott and Charles Dickens. Eventually, he tired of lecturing and turned from the public eye to writing. A master of most European languages, he knew Swedish, Danish, and even Finnish.

His poetry has been critiqued as too conventional and didactic. Sometimes he wrote hurriedly, writing "The Saga of King Olaf" in fifteen days and "Judas Maccabeus" in eleven days. The English hexameter was his stock in trade. His fiery nationalism is particularly evident in *Tales of a Wayside Inn.* He was charged to be a plagiarist by Poe and by the transcendentalist Margaret Fuller (1810–1850).[4] Something of his genius and later loneliness are reflected in *Tales of a Wayside Inn*:

> Ships that pass in the night, and speak to each other in passing,
> Only a signal shown and a distant voice in the darkness;
> So on the ocean of life, we pass and speak to one another,
> Only a look and a voice, then darkness again and a silence.

Longfellow remained a Unitarian, according to one daughter.[5] Fanny was a Unitarian. His father had been a classmate of William Ellery Channing (1780–1842). Channing's Unitarianism was the high Arianism that celebrated Jesus the model. Longfellow was exposed to orthodoxy at Bowdoin College, but he remained "by nature and education a Pelagian."[6] He professed a bias against dogma and theology. By-products of Christianity can be discerned in a poem such as "Blind Bartimeus."

There is no "personal or present Christ" in Longfellow's work.[7] The Bible seems to mean less to him than do the church fathers. He still was shocked by the heterodox views on the atonement of Horace Bushnell (1802–1876).[8] He encouraged his daughter Edith when she became an Episcopalian. He negatively portrayed the Puritan minister in "The Birds of Killingworth," but he was positive toward the Catholic missionary in "The Song of Hiawatha." He liked the Christian Harriet Beecher Stowe (1811–1896) but was taken aback by her brother, Henry Ward Beecher (1813–1887). He was interested in animal magnetism and spiritualism, but would not endorse Mary Baker Eddy (1821–1910) in *Science and Health, with a Key to the Scriptures*.

Longfellow's technical skills increased, but his creative spirit waned.[9] He aspired to write a religious classic as had Dante and issued his *Christus* toward the end of his life. The poem bears witness to Christian facts without heart and without a sense of reality. "The Children's Hour" was more popular and significant than was his mammoth religious work. He did not have deep spiritual wells upon which to draw. The last lines of his unfinished "Michael Angelo" fit him:

> Life hath become to me
> An empty theater, its lights extinguished,
> The music silent and the actors gone;
> And I sit musing on the scene
> That once have been. I am so old that Death
> Oft plucks me by the cloak, to come with him;
> And some day like this lamp, shall I fall down,
> And my last spark of life will be extinguished.
> Ah me! Ah me! what darkness of despair!
> So near to death, and yet so far from God.

---

1. *The Complete Poetical Works of Henry Wadsworth Longfellow* (Boston: Houghton, Mifflin, 1882).

2. Edward Wagenknecht, *Henry Wadsworth Longfellow: Portrait of an American Humanist* (New York: Oxford University Press, 1966), 38.

3. Ibid., 66.

4. Ibid., 143. He did use other people's work as resources, as in "Paul Revere's Ride" and "The Three Kings."

5. Ibid., 193. Longfellow was a tenderhearted father. His great trial was Charley, who ran away to war.

6. Strong, *American Poets and Their Theology*, 223.

7. Ibid., 236. How quickly the early church lost the sense of Christ the Lord and His atoning work. See Thomas F. Torrance, *The Doctrine of Grace in the Apostolic Fathers* (Grand Rapids: Eerdmans, 1948), 133ff.

8. Wagenknecht, *Henry Wadsworth Longfellow: Portrait of an American Humanist*, 194. Horace Bushnell abandoned the substitutionary atonement for moral influence.

9. Strong, *American Poets and Their Theology*, 231. He also wrote doggerel: "There was a little girl who had a little curl."

8.1.6 WHITMAN, MOCKER

> I celebrate myself, and sing myself,
> And what I assume you shall assume.
> Walt Whitman, a kosmos, of Manhattan the son,
> Turbulent, fleshy, sensual, drinking and breeding,
> No sentimentalist, no stander above men and women
> Or apart from them, the spread of my own body, or any part of it,
> No more modest than immodest
>
> Divine am I inside and out, and I make holy
> Whatever I touch or am touch'd from,
> The scent of these arm-pits aroma finer than prayer,
> The head more than churches, bibles and all creeds.
> If I worship one thing more than another it shall be the
> Translucent mould of me it shall be you!
>
> —Walt Whitman
> *Leaves of Grass*

Acclaimed by some to be the quintessential ideal of an American poet, yet admired more perhaps in Europe than in America, Walt Whitman (1819–1892) was undoubtedly a poetic revolutionary and a genius. Yet he carried Emerson's gospel of the self to its logical and shocking conclusion. Emerson was in raptures with the publication of *Leaves of Grass* in 1855, and while Whitman and he had serious tensions later, he saw Whitman as his heir in proclaiming his all-embracing individualism and secular religion.

Whitman, who shortened his name to Walt to differentiate himself from his father and to indicate his emancipation, was born on Long Island and raised in Brooklyn where his father was a builder. He set himself to exploding all conventions. On his mother's side, he was descended from the Hicksite Quakers who denied the deity of Christ and the inspiration of the Scriptures.

Even though Brooklyn was filled with good churches and able preachers, Whitman found no preacher appealing except for Henry Ward Beecher. He was particularly taken with Beecher's statement: "Do you suppose I study musty old books when I want to preach? I study you. When I want to deliver a discourse on theology, I study you!"[1] The rakish young man worked in print shops and taught school in West Babylon, New York. But then he was accused of sodomy, tarred and feathered, and run out of town. The Presbyterian pastor in the community denounced him, and the matter was referred to later as "Walt's trouble."[2]

He edited the *Brooklyn Eagle* from 1846 to 1848, but he did not stay with that or anything else very long. The one novel he wrote, *Franklin Evans,* ironically had a temperance theme. He purposed to start a new religion and projected that *Leaves of Grass* would be its Bible.[3] He was obsessed with death ("O mystery of Death—I pant for the time when I shall solve you"). His thinking was shaped by Kantian subjectivism, naturalistic evolution, phrenology, and spiritism. The mystic eroticism of Swedenborgianism was vastly appealing to him. That the "new theologies bring forth man" is apparent in Whitman.[4]

Leaves of Grass appeared in 1855, and he continually added to it into the 1890s. But it was not well received. Whitman had revolted against rhyme and meter in his blank verse. The work engendered more controversy for its overt sexual themes. It glorified the physical. Emerson urged some reticence about his own body, but for Whitman, impulse was divine, and the obscene was to be exalted. Whittier called *Leaves of Grass* a "phallic frenzy." Augustus Hopkins Strong well points out that Whitman had no sense of proportion because he had no standard for judgment. "We might as well give up Handel and Beethoven and go back to the music of tom-toms."[5] He is like Jean-Jacques Rousseau (1712–1778), who also preached a gospel of license. Many talk about the work who have never read it to see how it embodies a sick narcissism.[6]

Ambivalent about slavery, he did go to Washington to minister to a wounded brother and worked in the hospitals during the war. He also held government jobs, which explains his support for Andrew Johnson during the scandals leading to his impeachment trial. His boundless egotism and fanatic independence were modified in Washington because of economic realities. After 1873 he moved to Camden, New Jersey.[7] The Bohemian who had bragged about his six children born out of wedlock, became "the good, gray poet," even expurgating some eroticism from his poetry. He suffered a series of strokes, which debilitated him.

Several of his poems are striking, including his ode to Abraham Lincoln, "O Captain! My Captain!" and his "When Lilacs Late in the Dooryard Bloom'd."

Whitman never felt the need for Christ. He shared: "I have never had any particular religious experiences—never felt that I needed to be saved—never felt the need of spiritual regeneration—never had any fear of hell or distrust of the scheme of the universe. I always felt that it was perfectly right and for the best."[8]

Because he felt Christ and Satan and Hercules and Brahma and Saturn were of one kind, Strong rightly describes him "as without God and without hope," one whom "God gave up to a reprobate mind."[9]

---

1. David S. Reynolds, *Walt Whitman's America: A Cultural Biography* (New York: Knopf, 1995), 173.

2. Ibid., 70. His new writings of this time resonate with personal trauma, trying "to purge the demons."

3. Ibid., 238. Yet his new religion, in all of its deistic perspectives, provided no stable explanation for his questions.

4. Ibid., 255. Beecher's showmanship and secularization were emblematic of America's growing popular religion.

5. Strong, *American Poets and Their Theology*, 433.

6. For an important social commentary on self-worship, see Paul C. Vitz, *Psychology as Religion: The Cult of Self-Worship* (1977, repr. ed., Grand Rapids: Eerdmans, 1994). Vitz discusses Rousseau's assumptions about natural human goodness.

7. Horace Traubel, *With Walt Whitman in Camden: April 8–September 14, 1889* (Carbondale, Ill.: Southern Illinois University, 1964).

8. Strong, *American Poets and Their Theology*, 455.

9. Ibid., 469. Whitman's laxity of personal belief shows the disaster of antinomian liberty.

8.1.7 Poe, Sufferer

> "Prophet!" said I, "Thing of evil!—prophet still, if bird or devil!—
> Whether Tempter sent, or whether tempest tossed thee here ashore,
> Desolate yet all undaunted, on this desert land enchanted—
> On this home by Horror haunted—tell me truly, I implore—
> Is there-is there balm in Gilead?—tell me—tell me, I implore!"
> Quoth the Raven, "Nevermore."
>
> —Edgar Allan Poe
> "The Raven"

"Horror was his true element, primordial horror" is descriptive of Edgar Allan Poe (1809–1849) in one of his ablest biographers, Frances Winwar.[1] *The Haunted Palace* is one of the eerie encapsulizations of Poe's life. He was born into a prominent Boston family—his grandfather was an Irish immigrant who served as a colonial General in the American Revolution. His parents were actors, his father a drunkard and his mother morally frail. Both were dead by Poe's second birthday, and he was raised by Mr. and Mrs. John Allan of Richmond, Virginia, who never legally adopted him (but from whom he took his middle name). He had upper-class exposure when he lived with the Allans in England for five years and attended a classical academy. Upon returning, he had a gifted private tutor and studied at the University of Virginia and the West Point Military Academy.

His life seemed filled with promise, but drinking and debts resulting from his lifestyle alienated him from the Allans, who left nothing for him in their will.

Poe tried the military and took refuge with his natural father's sister in Baltimore. Nothing worked. His life was consistently a "calendar of poverty, sickness, madness, drink, dope and fornication." Yet he was a master of the short story—for example, "The Gold Bug." He originated the suspense novel in the mode of the mystery in such pieces as "The Mystery of Marie Roget." He probably exceeds all of his rivals in the dramaturgy of death in "The Cask of Amontillado" and "The Fall of the House of Usher," as well as the immortal "The Pit and the Pendulum."[2] His literary criticism was the first in America and was advanced in his *The Philosophy of Composition* and other works in which he viciously and violently attacks Longfellow.

Yet his poetry, particularly "The Raven," brought him to fame in 1845. T. S. Eliot was right that Poe wrote few poems, yet they "stick to our minds." He was a master of technique and passion. In only about one hundred pages of verse, he made an impact on all generations.

What young person in school has not shuddered at the onomatopoeia of "the silken, sad, uncertain rustling of each purple curtain" in "The Raven." This haunting poem is Poe's commentary on his own religionless philosophy. He leaves his readers perched on the edge of nothingness. Life and death are illusions.[3]

Totally untouched by Puritanism, Poe aspired to be a philosophic writer. We see his total subjectivity in his earliest poems, "Tamerlane" and "Al Aaraaf." Like Shelley, he denounces God (calling himself an atheist of the heart rather than the head) and then makes himself God. He followed Immanuel Kant (1724–1804) and Coleridge in accepting the human mind as creator. In this he followed very much the thinking of Emerson and Bushnell.[4] He did not express any concern about evil, drawing on his liberation from any idea of original sin. He sneered at James Fenimore Cooper (1789–1851) for his moral saws and "outright sermons." His writing had no moral and spiritual considerations. He judged the Christian view of death to be "stale," so he eroticized death and rationalized the apocalyptic context of life's future. Strong calls him "a victim of his own appetites." In "Eureka," which he wrote the year before his death, his absolute materialism and self-deification[5] are unmistakable.

He married his thirteen-year-old cousin, who soon died of tuberculosis and is memorialized in his moving "Annabel Lee."[6] He struggled on for two years after her death. After a series of heavy drinking bouts and attempted suicides, he was found unconscious by his friends and died at the end of 1849. Poe has been known as "the wild poet," or some have called him "the poet of the outcast soul." His literary executor, Griswold, wrote:

> He seemed, except when some fitful pursuit subjugated his will and engrossed his faculties, always to bear the memory of some controlling sorrow. The remarkable poem of "The Raven" was probably much more nearly than has been supposed, even by those who were intimate with him, a reflection and an echo of his own history. He was that bird's "unhappy master whom unmerciful Disaster followed fast and followed faster till his songs one burden bore of 'Never—nevermore.'"[7]

D. H. Lawrence said he believed that Poe was "concerned with the disintegrative processes of his own psyche."[8] He had no moorings beyond himself and his own resources and strength. This is a rope of sand to be sure. He renounced the idea of resurrection and final judgment. Some see his quest as the unending search for his mother. But it is more than that. In his hypostasis of the self, he has excluded the reality of the transcendent God from his life.

1. Frances Winwar, *The Haunted Palace: A Life of Edgar Allan Poe* (New York: Harper, 1965). Poe died in despair. He believed that "after dying, we become God—my whole nature revolts at the idea there is any Being in the Universe superior to myself" (Kenneth Silverman, *Edgar A. Poe: Mournful and Never-ending Remembrance* [New York: Harper/Collins, 1991], 340). Silverman's is the best biography now in print.

2. Edward H. Davidson, *Poe: A Critical Study* (Cambridge, Mass.: Belknap/Harvard University Press, 1966), 104.

3. Ibid., 103. A Romantic Idealist, Poe allows the poet to masquerade as God. He felt the "didactic" to be heretical.

4. Ibid., 68. He borrows from Milton but "bends all external reality to his own will."

5. Strong, *American Poets and Their Theology,* 187.

6. An excellent sampling of Poe is in Harry Hayden Clark's *Major American Poets* (New York: American Book, 1936).

7. Strong, *American Poets and Their Theology,* 203. Strong reports that in Poe's last conscious moment, "He moved his head gently, uttered the words 'Lord, help my poor soul!' and expired" (181). This could point to a deathbed conversion, but probably shows only fear of dying without God.

8. D. H. Lawrence, "Edgar Allan Poe" in *Edgar Allan Poe,* ed. Harold Bloom (New York: Chelsea House, 1985), 21.

8.1.8 LOWELL, RACONTEUR

Once to every man and nation comes the moment
    to decide,
In the strife of truth with falsehood, for the good or
    evil side;
Some great cause, God's new Messiah, offering
    each the bloom or blight,
And the choice goes by forever 'twixt that darkness
    and that light.

Though the cause of evil prosper, yet 'tis truth
    alone is strong:
Though her portion be the scaffold, and upon the
    throne be wrong;
Yet that scaffold sways the future, and, behind the
    dim unknown,
Standeth God within the shadow keeping watch
    above His own.

—James Russell Lowell
"The Present Crisis"

From one of the great Brahmin families of New England, James Russell Lowell (1819–1891) came from stock that furnished educators, politicians, and poets, including such noteworthy writers as Amy Lowell and Robert Lowell.

280 The Company of the Creative

At first highly touted by critics, but now less appreciated, Lowell never seemed to realize his promise. Perhaps he attempted too much—he made not one but one thousand impressions. Biographer Edward Wagenknecht summarized the poet's failing that "he lacks that last touch of genius—that 'St. Elmo's Fire.'"[1] His output was voluminous.

Apart from poetry, Lowell had a distinguished career. He followed Longfellow as professor of modern languages at Harvard. He served as ambassador to Spain and also to Britain's Court of St. James. He edited *Atlantic Monthly* and *North American Review,* both influential publications. But he considered his chief calling to be that of a poet. He was a voracious reader. In his various collections of verse, he makes thirteen hundred references to the classics and three hundred to the Bible.[2] Great literature was his first love.

Many consider his popular "The Vision of Sir Launfal" with its couplet, "What is so rare as a day in June? Then if ever come perfect days," to be his finest work. His *Biglow Papers* described New England life from a Yankee perspective.

He was born in Elmwood, the Lowell family domicile. His father was a Congregational minister who took no stand in the Trinitarian/Unitarian battle, preferring just to preach joy.[3] His mother was a teller of tales, but she was afflicted with "a darkened mind." Her son likewise was afflicted by bipolar, or what is popularly called "manic-depressive," disorder.

James Russell studied at a private academy and did not work hard at Harvard where he began his studies at age fifteen. He considered the ministry but went into law; but it was writing, not law, that satisfied him.

Two wives (the first was a Transcendentalist/Unitarian and the second a Swedenborgian) preceded him in death. He often was financially pressed, partly because of his care of a great old house that could not be heated, and partly because he was excessively generous. In keeping with his mental disorder, euphoric humor was frequently followed by suicidal impulses. He felt he was "a kind of twin—divided between grave and gay." He also suffered from chronic gout and various physical maladies.[4]

Lowell was a chronic smoker and intemperate in his habits. Occasionally he went on drinking binges. He was slight in build, fastidious in dress, "not easily accessible," shy, and plagued by feelings of inferiority. Said a researcher into his life, he had not the "stuff of which lions are made."

He vowed to read a chapter in the Bible daily and claimed to be a Christian, but in his ambivalent faith he identified himself spasmodically as a Congregationalist or an Episcopalian. He had no time for François Voltaire (1694–1778) but loved Dante (1265–1321) and John Milton (1608–1674). He read Henry Fielding's (1707–1754) *Tom Jones* annually. He was strong on Walter Scott (1771–1832) but oddly didn't read Charles Dickens's (1812–1870) *David Copperfield* until 1887. On meeting Emerson, he observed, "He is a good-natured man in spite of his doctrines."[5] He thought Emerson's "Divinity School Address" was "irreverent and muddleheaded." He highly valued his Puritan forebears but regretted that the Puritans had divorced the church from art.[6]

As a poet, he was careful and exacting. Some characteristic examples of his craftsmanship include "Under the Willows," "To a Dandelion," and "A Good Word for Winter." In "The Search," he disavows pantheism (he was always uneasy with Rousseau's and Thoreau's identification with nature).[7] His tribute to Lincoln in "Commemoration Ode" is one of the best. Like Longfellow, he aspired to write a religious classic (on the order of Dante's). In "Cathedral: A Day at Chartres," his love for the Gothic and some aversion for Protestant theology surface. Here most clearly, we see he is embedded in an immanence that excludes any element of transcendence. We have a bland theism but no Christianity. No miracle . . . no revelation . . . no mediator . . . no propitiation. "Every man is his own Melchizedec."[8] He has no expectation of reunion with his departed loved ones. He did not believe in divine inspiration of Scripture: "I have wondered whether you believed in the divine inspiration of the Hebrew prophets. Do you? I don't."[9]

Lowell has been an inspiration to many. In "Cathedral" can be sensed a mysticism, rather than any "faith once for all delivered to the saints."[12] He is not theological, but he urges a high moral standard upon us. He drinks at the fountain, but he does not acknowledge the Source. Still we identify with his sentiments as expressed in "International Copyright":

> In vain we call old notions fudge,
> And bend our conscience to our dealing;
> The Ten Commandments will not budge,
> And stealing will continue stealing.

---

1. Edward Wagenknecht, *James Russell Lowell: Portrait of a Many-Sided Man* (New York: Oxford University Press, 1971), 6.
2. Ibid., 105. Sources were very important for Lowell but references to his theology, best represented in "The Courtin'," are exceedingly vague.
3. Ibid., 9, 10. Perhaps his father's influence explains why one senses more feeling than thought in Lowell's work.
4. Ibid., 43. Confidence in "inevitable progress" is stronger in his earlier poems, but it perceptibly begins to wane.
5. Strong, *American Poets and Their Theology*, 270.
6. Wagenknecht, *James Russell Lowell: Portrait of a Many-Sided Man*, 162.
7. This would be a good time to dip into Henry David Thoreau's *Walden Pond*, a classic recital of Thoreau's two years living at the famous pond, telescoped into a year of narrative. Thoreau was very close to Emerson and his circle.
8. *American Poets and Their Theology*. Strong contrasts Lowell's "Cathedral" with Browning's "Saul."
9. Ibid., 305. Although he denied divine revelation, he would affirm the inspiration of all human beings.
10. Ibid., 309. Penitence and the cross have no positive place in Lowell's thinking.
11. *Portrait of a Many-Sided Man*, 195, 213. Lowell personifies the spirit of Schleiermachian liberalism.
12. Ibid., 208.

8.1.9 DICKINSON, SEEKER

> And "Jesus"! Where is Jesus gone?
> They say that Jesus—always came—
> Perhaps he doesn't know the House—
> This way, Jesus, Let him pass!
>
> —Emily Dickinson
> "Poem 158"

> Some keep the Sabbath going to Church
> I keep it, staying at Home
> With a Bobolink for a Chorister
> And an Orchard, for a Dome!
> God preaches, a Noted Clergyman,
> And the sermon is never long,
> So instead of getting to Heaven at last
> I'm going, all along.
>
> —"Poem 324"

Rated by Ivor Winters as "one of the greatest lyric poets of all time" and undoubtedly the great American poetess, Emily Dickinson (1830–1886) continues to fulfill and to frustrate readers and scholars. Of her more than eighteen hundred pieces, only a handful were published during her life, and those anonymously. Her sister Lavinia found a stash of manuscripts after her death. These were edited and published over a period of years.[1] Most are four-line pieces in aphoristic style. Some of her epigrammatic sayings have been organized into the "new" poems.[2]

Emily Dickinson was born in Amherst, Massachusetts, into a post-Puritan tradition when the influence of Jonathan Edwards's Calvinism had yielded to Ralph Waldo Emerson. Her father was a prominent churchman, attorney/politician, and treasurer of Amherst College. His was a dominating personality. She attended Amherst Academy for three years and then Mount Holyoke for a year.

In 1854 she apparently fell in love with a married minister. After a series of such disappointments in love, Emily began a pattern of withdrawal from society. Neither she nor her sister Lavinia ever married. Emily always dressed in white and for fifteen years ventured only a few steps from her parental home. Many family friends never saw her. She stayed upstairs listening to what transpired but never put in an appearance.

When revival meetings were held in the family church, she was the only member of her family who did not go forward to receive Christ. "Christ is calling everyone here, all my companions have answered . . . and I am standing alone in rebellion and growing very careless," she wrote.[3] She shows the Puritan penchant for rigorous self-examination and the influence of "Scripture, impassioned sermons and the sonorous hymns of Isaac Watts."[4]

Her most productive time of writing was the four dark and difficult years of the Civil War, during which she wrote half of her output. These were poems of love, death, and immortality. Her work is replete with symbols, such as the sun (used 170 times); the sea (122 times); noon (seventy-six times).[5]

There is agony in her words. What was it that "a plank in reason broke?"[6] She seemed very close to psychosis. The death of a friend devastated her when she was at the Academy, and she had to leave school for a while. Her mother was apparently a very deeply depressed hypochondriac, and the hypersensitive Emily had a ravenous but unfilled longing for love and tenderness.[7] "I never had a mother," she claimed. She admired but did not particularly like her father. He always screened her letters before she could read them. Not surprisingly, she remained very immature into her twenties. Her brother's marriage was a catastrophe. Even when her father was converted, there was a kind of proud defensiveness, so that the pastor said, "You want to come to Christ as a lawyer, but you must come to Him as a sinner—Get down on your knees."[8]

Although she did not feel close to her father, she mourned heavily for him for two years after his death and dreamed of him every night. He had made her world a very frightening place. She continued to be frightened all of her life. Once she made two trips to Cambridge because of eye problems, but she could never allow the doctor to examine her.

"I read my Bible sometimes," she remarked.[9] In a state of virtual collapse, she insisted on closing all the windows at night and leaving a light burning. In this time, she wrote her "volcano" poems (like "Poem 1677"), her "sea" poems ("378" and "1123"), and her love poems (such as "356," "430," and "508"). In 1867 she returned home, never to venture out again. She maintained contacts outside her tiny world. She corresponded with many people and sent gifts.

After the death of their parents, the two sisters were cared for by two servants, and the house was shuttered. Emily increasingly had "attacks of nervous prostrations" and apparently died of Bright's Disease (a cause of kidney failure) in 1886. Lavinia was a kind of surrogate mother to Emily to the last, and it was Lavinia who arranged publication of the works found after Emily's death.[10]

Her style and thinking are unconventional, heedless of the standards of her times. She reflects deep spiritual wrestling, misery that spawned intense creativity. She held back from commitment to Christ. She said that she loved the world too much, writing: "I feel that the world holds a predominant place in my affections. I do not feel that I could give up all for Christ."[11] She was honest enough to reject pretense. She would not live a charade.

Three divergent approaches were made in the late twentieth century to Emily Dickinson's life. Judith Farr wrote a novel about her life in *I Never Came to You in White*,[12] through the vehicle of a series of fictional letters. Jane Langton's delightful *Emily Dickinson is Dead*[13] is a delightful novel of suspense set at an Emily Dickinson Memorial Symposium. A study by evangelical scholar Roger Lundin, *Emily Dickinson and the Art of Belief*, is superb.[14] He concludes that she was "eccentrically Trinitarian," yet mesmerized by Emerson.

1. Readers can dip in anywhere and find sparkling challenges in Thomas H. Johnson, ed., *The Complete Poems of Emily Dickinson* (Boston: Little, Brown, 1951). For example, "Poem 1545" begins, "The Bible is an antique Volume."
2. William H. Shurr, ed., *New Poems of Emily Dickinson* (Chapel Hill, N.C.: University of North Carolina Press, 1994).
3. Thomas Becknell, "The Ache for Faith," *Christianity Today,* 8 August 1986, 23. Dickinson never experienced any certainty about her standing with God.
4. Ibid., 24. She wrote that she would never stand up for Christ, only stoop over with her eyes to the ground.
5. John Cody, *After Great Pain: The Inner Life of Emily Dickinson* (Cambridge: Belknap/Harvard, 1971), 7.
6. Two typical approaches to Dickinson are seen in the incautious John Evangelist Walsh, *This Brief Tragedy: Unraveling the Todd-Dickinson Affair* (New York: Grove Weidenfelt, 1991) and the cautious, Roger Lundin, "Whose Emily Dickinson?" *Books and Culture,* July/August 1996, 11ff.
7. Cody, *After Great Pain,* 39. There was great turbulence in her family—five family deaths in eighteen years.
8. Ibid., 66. There was something "very over-sized" about her extremely successful father. He wasn't home much.
9. Ibid., 251. Yet she rather defiantly says, "I did not give and become a Christian."
10. Ibid., 465.
11. Ibid., 494. She had a strong aversion to sexuality and saw men as rivals at worst, older brothers at best.
12. Boston: Houghton Mifflin, 1997.
13. New York: Penguin, 1984.
14. Grand Rapids: Eerdmans, 1998.

8.1.10 LANIER, SOUTHERNER

As the marsh-hen secretly builds on the watery sod,
Behold I will built me a nest on the greatness of God:
I will fly in the greatness of God as the marsh-hen flies
In the freedom that fills all the space 'twixt the marsh and the skies:
By so many roots as the marsh-grass sends in the sod
I will heartily lay me a-hold on the greatness of God:
Oh, like to the greatness of God is the greatness within
The range of the marshes, the liberal marshes of Glynn.

—Sidney Lanier
Marsh Hymns

A true son of the South, Sidney Lanier (1842–1881) has been praised as one of the great American poets and maligned by some as prominent as Allen Tate and Robert Penn Warren for a fawning nationalism. Much was compressed into a few years of his life, and the all-too-rare Christian accents in a major American poet are refreshing.

Lanier was born in Macon, Georgia, and raised in the home of a Huguenot lawyer and his Scottish-Irish wife. Sidney became an accomplished musician, choosing to focus on the flute at the behest of his father. He was raised a Presbyterian and at fifteen entered the Methodist Oglethorp College where he graduated at the head of his class in 1860. At college, he professed personal faith in Christ and never swerved from this commitment.[1]

He and his brother joined the Macon Volunteers at the outbreak of the Civil War. He had many harrowing experiences in the war including the Seven Days' Battle near Petersburg, Virginia, 1862, after which he helped shovel six hundred Union fatalities into a bombed-out crater near Petersburg. In 1864 he was captured on a blockade running ship and imprisoned at Point Lookout, Maryland. Here he apparently contracted the tuberculosis that plagued him the rest of his life. After the war, he crawled home to Macon, where he married Mary and worked as a clerk, a schoolteacher, and in law with his father.

He also wrote a rather discursive novel, *Tiger Lilies,* which was, nevertheless, widely read at the time. Totally dedicated to music, he was Romantic in his inclinations, a champion of chivalry and lady-worship, for which he was accused of "Sir Walter Scottism." He believed strongly in an innate moral sense and human responsibility for his actions after the fall.[2]

Not surprisingly, his postwar poetry was pessimistic. *The Jacquerie* had considerable rhetorical embellishment and sermonizing. At one point, the Franciscan friar John preaches a memorable sermon out of Revelation 6 on the seals. The preacher indicts war, praises the martyrs, and calls for a "vast undoing of things."[3] "Corn" is the first great agricultural poem on the American scene. Some of his best poetry uses regional dialects.

Even when he felt very low, he had the sense of the everlasting arms: "Of course I have my keen sorrows, momentarily more keen than I would like any one to know; but I thank God that in a knowledge of Him and of myself which cometh to me daily in fresh revelations, I have a steadfast firmament in blue, in which all clouds soon dissolve."[4]

He hated what he called "the spider-web of materialism," and celebrated an economy that would be mindful of the impoverished. We are not surprised at the musicality of his verse and observe with wonder "The Symphony," in which the strings, flute, and other instruments can be picked out from the words and cadence of the verse. In 1875 he was chosen to write the "Centennial Meditation" for Philadelphia, and while critics panned it, the people loved it. He actually became a lecturer in literature at Johns Hopkins University and first flautist for the Baltimore Symphony Orchestra. Word and rhythm blend in "Psalm of the West" and the remarkable "Song of the Chattahoochee," with its staccato rhythm of "run the rapid."[5] *Marsh Hymns* is musical verse at its best!

In confessing his faith, Lanier's "Resurrection" points to Christ as the resurrection and the life. In "Remonstrance," he pledges his love to his Lord "more fathoms deep than there is line to sound with." He comes to grips with the problem of evil in "Acknowledgment." In "The Crystal," he sees the uniqueness of Christ. These themes have rarely been treated by principle American poets before or since.

Forgiveness was a final theme for Lanier as he approached his own death. The two poems he wrote in the last two months of his tuberculosis-tortured life are both remarkable. "A Ballad of Trees and the Master" is about Gethsemane:

> Into the woods my Master went,
> Clean forspent, forspent.
> Into the woods my Master came,
> Forspent with love and shame.
> But the olives they were not blind to Him,
> The little gray leaves were kind to Him:
> The thorn-tree had a mind to Him
> When into the woods He came.
> Out of the woods my Master went,
> And He was well content.
> Out of the woods my Master came,
> Content with death and shame.

He dictated the mystical "Sunrise" while burning with 104-degree fever, as his scorched and seared lungs gave out.[6] His wife recorded the experience: "We are left alone (August 29th) with one another. On the last night of the summer comes a change. His love and immortal patience will hold off the destroyer of our summer yet one more week, until the forenoon of September 7th, and then falls the frost, and that unfaltering will renders its supreme submission to the adored will of God."

---

1. *American Poets and Their Theology,* 375.
2. Jack De Bellis, *Sidney Lanier* (New York: Twayne, 1972), 20, 40. He was deeply into feeling as a poet.
3. Ibid., 41. He loved German literature through Carlyle but ultimately dismissed both Kant and Goethe as guides.
4. *American Poets and Their Theology,* 382. His very striking love poems bespeak his beautiful marriage with Mary.
5. De Bellis, *Sidney Lanier,* 105. It seems strange that the "Southern Renaissance" Movement disdained Lanier.
6. *American Poets and Their Theology,* 416. Lanier died at the age of thirty-nine.

8.2   AMERICA'S POETIC PILLARS

Comparing a Lanier with a Whitman or a Holmes or even a Dickinson, allows one to make an overall observation about early-American Puritanism in America and its critics. That observation was best stated by cultural and evangelical theologian Mark Noll of Wheaton College: "While others preached self-reliance and sang the song of the self, Jonathan Edwards drove nearer the truth—that nothing can be saved without confronting its own damnation, that the way to gain one's life is to lose it."

In surveying the surges and swells, the valleys and vicissitudes that comprise the cultural history of the United States and Canada, some have tended to overstate the Christian tilt of her early leaders and people.[1] Others, marking the general tone of materialism and self-sufficiency that evidently characterized a majority of Americans from the American Revolution into the nineteenth and twentieth centuries, have seen mainly rebellion and revolt against God and His Word.[2] Threads of both faith and faithlessness are woven into this fabric, a weaving that can be sensed in poetry.

---

1. John Eidsmoe, *Christianity and the Constitution: The Faith of the Founding Fathers* (Grand Rapids: Baker, 1987).
2. Steven J. Keillor, *This Rebellious House: American History and the Truth of Christianity* (Downers Grove, Ill.: InterVarsity, 1997).

8.2.1 ROBINSON, AUSTERE YANKEE

> Friendless and faint, with martyred steps and slow,
> Faint for the flesh, but for the spirit free,
> Stung by the mob that comes along to see the show,
> The Master toiled along to Calvary;
> We gibed him, as he went, with houndish glee,
> Till his dimmed eyes for us did overflow
> We cursed his vengeless hands thrice wretchedly,
> And this was nineteen hundred years ago.
> —Edwin Arlington Robinson
> "Calvary"

Though not a Christian, Edwin Arlington Robinson (1869–1935) was captivated by the cross of Christ, as have been Gore Vidal, Norman Mailer, and other unlikely writers. In a time of shifting values, Robinson had an "anti-absolutist temper" and yet was an intellectual and a classicist with "a nineteenth century tone."[1] His twenty volumes of poetry were almost obscured "by the experimental poets of the twentieth century," but after age fifty, he seemed to come into his own, winning three Pulitzer Prizes and achieving considerable notice and good sales of his work.[2] In the poetic renaissance that began in about 1912, Frost and Robinson were more traditional, opposing the poetic posturing of Thomas Bailey Aldrich and R. W. Gilder and refusing to follow Dickinson and Whitman into the stream of Stephen Crane and Carl Sandburg. A master stylist, he did pioneer the break with certain outworn symbols.[3]

Robinson was born in Head Tide, Maine, but raised in Gardiner, Maine, his home for twenty-seven years. His parents were older, and he characterized them as "the best and kindliest of all parents."[4] Puritanism was really no longer "a coherent religious force" in New England but was in "stages of decay." Robinson had dispensed with the "acceptances of the eighteenth century" without the bitterness of others. He was by affiliation a Congregationalist Unitarian and by persuasion an

Emersonian gnostic. He came under the spell of words, reading Shakespeare by age seven. Although he virtually knew Dickens by heart and viewed Thackeray's *Pendennis* as his favorite, he confessed that "I was addicted to poetry."[5] Bryant and especially Tennyson shaped him.

He wrote at age eleven and after high school translated Horace and Vergil and explored some French forms. After high school, there were shadows, particularly his father's aging and his older physician brother's drug and alcohol abuse. He attended Harvard for two years but struggled with deafness and ear surgery. Retiring, he never married and struggled with a sense of failure. His brother Herman married the girl he loved. He developed eye trouble and various "mental disturbances."[6] He went into times of deep skepticism, rejected orthodoxy, and came out clinging to the philosophic idealism of Harvard's Josiah Royce. He tasted of Christian Science and dabbled in Carlyle and Swedenborgianism. He stated that he didn't have "enough stamina" to be a Christian.[7] Settling on a horizontalized Emersonian "asceticism of spirit," he expresses in "The Man Against the Sky" his essential problem of faith. This piece is built around Exodus 3, Daniel 3, and Revelation 16, 20. He couldn't expunge scriptural reference (just as Robert Lowell could never get away from Jonathan Edwards's "Sinners in the Hands of an Angry God"). We can hear his heart in this wrenching expression, "Doubt is certain, disbelief plausible, despair sympathetic and hope obscure." Little wonder that he was drawn to Cowper's poetry.

He made unsuccessful forays into prose and drama, returning to a "constant inclination to write verse."[8] He worked as a secretary and as a New York subway time checker fours a day. He got some financial relief when President Theodore Roosevelt obtained a post for him in the U.S. Customs House in New York. In this time, he began to drink heavily. Finding World War I distasteful, he turned his back on the modern world. He died of cancer of the pancreas in 1935.

Robinson was a great poet. His poems on "Erasmus" and "The Gift of God" (on unmerited love) are outstanding. His Arthurian trilogy lacks something, but an ability to portray human personality is seen in his creation of Tilbury Towne, the Gardiner, Maine, from whence he had come.[9] The alcoholic Miniver Cheever is certainly himself. Other characters, such as Richard Cory and Luke Havergal, leap off the page. "Sisera," "The Three Taverns" (on Paul's approach to Rome), "Lazarus," and "Nicodemus" show Bible knowledge—but they also trace his movement from faith through doubt to denial. "The Wandering Jew," with its picture of the Jew's "old, unyielding eyes," is striking.[10] He describes disappointed men. "The old human swamp" depicts "every man trying to cope with his demon." No redemption perspective relieves the human predicament.[11]

---

1. William Rose Benet, *Benet's Reader's Encyclopedia,* 3d ed. (New York: Harper and Row, 1987), 835.

2. Wallace L. Anderson, *Edward Arlington Robinson: A Critical Introduction* (Cambridge, Mass.: Harvard, 1968), vii.

3. Ibid., 20. Robinson's view was that a vacuum in poetry existed: "The country needs a poet!" (5).

4. Ibid., 26. His father was a successful state legislator and made and lost his fortune in the timber business.

5. Ibid., 22, 29. He especially liked *David Copperfield* and *Great Expectations*.

6. Ibid., 48. His classmates at Harvard regarded him as lonely and melancholy.

7. Ibid., 54. The great debate over science and religion left him limp and doubtful, as it did Mark Twain. Henry Ward Beecher opined that "No man can know the theology of the nineteenth century who has not read Swedenborg." Of course Swedenborg rejected original sin, the Trinity, the atonement, and salvation by faith. He was a Unitarian. Robinson was much influenced by this cult, but it did not prove to be enough for him (62).

8. Ellsworth Barnard, ed., *Edwin Arlington Robinson: Centenary Essays* (Athens: University of Georgia, 1969), 158.

9. Anderson, *Robinson: A Critical Introduction,* 74. The Tilbury Towne people are in *Children of the Night,* a work that is aptly titled for its spiritual darkness.

10. Roy Harvey Pierce, "The Old Poetry and the New: Robinson" in Harold Bloom, ed., *Edwin Arlington Robinson* (New York: Chelsea House, 1988), 28. Of the Jew: "In vain . . . the Second Coming came and went. . . ."

11. Josephine Miles, "Robinson and the Years Ahead," in Bloom, ed., *Edwin Arlington Robinson,* 134. A close friend of Robinson prophesied that his voice "will go on thundering down the ages." To study his legacy is important for a fuller understanding of those who came after him.

8.2.2 RILEY, HOMESPUN HOOSIER

Ah! who shall look backward with scorn and derision
And scoff the old book though it uselessly lies
In the dust of the past, while this newer revision
Lisps on of a hope and a home in the skies?
Shall the voice of the Master be stifled and riven?
Shall we hear but a tithe of the words He has said,
When so long he has, listening, leaned out of Heaven
To hear the old Bible my grandfather read?
The old-fashioned Bible—
The dust-covered Bible—
The leather-bound Bible my grandfather read.

—James Whitcomb Riley
"The Old-Fashioned Bible"

He wrote more than one thousand poems and considerable prose and, notwithstanding his "marked eccentricities," was the most popular American poet from the 1880s into the early twentieth century. He was known as "the people's laureate," and although "amateurish" stylistically, he was immensely popular throughout the English-speaking world. He was the wealthiest American writer of his time.

James Whitcomb Riley (1846–1916) was born the third of six children in the three hundred-inhabitant town of Greenfield, Indiana. His father was a lawyer, and his mother, who had great skill in rhymes, died when he was twenty. He was of Dutch Huguenot and Quaker extraction. His maternal grandfather was a frontier preacher widely known at camp meetings.[1] There were Methodist, Presbyterian, and Christian churches in Greenfield, but Swedenborgianism mixed in, through the influence of the famous Johnny ("Appleseed") Chapman (1774–1845). When his mother died, young Riley "had a vision of his mother in a Swedenborgian heaven, growing younger as Johnny Appleseed had promised."[2] Throughout his life, he was a nominal Methodist who had been thoroughly bored in Sunday school. His credo was the "American success ethic." As he expressed this ethic, it went like this: "I believe a man prays when he does well. I believe he worships God when his work is on a high plane; when his attitude toward his fellowmen is right, I guess God is pleased with him."[3]

"Formal theology never bothered him much," his biographer observes. He was influenced by Robert G. Ingersoll (1833–1899), although he could not go along with Ingersoll's militant agnosticism.[4] As a very young man, he was a Bible agent but could not sell a single Bible. He was a newspaper writer who was catapulted to negative public notice when some of his early poetry, written in the style of and represented to be Poe, was exposed. Rebounding, he started to write for himself (and under the pseudonym Benj. F. Johnson of Boone). His "Little Orphant Annie," "The Old Swimmin' Hole," and "When the Frost Is on the Punkin'" became legendary. Much of his writing was in Hoosier dialect. The writing was personable, if not cerebral.[5] He wrote in "the twilight of an age" and furthered "the myth of the American Eden." If you want to understand communication at this time on the American scene, you must dip into his newspaper column, "The Rhyme Wagon" and feel "the simple sentiments that came from his heart." One book alone sold more than a half million copies.[6]

He became a feverishly popular lecturer and performer on the Lyceum and Chautauqua platforms. So "whimsical and droll," he was by all accounts a better actor than poet.[7] His emotive monologue "Willie" was always a hit. He celebrated "the flurry of farm activity" and sentimentalized death. In 1881 he took the stage at Tremont Temple, Boston, where Dickens read, and with his zither regaled even Longfellow.[8] Always a victim of acute stage-fright, he had the appearance of a "benign English bishop," with his handsome gold-headed walking stick. He appeared with Samuel Clemens in Madison Square Garden and had a lasting friendship with Joel Chandler Harris of "Uncle Remus" fame.

He makes no effort to delve into "the darker places of the soul," as would Sinclair Lewis a generation later.[9] At his best, he is a descendant of John Greenleaf Whittier. Eugene Field and Theodore Dreiser liked his work, although Riley did not like the violent and seamy side of life Dreiser explored. He had sharp disagreements with Matthew Arnold and thought Henry James a snob. Benjamin Harrison was a good friend and Rudyard Kipling praised him. William Lyon Phelps (1865–1943) of Yale was also a booster. Little read today, he was a significant fixture in his time.

He had several triumphant overseas tours and was on the road almost constantly. But Riley never married and was often ill and drank heavily. In his moral life, the poet rejected Jesus Christ, but dozens of his poems have biblical themes.

He wrote appropriate holiday remembrances for Christmas and Easter on "The Wandering Jew," "The Prayer Perfect," "The Christ," "We Must Believe," and "Conscience."[10] He died at age sixty-six after strokes in Indianapolis where he had lived so long, in the heart of his beloved Indiana. Booth Tarkington and Hamlin Garland, noted writers, were his last visitors.

---

1. Richard Crowder, *Those Innocent Years: The Legacy and Inheritance of a Hero of the Victorian Era* (Indianapolis: Bobbs-Merrill, 1957), 22. One of Riley's heroes was the great Norwegian violinist, Ole Bull.
2. Ibid., 23, 51. The Methodist Church record shows: "Dropped. Never received into full connection" (66).
3. Ibid., 164.
4. Ibid., 218. Riley was expert in German dialect as well as Midwestern twang.
5. Ibid., 159.
6. Donald Culross Peattie, ed., *The Complete Poetical Works of James Whitcomb Riley* (Indianapolis: Bobbs-Merrill, 1937). Peattie makes the case that Riley was more than a versifier but "the poet of Midwest nature."
7. *Those Innocent Years,* 217, 102. From his earliest years, Riley was an avid reader and loved such pieces as *Moby Dick* and *Tom Jones.* Dickens and Burns had strong influence in Riley's life.
8. Ibid., 106.
9. Frank N. McGill, ed., *A Critical Survey of Poetry* (Pasadena, Calif.: Salems, 1992), 2762.
10. Riley stoutly opposed spiritualism and affirmed the immortality of the human soul.

8.2.3 SANDBURG, SWEDISH-AMERICAN WANDERER

> I shall foot it
> Down the roadway in the dusk,
> Where shapes of hunger wander
> And the fugitives of pain go by.
>
> —Carl Sandburg
> "The Road and the End"

A maverick and literary outsider, yet popular as "the people's poet," Carl Sandburg (1878–1967) migrated among many literary genres with aplomb. Robert Frost described Sandburg's free-verse as "playing tennis without a net," and other critics called him "a superficial and undisciplined poet" and a "careless biographer."

Yet he was a survivor and highly honored in his later years. He made his mark and must be read. For the Christian reader, he has tragic significance.[1]

This rough-hewn poet was born Carl August Sandburg in Galesburg, Illinois, the son of August and Clara Sandburg, immigrants from Sweden. Stern and hardworking as a railroad blacksmith, August Sandburg was steeped in the Swedish Bible. Escaping the Swedish ghetto, young Carl ventured to the Seminary Street Mission's Christian Endeavor Society, where he abysmally failed in his first declamatory experience.[2] Although painfully shy, he did muster the courage to escort a girl from a revival meeting. Staunch Republicans, his parents and their children were victimized by pastoral scandal at their Swedish Lutheran Church:

> The young Swedish-American Charlie Sandburg (as he called himself) was so disillusioned by a minister who was a hypocrite and fraud that he never again affiliated with any organized church. August, a reverent and devout churchman, was deeply shaken by the schism. The Elim Church was defunct, but he and Clara no longer felt at home in the old First Swedish Lutheran Church, and from that time on attended church services randomly, often at the Swedish Methodist Church, reading their Bible at home and privately keeping "to a faith that served them to the end."[3]

Encouraged by his mother to read and study (Dickens and Twain being his favorites), Sandburg had to leave school after eighth grade to bolster the family's finances. In these stark and bleak years, the seeds of socialism were sown, and he also discovered his love for music, which would become so commanding a factor in his later life. He considered suicide more than once during these arduous times and intermittently traveled as a hobo. He enlisted in Illinois Company C during the Spanish-American War and served briefly in Cuba.[4] Arresting his drift, he became a fireman in Galesburg and studied four years at Lombard College (a small Universalist school). Here he discovered Browning (the first to grip him) and then Walt Whitman, who must be seen as the decisive influence in his poetry and thinking. Although William James (1842–1910), Charles Lamb (1775–1834), and John Ruskin (1819–1900) were heroes, Upton Sinclair (1878–1968), the "muckraker," was his model.[5]

Aspiring to write a biography of Swedish King Charles XII, Sandburg traveled house to house in Wisconsin selling stereoptical equipment. His eyes were always troublesome. His heroes at this time were Jack London (1876–1916) "the Revolutionist" and William E. Henley (1849–1903) in his free-verse style. *Reckless Ecstasy* is the title of his first collection. He began to do investigative reporting for the Chicago Daily News and other papers. Although he could not totally escape his religious rootage (he wrote to himself "Take up your cross and go the thorn way"), he nonetheless had hostile tangles with the well-known Chicago preacher Frank Gunsaulus, and he took jabs at Billy Sunday (1862–1935) in both prose and poetry. Spiritually at this time clearly he had "embraced the ideal of the God within" as his guiding star.[6]

He also broke ties with his parents. With all of the rifts and estrangement from family, it is significant that he dedicated his work on Lincoln "To August and Clara Sandburg: Workers on the Illinois Prairie."

Although he always felt the lure of the open road, Milwaukee and then Chicago became the hub of his endless roaming. He was taken by the naturalism of Thomas Hardy (1840–1928) and James Joyce (1882–1941) and then by the "Decadence Movement" of Oscar Wilde (1854–1900). Now working the Lyceum circuit, he would study religious orators, such as Henry Ward Beecher, but he expressed contempt for organized religion. At this time, he met Lilian Steichen, sister of the renown photographer, daughter of immigrants from Luxembourg, and a lapsed Roman Catholic.

He married his beloved "Paula" in 1908. Though she was an ardent feminist, she was the ballast in the marriage, the child-rearer, and a world-class breeder of prize goats.[7] To keep food on the table, Sandburg worked in a department store, lectured for the Tuberculosis Society, and served as secretary to the new socialist mayor of Milwaukee. Later moving to the Ravenswood neighborhood in Chicago, Carl and Paula had three daughters.[8] At this time, he wrote both "Chicago" and "Fog," two of his best-known works. While his expression is formless, his very formlessness has form. His poetry is somber and cynical.[9] Harriet Monroe of *Poetry* Magazine encouraged him. When his life was collapsing around him, he reveled in a visit by William Butler Yeats (1865–1939) from Ireland.[10] He was drawn to such kindred spirits as Theodore Dreiser and Ezra Pound. Countering the New England concentration, Sandburg drew Vachel Lindsay, Edgar Lee Masters, and Sinclair Lewis into a Midwestern cluster.

A raucous realist, Sandburg's poetry was seen by many as excessively brutal. But this was the real world in the stockyards and sweatshops of Chicago. We hear a brawling sound in much of what he wrote. One critic went so far as to call Sandburg's work "sadistic," yet he could be tender, as when he wrote to a couple who had lost their little boy that "life is a series of things that vanish."[11]

He always dabbled in radical politics, but his war poetry during World War I was powerfully patriotic. He was seldom home and was a notorious womanizer, even in advanced years. In "Liars," written after World War I, he was crass and profane. His machine-gun repetition is haunting. For years he was movie reviewer for the Chicago Daily News. His resonant voice and guitar drew thousands to his lectures.[12]

Always on the trail of "right words," he wrote widely-praised children's stories, the first of which was called *Rootabaga Stories*. Interestingly, in handling his family grief, he read the book of Job. In the twenties, he began his studies in Lincoln, with whom he identified profoundly (he saw Lincoln's love for the Bible as paralleling his own fascination with his father's Swedish Bible). His *Lincoln: The Prairie Years* and *Lincoln: The War Years* were a great financial success if not critically acclaimed. Poet and critic Amy Lowell (1874–1925) wondered if Sandburg were more a propagandist than a poet. But she missed the point that Sandburg had a passion to communicate what he felt was truth to the common people.[13] In "The People, Yes," he does share his concern and burden for the truth as understood and felt:

> Can you bewilder men by the millions
> with transfusions of your own passions,
> mixed with lies and half-lies,
> texts torn from contexts,
> and then look for peace, quiet, good will
> between nation and nation, race and race,
> between class and class.[14]

After the Second World War, the "eternal hobo" moved from Chicago to Connemara, North Carolina. Here he attempted his only novel, *Remembrance Rock,* intended as the foundation for a movie adaptation that never happened. It was over-written and chaotic. His characters were trapped in his allegory.[15] He spent four and a half years on it. These were years of public honors and private sorrows. A long estrangement from their daughter Helga devastated the aging Sandburgs. He won the Pulitzer Prize for poetry, though never the Nobel Prize.[16]

"Everyone is a child of God" was his vague and impersonal basis for a worldview. He was not biblically illiterate.[17] He actually worked a year and a half on the movie version of *The Greatest Story Ever Told* (the life of Jesus). In a poem he read on Boston Common at the behest of his good friend, Archibald MacLeish, he turned to Acts 17:26 for his motif. As time drew short, he seems to have been assailed by doubts. "Has ever been a man praying?" he inquired in "Shadows Fall Blue on the Mountain" at age eighty-one.[18] He had fears before entering the valley of the shadow, his decline aggravated by his drinking. His daughter Helga related later that he was finally able to stop smoking. "I went to the feet of Jesus and quit smoking," he said.[19]

His funeral was held in the local Episcopal church, conducted by Unitarians who read from Whitman and Sandburg. The Hound of Heaven had pursued, but there is no evidence that the lost was ever found.

Moving background to Carl Sandburg's roots can be delved from Ole Rolvaag's trilogy on Norwegian immigrants in North Dakota: *Giants in the Earth, Peder Victorious,* and *Their Father's God.* Rolvaag was an immigrant and taught at the Norwegian Lutheran St. Olaf College in Northfield, Minnesota. A comparable work on the Swedish migration to Minnesota was written by Swedish novelist Vilhelm Moberg. His books, particularly *Emigrants* (1951), are stirring and have made fine cinema.[20]

---

1. Penelope Niven, *Carl Sandburg: A Biography* (New York: Scribner's, 1991), 2.
2. Ibid., 6. Galesburg was a town dominated by Swedish immigrants and by Knox College.
3. Ibid., 16. Little read today, he was a significant fixture in his time.
4. Ibid., 66.
5. He tried out for the U.S. Military Academy at West Point, N.Y., and competed for placement alongside Douglas MacArthur. Needless to say, it was MacArthur, not Sandburg, who made the grade (52).
6. Ibid., 115.
7. Ibid., 177. Sandburg had an aversion to anarchy but did assist in socialist political efforts in Wisconsin. For a more dire view of Sandburg's radical politics, see Philip R. Yannella, *The Other Carl Sandburg* (University, Miss.: University of Mississippi Press, 1994). Explores his Swedish adventure of 1918. Was he a "tub-thumping Wobbly?"
8. The Sandburg's oldest daughter, Margaret, was a severe epileptic; Janet was retarded. Their last-born, Helga, rebelled as an adult, was thrice-divorced, and ultimately became an acknowledged writer in her own right. Eventually, Helga and her two children ended their rift with her old parents.

9. Niven, *Carl Sandburg,* 224. Sandburg did address "big issues" in his "tradition-shattering" poetry.

10. Harriet Monroe, "Of Poets, by Poets and for Poets," *Chicago Tribune,* 16 June 1996, 18.

11. Niven, *Carl Sandburg,* 329. Sandburg wrote sensitively of Chicago's "Black Belt" and the race riots.

12. Ibid., 380. His work as a platform entertainer was done chiefly out of financial need. His writing later became more profitable.

13. Sandburg became one of the foremost authorities on American ballads. Cf. his *The New American Songbag* (1950).

14. Section 102.

15. Niven, *Carl Sandburg,* 585.

16. Ibid., 622. Sandburg described his as "the poetry of the fireside," not "the poetry of the academy."

17. The Sandburgs did have their daughters baptized by a Lutheran (Evangelical Lutheran Church) minister. Ibid., 465.

18. Ibid., 677. "I fear what my shadow tells me," he writes.

19. Helga Sandburg, *A Great and Glorious Romance: the Story of Carl Sandburg and Lilian Steichen* (New York: Harcourt Brace, 1978). Helga was prolific and also wrote, as did her father, in many literary genres.

20. The film version was *The Emigrants,* parts 1, 2.

8.2.4 FROST, AMERICAN COLOR-BEARER

We make ourselves a place apart
Behind light words that tease and flout,
But oh, the agitated heart
Till someone really find us out.

'Tis pity if the case require
(Or so we say) that in the end
We speak the literal to inspire
The understanding of a friend.

But so with all, from babes that play
At hide-and-seek to God afar,
So all who hide too well away
Must speak and tell us where they are.

—Robert Frost
"Revelation"

Severed from their religious roots, American writers Emerson, Whitman, Dickinson, and Frost face a relentless quest for faith, according to literary critic Alfred Kazin.[1] Robert Frost (1874–1963) is difficult to categorize in this. He has been described as "a powerful and disturbing voice." Some rank him first among poets of his generation. Treatments ranging from hagiography[2] to Lawrence

Thompson's three-volume villification. The latter is, according to Jeffrey Meyers, a "rabid bias against Frost."[3] The little old white-haired man who read at John F. Kennedy's windswept Inauguration left some four hundred pieces in eleven volumes. Four times a winner of the Pulitzer Prize, Frost's work is worth perusing.[4]

Named after the great Southern Civil War general, Robert E. Lee, Frost had New England roots but was born in San Francisco. His father was an often violent and hard-drinking newspaper man with a Harvard degree, who died when Robert was only eleven. His overprotective mother, a Scottish woman of illegitimate birth, was forced to go back East and for some time raised her two children on $400 a year. She read her son Bible stories and Jane Porter's *The Scottish Chiefs*. Frost loved to read Burns and Walter Scott. He excelled in Latin and Greek, and the influence of the classics is a strong factor in his conservative style.

He fell in love with his high school covaledictorian, Elinor White, the daughter of a Universalist minister. When she turned him down, he disappeared into the Dismal Swamp along the Virginia/North Carolina border to punish her. Later they married and had six children. Two died early, leaving embittered parents. Elinor renounced all faith. The other four were called by Louis Untermeyer, a close friend, "the most obnoxious and unattractive children" he had ever seen. One daughter became insane and had to be institutionalized, as had been Frost's own sister. He spoke of "incipient insanity" in the family. His son Carol took his own life. Daughter Lesley deeply resented her parents.[5]

Frost attended Dartmouth and Harvard but was graduated from neither. With the assistance of his grandfather, he bought a little farm in Derry, New Hampshire, but he really wanted to be a poet.[6] Never part of a local church, he sometimes called himself "an Old Testament Christian." He did not smoke, and he hated liquor. He expressed total lack of belief in the supernatural and opined that "There is nothing after this." He read the Bible but moved from a James "will to believe" to skepticism, nihilism, and finally mockery. Peter Stanlis has attempted to rehabilitate some respectable religion in Frost but is unconvincing.[7]

The isolation of life on the Derry farm marked his emerging poetic skill with a rugged individualism. He was rough and socially maladroit. His father had turned a pistol on him, and now he was known to use a pistol to bring his own rebellious child to heel. From 1906 to 1912, he taught in a school. He lived in England from 1912 to 1914 but found the English caste system distasteful. He found a positive reception of his poetry in America at his return. He lectured, interspersed with teaching at Amherst and the University of Michigan. "Barding around," he called it. He was a great performer.

Facing family tragedies and crises, he moved his family to Key West, Florida. Elinor died there, at a time when they were not speaking to one another. As a result, Robert carried feelings of guilt. He had an extended affair with Kay Morrison, a married woman who later became his secretary and manager.

As his life was in ruins, he entered a time of public honors. His poetry books sold a million copies before he died in 1965.

His poetry was "full of darkness" as he often admitted, and yet there was also wry humor and rich insights and an enduring optimism. He frequently alludes to the Bible. Emerson, Wordsworth, and Kipling influenced him, along with Browning's dramatic monologues. He adapted the ballads of Hardy for his own purposes. Biographer Jeffrey Meyers is correct in his assessment that Frost was modern but not modernistic. He still wanted to hold onto many of the rules of classic poetic formation. In his English sojourn, he was drawn more to Yeats than to Ezra Pound's "vulgar self-promotion." Ironically, D. H. Lawrence complained of Frost's own "puerile self-magnification."[8]

He was a great storyteller, using powerful narrative, and had a gift for "repetition and closure." He disliked the opaque novel and all literary obscurity. He appreciated a sense of decorum in art and condemned the tendency of some artists toward a Whitmanesque glorification of homosexuality.[9] He was a Romantic who used irony superbly. John Crowe Ransom considered him among the five great poets of own time, along with Hardy, Yeats, Robinson, and Eliot. His two masques, "A Masque of Reason" (on Job) and "A Masque of Mercy" (on Jonah) are weak, in that he comes to the problem of evil without any real insight. Some believe that his sonnet "Design" is his greatest, although it is disturbing from a philosophical viewpoint. God as designer is displaced.[10]

"The Road Less Traveled" is thoughtful, and "Mending Wall" fits so well with Ephesians 2:11–22. Other examples of Frost's genius are "Prayer in Spring," "Dust of Snow," "Lodged," "Birches," and "The Gift Outright," which he read at the Kennedy inaugural. "Directive" quotes from the gospel of Mark. Poetry is compression. It carries value in the inventory of every merchant of words. As in Anton Chekhov, the Russian playwright, the art is well concealed. Frost's recurring themes are isolation, extinction, and the final limitation of humankind. He goes far toward truth without knowing truth's Source.

---

1. Alfred Kazin, *God and the American Writer* (New York: Knopf, 1997). Kazin himself writes from the presupposition that the search for God is always vain.

2. An example of hagiography would be Joseph Brodsky, Seamus Heaney, and Derek Walcot, *Homage to Robert Frost* (New York: Farr, Strauss and Giroux, 1997). Three Nobel laureates pay high tribute to the enduring work of Robert Frost.

3. Jeffrey Meyers, *Robert Frost: A Biography* (Boston: Houghton-Mifflin, 1996). A fine, balanced study. Lawrence Thompson's two volumes, and the third volume finished by R. H. Winnick, are published by Holt, Rinehart and Winston. The first volume, *Robert Frost: The Early Years (1874–1915)* was published in 1966.

4. A good anthology is Edward Connery Lathem, ed., *The Poetry of Robert Frost* (New York: Holt, Rinehart and Winston, 1967).

5. Meyers, *Robert Frost,* 40.

6. Ibid., 41.

7. Peter J. Stanlis, "Robert Frost: Social and Political Conservative," *Chronicles of Culture,* August 1992, 19ff.

8. Meyers, *Robert Frost,* 69. Frost once told Untermeyer, "There's room for only one person at the top—and I mean that person to be me" (144).

9. Ibid., 94. A stickler for morality at his roots, Frost allied himself while in Britain with the Georgians.

10. Ibid., 318. After age seventy-five, his honors increased but his "poetry declined." "I am pretty me-sick" he complained.

8.2.5 LINDSAY, PERIPATETIC PREACHER

> And when Booth halted by the curb for prayer
> He saw his Master thro' the flag-filled air.
> Christ came gently with a robe and crown
> For Booth the soldier, while the throng knelt down.
> He saw King Jesus. They were face-to-face,
> And he knelt a-weeping in that holy place.
> Are you washed in the blood of the Lamb?
>
> —Vachel Lindsay
> "General Booth Enters into Heaven"

Some Salvationists and other conservative Christians thought the march-like description of General William Booth (1829–1912), "sung to the tune of 'The Blood of the Lamb' with indicated instruments" (including the "Bass drum beaten loudly") to be somewhat irreverent. But this is truly a dramatic tribute to Booth and the Salvation Army. The picture of the "walking lepers" and the "lurching bravos" is powerful. Nicholas Vachel Lindsay (1879–1931) was born in Springfield, Illinois. His parents were devout members of the Disciples of Christ, or Campbellite Movement. Jessie Rittenhouse described a stay with the Lindsays. After breakfast, a chapter of the Bible was read. Then father, mother, son, and maidservant got on their knees facing their chairs while Mrs. Lindsay prayed.[1] Vachel's mother was an aggressive woman who encouraged her son culturally and spiritually but may also have kept him from marriage.[2] Lindsay transformed the Campbellite vision of Christian unity into a vision for one world religion.

His father was a doctor, and young Lindsay attended Hiram College in the interest of following in his father's footsteps. Then he decided to be an artist and attended the Art Institute of Chicago. He did work as a cartoonist. Harriet Monroe of *Poetry* Magazine spotted some of his early poetry and invited him to read for the Cliff-Dwellers Literary Society in Chicago. He read "General Booth" for them and suddenly was famous. When Yeats came to Chicago, he read his noisy "Congo."[3] He never made much money from his writing but traveled about reading them in dramatic fashion. He lectured for the YMCA and the Anti-Saloon League. He had a deep rolling voice and often would exchange a program of poetry for a night's shelter. He never escaped his evangelical upbringing.

While many intellectuals went abroad at this time, Lindsay stayed in Springfield and proposed a "gospel" for America, built upon his "freshly conceived bases of religion, equality and beauty." "I am knocking on the door of America with a dream in my hand," he said.[4] The dream had millennial overtones and reverberated with his admiration of William Jennings Bryan (1860–1925). Louis Untermeyer called him a "rhyming John the Baptist, singing to convert the heathen." Others called it "Mid-American evangelism" or "messianic delusion."[5]

In 1914 he published a book, *Adventures While Preaching the Gospel of Beauty.* Unfortunately, this was not the Christian gospel, but rather the social gospel within Lindsay's own bizarre vision of ecumenism.

He wrote a tribute, "In Praise of Johnny Appleseed," which again carries Swedenborgian overtones. He was drawn to the "Science of Correspondences," which came out of Swedenborg's highly-touted escorted tour of heaven and hell.[6] H. L. Mencken dismissed him snidely as "the only person in *Who's Who* who gave his religious affiliation." That religious affiliation had a Marxist tinge, and Lindsay voted socialist. The only conventional employment he ever held was three months as a sorter in the Marshall Field's Toy Department and three months as a porter in a gas-tubing factory in New York City. He hoped his "The Golden Book of Springfield," a contrast of 1918 and 2018 in mid-America, would be his break-through. It met with a tepid public reception.

In 1925 when he was forty-five, he married Elizabeth Connor, an English teacher half his age, the daughter of an Independent Presbyterian minister. But the strains of marriage seemed more than he could take, and he became increasingly paranoid, with delusions, especially about his wife. He took his own life by poison on December 5, 1931.

Many anthologies still carry some of his poems, such as "The Unpardonable Sin" (on the irony of "Christian" nations fighting each other in World War I) or "Abraham Lincoln Walks at Midnight." His jazz-like poetry is at times reminiscent of Carl Sandburg's, with crushing intensity of feeling.[7]

---

1. Ann Massa, *Vachel Lindsay: Fieldworker for the American Dream* (Bloomington, Ind.: Indiana University Press, 1970), 26. There is much evidence of a residual faith in Lindsay but little evidence that he accepted it as his own.
2. Ibid., 5.
3. Harriet Monroe, "Of Poets, by Poets, for Poets," *Chicago Tribute Magazine,* 16 July 1996, 18ff.
4. Eleanor Ruggles, *The West-Going Heart* (New York: Norton, 1966).
5. Ibid., 25. Lindsay had missionary passion: "I have a world to save and I must prepare, prepare" (60).
6. Ibid., 53ff. Swedenborg had no doctrine of sin and saw God as essentially a man. It was appealing to Americans.
7. Ibid., 85. Other poems of significance: "The Eagle That Is Forgotten" and "The Chinese Nightingale." As Sandburg, Lindsay had a great admiration for Abraham Lincoln.

8.2.6 JOHNSON AND HUGHES, ANGUISHED PROTESTERS

> And now, O Lord, this man of God,
> Who breaks the bread of life this morning—
> Shadow him in the hollow of thy hand,
> And keep him out of the gunshot of the devil.

Take him, Lord—this morning—
Wash him with hyssop inside and out,
Hang him up and drain him dry of sin.
Pin his ears to the wisdom-post,
And make his words sledge hammers of truth—
Beating on the iron heart of sin.

—James Weldon Johnson
God's Trombones

North America's largest racial minority has a heritage of poetic expression stretching from the earliest plantation slaves to Maya Angelou (1928–), who read at William Clinton's inauguration as U.S. President in 1993. Angelou was the best-known living American poet at the close of the twentieth century. Several poets afford insight into the suffering and triumphs of African-Americans and black Americans with a Pacific islands heritage.

James Weldon Johnson (1871–1938) was born in Jacksonville, Florida. His father was a headwaiter, and his mother was a native of the Bahamas. After law school, Johnson was the first black person to be admitted to the Florida bar. He was a founder of the National Association for the Advancement of Colored People and served as the organization's longtime secretary. A Republican, he campaigned for Teddy Roosevelt and was a diplomatic envoy to both Venezuela and Nicaragua. As an anthologist, he gathered verses and spirituals by black poets, which had been little known or appreciated in literary circles. His best known work is *God's Trombones,* which is seven sermons in verse. Johnson's introductory analysis of black preaching and the black American church is informative.[1]

Although choosing not to use dialect in the sermons, Johnson captures something of the syncopation of the preaching and the flavor of the setting, although the reader must supply antiphonal responses or "hooping." He quotes one brother who, having read a cryptic passage, took off his glasses and announced: "Brothers and sisters, this morning—I intend to explain the unexplainable—find out the undefinable—ponder over the imponderable—and unscrew the inscrutable."[2] Particularly noteworthy in this collection are the sermons on the prodigal son and the crucifixion of Jesus.

Of another vintage altogether is Langston Hughes (1902–1967), who was born in Joplin, Missouri, and educated at Lincoln College in Pennsylvania. His parents were middle-class but divorced, and he lived part of the time with his father, who had chosen to live in Mexico to escape racial segregation and prejudice in the United States. As a result, Langston was proficient in English and Spanish. Often lonely and confused, he spent time also with his mother's family in Washington, D.C., but moved to New York, where he was associated with the "Harlem Renaissance."

Lindsay had an influence on Hughes, particularly in his jazz-poetry. Sandburg was his "guiding star."[3] He was a gifted writer for both children and adults. We hear his heart in a response to the beating of blacks by a gang of white toughs:

I do not hate you,
For your faces are beautiful, too.

I do not hate you,
Your faces are whirling lights of loveliness and splendor, too.
Yet why do you torture me,
O, white strong ones,
Why do you torture me?[4]

Hughes claimed he wrote his best poetry when he felt the worst and his worst poetry when he felt the best. His "blues poetry" is peerless. "Prayer Meeting" and "Feet o' Jesus" interpret the black religious experience. His own religious experience had been in the African Methodist Episcopal Church, but it is difficult to discern whether either Johnson or Hughes experienced anything from their religion more than a cultural overlay, which is the danger of ethnic religion.

Whatever their own faith, these poets and their successors have a message that is imperative for all races to hear.

---

1. James Weldon Johnson, *God's Trombones: Seven Negro Sermons in Verse* (New York: Viking Compass, 1927).
2. Ibid., 4ff. The pattern of the black sermon moved from creation to redemption in Christ to the judgment day. Johnson was married in 1910, but he had no children when he died in a train-automobile accident.
3. Donald C. Dickinson, *A Bio-bibliography of Langston Hughes* (New York: Archon, 1972), 11. Hughes has given us some superb autobiography including the story of his life in the 1930s, *I Wonder As I Wander* (New York: Hill and Wang, 1956). A versatile writer, Hughes wrote fiction and plays. He never married.
4. Raymond Smith, "Hughes: Evolution of the Poetic Persona," in Harold Bloom, ed., *Langston Hughes* (New York: Crescent House, 1989), 53. His collections, *The Weary Blues, Fine Clothes to the Jews,* and other volumes, are outstanding literary accomplishments of the twentieth century. A significant anthology is Michael Popkin, ed., *Modern Black Writers* (New York: Frederick Ungar, 1978).

8.2.7 MASTERS, TROUBLED LAWYER

I had no objection at all
To seeing my household effects at auction
On the village square.
It gave my beloved flock the chance
To get something which had belonged to me
For a memorial.
But that trunk which was struck off
To Burchard, the grog-keeper!
Do you know it contained the manuscripts
Of a life-time of sermons?
And he burned them as waste paper.

—Edgar Lee Masters
"Rev. Abner Peet" in *Spoon River Anthology*

Unnoticed until 1915, when *Spoon River Anthology* made a tremendous splash, Edgar Lee Masters (1869–1950) is a provocative early-twentieth-century poet. Born in Garnett, Kansas, the oldest of four children, Masters grew up in the Springfield, Illinois area. No definitive biography has yet been written. His mother was the daughter of a Methodist minister. The family actually lived in Lewiston, Ill., on the Spoon River and Petersburg, Ill., on the Sangamon. Young Masters studied the classics at Knox College in Galesburg, Ill. He became a successful Chicago attorney. He married, had three children, and then divorced. After he moved to New York City, he married a woman in 1926 who was thirty-one years younger than he. They had one son. They too separated but were reunited in his last years.

Masters was part of the Chicago literary renaissance with Dreiser, Lindsay, and Sandburg, among others.[1] Browning was important to the style of Masters, as was Thomas Hardy. Although he subsequently wrote three good novels and a biography critical of Abraham Lincoln, his brilliant stroke was a "collection" of 210 epitaphs from the cemetery in Spoon River. These free-verse poems tell the story of the community and of Masters himself. As John Hollander observes, "Underlying all of the patterns of relation among the individual portraits is the tangle of lines of power emanating from the banker Rhodes and his judicial, clerical and journalistic deputies."[2] The fools, drunkards, and failures come first. They subtly link with the power moguls of the community. This is poetry for those who love people. The names are of interest, for example "Hod Putt," the first to be described. The tragedy of Dr. Meyers, the appeal of Father Malloy, the tenderness of Anne Rutledge, and the secret of Deacon Taylor are alluring. Angles and tangles and secrets rise from the grave when these characters tell the truth. Many have seen in this work the exposure of hypocrisy in small-town America. If that was his intent, we didn't need Masters to tell us that human beings in small towns are also sinners.

Masters never got over his grouchiness. The last of those described was Webster Ford, undoubtedly Masters himself. In Webster, there is no glimmer of redemption.

---

1. "Of Poets, by Poets, for Poets," 18ff.
2. John Hollander, introduction to Edgar Lee Masters, *Spoon River Anthology* (New York: Signet Classics, 1992), xix.

8.2.8 ST. VINCENT MILLAY, HUMANIST CRUSADER

> If there were balm in Gilead, I would go
> To Gilead for your wounds, unhappy land,
> Gather your balsam there, and with this hand,
> Made deft by pity, cleanse and bind and sew
> And drench with healing, that your strength might grow,
> (Though love be outlawed, kindness contraband)
> And you, O proud and felled, again might stand;
> But where to look for balm, I do not know.
> The oils and herbs of mercy are so few;

Honour's for sale; allegiance has its price;
The barking of a fox has bought us all;
We save our skins a craven hour or two.—
While Peter warms him in the servants' hall
The thorns are platted and the cock crows twice.

—Edna St. Vincent Millay
Sonnet 132, "Czecho-Slovakia"

A precocious child catapulted to poetic notice by her remarkable "Renascence," which was written as a student at Vassar College, Edna St. Vincent Millay (1892–1950) wrote critically appreciated short stories and plays and even acted in some of her own theatrical works. In her writing can be detected the influence of Whitman and Lindsay, Tennyson and A. E. Housman (1859–1936). While her life is a spiritual tragedy, St. Vincent Millay will probably be remembered always as the leading American poetess of the twentieth century. She was the first woman to win the Pulitzer Prize in poetry (1923). Her elegant clarity, freshness, and energy edge past the style of Sara Teasdale (1884–1933). Her spacious poetry invites relaxed and thoughtful perusal.[1]

She was born in Rockland, Maine, to parents who divorced when she was but a child. Her father was successively a teacher, a school principal, and a superintendent, but he had a gambling addiction. Her mother was a practical nurse who motivated her three daughters to music and education. The redhead everyone called "Vincent" was exposed to the cultural spiritual heritage of North America at the turn of the century, but she became "an agnostic, self-conscious modern, cut off from traditional religion and standing alone in the midst of the indifferent universe that Thomas Hardy and A. E. Housman presented."[2]

After being graduated from Vassar, she lived a bohemian lifestyle and joined an acting company in New York City's Greenwich Village. She had liaisons and brief torrid affairs with well-known literary figures, among them John Reed and Edmund Wilson. She drifted about Europe and into Albania. She became pregnant and had an abortion. All of this inevitably led to an emotional collapse in the mixed-up young woman.[3]

A modicum of stability came into her life when she married the Dutch-Irish Eugen Boissevain in 1923. A disciple of Carl Jung (1875–1961), Eugen loved and cared for her. She continued to write high-calibre poetry, did reading tours, and wrote an opera. She espoused liberal causes like the murder conviction and subsequent execution of anarchists Nicola Sacco and Bartolomeo Vanzetti.[4] Her husband allowed her sexual freedom, but they both drank too much, with a dulling effect on creativity. She suffered a second emotional collapse in 1944 and could no longer write. When her husband died in 1949, she spent most of the rest of her life drunk at Steepletop, their estate in New York, where she died in 1950.

In her earliest work, St. Vincent Millay yearns, "Give me new birth." But she looked for that rebirth in radical humanism, rather than divine grace:

All sin was of my sinning, all
Atoning mine, and mine the gall

> Of all regret. Mine was the weight
> Of every brooded wrong, the hate
> That stood behind each envious thrust,
> Mine every greed, mine every lust.

Her short stories were "beautifully written, after a flippant fashion," according to biographer and critic Norman Brittin. Her poetry escapes "enjambment," which she feared above all else. She experimented with rhythms, and her words stimulate the imagination visually. She loads her art with considerable alliteration and assonance.

As in the example above, there are glimpses of spiritual insight in her thought. She sees in human beings "a bad cell," and in Sonnet 16 concedes that there is "a wild disorder" in human nature. In Sonnet 17, she acknowledges greed "as the great betrayer." In a rather unique seven-person dialogue, she does discuss religion in "Conversation at Mid-Night." Is this a hark-back to Christ's late-night conversation with Nicodemus? But while she may see the issues in some sense, she perceives no real solution. The sonnet on "balm in Gilead" at the head of this essay aches over Hitler's invasion of Czechoslovakia, but she knows of no "balm in Gilead" to heal.

Her later poetry has a persistent note of regret and mourning. Mortality hangs heavy. In "Dirge Without Music," all persons go "into the darkness." She cannot accept this but has no alternative. She did not forswear all Christian symbols, as in "Christmas Canticle" and "Jesus to His Disciples." Her odd little piece, "To a Calvinist in Bali" shows repressed guilt. She was loved, but her estimation among critics has had ups and downs. Her poetry is artistically superb and in content, she illustrates the implications of Christlessness.

Other poets to read are Cincinnatus "Joaquin" Miller (1837–1913), especially his "Columbus" with its dauntless "Sail on, sail on," and Joyce Kilmer (1886–1918) and his magnificent "Trees." The social protest of Charles Edwin Markham (1852–1940) in "The Man with the Hoe" (inspired by Jean Millet's [1642?–1679] painting) and the outrageous couplets of Ogden Nash (1902–1971) beg for attention.[5] E. e. Cummings (1894–1962) is another "only-in-America" phenomenon. His abandonment of traditional punctuation and unconventional formatting has driven printers crazy.[6] Other poets of spiritual stature should include Vassar Miller and Mona Van Duyn (both of whom are deeply indebted to the English metaphysical poets), as well as the late-twentieth-century contemporaries Madeline L'Engle and Luci Shaw. John Updike is a Barthian Presbyterian best known for his fiction.[7] His opening lines in "Seven Stanzas at Easter" are great:

> Make no mistake: if he rose at all
> it was as His body;
> if the cells' dissolution did not reverse,
>   the molecules reknit,
>   the amino acids rekindle,
> the Church will fail.

1. Norma Millay, ed., *Collected Poems of Edna St. Vincent Millay* (New York: Book-of-the-Month Club, 1990).
2. Norman A. Brittin, *Edna St. Vincent Millay* (Boston: Thayne, 1982).
3. Ibid., 14. Brittin points out her similarity to the romantic irony of Heinrich Heine and Byron. Some hear in her work the reverberations of G. M. Hopkins.
4. Ibid., 26. She also was a strong advocate of feminist causes.
5. Nash's couplet "How odd of God, to choose the Jews" is the wry humor he did so well.
6. e. e. cummings, *Collected Poems 1922–1938* (New York: Book-of-the-Month Club, 1990).
7. Updike's work was analyzed quite positively by Alice and Kenneth Hamilton in *The Elements of John Updike* (Grand Rapids: Eerdmans, 1970). This is the Kenneth Hamilton who gave us the incisive *Revolt Against Heaven: An Enquiry into Anti-Supernaturalism* (Grand Rapids: Eerdmans, 1965). I cannot read the earlier "Rabbit Angstrom" novels because of the language and imagery. The more recent *In the Beauty of the Lilies* (New York: Fawcett/Columbine, 1996) is quite good, depicting a minister's loss of faith and the consequences for his family. Another novel, *Toward the End of Time* (New York: Knopf, 1997), is set in the twenty-first century and is apocalyptic.

CHAPTER NINE

Sifting the Amazing Trove of British Fiction

While the novel form has ancient, worldwide antecedents, the British novel has given the world its strongest examples of the medium.[1] British Christians have produced some of the best examples. "Fiction is a window into the soul of a nation," Andrew L. Drummond argues in his erudite study of the novel form. From an English religious perspective, it is the various grades of popular fiction that accurately mirror life in the church, whether the Church of England, Roman Catholicism, or among the dissenting Protestants.[2]

Elizabeth Jay observes the connection between the novel and the Church of England, which bore so many of the great writers of the nineteenth and early twentieth centuries. Jay quotes William E. Gladstone's characterization of evangelicals "who aimed at bringing back, on a large scale, and by an aggressive movement, the Cross, and all that the Cross essentially implies."[3] This describes a pervasive impact on all society, including the arts. Jay quotes the evangelical leader Lord Shaftesbury's plea in this regard: "Depend on it, my friends, that there is no security whatever except in standing upon the faith of our fathers, and saying with them that the Blessed old Book is 'God's Word written' from the very first syllable down to the very last, and from the last back to the first."[4] We would not suggest that all English writers, or all Anglican or Nonconformist English writers, wrote out of an evangelical Christian perspective, though the movement produced a great burst of creativity. Most important, however, it so pervaded English thinking and reform movements that even unbelievers could not avoid standing in the shadow of the Cross.

---

1. Margaret Anne Doody, *The True Story of the Novel* (New Brunswick, N.J.: Rutgers University Press, 1996).

2. Andrew L. Drummond, *The Churches in English Fiction* (Leicester: Edgar Backus, 1950).
3. Elizabeth Jay, *The Religion of the Heart: Anglican Evangelicalism in the 19th Century Novel* (Oxford: Clarendon, 1979), 31. Professor Jay really delves into the doctrinal substrata of the arts with skill and insight.
4. Ibid. Shaftesbury was a courageous champion of the evangelical cause, particularly in his benevolent associations. Writers, in this as in other genres of literature, are all over the faith spectrum at the opposite extreme from Shaftesbury. William Makepeace Thackeray mounted a wild assault upon sermons and preachers. Thackery had few evangelical friends indeed.

9.1   PRECURSORS OF THE CLASSIC ENGLISH NOVEL

A good book always leads you to love or reverence something with your whole heart.

—John Ruskin

T. S. Eliot, in his essay "Religion and Literature," traces three eras in the English novel. In the first period, novelists took the existence of Christianity for granted and hence did not focus on it. Writers in this era include the proto-novelist/playwright Henry Fielding (1707–1754) and the first generation of true novel writers, Charles Dickens (1812–1870) and William Makepeace Thackeray (1811–1863).[1] Thackeray ushered in the transition to a less faith-centered life. After the evangelical ascendancy of the early 1800s, Thackeray's characterizations were "a wild assault upon sermons and preachers."[2]

In the second period were novelists who doubted, worried, or even contested the faith, such as George Eliot (1819–1880), George Meredith (1828–1909), and Thomas Hardy (1840–1928). In the third era came writers who had not heard of Christian faith as anything but an anachronism. Stephen Tanner suggests that a fourth category should be added: Those so anti-theological that they assert that nothing of religious faith or values can be communicated.[3]

We will take these periods in their turn, beginning with the earliest novelists, who do acknowledge the truth of Christianity or at least assume the centrality of the faith in their society.

---

1. Stephen L. Tanner, "Religion and Critical Theory," *Chronicles of Culture,* July 1990, 51ff.
2. *Religion of the Heart,* 31.
3. Analyzed by Tanner in "Religion and Critical Theory."

9.1.1   FIELDING, SATIRICAL MAGISTRATE

We read Fielding for more than reasons of historic interest. He wrote excellent drama and a skillful work of period fiction. Henry Fielding was the son of a general. He attended Leyden University and returned home to write plays. *Tom Thumb* was perhaps his best dramatic work. It was said that *Tom Thumb* made

Jonathan Swift laugh for only the second time in his life. Fielding studied the law and became judicial magistrate for Middlesex and Westminster shires.

In 1743 he published *Tom Jones: A Foundling.*[1] The big question about this novel has been whether it has a brilliant plot or no plot at all. Squire Allworthy returns from a long trip to find a baby in his bed. Thinking that the baby boy is the son of the servant Jenny Jones, he names the child Tom Jones and determines to raise him. Tom's rival is young Blifil, son of the squire's sister and her husband. Tom is banished and ultimately marries the beautiful Sophia after much struggle.

Fielding referred to himself as "a Christian writer,"[2] but Christianity is a thin veneer over the society he describes. The squire kneels to pray and employs a clergyman, the Rev. Thwakum, and a philosopher, Mr. Square. Both make suitable contributions to the two young men being raised in the household. Those outside the Church of England are presented in a particularly harsh light, especially Quakers, although the Presbyterian opposition to puppet shows does not sit well. Much action takes place in the tavern at the Sign of the Bell, which is operated by George Whitefield's brother and is the occasion for a poke at the Methodists. Reference is made in the puppet show to Jepthah's brash vow as set forth in the book of Judges. For the modern reader, the author's quaint but overwrought dialogue with his readers wears thin.

Fielding eventually moved to Portugal for his health and wrote about this country, where he died at the age of forty-seven.

----

1. Henry Fielding, *Tom Jones: A Foundling,* in Great Books of the Western World, vol. 37 (Chicago: University of Chicago, 1952).
2. Ibid., 152.

9.1.2 STERNE, CONTROVERSIAL CLERGYMAN

From the same generation as Fielding, another story found its way into the Great Books of the Western World series.[1] This early novel came from an unlikely source, a rather laid-back country cleric. Laurence Sterne (1713–1768) was born in Ireland, the son of an English soldier. The child's mother seems to have been indifferent toward him, but a cousin made it possible for him to study at Cambridge, where he received both his B.A. and M.A. Through the mediation of an uncle, he was appointed to a curacy in Sutton-in-the-Forest in Yorkshire.

Here in 1759, he began *Tristam Shandy.* The story brought immediate censure on moral and literary grounds from the three literary giants of the day, Oliver Goldsmith (1730–1774), Samuel Johnson (1709–1784), and Samuel Richardson (1689–1761). But as with many works the critics have hated, the book-reading public loved it. Ostensibly his own story and that of his relatives, the work is outrageously funny in its characterizations of Uncle Toby, Corporal Trim, and the papist, Dr. Slop. Reverend Yorick claims descent from the Yorick in Shakespeare. He is a convinced Lockean and desperately desires to preach from the heart. There are even examples of Whitefield's disciples.

Nine volumes of *Shandy* were issued in two-chapter installments before the consumptive author died at age fifty-five. The story was cut off when the hero of the novel is still only an infant.

---

1. Laurence Sterne, *Tristam Shandy,* in Great Books of the Western World, vol. 36 (Chicago: University of Chicago, 1952).

9.1.3 GOLDSMITH, INCREDIBLE DRIFTER

Already noted among the early dramatists (see 6.1.6), Goldsmith must be allotted mention because of his epochal early novel, *The Vicar of Wakefield.*[1] Goldsmith wrote the piece on the insistence of Samuel Johnson, in order that he might pay his rent. Because of the acclaim he received, he turned his hand to plays, most successfully. The author and hero is the vicar, Dr. Primrose, who seems gullible, yet is courageous and loyal. He preaches a notable sermon in jail where he is imprisoned for debt.

Still, Goldsmith is writing about human relationships. God is not much in the picture. Walter Scott wrote of the vicar: "Though each touch shows that he is made of mortal mould and is full of human frailties, the effect of the whole is to reconcile us to human nature."

---

1. Oliver Goldsmith, *The Vicar of Wakefield* (New York: Pocket Books, 1957).

9.1.4 DEFOE, PROLIFIC PAMPHLETEER

Daniel Defoe (1630–1731) wrote more than four hundred books and tracts and was deeply immersed in the political issue of his time. On occasion, he was imprisoned and pilloried for his satirical writings. His *Robinson Crusoe* is about a man who is shipwrecked and stranded for almost thirty years on an island in the Atlantic off the northeast coast of South America.[1] This story captivated many readers, young and old, and led to a similar story *The Swiss Family Robinson,* written by the Swiss writer and philosopher J. R. Wyss.[2]

Defoe's depiction has a Christian frame-of-reference. The shipwrecked man finds three Bibles in the wrecked ship as he scrounges material and provisions. Though he has not previously been a religious man, he is moved by God's providence. He observes the Sabbath, reads Scripture, and prays during the earthquake and the storm. When he rescues Friday, he leads him to a saving knowledge of Christ. Christian faith is presented as being as natural as the air people breathe.

---

1. Daniel Defoe, *Robinson Crusoe* (Philadelphia: John C. Winston, 1957), 211ff. The story is loosely based on the experiences of Alexander Selkirk, who was shipwrecked off Chile. Defoe was a founder of the fictional adventure genre. We are blessed by a

recent and riveting study by Richard West, *Daniel Defoe: The Life and Strange, Surprising Adventures* (New York: Carroll and Graf, 1998). Shows Defoe was a dissenter "but no prude."
2. The Wyss version, written in 1813, tells of a Swiss clergyman who is marooned with his wife and four sons.

9.2 PRACTITIONERS OF THE CLASSIC ENGLISH NOVEL

Poets set out seriously to describe the indescribable. That is the whole business of literature, and it is a hard row to hoe.
                                                    —G. K. Chesterton (1874–1936)

Christian faith never stirred far below the surface in the English novel. Preaching and revival are part of the warp and woof of a daily life governed by the commandments.[1] But there is a vast difference between subscription to Christian values and a personal relationship with Jesus Christ. The themes are everywhere, as we shall soon be reminded.[2] The fabric is of a complex weave. This is partly the reason many conservatives looked askance at any fiction. George Borrow of *The Bible in Spain* fame was very critical of Walter Scott's fiction and its promotion of the papacy.[3] But not all Christians felt this way. Hannah More used fiction to evangelistic purpose in her 2 million tracts. The venerable minister Rowland Hill wrote the fictional *Village Dialogues*.

---

1. See this life through the eyes of leading clerics in chap. 8, David L. Larsen, *The Company of the Preachers* (Grand Rapids: Kregel, 1998).
2. This is even more characteristic of the Victorian era. See Robert Lee Wolff, *Gains and Losses: Novels of Faith and Doubt in Victorian England* (New York: Garland, 1977); and Barry Qualls, *The Secular Pilgrims of Victorian Fiction* (Cambridge: Cambridge University Press, 1982). Qualls describes the intricate relationship among church, personal faith, and social religiosity as "labyrinthine tortuosities."
3. Andrew L. Drummond, *The Churches in English Fiction* (Leicester: Edgar Backus, 1950), 6f.

9.2.1 SCOTT, PILLAR OF VENERABILITY

Scott understood and nobody has better illustrated by example, the true mode of connecting past and present.
                                                    —Leslie Stephen

Called "the wizard of the north," Walter Scott (1771–1832) was the most popular writer of his time. An early Romanticist, he pioneered the historical novel. His father was an attorney from the Welsh border country, a strict Presbyterian whose hobby was the study of Presbyterian history. His parents were members of Grayfriars Church in Edinburgh, where John Erskine was the honored pastor, an evangelical leader, a warm friend of Whitefield, and an ardent proponent of world missions. Scott was born in Edinburgh, and at eighteen months was afflicted with a bone disease that left him with a pronounced limp.

Due to his physical limitations, he preferred reading to playing with the other boys and developed a phenomenal memory. He took legal training at the University of Edinburgh where Enlightenment teaching influenced him to moderate views and membership in the Scottish Episcopal Church. He shrank from the zeal of the Scottish Presbyterians.

Obtaining income from his law practice and from his position as clerk of the Court of Session, Scott developed his writing, particularly poetry celebrating Scottish history and heroes. *The Lay of the Last Minstrel* and *The Lady of the Lake* were his most popular poetic compositions. But the surging popularity of George Byron (1788–1824) beckoned him toward the novel. He also had a total fixation on Shakespeare and the theatre.

All students of Scott prescribe discrimination in selecting readings from Scott, because he wrote quickly, with much ease, and often carelessly. Some have accused him of jotting down his novels while in court. He always carried an intense burden for the poor, anticipating Dickens.[1] A restless soul, he often read *The Pilgrim's Progress* instead of going to church.

In 1825 he suffered financial collapse and wrote compulsively to pay his debts and preserve Abbotsford, the baronial estate he had built up.[2] He had a stroke in 1830 and died two years later, hoping for immortality, believing in "a beneficent Creator," but not articulating any Christian faith.[3]

The novels deserving attention include:

Waverley (1814): A story of the horrors of war. A young Englishman joins the Jacobite Rebellion in the Highlands. Scott is ever the master of dialogue.

Guy Mannering (1815): The well-drawn characters are more outstanding than the plot about a young man in the days of George III, perhaps because the entire novel was written in six weeks.

Rob Roy (1818): Dramatic story of the outlaw was made into a major motion picture in the 1990s.

Old Mortality (1826): The character list included Preacher Kettledrummle, whose sermon had fifteen heads, each with seven points of application.

The Heart of Midlothian (1818): Critics judge this story from the jail riots in 1736 to be his best work.

Ivanhoe (1830): This favorite among the young boys shows Scott's neglect of his sources. Rebecca, the medieval Jewess, talks to Rowena and the Templar as if they were gentry of the late 1700s.

Kenilworth (1821): A fascinating portrayal set in days of Elizabeth I.

The Talisman (1825): A tale of the Crusades.

Quentin Durward (1823): This portrait of Louis XI is a most original work.

Scott's crafting was based on his conviction that "Unless a novel makes a pattern, it is no more than a set of anecdotes."[4] Scott was widely read around the world and immensely popular in the British Isles. Scott has shaped generations of novelists and, in particular, was a model for Honoré de Balzac (1799–1850) and Leo Tolstoy Sr. (1828–1910). The reading of Scott is always entertaining and affords us important insights into the Scottish persona and character.

▨ **A recent incarnation** of Walter Scott can be found in Jean Plaidy, whose dozens of carefully constructed historical novels are organized in such series as The Norman Trilogy, Plantagenet Series, Tudor Novels, and the Queen Victoria Series. Another historical fiction writer of note, Maurice Edelman, M.P., has written us marvelous novels on Victorian themes: *Disraeli in Love* and *Disraeli Rising,* among them.

---

1. A. O. J. Cockshut, *The Achievement of Walter Scott* (New York: New York University, 1969), 24, 41. Scott wrote fourteen novels in six years.
2. Abbotsford on the River Tweed is a fascinating tour stop. Some descendants of the author still live in the private quarters.
3. David Daiches, *Sir Walter Scott and His World* (London: Thames and Hudson, 1971), 125. Scott never shows us any of the deep spiritual turmoil that caused him to turn from the Father's faith.
4. *The Achievement of Walter Scott,* 29. Scott declined an offer of the Poet Laureate-ship for Britain in 1813.

9.2.2 AUSTEN, FAVORITE OF GENERATIONS

Let other pens dwell on guilt and misery—I quit such odious subjects as soon as I can.

My books are my children.

—Jane Austen

Jane Austen (1775–1817) was the first woman novelist in England and perhaps the one who gave the novel its developed form. She was the seventh of eight children born into a clergyman's home in Steventon, fifty miles southwest of London. Her father, the Rev. George Austen, was a scholar, her mother wrote verse, and her brothers edited a satirical magazine. Literature was read aloud in the home, so she grew up in the presence of Shakespeare, Pope, Addison, and Johnson. Her matrix was not the literary salons of London, but the gentry among whom she was born. It was a stratified society of squires and parsons, of charming soldiers, and maidens in search of husbands in the best social class possible. The watchword in this polite society was good sense and good taste.

Curiously, Austen enjoyed a renaissance in the late 1900s, with lavish productions of her works for television and cinema. Her books were perennially the bases for films. Jane Austen has been a hot item, though she wrote to entertain her family and was not a writer of note in her own lifetime.[1]

A shy person, she never had confidence in her own writing. She was devoutly religious; Roger Gard describes her faith as "firm but unobtrusive Anglicanism."[2] She naturally was not greatly drawn to evangelical piety because of a general evangelical reserve about the writing of fiction. As her brief life was drawing to a close (she died of Addison's Disease), she gave herself more and more to prayer. Her sympathy for evangelicals grew as is reflected in lines she wrote: "I am by no means persuaded that we ought not all to be Evangelicals, and am at least convinced that those who act so, from reason and feeling must the happiest and safest."[3] Still, she was critical of William Cowper (1731–1800), her father's favorite poet, for his absorption with conversion and regeneration.

When her father retired and Jane's brother James succeeded him at Steventon, the family moved to beautiful Bath, especially for the health of her ailing mother. For the young woman, these were wrenching years. Several near-engagements, including one to a clergyman, did not materialize. Her father's death cut off income and further constricted the lives of the little family. The quirk of English law that women could not own or inherit property is part of the plots for both *Pride and Prejudice* and *Sense and Sensibility*.

The family settled in Chawton Cottage on her brother Edward's estate in a very modest situation (without even a carriage). Here she began her productive literary time, writing six novels in seven and one-half years.

William Lyon Phelps of Yale said: "Jane Austen is one of the supreme literary artists of the world. *Pride and Prejudice* is her masterpiece."[4] *Pride and Prejudice* was the fashionable novel of 1813, but literary popularity did not change her life because she was not known.

She does not refer to the French Revolution or the Napoléonic Wars, but this gives her work a timelessness in its appeal. She admits her readers into a sheltered world of gracious civility, where, as a newspaper and magazine writer considered:

> Maybe the overriding pleasure in reading or watching characters created by Austen is the unaffected and absolute acknowledgment of the importance of marriage and a keen understanding of the universal emotional and economic underpinnings of that institution. It helps, of course, that she writes with a deft hand and a classic perception that all is not necessarily perfect in the manners and morals of courtship.[5]

There is not a scene in Austen's books in which a woman is not present. *Pride and Prejudice* and *Emma,* her last book, are set in the southern English countryside. *Sense and Sensibility* is a comic romantic tangle, and *Persuasion* tells about a highly convoluted and elongated courtship. *Northanger Abbey* chronicles a young woman's romance with a clergyman, and *Mansfield Park* is about a poor relation's romance. All describe a life that can be painful and unfair, but also is humorous, wholesome, and good.

Building on Jane Austen's popularity, modern authors have given some interesting reading. Stephanie Barron has given us a superb mystery, *Jane and the Unpleasantness at Scargrave Manor.*[6] Some very good novels of suspense in the Victorian suspense genre are by Anne Perry. This describes the era after the death of Austen, in which England is poised on the edge of societal change. In one series, Perry's lead characters are Inspector Thomas Pitt of the Bow Street Police Division and his outspoken wife, Charlotte. An example of this series is *Farrier's Lane.*[7] The other series presents criminal investigator William Monk. *The Silent Cry*[8] is enthralling. Possibly Perry was drawn to crime mysteries after a rather sensational crime touched her own family when she was a child in New Zealand.[9]

314 THE COMPANY OF THE CREATIVE

1. David Cecil, *A Portrait of Jane Austen* (New York: Hill and Wang, 1978), 15, 17.
2. Roger Gard, *Jane Austen's Novels* (New Haven, Conn.: Yale University Press, 1992), 6.
3. Cecil, *A Portrait of Jane Austen,* 193. Jane Austen did really believe in the fall.
4. Jane Austen, *Pride and Prejudice* (New York: Pocket Books, 1956).
5. Suzanne Fields, "Losing It at the Movies with Jane Austen," *Insight,* 25 March 1996, 48.
6. New York: Bantam, 1996.
7. New York: Fawcett Columbine, 1996.
8. New York: Fawcett Columbine, 1997.
9. "Author Faces Up to a Long, Dark Secret," *The New York Times*, 14 February 1995, C-1. The story is that she and her best friend (at ages fifteen and sixteen, respectively) murdered her friend's mother.

9.2.3 THACKERAY, CYNIC OF THE SNOBBISH

> What I want to make is a set of people living without God in the world (only that is a cant phrase), greedy, pompous men, perfectly self-satisfied for the most part, and at ease about their superior virtue. Dobbins and poor Briggs are the only people with real humility as yet. Amelia's is to come.
>
> —William Makepeace Thackeray
> commenting on *Vanity Fair*

Henry James dismissed William Makepeace Thackeray (1811–1863) as a writer without ideas, but George Eliot called him "the most powerful of living novelists." Chesterton held that he was always interesting, "even in the passages which are bad." Anthony Trollope (1815–1882) alleged that Thackeray "knows what he means and knows all that he means." Thackeray towers in literature if not in the estimation of James, but less is known about him than about many other nineteenth-century writers. This is partly because his family was reluctant to cooperate with biographers. Thackeray complements Dickens, who looked at the lower classes in society. Thackeray pictured the upper and middle classes.

Born in India, Thackeray was sent home to school in England at age six after his father died. His school days were unhappy. He was inept at physical games and inclined to stay to himself and write. At Trinity College in Cambridge, his acquaintances included Frederick Tennyson, Richard Trench, and Henry Alford, but he did not complete requirements for graduation. He lost his inheritance, tried law and painting, then rather lightheartedly took up writing. Meanwhile, he drank, gambled, and "fluttered from one foible to another."[1] Tall at six feet three inches and well-built with a misshapen nose, he was affable but not a good speaker like Dickens or Edward Bulwer-Lytton (1803–1873). He offended others with his tart wit, so he frequently penned himself into hot water.

Thackeray married Isabella Shawe in 1836. They had three daughters, but his wife developed a mental illness, from which she was never to recover. She survived her husband by thirty years. Thackeray recklessly abused his health all his life, and his biographer observed that no one ever paid more dearly for sowing wild oats when he was young.[2] Thackeray drove himself in his writing for magazines and papers, desperately trying to lift himself out of his impecunious ways.

The result was a bitter harshness in his style. His reviewing was concise and often caustic. Max Müller quipped that he used plenty of "vinegar and cayenne pepper." He and Dickens were fierce competitors and never acknowledged each other until they became friends. In religion, he was skeptical. His mother became religious after William was an adult, and she taught his daughters the Bible. But he retained a "lasting distaste for evangelical dogma." Though he said he believed in God, he was basically an agnostic fatalist.[3]

Reflective and melancholy, remorseful for his rash outbursts, he could be tender but never morose. He was drawn to women and had a particularly difficult romance with Jane Brookfield, the wife of a fashionable preacher.

When he was thirty-six, he wrote his masterpiece, *Vanity Fair*. Needing money to provide for his daughters as his health began to fail, he started *Pendennis* (an uneven novel) within weeks after finishing *Vanity Fair*. He wrote some popular travel books. *Henry Esmond* is a magnificent historical novel that reconstructs the atmosphere of Queen Anne's reign.[4] This is one book he did not serialize, and it is the best example of his style in simulating the prose of the 1700s. Thackeray takes his readers aside and shares with them some insights and comments.[5] *The Virginians* is the sequel to *Henry Esmond* as the principles colonize the new world. He made several trips to America, lectured impressively on "English humorists in the 18th century" and was narrowly defeated when he ran for Parliament.

Increasingly, he was ill and despondent and, after a serious bout with spasms, died on Christmas Eve, 1863, at the age of fifty-two. He was reconciled to Dickens shortly before he died. His youngest daughter married Leslie Stephen and became the mother of Virginia Woolf. His natural style had a marked influence on the writers who followed him. No female character has ever been developed with more power and brilliance than that of Becky Sharpe in *Vanity Fair*.

There is greatness in Thackeray, but also such tragedy and difficulty in his complex life. I would wish he might have gone at least once to hear Charles Spurgeon at the Metropolitan Tabernacle.

---

1. Malcolm Elwin, *Thackeray: A Personality* (New York: Russell and Russell, 1932, 1966), 56.
2. Ibid., 56, 81.
3. Ibid., 164.
4. Lionel Stephenson, ed., *Thackeray's Henry Esmond* (New York: Harper, 1950).
5. Mario Praz, "Thackeray as Preacher," in *Thackeray: A Collection of Critical Essays* (Englewood Cliffs, N.J.: Prentice-Hall, 1968).

9.2.4 Trollope, Champion of the Status Quo

Have you ever read the novels of Anthony Trollope? They precisely fit my taste.

—Nathaniel Hawthorne

Had I written an epic about clergymen, I would have taken St. Paul for my model; but describing, as I have endeavored to do, such clergymen as I see around me, I could not venture to be transcendental.

—Anthony Trollope
The Last Chronicle of Barset

I have written much of clergymen, but in doing so I have endeavored to portray them as they bear on our social life rather than to describe the mode and working of their professional careers. Had I done the latter I could hardly have steered clear of subjects on which it has not been my intention to pronounce an opinion, and I should have laden my fiction with sermons or I should have degraded my sermons into fiction.

—*Framley Parsonage*

Anthony Trollope (1815–1882) has never been considered in the front rank of Victorian novelists, but he had a considerable renaissance of interest in the late twentieth century.

A memorial tablet was dedicated to him in Poets' Corner of Westminster Abbey, though not until 1963. The Trollope Society flourishes in England and the United States. John Hall maintains that "Trollope is read and bought by more people than any other major Victorian novelist."[1] Trollope wrote sixty-seven books, of which forty-seven were novels. He wrote five collections of short stories, four large travel books, three biographies, and four books of sketches. In his autobiography, Trollope concedes that if he had written less he would have written better. By comparison, Thackeray wrote eight novels.

A gifted writer like Frederick Buechner allows that Trollope is

the only fiction writer that I like reading right now, and that I read continually—my wife and I have this thing about him; we read aloud in the car. He's a marvelous novelist in every way. He's very humble in that, unlike many writers, he makes no effort to be a great stylist. He doesn't keep intruding into the story the way Dickens does. He just lets his characters be who they are. . . . Trollope just goes his gorgeous, quiet way. Not always that quiet, either. He has a dark, almost Dostoevskian side to him, too.[2]

Stanley Hauerwas of Duke University builds several essays around Trollope in his *Dispatches from the Front: Theological Engagements with the Secular.* Hauerwas explains that "I use Trollope because I love to read Trollope."[3]

Many English read Trollope during the "blitz" bombings of the Battle of Britain in World War II. Trollope wrote about the "peaceful world" of Barsetshire that was gone forever. Trollope was a relativist who liked order and decorum. He built a dream cathedral city with its clergy in tension over the threat of reform. Ruth apRoberts is right that "he is staunchly loyal to the Church of England because he is so non-committal."[4] The student of Victorian preaching needs to read Trollope for insights into the masses who sought preservation, not transformation, whose watchwords were: "Beware of explosive agents!"[5] Trollope ran unsuccessfully for Parliament on the same conservative philosophy with which he wrote. He was uneasy over the ferment of his times and advocated "running the reforming rascals out of town."[6] Both high and low church innovations threatened his beloved status quo.

Trollope was born in Russell Square, London. His father was a "disputacious barrister" lurching toward financial ruin. His mother was a well-known writer who vehemently attacked low-church evangelicals in her novel *The Vicar of Wrexhill*.[7] After day-school at Harrow, young Trollope took a position with the General Post Office and served in Ireland. He traveled around the world in his job, negotiating postal treaties. *The Small House at Allington* was written in America. It was he who introduced pillar boxes as a convenience for people to deposit their mail.[8] In 1844 he married in Ireland. His first several novels were Anglo-Irish and not much noticed.

He was a disciplined and speedy writer. He wrote from 5:30 until 8:30 each morning at the rate of one thousand words an hour before leaving for work. He alternated six Barsetshire novels with other works. Known for attention to the commonplace, his plots are simple yet inventive and humorous in development.

The beginner should start with *The Warden* and *Barchester Towers,* the first two of the six ecclesiastically oriented Chronicles of Barsetshire. The addicted can go on to choose among the six volumes on politics in the Palliser series, starting with *Can You Forgive Her?* Tolstoy read *The Prime Minister* while writing *Anna Karenina* (1877).

The leading character in the early Chronicles is the Reverend Septimus Harding, warden of Hiram's Hospital and precentor (director of music) at the cathedral. He is a cellist extraordinaire and a man of unblemished character. His stipend is challenged by a young reformer, John Bold, and by *The Jupiter* (obviously modeled on *The London Times*). Two Londoners are also troublemakers. These are thinly disguised fictionalizations of Charles Dickens and Thomas Carlyle. Other antagonists are the low-church evangelical, Obadiah Slope, with his "moist, sweaty palm" and Mrs. Proudie, the bishop's domineering wife. Evangelicals, Trollope thinks, are "too flashy and emotional" and thus upsetting. The Anglo-Catholics have similar faults.

Harding resigns after a memorable trip to London, though the suit against him is withdrawn. Harding, like Trollope, is more interested in peace and quiet than in theology. He likes easygoing and idle churchmen who love to hunt. Harding's worldly son-in-law, Archdeacon Grantley, is such a broad-minded cleric.

Henry James wrote: "Trollope did not write for posterity; he wrote for the day, the moment; but these are just the writers whom posterity is apt to put into its pocket."

Another Victorian stellar light is Edward Bulwer-Lytton. Particularly good is his *The Last Days of Pompeii,* a romance set in the days of the eruption of Mount Vesuvius in A.D. 79. Bulwer-Lytton served in Parliament for fifteen years and was Colonial Secretary. His are well-researched historical novels given the resources and state of archaeology of the day. The reading is a bit arduous by today's fiction standards.

1. In *Trollopiana,* publication of the Trollope Society, No. 21, May 1993, 3.
2. Interview with Frederick Buechner, *The Christian Century,* 16 November 1983, 1044.
3. Quoted in a review by Max Stackhouse, *The Christian Century,* 18 October 1995, 962.
4. Ruth apRoberts, *The Moral Trollope* (Athens, Ohio: University of Ohio Press, 1971), 126.
5. James Kinkaid, *"The Warden* and *Barchester Towers:* The Pastoral Defined," in *Anthony Trollope's* Barchester Towers *and* The Warden, ed. Harold Bloom (New York: Chelsea House, 1988), 71, 77.
6. Ibid., 66.
7. A rollicking biography of Trollope's novelist mother is Pamela Neville-Sington, *Fanny Trollope: The Life and Adventures of a Clever Woman* (New York: Viking, 1998). She was a funny woman, like Trollope's famous character Glencora Palliser in his justly famous "Palliser" novels out of the political sphere.
8. We are greatly enriched by two recent biographies of Trollope, N. John Hall, *Trollope* (Oxford: Oxford University Press, 1991); and Victoria Glendinning, *Anthony Trollope* (New York: Knopf, 1993). The latter is the first major treatment by a woman. She brings interesting insights into Trollope's able depiction of strong women in the battle of the sexes.

9.2.5 DICKENS, SOCIAL CRUSADER

Want is so general, distress so great and poverty so rampant—it is, in a word, so hard for the Million to live by any means. . . . We have come to this absurd, this dangerous, this monstrous pass that the dishonest felon, is, in respect of cleanliness, order, diet and accommodation, better provided for, and taken care of, than the honest pauper.

—Charles Dickens

"It is certainly very cold," said Peggoty, "Everybody must feel it so."
"I feel it more than other people," said Mrs. Gummidge.

"I was destined to be unlucky in life [said young Davy]."

—Charles Dickens
David Copperfield

Charles Dickens (1812–1870) is the most popular and influential novelist of all time. His *A Christmas Carol,* written at a time of genuine financial need for his wife and nine children, continues to play before packed audiences around the world each Christmas. When Fëdor Dostoevsky (1821–1881) was exiled to Siberia in 1849, his request was to be able to receive copies of the novels of Charles Dickens.

"Is Little Nell dead?" was a burning question of the populace when Dickens's novels were published serially throughout the English-speaking world. His fifteen novels addressed painful issues of the dark side of the Industrial Revolution and

Victorian English society. They aroused action leading particularly to improved conditions for children. The two thousand characters in his books are a treasure of varied individuals. T. A. Jackson has even given a Marxian interpretation that applauds Dickens and his writings.[1]

Dickens was born in Portsmouth, the son of a naval clerk and the second of eight children. His father was in and out of debtor's prison, hence the vivid descriptions of Little Dorritt and Marshalsea Prison. Embittered that neither of his parents had him educated, he caricatured his father in the person of Wilkins Micawber, who was always waiting for things "to turn up" and who eventually fled his debts and migrated to Australia.

When he was ten, Charles went to work in a warehouse pasting labels on blacking jars. He had only brief schooling under an Oxford student and Baptist minister, William Giles.[2] His childhood was a nightmare. He taught himself shorthand and ultimately became a newspaper reporter on the House of Commons beat. His first published work was *Sketches by Boz* (1836), and his real breakthrough came in the series of stories we now know as *Pickwick Papers*. Samuel Pickwick, Mr. Wardle, and the servant Sam Weller (of "You sir, are a humbug" fame) propelled the work to astonishing success.

At this time, Dickens married Catherine Hogarth with whom he parented nine children. Their relationship was never strong, however, and finally he separated from her. Dickens traveled abroad extensively, touring America twice with a program of readings from his books. In addition to his fiction, he wrote several travel books and experimented—unsuccessfully—with drama. He died after a massive stroke when he was only fifty-eight years old.

Writing never came easily. "Dickens agonized over his plots, suffered with his characters and knew black despair when ideas failed to come on his endless walks," wrote John Mortimer. One night while writing *A Christmas Carol,* he walked fifteen or twenty miles "about the black streets of London . . . when all the good folks had gone to bed."[3]

He was a nominal Anglican and his clergy characters, from the Rev. Stiggins to Canon Crispsparkle, are unattractive figures. The Milveys in *Our Mutual Friend* may be the most favorable portrayals. The hypocritical, oily Mr. Chadband in *Bleak House* shows us Dickens's animus toward evangelicals. Dickens did write *The Life of Our Lord* for his children. Unlike Thomas Jefferson's edited New Testament, the Dickens version does not omit the resurrection and miracles.[4]

The Dickens corpus holds many novels, each with intricate layers of plot. *Oliver Twist* is a good place to begin, with the thieving Oliver, the Artful Dodger, and kindly Mr. Brownlow. The most effectively plotted must be *Great Expectations,* which sets forth "the folly of a spendthrift youth" with Pip, Estella, and the insane Miss Havisham.

Our Mutual Friend is classic fiction at its finest, with the portrayal of the Podsnaps and "podsnappery" and an underlying warning about the unwillingness to face facts.

Bleak House critiques the judicial process. It has so many biblical references that one critic argues it is Dickens's "major fictional attempt to wrestle with the relevance of his own religious tradition for his times."[5] It also gives us Mrs. Jellyby's view of missions.

Prayer is a curious subtheme in the one historical novel Dickens wrote, *A Tale of Two Cities*. In this story of the French Revolution, Jeremiah Cruncher's wife gives way to what her husband calls "flopping."[6] Although Dickens was influenced by Bunyan, he lost faith in the supernatural.[7]

But who can rival Steerforth and Aunt Betsy Trotwood in *David Copperfield?* Or the repentance of Dombey? Or the deterioration of Boffin? Or the characterizations of the beautiful Esther Summerson and the wretched Mrs. Gamp? Or Harold Skimpole or Mr. Dick or Mr. Jaggers? Such characterizations are memorable and enriching.

---

1. T. A. Jackson, *Charles Dickens: The Progress of a Radical* (New York: International, 1987).
2. Fred Kaplan, *Dickens: A Biography* (New York: William Morrow, 1988). Edgar Johnson's two volume biography may still be the best, *Charles Dickens: His Tragedy and Triumph* (New York: Simon and Schuster, 1952). Kaplan the academic has given a splendid treatment. So has Peter Ackroyd in *Dickens* (New York: Harper/Collins, 1990). Ackroyd said his version is "innocent of post-structuralist suspicions." Additional tools are Angus Wilson, *The World of Charles Dickens* (New York: Viking, 1970) and Michael and Mollie Pickwick, *The Charles Dickens Encyclopedia* (New York: Scribner's, 1973). Note also a beautiful article by Richard W. Long, "The England of Charles Dickens," *National Geographic,* April 1974, 443–83.
3. John Mortimer, "Poorhouses, Pamphlets and Marley's Ghost," *The New York Times,* 24 December 1993, A13.
4. Charles Dickens, *The Life of Our Lord* (New York: Simon and Schuster, 1934). This book is not included in the standard edition of Dickens's complete works.
5. Janet Karsten Larson, "Is It Bleaker Than We Think?" *The Christian Century,* 29 January 1986, 87ff.
6. Charles Dickens, *A Tale of Two Cities* (New York: Peter Fenelon Collier, n.d.), 62, 403. This citation is from my own heirloom set of Dickens, bequeathed by my maternal grandfather. He traded his fiddle for it so that his wife and children might have good books to read when he staked a claim in Idaho early in the twentieth century.
7. Barry Qualls, *The Secular Pilgrims of Victorian Fiction* (Cambridge: Cambridge University Press, 1982). Sobering.
8. New York: Knopf, 1995.

9.2.6 ELIOT, REBEL WITH A CAUSE

There are days when I think of George Eliot and her Lydgate, and I come to the conclusion that lots of us doctors fool ourselves very easily, and that's what *Middlemarch* has to say to me now, just as it did back then. But maybe there's hope. I remember the end of the novel, when she pointed out that you never do know how a life will turn out (I'm sure paraphrasing!) Well, maybe my friend, Lydgate will help me turn the corner—go after what I think is right for me to do, for the sake of my wife and son, and for my own sake, too. I'd hate to end up a driven, driven "success," who is bored by what he does, but is always postponing any moral confrontation with himself!

—A student of Dr. Robert Coles of Harvard,
after medical students were assigned to read *Middlemarch*

Some have argued that George Eliot's *Middlemarch* is the single greatest English novel. Paul Johnson, the English historian, describes Eliot as "the most influential woman writer in the 19th century."[1] She captures the "discontinuities, contradictions and bewilderments of the Victorian age" in a lucid way.[2] Her complex plots pack tremendous punch. Frederick Karl calls his fine biographical study, *George Eliot: Voice of a Century*.[3] Her spiritual pilgrimage is a classic journey from certitude to skepticism. Her lifestyle scandalized her own family and required her to live under a shadow.

George Eliot was the pen name for Mary Ann (or Marian) Evans (1819–1880), who was born in Warwickshire. Her father was a farmer who served as an estate agent. He was a devout, conservative member of the Church of England. Mary Ann's brother Samuel converted to Methodism (and his wife became the model for the preaching woman in *Adam Bede*). Mary Ann attended several girls' schools, at one of which her governess was Marie Lewis, a "strong evangelical" with appropriate Puritan austerity. While at school in Coventry, she attended Cow Lane Baptist Chapel. She organized prayer meetings and read and wrote evangelical poetry.[4] Her best known poem from this time was "O May I Join the Choir Invisible." But a drastic change was coming.

After her mother died, she took over management of the home. She read Scott, Wordsworth, and Coleridge, and struggled with depression. She had many discussions with her Methodist aunt. Later she would say, "I used to pray so much—now I hardly ever pray." She still believed in abstinence rather than moderation and did not attend the theatre.[5] She loved evangelical writer Hannah More (1745–1833), Archbishop Robert Leighton of Glasgow (1611–1684), and ardent preacher Joseph Milner (1744–1797).

At first she remained in "evangelical and dissenting circles" when she moved to Coventry. However, the preaching in her new church was a disappointment. "Though we hear the truth, yet it is not recommended by the mode of its delivery."[6] Suddenly she became interested in phrenology, the pseudoscience of judging intelligence by the shape of the head. She was personally lonely, and in her writings made fewer and fewer biblical references. Her doubts grew until she rejected Christianity. Instead, Evans devoured Unitarian books, along with the work of David Hume (1711–1776) and Friedrich Schleiermacher (1768–1834).[7] She retained some sort of confession of God and Jesus but now she was translating into English the crude denial of the historicity of Christ, *Leben Jesu* by David Strauss (1808–1874).

She found identity with other unbelievers in a gathering of freethinkers called the Rosehill Meetings. At last, she ceased attending church and made a painful break with her father before he died in 1849.

She now began a series of affairs with men, including the philosopher Herbert Spencer (1820–1903). Spencer introduced her to Comtean atheist George Lewes (1817–1878), with whom she lived until his death. He never divorced his first wife so that he and Evans could marry.[8] Evans feared public disapprobation, and her lifestyle became so notorious that she was not forgiven by many of her readers. She worked on various periodicals and wrote vicious, mocking attacks against evangelicals.[9] She and Lewes traveled widely, remaining restless and unfulfilled.

Lewes first suggested that she write fiction.[10] She had publicly committed herself against Charles Kingsley with his "hortatory tone" and his willingness to "drop the homily in." Her first work of fiction, *Scenes of Clerical Life,* expose an ever-unattractive clergy. Rev. Amos Barton is influenced by Charles Simeon and is "as evangelical as an Independent Chapel."

She had no peer in her writing about rural England. Her first significant novel, *Adam Bede,* is "full of the breath of cows and the scent of hay." The book was immediately popular, and reviewers wondered who this George Eliot might be. Dickens, to his credit, quickly concluded from the writing style that "he" was a "she."

The plot of *Adam Bede* is built on the premise that human choices have consequences. Lovable Adam Bede is romantically attached to pretty Hetty Sorrel. But Hetty is seduced and impregnated by a gentleman. So Adam rejects her and finally marries the Methodist preacher Dinah Morris. Both Evans and her father seem to be represented in the story's hero.[11] Even more autobiographical is *The Mill on the Floss*. Tom Tolliver is like the author's estranged brother, Isaac. These are gripping stories, sparklingly told. *Silas Marner* is a briefer work, telling how little Eppie changes the life of Silas, the isolated old weaver in Ravelow.[12] In what may be her greatest novel, *Middlemarch,* the canvas is more intricately painted with four plots. There is much sorrow and gloom, since Eliot herself is in depression. *Middlemarch* also is a call for reform of the medical profession. It has a wonderful circle of characters: Dorothea and her older husband, Causebon, his second cousin Will Ladislaw, the younger Vincey's and their Uncle Featherstone, the evangelical banker Bulstrode. The question always is: Why did the author allow her heroine, Dorothea, to fail?

Her only historical novel as such was *Romolo,* set in medieval Florence and focusing on the pre-Luther reformer and social crusading preacher, Girolamo Savonarola (1452–1498). Her last work, *Daniel Deronda,* is ponderous and deals with the unexpected subject of Jewish history and prophecy. Old Mordecai has a vision for a Jewish state in Palestine, which makes the book a pre-Zionist landmark.[13]

These and other novels are just some of the best writing ever done in English. No wonder they endure and thrive. Both England and North American markets were immediately enthralled with them. Her fame dipped around the turn of the century, but then she was rediscovered and maintained a large literary and popular following. During the 1990s, high-quality British television productions filmed *The Mill on the Floss* and *Middlemarch*.

In 1878 Lewes died, and Evans was too feeble to attend the funeral. She took his name after his death, but in his will she is listed, "Mary Ann Evans, Spinster."

Curiously after all of her pooh-poohing of the afterlife, she spent much time at his grave and reported a spiritual visitation there. She and her brother reestablished their relationship, and she became engaged to a young clergyman, John Cross, who was twenty years her junior. They were married in 1880, and she died later that year.

How close to, and yet so far from, the living Christ was George Eliot and many of the other great writers.

1. Paul Johnson, *The Birth of the Modern: World Society 1815–1830* (New York: HarperCollins, 1991), 480.
2. Rosemary Ashton, *George Eliot: A Life* (New York: Clarendon, 1996), 9.
3. Frederich R. Karl and George Eliot, *Voice of a Century* (New York: Norton, 1995). Another very fine piece of work.
4. Ibid., 31, 36. Karl observes: "She wanted a Christianity with her own kind of Christ."
5. Ashton, *George Eliot: A Life,* 26.
6. Ibid., 34, 51. Eliot consciously used Kant's investigative technique. Such leads her toward skepticism. "I no longer believe in the Divine authority of the Old and New Testaments" she clearly said (44). George Eliot did not relish "the ecstasies of the twice-born." Cf. Andrew L. Drummond, *The Churches in English Fiction,* 28.
7. Ibid., 35.
8. Rosemary Ashton, *G. H. Lewes: A Life* (New York: Clarendon, 1992). Lewes wrote scientific materials.
9. Ashton, *George Eliot: A Life,* 144ff. Her writing developed a sharpness, "brilliance with a cutting edge."
10. Ibid., 147. Lewes dedicated himself to shielding her from criticism.
11. George Eliot, *Adam Bede* (New York: Pocket Library, 1956). These modest paperbacks are inexpensive.
12. George Eliot, *Silas Marner* (New York: Pocket Library, 1955). Another classic built off the same theme is Johanna Spyri's beautiful Swiss mountain novel, *Heidi,* in which the little girl softens the old uncle's heart.
13. George Eliot, *Daniel Deronda* (New York: Harper Torchbook, 1960). She wrote this as Disraeli came to power.

9.2.7 KINGSLEY, ADVENTUROUS PARSON

God forgive me if I am wrong, but I look forward to it [heaven] with an intense and reverent curiosity.

—Charles Kingsley

How beautiful God is!

—deathbed whisper overheard by Kingsley's daughter

The "muscular Christianity" enthusiastically advocated by Charles Kingsley (1819–1875) is a vibrant, hardy faith that does not hesitate to become wholeheartedly involved in the needs of society. Its promoter was born into an evangelical manse and there preached his first sermon at the age of four.[1] After taking his Cambridge degree, at twenty-three he assumed the curacy at Eversley, Hampshire, where he gave himself for thirty-three years until his death. This neglected rural parish thrived under the strong preaching and pastoral labors of the Kingsleys.

One day a week, Kingsley would travel to Cambridge, where he was first professor of English literature and composition and then chair of the Modern History Department. His critical essays on the radical skepticism of David Strauss on the one hand and the high church extremism of the Tractarians on the other led him into writing. He carried on a duel in print with John Henry Newman (1801–1890). It was in response to an 1864 attack from Kingsley that Newman wrote the autobiographical *Apologia pro vita sua,* which started his rise to cardinal in the Roman Catholic Church. Kingsley was a prolific writer of novels, poetry, and drama that expressed his strong ideas about a more responsible society. Carlyle and F. D. Maurice were the voices that called him.[2]

One of the great sea stories of the ages is told in *Westward Ho!* set in the days of Queen Elizabeth I (1533–1603).[3] *The Water Babies* shares the plight of Tom, the little chimney sweep, which deeply moved the social reformer Anthony Ashley Cooper, Earl of Shaftesbury (1801–1885). *Alton Locke* deals critically with Christian socialism and was commended by Carlyle as a "new explosive or red-hot shell against the devil's dung-heap."[4] *Hypatia* is set in the context of the second-century conflict between early Christianity and Alexandrian philosophy. *Village Sermons* recommended Kingsley as a strong Bible preacher. The book may have been one reason he was named canon of Chester and then of Westminster. These were largely honorary positions but gave regular access to these cathedral pulpits.

He also served as chaplain to Queen Victoria, but in these unrelenting duties and demands his focus was clear: "I have to preach Jesus Christ and Him crucified, and to be instant in that, in season and out of season, and at all risks."[5] The depth and breadth of Charles Kingsley's sympathies and his loyalty to the gospel of Christ should inspire men and women of faith in every generation.

---

1. See Larsen, *The Company of the Preachers,* 9.3.7.
2. Fanny Kingsley, ed., *Charles Kingsley: His Letters and Memories of His Life,* 2 vols. (London: Kegan Paul, 1882). There is much on the battle between Kingsley and the Tractarians. Some comes from Kingsley himself. The title character in *Alton Locke* is very dubious about the Anglo-Catholics in the Church of England. See John Shelton Reed, *Glorious Battle: The Cultural Politics of Victorian Anglo-Catholicism* (Nashville: Vanderbilt, 1996). He wrote a long poem, "The Saints Tragedy," against clerical celibacy. He was opposed to anything Romish. The Rev. Harry Jones reported that even "the sight of the red edge on his hymnbook would produce a deep inarticulate growl from all parts of the building." Catholic hymn books usually were decorated with a red edge.
3. Favorite sea stories would have to include Richard Dana, *Two Years Before the Mast;* Frank Bullen, *The Cruise of the Cachelot;* the Captain Hornblower stories; and the brilliant Patrick O'Brian series of novels featuring the characters Aubrey and Maturin.

The first of the latter books was published in 1987. Worth mentioning also for the "salts" are Robert Cushman Murphy's *Logbook for Grace* (about whaling) and Richard Hughes's *In Hazard*. It stands with Joseph Conrad's *Typhoon* among the best stories of storms at sea.

4. Johnstone G. Patrick, "A Fighter for the Faith: Centenary Salute to Charles Kingsley," *Life of Faith,* 25 January 1975, 3.

5. Ibid. Kingsley was a prodigious walker. As an undergraduate, he could walk fifty-two miles in a day.

9.2.8 STEVENSON, RECKLESS SCOTSMAN

A figure came out that I cannot do justice to. Imagine a man so thin and emaciated that he looked like a bundle of sticks in a bag, with a head and eyes morbidly intelligent and restless. He was costumed in a dirty striped cotton pyjamas, the baggy legs tucked into coarse knit woolen stockings, one of which was bright brown in color, the other a purplish dark tone. . . . When conversation fairly began, though I could not forget the dirt and the discomfort, I found Stevenson extremely entertaining. He has the nervous restlessness of his disease, and although he said he was unusually well, I half expected to see him drop with a hemorrhage at any moment, for he cannot be quiet, but sits down, jumps up, darts off and flies back, at every sentence he utters, and his eyes and features gleam with a hectic glow.

—Henry Adams, describing an 1890 visit
with Robert Louis Stevenson in Samoa.

Though relatively brief, the life of Robert Louis Stevenson (1850–1894) was intense and remarkably productive. In his great gift of description, he spoke about "people who sit on the threshold of their personalities," but he was not one of them. As described above, he was tall and gaunt. His family traced back to seventeenth-century Puritans. Stevenson men were prominent and successful engineers; Robert's father, Thomas, was known for building lighthouses on the rocky Scottish coast. He was a strict Presbyterian and a "stern and unbending Tory," a combination which set off many clashes with his son. Mrs. Stevenson was from the accomplished Balfour family of writers, scientists, and politicians. Her personality was the opposite from that of her husband. Unfortunately, she inherited a pulmonary weakness that made the family susceptible to tuberculin infection. She was allowed only one pregnancy and lived for that son, who also contracted tuberculosis.[1]

Like his mother, Robert was in fragile health and was under the continuing care of "Nurse Cunningham," a descendent of Scottish Covenanters by family and conviction. She read from the Bible and *The Pilgrim's Progress*. He later dedicated *A Child's Garden of Verses* to his nurse. He had only irregular formal education until he went to the University of Edinburgh to study engineering, but then switched to law. He never practiced, since he wanted only to write. He also defected from orthodoxy, moving gradually to agnosticism and then atheism, to the consternation of his excommunicating father.[2]

It was a volatile time in his life, during which his best friend was the future journalist poet William Ernest Henley (1849–1903), who would write the sullenly defiant "Invictus." Stevenson seldom attended lectures at the university, and he contracted syphilis. Always fighting tuberculosis, he repeatedly went to southern France through the generosity of his parents. He fell in love with and married a woman who already was legally married and was eleven years his senior. This was a "final outrage against Puritan orthodoxy."[3]

The rest of Stevenson's life was spent in a vain search for the climate and conditions that could arrest his disease. They traveled to the United States and lived in San Francisco and Monterey in the California highlands. Here, to entertain his stepson, he drew the outline of an island on a big sheet of paper and announced "Here is Treasure Island." The story of Jimmy Hawkins and Long John Silver was not popular when serialized, but as a book it brought instant fame and considerable monetary reward to its author. *Treasure Island* has remained one of the most widely read and loved books.[4] A similar novel, *Kidnapped,* is about the Highlanders, as is its sequel, *Catriona.*

Stevenson and his wife returned to England and lived for a few relatively tranquil years at Bournemouth on the English Channel. There, based on a dream, he wrote *The Strange Case of Dr. Jekyll and Mr. Hyde.* The story perhaps reflected something of the duality of his own struggle. It is haunting but brilliant.[5]

One of his best-drawn figures, Adam Weit in *Weir of Hermiston,* embodies the harshness Stevenson saw in Calvinism.[6] This was his last book.

The Stevensons emigrated to the Adirondacks of New York State, then turned to the South Pacific. Enroute they visited the leper colony on the Hawaiian island of Molokai. Father Joseph Damien (1840–1889) had recently died, and Stevenson wrote a fiery defense of the Belgian priest's selfless mission among the lepers. They settled in Samoa, where Stevenson lived as a planter. He also wrote and became involved in the affairs of the natives. In the end, he died of a brain hemorrhage, more from overwork than as a direct result of his tuberculosis.

Stevenson wrote an amazing variety of works. His poetry has been widely popular, while his six plays were disasters. Thirty short stories probably represent Stevenson's best writing, although several of his novels are classics. He wrote essays and seven books of travel, one of the most interesting of which is *Travels with a Donkey in the Cevennes* [a mountain range in France].[7] He describes his contact with the Plymouth Brethren in this unexpected place.

Stevenson renounced Christianity, but he never fully escaped the living God of his fathers or the Scriptures in which he had been nurtured. He was like Tolstoy, wanting Jesus but not the supernatural Christ. In a striking essay he suggestively entitled "A Christmas Sermon," Stevenson makes only a few passing references to Christ. He observes that "Christ's sayings on the point are hard to reconcile with each other and (the most of them) hard to accept."[8]

He had consumed much of Walt Whitman and Henry David Thoreau, so that he had little appetite for the gospel.[9] As with the schizophrenic Jekyll and Hyde, there was the attractive in Stevenson and that which was monstrous. The Samoans adored the *Tusitala* or "Teller of Tales." Sixty of them carried his body to a burial place on the summit of Mount Vaea.

1. Frank McLynn, *Robert Louis Stevenson: A Biography* (New York: Random House, 1994). Interesting analysis.

2. Saze Commins, ed., introduction to *Selected Writings of Robert Louis Stevenson* (New York: Modern Library, 1947), xi. The family home in New Town at 17 Heriot Row can be seen as a landmark in Edinburgh.

3. Ibid., xiii.

4. Ibid., xvii. Though uneven as a novelist, Stevenson had a clear style, dynamic plots, and vividly drawn characters.

5. Ibid., xviii. Stevenson conveys a sense of the supernatural in an effective way and is perceptive for the time in his psychological insights.

6. Ibid., xxvi. Stevenson acknowledged his debt in *Weir of Hermiston* to theologian Samuel Rutherford's (1600–1661) letters and religious writer Henry Scougal (1650–1678).

7. Robert Louis Stevenson, *Travels with a Donkey in the Cevennes,* in *Selected Writings,* 994ff.

8. Robert Louis Stevenson, "A Christmas Sermon" (repr. ed., London: Chatto and Windus, 1906).

9. Robert Louis Stevenson, *Familiar Studies* (repr. ed., New York: P. F. Collier, 1912), VII, 61–83, 84–109. See an interesting book by the noted Scottish preacher and homiletician John Kelman, *The Faith of Robert Louis Stevenson* (Edinburgh: Oliphant Anderson, 1903).

9.2.9 THE BRONTËS, PRODIGIES OF THE PARSONAGE

No writer or group of writers, has caught the imagination of the public as that strange, unsociable family who lived more than a hundred years ago in a place even then described as bleak and remote. So much indeed has been written that one tends to lose sight of the fact that the Brontës were living people who loved and laughed, ate their dinners and grumbled about the cost of living.

—Maureen Peters
The Enigma of the Brontës[1]

The talented trio of Charlotte (1816–1855), Emily (1818–1848), and Anne (1820–1849) Brontë wrote an array of the most remarkable fiction and now claim our attention. Their father, the Rev. Patrick Brontë (1777–1861), was born in lean circumstances in Ireland of an illiterate father. He became village schoolmaster. One of his employers, the Rev. Thomas Tigue, encouraged him to go to England and then to Cambridge, where he became something of a Greek scholar. Sponsored by William Wilberforce (1759–1833; see 5.8), Brontë was ordained in the Church of England in 1806 and served several curacies. At Hartshead near Bradford, he met and married Maria Branwell. They had six children. In 1820 Brontë took the pulpit at Haworth, one of the leading evangelical parishes. Here the dynamic preacher and associate of the Wesleys, William Grimshaw (1708–1763), had held forth. Brontë preached with vigor until advanced age. The sisters surely had an evangelical background.[2]

When Mrs. Brontë died in 1821, her strict Methodist sister, Elizabeth Branwell, came as housekeeper.[3] She was a formative influence and shaped the family's reading habits with massive doses of *The Pilgrim's Progress* and other evangelical staples. Surrounded by "misty moors" and a quaint cemetery, the children broke the monotony of their lives by imagining adventures in the Kingdom of Gondal.

Their brother Branwell (1818–1848) was the doted-upon favorite of the girls, but he later developed alcohol and drug addictions. The four oldest girls, Maria, Elizabeth, Charlotte, and Emily, were sent away to Cowan Bridge School, where Maria and Elizabeth died in an outbreak of fever. Charlotte used the oppressive atmosphere of this school as a model for her characterization of Lowood School in *Jane Eyre*. Charlotte later attended and ultimately taught at Roe Head School. To qualify to teach, she and Emily went to Belgium to study at Constantine Heger's academy through the generosity of Aunt Branwell, and Charlotte developed a deep attachment to the headmaster.[4]

They first published under assumed names. Charlotte was the most educated of the sisters, and her novel *Jane Eyre* has been a durable classic. It has had several film adaptations. When it was first published, the love story of the young governess Jane Eyre and the brooding landowner Edward Rochester shocked Victorian sensibilities. The mysteries hidden within Thornfield's manor house, the ancestral abode, are indeed shocking.[5]

Emily, probably the most brilliant, is known only for her one novel, *Wuthering Heights*. Set on the moors, this striking study has what some call "a mystical intensity." Emily was the sister who loved dogs and the outdoors, but she caught cold at her brother's funeral and died within a few months at the age of thirty.[6] Anne did not live even this long, and her two novels were not of the quality of her sisters'. They are always mentioned chiefly because she was part of the triad.

Charlotte had some exposure as a celebrity in London. She met Thackeray and Matthew Arnold (1822–1888). She lived long enough to marry Arthur Bell Nichols, one of her father's curates, but in 1855 she also succumbed to the tubercular curse that had decimated the family. Patrick Brontë survived his entire family. He was eccentric and carried a loaded pistol everywhere, but he was a great blessed parish preacher who lovingly raised his motherless children and gave himself unsparingly for the poor.[7]

The Brontë novels are all sympathetic to the church and clergy. Their evangelical beliefs are not clear from anything they wrote, but their personal tragedy does not tincture their work with bitterness or anger. Charlotte speaks of "the world-redeeming creed of Christ" in her introduction to *Jane Eyre*. The biblical world was inseparable from their lives.

If you had visited London in 1859 or later you might have worshiped at the Metropolitan Tabernacle south of the river and heard Charles Haddon Spurgeon (1834–1892), or you might have listened to Dean H. P. Liddon (1829–1890) at St. Paul's, or Joseph Parker (1830–1902) at City Temple, Holborn Viaduct.[8] Good biographies of one or more of these preachers will show the cultural interaction that stimulated Bible teaching in this remarkable era. One such volume is Lewis Drummond's commanding *Spurgeon: Prince of Preachers*.[9] A powerful account.

1. New York: St. Martin's, 1974.
2. A. Skevington Wood, "Father of the Brontes: Evangelical Influence on English Literature," in *Life of Faith*, 19 March 1977, 3. Some argue that their passionate and realistic romanticism derives in part from the Great Awakening, out of which their lives emerged.
3. Lyndall Gordon, *Charlotte Bronte: A Passionate Life* (New York: W. W. Norton, 1994), 6. One of the best biographies written on any of the sisters.
4. Peters, *The Enigma of the Brontes*, 86ff.
5. Charlotte Brontë, *Jane Eyre* (New York: Pocket Books, 1956). The book ends: "Even so, come quickly, Lord Jesus."
6. Katherine Frank, *A Chainless Soul: A Life of Emily Bronte* (Boston: Houghton/Mifflin, 1990). Emily remains the most mysterious Brontë.
7. Juliet Barker, *The Brontes* (New York: St. Martin's, 1995). This is a massive work of 1,003 pages.
8. For more on these men see *The Company of the Preachers*, 10.6.4 (Spurgeon), 10.6.6 (Liddon), and 10.6.5 (Parker).
9. Grand Rapids: Kregel, 1992.

9.2.10 MacDonald, Minister in Denial

> But with doctrines, and what men commonly call "theology," I do not care to become involved. . . . I believe that Jesus Christ is our atonement (at-one-ment), that through him we are conciled to, made one with God. There is not one word in the New Testament about reconciling God to us. . . . He makes us make atonement.
> —George MacDonald
> *Unspoken Sermons*

> Ian argues with his mother against substitutionary atonement, rejecting the idea that God's justice demands satisfaction: "Did Jesus deserve punishment? If not, then to punish him was to wrong him . . . not through an old-covenant sacrifice of the innocent for the guilty."
> —*The Highlander's Last Song*

George MacDonald (1824–1905) was born in rural Aberdeenshire and studied science at Aberdeen. His mother died when he was a child, and he had a troubled relationship with his father. He renounced his father's Calvinist faith. Entering the Congregational ministry, he served a parish at Arundel, but his universalistic view of salvation got him into hot water.[1] He preached in Manchester supplementing his meager income by writing. Finally he moved to London to write. The widow of Byron gave financial assistance. He was close to Maurice and Ruskin and knew Dickens, Carlyle, and Trollope. He exerted great influence on C. S. Lewis and the Lewis literary sphere. Lewis has been accused of being caught in MacDonald's heresies, but this is usually charged of his fantasy allegories, rather than his theological essays. The Narnia Chronicles by Lewis particularly draws on his style and ideas. So does T. S. Eliot's wasteland motif.

Joining the Church of England, MacDonald moved to Italy. In 1873 he toured and lectured through America. MacDonald was Christo-centric, but he was profoundly influenced by the German pietistic mysticism of William Blake (1757–1827), Emanuel Swedenborg (1688–1772), and Jakob Böhme (1575–1624). He denied the substitutionary atonement and became a universalist, denying that hell is eternal and believing that the devil will be converted.[2]

His juvenile fantasy is very well done and the prototype of the work that others went on to do. He also wrote twenty-nine realistic novels of the "they lived happily forever after" type. As originally written they were ponderous, with sentences running 100 to 150 words and some in excess of 200 words. The dialogues were heavy in dialect. Fortunately toward the end of the 1900s, Michael R. Phillips recast the novels in simplified language.[3] The novels are some of the best preacher stories ever transcribed. They shed much light on Scottish history, culture, and the Church of Scotland. *The Curate's Awakening* grapples with true piety in the life of the preacher, particularly the problems of pretense and plagiarism. *The Minister's Restoration* traces a poignant path of confession and repentance for the pastor caught up in sin.[4]

The writing and the sermons that survive show that George MacDonald was creative and thoughtful but sadly influenced by the increasing inroads of doubt and denial.[5]

---

1. Richard H. Reis, *George MacDonald* (New York: Twayne, 1972). See also Michael Phillips, *George MacDonald: Scotland's Beloved Storyteller* (Minneapolis: Bethany, 1987); and Rolland Hein, *George MacDonald: Victorian Mythmaker* (Nashville: Star Song, 1993).
2. Michael R. Phillips, ed., *George MacDonald: Discovering the Character of God* (Minneapolis: Bethany House, 1989).
3. Ibid.
4. George MacDonald, *The Curate's Awakening* (Minneapolis: Bethany House, 1985); and *The Minister's Restoration* (Minneapolis: Bethany House, 1988).
5. Rolland Hein, ed., *George MacDonald, Creation in Christ* (1871; repr. ed., Wheaton, Ill.: Shaw, 1976).

9.2.11 HARDY, BRILLIANT BACKSLIDER

If all hearts were open and all desires known—as they would be if people showed their souls—how many gapings, sighings, clenched fists, knotted brows, broad grins, and red eyes would we see in the market-place.
—Thomas Hardy diary entry, 8 August 1908

One of the late Victorian novelists and poets of stature, Thomas Hardy (1840–1928) was a thoroughgoing naturalist and determinist. Hardy's spiritual degradation is an illustration of the philosophical depths to which the nineteenth-century Enlightenment currents of Darwinianism and materialism led that generation.

He began within a devout family. The Hardys traced their lineage to the ancient Norman invaders of Britain. Thomas was born near Dorcester, one of four children born to a master cement mason and musician. He attended a religious academy and by age fifteen years was teaching Sunday school. Students of Hardy agree that he knew the Bible better than any other Victorian author.[1] He always attended church and felt a call to holy orders at one time.[2] He worked for a church architect for awhile and counted the Baptist leader Henry Robert Brastow among his best friends. He had ties with the Moule family. The patriarch of this family was the Rev. Henry Moule, vicar of Fordington, Dorchester, who was influenced by Charles Simeon at Cambridge. His five sons included Handley, the future bishop of Durham. Handley's brothers Henry Joseph and Horace were Hardy's good friends.

Hardy was a bookish young man. Though he worked long hours when he moved to London, he found time to learn Latin and Greek in order to read the New Testament. He also began to read Newman and Charles Darwin's newly published *The Origin of Species*. Darwin and positivistic influences began to incline him toward a deistic belief that God must be indifferent to the existence of his creatures. Soon he became an overt unbeliever,[3] though he attended church and took the Lord's Supper until his dying day. Henry J. Moule wrote a poem bemoaning his friend's lack of faith.[4]

What led to the lapse of this promising Bible student? It would seem that several factors were operative including his supercilious pastor. Gerald Brenan makes the sad observation that "the Victorian bishops and clergymen are the real fathers of atheism in the Church of England."[5] Hardy also seemed to begin his drift from the point of a weak notion of biblical authority.[6] He began to caricature the Baptists and in his early poetry speaks about being "God-forsaken." In 1874 he married the devoutly Christian Emma, who was acutely pained when he wrote such a poem as "The Funeral of God." Hardy wanted Jesus without dogma. He felt that theological lumber discredited Christianity, and he rejected biblical supernaturalism. Still he refused to be included in *The Biographical Dictionary of Modern Rationalists* (1920).[7]

While some of his poetry is impressive, Hardy is known for his eleven novels, many set in the mythical Wessex (in reality Dorset). The west country of England was robustly Methodist. He attacks uncritical Victorian optimism.

Hardy's writing style is often awkward, but he is skilled in opening his characters' hearts to the reader. He uses the strong language of the Bible and Shakespeare. In fact, he can't get away from biblical categories and cadences. Writers from Fielding to Thackeray had been turning toward the large unit of society itself. Hardy writes of the individual, often the lonely soul.[8] His presentation of women in this Victorian time is amazingly powerful. He is a skilled writer of fiction and shares "the speech and song of the peasantry," folk identity, those "into whose souls the iron has entered."

The Return of the Native is probably his best-known work, portraying Clem Yeobright's return to Egdon Heath. He had come back to be a teacher and help the country folk, but Eustacia Vye saw other possibilities.[9] Interestingly, Clem finally becomes an itinerant preacher. I incline to feel that *Tess of the d'Urbervilles* is his best work. Here Angel Clare enters the story to represent "the impotence of Christian idealism."[10] Tess is Hardy's masterpiece, and she marries Clare. Then Alec d'Urberville reappears as a ranter, a self-ordained preacher, and Tess launches a zealous effort to demolish his doctrine. Hardy's characters seem to be controlled by forces and furies they cannot resist. At this time, Hardy's own marriage drifted into "irreversible estrangement"[11] and then divorce, largely because his immoral lifestyle was becoming notorious. A faithful version of *Tess of the d'Urbervilles* was a British television release in 1998.

In *Far from the Madding Crowd,* we meet another strong woman, Bathsheba Everdene, who passes by dear Gabriel Oak to marry the reckless Sergeant Troy, and then William Boldwood who murders Troy. There is a rawness in this realism that shocks and stuns, but the author is presenting things as they are.

Hardy's last novel was almost too much for the British public. *Jude the Obscure* is about confused and changing partnerships. Desmond Hawkins believes that Hardy was beginning to doubt his doubts, and he now confessed "the farther I get, the less sure I am."[12] But there does not seem to be any great difference in the philosophy of *Jude the Obscure* than there was in Hardy's most developed plot for *The Mayor of Casterbridge.* The story's connecting tissues have become irrational or nonexistent. Christ, the cohesive connector of all things, has been dismissed from the universe (cf. Col. 1:17).

In Hardy, we can keenly sense "the great interplay between the human and the non-human." But who and what sorts of forces are involved in this interplay? Hardy was in no position to say. He had cut himself off from his transcendental moorings.

He died in 1928 and was buried in Poets' Corner, Westminster Abbey.

---

1. Martin Seymour-Smith, *Hardy: A Biography* (New York: St. Martin's, 1994), 28ff.; and Desmond Hawkins, *Hardy: Novelist and Poet* (New York: Barnes and Noble, 1976), 17.
2. Seymour-Smith, *Hardy: A Biography,* 29.
3. Ibid., 30. By 1881, when he wrote his worst novel, *A Laodicean,* he was vicious in his caricature of a Baptist minister.
4. Ibid., 43ff. A brother of Henry went to China as a missionary. His son was Cambridge scholar C. F. D. Moule.
5. Gerald Brenan, *Thoughts in a Dry Season* (Cambridge: Cambridge University Press, 1978), 27. C. S. Lewis makes a similar point when his tempter in *The World's Last Night* rather shrewdly observes: "It will be an ill day for us if what most humans mean by religion ever vanishes from the earth. . . . Nowhere do we tempt so successfully as on the very steps of the altar" (New York: Harcourt Brace, 1960).
6. Seymour-Smith, *Hardy: A Biography,* 30.
7. Ibid., 117.
8. Hawkins, *Hardy: Novelist and Poet,* 214.
9. Thomas Hardy, *The Return of the Native* (New York: The Pocket Library, 1954).
10. Hawkins, *Hardy: Novelist and Poet,* 127.
11. Ibid., 140. His second wife was Florence Henniker, but there were liaisons with other women.
12. Ibid., 163. Sue, the intelligent and strong woman in *Jude the Obscure,* is a dedicated worshiper.

9.2.12 JAMES, DEBONAIR EXPATRIATE

In deciding to become what he called a "cosmopolite," James abandoned his homeland and refused the wishes of his eccentric, stifling family. He remade himself, in the grand American tradition of willed metamorphosis, as an almost-European. He was too reflective, and too pragmatic, not to contemplate what he lost in the process. His canny grasp of the anxieties of freedom and the perils of choice make him—oddly enough given his fustian image—more attuned to today's climate of exhausting and ever proliferating options than a modernist romantic like F. Scott Fitzgerald.

—Laura Miller[1]

Another writer whose works gained a cinematic rediscovery at the end of the twentieth century was Henry James (1843–1916), an appealing immigrant from the U.S. whose novels *The Portrait of a Lady, Washington Square,* and *The Wings of the Dove* have been remade as appealing feature films. James is an important figure in the development of the novel. Born in New York City and enrolled in Harvard Law School, he was from a distinguished family with Presbyterian roots in Northern Ireland. His father, Henry Sr., rebelled from those roots all his life, especially after he lost a leg in a fire.

Senior Henry was graduated from Union College in Schenectady and started but dropped out of Princeton Theological Seminary. Exposed to the Sandemannian heresy in England during his impulsive journeying, he found solace during a time of nervous collapse in the "vastations" of Swedenborgianism. His view became close to that of Emerson.[2] His son William avoided cutting himself off from all belief (see *The Will to Believe*) and indulged in psychic research.

Among six children, Henry Jr. was most closely bonded to his older brother William, the famous Stanford/Harvard psychiatrist. The two suffered much in service during the Civil War. Their sister Alice was subjected to "hallucinatory invasions." The family was churchless and their worship was almost pagan, because "to have all the churches and all the religions was really to have none."[3]

Henry vowed never to marry, and his heroes don't understand or know how to approach women.[4] In considerable lassitude, Henry departed for Europe in 1869 and lived abroad for the rest of his life, finally becoming a British subject.

His plays didn't do well, but they influenced his highly dramatic novels, which started with a person and admitted only the perspectives of that person in what he called "stream of consciousness" writing. He enacts "a steady controlled sea swell toward the objective."[5] The emphasis on the person's own feelings and thoughts often led to a slack story line. William complained to his brother, "You have reversed the traditional canon of story-telling, by not telling the story."[6]

Henry referred to himself as "that queer monster, the artist, an obstinate finality," but nevertheless each novel presents a probing study of human nature. *Washington Square* is set in New York City and is probably the greatest novel ever written to portray parental overcontrol. *The Portrait of a Lady* wrestles with the legitimate desire for freedom. *The American, Daisy Miller,* and *The Europeans* are earlier novels, less elaborate in style but still engaging. *The Bostonians* was written after a trip home, and *The Princess Cassamassi* developed in the melancholy after his parents died.

At fifty, he was ill with gout and very depressed when Henrik Ibsen's (1828–1906) use of "symbolic power" challenged him.[7] He lingered near the "black abyss" and even tried visiting the Archbishop of Canterbury, E. W. Benson.[8] His *Turn of the Screw* involves ghosts whose reality seems undeniable. This plot surely drew on William's psychic research and the fact that a brother, Robertson, was a spiritualist. James also wrote a love story, *The Wings of the Dove,* at about the time he had a close relationship with the American writer Edith Wharton (1862–1937), whom he met in 1903.

Life declined for James in the twentieth century. He was emotionally unhinged by his heart flurries and an attack of shingles. He was depressed by the horrible nightmare of war and the bewildering treachery of his associate, H. G. Wells. An unkind biography of James by Wells's paramour, Rebecca West, concluded that James was "without moral balance."[9] His thinking was confused as death approached in 1916. His hopelessness was inevitable after the essay he had earlier written, "Is There a Life After Death?" He answered in the negative.[10]

The family was so brilliant and gifted but spiritually adrift. Even Henry James's "undiminished creativity" could not compensate for the lack of spiritual substance and hope. James's friend, historian Henry Adams (1838–1918), may have put at least a part of the problem into view when he wrote autobiographically that "Harvard College and Unitarianism kept us all shallow."[11]

---

1. "Bookend," *The New York Times Book Review,* 7 July 1997, 31.
2. R. W. B. Lewis, *The Jameses* (New York: Farrar, Strauss and Giroux, 1991). A remarkable study of the family.
3. Leon Edel, *Henry James: A Life* (New York: Harper, 1985), 35–36. Old Aunt Kate was a "palpable" presence among the old spiritual underpinnings. Henry, who was close to his sister Alice, escorted his sister and aunt around Europe often.
4. Ibid., 85. James was described as having "a portentous corpulence," but, though stout and bald, he was not unattractive.
5. Lewis, *The Jameses,* 506. When William married Alice Gibbens in 1878, the brothers pulled apart somewhat.
6. Ibid., 514. In 1906 William was visiting professor at Stanford during the San Francisco quake.
7. Edel, *Henry James,* 404. James knew and was influenced by Oscar Wilde, George Bernard Shaw, Rudyard Kipling, and other important literary figures of the late 1800s and early 1900s.
8. Archbishop Benson's son, E. F. Benson, wrote the lampoon of British society, *Dodo,* which caused quite a stir.
9. Lovat Dickson, *H. G. Wells: His Turbulent Life and Times* (New York: Athenaeum, 1969), 258. Probably the actions of Wells were caused by his jealousy.
10. Edel, *Henry James,* 717.
11. Ibid., 567.

9.2.13 WARD, LAST OF THE VICTORIANS

> "And to think," she said, shuddering a little, "that there are men and
> women who in the face of it can still refuse Christ and the Cross, can
> still say this life is all! How can they live—how dare they live?"
>
> —Mrs. Humphrey Ward
> Catherine in *Robert Elsmere*

When Mrs. Humphry Ward (1851–1920) died, Virginia Woolf commented that "she was merely a woman of straw after all—shovelled into the grave and already forgotten." Henry James liked Mrs. Ward. She was, after all, the granddaughter of Thomas Arnold of Rugby and the niece of Matthew Arnold. But James thought her novels were no art.[1] She loved Spanish and became something of an expert in Spanish literature.[2]

She did write poorly, and she was incredibly priggish, according to her biographer. But she also was a popular phenomenon whose bestsellers exerted wide influence.

Her father, Thomas, was a school inspector in New Zealand and Tasmania who married a Tasmanian, Julia Sorrell. He had become a Roman Catholic, and when he returned to England, he obtained a teaching job at Dublin University through John Henry Newman.[3] Mary Arnold spent most of her childhood apart from her parents. She was poorly educated but loved Bulwer-Lytton and Jane Porter's *The Scottish Chiefs*.[4] A precocious child, she wrote her first surviving story at age thirteen.

She broke into print with her first novel when she was nineteen. In 1870 she married Humphry Ward, the son of a hard-drinking Church of England clergyman who had a "saintly wife with Wesleyan highmindedness." Unfortunately, Humphry took after his father and gave his wife little cooperation as she raised their three children. He was a gambler and a spendthrift.[5]

To support her family, she became a fiction-producing machine. Often awkward, her novels were panned in reviews but had a large readership. She had surges of creativity and, up to 1900, was the highest paid English woman. She always had a remarkable hold on the American literary market. Her best work, *Robert Elsmere,* was the best-selling novel of the nineteenth century by any author. It brought phenomenal sales on both sides of the Atlantic.

Plagued with ill health, she did not grow in artistic strength.[6] At the time of her major collapse in 1906, she was the most famous living novelist in England. She did triumphant tours of America as a semi-invalid, but her private world was falling apart. Her son Arnold was an inveterate gambler. One bright spot was the marriage of a daughter to the eminent Cambridge historian G. M. Trevelyan.

Little wonder with the stresses of her life that she was not a creative thinker. Ward continually struggled for a solid religious faith. She was always learning on the fringes of Oxford and was close to Greek scholar Benjamin Jowett and the idealist philosopher T. H. Green. Both affirmed God but undercut supernatural revelation.[7]

She fought for women's halls at Oxford and was a founder of Somerville College. She became a militant anti-suffragite but always was known publicly by her husband's name.

The Ward book that should be read is *Robert Elsmere,* which came into being between 1884 and 1888. Prime Minister W. E. Gladstone (1809–1898) was obsessed with the book and urged that it be read, although he was troubled by the young clergyman's renunciation of Christianity and the Church of England.[8] Gladstone could not understand why Elsmere did not fight for his belief system, understanding that to deny miracles automatically denies the bodily resurrection of Christ. But the book reflected the author's own doubts about miracles and the resurrection.

Robert Elsmere is an Oxford graduate and visits his cousin, a vicar's wife, as he is about to be ordained and take up ministry at Murewell. He marries Catherine, daughter of an evangelical Church of England rector, who lives in the "old ideas" and becomes increasingly concerned about the influence of her husband's old tutor, who has thrown faith overboard.[9] Though plagued with doubts about the Pentateuch and the date of Daniel, he continues to preach well. Soon his doubts spread to include the Gospels and the saving gospel.

Notwithstanding Catherine's prayers and passion, they finally separate; her faith does not falter.[10] Here is the battle for Christian supernaturalism during the late 1800s against the appeal of the social gospel and rationalism and higher criticism.[11] Though Ward seems to celebrate Elsmere's quasi-Unitarianism, there is a sense of tragedy in his infidelity. One can sense why this book was so popular in Britain and especially the United States.

---

1. Leon Edel, *Henry James: A Life* (New York: Harper, 1985), 294. James and Mrs. Ward maintained a thirty-five-year friendship. Mary Arnold Ward was similar in background and influence to Charlotte Yonge (1823–1901), who also was educated by her Church of England minister father. Yonge's novel, *The Heir of Redclyffe,* was the means by which Abraham Kuyper, who would be a distinguished Dutch preacher and theologian and prime minister of the Netherlands, came to Christ. It is escapist fiction, whose hero is a gentleman-saint.

2. She not only wrote novels (failing at drama) but did considerable translation from French and Spanish.

3. Her father returned to the Church of England at a point but then reverted to Roman Catholicism. Her brothers all lived disastrously unsuccessful lives. Her sister Julia did marry T. H. Huxley's son Leonard and was the mother of Aldous Huxley.

4. John Sutherland, *Mrs. Humphry Ward: Eminent Victorian, Preeminent Edwardian* (Oxford, Clarendon, 1990), 19.

5. Ibid., 43. Arnold never could provide for his family.

6. Ibid., 63. Ill health and overwork moved Ward into a collapse cycle. One reason for her poor writing was a tendency to overuse melodrama.

7. Ibid., 212.

8. Ibid., 124.

9. Mrs. Humphry Ward, *Robert Elsmere* (New York: Hurst and Co., 1888), 191.

10. Ibid., 507.

11. Ibid., 219. The book faces the problem of religious liberals who lack an authoritative Bible—knowing what to preach (74).

9.3   PERPETUATORS OF THE CLASSIC ENGLISH NOVEL

Never say you know the last word about any human heart.
—Henry James

A bright and sunny optimism warmed hearts as the new century dawned. Yet soon it was painfully obvious that human intellectual process and the accomplishments of science had not ushered in the golden age. The twentieth century would be Europe's worst. There were eminent Edwardians and Georgians, but the buildup toward World War I was just the beginning of forces that changed the English literary scene forever.[1] Yet the novel is the form of fiction that helps explain English society in the midst of catastrophic social revolution. No one has painted the picture for us any better than Barbara Tuchman, whose work is always probing and thought-provoking. Tuchman shows how Darwin's findings gave theoretical justification for the inevitability and nobility of war and how "the survival of the fittest" allowed a rationalization for colonial imperialism. But, then, so did Christian missions.[2]

---

1. A fine set of personal sketches from this remarkable time is provided in A. G. Gardiner, *Prophets, Priests and Kings* (London: J. M. Dent, 1914).
2. Barbara W. Tuchman, *The Proud Tower: A Portrait of the World Before the War 1890–1914* (New York: Macmillan, 1962).

9.3.1   Galsworthy, Solicitor with Second Thoughts

What is continually apparent is how closely the most famous of Galsworthy's works, *The Forsyte Saga,* which traces a family from the Victorian age through the complexities of life following World War I, is a reflection of Galsworthy's own life, particularly his symbiotic relationship with Ada, for ten years his mistress and finally his wife and collaborator.
—Dudley Barker

John Galsworthy (1867–1933) is a major British novelist and dramatist, whose works on English manners examine life amid the upper middle classes before and after World War I. The winner of the Nobel Prize for Literature in 1932 was born in Surrey in a Victorian paradise. He was an unmotivated attorney, living off his very successful father, until he met Joseph Conrad (see 9.3.3) on a sea voyage and acted on Conrad's suggestion that he write. His father, old John Galsworthy, is very much like old Jolyon, builder of the Forsyte family, a descendent of farmers, and the maker of a fortune.

Young Galsworthy's hot temper cut him off from friends, and he could never keep out of his novels his dislike for his mother. He couldn't understand why she went to church even when she was ill.[1] She left his father just as Irene left Soames Forsyte.

He lived in rebellion against Victorian life and faith. Through his Oxford studies he became increasingly agnostic.[2] He had an extended liaison with Ada, breaking up her marriage to his cousin. He struggled in his writing for years, and he and Ada were not accepted in society.

After his father died, John and Ada were married and began the long process of rehabilitating their reputations. *The Man of Property* inaugurated the Forsyte Saga series, for which Galsworthy is now remembered, but at the time it did not make a strong impression.

Although Soames Forsyte is often his mouthpiece, Galsworthy is critical of the materialistic values and mores of this patrician. He turns the blade on religion, as in his argument that there is "utter disharmony between the Christian religion and English character."[3] He seems to idealize a woman who is "unburdened with a moral sense."[4]

The Forsyte Saga consists of three trilogies. Galsworthy deals in a hardened, cynical spirit with issues of divorce, honor, the law, the neglect of parents, childless marriages (as his own), and financial woes. He is a master of the complicated plot, brief introduction, skilled portraits of personality, moving interior dialogue, and variety and lyricism.[5] In each of the nine volumes, one finds the family tree for this remarkable clan. The last sentence of *The Patrician* seems to summarize the author's spiritual dilemma: "All are in bondage to their own natures, and what a man has most desired shall in the end enslave him."

Although the Galsworthys were devoted to each other and had become wealthy, Ada became neurotic and unhappy. The couple traveled restlessly. He predicted that World War I would be the end of Christianity.[6] Yet when he comes to the end of his 750,000 words, he has reversed course in many respects. At one time, he seemed opposed to Christian standards of marriage. Author and university lecturer in the classics Arthur Quiller-Couch (1863–1944) viewed his direction as "loose in indulgence."[7]

By 1928 Galsworthy was far more sentimental and traditional. He had become impatient with the younger generation for their incessant pressing of society's parameters.[8] *Swan Song* ends with the death of Soames. So popular was the series by now that this fictional character's death earned an obituary in *The Times of London*.[9] When Galsworthy himself died of a brain tumor in 1933, he was refused burial in Westminster Abbey, although a memorial service was held there.

Had the processes of aging changed the writer's perspective, or had he found his autonomous selfishness to be dissatisfying? He never softened his opposition toward Christianity, but clearly he was disillusioned with his faithlessness. This was the society to which F. B. Meyer (1847–1929) and G. Campbell Morgan (1863–1945) preached.

---

1. Dudley Barker, *The Man of Principle: A Biography of John Galsworthy* (New York: Stein and Day, 1963), 21–22.
2. Ibid., 42. He was very critical of the ruling class early on, feeling deeply the poverty around London.
3. Ibid., 120. Anything like Christianity seemed too closely aligned with the establishment, which he detested.

4. Ibid., 121. His close friends, such as Shaw, Joseph Conrad, and John Masefield, adopted lifestyles that were as licentious.
5. One would not say that Galsworthy was highly imaginative, but he was an astute observer. Some of these thoughts are from notes attributed to Alec Frechet, but I have been unable to trace their source.
6. *The Man of Principle,* 169. Some of his writing was just "bad stuff," especially the short stories and some of the plays.
7. Ibid., 158. In *A Saint's Progress,* he scorns organized religions (182) in his characterization of a clergyman concerned for "the conventions of morality."
8. Ibid., 218. Soames moves into "the brittle life of the 1920s" with his Victorian standards.
9. John Galsworthy, *Swan Song* (New York: Scribner's, 1928, 1956).

9.3.2 Forster, the Gulling of a Genius

> It is private life that holds out the mirror to infinity; personal intercourse, and that alone, that ever hints at a personality beyond our daily vision.
> —E. M. Forster
> *Howard's End*

> The novel warns against conventional religious faith, asking "Will it really profit us so much if we save our souls and lose the whole world," thus reversing the biblical question of Matthew 16:26. Nevertheless, *The Longest Journey* insists on the individual's duty to restate "questions that have been stated at the beginning of the world," to regard life as a matter of importance, to embrace a Hegelian secular spirituality.
> —Claude J. Summers
> about *The Longest Journey*

E. M. Forster or "Morgan" (1879–1970) was raised in comfortable circumstances in London. His father was a successful architect who died of tuberculosis the year following his son's birth. His mother remained her son's devoted companion through his life. This precocious child was "cosseted by a host of female relatives," chief of whom was his great-aunt, Marianne Thornton. Thornton was of the so-called "Clapham Sect" of evangelical Anglicans (see 5.8), who clustered around Wilberforce.[1] At her death, she left her nephew financially secure, but he did not receive her legacy of a warm, earnest testimony to Christ.

Such total female domination was of course not healthy. It helps explain the gender confusion Forster experienced later.

Young Morgan's experience at school was almost totally negative, and he carried considerable anger against what he saw as hypocrisy and cant in the establishment. In his years at King's College, Cambridge, he was profoundly influenced by the militant atheist Nathaniel Wedd. Forster became contemptuous of all convention including gender roles, although he frequently needed and had female companionship. He became an unrepentant agnostic.

After Cambridge, he began to write novels and short stories, developing the "Forsterian voice," stimulated by the Bloomsbury Group. He wrote four outstanding novels between 1905 and 1910. He was always terrified of becoming sterile as a writer, and as his deviant lifestyle became hardened, his creativity seemed to wither. In his last forty-six years, he wrote nothing. He mistakenly thought that sexual license would be liberating, but in fact it was stultifying.

In 1912 he visited India, which prepared him for *A Passage to India*. During World War I, he worked in Egypt as a Red Cross helper. He was a friend of T. E. Lawrence "of Arabia," but Lawrence's strong Christian views did not seem to make a mark on him.[2]

After his mother's death in 1945, he returned to India and visited America. Although honored as the greatest living English novelist for about two decades, his final years were quiet. He died at Coventry in 1970.

His six novels give a vision of what his genius was and could have been. Four of them have been made into outstanding films. They give an incomparable "feel" of their times and are very well worth reading:

Where Angels Fear to Tread (1905) is a study of salvation but goes no higher than Hegelian secular spirituality.[3] A few Wordsworthian moments of transcendence are allowed. Of the main character, Philip, Forster relates: "Quietly and without hysterical prayers or banging of drums, he underwent conversion, he was saved."[4] Repeated use of the word *saved* is intriguing, but Forster means no more by it than Philip's improvement. The action takes place between England and Italy.

The Longest Journey (1907) is less controlled and unwieldy. But in the stages of the life of Rickie Elliot, the Hegelian pattern is evident. Water imagery is pervasive. While traditional marriage is repudiated, there is an effort to find symbols of redemption. Christianity is disparaged, yet it is clear Forster desires that "the Beloved should rise from the dead."[5]

The most popular of his works must be *Howard's End* (1910). A plea for connection and reconciliation, this work is "among the most important novels between the death of Queen Victoria and World War I." Forster trumpets (prematurely, it turned out) the triumph of liberal humanism. He is convinced that salvation is latent in the soul of every man. The characters are outstanding. Described as "restrained poetry," this is Forster at his literary best. The search is for "something beyond the gray," but peace is elusive.[6]

A Room with a View (1908) is charming. This is probably the best loved of his novels and shows the influence of Jane Austen. Set largely in Florence in Italy at the Pension Bertolini, the plot advances in three scenes. The theme is "the holiness of direct desire." In his usual attack on Christian convention, he advances the idea that Christianity inhibits. The sunniest of his novels, there is even a celebration of heterosexual love and marriage. Still, repression is the villain.

One of the great novels in English is certainly *A Passage to India* (1924).[7] Forster despised colonial imperialism and is especially good in exposing the repulsive superiority complex of many Anglo-Indians. The theme is essentially the loneliness of the human situation. Forster seems less certain about the critical issues. Limitations of liberal secular humanism begin to show. The book questions the possibility of the existence of truth at all. Forster's characters still do a lot of God-talk. He reaches out to Hinduism because it is less dogmatic than Christianity.[8] But the reader is left with powerful ambiguity. What remains and what abides?

For his own funeral, Forster had appropriately forbidden any hints of religious ceremony. In this he was at least honest. His body was cremated as Beethoven's Fifth Symphony was played.

For another kind of look at upper-class English life, try some of the almost farcical satirical parodies of Sir Pelham Grenville (P. G.) Wodehouse (1881–1975), who has given us such characters as Bertie Wooster and his valet, Jeeves, Lord Emsworth and his prize pig Empress, and Sir Galahad Throop. These are outrageously funny but with a sharp edge. Caught in France by the Germans at the outset of World War II, Wodehouse made some naïve pro-Nazi broadcasts to secure his freedom and was unwelcome in Britain. He moved to the United States. The hard feelings eventually softened after the war, and he was knighted shortly before his death in 1975. A fine biographical treatment is by Frances Donaldson.[9] A good starting point with this author is *The Inimitable Jeeves*.[10] Many titles are available at this writing, as well as tapes of some of the British Broadcasting Corporation's television productions.

---

1. Claude J. Summers, *E. M. Forster* (New York: Frederick Ungar, 1983), 2.
2. Ibid., 16. The best on Lawrence is undoubtedly, Jeremy Wilson, *Lawrence* (New York: Athenaeum, 1990). Summers concedes that there was never a physical relationship because of Lawrence's "abhorrence of the physical."
3. Ibid., 27, 44. The repeated return to the concept of salvation is curious. Christ is truly "the desire of all nations."
4. Ibid., 63. Even though Christianity is reviled, salvation is found in the biblical law of love: "Let us love one another" (69).
5. Ibid., 105. This is a metaphysical novel, exposing the shallowness of materialistic fixation.
6. Ibid. 138. Keenly argues that individual idiosyncrasies are an important part of the battle against sameness.
7. Besides Kipling and Forster, great fiction about India must include Paul Scott's *Raj Quartet* (1942–47).
8. Ibid., 203ff. "Every system of belief is undercut in this novel" (191) leaving an ominous vacuum waiting to be filled by something else.
9. New York: Alfred Knopf, 1982.
10. London: Penguin, 1924.

9.3.3 Conrad, Prolific Pole

My mind struggles with a strange sort of torpor, struggles desperately while the sands are running out—and there is nothing done; nothing of what one desires to do.

—Joseph Conrad

Joseph Conrad (1857–1924) had as his objective in writing to use the power of the written word to make people "feel" and so to truly see. His narrative style is clean, clear, and worth emulating. Conrad was born Józef Teodor Konrad Korzeniowski in Polish Ukraine, where orthodoxy was almost a universal faith before formation of the USSR. His father, Apollo, wrote purgatorial poems of a semireligious nature.[1] He lost his mother early and two years later, his father while they were living in Cracow. He learned seamanship while in Marseilles (1874–78) and made three voyages to the Caribbean. He sailed on a British ship (1878–86) and became a British subject in 1886. He made eastern voyages (1886–89) and went into the Congo in 1890.

At one point in his travels, he attempted suicide after losing his money. Through his whole life, he suffered from neurotic and even psychotic depression.[2] He used not only his native Polish and other languages from his early years, but he was exceedingly fluent in French and English and wrote in English.

His periodic references to God and invocations of deity are in keeping with the conventions of the time. Although his statements tend to be contradictory, he is a skeptic—virtually an atheist—despite his claim that he was a nominal Roman Catholic. He had a problem with identity and didn't have "anyone close to lean on and have confidence in."[3] He claimed that "from the age of fourteen, I always disliked the Christian religion, its doctrines, ceremonies and festivals."[4] He would deride "the Bethlehem legend. . . . Nobody, not a single bishop, believes in it. The business in the stable is not convincing."

This product of the Enlightenment wrote in the Romantic tradition. He loved François-Marie Voltaire (1694–1778) and Jean-Jacques Rousseau (1712–1778). He modeled himself after Dostoevsky. He was much influenced by Guy de Maupassant (1850–1893), the great short-story writer.[5] He had met Galsworthy at sea and nudged him to write, and John Galsworthy regularly subsidized him until his uncle died and he became more financially comfortable. Gustav Flaubert (1821–1880), Henry James (1879–1947), and Ivan Turgenev (1818–1883) were also his heroes (he couldn't stand Leo Tolstoy [1828–1910], particularly in his defense of deathbed conversion). Conrad liked Bertrand Russell's (1872–1970) philosophy. He, as Russell, found "Christianity distasteful."[6]

In 1896 he married Jessie George. Thereafter he had something of a literary breakthrough and associated with Ford Maddox Ford (1873–1939), the well-known writer and editor, who represented Conrad in his novel *The Simple Life Limited* as "possibly Polish, possibly Lithuanian, possibly a little Russian Jew," who settled in England after a life of travel to become a writer.[7]

In 1900 Conrad finished his greatest novel, *Lord Jim*. The author of so many novels and short-stories, Conrad is at his best in this novel about a young naval officer who took to the lifeboats when his ship was sinking with eight hundred Muslim pilgrims. The ship is saved, and Jim's cowardice is known. He becomes a wandering moral outcast, spending his life in attempts to atone for what he had done. He finally achieves some honor as he goes stoically to his death in the East Indies. Again and again, in the agonies of Jim's efforts at auto-atonement, we ask: "What can wash away my sin?"

Conrad knew his own moral failures in a series of extramarital affairs. He also knew physical and mental pain, as he was continually afflicted with gout and was the victim of frequent episodes of nervous collapse. After 1912 there is a noticeable decline in the quantity and quality in his work. From 1919 to 1924, he did travel to the U.S. and attract some notoriety. He was one of the first to recognize the French writer Marcel Proust (1871–1922). Lawrence praised his "rhythmical, suggestive, incantatory" style. H. G. Wells (1866–1946) recorded this description:

> He was rather short and round-shouldered with his head as it were sunk into his body. He had a dark retreating face with a very carefully trimmed and pointed beard, a trouble-wrinkled forehead and very troubled dark eyes, and the gestures of his hands and arms were from the shoulders and very Oriental indeed. He spoke English strangely. Not badly altogether; he would supplement his vocabulary—especially if he were discussing cultural or political matters—with French words; but with certain oddities. He had learnt to read English long before he spoke it and he had formed wrong sound impressions of many familiar words.[8]

He died of a heart attack at age sixty-six in 1924. In great incongruity, his funeral was conducted according to the rites of the Roman Catholic Church.[9]

---

1. Zdzislaw Najder, *Joseph Conrad: A Chronicle* (New Brunswick: Rutgers, 1983), 10. This vast study of 647 pages is the classic source. Another rich study that is even more recent is Jeffrey Meyers, *Joseph Conrad* (New York: Scribner's, 1991).
2. He was an extremely nervous person, often giving the impression of someone undergoing shell-shocked nervous trauma.
3. Ibid., 227.
4. Ibid., 287. He did seem to retain his church's view on "the unchangeability of man's flawed nature" (220).
5. Meyers observes that Conrad had special knack for the "psychological scene." Guy de Maupassant, a pupil of Flaubert, became a leading writer of short stories. See the Dell edition of his stories, published in 1959. His "The Necklace" is one of the greatest short stories ever written.
6. Najder, *Joseph Conrad: A Chronicle,* 392.
7. Ibid., 244. Conrad and Ford broke sharply at one point, and Ford's novel came shortly thereafter. Robert J. Andreach argues that Conrad sought to slay Christianity as "a salvation scheme," while Ford wanted to do away only with a doctrinally defined form of Christianity. In any event, neither succeeded in revitalizing "the dead god." See Andreach's *The Slain and Resurrected God* (New York: New York University Press, 1970), 210.
8. Ibid., 244. Wells thought Conrad was an "alienation against English culture," a "shifty-eyed Philistine."
9. Ibid., 490. As with Forster, there was a marked decline and diffusion as life drew toward its close. There could be no cohesive center, as in Colossians 1:17: "And in [Christ], all things hold together."

9.3.4 ORWELL, PESSIMISTIC PROPHET

> Western civilization, unlike Oriental civilizations, was founded partly on
> the belief in individual immortality. If one looks at the Christian reli-
> gion from the outside, this belief appears far more important than belief
> in God. The Western conception of good and evil is very difficult to sepa-
> rate from it.
>
> One cannot have any worthwhile picture of the future unless one re-
> alizes how much we have lost by the decay of Christianity. . . . I do not
> want the belief in life after death to return, and in any case it is not likely
> to return. What I do point out is that its disappearance has left a big hole,
> and that we ought to take notice of the fact.
>
> —George Orwell

The deft pen of Eric Blair—who is known almost exclusively by his pen name
of George Orwell (1903–1950)—has produced *Animal Farm* and *1984,* two books
of political satire without peer in the twentieth century. Blair was born to British
civil servants in India but raised in Oxfordshire. He was educated on scholarship at the elite schools of St. Cyprian's and Eton, but he could not afford to go
on to Oxford. These were difficult and lonely years for the young man, and he
claimed he was beaten at St. Cyprian's for mistranslating a Latin sentence.[1] He
entered the Royal Indian Police and served five years in Burma. Some of the
"feel" of those years can be ascertained by reading his immensely attractive *Burmese Days.*[2] He was very critical of the feelings of superiority he saw among
many British in the colonial governments and church missions.

Struck down with dengue fever, he decided to resign from the service and go
back to England where he could write. He already showed early symptoms of
the consumption that would take his life. His battle with tuberculosis was not
helped by his chain-smoking. In his Romantic fatalism and satiric humor, one
can see the influence of Conrad, Forster, A. E. Housman (1859–1936), and
W. Somerset Maugham (1874–1965). Somewhat under the spell of James Joyce's
(1882–1941) *Ulysses,* he wrote *The Clergyman's Daughter.* This is an implau-
sible story of Dorothy Hare, the daughter of a nincompoop of an Anglican rector. At this juncture, he heeded the counsel of fellow socialist Storm Jameson,
who urged that "the narrative must be sharp, compressed, concrete."[3] He had a
great burden for the poor and unemployed in the North and gave vent to his feelings in *The Road to Wigan Pier.* At thirty-three, he married Eileen O'Shaughnessy
in a traditional Church of England service, then left to fight the Fascists in Spain.
He was wounded and almost put to death in Spain and recuperated in Marrakech,
Morocco. Out of these experiences came the commercially abysmal *Homage to
Catalonia.*

He and his often depressed wife read Dickens aloud to each other and especially loved *Our Mutual Friend,* though he faulted Dickens for "cloying sentimentality, overreliance on character types, hopelessly unrealistic endings and avoidance
of genuine tragedy."[4] He and his wife adopted a son, Richard. It was then he wrote
his barbed *Animal Farm* as a condemnation of Stalin's betrayal of the masses.

Orwell lived with the regret that he had never had the time to become truly close to Eileen before she died in surgery. This time of grief became a fertile period of writing; he produced 130 articles and reviews and wrote *1984* on the wild island of Jura off Scotland.

Already sick and dying, he married again shortly before his death at age forty-seven. His widow, Sonia, turned Richard over to Orwell's sister and drifted into alcoholism. Powell and Muggeridge arranged a Church of England funeral service.

As Aldous Huxley's *Brave New World, 1984* projects a negative utopia. Orwell hated totalitarianism but saw Western democracies on the slippery slope in which a bleak prosperity is possible at the price of complete control over human actions and thoughts. Christians have always found this tale, with its worship of the seemingly all-knowing "Big Brother," as frighteningly close to the prophetic narrative in Revelation 13.[5] The saddest feature of the Orwellian world is the total absence of religion. Christianity is now dead; the soul had been cut away.[6] Orwell saw the failure of both the kingdoms of God and Marx. Evelyn Waugh wrote him, protesting:

> Your metaphysics are wrong. . . . You deny the soul's existence (at least Winston does) and can only contrast matter with reason and will. It is now apparent that matter can control reason and will under certain circumstances. So you are left with nothing but matter. . . . But what makes your version spurious to me is the disappearance of the Church. I wrote to you once that you seemed unaware of its existence now when it is everywhere manifest. Disregard all the supernatural implications if you like, but you must admit its unique character as a social and historical institution. I believe it is inextinguishable, though of course it can be extinguished in a certain place for a certain time. Even that is rarer than you might think.[7]

If human beings are left to our own recourse, then this pessimistic prophet has looked ahead to the certain totalitarian result in *1984*. When Christ and the supernatural gospel are ignored or omitted, the end is the dehumanization of materialism.

---

1. Michael Shelden, *Orwell: The Authorized Biography* (New York: Harper/Collins, 1991), 29.
2. New York: Harcourt Brace, 1934. Malcolm Muggeridge says this is Orwell's best novel.
3. Shelden, *Orwell,* 230.
4. Ibid., 313.
5. George Orwell, *Nineteen Eighty-Four* (New York: Harcourt Brace, 1949), 16–17.
6. Alvaro de Silva, "Orwell and Religion," in *Chronicles of Culture,* December 1986, 18.
7. Ibid., 19. There is no glimmer of the immortality of the soul, no supernatural faith, and no church in an Orwellian society.

9.3.5 MAUGHAM, HIGH-BORN HEDONIST

Only the mediocre man is always at his best.
I'm glad I don't believe in God. When I look at the misery of the world
and its bitterness, I think that no belief can be more ignoble.
—W. Somerset Maugham

William Somerset Maugham (1874–1965) was thought by many literary scholars of his time to be the greatest living novelist, and his work *Of Human Bondage* to be the greatest novel. Maugham was accomplished in creating novels, plays, and short stories.[1]

He was born in Paris where his father worked for the British diplomatic corps. Both of his parents died when he was quite young, and when he was in his eighties Maugham testified that he still felt the wound. "Willie" was entrusted to his father's brother, the Rev. Henry Maugham, vicar of the thirteenth-century All Saints' Church in Whitstable. This Victorian clergyman and his rigid German wife had no children of their own and were not prepared to raise a young boy. The home was very strict, although later Maugham admitted he had unfairly criticized the couple who cared for him.[2] The home was full of books, and Willie spent much time with them (as did Philip in the semi-autobiographical *Of Human Bondage*). Young Maugham had a serious stuttering problem and resorted to prayer as a cure. When healing did not come, he was disillusioned and angry.[3] He also was bewildered by the endless disputes between the established Church and dissenters. His uncle was high-church in orientation. He yearned to be freed from "the irksome conventions of the vicarage," and happily went off to the King's School in Canterbury. Still, his dislike for games and his shyness left him lonely and afraid.

Considering his speech handicap, it seems odd that his uncle wanted him to prepare for the church, but Maugham successfully argued he needed time away to think. He spent a memorable year in Heidelberg, Germany. Exposed here to the philosophy of Arthur Schopenhauer (1788–1860) and writer Henrik Ibsen, "I cast off the misfit mantle of Christianity."

He took a stab at being a chartered accountant but finally decided to become a medical doctor and spent five years at St. Thomas Hospital in London, where he assisted in sixty-three childbirths. He never really practiced medicine, but wandered through Spain and Italy; no other modern writer has been as widely traveled. While in Paris, "at the center of electric new movements in art and literature,"[4] he began to write plays.

His breakthrough came in 1908. His early writing was quite biographical, as in *Of Human Bondage,* where the central figure, young Philip Carey, has a club foot to parallel Willie's speech defect. Philip wants to be an artist, but his unsympathetic uncle and aunt, who raise him in a vicarage, disapprove.[5] The famous digressions on art, particularly on El Greco (c. 1541–1614), the Greek-Spanish genius of Toledo, surprise the reader by flowing easily with the narrative. Maugham's clear, clean flow is amazing. Young Carey has a distracting love affair with Mildred, a waitress, but finally gives up and becomes a country doctor.[6]

Maugham started the book in 1912 and finished it in 1914, reading the proofs within the sound of artillery in Belgium. He served with the Red Cross in France and then as a British Intelligence agent in Geneva, with highly secret missions to the United States, the South Seas, and Russia. His earlier novels, *Liza of Lambeth* and *Mrs. Craddock,* came out of the slum conditions he observed while a medical student; *Ashenden, or the British Agent* (1928) of course reflects his intelligence work.

One of his best books is a satire on British literary life that raised a firestorm because of the perception that it was an attack on Thomas Hardy and others. *Moon and Sixpence* is a skillful novel about the French artist Paul Gauguin (1848–1903).

In 1916 Maugham married and had one daughter, Lisa, but this marriage ended in divorce. In 1938 he visited India and was genuinely touched by Hindu mysticism. The result was *The Razor's Edge* about Larry Darrell, a Chicago war veteran who converts to Hinduism and leaves all to pursue a holy life. The general criticism of this book is that its hero is more of a phenomenon than a person.

In the Second World War, he wrote propaganda for Britain and was roundly denounced by the Nazis. While waiting for assignment, he devoted himself to the study of Edmund Burke (see 5.7). He lived for a while in South Carolina and marveled at the American love for oratory and susceptibility to emotional persuasion. After the war, he settled again in southern France where he was an honored figure until his death.

In *Of Human Bondage,* Philip is liberated when he concludes that all of his life, be it his degrading passion for Mildred or his abandonment of a career in medicine, has no meaning at all.[7] Maugham was a confirmed hedonist. Idealism, he believed, led only to hypocrisy, so he rejected the concept of altruism. This is very curious and makes us wonder why he was so generous in providing scholarships for young writers. Building off Ralph Waldo Emerson's (1803–1882) "Self Reliance," he believed there is no moral code, that human beings can only reconcile with themselves. Mistakes are irremediable; missing is the meaning of Christ's atonement.[8]

The ending of *Of Human Bondage* is weak, evaporating into what Maugham conceded was a kind of "wish-fulfillment." Actually, he wrote some very poor things, although some short stories are apt, particularly "Miss Thompson," which was dramatized as *Rain.* This story depicts the endless downpours of the South Seas and the Davidsons, missionaries whom he delighted to impale mercilessly by having the missionary seduce his convert, the young tart Sadie Thompson. Graham Greene loved to quote the Rev. Davidson's words: "When we went there they had no sense of sin at all. They broke the commandments one after the other and never knew they were doing wrong. And I think that was the most difficult part of my work, to instill into the natives the sense of sin."[9] Would Maugham have been so sanguine about the premissionary islanders had he been cooked for one of their sacrificial feasts?

As he survived into his nineties, Maugham spoke of himself as "an extinct volcano." Now he carried "the burden of his memories." He had become less boisterous. His one desire was, "Save me from all of these people." He seemed a man without roots. In his last published work, an aged writer sees the face of

Christ come to life in a painting and turns to face him. Was he himself encountering the piercing eyes of Christ? There is no record that he did anything but avert his own eyes from such a gaze.

Examples of the obsession of unbelievers with faith is seen in Gore Vidal's *Golgotha* and Norman Mailer's *The Gospel According to the Son*. In the visual arts are similar religious themes by modernist painters Richard Diebenkorn and Stanley Spencer.[10] Modern artists, including Maugham, cannot obliterate the imbedded image of the person and work of the living Christ.

---

1. Richard A. Cordell, *Somerset Maugham: A Writer for All Seasons* (Bloomington, Ind.: Indiana University Press, 1961). See also, Robert Calder, *The Life of W. Somerset Maugham* (New York: St. Martin's, 1989). A beautifully illustrated treatment is Anthony Curtis, *Somerset Maugham* (New York: Macmillan, 1977).
2. Ibid., 21.
3. Ibid., 92. A similar story of disappointment in prayer and resulting unbelief is found in the experience of Will Durant.
4. Ibid., 24, 39. His early life in France established a life affection for the country. He also fell in love with Miguel de Cervantes (1547–1616).
5. W. Somerset Maugham, *Of Human Bondage* (1915; repr. ed., New York: Pocket Books, 1950). Few authors have as consistently and cleverly concealed real persons in their fictional characters.
6. Ibid., 30. Maugham never experienced the poverty that Philip Carey knew.
7. Cordell, *Somerset Maugham*, 53.
8. Ibid., 61. It is interesting to put his cynicism, misogyny, and hedonism into this worldview.
9. Ibid., 173.
10. "God Is in the Vectors," in *Time*, 8 December 1997; and *Insight*, 1 December 1997. See Spencer's extraordinary work, "The Crucifixion."

9.3.6 JOYCE, RAMBUNCTIOUS RADICAL

I will not serve that in which I no longer believe, whether it call itself my home, my fatherland, or my church: and I will try to express myself in some mode of life or art as freely as I can, using for my defense the only arms I allow myself to use—silence, exile and cunning.

—James Joyce
Portrait of the Artist as a Young Man

The young artist in James Joyce's (1882–1941) autobiographical novel asserts his identity and independence at the end of each chapter. Here is an autonomous modern man, living at the center of his own universe. God and other people are ultimately irrelevant. Joyce's plot in *Portrait of the Artist as a Young Man* is as directionless as the artist. Clear narrative progression has been rejected in favor of a rambling, diffuse "stream of consciousness" flow that defies all convention. Joyce had an inordinate influence on other writers as he led a revolt against plot, character treatment, and all notions of style. It was a retracing in literature of the path of Adam and Eve in their rebellion against form and order, as well as the path of each of Adam's children (Isa. 53:6). The consequence is seen in the flowering of shapeless and formless modern art, the cacophony and dissonance of much modern music and in the theatre of the absurd.[1] One senses the ghost of Immanuel Kant (1724–1804) hovering gleefully over the final stages of the skepticism about truth he fostered.

One of Joyce's biographers, Richard Ellmann, claims that "we are still learning to be James Joyce's contemporaries."[2] In his earlier short stories, *Dubliners* and in *Portrait* where he shares how he got off the rails, Joyce is still coherent. But the works regarded as his masterpieces, the massive *Ulysses* and *Finnegan's Wake,* embody modernism. The writer irreverently goes off alone. *Ulysses,* so called because of its studied parallels with Homer's classic, is the landmark epic of the city of Dublin. Stephen Dedalus, the artist introduced in *Portrait,* meets the Jewish advertising man Leopold Bloom in a maternity hospital. Together they wander about Dublin for eighteen hours. Joyce began the work in 1922 and worked on it seven years. The book created a furor and became more popular and influential after U.S. Postal authorities banned its distribution through the mail as obscene literature.[3] In *Ulysses,* we are viewing the collapse of the old order. Similar stories have been articulated by others, but always before there has been some kind of hope of redemption; Joyce allows none. Evangelical social critic Francis Schaeffer describes this modernist track in literature as "the line of despair" and "the horror of a great darkness."[4]

There are spiritual overtones to *Ulysses.* In preparing for his performance of the role of Bloom, Anthony Quinn interpreted the advertising man as Joyce's replication of the Holy Spirit in a modernist frame of reference. T. S. Eliot saw *Ulysses* as describing the destruction of civilization.

Finnegan's Wake gives us the cycloramic view of the rise and fall of human history in language so idiosyncratic as to be virtually incomprehensible. The central figure is a Protestant Irishman of Scandinavian descent who frets because he is accused of accosting either a male or a female in Phoenix Park. The novel, which took seventeen years to write, is entirely circular and ends with an unfinished sentence. Joyce totally repudiates any biblical idea of history as linear. He admits no eschatology. He regards any notion that the cross of Christ is unique as anathema.

Given the worldview expressed in *Finnegan's Wake,* it is perhaps not surprising that the great champion of James Joyce is the mad American poet, Ezra Pound, who collaborated with Hitler.

More than a quick dip into such a mass of meaninglessness is fruitless, but thoughtful students should study carefully *Portrait of the Artist as a Young Man.* Here Joyce tells his own story, although in a distorted fashion. Joyce was thirty-three when he wrote *Portrait* and clearly considered himself a Christ-figure.

Joyce was the oldest of ten children. He was graduated from the Jesuit University College of Ireland in 1902, majoring in modern languages. He fell in love with Nora Barnacle, an uneducated chambermaid, and with her fled Ireland for the Continent. They lived with their two children in Trieste, Rome,

Zurich, and Paris, though they were not married until he had become virtually blind. Always a heavy drinker, he wrote in an atmosphere of reduced mental and spiritual as well as physical visibility. His pseudo-Darwinian determinism left a much reduced God, who was like Joyce's own father—errant, irascible, loving.[5]

In *Portrait,* Joyce's staunch Roman Catholic upbringing can be seen stimulating his guilty longing for absolution.[6] The author refused his dying mother's request to kneel and pray by her bed. The behavior, like the work, was that of a spiritual wanderer, a vagrant who has led many in his ways. It is one cause of the despair of the late twentieth century that the weary modernist road of Joyce had no resting places.

The horrors and futility of the First World War are felt over the pages of the massive chronicles by C. P. Snow and Anthony Powell. This horrific story is told more poignantly in Erich Remarque's *All Quiet on the Western Front* and in the Spanish novelist Vicente Blasco Ibanez's moving work *The Four Horsemen of the Apocalypse,* which was made into a movie starring Rudolph Valentino in 1918, soon after the Armistice. The strongly Republican Ibanez fled Spain and lived in South American exile. Ernest Hemingway's *A Farewell to Arms* is the great American novel on World War I.

---

1. No one has treated these themes more popularly than Francis Schaeffer in *The God Who Is There* (Downers Grove, Ill.: InterVarsity, 1968), 13ff. Schaeffer argues that the drug culture and existentialism are parallel responses.
2. Quoted in James Joyce, introduction to *Portrait of the Artist as a Young Man* (1916; repr. ed., New York: Time, 1964), vii.
3. John Gross, *James Joyce* (New York: Viking, 1970), 2, 4. There is a sordid "sexual and scatological frankness" in these works.
4. Ibid., 80. We can admire Joyce's "linguistic exuberance," but he cuts himself off from community by his opaqueness. Nihilism in Joyce or in Friedrich Nietzsche is chaos, confusion, and consternation.
5. Ibid., 17. Maugham amused himself by creating a mock theology in which his father was enthroned as God.
6. *Portrait of the Artist,* 127ff. In Maugham's story, Father Arnall preaches a remarkable sermon on hell, which gives a clear statement on sin and salvation, but "they would not hear." Reading this sermon actually led to the conversion of Thomas Merton, the Trappist monk whose life is recounted in *The Seven Story Mountain* (New York: Harcourt Brace, 1945). An absolutely gripping biography of Merton is Michael Mott, *The Seven-Story Mountains of Thomas Merton* (Boston: Houghton, Mifflin, 1984). See also Gross, *James Joyce,* 24.

9.3.7 WAUGH, CREATIVE CURMUDGEON

Civilization—and by this I do not mean talking cinemas and tinned food, nor even surgery and hygienic houses, but the whole moral and artistic civilization of Europe—has not in itself the power of survival. It came into being through Christianity, and without it has no significance or power to command allegiance. . . . It is no longer possible, as it was in the time of Gibbon, to accept the benefits of civilization and at the same time deny the supernatural basis on which it rests. . . . [Christianity] is in greater need of combative strength than it has been for centuries.

—Evelyn Waugh

A curmudgeon is a "churl, an ill-natured and cantankerous man."[1] Evelyn Waugh (1903–1966) surely was all of this. He has been described as a brilliant satirist and one of the twentieth century's funniest writers,[2] a world-class eccentric, a gifted crank, a displaced person, "outrageously politically incorrect," a shameless social climber, and a colossal snob. He was considered prickly, recklessly brave, and fecklessly undisciplined.

This tempestuous misanthrope was born into the home of middle-class "vestigial Anglicans." His father, Arthur, was a book publisher. Alec, his older brother, was disgraced in a school sexual scandal but went on to be the noted writer of *Island in the Sun* (1956).

A primary influence on young Evelyn was his nurse, Lucy, who was "strictly chapel in religion." She read her King James Bible through every six months.[3] From her, he gained a fierce dedication to truth. In boarding school at thirteen, he was a misfit. Already he was passionately interested in religion and loyal to the very theatrical pastor near his Hampstead Garden home.[4]

Waugh's crisis in faith came while his brother was fighting in France during World War I. He almost entirely stopped reading his beloved King James Bible and the *Book of Common Prayer*. He had lost faith both in his father and in God. This is coincident with a time of gender confusion and some homosexual practices, for which English public boarding schools were infamous. He became suicidal. Alcohol was a problem throughout his life.[5]

As early as age seven, he wrote a five-hundred-page novel. His interest shifted to art and the making of book covers. He won the poetry prize before matriculating at his beloved Oxford. His long friendships with Harold Acton, Anthony Powell, and Graham Greene date from this time.

He finished Oxford with a dismal record and began a brief career as a schoolmaster. Often depressed and an insomniac, he did write his early work on the pre-Raphaelite artists and a biography of Dante Rossetti. Sacked from his school jobs because of chronic drunkenness, he wrote such early and popular works as *Decline and Fall* and *Vile Bodies* (from Phil. 3:21), which sharply satirized fashionable English society. In 1928 he married Evelyn Gardner in St. Paul's, Portman Square, but she left him for another man. Some saw a new hardness and bitterness in his writing from this time, and truly his black humor is not very appealing. This deep wound and his love for classical art led him into the Roman Catholic Church in 1930. The priest who instructed him was the well-known Martin D'Arcy.[6] His parents were distressed and many vilified him for becoming a papist, but like many converts he was fervent and "perhaps too literal about the Last Things and the message of the Gospel" according to a birthright Catholic.[7]

Waugh traveled to Ethiopia for Haile Selessie's coronation in 1930 and, out of the trip, produced several more of an impressive series of travel books. He was almost reactionary in his politics, early favorable to Hitler and anti-Semitic like his friends Hilaire Belloc (1870–1953) and G. K. Chesterton (1874–1936). In his novel of this period, *A Handful of Dust* (with apologies to T. S. Eliot), as per usual the victim becomes the hero. This piece tells the story of Tony Last's trip to South America. Waugh also ventured into Tudor history with a splendid biography, Edmund Campion, the Roman Catholic martyr. He was very close to Msgr. Ronald Knox, the Bible translator and author of the scholarly *Enthusiasm,* which was dedicated to Waugh. At this time, he started on a novel, *Helena,* the mother of the Emperor Constantine, which ultimately became a very significant work.

Critics like Cyril Connolly were "vicious in their attacks on his work."[8] After a long delay, his first marriage was annulled and in 1937, he married Laura Herbert, also a convert to Catholicism, with whom he had six children.[9] Waugh was atrocious in all of his interpersonal relationships and tended to bully everyone. He was almost anarchic during the 1920s and 1930s.

With the advent of the Second World War, he entered the Royal Marines. He was able to write some war books, *Put Out More Flags* and *Work Suspended.* He was overseas much of the war, actively involved in the abortive effort to take Dakar in North Africa and in the British fiasco on Crete. He was stationed in Egypt for a time and worked with Randolph Churchill in Yugoslavia to sort out the tangled affairs of Marshal Josip Broz Tito's new government after the war. Waugh was almost court-martialed because of his criticism for Tito's hostility toward Roman Catholics in Croatia (many of whom had been Nazi collaborators). The future bloody history of Croatia, especially after the fall of the Soviet Union, vindicated Waugh's concern.[10]

Also out of the war came his masterpiece, *Brideshead Revisited.* This moving narrative was very popular, particularly in North America. A BBC production was regarded as one of the best novel adaptations of the late twentieth century. *Brideshead Revisited* tells the story of an old Roman Catholic family, the Flytes of Brideshead. The narrator, Charles Ryder, reflects on this family's prewar experiences. While the story revolves around youthful indiscretions, and youthful and mature love, Sykes maintains that the theme is "last things." These ultimate issues include how to face death, Christian truths, and the claims of the Roman Catholic Church.[11]

Brideshead's Charles Ryder is weak in a different way than is his rigid father. The scenes of life in Oxford, the characterization of Mr. Samgrass of All Souls, the decay of Sebastian, the strength of Lady Marchmain, the contrast between the women in Ryder's life, and the charm of his little sister Cordelia together make this an extraordinary study of English life in the era of G. Campbell Morgan, William Sangster, and Dinsdale Young.

Waugh intrigues us with his "sleepless curiosity about words."[12] At times he shows the influence of Wodehouse, whose champion he was to become after the war. He visited Los Angeles and wrote *The Loved One* after seeing Forest Lawn, the unique cemetery which he thought encapsulated America. He could do brilliant dialogue and used metaphor with consummate effect. Yet he gave way to ungovernable rages at friends and waitresses. His vicious temper became more ferocious as he grew older.[13] His wartime trilogy, *Sword of Honour*, is uneven, displaying some of his best and some of his worst writing. In *Men at Arms, Officers and Gentlemen*, and *Unconditional Surrender*, we meet the hero, Guy Crouchback and his father, Gervase, who had the maxim, "Quantitative judgments don't apply."[14]

Sometimes he got along better with a strong person who was diametrically opposed to him, as when he lunched with Catholic socialist Dorothy Day in Greenwich Village.[15] He indulged in much self-analysis about his own delusions in the autobiographical *The Ordeal of Gilbert Pinfold*. Gilbert Pinfold's incessant drinking and the drugs he took for insomnia impaired his memory. He feared his mind was beginning to give way.[16] Tormented by demons, he seeks exorcism. Then he rises up out of his torpor and tries rejuvenation therapy. Soon the persecution mania returns to plague him. His "emotional capriciousness" appall all around him. Waugh's last work was *Basil Seal Rides Again* and dealt with fatigue.

In 1964 Waugh had his teeth extracted and never seemed to recover. He was now altogether an angry old man, and when Sykes saw him for the last time, he thought he looked ten years older than his age.[17] I have found Waugh to be a significant window into the soul of a troubled and tormented human being as well as a remarkably revealing window into the times in which he lived. He could be legalistic and rigid. With his ear trumpet, he marched through his societal setting.

---

1. *Webster's New Collegiate Dictionary*, s.v. "curmudgeon."
2. George Wiegel, "St. Evelyn Waugh," *First Things*, May 1993, 31ff.
3. Christopher Sykes, *Evelyn Waugh: A Biography* (Boston: Little, Brown, 1975), 9. Sykes was long a friend of the Waugh family, and his was the family-authorized biography. The massive two-volume study by Martin Stannard, *Evelyn Waugh: The Early Years* and *Evelyn Waugh: The Later Years*, is the most detailed and accurate at every point. New York: Norton, 1987, 1992. A strong work.
4. Ibid., 11. Always high church in his Anglican days, Waugh loved chapel services at school.
5. Ibid., 36. "I led as pure a life as any Christian in the place, always excepting conversation, of course" (32).
6. See M. C. D'Arcy, *The Mind and Heart of Love* (New York: Meridian, 1956). Written to counter de Rougemont's *Passion and Society*. D'Arcy well argues that *eros* and *agape* are not incompatible and together enrich the soul.
7. Sykes, *Evelyn Waugh*, 108. Waugh had great problems with all of the changes taking place in Catholicism.
8. Ibid., 139. Connolly was ruthless but his premise in criticism was always: "I stay very close to the text." See Clive Fisher, *Cyril Connolly: The Life and Times of England's Most Controversial Literary Critic* (New York: St. Martin's, 1995). Connolly admitted, "I have always disliked myself at any given moment."
9. Waugh's oldest son, Auberon (b. 1939), is himself an author; his *Consider the Lilies* is about Anglican clergy.
10. The English writer Olivia Manning gave us *The Balkan Trilogy* about life in Bucharest

in its last days before Hitler's conquest. In her series *The Levant Trilogy,* Guy Pringle and his wife are in Egypt and Palestine. These are gripping war stories. See also Fitzroy Maclean, *Eastern Approaches* (Boston: Little, Brown, 1949), 484.

11. Sykes, *Evelyn Waugh,* 248.

12. Ibid., 314.

13. Charlotte Mosley, ed., *The Letters of Nancy Mitford and Evelyn Waugh* (Boston: Houghton Mifflin, 1996). At the end he wrote: "I am full of regret for failures in gratitude and patience and service and that has made me think of my failures towards all I love. . . . Please . . . believe always in my love."

14. Wiegel, "St. Evelyn Waugh," 36. Wiegel affirms that Waugh was probably the finest English craftsman since Henry James. Purgatory obsessed him, and he was a firm believer in a literal hell as described in the Bible.

15. A choice study of Dorothy Day is to be found in the Radcliffe Biography series, *Dorothy Day: A Radical Devotion,* written by Robert Coles, a Harvard psychiatrist who has written helpful studies on children.

16. Sykes, *Evelyn Waugh,* 360. *The Ordeal of Gilbert Pinfold* is written in novel form, but it is a thinly disguised autobiography.

17. Ibid., 444. Waugh wrote Orwell about *1984:* "Men who have loved a crucified God need never think of torture as all-powerful." The substance in Waugh makes him worthwhile. He made a wrong turn in seeking the solution to the human predicament but approximates the answer.

9.4   PRESERVERS OF THE CLASSIC ENGLISH NOVEL

The twentieth century is the worst century Europe has ever had.
                                                                —Isaiah Berlin

"The West appears to have said its definitive farewell to a Christian culture," observes philosopher Louis Dupré. He is undeniably correct that "culture as a whole has become secular in a way that it never has before," but Dupré takes refuge in mysticism, quoting with approbation Karl Rahner's (1904–1984) remark that "Christianity in the future will be mystical or it will not be at all."[1] With big boosts from Ezra Pound (1885–1972) and Joyce, many writers have thrown over rationality for radical subjectivity; no more Aristotelian beginning, middle, and end. But this shunning of the cognitive is proving disastrous. Social critic Christopher Lasch has given a scathing analysis of the lack of progress under the new rules of the game.[2] Cleanth Brooks remarks that this modernism sets an advocate of pedophilia, Michel Foucault, as the ideal for university English studies.[3] But some important recent novelists take more reassuring positions.

1. "Seeking Christian Interiority: An Interview with Louis Dupré," *The Christian Century,* 16 July 1997, 654–55. Dupré sees "massive apostasies" in the United States and Western Europe.

2. Christopher Lasch, *The True and Only Heaven: Progress and Its Critics* (New York: Norton, 1990).

3. Cleanth Brooks, *Community, Religion and Literature: Essays* (Columbia, Mo.: University of Missouri Press, 1995). R. V. Young, "A Review of Cleanth Brooks and the Rise of Modern Criticism," *First Things*, April 1997, 50ff. The onset of postmodernism and its pluralism (or what popular culture analyst Ken Meyers calls "post-human" society) is provocatively analyzed in D. A. Carson, *The Gagging of God* (Grand Rapids: Zondervan, 1996).

9.4.1 SNOW, SOPHISTICATED SCIENTIST

She needed me as an adult man, her son, her like, her equal. She made her demands: without knowing it, I resisted. All I knew was that, sitting with her by the fire or at her bedside when she was ill, my quick light speech fled from me. I was often curt, as I never should have been to a stranger. I was often hard. Yet, away from her presence, I used to pray elaborately and passionately that she might become well, be happy, and gain all her desires. Of all the prayers of my childhood, those were the ones that I urged most desperately to God.

—C. P. Snow
Time of Hope

Charles Percy Snow (1905–1980) is significant for several reasons, most unusual of which is that he came from the lower middle-class. Born in Leicester in the industrial midlands, his father worked in a boot factory and was an organist. Charles went far beyond the factory. He did doctoral work in physics and taught in the university. He made positive contributions in the field of infrared spectroscopy. He entered civil service in 1959 and was a consultant on nuclear projects. He was successively Dr. Snow, then Sir Snow, then Lord Snow. In 1959 he gave the Rede Lectures at Cambridge, which were published as *The Two Cultures and the Scientific Revolution*. His thesis was that the humanities (which he called literary and artistic culture) had become estranged from scientific culture. His provocative call was for a holistic approach to these disciplines. His own life was a practical experiment in bridging just that chasm.

In an early novel, he describes Lewis Eliot's mother as a person who "had an eye for truth."[1] In that all truth is God's truth we can identify with this quest.[2] He felt that the antinovels of Joyce and Virginia Woolf exacerbated the intellectual alienation. On the threshold of the 1960s, this was nearly literary heresy. Critics called him too conservative and old-fashioned. He was concerned about communication and loved Tolstoy, Dostoevsky, Dickens, and Trollope. In 1950 he had married novelist Pamela Hansford Johnson.

So Snow admired and emulated the realistic novel, and his writing style is plain and unadorned.[3] Though he might be dismissed as a novelist of the establishment, he was remarkably perceptive in identifying critical issues in society.

He was at bottom "a pious agnostic." His paternal grandfather was Charles Bradlaugh, an atheist.[4] Even though his father was long an organist at St. James in Aylstone Park, Leicester, it was his mother who was deeply religious. She was also a High Tory in politics and a Rechabite (Jeremiah 35). Clergy never made a positive impression on young Snow, and no one gave him teaching on the Bible and prayer. Not even Canon Charles Raven at Cambridge, the don who was writing and lecturing in science and religion, spoke persuasively to him.[5] Snow was a tolerant and easygoing man who was more detached from vital Christianity than hostile to it. He did believe in original sin—this was an irrefutable reality.[6] But he did not believe in salvation or the afterlife. As his brother observes: "He had never for a moment believed in any form of theological salvation, though he liked to think that his behaviour conformed to Christian ideals, making conscious efforts to love his friends and forgive his enemies. If that sounded sanctimonious he would say that he would have been a better man if he had followed the ideals more strictly."[7]

In the *Strangers and Brothers* series, Jack Cotery, trying to convert Lewis Eliot and George Passant, has a kind of "cosmic faith" in which he urges Eliot, "Let the winds of life blow through you. Live by the flow of your instincts. Salvation through freedom."[8] Eliot could not accept human perfectibility.

Snow was inclined to draw on his college days for plots in his novels and stories. From the beginning of his published works, he is testing out themes that ultimately find their way into the *Strangers and Brothers* series. In 1935 he had the idea of writing a series featuring himself in the person of the central figure, Lewis Eliot.[9]

This series picks up the panorama of English life where Galsworthy put it down. Working professional people grapple with issues and questions. Like Snow, the fictional Lewis Eliot came from nowhere (although Eliot went into law rather than science). The earliest years are chronicled in *Time of Hope,* where Eliot verbalizes his hopes: "I want to see a better world; I want success; I want love."[10] We hear Snow when Eliot is pressed by his friend Sheila to explain his beliefs: "I told her that I had no faith in any of the faiths. For me, there was something which took their place; I wanted to find some of the truths about human beings."[11] These eleven volumes by this physically and mentally profound person are worth reading and extremely enjoyable. If you want only to sample the finest of the wheat, read *Time of Hope, The Masters* (such insight into the university struggles for power), *The Affair,* and *Last Things,* the last of which lacks structure and plot. But apart from faith, what is the source for a true last-things perspective?

For a fresh look at English parish life in a small southern village, enjoy reading Miss Read's (Dora Jessie Saint, 1913–) *Affairs at Thrush Green.* Set in the Cotswolds, this book and others in the series were written by a onetime school teacher who has the "knack." The Rev. Charles Henstock and his wife Dimity take the living at Lulling. The plots are simple, the characters are "alive," and the delights are legion.

---

1. C. P. Snow, *Time of Hope* (New York: Scribner's, 1949), 77. His mother had faith in the reality of an afterlife (78).

2. Scientism is bluster, as is shown in Anthony Standen, *Science Is a Sacred Cow* (New York: E. P. Dutton, 1950).

3. David Shusterman, *C. P. Snow* (Boston: Twayne, 1975), 32ff. *Time of Hope* has fewer subplots than some earlier works and more unity and intensity (65).

4. Bradlaugh is treated in Henry Lewis, *Modern Rationalism As Seen at Work in Its Bibliographies* (London: SPCK, 1913). Since the day Bradlaugh predicted the demise of the Bible, his own book was never reprinted, but Great Britain has published 500 million copies of Scripture, and the Bible has been translated into another 500 languages.

5. Philip Snow, *Stranger and Brother: A Portrait of C. P. Snow* (New York: Scribner's, 1982), 40. Raven appears as Paul Jago in *The Masters*. Raven will also be seen in the novels of Susan Howatch.

6. Shusterman, *C. P. Snow*, 131. The holocaust is the clincher for Eliot. A "horror" is built into each of us.

7. *Stranger and Brother*, 134. Both Snow and Eliot had eye surgery. Awakening after surgery, Snow says: "Now I know what the after-life is. There isn't one."

8. Shusterman, *C. P. Snow*, 131. Religion is complex in Snow's work.

9. Snow, *Stranger and Brother*, 37. He originally projected a series that would take him up to twenty years to write.

10. *Time of Hope*, 107.

11. Ibid., 232–33. Although Snow, unlike Eliot, did not divorce his wife, he had a mistress (182).

9.4.2 GREENE, CARNAL CONVERT

> If anybody ever tries to write a biography of me, how complicated they are going to find it and how misled they are going to be.
>
> —Graham Greene

In the earlier days, many of us were magnetically drawn to the profuse writings of Graham Greene (1904–1991) because of their strong religious dimension. So able to heighten suspense in his fiction, Greene knew how to depict sin. According to a description of his work in his one-volume edition of short stories: "Known for his uncanny gift of seeking out the evil hidden in the human heart, Greene creates a dark, violent world of men and women hounded by desires over which they have no control."[1]

His themes were sin and salvation, conscience and grace, and the search for God. And in 1926, after he had converted to Catholicism to marry a Catholic girl, Vivien, Greene became an ardent convert and a Catholic journalist.[2] Perhaps his best novel epitomizes this personal casting about for the divine. In *The Power and the Glory*, a "whiskey priest" fathers a child and now finds himself the only priest—God's only representative—in totalitarian Tabasco, Mexico. Editors of *Time* wrote the introduction to the book. They made the observation that "it is not necessary to subscribe to Graham Greene's theology to realize that he has written about the final confrontation: Man in the presence of God."[3]

Greene was raised in the womb of the school at Berkhamsted near London, where his father was a Church of England headmaster. He was a moody, somewhat dejected child who hated school, lived in fear of the rougher boys, and would flee to the forest whenever possible. Beginning at age fourteen, he made serial efforts at suicide. His parents put him into psychoanalysis, and he actually lived with the analyst for a while. Even after all the help, he tried to commit suicide six times playing "Russian roulette."[4]

He was also bored at Oxford but began to write. He had been a voracious reader in childhood, starting with G. A. Henty and Rider Haggard and moving on to John Buchan and Joseph Conrad.[5] His early novels he called "entertainments." He had something so special going with his very precise use of words and clear flowing style. But did he really believe in God? He himself raises that question.[6] Norman Sherry, his recent biographer, lays the evidence out: "Here is a man whose nature craved constant excitement and whose temperament cast him into moods of despair and chronic ennui, who sought release in drink and drugs, and in sex with prostitutes and accommodating acquaintances on several continents."[7]

He wrote for *The Times of London* and, during World War II, did a stint for the Ministry of Information and then, in his best years, was engaged with British Intelligence (MI6) in West Africa and then Portugal. His boss was Kim Philby, who at some point became an agent for the Soviet Union. The relationship between Greene and Philby has been a matter of intense interest. Some of his best friends in this time were Malcolm Muggeridge, George Orwell, and Anthony Powell.

He had numerous affairs, most notoriously with Catherine Walson, a married woman with five children. Greene had two children himself, yet left his wife in 1947. At the time, he said he felt "abandoned by God." A heavy drinker with a passion for opium, he was "the most famous and pursued writer in England." He literally became a death seeker in bizarre and violent places such as Vietnam, Malaya, and Kenya. He wrote remarkable books set in these unlikely places. *Time* magazine captioned a cover story about him in 1951 "Adultery Leads to Sainthood."[8]

In this McCarthy era, he was of suspect politics and had visa problems entering the United States. An anti-American book, *The Quiet America,* came out in 1955. During this time, he lurched away from even speaking about God. As he put it: "It will be fun to write about politics for a change, and not always about God."[9] But this would be, as Evelyn Waugh observed, like Wodehouse dropping Jeeves.

To everyone's surprise, he never won the Nobel Prize. Artur Lundqvist of the Nobel Committee was said to hate him personally. Such books as *Journey Without Maps, Traveling with My Aunt, Brighton Rock, Our Man in Havana,* and *Stamboul Train* are certainly of Nobel Prize caliber.

A telling later work of Greene's is *Burnt-Out Case* (1960). The story involves Querry, a world-famous architect, who becomes emotionally "burned out" and leaves his stressful life for refuge in a Congolese leper village. There he makes progress toward a cure for leprosy until the popular English journalist Montagu Parkinson interrupts it all. This is a parable about human life seen as Alexander Pope described it, "that long disease." This is a deeply moving book, in which we sense tremors of the genius of Greene.[10]

He spent the last thirty years of his life in Antibes off the French Mediterranean coast, separated but not divorced from his wife, writing three hundred words a day. In its obituary article, *Time* reminds us that here it was he wrote the opening sentence of the second volume of his autobiography: "What a long road it has been."[11]

1. Graham Greene, *Nineteen Stories* (New York: Lion, 1949, 1955). Sigmund Freud also saw the sludge deep in the human mind. Early on he said: "I have always been preoccupied with the mystery of sin. It is always the foundation of my books." This preoccupation later evaporated in favor of politics; see Henry J. Donaghy, ed., *Conversations with Graham Greene* (University, Miss.: University Press of Mississippi, 1992). According to T. S. Eliot, "before 1930 writers had no sense of original sin."
2. In Erich Fromm, *Escape from Freedom* (1941).
3. Graham Greene, *The Power and the Glory* (New York: Viking, 1940), x. The Vatican was not happy about this book.
4. Graham Greene, *A Sort of Life* (London: Penguin, 1970), 94. This is the first of a two-volume autobiography.
5. G. A. Henty (1832–1902), a Victorian historian, wrote books for boys that many of us read, to our intense entertainment and instruction. He told tales of colonial India, Africa, South America, the fall of Jerusalem, and the invasion of Britain.
6. *A Sort of Life,* 120. Greene gives a moving warning about a love too great for words (144).
7. Terence Brown, "Review: *The Life of Graham Greene, II,*" *The New York Times Book Review,* 26 February 1995, 9. Brown describes Greene's emotional life as "a farrago of entanglements."
8. Norman Sherry, *The Life of Graham Greene, II* (New York: Viking, 1994), 292. In later life, he "scotched the idea of sexual sin." So what had been a great strength in his writing became severely truncated.
9. Ibid., 437.
10. "A Life on the World's Edge: Graham Greene (1904–1991)," *Time,* 15 April 1991, 68.
11. Ibid., 68. Early on there was a kind of redemption, but it dwindled over time.

9.4.3 Lewis, Apostle to Skeptics

> We are half-hearted creatures, fooling about with drink and sex and ambition when infinite joy is offered us, like an ignorant child who wants to go on making mud pies in a slum because he cannot imagine what is meant by the offer of a holiday at the sea.
> —C. S. Lewis in a sermon preached at Oxford

> In a toast to God at Tempter's Training College: "It will be an ill day for us if what most humans mean by religion ever vanishes from the earth. Nowhere do we tempt so successfully as on the very steps of the altar."
> —*The World's Last Night*

Called "the Apostle to the Skeptics" by Chad Walsh, Clive Staples Lewis (1898–1963) became the chief popular Christian apologist of the twentieth century. In addition to his own considerable body of writings in multiple disciplines, a mountain of critical literature has risen about his work. In the mid-1990s, there was even a biographical film that became a major motion picture, "Shadowlands," with Anthony Hopkins playing the writer. His ancestors came from the hills of Wales to settle in Belfast, Northern Ireland, where his bookish father was a solicitor. His mother, the daughter of a clergyman, taught her prodigy son French and Latin before he was nine. Then she died, beginning a dark and difficult passage to premature adulthood for young Lewis and his brother, Warren.[1]

Lewis was sent to England for school where a tutor's beatings led him to atheism, but where he devoured literature of all kinds. His favorite teacher at Chartres was "a high atheist" who lived in *The Golden Bough* and the writings of philosopher Arthur Schopenhauer (1788–1860). At this time, he also discovered George MacDonald, who would play an influential role in his later theology and writing. His studies at Oxford were interrupted by war duty in France, where he was severely wounded.[2] He returned to finish at Oxford and was elected as a fellow of Magdalen College in 1925. God was working through a network of influences that first led to his conversion to theism in 1929 and, shortly thereafter, to belief in Christ as the Son of God while riding in a sidecar on his way to Whipsnade Zoo.[3] The "hound of heaven" had found his quarry.

For almost thirty years, Lewis was a tutor at Oxford and turned out an incredible stream of works, but his Christian convictions offended many peers, and he never achieved a professorship. His first book, *The Pilgrim's Regress,* was published in 1933 as a modern-day Bunyanesque interpretation of Ecclesiastes. In his book, the lands of Puritania and Hegeliana (where Mr. Enlightenment is the villain) are equally unappealing to Lewis. *The Screwtape Letters* (1945) became one of his most widely read pieces, followed by *The Great Divorce* (1946), about a busload of residents of hell who are given the opportunity to explore the outskirts of heaven. That most are unwilling to enter heaven when given the opportunity is Lewis's great parabolic defense of free moral agency.

Lewis's apologetic masterpiece was *Mere Christianity* (1952), which led Charles Colson, Sheldon Vanauken, and a host of others to Christ. Lewis advances on the premise that Christianity is reasonable. He puts Christ forward as legend, liar, or Lord in the confidence that there is sufficient evidence for the historicity of Christ to take the gospel accounts as accurate.

Some of his critics speak disparagingly of his Christian philosophical works, particularly *The Problem of Pain* and *Miracles,* as excessively rationalistic, but Lewis is only insisting in these volumes that both reason and faith must be included in the equation and that anyone who does not believe in rational communication is in fact ruling out all communication.[4] His work on moral education, *The Abolition of Man,* is a devastating attack on modern philosophy, and even his more devotional *Reflections on the Psalms* has the intellectual depth and integrity to contribute to Christian apologetics.

An odd and highly creative collection of intellectual writers and apologists gathered around the Oxford circle of Lewis in the late 1940s and 1950s. Called the Inklings, the group included Arthur Owen Barfield, before Barfield became caught up in theosophy; and fantasy writer J. R. R. Tolkien, a Roman Catholic whose fantasy trilogy *Lord of the Rings* is essentially pre-evangelism Christian thought. Another member was Charles Williams, author of supernatural thrillers.[5] Their stand for Christian supernaturalism was sorely needed in the post-

World War II malaise. Lewis saw the disaster being wrought in the church by "theological modernism." He stood staunchly for the authority of the Scripture against the theologies of Rudolf Bultmann (1884–1976) and others, repeatedly calling Christians back to their Bibles.

Some critics have questioned the orthodoxy of Lewis. Any problems he has are not in the basic areas of the faith, for he ascribes unexceptionally to the Nicene, Athanasian, and Apostles' Creeds.[6] He does nuance depravity in a Roman Catholic direction, which is not unusual among Anglicans, and therefore he may have weak views of penal substitution in the atonement and of forensic justification. In his view of the end times, Lewis looked for some great catastrophe to be imminent in human history, believing the Second Coming might be the next great event.[7]

Perhaps an overall theme of Lewis's message is that there is a universal human longing for joy. He calls this "the inconsolable secret" in every human breast. Many feel his greatest novel is *Till We Have Faces,* where he wrestles with the problem of evil and the efficacy of prayer, a subject further treated in *Letters to Malcolm. Till We Have Faces* rewrites the Greek myth of Persephone to show how healing comes through sacrifice and not self-indulgence.[8]

Not so deep but filled with his thought are the seven books in The Narnia Chronicles. Ostensibly for children, these stories have equal appeal to adults who love the literature of fantasy.

By the mid-1950s, Lewis occupied the prestigious chair of medieval and Renaissance English at Cambridge University. His scholarly works on medieval literature had found wide acceptance, and he had mastered Anglo-Saxon language.

This is not to say that Lewis made none of the bad decisions and mistakes that have been criticized in other authors in this survey. Some biographers have tended to be superficially hagiographic, elevating Lewis in ways he would find most distressing.[9] An occasion when Lewis seemed more pragmatic than consistent in his ethics was in his romance with the American Jewish divorcée, Joy Davidman. Did he here adhere to his own articulated renunciation of divorce: "There is no getting away from it: The Christian rule is 'Either marriage, with complete faithfulness to your partner, or else total abstinence.'"

Davidman was a fine writer herself (e.g., *Smoke from the Mountain,* which dealt with the Ten Commandments), and while their 1956 marriage began as a convenience to enable Davidman to satisfy English immigration rules, it became a passionate love. Her extended bout with cancer and Lewis's devastation as she died after only three years together are voiced in the classic *A Grief Observed.* His own sudden death at sixty-four, though overshadowed at the time by the assassination of John Kennedy on the same day, left all the literary community acutely bereaved.

Among his great variety of works, communicators who sense a need to resuscitate their imaginations might want to study the allegorical theology of Lewis's "space trilogy," a Gothic-Romantic view of salvation history in three interrelated stories. *Out of the Silent Planet* is set on Malacandra (Mars), where the forces of evil are held in check; and *Perelandra* imagines life on an unfallen world (Venus), which has come under demonic attack. But I think the best is *That Hideous Strength,* in which the cosmic conflict between good and evil, God and Satan, comes to a climax on Earth in Lewis's view of what the dynamics of the great tribulation might look like. Here "the real man" is at last presented, the Anti-christ, in a conspiracy of evil scientists to Satanize England.[10] Called "A Modern Fairy-Tale for Grown-ups," this set will appeal more to some than to others, but it affords an immense stimulation for all who read it with care.

Remember the children, for whom there are rich sources of imagery. In *The Wind in the Willows*, Kenneth Grahame, a lonely banker, set out to construct an ideal model of the "good life" for his own handicapped child. Inspired by Grahame's work, A. A. Milne wrote the Winnie-the-Pooh books. Ann Thwaite's fine biography, *A. A. Milne*,[11] explores the troubled relationship between Milne and his real son, Christopher Robin. Reassuringly, J. M. Barrie's (the author of *Peter Pan*) treatise on smoking has now been reissued: *My Lady Nicotine: A Study in Smoke*.[12] These essays originally were written for newspaper publication. A fine new biography of Lewis Carroll, who wrote *Alice in Wonderland*, has been given by Morton N. Cohen.[13]

1. George Sayer, *Jack: C. S. Lewis and His Times* (New York: Harper, 1988). One of Lewis's closest friends treats his father, Janie Moore, and Joy Davidman more kindly than have some. His alcoholic brother, Warren, is seen in a bad light.

2. Clyde S. Kilby, *The Christian World of C. S. Lewis* (Grand Rapids: Eerdmans, 1964), 17.

3. C. S. Lewis, *Surprised by Joy: The Shape of My Early Life* (London: Fontana, 1955). The *preparatio evangelica* for it shows the steps toward full commitment.

4. Ralph G. Wood, "The Baptized Imagination: C. S. Lewis's Fictional Apologetics," *The Christian Century*, 30 August–6 September 1995, 812ff. Wood is irritated by the "didactic arguments" of Lewis.

5. Charles Williams's best-known work is *The Descent of the Dove: A History of the Holy Spirit in the Church* (New York: Meridian, 1955). His supernatural novels include *War in Heaven, Descent into Hell*, and *All Hallow's Eve*.

6. Clyde S. Kilby, "C. S. Lewis: Everyman's Theologian," *Christianity Today*, 3 January 1964, 13.

7. Ibid. Aslan, who represents Christ in Narnia, is a mighty lion who both wounds and heals.

8. C. S. Lewis, *Till We Have Faces* (New York: Harcourt Brace, 1956). I would not agree with T. S. Matthews who writes in the introduction to one edition of this work that "there is not a trace of Christian propaganda in this book." Calvary permeates the story.

9. A. N. Wilson, *C. S. Lewis: A Biography* (New York: Fawcett Columbine, 1990). Wilson, whose very critical books on Christ and the apostle Paul are disappointing, has nonetheless given a very open work on Lewis, probing into the many years Lewis lived in the home of Mrs. Janie Moore. Sixteen years his senior and mother of a dear friend who was killed in France, Mrs. Moore was doubtless a mother figure for Lewis. There has been speculation that she was also his lover. Wilson's novels contain some very positive surprises, especially his trilogy on the Lampitt family, *Incline Our Hearts, A Bottle in the Smoke*, and *Daughters of Albion*. His *Gentlemen in England* has a wonderful conversion story (61).

10. C. S. Lewis, *That Hideous Strength* (New York: Macmillan, 1946), 203.
11. New York: Random House, 1990.
12. Moscow, Idaho: Thornbush Anthologies, 1997.
13. *Lewis Carroll* (New York: Knopf, 1995).

9.4.4 POWELL, CRAFTY CONSERVATIVE

> You have to appreciate that, after six years of war, I made up my mind that I was going to write a very long book. I came to the conclusion that if people write a book in about 10 or 12 volumes, there's bound to be somebody who really represents what they think and the way they look at life, and it seemed to me, after a good deal of thought, that if you wrote in the first person—strange as it may seem—it was less egotistical than writing in the third person and describing somebody all the time who is really yourself. Over and above that, there is the question of saying "I" and narrativing a lot of things which I hadn't done. There are two personae, your own point of view and the things that have happened to you, and the fictional as well. You have to merge those together in a tolerable way. I think that is, roughly speaking, what is called art. That is what writing a novel means.
>
> —Anthony Powell

"The century's best novel?" is how one reviewer greeted the announcement that Anthony Powell's twelve volume series, "A Dance to the Music of Time," was being reissued by the University of Chicago Press.[1] Powell (pronounced "pø–el") was born in London in 1905, the son of an army officer. He attended Eton and Oxford (B.A. 1926, M.A. 1944) and went to work for Duckworth Publishers. In 1934 he married Lady Violet Pakenham of the Earl of Longford family, and they had two sons. In 1936 he tried his hand at Hollywood scriptwriting.

During the war, Powell served with British Intelligence as liaison officer between Britain and governments under German occupation. After the war, he worked for the *Times Literary Supplement* and *Punch*. In the early 1950s, he retired from journalism to devote his time to writing novels.[2] His first work, *Afternoon Men,* was published in 1931. His objective was to utilize new techniques but to retain the classic objectives of fiction—to instruct and entertain.[3] Although he wrote biography and many essays,[4] as well as a four-part set of memoirs (really well worth reading),[5] his climactic opus was the twelve-volume "Dance" of almost three thousand pages and one million words.

This mammoth set of novels is definitely Proustian (according to the style of Marcel Proust) in its psychological analysis of characters, though it is not all detailed description. There is a strong Kipling loyalty to past values. Powell resumes the critique of society that Galsworthy began and Snow continued.

The books follow the life of Nicholas Jenkins and share one hundred characters in slow motion.[6] The first trilogy starts with *A Question of Upbringing* and carries us from the character's early years to England's economic slump of 1932. Powell's satire is delightfully funny as he pokes holes in the airs of the British left. He hates pretension in life and in art. Like Powell in many ways, Jenkins was from a career military family and went into the publishing business.

Perhaps it is true that "Powell is the historian of a vanishing civilization and of a social order on the verge of extinction."[7] Still as one reviewer puts it, "No books ever made me feel more as if I were living someone else's life with him."[8] Powell presents a period piece with a great love for genealogical "roots." The characters are caricatures of life: Widmerpool, the quintessential modern; Charles Stringham, the inebriate; Pamela Flitton, the serial polygamist; and Sir Magnus Donners, the tycoon.

By the era described in the third trilogy, Powell has reached the war years. If one reads only a part of the work, a fascinating volume is *The Valley of Bones,* describing life in the Welsh infantry in the dark early days of World War II. A moving segment is the sermon of Chaplain Popkiss to the troops from Ezekiel 37, which gives the book its title. "Journey with me—journey with me," the chaplain proclaims, describing the nation. "They are our bones that await the noise and the mighty shaking, the gift of the four winds of which the prophet of old did tell."[9]

Conservative as Powell is on so many issues and while his characters sing "Guide Me, O Thou Great Jehovah," it is very difficult to know where Anthony Powell stands in regard to the spiritual verities. He is nominally Anglican, and he readily critiques offbeat religious movements. He is far more reticent to tell us what is he for.

1. John Russell, "Review: *A Dance to the Music of Time,*" *Chicago Tribune Books,* 28 May 1995, 1ff.
2. Jeremy Treglown, "Class Act—Anthony Powell, Chronicler of an Era, at Ninety," *The New Yorker,* 18 December 1995, 106ff. This engaging description of a visit to the Powells includes both an interview with them and an evaluation.
3. "Anthony Powell" on the occasion of being awarded the Ingersoll Prize, *Chronicles of Culture,* December 1984, 4.
4. Anthony Powell, *Miscellaneous Verdicts: Writings on Writers 1946–1989* (Chicago: University of Chicago Press, 1990). Powell's essays review the works of classic and contemporary writers.
5. The collected memoir in four volumes, *To Keep the Ball Rolling* (New York: Holt, Rinehart, 1976), abounds with insights on many interesting people.
6. John Russell, *Anthony Powell: A Quintet, Sextet and War* (Bloomington, Ind.: Indiana University Press, 1970). This is the standard study on Powell. Russell feels Powell's early prose is a little limp but that it firms up as his career advances.
7. "Anthony Powell," 4. See also his acceptance address for the Ingersoll Award, entitled "Literature and the Real Person," *Chronicles of Culture,* January 1985.
8. Barbara Wallraff, "Life's Choreographer—A Dance to the Music of Time," *Atlantic Monthly,* January 1996. I am grateful to Dr. Dorrington Little Jr., and his father Dorrington Little, Sr., for broadening my appreciation of Powell.
9. Anthony Powell, *The Valley of Bones* (Boston: Little, Brown, 1964), 38f.

9.4.5 PYM, SPIFLICATED[1] SPINSTER

> Oh, pray for the Church of England.
>
> —Barbara Pym

Born in Oswestry, England, into a comfortable parish where her lawyer father sang bass in the choir and her mother was the assistant organist, Barbara Mary Pym Crampton (1913–1980) lived and breathed the Church of England. She likewise breathed literature. As early as age twelve, she wrote "poems and parodies." She studied English at Oxford. While there, she began in 1932 a diary that has told us more about her than is available on most writers.[2]

Barbara had a passionate romance with a fellow student, Henry Harvey, but he married a Danish woman. Deeply disappointed, she nevertheless corresponded with the couple. She managed her "sweet revenge on Harvey" by including in her novels a self-important archdeacon who preaches sermons from the minor poets that his congregation never understands. He overuses Harvey's favorite phrase, "remarkably fine."[3] Ultimately sharing a home with her sister Hilary and some cats, Barbara wrote her first novel at Oxford, *Some Tame Gazelle,* in which she and her sister are two aged spinsters in a small village, who take tea, talk much church, and belatedly realize that life has passed them by.[4] Her publisher advised her to be more wicked.

During the war, she served in the censorship office and then in the Wrens (Women's Royal Naval Service) with duty in Naples. She also followed the publisher's advice in brief but intense romantic interludes that fell short of marriage. At thirty-one, she realized she might never marry, so she began what would become six novels between 1950 and 1961. She also worked as editor of *Africa,* an anthropological review. Her work remained tame in a literary world enamored with torrid potboilers. She was rejected by twenty-one publishers. "I wonder what could possibly be too daring to publish nowadays?" she pondered.[5] Her works were satirical as she faithfully "depicts the decline of a world larger than the self."[6] We sense through her pen that things are gray and grim in postwar Britain.

In 1977 two literary figures, Phillip Larkin and Lord David Cecil, named Barbara Pym "one of the most underrated writers of the twentieth century." People began to read her, and she began to write again, but cancer slowed her production, and she died in 1980. It is good to read her novels in order. She makes charming "off-hand and oblique references" to characters from earlier contexts.[7] She had felt that "the position of the unmarried woman is of no interest to the reader of modern fiction," but her work and its acceptance has quite quashed that idea.

Her rectors, canons, vicars, and clergy wives are a riot! In *Gazelle,* the aging Belinda Bede still carries the torch for Archdeacon Henry Hoccleve, "a pompous light-weight, long married to someone else."[8] There is continual apprehension about high church Anglicans who would send "half the congregation to Rome." In this author's sights is a folk religion built upon the jumble sale at church. But no aspect of church life, from music and liturgy to preaching, escapes her pointed attention. Early on in the novels, Ovaltine, the drink of Barbara and her sister, dominates the homes of her characters. But as time goes on, liquor becomes more common. The books abound with genteel, educated people who don't dress or eat well and who have to scrimp and scrounge to get by. Lyles observes that Pym "amuses us with her cheerful spirit and wry observations to the last, her faith sustaining her as she pondered the mysteries of life and death."[9]

Don't overlook other Englishwomen writers, such as Ivy Compton-Burnett (1892–1969), whose novels are set at the end of the nineteenth century in large country homes. Anthony Powell believed Compton-Burnett the best woman novelist of her time. My favorite among her books is *A God and His Gifts*. Also good is Angela Threlkell. Such Threlkell works as *Pomfret Towers* update Trollope's clergy novels in Barsetshire. Not to be overlooked is Marian Chesney who wrote one book on each of her six sisters. These are much lighter, but not lacking insight.

---

1. I.e., somewhat bewildered.
2. Hazel Holt and Hilary Pym, eds., *A Very Private Eye: An Autobiography in Diaries and Letters* (New York: Dutton, 1984).
3. Jean Caffey Lyles, "Pym's Cup: Anglicans and Anthropologists," *The Christian Century,* 21–28 May 1986, 520.
4. Ibid. Hazel Holt, an associate, remembered Barbara sometimes forgot what was real and what was not. She quotes Pym: "I couldn't ask W if his mother were better because I couldn't remember if we invented her."
5. Jane S. Shaw, "Barbara Pym's Unsentimental Eye," *Chronicles of Culture,* July 1988, 18.
6. Ibid. Her characters know their times, but they tend to hang back from taking part in those times. Writes Shaw: "They are observers and interpreters (though less than fully articulate). . . . They worry" (19). That doesn't mean she approves of such introversion. Pym scorns Rupert Stonebird, an anthropologist in *An Unsuitable Attachment,* who at age sixteen had buried his conscience. Now that conscience is revived, "not about the fundamentals of belief and morality but about such comparative trivialities as whether or not one should attend the church bazaar."
7. "Pym's Cup: Anglicans and Anthropologists," 521.
8. "Barbara Pym's Unsentimental Eye," 19. The "low status of women" and "the dissatisfaction of clergy wives" are pervasive.
9. "Pym's Cup," 522. This literature is relevant because there are a lot of Pym's people about us.

9.4.6 SPARK, CRUSADING CONSERVATIVE

Either the whole life is unified under God or everything falls apart.
—Muriel Spark

Q. What are the four last things to be ever remembered?
A. The four last things to be remembered are Death,
Judgment, Hell and Heaven.

—Muriel Spark
"The Penny Catechism" in *Momento Mori*

When she was almost forty years old, Muriel Spark began to write serious fiction. Since then she has written about one novel a year. Winner of the Ingersoll Foundation's T. S. Eliot Award for 1992, she is recognized as "one of the most urbane critics of modern life."[1] Her novels tend to be short, with "occasionally nasty wit." She seeks to return to the eternal view, since "she takes the existence of God so seriously that everything else becomes a joke by comparison."[2]

Born Muriel Camberg in Edinburgh, Scotland, in 1918, her father was Jewish and her mother an elegant English Presbyterian. Her teacher at school, Christina Kay, appears later in Spark's most popular novel, *The Prime of Miss Jean Brodie,* which was adapted to the screen soon after its publication in the 1960s.

Business college did not satisfy Muriel, and at age nineteen she rebelled against her parents and went to Rhodesia to marry S. O. Spark, a troubled man ten years older than she. In 1938 she and her son, Robin, fled the relationship. During the war, she worked for the Foreign Office, censoring and in some cases distorting for propaganda purposes the news to be broadcast to the Continent.[3]

She began to write poetry and showed the influence of Max Beerbohm (1872–1956), Marcel Proust, and the style of John Henry Newman. She lived in New York and then in Rome, the latter because in 1954 she had become a zealous convert from Anglo-Catholicism to Roman Catholicism. Faith seemed to provide the structure and frame of reference for the flow of fiction that began with her first novel, *The Comforters,* based on the book of Job and parallel to the time of misdirection in her own life.[4] *The Abbess of Crewe* is about a scandal and power struggle inside a Catholic Abbey. Her most ambitious book, *The Mandlebaum Gate,* explores the fragmentation of modern life over against the background of a divided Jerusalem and the trial of Adolph Eichmann. This work really combines thrills and theology.[5]

Like Dickens, she takes up one controversial issue in each novel. Her solution is to seek the unifying worldview of historic Christianity that she believes can alone restore wholeness.[6] In *Reality and Dreams,* she shows how a film director's egocentricity rends his own well-being and the lives of others as well.

Her masterpiece may be *Momento Mori* (Lat., "Remember, You Must Die"). This 1959 publication tackles issues of aging and approaching death.[7] Lettie Colston repeatedly picks up her telephone and hears a man's voice intone: "Remember, you must die." All of the senescent characters come to life as they are dogged by a relentless persecutor. Critic V. S. Pritchett appreciated the insight of Guy Leet, as he visits his sweetheart of many years before: "'How banal and boring,' Guy thought, 'do the most interesting people become when they are touched by a little bit of guilt.'"[8]

With her darkening vision of human nature and its shadows, I could wish Spark had let the light shine through to some of her characters.

---

1. Ian Boyd, "Sacramental Parodies: G. K. Chesterton and Muriel Spark Confront the Spiritualists," *Chronicles of Culture,* December 1996, 14. She addresses "the solipsistic nightmare of modernity."

2. Penelope Mesic, "Muriel Spark's Dark Delights," *Chicago Tribune Books,* 1 July 1995, 14.1.

3. Muriel Spark, *Curriculum Vitae* (Boston: Houghton Mifflin, 1993). Sparks's autobiography is well reviewed by Frank Brownlow in "A Documented Life," *Chronicles of Culture,* June 1994, 30.
4. Velma Bourgeois Richmond, *Muriel Spark* (New York: Frederick Ungar, 1984), 7. "The purpose of art is to give pleasure" (178). But the writings of Spark clearly go beyond art for the sake of pleasure.
5. Ibid., 104. The theology is vigorous, but it is more divine providence than redemption.
6. "Sacramental Parodies," 14. Spark, like Chesterton, sees a sacramental unity to life, rather than the dualism of "spiritualists."
7. Muriel Spark, *Momento Mori* (New York: Lippincott, 1958). The other very effective work on gerontological issues is James A. Michener, *Recessional* (New York: Fawcett Crest, 1994). Michener's is a good story.
8. V. S. Pritchett, introduction to *Momento Mori,* Lippincott edition, xvii, about "the great censored subject."

9.4.7 SAYERS, SURPRISING, STRANGE, AND SOUND

The Christian faith is the most exciting drama that ever staggered the imagination of man—and the dogma is the drama. That drama is summarized quite clearly in the creeds of the Church, and if we think it dull it is because either we have never really read those amazing documents or have recited them so often and so mechanically as to have lost all sense of their meaning. The plot pivots upon a single character, and the whole action is the answer to a single problem: What think ye of Christ?

I believe it to be a grave mistake to present Christianity as something charming and popular with no offense in it. . . . We cannot blink the fact that gentle Jesus meek and mild was so stiff in His opinions and so inflammatory in His language that He was thrown out of church, stoned, hunted from place to place, and finally gibbeted as a firebrand and a public danger. Whatever His peace was, it was not the peace of an amiable indifference.

The point made . . . is that the story of the Crucified God appears irrelevant because people nowadays have no sense of sin. That, of course, is literally the crux. . . . I'm a very poor person to appreciate modern man's feelings on all this, because I can't think of any personal misfortunes that have befallen me which were not, in one way or another, my own fault. . . . I mean that I know jolly well that if anything unpleasant happened in my life I had usually "asked for it." Consequently, when I talk about carrying the sins of the world, I'm going outside my experience—anything I have to put up with looks to me like the direct punishment of my own sins, and not to leave much margin over for redeeming other people's! But I do see that most people today look upon themselves as the victims of undeserved misfortune, which they . . . have done nothing to provoke. Contemporary literature and thought seems to me to be steeped in self-pity.

—Dorothy L. Sayers

Dorothy Leigh Sayers (1893–1957) wrote twenty fabulous Lord Peter Wimsey mysteries, fine poetry, significant theological essays, delightful books for children, and some of the most forceful Dante translation and interpretation. C. S. Lewis called her "one of the great English letter-writers." Sayers was the only child born to an Anglican rector in Oxford, who was headmaster of Christchurch Cathedral Choir School. Her father was past forty when she was born, and, as she said, "dullness seemed his only failing."[1]

The family relocated in 1897 to Bluntisham Rectory, an isolated parish in Huntingdonshire. At six, she was tutored in Latin and, by fifteen, she was fluent in French and competent in German. In 1912 at Oxford, she read romance languages and sang with the Bach Choir. She was one of the first women to take degrees from Oxford, earning her B.A. and M.A. with first-class honors.

After Oxford, she tried teaching, reading copy at Blackwell's publishing house, and working as a secretary at a school in France and for Benson's, the most prestigious advertising firm in London. She also began writing detective fiction about "Lord Peter." Typical of this series is *Comedy of Manners,* in which her highborn sleuth (as Wyston Auden observed) brought far "more energy and erudition to his conversation than the situation required."[2]

Her personal life did not fare as well. Sayers had many romances—none of which succeeded in winning her heart. She claimed, "I must love Christ, for there is no one else."[3] She received a proposal of marriage from Anglican theologian Leonard Hodgson.[4] On the rebound from a relationship with a Russian-born American, she was impregnated by someone she didn't "care twopence for." She never publicly acknowledged her son, John Anthony, who was born in 1924 and raised by her cousin. In 1925 she married a divorced man, Oswald Atherton Fleming. He was a heavy-drinker and opposed his wife's wish that her son might live with them.[5] In all of this turbulence—and despite her tidal waves of interest in psychoanalysis, science, and spiritualism—Sayers found strength in Christ.

She also was sustained, psychologically and monetarily, by her writing, including outstanding plays such as *The Zeal of Thy House* written for Canterbury Cathedral (as was T. S. Eliot's *Murder in the Cathedral*). She wrote such wartime broadcast features as "The Greatest Story Ever Staged" and a twelve part series on the life of Christ called *The Man Born to Be King.* She was soon recognized as a significant Christian apologist. At this time, she also wrote *The Mind of the Maker,* a most refreshing study of creativity. George Bell, Bishop of Chichester, spoke of her work as one of the greatest evangelistic outreaches of the century.

E. L. Mascall, the distinguished mathematician and theologian, advanced the thesis: "Her central concern is clear and it is supported by almost everything she wrote about religion. It is that, when all is said and done, the only really relevant reason for accepted Christianity is that you are convinced that it is true; not that it is comfortable or uncomfortable, interesting or uninteresting, profitable or unprofitable, or what have you, but simply that it is true."[6]

Because of her insistence that Christianity does involve the intellect and the mind and certain propositions that are true, "The dogmatic pattern" was her "gateway to the mysteries beyond."[7] Hers was an advocacy for a "passionate intellect." She saw the historic creeds as "short-hand" for the divinely-inspired text and that beneath them was "the unchanging Bible."[8] Hence her collected essays, *Creed or Chaos?* showed that pious feelings, "inner light," and "vague cosmic worship" could not suffice.

In recognition of her work, she was offered a Lambeth Doctor of Divinity but refused it. She later accepted an honorary degree of Doctor of Literature from Durham. Charles Williams had introduced her to Dante, opening a new venue of challenge.

By this time, her husband had died, and she was fatigued from overwork. She was grossly overweight and suffering the effects of lifelong smoking. One reporter described her as "a great shy, short-sighted hulk of a woman, cut off in her later years by deafness."[9] She died suddenly in 1957.

One of the best indications of Sayers dedication to her craft was her extensive research for each mystery. For example, after bells figured prominently in one of the Lord Peter books, the Campanological (bell-ringing) Society offered her a vice-presidency in their organization. What a remarkable and refreshing writer.

Speaking of "super sleuths," just about everyone knows Agatha Christie's Belgian detective, Hercule Poirot, and the nosy spinster, Miss Jane Marple. These mysteries are good for just-before-sleep relaxation. Check also the P. D. James novels featuring Adam Dalgliesh, as well as the consistent writers Ruth Rendell, John Buchan, and Josephine Tey. Tey may write the most elegant prose of them all. Don't overlook Ngaio Marsh, a New Zealander, whose Inspector Roderick Alleyn mystries are set in England. This is an important genre.

1. David Coomes, *Dorothy L. Sayers: A Careless Rage for Life* (Batavia, Ill.: Lion, 1992), 27. Coomes is a BBC producer.
2. Carolyn Heilbrun, "Sayers, Lord Peter and God," *The American Scholar* 37, no. 2 (spring 1968). Reprinted in the collection of all twenty Wimsey stories, Dorothy L. Sayers, *Lord Peter* (New York: Avon, 1972), 457. An unfinished Wimsey novel, *Thrones, Dominations,* was later finished by Jill Paton Walsh and published by St. Martin's in 1998, along with volume 2 of her journals.
3. Janet Hitchman, *Such a Strange Lady* (New York: Avon, 1975), 35. She early on wrote a play, "The Mocking of Christ."
4. Hodgson is best known for his very able Croall Lectures, 1942–43, *The Doctrine of the Trinity* (New York: Scribner's, 1944). He strongly emphasized the work of the Holy Spirit in preaching (38ff.). He mentions Sayers on page 230.
5. *Careless Rage for Life,* 92.
6. Ibid., 214.
7. Peter S. Hawkins, "In Love with the Pattern," *The Christian Century,* 18–25 May 1994, 529. Sayers was seeing so much theological controversy and change during her lifetime that she strongly strove to illuminate and defend the core dogma of Christianity. Her position: "Christianity is a rational explanation of the universe . . . steeped in a drastic and uncompromising realism."
8. *Careless Rage for Life,* 213.
9. *Such a Strange Lady,* 177.

9.4.8 Murdoch, Provocative Professor

> We live in an age in which the dogmas, images and precepts of religion have lost much of their power. We are also heirs of the Enlightenment, Romanticism and the Liberal tradition. These are the elements of our dilemma: whose chief feature, in my view, is that we have been left with far too shallow and flimsy an idea of human personality.
>
> —Iris Murdoch

> He had by now ceased to believe in God or in the divinity of Christ, but he believed in prayer.
>
> —Iris Murdoch,
> of Father McAlister in *The Book and the Brotherhood*

> Murdoch's Good is what the poet Wallace Stevens called a "supreme fiction": a story, a metanarrative, by which we can direct our lives, and the origin of which is our own creative imagination. If as Jean-François Lyotard has claimed, postmodernism may be defined in a phrase as "incredulity toward metanarratives," then Iris Murdoch (like Stevens) is a modernist; that is to say, one whose incredulity is limited to metanarratives written by others.
>
> —Alan Jacobs

An Irish-born novelist, playwright, and poet, Iris Murdoch (1919–) was a formidable figure on the twentieth-century literary landscape if only for the quality and quantity of output. She produced at the rate of one novel a year.[1] Beyond that, she was for many years fellow and tutor in philosophy in St. Anne's College, Oxford, and Gifford Lecturer in 1982 on "Metaphysics as a Guide to Morals."[2] She wrote a number of hefty philosophic tomes, notably defending Platonism. Her novels are long and complex and usually begin with a striking dissonance, but, as Roger Lundin says, she is "an exuberant story-teller."[3] As we would expect, she interacts with philosophical and theological issues.[4]

As a Platonist, she sets the idea of "the Good" at the apex of the hierarchy of concepts. God is subservient and subordinate to this idea of the Good, hence she says, "We can lose God but not Good." Evil in her system is the inevitable consequence of "misinformation about or a misconception of the Good." Conversely, to rightly know the Good is to do the Good.[5] Alan Jacobs points out her lack of any notion of the will. In an effort to sustain some kind of moral responsibility, she seeks to rehabilitate Kant's sense of duty. She would preserve certain Christian values, such as the infinite worth of the individual and the need for altruism in the moral struggle, but she wants to peel away the theology that gives rise to these values.

"Murdoch seeks to salvage the aesthetic riches of the Christian tradition and to do so through the glorious ambiguities of art," Lundin notes. In this she is following the paths of Friedrich Schleiermacher (1768–1834) and Ralph Waldo

Emerson (1803–1882).[6] The Enlightenment, she believes, has made classical orthodoxy untenable to any person of intellectual honesty. Lundin shows how Murdoch, as Reinhold Niebuhr, will admit to the significance of biblical symbols. But the symbols serve no purpose but application to attitudes and behavior. Behind the symbols stands only the myths of God in Christ. At the bottom of Murdoch's worldview there is no ultimate, controlling truth.

Thus she puzzles over Paul's certitude about the bodily resurrection of Christ. In a typical later work, *The Book and the Brotherhood,* she shows us characters who "are torn between their attraction to the moral legacy of Christianity and their guilty sense that they have no right to cling to a heritage they do not believe in."[7] In a much earlier novel, *The Bell* (1958), she shows two opposing types of moral and spiritual conviction. She casts a jaundiced eye toward any belief in the divine Savior, the atonement, or the resurrection.[8]

Iris Murdoch is an important writer of the twentieth century, not only because of her background but also because of the shape and contour of her unbelief.

Two English writers worth pursuing are William Golding (1911–1993), winner of the 1983 Nobel Prize for Literature, and Joyce Cary (1888–1957). Golding developed one of the most haunting reflections of the innate depravity of fallen humanity in *Lord of the Flies* (1955). His other work (e.g., *The Spire,* 1964) is also almost parabolic. Cary worked in Nigeria for the British and produced what is arguably the best novel about Africa, *Mister Johnson.* His Dickensian *The Horse's Mouth,* the story of a character named Gully Jimson, is part of a remarkable trilogy. He knows how to make people come alive.

---

1. A stirring record of Murdoch's degeneration into dementia is given by her husband, distinguished critic and author John Bayley, in *Elegy for Iris* (New York: St. Martin's, 1998). Powerful scenes from the book were excerpted in *New Yorker,* 27 July 1998, 44ff.
2. The Gifford Lectures in Scotland continue to be among the most prestigious. Among the most significant series was Reinhold Niebuhr's *Human Nature and Destiny.* His classic analysis of original sin is penetrating. Unfortunately, he had very little to offer in terms of solution, hence volume 2 is seldom touched.
3. Roger Lundin, "Murdoch's Magic: The Consolations of Fiction," *The Christian Century,* 18–25 May 1988, 499.
4. Alan Jacobs, "Go(o)d in Iris Murdoch," *First Things,* February 1995, 32.
5. Ibid., 32. Even the murderer in *The Green Knight* seems "more confused than malicious" (33). This conception is not true to reality.
6. Lundin, "Murdoch's Magic," 499. Since ethical values have been rooted in religion, what happens when religion is gone?
7. Iris Murdoch, *The Book and the Brotherhood* (New York: Viking, 1988). Many religious figures inhabit this story, but most are lapsed.
8. Iris Murdoch, *The Bell* (London: Chatto and Windus, 1979). *The Bell* is about a religious community in Gloucestershire. Toby claimed "not I but Christ" (144), and Michael lost his faith (312). The community dissolved.

9.4.9 HOWATCH, CHRONICLER OF CLERGY CRISIS

I am not interested in writing about people who experience great angst and end up with great doubts about the faith. That theme has been done to death. Graham Greene is the expert on that. My clergymen know that God is there. The problem is that they get alienated from Him, put off from Him, because they themselves are not right, they are not integrated properly, there's something wrong in their past that is affecting their present and future. We all have to straighten ourselves out as we grow up.

—Susan Howatch

Susan Howatch (1940–) wrote the most theologically erudite and suspenseful series on Church of England clergy, after a drastic turn in her life. Howatch took a law degree from London University. For eleven years, she lived in Ireland and the U.S. Her early novels, *Penmarric* and *The Wheel of Fortune,* were bestsellers, making her a wealthy member of the jet-set. But in 1983, she suddenly became appalled with the meaningless luxury of her life. "God seized me by the scruff of the neck, slammed me against the nearest wall, and shook me until my teeth rattled."[1] Although raised religiously, she was uninterested until her conversion. Eventually she started writing about frankly flawed clergy while staying close to her home overlooking Salisbury Cathedral. Now she lives near Westminster Abbey in London, where she worships every day.[2]

Her six-volume series on the clergy and their conflicts has a frankly evangelistic purpose. She failed in one marriage before her changed life, and so she does not write from a sheltered cove as she depicts the conservative Charles Ashworth, the liberal Neville Aysgarth, and the mystic Jonathan Darrow. Their lives are intertwined around the theologies of true-life thinkers Michael Ramsay, John A. T. Robinson, Charles Raven, William Inge, and Friedrich Von Hügel.

The Howatch clergy struggle with money, sex, and power, but there is hope because "God's loving power redeems, indeed resurrects" these people.[3] The action covers the tumultuous times in the Church of England between 1937 and 1969 in *Glittering Images, Glamorous Powers, Ultimate Prizes, Scandalous Risks, Mystical Paths,* and *Absolute Truths.* These probing novels are graphic and vivid about battles faced by vulnerable men and women. They remind some critics of good spy novels, so that Howatch has sometimes been called "the ecclesiastical le Carre."[4] As the books come down the stretch, they give us a flavor of the swirling sixties.

In *Absolute Truths,* Ashworth's wife dies, and he is left perplexed by the ambivalence of his life spent in ministry:

I think I did finally make a success of that Starbridge bishopric—a spiritual success instead of merely a worldly one. In worldly terms it was said that I went soft, lost my edge, became fuzzy on dogma, but in fact all that happened was that I stopped proclaiming the absolute truth of Charles Ashworth and started proclaiming the absolute truths of Jesus Christ. This annoyed the liberals, since they felt that now that I was less

> authoritarian I should join their ranks, and it annoyed conservatives even
> more because they felt I had sold out to the liberals, but then I found I
> could live very happily with myself as a conservative liberal—or should
> I say a liberal conservative? Jon [Darrow] suggested that God was not
> annoyed at all, and that God, in the end, was the one who mattered.

The original series concluded in 1994, but a few years later, Howatch's fans were elated that another title, *The Wonder Worker,* had appeared, this time dealing with Nicholas Darrow, a young priest with extraordinary powers. Not intended to be quite so theological, *The Wonder Worker* was significant as high-quality prose with profound theological and practical implications.[5]

While in this glorious garden, don't pass John Mortimer, the barrister whose *Rumpole of the Bailey* has regaled reading and BBC television audiences. Mortimer also wrote a superb novel *Paradise Regained.* Similar in appeal is Joanna Trollope, whose book *The Rector's Wife* was produced for public television's "Masterpiece Theater" series. Trollope has been called by some "the new Jane Austen" and likened to Barbara Pym. Genetically she takes the British novel full circle, for she is a descendant of Anthony Trollope. One of the finest writers in the Irish renaissance at the end of the twentieth century is Maeve Binchy, who writes about Dublin and matters Irish. She makes one weep with concern over the people she describes. Among a long list of novels is *Evening Class.*[6] Almost as good are Edna O'Brien, mystery writer Daniel Binchy, and suspense weaver Bartholomew Gill.

---

1. "Interview with Susan Howatch," *The Door,* May–June 1994, 7. Howatch has sold more than 20 million novels, making her a wealthy writer.
2. Ibid., 8. She recently endowed a lectureship at Cambridge on the relationship between theology and science.
3. Lawrence W. Farris, "A Review of Absolute Truths," *The Christian Century,* 25 October 1995, 994.
4. John le Carré has written some of the finest spy stories, mostly featuring the British espionage mastermind, George Smiley. In *The Little Drummer Girl* (New York: Knopf, 1983) he left Smiley for a novel on Israeli infiltration of Palestinian terrorists.
5. Susan Howatch, *The Wonder Worker* (New York: Knopf, 1997).
6. New York: Delacorte, 1996.

CHAPTER TEN

Examining the Startling Surges in American Fiction

From the Mayflower Compact and the Puritan concept of the colonies as "a city set on a hill," a society set ablaze for God, clearly something special was happening on the North American shores. The American sense of "manifest destiny" has made the country vulnerable to the Emersonian "self-reliance" and philosophic pragmatism as a worldview. Pelagianism or self-salvation got a fresh and forceful start on the North American continent.

The thirty-six-year-old French civil servant Alexis de Tocqueville (1805–1859) made a nine-month tour of the United States in 1831, studying American penal systems. He also filled fourteen notebooks with his impressions about the country, its government, social fabric, and popular spirit. Several years later, he published his measured evaluation as *Démocratie en Amérique (Democracy in America)*.

Looking now at a nation in which the bloom was off revolutionary ardor, he was impressed by what he saw of American idealism, a well-informed elite, great concern for physical well-being, and a commendable individualism.

While he was an apostate Roman Catholic, he spoke much of the importance of religion and hoped the United States would take ultimate refuge in religion and the moral law.[1] He expressed concern about militarism, the growth of power in the executive branch, and government by far-flung and ponderous bureaucracy. The government was effective, but not very efficient. He saw peril in the tyranny of the majority and signs of a people who were frightened into conformity. Among the count's insights was a harsh critique of the American institution of slavery and a farsighted belief that one day America and Russia would divide the world.

De Tocqueville decried the decline of genuine moral community and rampant individualism that disguised an underlying selfishness. A quarter-century later, this spirit would be epitomized by Walt Whitman (1819–1892).

1. For a fascinating replay of Tocqueville's trip, see Richard Reeves, *Journey in Search of Democracy in America* (New York: Simon and Schuster, 1982), as well as the LTV Corporation symposium *Tocqueville's America* (Dallas: LTV Corp., 1982).

10.1 FOUNDERS AND FRAMERS OF AMERICAN FICTION

We shall be as a city upon a hill, the eyes of all people are upon us.
—John Winthrop, 1630

Peter Shaw warns us in *Recovering American Literature* of the dangerous tendency in every strong society to subordinate literary excellence and authorial purpose to political correctness.[1] Shaw's warning is important in view of the disturbing trend to advance a political agenda that condemns out of hand *The Adventures of Huckleberry Finn* or turns *The Bostonians* or *Moby Dick* into an exposé of capitalism or some other sort of political treatise.

To avoid the danger of reading today's agenda into the writings of earlier times, it is good to see that the men and women who take pen in hand are very much framed by their own context and world society. Early North American writers had three distinctive influences. They lived in an interesting but also a harsh and dangerous environment. They also were greatly influenced by their European connections. One of the first American fiction writers of note, Washington Irving (1783–1859), for example, wrote about his travels abroad. *The Legends of the Alhambra* was written while he was U.S. Ambassador to Spain. He also wrote about frontier experience, but not very reflectively. His character Rip Van Winkle, who slept for twenty years, was based on a folk tale.

The third influence was religious. Links between continents were significant, but a sturdy and individual approach to faith made indigenous American literary a thing apart. The Puritans were amazingly productive writers, but they were suspicious of some forms of the humanities, particularly religious art, instrumental music by the organ, drama, and the novel. Awakenings, social reforms, and reactions to European philosophy—these and other influences profoundly affected American literature and were profoundly religious at their roots.

1. Peter Shaw, "Don't Read Politics into American Literature," *Insight,* 23 May 1994, 18ff.

10.1.1 COOPER, FRONTIERSMAN

The pale faces are masters of the earth, and the time of the red men has not yet come again. My day has been too long. . . . I have lived to see the last warrior of the wise race of Mohicans.
—James Fennimore Cooper,
Chief Tamenund's final lament in *The Last of the Mohicans*

His eye alone, which glistened like a fiery star amid lowering clouds, was to be seen in its state of native wildness. For a single instant, his searching and yet weary glance met the wondering look of the other, and then changing its direction, partly in cunning, and partly in disdain, it remained fixed, as if penetrating the distant air.

—James Fennimore Cooper,
description of Indian runner in *The Last of the Mohicans*

Though in a sense he passed out of vogue even in his life and has never really been readmitted to the citadel of respectability, James Fenimore Cooper (1789–1851) was the first significant American novelist. I read *The Leather-Stocking Tales* when I was a boy, and the impressions of the frontier were deep and durable. William Lyon Phelps called him "the most important man of letters ever connected with Yale." Cooper staged a minor comeback at the end of the twentieth century when *The Last of the Mohicans* (1992) was a major feature film. We were reintroduced to the hero of the five novels in the series, Natty Bumpo, and his companion, Chingachgook. Cooper actually lived at the time when native Americans were withdrawing; yet, as Mark Twain said, Cooper wrote poorly about his own society and best about the Indians whom he did not really know. His "admirable aborigines" were highly admired in Europe, where Cooper and his family lived for seven years and where his novels were very popular.[1]

He was born in Burlington, New Jersey, into the wealthy home of Judge William Cooper. When James was fourteen, his father resettled his family in the new community he was founding—Cooperstown, New York. William already was a fifth-generation American of Quaker ancestry, a strong Federalist who served two terms in Congress. He sent his son James to the village school. Because the family was active in the Episcopal Church, James attended St. Peter's School in Albany.[2] He was admitted to Yale but expelled for a prank after only a year. Timothy Dwight, the able preacher, revival promoter, and president of Yale, did have a marked influence on Cooper's thinking.

Cooper served in the American Navy until 1812. He then married Susan Delancy, who had inherited considerable property. With this wealth, he could live as a gentleman farmer and vestryman at the Episcopal Church, raise his family, and begin to write. Reading aloud to his wife and children on one occasion, he threw down the book, exclaiming, "I could write a better book." And he did—*Precaution,* his first novel. While that first effort was not a commercial success, his next efforts, *The Pioneers* and *The Pathfinder,* were successful. He patterned his writing after that of Jane Austen (1775–1817).

His story line is often a bit plodding, and he preaches about America and her problems as he sees them. He was described as "a fine looking man, with a large manly figure, rather tall and stout, with a full broad forehead, strong features, lips full, firm and determined, with large, clear, gray eyes."[3]

Cooper loved New York City and regularly attended The Bread and Cheese Club of writers, where he hobnobbed with William Cullen Bryant (1794–1878) and Daniel Webster (1782–1852), the distinguished orator and statesman.[4] Cooper was present at the dedication of the Erie Canal. Seeking a better education for his children, he lived in France and England (1826–33), where he met Sir Walter Scott (1771–1832) and was a constant defender of the much maligned Marie du Motier, Marquis de Lafayette (1757–1834). In Europe, he wrote his novel *Red Rover* on the sea and a European medieval trilogy. He deals with the impact of Lutheranism in central Europe in a thinly disguised political critique of the old European order.[5]

When he returned to the United States, he found many things had changed, and his tendency toward elitism was out of joint amid Jacksonian populism. Yet Cooper could not, or did not want to, find new models for his work.[6] He tended to be defensive and litigious. He filed and won libel suits against his critics. He and his good friend, Samuel F. B. Morse (1791–1872), commiserated about the trends. He was at war with the press and the masses.[7]

He wrote more than fifty books, including some social satire and the first American sea stories. But his lasting monument is the five novels in *The Leather-Stocking Tales: The Pioneers, The Last of the Mohicans, The Prairie, The Pathfinder,* and *The Deerslayer*. These volumes cover a sixty-year period of frontier life from the French and Indian War through the opening and settlement of the Great Plains. I think we have nothing finer on the subject; I recommend reading one of these stories aloud to a son or grandson.

One of Cooper's antiheroes is a hermit trapper, who hunts scalps for bounty until he himself is scalped and faces death with a great fear of hell. In this memorable sequence in *The Deerslayer*, Cooper observed: "We live in a world of transgressions and selfishness and no pictures that represent us otherwise can be true."[8] Cooper was not a very articulate person on things theological, but as he grew older, there was a perceptible "gradual strengthening of religious conviction."[9] Part of his struggle was his dislike for New Englanders and their "crabbed ways." While he shared the general view of divine providence, which informed Puritan thinking, he worried that their wrong-headed "rational means to liberty" would become a disruption. We must take into account that James Fenimore Cooper was a Federalist and Anglican.[10]

---

1. Richard Brookhiser, "Deerslayer Helped Define Us All," *Time,* 9 November 1992, 92. Another wonderful source on Cooper is James Franklin Beard, ed., *The Letters and Journals of James Fenimore Cooper* (Cambridge, Mass.: Belknap, 1960). Although he never really lived on the frontier himself, he made a trip to Niagara, N.Y., which was very much the American frontier in the early nineteenth century. This was the geographical background for *The Pathfinder*.
2. Robert E. Spiller, *Fenimore Cooper: Critic of His Times* (New York: Russell and Russell, 1963), 32.
3. Ibid., 291.
4. See the fine study, Robert V. Remini, *Daniel Webster: The Man and His Time* (New York: Norton, 1997).
5. Spiller, *Cooper: Critic of His Times,* 219.
6. Ibid., 208.
7. As a champion of "social ascendancy," Cooper fretted about man "in the mass."

8. "Deerslayer Helped Define Us All," 92. He believed in one moral standard and one Judge.
9. *Critic of His Times,* 291. Cooper was not part of the frontier camp meeting and brush arbor revival experience.
10. William Raymond Smith, "The Dark Face of God," *The Christian Century,* 18 May 1960, 600ff. Smith points out Cooper's criticism of the invasive press and of the fanaticism of the New England "ancestors." Though somewhat pessimistic, he believed democracy to be the best option. The Episcopal Church appealed to his "elitism," whereas Puritanism seemed to favor the middle-class.

10.1.2 HAWTHORNE, NEO-PURITAN

The minister might stand there, if it so pleased him, until morning should redden in the east, without other risk than that the dank and chill night air would creep into his frame and stiffen his joints with rheumatism, and clog his throat with catarrh and cough, thereby defrauding the expectant audience of tomorrow' prayer and sermon. No eye could see him, save that ever-wakeful one which had seen him in his closet wielding the bloody scourge. Why, then, had he come hither? Was it but the mockery of penitence? A mockery indeed, but in which his soul trifled with itself! A mockery, at which angels blushed and wept, while fiends rejoiced with jeering laughter! . . . Crime is for the iron-nerved, who have their choice either to endure it, or, if it is pressed too hard, to exert their fierce and savage strength for a good purpose, and fling it off at once! This feeble and most sensitive of spirits could do neither, yet continually did one thing or another which intertwined, in the same inextricable knot, the agony of heaven-defying guilt and vain repentance.

—Nathaniel Hawthorne
Dimmesdale on the scaffold in *The Scarlet Letter*

Is *The Scarlet Letter* indeed, as Harold Bloom enthused, the finest piece of imaginative literature in the nineteenth century? Was Andrew Lang correct in seeing Hawthorne as the greatest writer of prose fiction whom America has produced? Did Edgar Allan Poe overstate matters in saying that Hawthorne's genius had no rival "either in America or elsewhere?" While his greatest work, *The Scarlet Letter,* is highly symbolic, it is still moral realism with a vengeance. It must stand with Shakespeare's *MacBeth,* Dostoevsky's *Crime and Punishment,* and William Golding's *Lord of the Flies* as a poignant and powerful depiction of the disintegration of a human nature under the effects of guilt. Interestingly, he alone among the early American writers held a secure literary reputation during his own lifetime.

Nathaniel Hawthorne (1804–1864) was born in Salem, Massachusetts, into what had been a great New England family. His sea-captain father died when he was four, and his mother became a recluse. At age nine, Hawthorne became an invalid for two years and thereafter was also somewhat withdrawn. He loved to take lonely walks and told his mother of his desire to go to sea and never come back. Edwin Miller characterizes Hawthorne as a secretive author, hiding behind veils that he creates, much emphasizing "repression, non-communication, fear of tactile touch and gratification."[1] In 1821 he entered Bowdoin College in Maine, where two fellow students greatly influenced his life—Henry Wadsworth Longfellow (1807–1882) and future U.S. President Franklin Pierce (1804–1869).

It was while Hawthorne worked in the Salem Custom House that he fought his boredom by writing. His *Twice-Told Tales* was an early collection of short stories and essays. Hawthorne was a talented writer of the short story. Especially outstanding are "The Minister's Black Veil" and "Ethan Brand."[2] Before he was married in 1842, he flirted with communal living at the utopian experiment at Brook Farm, but he did settle down with Sophia Peabody in Concord when he was thirty-eight. There he hiked with Ralph Waldo Emerson (1803–1882) and enjoyed the company of Henry David Thoreau (1817–1862) and William Ellery Channing (1780–1842). At Concord, he wrote *The Scarlet Letter* (1850) and *The House of the Seven Gables* (1852).

President Franklin Pierce appointed Hawthorne as American consul in Liverpool, and he lived in Europe in that post for five years, followed by two more years in France and Italy. He penned his last published novel, *The Marble Faun,* while in England. He later wrote a biography of Pierce.[3] He returned to the United States in 1860, but by 1863 his imagination and energy were ebbing; Hawthorne died in Plymouth, New Hampshire, in 1864 at the age of sixty.

We have no reason to believe that his marriage to Sophia was not a good one; indeed his love letters are masterful. His son Julian quoted Herman Melville (1819–1891) that "there was some secret in his life" that was never disclosed.

His prose style was "decorous" and classic, very much like the styles of his models, John Bunyan (1628–1688) and Edmund Spenser (1552–1599). Unfortunately, he lacked Bunyan's faith. He felt a deep guilt that one of his forebears had been a judge at the Salem witchcraft trials.[4] He had "a qualified faith, sometimes" but found the way barricaded to the God of the Puritans. Both Hawthorne and Melville continued to believe in "the Calvinistic sense of innate depravity and original sin." They believed that the wrong in one generation lives on into the next. In telling the story of Hester[5] and Rev. Dimmesdale, Hawthorne portrays adultery as wrong.[6] His treatment of conscience is biblical.[7] Hawthorne never felt at home with Emerson and his "subjectivism," in part because Emerson denied original sin. Indeed Hawthorne saw Emerson as "that everlasting rejecter of all that is, and seeker for what he knows not."[8]

In *The Marble Faun,* Hawthorne explores the effect of a murder upon the people involved in the crime. His premise was that "Every crime destroys more Edens than our own." As his character Hilda exclaimed, "Now I understand how the sins of the generations past have created an atmosphere of sin for those who follow."[9] Longfellow, who was addicted to the Pelagian religion of Emersonian "self-reliance," said of *The Marble Faun,* "A wonderful book but it has the old dead pain which runs through all of Nathaniel Hawthorne's writings."[10] His satire is extremely negative and biting.[11]

Certainly Hawthorne carries a resentment against Puritanism generally. The wearing of an "A" for adultery is purely fictitious.[12] What is worse is how film makers savaged the original *Scarlet Letter* story in late-twentieth-century movies. One film has Hester and Dimmesdale riding off into the sunset with the scarlet "A" falling into the dust—while Indians destroy all of those dreadful Puritans. Of course now Hester is a heroine for refusing to admit adultery is wrong. [13]

Hawthorne knew and felt otherwise, so he allows the young artist Holgrave in *The House of the Seven Gables* to verbalize a more biblical and realistic confidence in a humble faith in the Lord.[14]

1. Edwin Haviland Miller, *Salem Is My Dwelling Place: A Life of Nathaniel Hawthorne* (Iowa City, Iowa: University of Iowa, 1991). A good biographical study.
2. He was a versatile writer, whose short stories are especially worth reading, for example "The Canterbury Pilgrim" about the Shaker village and religion.
3. H. Arthur Scott Trask, "Franklin Pierce and the Fight for the Old Union," *Chronicles of Culture,* October 1997, 33.
4. A very balanced analysis of the trials is Marion L. Starkey, *The Devil in Massachusetts* (New York: Time Reading Program, 1949). Arthur Miller's *The Crucible* in play and movie is a distortion of the Puritans and American beginnings. Well-reviewed by Marvin Olasky in "Witchhunts," *World,* 11 January 1997, 30. Note also the significant study by Elaine G. Breslaw, *Tituba: Reluctant Witch of Salem* (New York: New York University Press, 1996).
5. Edward Wagenknecht, *Nathaniel Hawthorne: Man and Writer* (New York: Oxford, 1961). Wagenknecht also argues the thoughtful thesis that Hester Prynne was the first significant female character in American literature. Cooper's women had been as "sappy as maples."
6. Harold Bloom, *Hester Prynne* (New York: Chelsea House, 1990), 4. The novel without redemption is like a Greek tragedy, but it stresses the importance of confession of sins. It does not present this confession as to God, however, which it must be.
7. E. Michael Jones, "The Dimmesdale Syndrome: Why Confession is a Necessity," *Culture Wars,* December 1995, 32.
8. Miller, *Salem is My Dwelling Place,* 248. "Byronic-looking Hawthorne," was often "stubbornly if elegantly negative."
9. Nathaniel Hawthorne, *The Marble Faun* (New York: Pocket Library, 1958), 173. Focus not on deed, but the motives.
10. Darrel Abel, *The Moral Picturesque: Studies in Hawthorne's Fiction* (Lafayette, Ind.: Purdue University Press, 1988).
11. Miller, *Salem Is My Dwelling Place,* 452. Hawthorne was very fond of the satire of Anthony Trollope (1815–1882). Both intrude into their narratives.
12. Leland Ryken, *Worldly Saints: The Puritans as They Really Were* (Grand Rapids: Zondervan, 1986), 188f.
13. "Hester Prynncesse," *Newsweek,* 4 April 1994, 58. The review openly calls for the end to negative thinking about adultery. This is increasingly the hue and cry of the media.
14. Nathaniel Hawthorne, *The House of the Seven Gables* (New York: Pocket Books, 1954). Cf. Hiromu Shimizu, "A Study on Nathaniel Hawthorne," in *Gumma University Cultural Science Series,* 9.8. This is excellent Christian insight.

10.1.3 MELVILLE, METAPHYSICIAN

> Nor was the pulpit itself without a trace of the same sea taste that had achieved the ladder and the picture. Its panelled front was in the likeness of a ship's bluff bows, and the Holy Bible rested on a projecting piece of scroll work, fashioned after a ship's fiddle-headed beak. What could be more full of meaning?—for the pulpit is ever this earth's foremost part; all the rest comes in its rear; the pulpit leads the world. From thence it is that the storm of God's quick wrath is first descried, and the bow must bear the earliest brunt. From thence it is that the God of breezes fair or foul is first invoked for favorable winds. Yes, the world's a ship on its passage out, and not a voyage complete; and the pulpit is its prow.
>
> —Herman Melville
> *Moby Dick*

When W. Somerset Maugham (1874–1965) was asked to select the ten greatest novels ever written, he chose four English, three French, two Russian, and one American—and the American novel was *Moby Dick*. Great Books of the Western World includes *Moby Dick* as one of very few novels in its canon. It is on most lists of the one hundred best books ever written. Its author was unrecognized while he lived, but for that one novel has been ranked (particularly since the 1920s) among the greatest American writers. The novel is symbolic and metaphysical and hard to understand. Is it really that good and that important? Are the accolades truly deserved?

Born in New York City, Herman Melville (1819–1891) was raised within a family that had known greatness and means. Two relatives had been heroes in the American Revolution.

His father, however, left the College of New Jersey and its Calvinist heritage to become a Unitarian. He also became enmeshed in shady business deals and died, ruined and mad, in 1832. His mother, like all of his Dutch ancestors, was a staunch Calvinist who moved her family back to Albany after her husband's death. Herman was not the favorite son and had to leave school to work. "Secret grief is the cannibal of its own heart," he wrote.[1]

Through the tangled affairs of his young life, Melville began to write, while drifting among jobs in a bank and on a farm and as a school teacher. He went to sea for four years aboard a whaling vessel. Finally sick of this life, he jumped ship in the South Seas and lived among the natives. After becoming involved in a mutiny and always in trouble, Melville finally sailed home in 1844 and tried the more settled life. He married Elizabeth Shaw, whose father became chief justice of the Massachusetts Supreme Court.

His seafaring life behind him, he now had leisure to read widely, with special fondness for William Shakespeare (1564–1616), Emerson, and William Makepeace Thackeray (1811–1863). He found writing therapeutic. Soon his own writing was gaining attention, although he was prone to "tedious digressions" and many "lapses of narrative convention." Frequently, he offended readers by voicing defiance at the laws of God and society. Yet, as one of his biographers put it, "The power that surged through him felt like demonic possession or religious ecstasy."[2]

He purchased a small farm near Pittsfield, Massachusetts, so that he might live near his friend Nathaniel Hawthorne. At the farm, he wrote *Moby Dick* (1851), which he dedicated to Hawthorne. Unfortunately, he quickly followed this book with *Pierre,* a pessimistic and personal book that ruined his reputation.[3] One critic remarked that the revolting nihilism of *Pierre* was like "tap-dancing in quick-sand."[4]

In an effort to extricate himself from this slough of despond, Melville began to write short stories, but he was drinking heavily. He had "ugly attacks" of depression, and his in-laws sent him on a long trip to Europe and the Middle East. He returned home to hibernate with his books and to drink. Again his in-laws sent him on a long trip, this time to the Pacific. He came home to the Civil War and the death of Judge Shaw, his father-in-law.

His sister, Augusta, taught Sunday school and had a burden for him "with missionary zeal." Few writers have been as familiar with and saturated with Scripture as Melville,[5] but "his quest for religious certainty had foundered in the Holy Land."[6]

He gave up the farm and spent the last thirty years of his life at 104 East 26th Street in New York. He did some writing and worked at the Customs House. He joined All Soul's Unitarian Church, which had become notorious when its pastor, Horatio Alger, was dismissed for molesting young boys.[7] By this time, Melville was "seriously out of control." He bullied his family, and his son committed suicide in their home. Although he made futile efforts at self-atonement, he died a brooding and bitter old man at seventy-two and was buried in the Bronx.

Probably no author has been as "lionized and as lambasted" as intensely as has Melville. He suffered mental conflict in trying to hold incompatible values. He was influenced by Longfellow's son-in-law, Richard Dana (1815–1882), the author of *Two Years Before the Mast* and a Burkean conservative. He read Jeremy Taylor's (1613–1667) *Holy Dying* and was thoroughly disgusted with the radical ideas trumpeted by Charles Darwin (1809–1882), Karl Marx (1818–1883), Ernest Renan (1823–1892), and David Strauss (1808–1874). He liked James Thomson (1700–1748) and William Blake (1757–1827). He wrote "Claret," a long and very bizarre poem on the Holy Land and the Cross.[8] He makes innumerable references to the Bible, but neither his mother's Calvinism nor transcendentalism satisfied him.[9] He found fault with Emerson's lack of compassion.

Melville brings James 1:7–8 to mind as the "double-minded man, unstable in all his ways." One day he wrote like an angel, and the next day he wrote like a demon. Hawthorne relates something of Melville's frame of mind from a Liverpool meeting in 1856:

> Melville, as he always does, began to reason of Providence and futurity, and of everything that lies beyond human ken, and informed me that he had "pretty well made up his mind to be annihilated": but still he does not seem to rest in that anticipation; and I think, will never rest until he gets hold of a definite belief. He can neither believe nor be comfortable in his unbelief; and he is too honest and courageous not to try to do one or the other. If he were a religious man, he would be one of the most truly religious and reverential; he has a very high and noble nature, and better worthy of immortality than most of us.[10]

Writing with immense vigor in *Moby Dick,* Melville fills the narrative with large amounts of material on whaling and whales. But what is the book about? It begins with the worship service in New Bedford for the seamen and what has been called "the greatest sermon in fiction," preached by Father Mapple on Jonah from the remarkable ship's prow pulpit.[11] But I think Bruce Lockerbie goes too far in describing *Moby Dick* as "a very great Christian novel, . . . the story of man's rebirth from the ways of death to the way of life." Others have understood *Moby Dick* to be a "romantic tragedy about Captain Ahab's sexual obsession with an enormous white whale" or "a picaresque comedy about sailing" or "a serio-comic grand opera . . . that leaves the narrator Ishmael alone in the ocean floating on the harpooner Queequeg's coffin."[12]

Certainly the book has deep apocalyptic overtones and would seem minimally to represent "man's search for meaning in a world of deceptive appearances," if not seeking "the redemption of America's blood-guilt."[13] Is not Ahab's obsession with the white whale (he says, "as white as the robes worn by the twenty-four elders in Revelation") a picture of original sin wanting to kill God and indicative of his own inner turmoil?[14]

Not published until thirty years after his death—and partly responsible for the recovery of his reputation—*Billy Budd* is the story of a seamen who is falsely accused and destroyed. We face here the mystery of sin and sorrow. Many see this novella as Melville's confession of his own guilt at the death of his favorite son and a passionate effort at self-atonement.[15] Everyone should read through *Moby Dick,* but undoubtedly *Billy Budd* will emerge as the "favorite Melville."

1. Laurie Robertson-Lorant, *Melville: A Biography* (New York: Clarkson Potter, 1996), 60. This fine study will stand until the completion of the series by the dean of Melville scholars, Herschel Parker, *Herman Melville.* The first volume, covering 1819–1851, was published in 1996 by Johns Hopkins University Press. Parker overwhelms us with the mass of detail he gathers.

2. Robertson-Lorant, *Melville: A Biography,* 176. Melville had "a manic intensity" or what has been called "a Dionysian wildness" about him (187).

3. Richard H. Brodhead, "The Book That Ruined Melville," *The New York Times Book Review,* 7 January 1996, 35.

4. Robertson-Lorant, *Melville: A Biography,* 315. Called "the greatest potboiler of all time," says "Virtue and vice are trash."

5. Nathalia Wright, *Melville's Use of the Bible* (New York: Octagon, 1969). On average, every seventh page of his prose had some biblical allusion.

6. Robertson-Lorant, *Melville: A Biography,* 399. Jerusalem was a "heart-sickening disappointment" (389).

7. Ibid., 510. Solitary most of the time, Horatio Alger unquestionably committed spousal abuse and mistreatment of the children.

8. Ibid., 552. There is no "lift of the resurrection" or movement from earth to heaven in the poem.

9. *Melville's Use of the Bible,* 77. Melville marked his Bible, which remains. He loved Wisdom Literature and the Gospels.

10. Hiromu Shimizu, *A Study on Herman Melville* (Tokyo: Gumma University Cultural Science Series, 11:1), 23.

11. D. Bruce Lockerbie, "The Greatest Sermon in Fiction," *Christianity Today,* 8 November 1963, 9ff. Lockerbie well argues that the book claims for the sermon "a lasting place" in literature.

12. J. Bottum, "Melville in Manhattan," *First Things,* October 1977, 48. Also analyzes the disaster of Pierre.

13. Robertson-Lorant, *Melville: A Biography,* 279. We remember that Father Mapple cried, "Root out sin!"

14. *Melville's Use of the Bible,* 30. *Moby Dick* has 250 biblical references and *Billy Budd* about 100.

15. F. W. Dillistone sees intimations of atonement here. It is true that the spar on which *Billy Budd* was suspended "was as a piece of the cross." See *The Novelist and the Passion Story* (New York: Sheed and Ward, 1960).

10.1.4 STOWE, "LITTLE" WOMAN

Mas'r, if you was sick, or in trouble, or dying, and I could save ye, I'd give ye my heart's blood; and, if taking every drop of blood in this poor old body would save your precious soul, I'd give 'em freely, as the Lord gave his for me. O Mas'r, don't bring this grat sin on your soul! It will hurt you more than 't will me! Do the worst you can, my troubles'll be over soon; but, if ye don't repent, yours won't never end!

—Harriet Beecher Stowe
Uncle Tom to cruel Simon Legree

So you're the little woman who started the big war.

—Alleged comment of President Abraham Lincoln
when introduced to Harriet Beecher Stowe

Uncle Tom's Cabin, though translated into forty-two languages, has been dismissed by some as "bad art." Whatever its literary qualities, it is significant historically and should be read by each generation. Scenes from this treatment of "Life Among the Lowly," such as Eliza's flight across the ice with her baby in her arms and the murder of Uncle Tom, indelibly etched the horrors of slavery into readers' minds. Millions have been stirred by this book.

Harriet Beecher Stowe (1811–1896) was the youngest of seven children born to Lyman Beecher, an eminent Congregational preacher in Litchfield, Connecticut, and his wife, Roxana, a woman who read French and the scientific articles in *The Edinburgh Review.*[1] Largely raised by relatives, "Hatty," as she was called, was converted at the age of thirteen in response to one of her father's sermons. She attended the Hartford Women's Seminary, which was directed by her older sister, Catherine, and she later taught rhetoric and composition at the school. Under five feet in stature, she was an ardent soul winner.

President of abolitionist Lane Theological Seminary and pastor of the Second Presbyterian Church in Cincinnati, Lyman Beecher's rejection of some historic

Calvinist doctrines and his social gospel revival preaching did not please the "Old School" wing of the Presbyterian Church. He was defended in two heresy trials by Salmon P. Chase (1808–1873), later chief justice of the U.S. Supreme Court. In 1836, the year the Presbyterian Church split into two denominations (partly over her father), Harriet married Calvin Stowe, a pessimistic and often explosively angry biblical scholar. Her brother Henry Ward Beecher (1813–1887) began his illustrious ministry in Plymouth Church, Brooklyn, New York, in 1847.[2] In 1850 Calvin and Harriet moved to Bowdoin College in Maine and later to Andover Seminary in the Boston area. Meanwhile, Harriet began to "test her voices" in various periodicals.

When President Millard Fillmore signed the Fugitive Slave Act as part of the Compromise of 1850, she was so enraged that she set herself to write a Christian drama exposing the vileness of slavery. Her *Uncle Tom's Cabin* was first published serially. It was her purpose "to persuade not by argument but by picture."[3] At a 10 percent royalty, she received $10,000 in the first three months of publication—the most ever received by a European or American author in so short a time. The book was exceedingly popular in England, where Charles Kingsley called it "the greatest novel ever written." A stream of other novels followed, including an *Atlantic Monthly* serial, *The Minister's Wooing,* which attacked the theology of Jonathan Edwards (1703–1758) and Samuel Hopkins (1721–1803). *Oldtown Folks* was written later in Florida. In *Lady Byron Vindicated,* she picked up the cudgel for Byron's wife in view of Byron's incestuous relationship with his sister.[4]

Mrs. Stowe was warmly received on a visit to England. At one dinner, she sat across the table from Charles Dickens (1812–1870). Her husband retired in 1863, and she was the sole support of her family for sixteen years.

Her style was inelegant, and she may have been somewhat paternalistic, as her critics tend to charge, but she was colorful and clear. She was evidently somewhat guided by the positive and negative examples of persuasion she heard from the pulpit, for "I have sat under preaching which didn't hit and didn't warm and didn't comfort."[5] A typical Beecherism is her tale of a preacher who found himself entangled suddenly in a thicket of accumulated clauses and who extricated himself by saying: "I have lost track of the nominative to my verb, but my brethren, one thing I know: I am bound for the Kingdom of Heaven!"

She crusaded against the free-love movement in feminism and stood by her brother Henry as charges of adultery rocked his career.[6] Her husband had a paralytic stroke in 1872 and died in 1886. Her own children went in every direction morally and spiritually—Fred disappeared in San Francisco, and Charlie became a Methodist Episcopal minister. She corresponded extensively with George Eliot (1819–1880) and dabbled in spiritualism, ultimately joining the Episcopal Church. After 1889, Stowe declined in health and died in 1896.

Her heart and soul are laid bare in *Uncle Tom's Cabin* where Uncle Tom urges St. Clare after Miss Eva's death to look away to Jesus. St. Clare wonders how Uncle Tom knows anything about it, but Tom responds that "fire is burning inside."[7] It is remarkable to consider how great a share her Christianity played in Stowe's leadership against the curse and tragedy of slavery through *Uncle Tom's Cabin.* Frank W. Boreham (1871–1959) underscored "the irresistible weight of Tom's testimony." Old Tom loved his precious Bible, and there is a clear symbiosis in the book and in historical fact between evangelical and slave Christianity. Tom reads Matthew 11:28 to the terrified women in the corn mill. "He walked through a hard world with nothing but the Bible to call his own."[8] "The Lord's brought me here and is going to take me home," Tom confidently affirms.[9] All that George Shelby could say in confronting Tom's death was: "What a thing it is to be a Christian."[10]

For supplemental reading in this era, try novels of Louisa May Alcott (1832–1888) whose father, Bronson Alcott, was a transcendentalist philosopher. Always poor, Louisa worked hard with her three sisters to keep the family afloat. Her popular *Little Women* bolstered the family's economy. It is the story of a hardy woman in New England who raised her daughters while her husband was away in the Civil War. The 1994 movie with Winona Ryder and Gabriel Burn returned this story to the public's attention. Jo March, one of the daughters, is Louisa herself. Both Emerson and Henry David Thoreau (1817–1862) were neighbors of the Alcotts in Concord. Thoreau's *Walden Pond* is a unique chronicle of a two-year, two-month, and two-day stay in a little cabin in which he argues "we need the tonic of the wilderness." Beautiful prose.

---

1. David L. Larsen, *The Company of the Preachers* (Grand Rapids: Kregel, 1998), 9.2.6.
2. Her brother Edward was pastor of Park Street Church in Boston. An amazing family!
3. Joan D. Hedrick, *Harriet Beecher Stowe: A Life* (New York: Oxford University Press, 1994), 218.
4. These three novels are included in The Library of America edition (New York: Oxford University Press, 1982). A storm of abuse and a physical collapse resulted from her advocacy of Lady Byron.
5. Hedrick, *Harriet Beecher Stowe: A Life,* 370. All of the Beechers moved toward the abolition movement before the war. Henry was close to Lincoln.
6. Ibid., 352. The double-standard in the Henry Ward Beecher controversy of 1872 is an abomination. She didn't see it.
7. F. W. Boreham, *The Gospel of Uncle Tom's Cabin* (London: Epworth, 1956), 24.
8. Ibid., 56.
9. Ibid., 66.
10. Ibid., 73.

10.1.5 CLEMENS, AMERICAN ICON

The minister gave out the hymn, and read it through with a relish, in a peculiar style which was much admired in that part of the country. His voice began on a medium key and climbed steadily up till it reached a certain point, where it bore with strong emphasis on the topmost word and then plunged down as if from a springboard. . . . After the hymn had been sung, the Rev. Mr. Sprague turned himself into a bulletin board and read off "notices" of meetings and societies and things till it seemed that the list would stretch out to the crack of doom. . . . And now the minister prayed. A good, generous prayer it was, and went into details. . . . The minister gave out his text and droned along monotonously through an argument that was so prosy that many a head by and by began to nod— and yet it was an argument that dealt in limitless fire and brimstone and thinned the predestined elect down to a company so small as to be hardly worth the saving. . . . Tom counted the pages of the sermon.

—"Mark Twain"
Tom Sawyer

Granted this is a caricature, but was Samuel Langhorne Clemens's experience as a boy in the Presbyterian Church in Hannibal, Missouri, anywhere close to such an unflattering description of the pulpiteer? Dull preachers have culpability to be sure. Clemens (1835–1910), who took the pen name Mark Twain from river parlance meaning "two fathoms deep," was born in Florida, Missouri. His father failed as a shopkeeper and land speculator, and he served as a justice of the peace. Until his father died in 1847, Samuel lived in "armed neutrality" with him. He felt closer to his "quirky" mother, but never built relationships with his siblings.[1] He lost not only his father but a brother and sister in death by the time he was twelve years of age.

Caught in the divided loyalties of Missouri in the conflicts leading to civil war, Clemens voted a proslavery ticket in 1860 and served briefly in the Confederate Army. He worked as a journeyman printer for eight years and as a Mississippi River pilot for four years. Then he went west to prospect for gold in Nevada. He worked as a newspaper reporter in Virginia City, where he wrote the short story that gave him fame, "The Celebrated Jumping Frog of Calaveras County."[2]

Not only did he begin to write but also he began to give humorous lectures. Artemis Ward (Charles Farrar Browne, 1834–1867) and Bret Harte (Francis Bret, 1836–1902) influenced him greatly at this time.

Travels in Asia and Europe provided the background for *Innocents Abroad*. That success gave him the financial freedom to marry Olivia Langdon of Elmira, New York. Livy was deeply religious and insisted that Clemens profess Christ before they married. Twain had weighed at one point whether he should become a river pilot or a preacher, but he had no religion. "In every storm he suffered agonies of remorse."[3] His "trained Presbyterian conscience" is heard in his quip, "I don't believe in hell but I'm afraid of it." He assured Livy that "I now claim that I am a Christian," but it remained obvious that he was not.[4]

As Mark Twain, Clemens wrote *Tom Sawyer* about a rascal boy who lived in a small town along the Mississippi River. Its income allowed the family to move in style to Hartford, Connecticut, where they lived from 1871 to 1891. The sequel to *Tom Sawyer, Huckleberry Finn,* was influenced by his friendship and travel with Joseph Twichell, a Congregational minister of Hartford. It is more serious and substantive than its predecessor.[5] But despite his reputation as a humorist and abundant writing success, Clemens became increasingly angry and bitter. He saw the deaths of his son and two of his three daughters, and Livy died in 1904. He could only say, "Goodbye, if we meet." He had dabbled with Christianity but never had a personal experience of Christ.

Maxwell Geismar calls Clemens "An American Prophet," but of what message?[6] His beloved wife had been a constant and a mainstay, but she was now gone. He fixated on the fall of our first parents and tried to exorcise his Puritan past. At one time, he was drawn to Christian Science and Mary Baker Glover Patterson Eddy (1821–1910), but this did not satisfy.[7] He made slashing attacks on all missionary effort and tried to hide his profanity and obscenity from his believing wife.[8] He became an advocate of sexual freedom and issued diatribes against Anglo-Saxon civilization. His more philosophic *The Mysterious Stranger* tells how a smooth Satan destroys a boy's scruples and morality. This work is "demonic, nihilistic and enigmatic." Clemens came to the place where he maligned Jesus Christ and denounced him as "more cruel than the cruel Jahweh of the Old Testament."[9] He even thought he would write a "Satan Bible." For him there was no God, no heaven, no hell. All is a dream.

He adamantly put down the pulpit. One critic quotes him from an otherwise unavailable article: "The gospel of Christ came filtered down to nineteenth century Americans through stage plays and through the despised novel and Christmas story, rather than from the drowsy pulpit."[10] Thus the gifted, influential, and universally acclaimed writer should be read for entertainment and insight into "the lost paradise of man," but he remains a tragic figure.

---

1. Andrew Hoffman, *Inventing Mark Twain: The Lives of Samuel Langhorne Clemens* (New York: Morrow, 1997). The thesis of this book is that Mark Twain was a clown mask for the real-life Clemens, who was a brooding, insecure racist.

2. I strongly recommend *The Complete Short Stories of Mark Twain* (New York: Bantam, 1956). The best is the 1902 teaser on whether a lie is ever justified, "Was It Heaven? Or Hell?" (474ff.). His writing exhibits a profound ignorance about the meaning of God's salvation.

3. Margaret Sanborn, *Mark Twain: The Bachelor Years* (New York: Doubleday, 1990), 50. When he was young, he prayed for gingerbread and then stole it. He always remained a skeptic.

4. Ibid., 421. Once in Keokuk, Iowa, a page of *Joan of Arc* blew across his path. She became one of his few heroes.

5. Russell Banks, "How a Clergyman from Hartford Freed Huckleberry Finn," *New York Times Book Review,* 18 June 1995. Twichell married the Clemenses, buried their dead, and was a best friend. He was close to liberal theologian and education theorist Horace Bushnell.

6. Maxwell Geismar, *Mark Twain: An American Prophet* (Boston: Houghton Mifflin, 1970). Like Twain, this biography is anti-Christian.

7. Ibid., 264. Twain is called "a pagan puritan," which is oxymoronic. He loved to hear Henry Ward Beecher preach.

8. Ibid., 420f. He thought the Bible was like an old drug store in which the same poisons always have sat on the shelves.

9. Ibid., 522. He loosed fusillades against "Biblical Teaching and Religious Practices."

10. Charles Lippy, *Being Religious American Style: A History of Popular Religiosity in the United States* (Westport, Conn.: Greenwood, 1994).

10.1.6 WHARTON, LITERARY VIXEN

I don't believe in God but I do believe in His saints.

—Edith Wharton

Properly called "the most distinguished woman author in the United States before 1940," Edith Wharton (1862–1937) was born to a very prominent society family in New York City. Her parents were nominal Episcopalians, and in their value system, breeding was everything, but Edith developed a religious interest—God was much in her thoughts during her early life.[1] She read much religious material indiscriminately, "particularly sermons of every kind of doctrinal persuasion."[2] Some of her early poetry was religious in a limited sort of way. She early achieved notice through her mastery of the short story. She became adept at satirizing high society in New York for its emptiness and falsity. In 1885 she married the Philadelphia blue blood, "Teddy" Wharton, but after 1903 he began to deteriorate from a debilitating mental disease. In 1905 she wrote *The House of Mirth,* which gave her opportunity for a psychologically acute lampoon of the manners and morals of high society. She struggled with depression and moved to Europe in 1912, returning to North America only once when she received an honorary doctorate from Yale University, the first woman to be so honored. Her savage portrait of Undine Sprague in *The Custom of the Country* showed her to be, in the words of her leading biographer, "demanding, imperious, devastating."[3]

In 1911 she wrote *Ethan Frome,* "her most read and most American novel," according to Harold Bloom. Ethan is a poor New England farmer who falls in love with Mattie, his wife's cousin, who comes to help him care for his hypochondriac wife. Ethan and Mattie try to escape their dilemma by running their bobsled into a tree, but both survive as cripples. Their roles reverse, and wife Zeena becomes the loving nurse, and Mattie the whimpering crone. This is the book that must be read.[4]

After age forty, Edith Wharton really began to write. Her various romantic entanglements and affairs had not satisfied her. By now she was a declared agnostic.[5] She had a long friendship with Henry James (1843–1916), who exerted considerable influence on her economy of words, her practice of limiting dialogue to the crucial scenes, and her fastidiousness in style.[6] She had a deep friendship with Bernard Berenson (1865–1959), the noted art critic.[7] Her *The Age of Innocence* won her a Pulitzer Prize in 1920. In later years, she had some decline in acceptability, as the trend was away from high society to Main Street and the world described by Sinclair Lewis (1885–1951). Wharton advocated the old social order. She called herself "the priestess of reason."

She became increasingly hostile to Christianity, although she did "discover" the New Testament after she had read Renan's higher-critical views. She confessed she had never really considered that Christ and his apostles might have been who they said they were.[8] She had become "an emphatic Nietzschian" (with some of the grimness of Friedrich Nietzsche's predecessor, Arthur Schopenhauer, 1788–1860) and an heir of a "terrible fatalism" out of her Emersonian heritage.[9]

This is tragedy taken beyond Hawthorne to a kind of sordid sadism. In the total vacuum of her years, she began to sniff about Roman Catholicism when she was much taken by St. Peter's in Rome.[10] It was then that she said, "I don't believe in God but I do believe in His saints." That is as far as she went. We get some nihilistic overtones in Wharton, which will become very much more pronounced and loudly stated in society quite shortly.

---

1. R. W. B. Lewis, *Edith Wharton: A Biography* (New York: Harper, 1975), 25. A solid and moving account. Lewis has an extended appendix on the issue of Edith Wharton's paternity.

2. Ibid., 25.

3. Harold Bloom, introduction to *Edith Wharton* (New York: Chelsea Books, 1986), 3.

4. Edith Wharton, *Ethan Frome* (New York: Scribner's, 1911, 1970). The book is less than one hundred pages long.

5. Lewis, *Edith Wharton,* 221. With this decision of nonbelief came a declaration that nothing was wrong with adultery. This was convenient self-justification, since she was an adulterer at the time.

6. Margaret B. McDowell, *Edith Wharton* (Boston: Twayne, 1976), 34. "A long and affectionate relationship."

7. Bernard Berenson's first wife was Mary Pearsall Smith, daughter of Robert Pearsall Smith, the reprobate Quaker "deeper-life" teacher, and his wife, Hannah Whithall Smith, who was devoted to God and the able author of *The Christian's Secret of a Happy Life.*

8. Lewis, *Edith Wharton,* 230f., 393. She detested the "conventions" and wanted to feel guiltless about her loose living.

9. Bloom, introduction to *Edith Wharton,* 4, 6. Applying this philosophy to her writing, Bloom writes, "An inner whiteness and blankness has crippled Ethan Frome."

10. Lewis, *Edith Wharton,* 510. Many of her friends wondered if she would convert to Catholicism, but she did not.

10.1.7 CRANE, WAYWARD SON

I used to like church and prayer meetings when I was a kid but that cooled off when I was thirteen or about that. . . . My brother Will told me not to believe in Hell.

I know what Saint Paul says, but I disagree with Saint Paul.

—Stephen Crane

Described as "a slight boyish figure, with a wisp of light hair and shining eyes which saw everything," Stephen Crane (1871–1900) was famous as a writer of novels, short stories, and poems at age twenty-four, but he was dead at twenty-eight. He made a deep impression and is regarded by some as "the first modern American writer," a pioneer as a literary "realist, impressionist, naturalist and symbolist."[1] Crane was born in Newark, New Jersey, but lived in many different locales as a boy since his father was a Methodist minister.

Methodist clergy abounded on both sides of his family, and his father actually left the Presbyterian Church because he could not accept infant damnation. Found in Stephen's effects was Jesse Peck's (d. 1880) sulfurous tract, "What Must I Do to Be Saved?"[2] It is true that in the holiness Methodist confines of Asbury Park and Ocean Grove, New Jersey, the opposition to worldly amusements was strong. The Cranes frequented this area, and Stephen lived there after his father's death. Rev. Crane was known for his fulmination against dancing, drinking, gambling, smoking, horse races, circuses, theatres, chess, billiards, baseball, and the reading of novels.[3]

Now as a widow, Mary Helen Peck Crane continued to write and speak in the gospel cause, but young Stephen revolted. He had professed conversion when his favorite older sister Agnes died in 1884, but now the youngest of fourteen children threw overboard the orthodoxy of his parents. Many who write about Crane viciously taunt "the obsolete orthodoxy" of Crane's day. This overlooks the points made by such historians as Garry Wills in *Under God* that much of the vitality of the American people in the late 1800s and early 1900s was in cultural sectors most influenced by the orthodox religious movements. This evangelistic fervor would be carried on by a series of well-known preachers of the like of Billy Graham (b. 1918) through the century.[4]

Crane rejected the religion in which he was raised because he intended to be "his own Master."[5] His brief flings at education at Lafayette College and Syracuse University were singularly undistinguished. At nineteen, he became a correspondent for the *New York Tribune* and wrote the most incredible series of sketches about the tramps of the Bowery in New York City. Out of this came his first novel, *Maggie: A Girl of the Streets*. He published this at his own expense, which is one reason it was largely ignored by critics. He was bitter in his criticism of the "hypocrite" Christian workers among the homeless.[6] In 1895 he wrote his masterpiece, *The Red Badge of Courage,* the great novel about the Civil War and the fears of a boy who must come of age on the battlefield. Hardly more than a short story, this brief book is well worth reading.

A gifted craftsman of irony, Crane wrote with psychological realism. Though he never smelled the smoke of battle, his description of the fears of Henry Fleming at the Battle of Chancellorsville is gripping, and his reconstruction of the action "uncannily accurate."[7] This is the story not of the fear of danger but of the fear of fear. Harold Bloom likens the great concluding movement to the work of Leo Tolstoy (1828–1910) in *War and Peace*.[8] This spare novel is "laden with verbs of perception."[9] Interestingly, when Henry looked back upon leaving home, he saw his mother kneeling in the potato patch praying, but he expunged the scene of Henry's mother presenting him with a Bible when he left.[10] Henry is "reborn" in the novel but not into new life in Christ. Rather, he grows out of the Christian group values (which the author detested) by accepting his own individuality.[11]

Crane veered from Christianity to a commonsense stoic humanism.[12] He despised dogma and ignored Christian eschatology. He retained a semblance of the Christian notion of fallenness, but he never acknowledged sin to be disobedience to God's commands.

Because he lived on the run as a well-known young journalist, Crane's writings after *The Red Badge of Courage* were of an inferior, second-rate quality. *The Blue Hotel* (1898) is again about fears and illusions and Swede's identification with storm and blizzard.[13]

Crane traveled to Cuba as a war correspondent and almost seemed to have a death-wish. He wrote from Greece about the Balkan War and there married Cora, the proprietor of a brothel he had visited in Jacksonville, Florida. They decided to live in England where he developed friendships with H. G. Wells, Joseph Conrad, James M. Barrie, Henry James, and Frederic Ware.[14] However, Crane soon died in England of tuberculosis. Although he died so young, he left behind work that is still read and admired.[15]

In Stephen Crane, we have the sad story of a prodigal who never came home.

1. William Rose Benet, *Benet's Reader's Encyclopedia*, 3d ed. (New York: Harper and Row, 1987), "Crane, Stephen."

2. Stanley Wertheim, "Stephen Crane and the Wrath of Jehovah," in *Stephen Crane*, ed. Harold Bloom (New York: Chelsea House, 1987), 41. His mother is "the prototype of the dogmatic but ineffectual maternal figure."

3. Ibid., 42. Wertheim is caustic, showing that Crane could not have been reconciled to the church.

4. Garry Wills, *Under God: Religion and American Politics* (New York: Simon and Schuster, 1990), 124.

5. Marston LaFrance, *A Reading of Stephen Crane* (Oxford: Clarendon, 1971), 8.

6. Ibid., 53. One study of Crane, Christopher Benfey's *The Double Life of Stephen Crane* (New York: Knopf, 1992), argues that *Maggie* is a premature novel in which Crane does not know his characters. A robust biography was published in Linda H. Davis, *Badge of Courage: The Life of Stephen Crane* (Boston: Houghton, Mifflin, 1998).

7. Bloom, introduction to *Stephen Crane*, 1.

8. Ibid., 4. Keeping in mind the massive scope of Tolstoy, Crane is a model of brevity.

9. James Nagel, "Stephen Crane and the Narrative Methods of Impressionism," in *Stephen Crane*, 84. His impressionistic style renders, rather than reports, action scenes.

10. Ibid., 123, 47. Very likely Crane represents his own struggle in the fearfulness of Henry Fleming in *Red Badge*.

11. Ibid., 125. In other words, there is psychological conversion in contradistinction to Christian conversion.

12. *Reading of Stephen Crane*, 149. The author cites a poem by Crane which is his "most complete denial of God" (141).

13. Ibid., 220. At this point, Crane was sick, hyperactive, and ill-prepared to write anything of high quality.

14. Harold Frederic (1856-1898) was also an expatriate Methodist whose study of the fall of a Methodist minister is a neglected minor classic: *The Damnation of Theron Ware* (1896; repr. ed., New York: Holt, Rinehart, 1958).

15. Max Herzberg, introduction to *The Red Badge of Courage* (New York: Washington Square, 1959), p. ix and following.

10.2 RADICALS AND REBELS OF AMERICAN FICTION

> We must distinguish between taste and fashion. Fashion, the love of change for its own sake, the desire for something new, is very transient; taste is something that springs from a deeper source.
>
> —T. S. Eliot

In a time when Jacques Derrida (b. 1930) and the deconstructionists denied that words have intrinsic meaning, artistic merit, or moral worth,[1] it is gratifying to read the authors who refused to give up the meaning content of the text. E. D. Hirsch Jr., argued that "texts have meaning," and Robert Alter of the University of California and his comrades in the Association of Literary Scholars and Critics refused to reduce imaginative writing to "the sum of its crimes against humanity, losing sight of the ambiguous and magical ways in which novels, poems and plays areally operate."[2] Similarly, Andrew Delbanco of Columbia University argued effectively for the viability of the "great books" and underscored the political and spiritual verities with which many American writers wrestled. "What's wrong with the book?" is only one question we ask of many.[3]

---

1. Milton J. Rosenberg, "L'Affaire De Man," *Chronicles of Culture,* July 1991, 35f.
2. Richard Lacayo, "War of Words—Are the Great Books Racist, Sexist, Homophobic?" *Time,* 1997, 92.
3. Andrew Delbanco, *Required Reading: Why Our American Classics Matter Now* (New York: Farrar, Strauss and Giroux, 1997). Delbanco has shown that the American Civil War was a cultural disaster, the great divide between cultures of faith and doubt. He maintains that both North and South went into the war believing in divine providence but emerged looking only to fate. Andrew Delbanco, *The Death of Satan: How Americans Have Lost the Sense of Evil* (New York: Farrar, Strauss, Giroux, 1995).

10.2.1 LONDON, REBEL WITH A CAUSE

> Ask people who know me today, what I am. A rough, savage fellow, they will say, who likes prizefights and brutalities, who has a clever turn of pen, a charlatan's smattering of art, and the inevitable deficiencies of the untrained, unrefined, self-made man which he strives with a fair measure of success to hide beneath an attitude of roughness and unconventionality. Do I endeavor to unconvince them? It's so much easier to leave their convictions alone.
>
> —letter from Jack London to Charmian Kittredge
> in 1903, early in their courtship

What is the difference between anything that is strong and fine and well-arranged—be it words or stones or trees or ideas or what not—and the same elements as they were in their unorganized weakness? Man—the brain of man, the effort that man had put into man's supreme task—organizing! That is the work of man, work that is worth a man's doing—to take something second-rate and chaotic and to put himself into it until it becomes orderly and first-rate and fine.

—Jack London in an interview six days before his death

When he died at forty of a drug overdose, John Griffith ("Jack") London (1876–1916) was already in decline. At age thirty-six, he had written twenty-eight books and 160 short stories, standing at that time as the most famous and highly paid writer in America.[1] He was born out-of-wedlock in San Francisco and raised by his mother, a devotee of spiritualism, in deep poverty. Selling newspapers at ten and working in a cannery at fourteen, he knew a rough-and-tumble life. His mother's religion left him with a deep struggle over the viability of any supernaturalism. He learned to rob oyster nets and rode the rails. He was loud and crude, typically fulminating against "the yellow peril" on the West Coast. After a particularly galling job in a laundry, he decided that he wanted to become a writer. He devoured Joseph Conrad, Rudyard Kipling, Herman Melville, Edgar Allen Poe, Charles Darwin, Sigmund Freud, and Nietzsche. Theodore Roosevelt became his model as "the apostle of a strenuous life."

London didn't particularly care to write, but he needed income. His own experiences in the Klondike stimulated his earliest works of "red-blooded realism." Although there is much that is obnoxious about Jack London, literary critic Charles Watson is right that he was "a serious and compelling writer."[2] He denied all metaphysics in favor of a frankly materialist position and became radical in his politics, a disciple of "superman socialism" or even Marxism.[3]

The Call of the Wild must be read as a part of Americana. Similar to *Black Beauty* in its alternating bad and good masters, this is really a story about society. The magnificent sled dog is caught in a tension between the call of his primitive roots versus the civilizing influence of good John Thornton. Starting as a more pampered domesticate, Buck the dog is drawn to the alternative. In keeping with the "new naturalism," London gives us a series of "ritualistic acts" that are almost mystical.[4] We sense demonic overtones in the story as Buck becomes "a ghost dog." This plot, along with London's later *White Fang,* is moved by Darwin's "survival of the fittest." It is nature "red with tooth and claw." London knew such violence, narrowly escaping death from drowning. He participated in violence of another sort when he left his wife and two young daughters for another woman.

The other work of London that should be read is *The Sea Wolf,* in which we meet the Danish sealing captain Wolf Larsen, London's most "fully imagined character."[5] Is Wolf the Ahab of Melville? Many accused London of plagiarism. Here we encounter again "the creed of brute strength," the perfect type of "Gothic hero-villain."[6] The demonic sense definitely intensifies, and London's advocacy of "overdeveloped masculinity" becomes heavy. The blasphemous Wolf Larsen is likened by London to the beast in the book of Revelation. Larsen loves power and control and hungers for knowledge.

In characterizing Larsen, London resorts to Hamlet's dilemma, the wisdom in Ecclesiastes, and the blunt crudity of Scandinavian mythology. London lays bare his struggle with primal melancholy. His bitter defiance is like that of Satan in *Paradise Lost*. From a biblical perspective, one wonders whether London was under demonic influence. His second wife observed that "his period of depression following the dissolution of his first marriage was associated in his mind with Nietzsche's 'long sickness' which ended with this death from tertiary syphilis."

Something Nietzschian permeates the story of the romantic triangle in *The Sea Wolf* and the death of the blinded Wolf Larsen. To the end Wolf, is angry, defiant, and indomitable. But the spiritual journey represented is intriguing— from Charles Darwin's brutal nature to Karl Marx's brutal society and finally to Sigmund Freud's brutal self. His novels and short stories present an individual-worshiping embodiment of something that has been a reality in American life.

1. Daniel Mark Epstein, "The Three Incarnations of Man: The Brave, the Wise and the Cynical," *Insight*, 12 December 1994, 26. This article reviews London's *Complete Short Stories* (repr. ed., Palo Alto: Stanford University Press, 1994).
2. Charles N. Watson Jr., *The Novels of Jack London: A Reappraisal* (Madison, Wis.: University of Wisconsin Press, 1983), x.
3. Ibid., 12. Kipling was another literary influence on London.
4. Ibid., 43. Francis Schaeffer adeptly shows how nihilism sometimes finds refuge in mysticism in *The God Who Is There* (Downers Grove, Ill.: InterVarsity, 1968), 55ff. Schaeffer calls this semantic mysticism "despair beyond despair." Because Schaeffer and others have pointed out the danger of mysticism toward monism, and there have been errors among Christians, mysticism had a bad reputation at the end of the twentieth century. Arthur L. Johnson fanned this overreaction in *Faith Misguided: Exposing the Dangers of Mysticism* (Chicago: Moody, 1988). But great Christians ever since the apostle Paul have rejoiced in a profound and biblical mysticism that centers around Christ. We should not let the errors of mystics steal away our proper "Christ-mysticism."
5. Ibid., 58. Wolf Larsen and his brother "Death" are always feuding.
6. Ibid., 60–61. Oaths of the characters are a sad testimony of Zolaesque naturalism (248).

10.2.2 DREISER, REBEL AGAINST HUMANITY

In fact, now that I looked back on my college year, I was irritated by the deprivations I had endured, the things in which I had not been included, the joys which many had had and which I had not. For I take no meaning from life other than the picture it presents to the eye—the pleasure and pain it gives to the body.

—Theodore Dreiser

So much of both positives or negatives in the life and writings of Theodore Dreiser (1871–1945) relates to the matrix out of which he emerged. He was the twelfth of thirteen children born within a very strict Roman Catholic family in Terre Haute, Indiana. Increasingly obsessed with his Roman Catholicism, John Dreiser failed in his business and abandoned his family.[1] Young Dreiser despised the economic system that brought such dysfunction to his family, and throughout his life, he felt a deep compassion for the disinherited and downtrodden folk who always found themselves outsiders.

He tended to moodiness to the extreme of a bipolar emotional temperament, leaving for Chicago to make his fortune in 1887. Through the generosity of a teacher, he attended Indiana University for a year, but he did not pursue his opportunity. He preferred the hurly-burly of a news writer's life. Notwithstanding his coarseness, boorish behavior, and superstitions (he turned briefly to yoga and to Christian Science),[2] he became part of the "Chicago group" of writers and was influential as an advocate of American naturalism.

Ultimately a member of the Communist Party in the U.S.A. and a defender of Stalin, Dreiser shows the influence of Nietzsche, Darwin, and Freud. He believed that life is a jungle and that man is an animal. He was a strict determinist. When Hurstwood in *Sister Carrie* is struggling with the temptation to steal from the safe, he equivocates, opening and shutting the safe door. With the money in his hand, he hears the click of the safe. Now he has no choice. He must take the money and dispose of it. Robert Penn Warren in his *Homage to Theodore Dreiser* cautions against overestimating the literary influences on Dreiser at the expense of what came out of the rough-and-tumble of his own instincts and living.[3]

Dreiser was the first non-Anglo-Saxon and the first non-Protestant novelist of account in North America. His first novel, *Sister Carrie* (1900) was a story of vice and was censored. His books are not really steamy or lurid, but he addressed aspects of human sexuality that had not been addressed in his day. He was a shameless womanizer, a weakness that played into the hands of critics who felt he should be shut down. He attributed his own conduct toward women to uncontrollable mechanistic instincts. He strongly argued for an author's right to demand an honest interpretation of his texts.[4]

He often bungled his writing stylistically, but he was so forceful and clear that he put it across. Carrie was "the first truly modern heroine in American literature," but, as all of Dreiser's major characters, Carrie exhibits "moral detachment" in a totally unrealistic way. This lack of any moral referent accounts for the dismal conclusions for which Dreiser is famous.

His next novel, *Jennie Gerhardt,* tells the story of the seduction of the young central figure by Senator Brander and then Lester Kane. Dreiser supplies no psychological insight in his studies of human nature, but he draws us along with his "great sense of the flow of life." He acknowledged that the "ghost of the Puritans would arise and gibber in the streets" at the sight of what Dreiser was producing.[5] In his frankly autobiographical and voluminous novel, *Genius,* James Lundquist supports his contention that there is much structural Victorianism even in this rebel.[6] The same could be said of his *Trilogy of Desire.* We are told that his chief image came from watching a lobster kill a squid in a store window. In this, his Cowperwood saga, there is so much philandering that not even the salacious critic Ford Maddox Ford could read beyond the eleventh seduction. Money, sex, and power had totally taken control.[7] In *The Bulwark,* Dreiser gives his classic statement on the disaster of religion. Solon Barnes, the central figure, was a

Quaker of high ideals who finally foundered on religion's lack of reality.[8] One of Dreiser's characters in a play expresses the mood: "It ain't my fault. I didn't make myself, did I?"

Some of his sharpest shafts aimed at Christianity are launched in his classic *An American Tragedy*. Based on an actual murder trial, this is the story of Clyde Griffith, the child of street-corner evangelists who operated the Door of Hope Mission. Clyde's father warned him of life's perils; indeed the book opens and closes with street preaching. Dreiser made a small fortune off this book and was drinking very heavily as he wrote it. This was his consummate hatchet job against "the naive tradition of evangelicalism in American life. . . . a tradition that had its manifestations in the 1920s in Billy Sunday revivalism, gospel missions, and fundamentalism of the sort made famous in the 1925 Scopes Monkey Trial."[9]

Clyde impregnates the hapless Roberta in his quest for excitement and then seeks the wealthy Sondra as his wife. He is accused of murdering Roberta; there is a deeply moving depiction of Clyde's trial, conviction, and execution representing the murderous society that Dreiser believed America had become. Like Marx, Dreiser saw religion only as "belief in an illusion" and the world as the "topsy-turvy" path of an endless pendulum swing.

He drifted increasingly leftward in works he refused to revise or sufficiently research, such as his *Dreiser Looks at Russia*. Though often banned, his works are still read, but it is little wonder that they are unrelievedly grim. A fitting picture of the dichotomy of American life in the century, Dreiser was buried in Forest Lawn cemetery in Los Angeles, next to the rodeo cowboy and western movie star Tom Mix.

---

1. James Lundquist, *Theodore Dreiser* (New York: Frederick Ungar, 1974), 3. He believed love to be an illusion.

2. Ibid., 106. He consulted fortune tellers, worried over omens, and believed that one could communicate with the spiritual world by using an Ouija board.

3. Ibid., 39. Robert Penn Warren, this Southern man of letters and the first American poet laureate, drifted toward the left. This descendent of William Penn should be read above all for his powerful *All the King's Men,* in which he makes Huey Long into Willie Stark. Stark tells the narrator that "he himself went to an old-fashioned Presbyterian Sunday School where in the old days they still taught some theology." Robert Drake, "Robert Penn Warren's Enormous Spider Web," *The Christian Century,* 22 November 1989, 1089f. *All the King's Men* is the great American political novel. See Joseph Blotner, *Robert Penn Warren: A Biography* (New York: Random House, 1996).

4. Ibid., 25. Dreiser was occasionally a sentimentalist. There is a duality to his nature.

5. Ibid., 50. Dreiser's realism was "social not sexual," and he handles sexual description clumsily (61).

6. Ibid., 60. "Dreiser's lovers always employ the bizarre language of Victorian romance."

7. For a strong statement of the Judeo-Christian view, see Richard J. Foster, *Money, Sex and Power* (New York: Harper and Row, 1985). After all of the barrage, the Christian stands only to face new and insidious foes today.

8. Lundquist, *Theodore Dreiser,* 73. Dreiser tries to show that religion brought the family all of its troubles, a superficial and unfair "straw man" tactic for demeaning faith.

9. See Sprague de Camp, *The Great Monkey Trial* (New York: Doubleday and Doran, 1969). This is my favorite treatment of the historic trial that was broadcast by WGN Radio of Chicago. Important background.

10.2.3 CATHER, REBEL AGAINST THE CODE

Any first-rate novel or story must have in it the strength of a dozen fairly good stories that have been sacrificed to it.

—Willa Cather
"On the Art of Fiction"

A surge of six significant novels she wrote from 1918 to 1931 fixed Willa Cather's place in literature (1873–1947). She was raised on the prairies of Nebraska, but shaped by the stateliness of Virginia where she was born. She came from very religious stock near Winchester, Virginia. With her husband and brother, who was Willa's grandfather, her great-aunt left the moderate Presbyterians to be a zealous, toe-tapping Baptist. Willa seemed to make a decision for Christ as a child, and she read the Bible and revered *The Pilgrim's Progress.*[1] The actual state of her spiritual life, however, is questionable.

With her parents and three siblings, eight-year-old Willa joined the extended family in Red Cloud in Webster County, Nebraska. The family became Episcopalian, the only church available. Willa was not confirmed in the Episcopal Church until 1922, but she was effectively educated by her two grandmothers. The Danes, Swedes, Bohemians, and Swiss lived near them and figure in her novels. She went on to Lincoln in 1891 and studied at the Latin School and then majored in English and classics at the University of Nebraska.

Unsure whether to pursue science or medicine, she set herself to be a writer. After graduation, she stayed one year in Red Cloud but became restless with its conventionality.[2] She went on to Pittsburgh, where she wrote for *The Home Monthly* and *The Leader.* In this citadel of Presbyterianism, she became disgusted because the Presbyterians offered "little encouragement to any artistic activity."[3] In 1911 she wrote her first novel, a work she later regretted greatly. Now in a strong revolt against "stern Presbyterianism," she and wealthy Isabel McClung, with whom she had been living, took a European tour. In 1912 she discovered the Pacific Southwest and began to write poetry.

For a time, she was very attracted to the Roman Catholic Church, "by the aura not the substance of Catholicism."[4] As Lionel Trilling puts it, "The Catholicism to which she turns is a Catholicism of culture, not doctrine."[5] She saw the white whale Moby Dick as Protestantism, while Catholicism was represented in the settled cultures. The focus of her religion then was art. There was a sensuous artistic richness in the liturgy and architecture of Catholicism. In *Death Comes for the Archbishop,* her interest is absorbed in the building of the cathedral.

Willa lived for forty years with Edith Lewis, moving to the Grosvenor Hotel in New York City where she edited *Maclure's* Magazine. Like many of her contemporaries, Cather often articulated the popular anti-Semitism. She regretted the passing of the old West, and, with the fabled western frontier individualist, she defied moral convention. She had a great aversion to heterosexuality, and her heroines are her best work.[6] Her women are mothers and daughters of men, but never lovers.[7] She consistently "invalidates sex," and symbols of emasculation abound. She herself had a dominating masculine personality. Opinions differ as to how overt her same-sex lifestyle was, but there is little doubt as to her stance.[8]

Cather was most deeply stirred by her appreciation of the Southwest prairies and a conservative reaction to the corrupted system and the relentless erosion of Western values. We sense this undercurrent of disapproval with modern society in A Lost Lady and The Professor's House. She liked Thomas Mann (1875–1955) because he looked back fondly to a time that had been long before.

She continued her fascination with eighteenth-century Southwest Catholicism until the death of her parents shocked her out of her preoccupation. Her last novel, Sapphira and the Slave Girl, moves back to Virginia and her Protestant past in the Church of England and Baptist communions.[9] In this final work, her character Henry Colbert attends a Baptist chapel and searches for Scriptures on the slavery issue.[10]

They have defects and lack central action, but her prairie novels from Nebraska ought to be read, including The Song of the Lark, My Antonia, and O Pioneers! They abound with Scandinavian dialect and the harsh world of the Kronbergs, Ericsen's, old Mrs. Svendsen, Ole the Swede, the Bergsons, Lina Lingard, and Antonia, who marries the Bohemian farmer.

Her classic is still Death Comes for the Archbishop (1927), the story of two French priests who come as missionaries to the Southwest. The inscription on Father Vaillant's signet ring, "Auspice Maria" ("by the favor of Mary") is on the title page of the book. We are especially drawn to Bishop Jean Marie Latour, who knows Kit Carson, among others. This bishop is of gentle birth but wears buckskin, faces lawlessness with a gun, and deals with wayward native clergy. While there is a glimmer of a missionary impetus and some Christian concern for the Navajos, it would seem this reader of The Pilgrim's Progress should have made a stronger statement.[11]

Cather was an enthusiast for Henry James (1879–1947), visited A. E. Housman (1859–1936) in Britain, and entertained Norwegian novelist Sigrid Undset (1882–1949). She grappled with inner spiritual issues and seemed to be wandering back toward her evangelical roots in her later years. Whether she had truly come to terms with God at her death is a matter of conjecture.

---

1. E. K. Brown, Willa Cather: A Critical Biography (New York: Knopf, 1953), 10.

2. Ibid., 47. My Antonia reflects enough of her resentment that it caused hard feelings in her home town.

3. Ibid., 77. She wrote: "There is no getting away from a Presbyterian environment, no getting around it, or behind it or above it." She went to Pittsburgh seeking "freedom," but found herself in a dreary round of daily work.

4. Harold E. Bloom, ed., introduction to *Willa Cather* (New York: Chelsea House, 1985), 2. At this time, Bloom observes, she "fulfills the overt program of Emersonian self-reliance." Hers is not a quest for grace.

5. Lionel Trilling, "Willa Cather," in *Willa Cather,* 10. This is a good example of aesthetic religion.

6. Ibid., 3. Bloom terms Cather's work as "the study of nostalgias."

7. Trilling, "Willa Cather," 13. Kazin speaks of her "elegiac traditionalism."

8. James Woodress, *Willa Cather: A Literary Life* (Lincoln: University of Nebraska, 1987) feels there never was anything physical, 141. Phyllis C. Robinson, *Willa: The Life of Willa Cather* (Garden City: Doubleday, 1983) is persuaded to the contrary. Cather does not address the subject in any of her published writings.

9. Morton D. Zabel, "Willa Cather: The Tone of Time," in *Willa Cather,* 46f. Brown calls these "Winter Memories."

10. Brown, *Willa Cather,* 315.

11. John J. Murphy, "Willa's Archbishop," in *Willa Cather,* 163. See *Death Comes for the Archbishop* (New York: Knopf, 1926, 1927).

10.2.4 LEWIS, REBEL AGAINST COMMUNITY

To understand America, it is merely necessary to understand Minnesota.
—Sinclair Lewis

In some ways he preferred New Thought to standard Protestantism. It was easier to play with. He had never been sure but that there might be something to the doctrines he had preached as an evangelist. Perhaps God really had dictated every word of the Bible. Perhaps there really was a hell of burning sulphur. Perhaps the Holy Ghost really was hovering around watching him and reporting. But he knew with serenity that all of his New Thoughts, his theosophical utterances, were pure and uncontaminated bunk.
—Lewis's description of Elmer Gantry

Harry Sinclair Lewis (1885–1951) was the youngest son of Edward J. Lewis, a country doctor who practiced in the small Western Minnesota town of Sauk Center. His mother died when he was six, but he was raised by a kind stepmother. However, intense sibling rivalry and a sense of being unloved, plus "the excruciating boredom of Sauk Center," left him restless.[1] He was bookish and went willingly to the mainline denominational church and Sunday school of his parents. "Red" persuaded his father that he should go to Oberlin College as a preparation for Yale. He was an indifferent student but worked as a janitor in the socialist colony where Upton Sinclair (1878–1968) exerted considerable and lasting influence on the young man.[2]

After being graduated from Yale in 1908, he traveled, worked briefly on a newspaper in Waterloo, Iowa, and consorted with Jack London and other radicals in a bohemian colony in Carmel, California. By then he was writing short stories and novels and had developed a "taste for the independent life."[3] A series of unhappy marriages, one with the journalist Dorothy Thompson, only deepened his frustration and fostered his excessive drinking habits. Thompson said of her former husband that "he drank because he wanted to." In 1920 *Main Street* was published, a novel set in Gopher Prairie, Minnesota—the Norse State. Carol Kennicott finds her town and her physician husband boring. She leaves for a while but then comes back in a kind of compromise with convention, such as Lewis himself always seemed to make. Minnesota talk and "the ragtimes and ricky-ticky rhythms of 1920s America" are all here.[4] While he felt it was futile to "buttress the old-time values" like religious fundamentalism, Lewis did truly love Minnesota and came back to it again and again. He memorized Minnesota's eighty-seven counties and their county seats.

In style, he shows the influence of Thoreau (whose *Walden* he always carried about with him), Walt Whitman (1819–1892), and Samuel Clemens (1835–1910). He wrote much that was just trash but interspliced some powerful novels about social class, such as *Babbitt* (1922), about moving to Zenith, the big city; *Arrowsmith* (1925), about medical practice and research in which his advisor was Paul De Kruif, the author of *Microbe-Hunters;* and *Dodsworth* (1929), about the unhappily married Sam Dodsworth, who finds romance in Europe. His books sold fabulously well, and he was the first American to win the Nobel Prize for Literature (1930). Still, he did not achieve emotional satisfaction and was afflicted with painful feelings of inferiority. His drinking bouts became more frequent and disruptive. Always tormented by skin lesions, he was an abysmally unhappy man who thought he could find and proclaim "moralities for a new time." But he didn't have his own life under control.[5]

His "most brutal attack on American standards" was his onslaught upon evangelical religion, *Elmer Gantry* (1927).[6] Made into movie versions and finally into a musical, this is a sordid tale of a football player turned fraudulent minister and his scandalous liaisons. Tracing the Baptist education of its hero, his evangelistic ministry, and then his rise into Methodism, the book begins with the lines "Elmer Gantry was drunk." Actually Lewis did extensive research for the book in the heartland of Kansas, first with a Methodist minister named William Stidger, and then with L. M. Birkhead, who had been raised a Baptist, served as a Methodist, and after attending Union Seminary in New York became an agnostic and a Unitarian preacher.[7]

But Lewis was an exile, a vagabond too undisciplined to lead us out of our wilderness. For one thing, this follower of H. G. Wells and Thomas Hardy had a tendency to overwrite. After his 1930 Nobel Prize, his quality plummeted. He has been described as a "one man *sturm und drang*" ("storm and stress"). He became a law to himself, endorsing the Nietzschean sexual mores, in which no one is bound by convention. In his last book, *The God-Seeker,* intended to be the first of a trilogy, we sense his anger and isolation and his "great contempt toward the Victorian missionary impulse." In his last years, he wandered about Europe and died in Rome, a lonely and bitter man.[8]

Elmer Gantry, though tawdry, is the influential work of Lewis that should be read, partly to understand a source of modern bias against Christian evangelists.

1. Mark Schorer, *Sinclair Lewis* (Minneapolis: University of Minnesota, 1963), 7.
2. Upton Sinclair wrote eighty books, including *The Jungle,* which led President Theodore Roosevelt to campaign for food purity laws. Sinclair's writing fits the sensationalized "muck-raking" appeal common in early 1900s urban journalism, a style that rubbed off on Lewis. Sinclair's *The Cup of Fury* stands with Charles Jackson's *Lost Weekend* as the most significant works on the tragedy of alcoholism.
3. James Lundquist, *Sinclair Lewis* (New York: Frederick Ungar, 1973), 9.
4. Ibid., 12. He could speak the cultural languages of both Eastern and Western U.S., much as another Minnesotan, Garrison Keillor, would late in the century.
5. Ibid., 23. He, Thomas Wolfe, and H. L. Mencken would drink so heavily that they would collapse at their own parties.
6. Schorer, *Sinclair Lewis,* 20. Gantry pontificates: "We shall yet make these United States a moral nation!"
7. Mark Schorer, "Afterword," in *Elmer Gantry,* by Sinclair Lewis (repr. ed., New York: Signet, 1980), 420ff. Birkhead founded "Sinclair Lewis's Sunday School Class," in which subjects like "The Holy Spirit" were discussed.
8. Lundquist, *Sinclair Lewis,* 107. In his Nobel Acceptance Address he took a nasty poke at William Dean Howells, the well-known critic, which reinforced his reputation as "the bad boy of national letters." Maxwell Geismar spoke of him as "the last frontier anarchist, with his desiccated visage, his rapier-like wit, his cold reptilian stare."

10.2.5 FITZGERALD, REBEL AGAINST CATHOLICISM

Again let me repeat that if you start any kind of a career following the footsteps of Cole Porter and Rodgers and Hart, it might be an excellent try. Sometimes I wish I had gone along with that gang, but I guess I am too much a moralist at heart, and really want to preach at people in some acceptable form rather than to entertain them.

—F. Scott Fitzgerald
letter to his daughter Scottie

Another Minnesotan, who sometimes has been called "the laureate of the Jazz Age," was Francis Scott Key Fitzgerald (1896–1940). He spoke both to and for his times. Fitzgerald was born in St. Paul into a devout Roman Catholic home. His mother had wealth but grieved the death of two daughters. The tragedy had caused a "branding effect" on the family psyche. As a very young person, he would pretend to be inebriated in outlandish places so he might identify with his heavy-drinking father. As part of fashionable St. Paul society, he attended St. Paul Academy and Newman School before going on to Princeton University. Ever in quest of a sense of identity, young Fitzgerald manifested "a defiant kind of autonomy."[1] He believed in the "limitless material promises of the American dream," so pervasive after World War I. Yet he was uneasy over the seductive qualities of that dream. He renounced his own foundation for truth, Catholicism, when he went to Princeton. He became close to Edmund Wilson, who would be an influential critic and writer.

While in the military, he met Zelda Sayre, daughter of an Alabama judge. They were married in 1920, over her father's objections to Fitzgerald because of his drinking. They lived a party life, and increasingly Zelda fell out of touch with reality. They had one daughter, then Zelda aborted her next baby, which caused Fitzgerald to suffer painful guilt.[2] While his gifted prose described the wild 1920s with "glittering characters, cynical and irresponsible, trying to turn life into an endless party,"[3] he had a sense that "something was desperately wrong" with this lifestyle. After Zelda's sexual unfaithfulness became known, the breach in their relationship was never repaired. They wandered back and forth between Europe and the U.S., and such friends as Ernest Hemingway livened up their existence. Despite her achievements in dance, Zelda attempted suicide on several occasions. There was just too much drinking, too much smoking, and too much arguing. She collapsed into schizophrenia and was in and out of hospitals for the rest of her life. He broke down in "psycho-neurotic depression" in 1934 and 1935, confessing his total emptiness. *Both Crack Up* (edited by Edmund Wilson) and *Tender Is the Night* come out of these wrenching experiences. *The Last Tycoon* was incomplete when he died of a heart attack in 1940 and, like all of his work, displays a pervasive sense of "transience and loss." He had never filled the vacuum left when he rejected his Irish Catholicism.

The Great Gatsby is probably his greatest novel and "the most penetrating depiction of life in America in the 1920s." It is brilliant and moving, yet elusive. Skillfully crafted and structured, the book uses a first-person narrator (as Joseph Conrad often did). The narrator, Nick Carraway, uncovers much corruption among the rich and the famous. Gatsby, a neighbor of Carraway, is an impressive host at glamorous parties for the rich set. He tells Nick that he has come back to reclaim Daisy, an old flame who is now the wife of the wealthy but cloddish Tom Buchanan. Carraway is weak, Daisy is without substance, and Gatsby, notwithstanding his noble death, is an "incoherent failure."[4] This grim story is T. S. Eliot's "wasteland." The "ineffable gaudiness" of this shallow world is all the more appalling, as only Gatsby's old father from the Midwestern farm and one other person attend his funeral. The dear old lines come to mind when we think of Gatsby and his creator, Fitzgerald, and the entire zeitgeist:

> If I gained the world and lost the Savior,
> Would my gain be worth the life-long strife;
> Are all earthly pleasure worth comparing
> For a moment with a Christ-filled life.
>
> —Anna Olander
> *Covenant Hymnal,* 1931 edition

For an unforgettable treatment of the Albany area of New York, try William Kennedy's "Albany Novels," starting with *Billy Phelan's Greatest Game,* then *Legs* and *Ironweed.* This Pulitzer Prize winner has also given us *Quinn's Book,* with a more remote background in the era. In *Ironweed,* we meet Francis Phelan, a man unable to forgive himself, who spends much time at the local rescue mission but never responds to the invitations he frequently hears. Said a reviewer, "Francis needs grace—but he asks for a turkey sandwich."[5]

1. Thomas J. Stavola, *Scott Fitzgerald: Crisis in an American Identity* (New York: Barnes and Noble, 1979), 34.

2. Benet, *Benet's Reader's Encyclopedia,* "Fitzgerald, F. Scott."

3. Ibid., 55. In this, he was much like his character Gatsby.

4. Ibid. Stavola sees *Gatsby* as a religious book, with his piercing short-story "Absolution" as its real introduction. Gatsby's quest led him into "a vast material wilderness of illusions." See also Ernest Lockridge, *Twentieth Century Interpretations of* The Great Gatsby (Englewood Cliffs, N.J.: Prentice-Hall, 1968), 83. Gatsby wins our grudging admiration, but he falls into egregious moral error.

5. *Christianity Today,* 13 May 1988, 63.

10.2.6 BUCK, REBEL IN STRANGE LANDS

> I am one of those unfortunate creatures who cannot function completely unless he (she) is writing, has written or is about to write a novel.
>
> —Pearl S. Buck

Pearl Buck (1892–1973) wrote more than seventy books, using virtually every literary genre. She was the most translated American author of her day, and everything she wrote seemed to make the best-seller lists. She won both the Pulitzer Prize and the Nobel Prize for Literature. Like John Hersey (1914–1993), whose *The Call* grapples with missions in China, and Henry Luce (1898–1967), founder of *Time* magazine, Pearl was the daughter of veteran China missionaries. She was a rebel who resented her parents and their Christianity. Yet she remains, as historian James Thompson observed, "the most influential Westerner to write about China since Marco Polo in the 13th century."

She was born in Hillsboro, West Virginia, and accompanied her parents to China. Her father, Absalom Sydenstricker, was one of six brothers (out of seven) who went into the ministry. Buck considered her father "a fanatic touched with apocalyptic fever," a "totally unreconstructed fundamentalist."[1] Ordained a Southern Presbyterian, he labored with his wife, Carie, even in the face of withering blasts against the motives and methods of missionary work. He learned several dialects of Chinese in order to preach to the people and became an authority on the language. He revised the Mandarin Old Testament. Pearl went back to China with her parents after the Boxer Rebellion and was raised there.

She returned to Lynchburg, Virginia, to study at Randolph-Macon College in 1914. Teaching at the University of Nanking, she met a Presbyterian agricultural missionary and graduate of Cornell University, John Lossing Buck. They were married in 1917. Their only child, Carol, born in 1920, was severely retarded, and Pearl Buck blamed her husband for the tragedy. She was increasingly critical of his research and ministry, as she was of her father's preaching. Always independent, she became more selfish and hostile to the missionary enterprise. She took a Chinese lover in the time before 1931 and the Japanese invasion of Manchuria.[2]

After she was saved by gunboats from the riots in Nanking, she began to write.

Her first novel, *East Wind, West Wind,* was immediately popular. In 1932 she returned to America, fell in love with her publisher, Richard Walsh, and married him. All of this contributed to splitting the Presbyterian Board of Missions into two competing bodies, one modernist or neoorthodox and one conservative. Buck found herself at the center of a vitriolic controversy, in which her father took after the latitudinarians, and she took up the cudgel against J. Gresham Machen (1881–1937), James Graham, and other conservatives.[3]

Her great trilogy on Chinese life, *The Good Earth, Sons,* and *A House Divided* was eagerly read, but not considered "great" literature by critics. However, no better exposure to rural Chinese life and the urgent need for the gospel of Christ can be found than in the lives of the farmer Wang Lung and his wife, O-lan, in *The Good Earth.* Her book about the war in China, *Dragon's Seed,* is a masterpiece. She wrote two and three books a year, and her husband "obediently" published them "as is." Some of her work is most worthwhile, such as *The Exile, Pavilion of Women, Peony* (about the Jewish colony at Kaifeng), and *The Living Reed* (about Korea).

She also had a liaison with Theodore Harris, who was forty years her junior, and an extended affair with ecumenical philosopher William Ernest Hocking of Harvard, the exponent of religious syncretism. She ultimately married Harris and put him in her will instead of her children, even though he was a drug smuggler, a child molester, and a financial crook. Her major biographer shows how Harris systematically enveloped her and alienated her from all of her friends. She finally retreated to Vermont. In her last illness with lung cancer in 1973, she called for the novels of Dickens.

---

1. Peter Conn, *Pearl S. Buck: A Cultural Biography* (New York: Cambridge University Press, 1996), 3. Her father developed a widely used correspondence course in preaching at Nanking University.
2. Ibid., 55. Carie was not happy on the field, particularly after two children died in China.
3. Ibid., 129, 134.

10.2.7 FAULKNER, REBEL WITHIN A CULTURE

She had been a big woman once but now her skeleton rose, draped loosely in unpadded skin that tightened again upon a paunch almost dropsical, as though muscle and tissue had been courage or fortitude which the days or the years had consumed until only the indomitable skeleton was left rising like a ruin or a landmark above the somnolent and impervious guts, and above that the collapsed face that gave the impression of the bones themselves being outside the flesh, lifted into the driving day with an expression at once fatalistic and of a child's astonished disappointment, until she turned and entered the house again and closed the door.

—William Faulkner
Dilsey in *The Sound and the Fury*

Another regional novelist, and this time from the buckle of the Bible Belt, is the Pulitzer and Nobel prizes winner William Faulkner (1897–1962). Born and raised in an old family in and around Oxford in northern Mississippi, Faulkner was only five feet, five inches tall. He wrote about the deep South in 119 novels and eighty short stories.[1] Not easy to read, he is fixated on the decline of the Southern aristocracy, their "lost innocence." An uneven writer, he wrote with a tragic intensity and a morbidity, using the James Joyce/Marcel Proust "stream of consciousness" technique. Therefore, he is often forbidding, and puts off readers by the violence of his depiction. Yet he deals with reality of life in a geographic area where nineteenth-century pietism was still "quite alive." He accepts Christian virtues as a given and yet was personally schizophrenic with respect to Christian faith.[2]

He joined the Canadian Air Force at the end of World War I, since he was too short for the U.S. military, but he saw no action. He briefly attended the University of Mississippi, Oxford. A very private person, he fed lustily on the poetry of Swinburne (7.4.4) and Housman (7.5.5).

In 1929 Faulkner married Estelle Oldham, a divorced woman with two children, to whom was born a daughter, Jill, in 1933. It was Jill who accompanied her father to Stockholm for his Nobel Prize acceptance speech in 1950. The death of an earlier child had led to a "notorious spree" of drinking and misbehavior.[3] He had been writing for some time and doing odd jobs to maintain economic viability. He even tried writing film scripts for the Hollywood studios without success. Halfway through his third novel, he decided to "create his own cosmos," and thus he invented Yoknapatawpha County with its county seat, Jefferson, 15,611 black residents and 6,298 white residents. This fictional stage was set eighty miles south of Memphis in the rolling pine hills of Mississippi.[4] Although Baptists actually predominate over the Presbyterians and Methodists, Presbyterians are prime movers in this world. Faulkner wanted the flavor of predestination and total depravity in large doses, and he wanted to emphasize the Scotch-Irish origin of the inhabitants.[5] In his *Light in August,* he attacks Protestant excess.

The Sound and the Fury (1929) is probably his best work, and the one volume I believe should be read. Behind this title borrowed from Macbeth, Faulkner tells about the Compson family, once rich landowners in Jefferson. The family has lost its ethical and spiritual center and is in ruins. No longer important, Mr. Compson is a heavy drinker with a philosophy of negation; Mrs. Compson is a hypochondriac and never really a mother to her children. Son Benji cannot speak and is regarded as *non compos mentis.* Quentin, a Harvard student, commits suicide in despondency over his sister Caddy's seduction and her hasty marriage and disappearance from their lives. Jason is one of the most vicious characters in all of literature.[6] In all of this, there is little trace of Christian doctrine, the church, or "formalized belief,"[7] except in the black cook, Dilsey, for whom the values of eternity are the guiding star of life. She is simple but whole.[8] For thirty years, she has been the real mother in the family, keeping things together. Although his record on matters racial is mottled, Faulkner gives a beautiful picture of Dilsey. She takes Benji to the black church on Easter where the black preacher from St. Louis preaches a magnificent sermon, which she shares and which only Benji, on this weekend of his thirty-third birthday, really hears.[9]

Faulkner claimed that Christianity had never hurt him and that "probably . . . within my own rights I'm a good Christian."[10] He was certainly no churchman but did mine the Bible for themes, all the while detesting people who submitted to its authority. Later, he gives another "take" on the Compsons in *Absalom, Absalom!* and in a famous trilogy shares the lives of the Snopes family. By this time, his writing is declining. His later *Fable* is an allegory of Christ's passion week. Again we confront the inescapable cross. Faulkner, with all of his trifling with the biblical heritage, which was so rich and rife in his culture, repudiates redeeming grace as impossible. He rejects all creeds, for "each man must be his own redeemer."[11] And yet *The Sound and the Fury* ends with Easter and the Resurrection.

---

1. All of Faulkner's major works were done in a ten-year period.
2. William Van O'Connor, *William Faulkner* (Minneapolis: University of Minnesota Press, 1959), 10. The exhaustive Faulkner resource is still Joseph Blotner's monumental two-volume study, *William Faulkner: A Biography* (New York: Random House, 1991). See also Thomas S. Hine's fine work, *William Faulkner and the Tangible Past* (Berkeley, Calif.: University of California Press, 1996).
3. Lewis Leary, *William Faulkner of Yoknapatawpha County* (New York: Crowell, 1973), 33.
4. "The Curse and the Hope," *Time,* 17 July 1964, 44ff. One of *Time's* best features on an author.
5. O'Connor, *William Faulkner,* 20.
6. Leary, *William Faulkner,* 54. After Mr. Compson dies, Jason as head of the family has Benji castrated. Caddy has been gone by this time for nineteen years.
7. Chilton Williamson Jr., "The Unsovereign Artist," *Chronicles of Culture,* December 1989, 36.
8. Leary, *William Faulkner,* 58.
9. Ibid., 62. See also William R. Mueller, *The Prophetic Voice in Modern Fiction* (New York: Association, 1959). The essential action in *The Sound and the Fury* takes place from Good Friday, April 6, to Easter Sunday, April 8, in 1929.
10. "The Unsovereign Artist," 38. Williamson shows that Faulkner did have a great love for, and knowledge of, the Old Testament.
11. Leary, *William Faulkner,* 199. Here is the echo of the Emersonian "autonomous man" so important to North Americans.

10.2.8 HEMINGWAY, REBEL WITH CLASHING CRESCENDO

If people bring so much courage to this world the world has to kill them to break them, so of course it kills them. The world breaks every one and afterward many are strong at the broken places. But those that will not break it kills. It kills the very good and the very gentle and the very brave impartially. If you are none of these you can be sure it will kill you, too, but there will be no special hurry.

—Ernest Hemingway
A Farewell to Arms

Another Pulitzer and Nobel prize winning novelist who commands center stage in American fiction is Ernest Hemingway (1899–1961). The Christian turns with aversion from much in Hemingway, but he has much to teach us. A Byronic hero, this artist-adventurer is the macho hunter and fisherman who strides forward in brash cacophony. His four unsuccessful marriages and his suicide make him a tragic figure, especially when we consider his roots and background. His spare writing style without the excess baggage of too many adjectives and adverbs uses powerful verbs and nouns to capture us. His testimony was: "I live in a vacuum that is as lonely as a radio tube when the battery is dead and there is no current to plug into."

Hemingway's grandparents studied at Wheaton College in the 1860s.[1] His paternal grandfather was general secretary of the YMCA in Oak Park, Illinois, a suburb just west of Chicago, and a friend of D. L. Moody. His father, Dr. Clarence "Ed" Hemingway, was a general practitioner in Oak Park who had wanted to go overseas as a medical missionary. He was rigid, "piercingly intelligent," and an outdoorsman. His wife, Grace, a Sunday school teacher and lover of beauty and flowers, gave up a career in opera for her husband and family, but she drew the line there. Ernest's maternal grandfather (Abba) lived in the home and conducted "strong" daily worship. He said of his grandson: "He'll be famous or in jail."[2]

His mother dressed him as a little girl until he was three. He deeply loved his father and "his unhypocritical life."[3] Raised in a conservative Congregational church, Ernest faithfully read his Bible and memorized Scripture. He rebelled mightily in high school, twice running away from home. He refused to go to college. Instead, he went to Kansas City to work as a journalist but didn't go to church. Reapplying a traditional Congregational Church line of reasoning to an extreme, he assured his mother in a letter, "not to worry. . . . I believe in God and Jesus Christ. . . . Creeds don't matter."[4]

Hemingway was wounded in the World War I Battle of Caporetto, Italy, where he was a volunteer ambulance driver.[5] He was one of 320,000 casualties, an enormous toll even for this bloody war. He came home shell-shocked and drinking to relieve the pain. He retreated to Northern Michigan to the family hideaway to write short stories. By age twenty-five, he had split with his parents. His mother would not see him and detested his divorces, his "filthy books," and just about everything else about him. His father, suffering from acute diabetes, shot himself. Ernest blamed his mother for the suicide. "I will not see her. . . . I hate her," he raged.[6] The bitterness was mutual. On one birthday, his mother mailed a birthday cake to him—enclosing the pistol his father had used to kill himself.

Officially he converted to Roman Catholicism after World War I, but he admitted he was a "rotten Catholic." Fiercely competitive, violently breaking one friendship after another, he lived increasingly in "a sense of hostile isolation." His literary output was small: six novels, a novella, and fifty-five short stories. Much influenced by Gertrude Stein and Ezra Pound, his style was "new and clean," evoking physical sensations, throbbing with the rhythms of the King James Bible.[7] Although Ahabesque at points, he is more in tune with the philosophies of Emerson and Whitman than with Melville and Hawthorne.[8]

Of special interest is *The Sun Also Rises* (1926), an autobiographical account of his empty, Bohemian existence in Spain, set against the running of the bulls at

Pamplona. Also excellent are *A Farewell to Arms* (1929), about the Italian campaign in World War I, and *For Whom the Bell Tolls* (1940), his most ambitious novel, about the Spanish Civil War. He had become thoroughly humanist, with no doctrine of sin and "no crazed need for redemption."[9]

The book that *must* be read is his novella, *The Old Man and the Sea,* which was made into a memorable movie starring Spencer Tracy. Written in Cuba near Havana, it is structurally simple, telling the story of the old fisherman, Santiago, and his three-day fishing expedition. He has failed to make a catch for eighty-four days, and his young friend, Manolin, is no longer allowed by his parents to go with him. Now, however, he ventures forth and catches a great marlin.

First published in *Life* Magazine and sold through Book-of-the-Month Club, the book is open to a variety of interpretations. Some see it as reflecting Hemingway's own lonely struggle. Others read it as picturing humanity's fight against natural forces. When William Faulkner read it, he exclaimed: "Hemingway has found God!"[10] Critic Gerry Brenner concedes that a Christian symbolism possibly surfaces in the work.[11] Certainly Christianity haunts Hemingway's background; Santiago in his ordeal does think of sin.[12] His wounded hands are prominent, and he makes an expression which "is just a noise such as a man might make, involuntarily, feeling the nail go through his hands and into the wood."[13]

Earl Rovit sees the passion of Christ in the bullfighting and prizefighting that loom in Hemingway's plots. "Today is Friday," observes Santiago.[14] In the distance of Ernest Hemingway's stories, we occasionally sense the distant baying of the "Hound of Heaven," and the rebel's forced turning to face the cross of Christ.

---

1. Daniel Pawley, "Ernest Hemingway: Tragedy of an Evangelical Family," *Christianity Today,* 23 November 1984, 20. This is a remarkably insightful study.

2. Ibid., 22. His brother Willoughby went to China as a medical missionary. Ernest, on the other hand, was diagnosed as a "manic-depressive." He seemed to lack conscience or moral code.

3. Ibid., 24. He spoke of his father as his "boyhood hero." His parents were stoutly against modern amusements. Their strongest language was "O rats!"

4. Ibid.

5. Ibid., 26.

6. Earl Rovit, *Ernest Hemingway* (Boston: Twayne, 1963), 20.

7. Ibid., 24–25.

8. Ibid., 169. His writing style can be characterized as "terse," with dramatic understatement and great dialogue. Hemingway's books have many layers and remind us of Robert Maynard Hutchins's dictum: The greater the book, the more divergent the possible interpretations.

9. Ibid., 122. At this stage of life, he didn't seem to need any help or anyone at all. He always regarded suicide as the abrogation of the rules, yet took his own life.

10. "Tragedy of an Evangelical Family," 27.

11. Gerry Brenner, *The Old Man and the Sea: Story of a Common Man* (New York: Twayne, 1991), 18, 37.

12. Ernest Hemingway, *The Old Man and the Sea* (New York: Scribner's, 1952), 105.

13. Ibid., 107. This work was for a long time staple fare in high school literature classes. Passing out of vogue now.
14. Rovit, *Ernest Hemingway*, 31. "I am a strange old man," Santiago says. This character has a mysterious tone.

10.2.9 STEINBECK, REBEL IN A TIME OF COLLAPSE

This you may say of man—when theories change and crash, when schools, philosophies, when narrow dark alleys of thought, national, religious, economic, grow and disintegrate, man reaches, stumbles forward, painfully, mistakenly sometimes. Having stepped forward, he may slip back, but only half a step, never the full step back.

—John Steinbeck

If I was still a preacher I'd say the arm of the Lord had struck. But now I don't know what's happened.

—John Steinbeck
Jim Casy in *The Grapes of Wrath*

Arguably the writer of the best stories published in the 1930s, John Steinbeck (1902–1968) was born in the great Salinas Valley, the lettuce capitol of the world, just south of the San Francisco Bay area in California. A regional writer who did his best work in California, he wrote novels of the proletariat—stories about the oppressed underdog. His *The Grapes of Wrath* is the great novel of the Depression.

A winner of the Pulitzer and Nobel prizes, Steinbeck is an example of a naturalistic author who would not commit himself to any cause. He rejected teleological thinking, believing that there is no purpose or goal toward which history is moving. He chooses not to think about what *ought to be* and concentrating on what *is*. Steinbeck's father was a prominent miller and the treasurer of Monterey County; his mother taught school. From 1920 to 1925, he attended Stanford University, majoring in marine biology, but he never took his degree. He wrote for the *Stanford Spectator* and, between intermittent bouts with his studies, "worked on ranches, joined a road-building gang, worked in the laboratory of a sugar-beet factory, and even helped build Madison Square Garden."[1]

His marriages failed, and his early work was not received positively. His first success, *Tortilla Flat* (1935), is about bums and loafers on the Monterey Peninsula. Steinbeck is at his best describing down-and-outers. The novel describes defeat and "a shrewd ribbing of those who live 'lives of quiet desperation' and whose undiscriminating response to the barbaric makes them even more despicable than the untutored savage."[2] He achieved notice for his bitterly ironic fable *Of Mice and Men* (1937). The work was shaped by the Arthurian legend. The Bible was a more formative influence on his next work, *The Grapes of Wrath*.

He experienced lean years and tried to regain his footing with *Cannery Row* (1945) and *East of Eden*. The latter seeks to trace the migration of his mother's people, the Hamiltons, in their move to the Salinas Valley. Consciously based on the Cain and Abel story in Genesis, the book wrestles with the issue of free will versus determinism. The action falters, though, because Steinbeck "cannot face unblinkingly the consequences of an unchecked lust for power."[3] He avoided reality with his characters and finally went back to being a news correspondent.

In all of his writing, he treats the middle-class roughly and makes no kind references to the organized church.[4]

The Grapes of Wrath is about the Joad family, "Okies" who flee to California from certain death in dust-bowl Oklahoma. The book has been called "The *Uncle Tom's Cabin* of the twentieth century." The Joads are not really upright or lovable people, but they are human beings. The family teeters on disintegration as they experience the death of Grandpa and Grandma (who is unceremoniously buried in the Mojave Desert). They arrive in Bakersfield and commence their scratch existence as sharecroppers, picking cotton. Jim Casy, the former preacher, is a kind of fulcrum in the action. Notice his initials are J. C., as are the initials of another Steinbeck character, Juan Chicoy, in *The Wayward Bus*.

Steinbeck stands in the Emerson and Whitman tradition and seems aware of the Hemingway shadow everywhere. Even his use of the Bible is rhythmical like Hemingway's.[5] Holding to a relativistic view of sin, Steinbeck unloads against the irrelevance of organized religion in general and the Salvation Army in particular.[6] Former orthodox preacher Jim Casy has given up the gospel for Emerson's "oversoul," as we hear:

> Ain't got the call no more. Got a lot of sinful idears—but they seem kinda sensible. Why do we got to hang it on God or Jesus? Maybe it's men an' all women we love; maybe that's the Holy Spirit—the human spirit— the whole shebang. Maybe all men got one big soul ever'body's apart of.[7]

Nowhere can the influence of Emerson be experienced more overtly. Steinbeck is easy to read and abounds with concrete metaphors. Yet his masterpiece epitomizes our dilemma. Will Rose of Sharon succeed Ma as the strong woman? Will the family survive? In his controversial final paragraphs, he does not give a clue. But how, with his naturalistic system, could he tell?

Some have seen much Christian symbolism, even the Eucharist, here.[8] If so, Steinbeck never got to the point when the elements of faith were more than literary motifs.

In this tradition, do not overlook J. D. Salinger (b. 1919), who wrote the powerful *Catcher in the Rye*[9] about a confused adolescent, Holden Caulfield, who went underground in New York City for forty-eight hours in a desperate effort to "find himself." In his *Franny and Zooey* (1961), he grapples with Jesus. Strangely, Salinger stopped writing and lived as a recluse from the mid-1960s. Another writer who bears observation is John Irving, whose surprising *The Prayer of Owen Meany*[10] includes the confession: "I am doomed to remember a boy with a wrecked voice— not because of his voice or because he was the smallest person I ever knew, or even because he was the instrument of my mother's death, but because he is the reason I believe in God; I am a Christian because of Owen Meany."[11]

1. Warren French, *John Steinbeck* (New York: Twayne, 1961), 21. Steinbeck was a private person.
2. Ibid., 61. Danny, the pseudo-hero, turns out to be a totally "anarchic personality."
3. Ibid., 156. A leading character, Cathy Trask, is a wayward wife and successful brothel-keeper, who in the end takes her own life (153).
4. Ibid., 56. Critics see Steinbeck's works as "marred by intense sentimentality."
5. Harold Bloom, ed., introduction to *John Steinbeck's* The Grapes of Wrath (New York: Chelsea House, 1988), 2.
6. French, *John Steinbeck,* 108f. In *The Wayward Bus,* the inscription on the bus "the great power of Jesus" has been painted over to read simply "Sweetheart" and also "repent" has faded on the rock. Christianity supplanted?
7. Frederic I. Carpenter, "The Philosophical Joads," in *John Steinbeck's* The Grapes of Wrath, 8. Erskine Caldwell's *Tobacco Road* is another very gut-grinding study. Impoverished Jeeter Lester and his family in Georgia are moving characters.
8. Mimi Reisel Gladstein, "The Indestructible Women: Ma Joad and Rose of Sharon," in *John Steinbeck's* The Grapes of Wrath, 124.
9. New York: Signet, 1945.
10. New York: William Morrow, 1989.
11. Ibid., 13. The book was basis for a film in the 1990s, *Simon Burch.*

10.3 STEADYING AND BALANCING INFLUENCES

That there had been an unimaginable, unprecedented moral degeneration, no one who looked at the facts could deny.

—Paul Johnson
Modern Times: The World from the Twenties to the Eighties

Culture as a whole has become secular in a way that it has never been before.

—Louis Dupré

Brilliant and acclaimed writers have shown us the Enlightenment influences of their nihilism and relativism. They are, for the most part, devotees of "the American religion," as the late Allan Bloom called it—"Emersonian gnosticism." This filters down to everyday life in the outlook of one John Tollefson, of whom Garrison Keillor writes in a recent novel:

In the midst of plenty, it occurs to John that his life lacks nobility and grace. A consumer of fine food and wine and a giver of good parties, he yet has no coherent life story. Compared to his great-grandfather John Tollefson, who finagled his way from Norway, he feels rootless, restless, joined in no struggle, with nothing at stake. The only true magnificence in his life is Alida, who eludes his courtship and gives him an impassioned speech about the pleasures of living alone.[1]

Strenuous protests against the absurdists, minimalists, and "K-Mart realists," who have dominated the writing of fiction since the 1960s, have been lodged by those who lament the lack of moral vision in today's literature.[2] We turn now to a company of novelists who register greater concern with "first things" in various ways.

---

1. Garrison Keillor, *Wobegon Boy* (New York: Viking, 1997), cover copy. Although Keillor has strayed from his evangelical roots, he is a consummate storyteller and worth reading or hearing on his Public Radio programs.
2. Such as Tom Wolfe in *The Bonfire of the Vanities*. Interesting resort to the imagery of Ecclesiastes in the Bible.

10.3.1 PERCY, DIAGNOSTICIAN

I need not warn you, I am sure, of the dangers of overacculturation. We know what happened to some of the mainline Protestant denominations who are attuned to the opinion polls, so to speak, and trim their sails accordingly as the winds of culture shift. Instead of serving as the yeast which leavens the cultural lump, they tend to disappear in the culture. By remaining faithful to its original commission, by serving people with love, especially the poor, the lonely and the dispossessed, and by not surrendering its doctrinal steadfastness, sometimes even the very contradiction of culture by which it serves as a sign, surely the Church serves culture best.

—Walker Percy
"Morality and Religion"

In a sense, a Southern regional writer Walker Percy (1916–1990) is in fact much larger than that.[1] He was convinced that significant poets and novelists write about God.[2] His friend, Shelby Foote, worried that Percy's faith as a Catholic convert subverted his art.[3] Philip Yancey quotes Percy as saying that "the Christian novelist nowadays is like a man who has found a treasure hidden in the attic of an old house, but he is writing for people who have moved out to the suburbs and who are bloody sick of the old house and everything in it."[4]

Percy was outspoken in his opposition to abortion. His faith in God is resolute, and he subscribes to orthodoxy. But one hankers for just a word about Christ the Redeemer. He wrote six apocalyptic novels and several pieces of nonfiction worthy of reading.

Percy was born in Birmingham, Alabama, into upper-class Southern society. The family had opposed secession but fought loyally for the Confederacy. His father died by his own hand, and his mother was killed in an auto accident. Young Walker pressed on to receive his M.D. from Columbia University's College of Physicians and Surgeons in New York City. His peers enlisted for the war in 1941, but Percy was confined to a tuberculosis sanitarium in Lake Saranac, New York, probably the result of performing autopsies on derelicts during his residency. As he convalesced, he grappled with the question of why sophisticated Germany would spawn the likes of Hitler. In his study, he discovered Søren Kierkegaard (1813–1855; see 5.14).

Percy wrote extensively on philosophy, psychiatry, and linguistics. After the war, he married, converted to Catholicism, and began to raise a family. He particularly devoted himself to his daughter Ann, who was deaf from childhood. He also taught at Loyola and Louisiana State.[5]

Combining Christian morality with great storytelling, Percy wrote satirical novels about the decay within Western culture and the symptomatic weariness, boredom, cynicism, and greed. Indeed, like Thomas Mann, he saw tuberculosis or consumption as "a metaphor for the state of western culture." In his striking novels *The Moviegoer, Lancelot,* and *The Last Gentleman,* the heroes show that the problem in culture is truly the projection of their own inner ruin.

Writing his first novel at age forty-five, Percy still had time to produce a rich trove. He incisively slashes away at the practitioners of scientism, behaviorists, and spiritualists. In Percy's final work, *The Thanatos Syndrome,* Father Rinaldo Smith shouts at Dr. Tom More:

> You are a member of the first generation of doctors in the history of medicine to turn their backs on the oath of Hippocrates and kill millions of old useless people, unborn children, born malformed children, for the good of mankind—and to do so without a single murmur from one of you. Not a single letter of protest in the August *New England Journal of Medicine.*[6]

In this book, Dr. More, a lapsed Catholic and a heavy drinker, has just come back to the Feliciana parish in Louisiana after serving two years in prison for selling amphetamines illegally. His wife, Ellen, is now a champion bridge player and a tongues-speaking charismatic. Percy still sees the Christian gospel of grace as offering hope. Soulless technology certainly does not have the answer.

My favorite of his novels, *The Second Coming,* continues the story of Will Barret, who first appeared in *The Last Gentleman.* Barret is an autobiographical character, who carries Percy's comparison of the late-twentieth-century West with the decadence and desperation of the Weimar Republic before Hitler's rise to power. This cultural diagnosis founded upon his "Judeo-Christian notion that humanity is more than an organism in an environment, more than an integrated personality, more even than a mature and creative individual. . . . He is a wayfarer and a pilgrim."

Percy endured "solitary funks and strange elations," but he stoutly held to the possibility of communication. In his more technical study, he believed with many neurologists that "the self is in the language area of the cortex."[7]

He also was one of the few observers who believed that anthropologist Margaret Mead (1901–1978) had been led far astray in *Coming of Age in Samoa,* when she described the people as innocent, happy, and Edenic until the coming of missions and technology. Later studies of Samoa and Mead's methodology proved Percy correct in this assessment. Rather they were (and are) as neurotic and sinful as anyone else and candidates for divine grace.[8] He urged amid stories of sexual scandals among evangelists during the late twentieth century that charlatans do not disprove the existence of God.[9]

Walker Percy was a spiritual voice among the twentieth century's arid bards; his presence is missed.

---

1. Other regional writers who exceed boundaries are the New Englanders John Cheever, *The Wapshot Chronicle* (New York: Harper, 1954); and John P. Marquand, *Wickford Point* (New York: Little, Brown, 1939) and *The Late George Apley* (New York: Little, Brown, 1936). Cheever deftly exposes the immorality in affluent suburbia. Marquant shows Boston "Brahmins" and their aristocratic and "Puritan" ways. Cheever never sought forgiveness. He never really asked God for help, although he tried to bow himself before him. Thus he always felt alone.

2. Patrick Samway, ed., *Signposts in a Strange Land* (Farrar, Strauss, 1991), 161.

3. Jay Tolson, ed., *The Correspondence of Shelby Foote and Walker Percy* (New York: Norton, 1997).

4. Philip Yancey, "A Whiff of Something Lethal," *Christianity Today,* 22 October 1990, 72.

5. The best biographies are Jay Tolson, *Pilgrim in the Ruins: A Life of Walker Percy* (New York: Simon and Schuster, 1992); and Patrick H. Samway, *Walker Percy: A Life* (New York: Farrar, Strauss, 1997).

6. From Walker Percy, *The Thanatos Syndrome* (New York: Farrar, 1987), 127–28.

7. Samway, *Walker Percy,* 391. Percy saw ours as "The time of *thanatos* (death)" both in and beyond our culture.

8. Ibid., 395. He loved to quote Churchill on democracy—"vicissitudinous, yes—but look at the alternatives."

9. Ibid., 159. Percy insists on pursuing deep spiritual and philosophical inquiries.

10.3.2 HURSTON, CLINICIAN

I have been in sorrow's kitchen and licked all the pots.

—Zora Neale Hurston

Writing from within the Western racial struggles of the twentieth century, Zora Neale Hurston (1901?–1960) represents an oppressed community with strong biblical and Christian affirmations. Hurston wrote before the turbulent civil rights days of the 1960s, but she was, despite her conservatism on segregation, a protowriter for the genre of African-American literature.[1] Hurston was part of the "Harlem Renaissance," to which we were introduced in Langston Hughes (8.2.6).

She was born in the all-black community of Eatonville in central Florida, where, through her early years, she listened to her father preach at Macedonia Baptist Church. She left home at age nine after her mother died and became a maid for a traveling troupe of actors. She finished high school in Baltimore and then studied at Howard University, finally graduating from Barnard College in 1928. Often she had only one dress and one pair of shoes.

She was accepted as protegé to the Columbia University anthropologist, Franz Boas, and gave herself to the study of African-American folkways. She was initiated into voodoo so she could better grasp its grassroots appeal. She received a Guggenheim Fellowship to study black customs in Jamaica and Haiti. Described by biographers as "a woman in the shadows," she was "without ideology."

Her four novels, two folklore studies (including an incomparable work called *Mules and Men*), and her autobiography are not lectures on the vexatious race problem. She does not write as a social visionary.[2] Rather she seems to be sitting on the porch of the general store listening to "the men-folks having a 'lying' session. That is, straining against each other in telling folk tales. God, Devil, Brer Rabbit, Brer Fox, Sis Cat, Brer Lion, Tiger, Buzzard, and all the woodfolk walked and talked like natural men."[3] Social activists faulted her conservative political stand. She was suspicious of communism, wrote favorably of the conservative Robert A. Taft (1889–1953), and condemned the U.S. Supreme Court's action in *Brown v. Board of Education*. She said the demand for interracial education demeaned the achievements of black teachers.

After a brief marriage, she returned to the South. She celebrated the wholeness and uniqueness of the black people even as she wrote of the "Negro farthest down." She was falsely accused in a morals case, and her great work on *Herod* was turned down by publishers.

This great storyteller came to a tragic end, without seeing her worth recognized. In her last days, she had no money and went uncared for, living alone with her dog in a block house after suffering a stroke. Malnutrition hastened her death. She was buried in an unmarked grave until Alice Walker discovered it and placed a stone. Something of a revival of Hurston as a novelist followed.

Two of her novels are particularly recommended. In *Jonah's Gourd Vine* (1934), we read of the rise and fall of a great black preacher, clearly patterned after her own father. "Rev-un" Pearson could really preach, but he was sorely tempted "by the enticements of the flesh."[4] In her vivid metaphysical style, Hurston helps us to hear the preacher's voice. We get something of his sermon on creation and his marvelous message on the "Wounds of Jesus" from Zechariah 13:6, which is very strong on Christ's death. He preached powerfully on the "dry bones" of Ezekiel 37.[5] Rev. Cozy gave a lecture not a sermon in attempting to displace Rev. Pearson. The black preacher is a poet, as well as the bearer of the Word. The community clings to him. Yet everyone knows that Lucy, Pearson's first wife, is really the strong figure.

Her *Moses, Man of the Mountain* is a great retelling of the Exodus story in the black vernacular (1939). But the other novel which must be read is *Their Eyes Were Watching God* (1937), which tells the story of Janie and her three husbands. Each of these husbands is a fascinating character, especially the last, Teacake.[6] Hurston has a way of walking right into our hearts.

The thirties were Hurston's meridian, and she found acceptance increasingly difficult. Yet there is such a commanding winsomeness, despite the poverty and obscurity. As her character Janie, she has learned that there are "two things everybody's got tuh do fuh theyselves. They got tuh go to God, and they got tuh find out about livin' fuh theyselves."[7]

█ **Also notable as a** later black woman novelist is Nobel Prize winning Toni Morrison (b. 1931).[8] Some of the best ethnic folk writing, however, describes the Latino community through the eyes of Oscar Hijuelos. His remarkable *Mr. Ives' Christmas* is the story of an exceedingly religious man of considerable success whose seventeen-year-old son is gunned down at Christmas time.[9] We feel New York City and many things Hispanic as this dear one seems overwhelmed with grief. He faces the young man who took his own son's life. This is a powerful and poignant work. Hijuelos is a major novelist.

---

1. For an invaluable survey of the height of the racial struggle in the United States, see Taylor Branch, *Pillar of Fire: America in the King Years 1963–65* (New York: Simon and Schuster, 1998). This is a sequel to Branch's work, *Parting of the Waters*.
2. Nick Aaron Ford, "A Meeting with Zora Neale Hurston," in *Zora Neale Hurston*, ed. Harold Bloom (New York: Chelsea House, 1986), 8. She said, "I have ceased to think in terms of race; I think only in terms of individuals."
3. Robert E. Hemenway, "That Which the Soul Lives By" in *Zora Neale Hurston*, 84. Hurston is the best-informed folklorist on pre-World War II black North America.
4. Larry Neal, "The Spirituality of *Jonah's Gourd Vine*," in *Zora Neale Hurston*, 26. Promiscuity finally destroys John Pearson.
5. Zora Neale Hurston, *Novels and Stories* (New York: Library of America, 1995), 133, 144.
6. Zora Neale Hurston, *Their Eyes Were Watching God* (New York: Harper and Row, 1937).
7. For an overview of the whole Southern cultural picture, see Christine Leigh Heyrman, *Southern Cross: The Beginnings of the Bible Belt* (New York: Knopf, 1997). She focuses on "the hot gospel" of the Baptists and Methodists.
8. For a review of *Paradise Found*, the most recent Toni Morrison novel at the time of this writing, see the coverage by Paul Gray in *Time*, 19 January 1998, 63ff.
9. New York: Harper/Collins, 1995.

10.3.3 O'CONNOR, PHYSICIAN

Push back against the age as hard as it pushes against you.
What people don't realize is how much religion costs. They think faith is a big electric blanket, when of course it is the cross.

—Flannery O'Connor

Alfred Kazin called her "the best woman writer of this time." (Mary) Flannery O'Connor (1925–1964) was born in Savannah, Georgia, and raised as a devout Catholic on a farm near Milledgeville. She was graduated from the Women's College of Georgia and then received her M.F.A. degree from the writing program at the University of Iowa in 1947. Here she read voraciously and began to write. Allen Tate told her to "write about what you know." The first six chapters of *Wise Blood* won her a prize and were her dissertation. Influential were T. S. Eliot,

William Faulkner, and Nathanael West.[1] After another year as a student assistant in Iowa City, she was invited to join a writer's colony near Saratoga Springs, New York; but in 1950, she returned to the farm in Georgia for good after a vicious onslaught of the hereditary autoimmune disease lupus erythematosus, a deterioration of the bones, that eventually took her life at age thirty-nine.

One cannot help but wonder what extended years might have seen in terms of production. Here is a writer who writes more as a Christian than as a Catholic. She is an example of "Southern Gothic," one who discerned "the orthodox virtues of backwoods preachers."[2] The South of which she writes is "Christ-haunted." She was blunt, with a vibrant streak of humor, yet doesn't spare reader sensibilities from jarring violence in each of her novels and short stories. The theme of her writing is "conversion," the precondition to which is often "loss" or disastrous difficulty.[3] Her literary output was not large, but she wrote unashamedly from the standpoint of "Christian orthodoxy," by which she meant that "the meaning of life is centered in our Redemption by Christ."[4] She writes as one who believes that absolute truth exists. She has been lionized and canonized as a sterling example of the Christian writer, the "Joan of Arc."[5]

She despised religious liberalism, feeling a much deeper affinity for Protestant fundamentalists than for Protestant liberals:

> One of the effects of modern liberal Protestantism has been gradually to turn religion into poetry and therapy, to make truth vaguer and vaguer and more and more relative, to banish intellectual distinctions, to depend on feeling instead of thought, and gradually to come to believe that God has no power, that he cannot communicate with us, cannot reveal himself to us, indeed has not done so and that religion is our own sweet invention.[6]

As Jill P. Baumgaertner observes, "In O'Connor's works one is always pushed back to the agonizing scandal of the cross."[7] Caroline Gordon, the Kentucky novelist, sent O'Connor's work to J. F. Powers, terming it "Kafkaesque." Powers wrote back that Kafka was not in O'Connor's league.[8]

High Blood is about Hazel Motes who established his automobile-based "Church of Truth Without Jesus Christ Crucified." Her novel *The Violent Bear It Away* is based on Matthew 11:12. This work traces the strange decadence of a family into three generations. Her short stories are sparklingly written but solemn.[9] We need to read this writer, who expressed amazement that so many of the *literati,* especially English professors and critics, knew so little about Christianity.

For a penetrating analysis of the course of the United States (and to a large extent Canada) at the end of the twentieth century, I would strongly recommend Professor Garry Wills's *Under God: Religion and American Politics.*[10] Wills states: "The Bible is not going to stop being the central book in our intellectual heritage."[11] He argues that the cultural foundation is evangelical Protestantism and that "an understanding of Christian prophecy will be more needed, not less, in the next few years."[12] Also rewarding is Paul Johnson, *A History of the American People.*[13]

1. Nathanael West wrote *The Day of the Locust* (1939), the classic description of Hollywood and filmmaking.
2. Patrick Samway, ed., *Signposts in a Strange Land* (New York: Farrar, Strauss, 1991), 159. Two other striking Southern writers are Harper Lee and her remarkable *To Kill a Mockingbird* (1960) and Marjorie Kinnan Rawlins, whose *The Yearling* and her autobiographical *Cross Creek* (1942) speak out of her life in the backwoods of Florida. Very dear.
3. Jill P. Baumgaertner, "'The Meaning Is in You': Flannery O'Connor in Her Letters," *The Christian Century*, 23 December 1987, 1172. For many of these years, she was on crutches and traveled only with excruciating pain.
4. Sally Fitzgerald, introduction to *Three by Flannery O'Connor* (New York: Signet, 1983), xxi.
5. James Calvin Schaap, "On Truth, Fiction and Being a Christian Writer," *The Christian Century*, 17 December 1997.
6. "'The Meaning Is in You,'" 1174. She greatly distrusted feelings in matters relating to faith.
7. Ibid., 1175. Her mother, who ran the farm, had a great influence on her daughter and carefully read all of her work.
8. J. F. Powers is another Roman Catholic writer. His short stories are outstanding. See *Lions, Harts, Leaping Does and Other Stories* (New York: Time Reading Program, 1963). Powers's *Wheat That Springeth Green* (New York: Knopf, 1988) is one of the better twentieth-century clergy novels. His writings also include the books of short stories *From the Presence of Grace* (1947) and *The Prince of Darkness* (1956).
9. The collection of O'Connor's short stories is *Three by Flannery O'Connor*. The lead story is "Everything That Rises Must Converge." These are just great.
10. New York: Simon and Schuster, 1990.
11. Ibid., 124.
12. Ibid., 24.
13. New York: Harper, 1998. We must not forget the Southern treasure Eudora Welty, storyteller extraordinaire. Just out is Ann Waldro's *Eudora: A Writer's Life* (New York: Doubleday, 1998).

10.3.4 HELPRIN, HISTORIAN

> Some people like to eat maggots. We in the West have a culture going back thousands of years, and it doesn't include eating maggots. We have certain tastes and assumptions we want met, and that goes for literature. In terms of the history of Western literature, this stuff (the minimalist school of writing) is a departure just as maggots would be if they were served at an inaugural dinner.
>
> —Mark Helprin

Reading much modern fiction is like eating maggots. The language is so crass and the obsession with sexuality so pronounced that there are more nutrients in the garbage dump. The altogether formless and shapeless literature "with no plot, no climax, no denouement; no beginning, no middle and no end" (Kenneth Tynan's description of Samuel Beckett's *Waiting for Godot*) would find its counterpart in some modern art, music, and cinema.[1] One instance of a gifted writer refusing to be a "pack writer" is the novelist, short story writer, and editor, Mark Helprin.[2]

Helprin grew up in New York City and obtained his B.A. and M.A. from Harvard University, doing postgraduate study at Magdalen College, Oxford University. He served with the Israeli army and air force. Besides his own three collections of short stories, *Ellis Island, A Dove of the East,* and *Refiner's Fire,* his novels *Winter's Tale* and *Memoir from an Antproof Case* are most worthwhile. The latter is the story of an aged American adventurer, Mr. "X," who lives in Brazil. The record of his infamous past is hidden in an eponymous "antproof case," which he guards with his Walther P-88. Helprin's soaring imagination and his ability to make the details of setting move us are evident in this saga, which one reviewer described as "the rise and fall of a crazed knight errant."

More ambitious is his 1991 *A Soldier of the Great War*,[3] on the life of an old Italian, Alessandro Guiliani. Guiliani served in the Italian military under Field Marshall Blasius Strassnitzky in World War I. The old soldier, now dying, travels seventy kilometers to the village of Monte Prato, accompanied by an illiterate seventeen-year-old boy. Along the way, he tells his life story. The character Rafi Foa affords significant insight into Jewish life in Italy in the twentieth century.[4]

Helprin is of the opinion that God's existence is not a matter of argument but apprehension, and he weaves ultimate issues into his focused narrative. *A Soldier of the Great War* ends with a grand line: "And then it all ran together, like a song."

---

1. Francis A. Schaeffer, *How Should We Then Live? The Rise and Decline of Western Thought and Culture* (Old Tappan, N.J.: Revell, 1976), 182ff. "Modern people are in trouble indeed," he concludes.
2. Mark Helprin, ed., *The Best American Short Stories, 1988* (New York: Houghton, Mifflin, 1988).
3. Mark Helprin, *A Soldier of the Great War* (New York: Harcourt Brace, Jovanovich, 1991).
4. Ibid., 144. See the book and film on Jews in Italy, Giorgio Bassani, *The Garden of the Finzi-Continis.*

10.4 FICTION IN THE HINTERLAND

Thus, the failure to read good books both enfeebles the vision and strengthens our most fatal tendency—the belief that the here and now is all there is.

—Allan Bloom
The Closing of the American Mind

Because the Chicago priest and best-selling author Andrew Greeley is a practitioner of the degenerate, almost pornographic, "washroom school of fiction," I bypass him for Malachi Martin's *Windswept House: A Vatican Novel.*[1]

An important genre of regional historical literature is the Western, with its rugged hero and frontier life. A trenchant spokesman for the created order (although I wish he had a deeper understanding of original sin) has been Kentucky writer Wendell Berry.[2] Berry emphasizes our stewardship of nature.

Edward Abbey was a powerful novelist of the American Southwest. His philosophic patter alienated him from the liberal establishment. Several of his novels were made into movies. *The Brave Cowboy* (1956) came out as *Lonely Are the Brave*. Ivan Doig's Montana Trilogy on the McCaskill family gives a sense of the "big sky" in *English Creek* (1984), *Dancing at the Rascal Fair* (1987), and *Ride with Me, Mariah Montana* (1990). There is much schmaltz in this genre, but Walter Van Tilburg Clark's *The Ox-Bow Incident* is a genuine classic.[3] The late Alexander Miller of Stanford advanced the notion that in the riding of the range we have "the eternal dialectic of pilgrimage and rest. . . . Man has to play the hand he's dealt," and the range war is a Holy War.[4]

The Ox-Bow Incident is set in the Nevada Territory of 1885. Clark, who lived in Nevada during his early years, expertly crafts the story of a lynch mob that tries to deal summarily with cattle rustlers. He observes, "I wouldn't mind it too much if readers were momentarily to feel—not think of but feel—the shadow of three crosses on Golgotha reaching across nearly 2000 years to cover the shadows made by three ropes in a high Sierra valley in 1885."[5]

Other names of classic Western genre authors are Eugene Manlove Rhodes, Ernest Haycox, and Max Brand.

---

1. New York: Doubleday, 1996. Malachi Martin takes a firm stand against some pervasive doctrinal trends in contemporary Catholicism such as "All are de facto saved in some sense." "But what about salvation, Paul?" (356). He has also written the very provocative *The Jesuits: The Society of Jesus and the Betrayal of the Roman Catholic Church* (New York: Simon and Schuster, 1987). Martin grapples with "the new unbelief" and the move away from the cross.
2. Wendell Berry, *Sex, Economy, Freedom and Community: Eight Essays* (New York: Pantheon, 1993).
3. Walter Van Tilburg Clark, *The Ox-Bow Incident* (New York: Random House, 1940).
4. Alexander Miller, "The 'Western'—A Theological Note," *The Christian Century*, 27 November 1957, 1409–10.
5. Van Tilburg Clark, introduction to *The Ox-Bow Incident*, xiv.

10.5 A CADRE OF UP-AND-COMING CONTRARIANS

Books are the gun powder of the mind.

—David Reisman

While much modern fiction is sheer tripe and not worth reading, it is fascinating to see how even the enemies of Christianity cannot ignore Christ and the cross.[1] The woundedness of the mainline denominations and the evangelical renaissance have opened new doors for evangelical expression.[2] While it is premature to see any contemporary literature as classic, there are some candidates.

Frederick Beuchner: The novels of this Presbyterian minister are most worthwhile: *The Book of Bebb,* about a mail-order evangelist; *Godric,* the story of an Anglo-Saxon monk; *The Final Beast,* the lives of a widowed minister and his two daughters; and *On the Road with the Archangel.*

Larry Woiwode: A member of the Orthodox Presbyterian denomination, Larry Woiwode is a master novelist of North Dakota. His reflections on the church, writing, and his own life are in a volume entitled *Acts.* His best work is found in *Poppa John, Beyond the Bedroom Wall,* and *Born Brothers.* He calls a sleeping church to awaken.

Jon Hassler: This Roman Catholic writer from Minnesota authentically describes small town life in *Staggerford, A Green Journey, Grand Opening, North of Hope,* and *Rookery Blues.* In his best, *Dear James,* the priest James says to Agatha: "Stories can move people, Agatha. I learned that in the pulpit. You can preach till the cows come home and not awaken a single soul, but the right story, well told, goes straight to the heart."

Louise Erdrich: Several writers have tried to describe and represent the American experience through the eyes of the continent's first residents. Louise Erdrich writes especially meaningfully about Native American experience.

Madeline L'Engle: A critically acclaimed New York City writer, Madeline L'Engle is a devout Episcopalian. She tends to concede too much to liberal biblical interpreters, but such pieces as *A Severed Wasp* and *Walking on Water* are choice. She has also given us some powerful autobiographical novels.

Annie Dillard: One of the very best novelists of the late-twentieth-century generation, Annie Dillard is at her best in *Pilgrim at Tinker Creek, Holy the Firm,* or *Teaching a Stone to Talk.* A lapsed Presbyterian, she is able to remember and vividly capture impressions of the old camp meeting days about as well as does anyone. Her later work indicates a return to her Christian roots.

Doris Betts: A Presbyterian who teaches at the University of North Carolina at Chapel Hill. Doris Betts was raised in the Associate Reformed Presbyterian Church. Titles such as *Souls Raised from the Dead, The River to Pickle Beach,* and *Heading West* are stimulating. The issues of faith, the authority of Scripture, and the nature of God are never far below the surface in these works.

Jan Karon: Such is the interest in her series of books on life in Mitford, North Carolina, that Jan Karon has almost become a cult figure. These stories about the Episcopal rector Tim Kavanagh and Cynthia, his fiancée, are wholesome and realistic. Start with *At Home in Mitford* and then move on to *A Light in the Window; Those High, Green Hills; On to Canaan;* and *A New Song.* She is a Christian and writes through the eyes and worldview of her faith.

Such works stand in stark contrast with the atheist **Ayn Rand,** whose novels, most notably *Atlas Shrugged,* push her atheistic "objectivist" philosophy. Regrettably, her individualism inspired a generation.

Frank Peretti, whose *This Present Darkness* doesn't quite make it, has a remarkable interview in *World,* 25 October 1997, 13ff.

1. Such enemies of the gospel as Gore Vidal in *Live from Golgotha* (1992) writes a scandalously revisionist version. Similarly the naughty Norman Mailer, in *The Gospel According to the Son* (1997), purports to give a first-person memoir of Christ. Not worth the time to read, except to note that neither of these writers can shake loose from the cross.
2. Mark A. Shibley, *Resurgent Evangelicalism in the United States: Mapping Cultural Change Since 1970* (Columbia: University of South Carolina, 1997). See also Ben J. Wattenberg, *The First Universal Nation* (New York: Free Press, 1991). This is a study of the surge of America as the only world power remaining in the 1990s with the end of the Eastern Bloc alliance of the USSR.

CHAPTER ELEVEN

Broadening the Search into World Literature

We turn from the U.S. and U.K. to a broad literary canvas. Oxford don Felipe Fernandez-Armesto argues that the last thousand years was dominated by the "Atlantic civilization," but this hegemony is disintegrating. The coming era will be dominated by lands around the "world ocean" of the Pacific.[1] The reason is Western skepticism about the possibility of objective reality has vitiated the culture.

Supporting this analysis, philosopher Louis Dupré of Yale University observes: "The West appears to have said its definitive farewell to a Christian culture."[2] He compares the "massive apostasies" of the last decades to the collapse of values in the time of Augustine (354–430). Correctly seeing Christianity as always beginning with "a personal conversion of the heart," Dupré summons us to the Scriptures and preachers to the objective task of preaching the Word.[3]

Given such a foreboding analysis, we must look carefully at the broader picture of the literary world.

---

1. Felipe Fernandez-Armesto, *A History of the Last Thousand Years* (New York: Scribner's, 1995).
2. "Seeking Christian Interiority: An Interview with Louis Dupré," *The Christian Century,* 16–23 July 1997, 654.
3. Ibid., 660.

11.1 OUT OF THE CANADIAN CAULDRON

Canada exists well within the orbit of Western civilization, yet it is unique, drawing on French, British, and American life and adding a perspective that is its own. This viewpoint is framed by the sheer mass of the land over which Canadians stretch from Atlantic to Pacific. Yet the population is relatively small and variegated. It is torn and straining ethnically. So American; so European; so beautiful and so richly endowed.

11.1.1 DAVIES, THE ORIGINAL CUNNING MAN

> In my opinion, the . . . society . . . from which the Bible is disappearing is a society which is moving toward barbarism. Because one of the elements of a civilized society is that it has a congruous body of common knowledge, generally of classical literature. And that is what the Bible was, quite apart from what it had to say on religious subjects, which was another thing. . . . There was a common frame or reference for conversation, oratory and opinion, right from the top of society to the bottom, and when somebody in parliament made a biblical reference, he was literally talking to a nation which understood him, not making a classical allusion which went over the heads of most of the people who might hear him. We have lost that great classical background.
>
> —Robertson Davies

A Canadian who writes about Canada, an accomplished actor in the Old Vic Company in England, a newspaper publisher, the first master of Massey College at the University of Toronto—William Robertson Davies (1913–1995) was the modern equivalent of a renaissance man of genius proportions. He was born in remote Thamesville, Ontario, the model for his fictional Deptford, where his father was a newspaper editor. Young Robertson aspired to an acting career and deliberately set for himself the appearance and role of an eccentric Edwardian.[1] One benefit of his acting career came when he was stage manager at the Old Vic and met Brenda Newbold. They enjoyed a happy lifelong marriage. By the time he was an elderly man, he looked like Santa Claus, but with a broad-brimmed hat, monocle, and walking stick.

Davies's university career commenced in Canada but continued at Oxford, where he moved from his native Calvinism to the Church of England. He was intrigued by Carl G. Jung, whose concept of "modern man in search of a soul" seemed promising to evangelicals who wanted to integrate faith into the social sciences. Jung was the son of a minister. Surely he saw a positive function for religion as did few of his analytic counterparts.

But it was soon evident that Jung's Kantian epistemology precluded any supernatural reality. Davies's faith lacked any authority, and he collected an eclectic group of writings to follow because Scripture wasn't enough. He was so Jungian at this point. He has been called "a writer of Christian apocrypha." Evangelicals who stood within the intelligentsia, including Davies, were left with pretty much of a pick-and-choose Christianity. "I had a very Calvinist bringing up, you know," he made clear.[2] However, he disliked the idea that "Christianity was free for everyone" and resisted the notion that one's beliefs can be nailed down and defended.

While he lamented the lack of theology in the churches, he resisted the spur of Christian orthodoxy to perfection.[3] He saw himself as "a moralist possessed by humor" and wrote twelve thousand words a week throughout his career and up to his death. He produced thirty books, eleven of which are novels. The latter included his Deptford, Salterton, and Cornish trilogies.

Each of these novels is well worth reading, and the collection bristles with characters who are cognizant of Christian frailties. One character in *Fifth Business* testifies: "I avoided the Catholic gush and the Protestant smirk." In the story of Frances Cornish in *What's Bred in the Bone,* for example, we meet "the hot, sweet Catholicism of his aunt, the stern and unyielding Presbyterianism of the cook and the lukewarm Anglicanism of his boarding school, 'the religion that never went too far.'" Cornish describes a generation of priests that pompously presents a total "lack of symbol and metaphor and with a zeal for abstraction drive mankind to a barren land of starved imagination."[4] Davies is obsessed with high church Anglicanism and cathedrals and Wesleyan preaching.

Such characters can give a spiritual spin to all of life. Science, says Cornish in *What's Bred in the Bone,* "has such a miserable vocabulary and such a pallid pack of images to offer us."[5] In his next to last work, he takes us to "the university," which he defines as a spiritual structure, inhabited by dead human beings, grouped in coherent communities. At the university, he confronts Emanuel Swedenborg, the Swedish scientist and cultic sage who foresaw nebular and magnetic theory, the machine gun, and airplane. He founded crystallography.[6]

Though he frequently makes reference in his writings to the traditional Canadian inferiority complex, he demonstrates in descriptions of his countrymen that they are a resilient and an accomplished people worthy of respect.

Davies, the consummate story teller, lived by the dictum of one of his characters in his last novel on Canadian life, *The Cunning Man*: "Never neglect the charms of narrative for the human heart." He urges his readers to invite great books into their lives.[7]

In *The Cunning Man,* we meet Dr. Jonathan Hullah, who likes the high church's liturgy. Dr. Hullah speaks for many bored parishioners who feel that

> the part of the service—and you can leave before it begins, but that might be thought rude—that gets my goat is the Sermon. Then you come down from all the splendour of the Prayer Book and the really super-prose of Cranmer to what some chap thinks it would be good for you to hear.[8]

Culturally, this is really a book about the transformation of old Toronto into an international metropolis. Ecclesiastically, Davies comments on the danger of antinomianism. Any author who reminds us that grace does not open the door to license has done us a service. He is one of the great writers of the twentieth century, one who has been sadly neglected at our own loss.

---

1. Judith Skelton Grant, *Robertson Davies: Man of Myth* (New York: Viking, 1995). "Artistic magic of the highest order."

2. Hap Erstein, "A True Canadian Renaissance Man," *Insight,* 17 September 1990, 57.

3. Martin Marty, ed., *Context,* 15 July 1989, 5. This movement away from the founda-
tional authority of the Bible helps explain today's biblical illiteracy.

4. Peter S. Hawkins, "Robertson Davies: Shaking Hands with the Devil," *The Christian Century,* 21 May 1986, 516.

5. Robertson Davies, *What's Bred in the Bone* (New York: Viking, 1986), 16.

6. Robertson Davies, *Murther and Walking Spirits* (New York: Viking, 1991).

7. Robertson Davies, "A Reading Lesson," *WQ,* spring 1993, 99. "Listen to the inner
music of a writer's words."

8. Robertson Davies, *The Cunning Man* (New York: Viking, 1994), 316. Davies plays
cosmic jokes on his characters.

11.1.2 RICHLER, ENTERPRISING ETHNIC

> Did you know that in every previous apocalyptic era there has been both
> a crisis of leadership and penchant for cross-dressing? That conspiracy
> theories, distrust of government, renewed religiosity and sex and gender
> flux are symptomatic of end-times throughout history?
>
> —Mark Kingwell
> *Dreams of Millennium*

A brilliant philosopher at the University of Toronto describes the Canadian mirror image of a "brink culture" often decried in the United States and Great Britain.
With "rationality out of fashion," Mark Kingwell analyzes an internet culture that
produces both a new elite and extraordinary anxiety.[1] Mordecai Richler (1931–),
who so visualizes this maelstrom, was born in Montreal and raised in the Jewish
ghetto there. Descended from Russian immigrants, he has lived in exile in Paris,
London, and Spain. He spent ten years as a Book-of-the-Month Club editor. He
can be called "enterprising" in that his contributions ranged through the spectrum
of literature, wherever he saw a market for his writing. He has written novels, short
stories, plays, three volumes of essays, and children's stories.

His highly-contested rise and rocky marriages produced a curious combination of humor and anger. He takes feisty, outrageous potshots at Canada, Quebec
separatism, *Quebecois* language laws, anti-Semitism (both among Gentiles and
Jews themselves), New Age spiritualism, Hollywood leftism, and feminism.[2]
Some of his best work comes in *The Apprenticeship of Duddy Kravitz,* which
gives priceless insights into Montreal's Jewish community through the eyes of a
young Montreal Jew who has a consuming ambition for land. This novel was made
into a film starring Richard Dreyfus and launched the megacareer of Richler. His
later *Solomon Gursky Was Here* is a 423-page saga "dense with a century and a
half of Canadian history." Richler covers four generations of Jewish-Canadian
history.[3] The central image of the book is the raven, a bird that can endure great
extremes of cold. His 1980 book, *Joshua Then and Now,* is vintage Richler and a
good place to begin. *Barney's Vision* presents a flamboyant sinner. Said one critic,
"the Ten Commandments and their discontents are what keeps the pages turning."[4]
The story's hero, Barney Panofsky, is the son of Montreal's first Jewish policeman,

and he calls his television production company Totally Unnecessary Productions. The subtext conveys "the unreliability of narrative and memory."[5] Barney has the sort of panache the Yiddish language might call *chutzpah*.

These are not calm waters, but they open windows into a world not so distant.

---

1. Mark Kingwell, *Dreams of Millennium: Report from a Culture on the Brink* (Toronto: Viking, 1996), 55.
2. Mark Shechner, "A Crumb-Bum Hero," *The Jerusalem Post,* 7 February 1998, 22.
3. Rick Marin, "Canada's Unlikely Hero-Novelist," in *Insight,* 25 June 1990, 62f.
4. R. Z. Sheppard, "Sinning Flamboyantly," *Time,* 22 December 1997, 88. Sheppard describes the inhabitants of Richler's works as such "raffish characters."
5. James Shapiro, "The Way He Was—or Was He?" *The New York Times Book Review,* 21 December 1997, 4.

11.2 FROM THE GERMAN GARDEN

Germany is always an intellectual and cultural force. Germans struggle with human imperfections. Yet in the twentieth century arts, Germany has been in something of a creative malaise.[1] The situation can be understood as a harvest of secularization and idolatrous nationalism.[2] Heisenberg's "uncertainty principle"[3] and its part in the German search for the atomic bomb epitomizes the German dilemma. But we must go back to an earlier Germany for a fuller understanding.

---

1. John Ardagh, *Germany and the Germans* (New York: Harper and Row, 1987). Great honor to aristocrats.
2. Owen Chadwick, *The Secularization of the European Mind in the 19th Century* (Cambridge: Cambridge, 1975).
3. Heisenberg's "uncertainty principle" rejected the mechanical models that had characterized scientific explanation of atomic structure. His theories founded the new models of quantum physics. The uncertainty principle states that the position and momentum of a subatomic particle is so much in flux and subject to change, that it cannot be determined for any point in time. Since all things are composed of these uncertain particles and behave much the same way, the implication is a philosophical relativism. Nothing can be said to be true about the physical world. There are ultimately no laws, only statistical probabilities. See Thomas Powers, *Heisenberg's War: The Secret History of the German Bomb* (New York: Knopf, 1993).

11.2.1 GOETHE, FATHER FIGURE

Everyone knows that of himself which he would not tell his dearest friend.
—Johann Wolfgang von Goethe

He who always striving makes the effort, Him we can save.
—the demons, *Faust,* part 2

Johann Wolfgang von Goethe (1749–1832) has drawn accolades: Germany's most famous writer; the greatest writer of Germany's "golden age of literature" in which the Renaissance finally came after a long winter of war; dean of German literature; the intellectual father of the nineteenth century. This highly lauded philosopher and novelist was born in a wealthy Frankfurt-am-Main home. His father was a judge and his mother the daughter of the mayor. He was close to his mother, Elizabeth, who was twenty-one years younger than his father. She supervised Johann's tutorial education. Religious instruction tended to be arid moralism.[1] His mother was a fervent pietist (the background that also produced Kant, Hegel, Schleiermacher, Bach, and Handel).[2] He writes to a fellow-student at the University of Leipzig where he studied law: "My mother has declared herself an open adherent of the group of the Pietists; my father knows and does not object. My sister has gone to the prayer meetings . . . and I'll probably end by going, too."[3]

Some of the conventicles met in their home, but Goethe was not drawn to the pietists in Strassbourg, where he finished his law course. He spoke of these evangelical Christians: "They are terrible bores—poor things."[4] When his mother's friend Frau von Klettenberg intimated that he needed to be reconciled to a deity, he said, "I had always imagined that I was on quite good terms with God; in fact, I rather fancied after a good many experiences that he was somewhat in my debt and that it was I who had to pardon Him for several circumstances."[5]

He became interested in literature and writing and while in Strassbourg met Johann von Herder (1744–1803), who introduced him to Shakespeare and biblical poetry.[6] He was taken with *The Vicar of Wakefield* (9.1.3).

He was described by a Danish diplomat:

> He is a slender young man of about my height. His color is pale; his nose big and aquiline; he has a longish face and medium black eyes and black hair. His expression is serious, even melancholy, although comic and laughing and satiric moods gleam through. He is very eloquent and produces a stream of witty notions. He seems to produce with extraordinary ease. He draws and paints, too.[7]

He came to compare Jesus with Benedict de Spinoza (1632–1677), and he called the latter a Christian, not an atheist. After translating the Song of Songs, he characterized it as "the most magnificent collection of love songs God ever created."[8] When he was in physical extremity, he read the book of Job.[9] He spoke of singing "psalms to the Lord" and referred to Luther's Shorter Catechism.

Yet he joined the Masons and was attracted to the Swedenborgian spirit universe.[10] He adamantly set himself against believing in the gospel miracle accounts, saying that "an audible voice from heaven would not convince him." He claimed to be not anti-Christian or un-Christian; he was simply non-Christian.[11]

Goethe wrote three thousand poems, such best-selling novels as *The Sorrows of Young Werther,* plays, intellectual treatises, and his own autobiography. He launched the *Sturm und Drang* (storm and stress) literary movement and accepted a position as a cabinet minister in tiny Weimar, which remained his home for the remainder of his life.[12]

In his wide travels, he associated with Napoléon Bonaparte (1769–1821) and other international leaders. He cultivated friendships with the literati, such as Johann Friedrich von Schiller (1759–1805), the great poet-dramatist and disciple of Immanuel Kant (1724–1804). He developed his interest in plants and wrote a treatise as well as on optics, architecture, and anatomy (discovering the intermaxillary bone). He spent twenty-two months in Italy (1786–88). He had one romantic affair after another and finally married Christine Vulpius after considerable scandal. Thomas Mann praised Goethe's narcissism as the complement to democracy.[13] Goethe's radical sexuality is consistent with Mann's "Schopenhaurean pessimism" and his admirable "no hopes and therefore no illusions."[14] This is not far from the Pelagianism of Emerson and North American philosophy.

What must be read in Goethe is his masterpiece on which he expended energy over a period of sixty years. He worked over the Faust legend (as Christopher Marlowe had in the sixteenth century and Thomas Mann later would in the twentieth). Goethe made of it one of the great epic poems of the Western world, along with Homer's *Iliad* and *Odyssey,* Vergil's *Aeneid,* Dante's *Divine Comedy,* and John Milton's *Paradise Lost.* Apparently there actually was a Dr. Faustus. The Lutheran Reformation theologian Philipp Melanchthon (1497–1560) claimed to have known him.[15]

The story concerns how Faust made a pact with the devil, Mephistopheles, promising his soul in exchange for power and pleasure. Here we see Goethe as a leader in German Romanticism. The bells and hymns of Easter Day ("heavenly tones") call Faust back from suicide to a recollection of "his childhood faith and joy."[16] Faust turns to the New Testament in his study and attempts to translate John 1, but makes "the word" to be "the deed." The key is action and striving as the way of salvation. Faust ruins both himself and Gretchen in sexual passion, and Part I ends in pathetic tragedy.

Unlike the original story, Goethe's *Faust* ends happily; human striving succeeds, and heaven is attained. The absence of a Savior for sin is deafening. Without a true salvation, Goethe's vaunted Romanticism stalls out into futility. In reality, self-salvation is unattainable. This makes Goethe's dying words at Weimar sadly ironic: *"Mehr Licht"* ("More light").

> **One of Germany's** premier poet-authors, Heinrich Heine (1797–1856), had considerable ambivalence toward Germany and his own Judaism. Viewing the latter as a misfortune, he was baptized as a Christian to gain an "entrance ticket to European culture." He spent time in Paris and knew Karl Marx and the anarchist Pierre-Joseph Proudhon (1809–1865). After studying Jewish history and suffering, he wrote *The Rabbi,* in which a character says: "Comrades in exile, nomads, my unhappy friends." After his baptism, he wrote: "I am now hated by Christian and Jew."[17] His *Book of Songs, The Harz Journey,* and *The Baths of Lucca* are worth probing; especially read his wrenching *Edom.*

---

1. Ludwig Lewisohn, *Goethe: The Story of a Man,* vol. 1 (New York: Farrar, Strauss, 1949), 8.

2. See David L. Larsen, *The Company of the Preachers* (Grand Rapids: Kregel, 1998), 6.4.2, 6.4.3.
3. *The Story of a Man,* 32. Goethe was not totally averse to preaching. He expressed a particularly positive reaction to a sermon in 1755 regarding the destruction of Lisbon, Portugal, by earthquake and tidal wave (6).
4. Ibid., 48.
5. Ibid., 32.
6. He received his Doctor of Laws at Strassbourg in 1771.
7. *The Story of a Man,* 87–88.
8. Goethe had an obsession with sexuality to which Song of Songs appealed. He had many frenzied affairs.
9. *The Story of a Man,* 126.
10. Ibid., 242. He was very open to all forms of culture and society.
11. Ibid., 256. The very sound of church bells across the street greatly irritated him. He was "on the run."
12. Ibid., 167. Goethe's influence on "world literature" (a term he coined) is traced in Fritz Strich's *Goethe and World Literature* (Westport, Conn.: Greenwood, 1971).
13. Mortimer Adler and Seymour Cain, *Imaginative Literature* (Chicago: Britannica, 1962), 2:113. Thomas Mann wrote a great novel about Goethe, his *The Beloved Returns.*
14. Ibid., 255. His mother never gave up her efforts to get her son into the fold.
15. Anthony Heilbut, *Thomas Mann: Eros and Literature* (New York: Knopf, 1996), 511, 513.
16. *Imaginative Literature,* 2:109.
17. See Jeffrey L. Sammons, *Heinrich Heine: A Modern Biography* (Princeton: Princeton University Press, 1979).

11.2.2 MANN, PRODUCTIVE PROPAGANDIST

> Belief? Unbelief? I hardly know one from the other. I really couldn't say if I consider myself a believer or an unbeliever. I have the deepest doubt or skepticism toward both positions.
>
> —Thomas Mann

By any consensus, Thomas Mann (1875–1955) is the mightiest German writer in the twentieth century. His life spanned an immensely eventful era in German history.[1]

He was born in Lubeck to a troubled, "artsy" family that was nurtured in "the kinder, gentler Calvinism" admixed with Pietism. Mann himself never exhibited any religious tendencies.[2] A poor student academically, he found refuge in the arts. The big formative influences on his life were Friedrich Nietzsche (1844–1900), Richard Wagner (1813–1883), and Arthur Schopenhauer (1788–1860). Always elegantly attired, he tried to cultivate an impressive speaking style, but was so sensitive to criticism that one bad review sent him to a sanitarium.[3]

His early stories showed him to be a master of the form and displayed "the ironic modes, perspectives and tones" that would mature in his later fiction.[4] *Buddenbrooks,* his first novel, was about Lubeck. The elder Buddenbrook, who was of the Enlightenment, mocked the Lutheran catechism, but his son, the Consul, absorbing the piety of his mother who was the guardian of the sacred text, was "a rigorous combination of capitalist principles and fundamentalist Christianity."[5] The book is "saturated with religious imagery" and reflects the vestigial remains of his own upbringing.

Both Thomas Mann and his author brother Heinrich wrestled with "doubts, self-contempt, unfulfilled longings and hypochondriacal sensitivity to criticism."[6] The war shook him deeply, and he was drawn to the pessimistic Oswald Spengler (1880–1936), who wrote *The Decline of the West*. He found in Walt Whitman (1819–1892) a kindred spirit and began to attend seances and write (particularly in *Death in Venice,* on the morality of dissipation) and behave in such a way that he became to some the symbol of German decadence. His brother made a brief foray into religion in a novel about a transformed life in Jesus, but Thomas Mann could only fault German Christians. He married Katia Pringsheim, a culturally converted Jewess who bore him six children and remained faithful to him for over fifty years of marriage, notwithstanding his bisexual lifestyle.[7]

His literary masterpiece (and undoubtedly one of the great works of fiction in all time) was *The Magic Mountain* (1924). This is the story of Hans Castorp's stay at Haus Berghof, a tuberculosis sanitorium in the Alps, and the brilliantly depicted international clientele that represents the diseased society of Europe before 1914. All of the options are explored, from psychoanalysis to freemasonry,[8] even to a Pentecostal revival. But "all of the ideologies are whistling in the dark."[9]

Mann won the Nobel Prize for Literature in 1929. A chance request of a Munich artist for Mann to pose as Joseph the ruler of Egypt for a painting inspired him to write a tetralogy on the life of Joseph. These books are a political retelling of Scripture, a kind of Eastern psychoanalysis.[10] One critic charged that Mann made an ancient text conform to his desires. In effect, he rewrote the Bible.[11]

Mann and his family fled Hitler's Germany for refuge in the United States. Joseph in the books is really Franklin Delano Roosevelt. The family became American citizens but turned sharply left politically and opposed the Cold War and taxes. Eventually they returned to Germany and Switzerland, where Mann died in 1955. Toward the end of his life, he had become embittered politically. When U.S. Congressman Richard Nixon orchestrated the investigation that led to an eventual perjury conviction for Alger Hiss in an espionage scandal, Mann called Nixon "the Hiss murderer" and named his dog Alger.

In writing his last book, *The Holy Sinner,* he wrote wistfully to a friend that the idea of grace was becoming very appealing to him.[12] *The Holy Sinner* is a "Christian" version of the Oedipus tragedy. The fictional Pope Gregorious is in fact married to his mother. Unlike Mann's other books, this action offers an escape from the dead-end alley. This is what he means by "grace." He had earlier written his own version of *Doctor Faustus.* "Isn't it pure grace," he said, "that after the consuming Faustus, I was able to bring off this little book [*The Holy Sinner*] of God-sent jests and diversions." Even with his avowed Goethean ambition, he had to acknowledge: "I have not enjoyed this life—but one must live one's life to the end as best one can."[13]

An unusual and gripping novel about Germany during and after the Hitler era is *Stones from the River* by Ursula Hegi.[14] Hegi is a German who lived through some of these years. She later moved to the United States. This is the story of Trudy Montag, a Zwerg or dwarf. She does not see another Zwerg until the circus comes to town. We feel Protestant-Catholic tension and the anguish of the Jews. Trudy and the townspeople really come alive.

---

1. Another contrasting family chronicle is Otto Friedrich, *Blood and Iron: From Bismarck to Hitler—the von Moltke Family's Impact on German History* (New York: Harper/Collins, 1995). The old patriarch, General Helmut Graf von Moltke (1800–1891), read his Bible every day (8) and was active in "a circle of devout Pietists" (103). A later figure, Wilhelm, turned to the Bible (335) and attempted to rally Christians to oppose Hitler. He claimed Isaiah 43:2 before his martyrdom in that cause (393).
2. *Eros and Literature*, 27. Like Nietzsche, he hated Luther for taking Christianity out of its institutional envelope and putting it into the heart where it was so difficult to eradicate.
3. Ibid., 45. Early on, he idolized Goethe the Romantic who had written on Faust and a youthful epic on Joseph.
4. Thomas Mann, ed., *Burton Pike: Six Early Stories* (Los Angeles: Sun and Moon Press, 1997). Serious communicators need to read short stories, which are more like sermons and lessons.
5. *Eros and Literature,* 105–6. Interestingly, Thomas in the novel flirts with Catholicism in a difficult time period.
6. Ibid., 206. Mann celebrated the "irrecoverable loss of standards" in a writer like Whitman.
7. Ibid., 463. Mann found in Katia a help-meet, a reader, a manager of the household affairs, etc. She became more.
8. Thomas Mann, *The Magic Mountain* (New York: Knopf, 1972), 515.
9. *Eros and Literature,* 514. This book affords him opportunity to explore the roots of modern life.
10. Ibid., 541. He was looking for "a myth adequate to an era poised on the lip of an abyss" 536.
11. Ibid., 583.
12. Ibid., 589. Mann's treatment of hell in *Doctor Faustus* is very interesting.
13. Ibid., 300. The agnostic Mann ends with Nietzsche, "Man is a sick deer." Another project, *The Joseph Tetralogy*, was a Book-of-the-Month Club selection. It is an idiosyncratic rewriting of the Bible.
14. New York: Scribner, 1994.

11.2.3 HESSE, EYES AND EARS OF THE EAST

Hesse's work—a divided self, dark and light, passionate and ironical, confessional and observing, dreaming and analytical, listening to the subterranean dreams of childhood with the ear of the critical mind.

—Mark Boulby

"Nature abhors a vacuum," we have frequently been told. In the moral and spiritual vacuum in Germany in the wake of the Enlightenment and the tragedies of the twentieth century, Hermann Hesse (1877–1962) turned to Eastern religion. In this, he followed the path taken by Nietzsche and others.

He was born in the heart of the Black Forest. The roots of his family had been in Lubeck and Estonia (a background similar to Mann's roots, which were portrayed in *Buddenbrooks;* see 11.2.2). Hesse's father, Johannes, felt the call of God to the ministry: "I resolved to study theology, . . . but gradually a yearning took possession of me to serve the Lord practically . . . and to follow his banner,"[1] he said. Johannes and his wife served four years on the Malabar Coast in India under the Basel Mission Society. Evangelical warmth and orthodoxy in the German-speaking world was centered in this society and the theological faculty in the University of Basel.[2] Ill-health forced them to return home.

Young Hesse chafed under what he felt was "the secluded, narrow pietistic horizon of the missionary society." He wanted to be a poet—and only a poet![3]

As expected, he went to seminary to prepare for the ministry, but he ran away in deep revolt. His parents apprenticed him to a towerclock factory; from thence he was self-educated. He was drawn to Goethe, Friedrich Schleiermacher (1768–1834), and the Romantics. His motto was shared in his first novel, *Demian*: "After all, I wanted only to attempt to live that which was trying to work its way out of me. Why was that so terribly difficult?"[4]

In full flight from the faith, Hesse replaced morality with aesthetics.[5] His relationship with his parents became strained. By now, he was keenly a disciple of Nietzsche and Schopenhauer. Narcissistic symbols abound in his works. He mocked the total abstinence from alcohol of his parental home. He wrote a strongly rebellious letter to his mother.[6]

Married three times, Hesse was a restless soul. He traveled to India in 1911 and was profoundly attracted to the Buddhists of Ceylon. Eastern mysticism fit nicely his psychoanalytic interests. After the collapse of his first marriage, he went into Jungian analysis. In *Demian,* the site of tension for the hero is confirmation class, where he gives a Gnostic interpretation to Bible stories. He praises the unrepentant thief![7] He sees the God of the Bible as including the devil within himself. He is indeed now on the road to self-knowledge and the new morality. "The true vocation for everyone is simply to arrive at himself."[8]

Sometimes called "the last knight of Romanticism," Hesse believed in no religious dogma. Occasionally, we catch a glimmer of Kantian moral will, but basically he is Eastern in his serenity, passivity, and quietism. His greatest work, *Siddhartha,* was started in 1919 and is the Buddhist-inspired search for reality. Siddhartha finds the river, but does it truly satisfy? This book made Hesse a cult hero. Many in the antiestablishment movements of the 1950s and 1960s adored him. The Nobel Prize was awarded in 1946.

In his novel *Steppenwolf,* the story of an actor named Harry Haller, he digs at conventional morality and concludes that one must overcome all inhibition.[9] He wrote poetry, political and social criticism. His words exude a "spicy sexuality."

The window into the soul of this influential thinker and writer is to be found in *Siddhartha.*[10] The underlying prophecy of this work is the imminent collapse of Christianity. Rather, as Siddhartha tries everything, including Buddhism, only death will ultimately end his search. Failing in his own search, Hesse lived in seclusion until his death.

■ **Another literary giant** from this era is certainly Franz Kafka (1883–1924), a German Jew born in Prague. Kafka truly lived a nightmare. He contracted tuberculosis and became severely mentally ill. Appropriate to these troubles, his works are a pageant of doom. His theme is alienation—a world without God. His theme is illustrated in the story of a man who was found fishing in a bath tub. He is told: "You're not going to catch any fish in there." His dismal response is: "I know it," and he continues fishing. His novels *The Trial* (1925) and *The Castle* (1926) show the harvest of nihilism. The post-World War II novels of Heinrich Boll disclose this same emptiness and deep disillusionment. By that time, existential hopelessness was becoming endemic. Kafka was awarded the Nobel Prize in 1972.

---

1. George Wallis Field, *Herman Hesse* (Boston: Twayne, 1970), 14. Hesse's maternal grandparents were pioneer missionaries in Malabar. His father's father was a physician.
2. David Larsen, *The Company of the Preachers* (Grand Rapids: Kregel, 1998), 9.4.2–4.4; 9.6.4.
3. Field, *Herman Hesse,* 15.
4. Ibid., 18. While at Maulbronn Seminary in 1892, an unsuccessful cure by a "well-known theologian and faith-healer, and an attempted suicide" led young Hesse to a crisis of credibility and he fled the scene. A complex phenomenon.
5. Ibid., 21. Hesse always had a great interest in music. He wrote a novella that featured Richard Wagner.
6. Ibid., 22, 26, 44. One of his characters says: "I felt within me overwhelming opposition to my father and toward everything he expected and demanded of you. . . . " This is certainly autobiographical. He wrote to his mother: "If I had all the 'Holy Ghost' you wish me, I would long since have become a great apostle."
7. Ibid., 44. This is the familiar bildungsroman form of the novel in which he is following Thomas Mann and others.
8. Ibid., 54. Of course Buddhism is in its essence exceedingly egoistic and self–centered.
9. Ibid., 97. Hesse long since became a Swiss citizen and was faulted by the Nazis for praising "the Jew Kafka."
10. Herman Hesse, *Siddhartha* (New York: Bantam, 151).

11.3 THE SCANDINAVIAN STREAM

In the beautiful Scandinavian countries, we sadly see the "collapse of the dream of the secular city."[1] The inroads of secularism and the "cradle-to-grave" government care of the welfare state have left once vigorous cultures limp and spiritually lifeless. Sweden became the least religious country in the world, followed closely by Denmark.[2] Even Norway and Finland show the symptoms of these suffocating influences. The newer literature shows it.

1. A remarkable study is found in Allan Carlson, *The Swedish Experiment in Family Politics: The Myrdals and the Interwar Population Crisis* (New Brunswick, N.J.: Transaction Publishers, 1990). Important updating of the earlier study by Roland Huntford is *The New Totalitarians* (New York: Stein and Day, 1972).
2. This study found India to be the most religious.

11.3.1 LAGERLÖF, THE OLD HEARTH AND HOME

There is a winnowing going on in the churches.
—Charles Haddon Spurgeon

Despite revival winds blowing over Scandinavia (with only Denmark generally excepted), the ravages of naturalism and German rationalism had a ruinous effect on Sweden above all. Protesting against these riptides and vainly trying to retain the Romantic voice (but with no clear recourse to historic Christianity) was Sweden's best-known writer, Selma Lagerlöf (1858–1940). She was from a large family, the older daughter born to Erik and Lovisa Lagerlöf, who were from the charming and lovely province of Värmland. Her father was from a long line of military men and her mother descended from generations of clergy.

At age three Selma had something like infantile paralysis and was in frail health thereafter. She went to Stockholm to study to be a school teacher and there attended the theatre for the first time. She was stimulated to write some poetry, though the poetic medium was never her strength. She taught school in Lands Krona in Dalarna. The family home at Mårbacka was sold after her father's death in a time of fiscal austerity.

She began to write and travel and her *Gösta Berlings Saga* about Swedish cavaliers and their ladies from folk stories in Värmland became very popular. Thomas Carlyle (1795–1881) was an early model, but she became more and more like Hans Christian Andersen of Denmark (1805–1875) as time went by.[1] She wrote two volumes of stories about Swedish life and culture, as seen through the eyes of young Nils Holgersson, who traveled around Sweden on the back of a goose. She also wrote *The Miracles of Anti-Christ* out of her travels to Sicily. With the proceeds of her writing, she repurchased the family home at Mårbacka, remodeled it and lived there until 1940 and her death. This place and "Ekeby," the estate in her novels at Rotternos in Värmland, are both delightful museums for tourists to visit. In 1909 she became the first woman to receive the Nobel Prize for Literature. She wrote two novels about Swedish farmers who emigrated to the Holy Land to wait for the Lord's coming, *Jerusalem I* and *Jerusalem II*.

To say she was appreciated by Scandinavians would be an understatement. Even a popular breakfast food was called Lagerlöf. Though a convinced pacifist, she gave her Nobel Gold Medal to the Finnish Defense Fund to support the heroic Finns in their struggle against Russian invasion. In accepting his Nobel Prize for Literature in 1980, Czeslaw Milosz, the Polish writer, gave extensive tribute to Lagerlöf and her work.

I am most fond of her trilogy, *The Ring of the Lowenskolds,* which basically tells the story of how inherited character traits were destroying a prominent family until the curse was removed by a peasant girl named Anna Sward.[2] There are religious undercurrents in this splendid study, but they are largely formal and institutional. Tragically, a living faith is not in evidence in Lagerlöf. In *The Holy City: Jerusalem II,* we get a further sense of the substratum of biblical tradition that was so very Swedish for so long. The scenes and sites of biblical lore are deeply moving in this masterpiece (especially the chapter on the area known as Gehenna, meaning the grave or hell in biblical symbolism).[3] Still in unexpected niches of the Lutheran State Church and the free churches there was cherished the light of the lamp of faith. Sadly, Selma Lagerlöf never apparently knew or cared about such matters. She may have had "an amiable weakness" for the supernatural, the wood nymphs, and so on, but she showed no interest in the supernatural Christ.

Another Nobel laureate from Sweden is Pär Lagerkvist (1891–1974), born in Vaxjo. He wrote remarkable pieces on Barabbas from the crucifixion, *Herod and Mariamne,* and *The Death of Ahasuerus.* Yet he was profoundly humanistic and had no personal system of belief. It seems that even the *literati* are continually drawn back to the Bible, though they reject all supernaturalism. A set of Swedish mysteries by Maj Sjowall and Per Wahloo features Detective Inspector Martin Beck of the Stockholm National Police. These seven books are far above average. Other Swedish writers, such as Kerstin Eckman, portray modern rural life, but they are consistently nihilistic. Lars Andersson shows some moral concern. Ingmar Bergman, son of a minister, has given a remarkable series of highly symbolic films that wrestle with religious issues. *Fanny and Alexander* (1983) is a richly woven study of intergenerational family life in a historic epoch. Olav Hartman's *Holy Masquerade* is the story of tension in a state-church parsonage. In this case, the pastor's wife is a skeptic.

---

1. Hans Christian Andersen, from Odense in Denmark, was an unmarried minstrel and storyteller of rare skill. His tales have been translated into eighty languages. Andersen traded barbs with Kierkegaard. See Helle Bering-Jensen, "Diversity of the Fairy Tale King," *Insight,* 20 March 1989, 61–63.
2. Selma Lagerlöf, *The Ring of the Lowenskolds* (New York: Literary Guild, 1931). An engaging story.
3. Selma Lagerlöf, *The Holy City: Jerusalem II* (Garden City: Doubleday, 1918), 129ff.

11.3.2 UNDSET, THE OLD HISTORY

For it is by grace are you saved, through faith—and this not of yourselves, it is the gift of God—not by works, so that no one can boast.
                                                              —Ephesians 2:8–9

Somehow the simple gospel and the plain way of salvation got lost for so many Scandinavians, notwithstanding such revivals as a powerful layman's movement that awakened Norway in the early 1800s under Hans Nielsen Hauge (1771–1824).

Sigrid Undset (1882–1949), though brilliant, is a case in point. She was a Norwegian born in Kallundborg, Denmark, the daughter of an archaeologist who specialized in medieval antiquities. When he died in 1893, she retained an interest in his field of expertise and wrote several massive historical works, the most popular of which is the trilogy *Kristin Lavransdatter.* This remarkable story follows a medieval woman in Norway through her youth, adulthood, and old age. The roughness and crudity of medieval Scandinavia comes alive as she considers these descendants of the Vikings.[1] In the final volume, *The Cross,* Kristin, who is the ultimate survivor, finds her world crumbling in turbulence and tempest and the black death raging on every side. The church is here and the sacraments, and she becomes a nun. Here is piety but no saving victory in a living Jesus.

Undset was married to a painter and raised six children, but she and her husband were divorced in 1925. She had turned from the more liberal, feminist circles in which she had moved and became a Roman Catholic in 1924. She lived in a restored house dating from A.D. 1000 and dressed as a medieval Norse matron. In 1928 she won the Nobel Prize for Literature. She spent the war years in the United States.

In another work, the four-volume *The Master of Hestviken,* she returns to the fourteenth century. There is no better way to grasp the issues and the quality of life in Scandinavia in the Middle Ages than to read Undset on the pomp and pageantry, the sights and sounds and smells.[2] She can tell a story well, with probing psychological insight into characters. The society is God-fearing but not grace-understanding. The hero is a proud, impulsive man of huge strength whose marriage and son envelop him.

Undset's spiritual journey ended in the Roman Catholic Church. In that she was joined by several among the *literati.*

A true son of the rocky Norwegian soil has been Knut Hamsun (1859–1952), born on a farm in Gudbrandsdal. He knew grinding poverty. Visiting the U.S. twice, he worked many kinds of jobs. His great novel, *Growth of the Soil,* is about life in northern Norway. He wrote many novels and was awarded the Nobel Prize for literature in 1920. He was a keen observer, remarking in his memoirs that the sermons he heard in America "did not contain theology but morality . . . they do not develop the mind, though they are entertaining." Other Norwegian writers of note included Bjornstjerne Bjornson, Jonas Lie and Alexander Kielland, who was refused a pension because of his attacks on the church. The Norwegian Lutheran Church has been the most pietistic.

---

1. The titles in the *Kristen Lavransdatter* series are *The Bridal Wreath, The Mistress of Husaby,* and *The Cross.* One relatively recent paperback edition was in 1978 by Bantam Books. These would be a wonderful library acquisition.
2. The *Master of Hestviken* titles are *The Axe, The Snake Pit, In the Wilderness,* and *The Son Avenger.* First published in 1920, the New American Library reprint edition was in 1956. This work opens a way to understand the Scandinavians.

11.3.3 DINESEN, FEARLESS FEMALE FARMER

I had a farm in Africa, at the foot of the Ngoing Hills. The equator runs across these highlands a hundred miles to the North, and the farm lay at an altitude of over 6000 feet. In the day-time you felt that you had got high up, near to the sun, but the early mornings and evenings were limpid and restful, and the nights were cold.

—Isak Dinesen

These are the opening lines of the well-known memoirs of Isak Dinesen, or the Baroness Karen Dinesen Blixen (1885–1962), published as *Out of Africa* and made into a very popular American movie by that title in 1985. She was born in Rungsted, Denmark into an aristocratic home. Her education was in the classics and at home. Her father and grandfather had been professional soldiers for the French. Her father had visited the United States and lived as a fur-trapper with the Indians. Karen did study art at the Danish Royal Academy and in Paris and began to write short stories.

Since one great disadvantage for Scandinavian writers is that their languages are spoken by so many and thus seldom translated, Isak Dinesen (her pen name) had the good fortune to write in both Danish and English. She married her cousin, the Baron, in 1914. And they were divorced in 1921, but not before he had given her syphilis. She stayed on in Kenya to run the farm until 1931, when she went bankrupt in a tumultuous drop of the price of coffee worldwide. Her writing on those years is enriched by a great love for Africans, particularly the Somali and Masai. This makes her memoirs an absolute necessity.[1]

But her short stories are enormously worthwhile, and I cite her fable "Babette's Feast," which was also made into a most memorable film. This story has great potential as an illustration of God's lavish grace. Babette has been chef in a fancy Parisian restaurant and takes a position with two elderly sisters in the wilds of Jutland in Denmark. These dour sisters are part of a joyless religious movement. When Babette wins the lottery, she prepares a banquet for the sisters, along with the faithful, and they partake of these incomparable gourmet delicacies with restraint, but they begin to mellow and free up to express some joy.

This piece is beautifully done. Dinesen hovers near to the supernatural in this story, as in many of her works, but hers was always an unsurrendered soul.[2]

Denmark, with all of the richness of its culture and its high standard of life, was little touched by the revivals that moved across Scandinavia in the nineteenth century. Dinesen epitomizes a diffidence toward the spiritual that so characterizes the Danish people.

Danish writers to notice must include Martin Andersen Nexo and his *Pella the Conqueror,* which addresses the oppression of workers. Peter Hoeg has also had a social message in his *Borderliners* (1994), in which he deals with the Danish school system. He constantly challenges the conventionality of Danish life. Other writers must include Herman Bang, whose *Katinka* is the search of a woman for love. Hans Scherfig also gives biting social commentary, as does William Heinesen. The Swedish-Finnish poetess, Edith Sodergran, can be read in English. This is a unique culture.

1. Isak Dinesen, *Out of Africa* (1937; repr. ed., New York: Random House, 1952).
2. Collections of Dinesen's short stories in English include *Seven Gothic Tales* (1934) and *Winter's Tales* (1942). "Babette's Feast" is found in Dinesen's *Anecdotes of Destiny* (repr. ed., New York: Vintage, 1988).

11.4 FROM THE FRENCH FAIR

Beautiful and enchanting France has ever been a fount of the arts. From the days of the conversion of Clovis, king of the Franks (d. 511), who wanted to put only one arm under the water in baptism,[1] through Bernard of Clairvaux (1090–1153) until the Reformation and John Calvin (1509–1564), France was in the vanguard of positive response to the gospel. Yet the encyclopedists and the Enlightenment crusaders, François-Marie Voltaire (1694–1778) and Jean-Jacques Rousseau (1712–1778) spawned such unbelief that France became and remains a pagan culture. There were waves of spiritual opportunity in the powerful preaching at the end of the Middle Ages and during the Reformation—and even among later court preachers, especially in the reign of Louis XIV (1638–1715).[2] But now France languishes in Europe's spiritual malaise.[3]

1. He allowed only one arm to be baptized, so he could kill with the other one.
2. Larissa Taylor, *Soldiers of Christ: Preaching in Late Medieval and Reformation France* (New York: Oxford University Press, 1992). See Larsen, *The Company of the Preachers* for an exposition of this amazing development.
3. John Newhouse, *Europe Adrift* (New York: Pantheon, 1997). Sadly, the social rot in the European spiritual fruit is to the core.

11.4.1 BEYLE, MOVER TO THE MODERN

It is a fact that cannot be denied: the wickedness of others becomes our own wickedness because it kindles something evil in our own hearts.
—Carl G. Jung, just after World War II

Addicted to Napoléon Bonaparte and Lord Byron, Marie-Henri Beyle (1783–1842), Stendhal by pen name, was the herald for a new French novel. This genre would draw strength from both realistic urges with romantic melodramatics.

Stendhal was astute at psychological analysis and probing. The quest for happiness and beauty were his highest good. Not appreciated while he lived, he has become more widely read.

He was born in the mountainous area in the city of Grenoble. His father was a highly successful attorney, and his mother was the daughter of a physician. She knew Dante's *Divine Comedy* by heart. His mother died when Henri was seven. His father was a rigid disciplinarian, but his maternal grandfather, who loved literature and had a large library, initiated the young man into vistas of imagination.[1] He went to Paris in 1799 to study for a life in science but contracted a disease in which he lost all of his hair (and thereafter wore a toupee). He took a position in the war ministry and was a dragoon in Napoléon's campaigns, including the disastrous retreat from Moscow. During the Bourbon Restoration, he lived in exile in Italy and began writing on a variety of themes using a *nom de plume,* Stendhal. Such claim to fame as he may have is largely due to two novels, *The Red and the Black,* written when he was forty-seven, and *The Charterhouse of Parma,* which he wrote in fifty-three days ("and it shows it," critiques Clifton Fadiman).[2] Fadiman sees Stendhal as a seminal writer in his psychological realism and quotes Nietzsche that Stendhal was "that remarkable anticipatory and forerunning man who with Napoléonic tempo traversed Europe, in fact several centuries of the European soul, as a . . . discoverer thereof."[3]

The book to read is *The Red and the Black,* which is probably partly autobiographical.[4] Julien Sorel, a young man from the provinces, is a peasant's son with driving ambition. He becomes a student of divinity, certainly an avenue to power in the Bourbon Restoration Period. The church as reflected in this action is inconsequential, traditional, and cultural. Julien has two great loves, the wife in the home where he is a tutor, and later the daughter of a nobleman. Fadiman well describes Julien as a lost soul, the classic outsider. Julien is an extraordinary creation and well worthy of study, but once he reaches the seminary the story becomes commonplace and disappointing. Julien mirrored his turbulent times, but sought no succor or resource in the Lord God.

1. Jonathan Keates, *Stendhal* (New York: Carroll and Graf, 1997). "He suffered from Romantic out-of-jointedness."
2. Clifton Fadiman, introduction to *The Red and the Black* (New York: Bantam, 1958), 2.
3. Ibid., 7. Stendhal prophesied: "I shall be understood in about 1880." It was so.
4. Ibid., Fadiman characterizes Stendhal as, like Alexis de Tocqueville, "a Great Ancestor," that is, a pioneer and formulator.

11.4.2 BALZAC, CREATOR OF CHARACTERS

I understand these people's ways, I espoused their way of life, I felt their rags on my shoulders, I walked with my feet in their tattered shoes; their desires and their distress penetrated my soul, or my soul passed into theirs. It was like a waking dream. With them I flew into a passion at the employers who tyrannized over them, or at the malicious trickery which compelled them to return many times before they were paid their wages. I entertained myself by giving up my own habits, by transmuting myself into somebody else in a kind of intoxication of my moral forces, and by playing this game as often as I liked. To whom do I owe this gift? Is it a kind of second sight? Is it a quality which by abuse can border on madness? I have never explored the sources of this power. I possessed it and I used it—and that was all.

—Honoré de Balzac
Facino Cane

Often likened to Charles Dickens because of the two thousand or more characters he sketched in quite a similar manner to Dickens, Honoré de Balzac (1799–1850) was born into an unhappy home in Tours. His father was a story teller, but his mother was chronically unhappy and very selfish. One of her children claimed "I never had a mother," and Honoré never felt accepted.[1] Honoré went to boarding school at Vendome but did not have a very positive experience there, living in the world of books rather than doing his studies. In 1816 he went to the Sorbonne to study law, but nothing could dissuade him from seeking to be a writer. He had read to his family by the hour, and he was determined to write a play called "Cromwell." He wrote with tremendous speed (he finished seventy-four novels), but love and fame eluded him throughout his life.

He had many affairs and liaisons. He had a "sparkling torrent of wit," but was coarse and clumsy. He looked like a man of the people. Biographer Stefan Zweig lists his none-too-flattering features: "His hair was like mane; his nose was short and compressed, furrowed at the tip and with broad nostrils like a lion. His forehead too was leonine and divided into two powerful bulges by a great cleft."[2] He was broad-shouldered and corpulent. Madame de Hanska, the Polish noblewoman he finally married just before his death, complained that "he put his knife into his mouth when he ate."

Business ineptitude kept him one step ahead of his creditors. Most of his erstwhile friends had deserted him until *The Chouans* (1829) became a celebrated work. He was often humiliated and snubbed but sought revenge through his novels. His practice of starving and then gorging himself contributed to his early death.[3]

Over twenty years he wrote his voluminous series *La Comédie Humaine (The Human Comedy),* which features a processional of farmers, military men, clergy, servants, and spinsters. This is a social history of France. Some of the novels in the series really ought to be read, such as *Eugénie Grandet* (1834), *Old Goriot* (1834), and *Cousin Pons* (1847). These exuberant novels reflect his craze for the aristocracy, but he never lost the common touch.[4] Driven by endless primitive superstition and much influenced by playwright François Rabelais (1483–1553), he tended to overdramatize, and his autobiographical data are just plain unreliable. It was said of him that "he preached chastity but changed women like he would change shirts."[5]

Religion is everywhere in his writings. He alleged: "I write in the light of two eternal verities, Religion and the Monarchy."[6] Priests, bishops and nuns abound, though biographer Felicien Marceau remarked that "his Catholicism is far from true Catholicism."[7] His religion was a contributory factor in his life. Earlier on there may have been a vague hostility, but his was adherence to the outer forms. He is sympathetic to the forty churchmen he portrays. In *Seraphita,* we sense a vague Swedenborgian mysticism.

Travel, inescapable debt, serial polygamy, and his overexertion at both work and play finally ended his life. He has a sense of sin but no awareness of redemption as a reality through Christ. Balzac speaks to us about the human situation without any hint of solution.

For an engaging delineation of the fourteenth-century French monarchy, see Maurice Druon (b. 1918), whose seven volumes (1955–77) are entitled Les Rois Maudits, and include such fine, fascinating studies as *The Iron King, The Strangled Queen, The Poisoned Crown,* and *The She-Wolf of France.*

1. Stefan Zweig, *Balzac* (New York: Viking, 1946), 9ff. In a sense, his life was lived in an attempt to escape his mother.
2. Ibid., 111. He failed in silver mining in Sardinia and as owner of the literary journal *Chronique de Paris.*
3. Ibid., 135ff. He incessantly traveled with women, including French woman novelist George Sand.
4. *Old Goriot* is about an old man who has given all of his money to his two daughters who won't attend his funeral.
5. Ibid., 134. Like Dickens, he shares them "warts and all," and perhaps with such bold strokes they are caricatures.
6. Felicien Marceau, *Balzac and His World* (trans. and repr. ed., New York: Orion, 1966), 432. A wondrous parade of people!
7. Ibid., 434. Far more insightful is the Erasmus Lecture of Jean-Marie Cardinal Lustiger, archbishop of Paris, in New York in 1996, *First Things,* October 1997, 38ff. Lustiger trumpets Christ and his Cross for our times. See Bruce Buursma, "West's 'Spiritual Crisis' Worries Paris Cardinal," *The Chicago Tribune,* 3 May 1986, 6.

11.4.3 DUMAS, TELLER OF TALL TALES

I have had many reverses in the course of my life . . . but I have always managed to recover.

—Alexandre Dumas

No novelist gripped me in my youth anymore than did Alexandre Dumas (1802–1870), whose swashbuckling *The Count of Monte Cristo* and *The Three Musketeers* continue to enthrall readers and moviegoers. His stupendous productivity (three hundred works bear his signature) caused some of his colleagues to suspect he was using ghost writers. From 1840 he did employ M. Maquet to do the groundwork for his books. He dedicated himself to the historical novel, "to exalt history to the height of fiction." Unfortunately, some of his historical data was fiction. Reality never hindered his story lines. His goal was to be the Walter Scott of France, and his works have intrigue, suspense, lively characters, and action.[1]

Dumas was born in Villers-Cotterets, the son of a general, as was Victor-Marie Hugo. His grandfather was a Norman nobleman who had married a native woman while on military assignment in Haiti. His father had been with Napoléon in Egypt but became a republican and died when Alexandre was only twelve. Like his father, Alexandre was always involved in the complex politics of the day. His mother struggled with hard times. Often the young boy was kept by his legal guardian, M. Collard, who grounded him in literature and, above all, the Bible.[2]

He had the wanderlust and never stayed long in any one place. He actually started seminary study for the priesthood but turned aside from that and went to Paris, where he became a clerk for the Duke of Orleans. Under the influence of Byron, Scott, Goethe, and Johann F. von Schiller (1759–1805), he started to write plays.

The Three Musketeers (1844), along with its sequels, embodies a raucous Romanticism. Based on historical personages, D'Artagnan and his three friends, Athos, Porthos, and Aramis serve together as bodyguards for Louis XIII. They spend much of their time in sword play with the dastardly agents of the Roman Church.

More compelling dramatically, *The Count of Monte Cristo* (also 1844) tells of Edmond Dantes, who is convicted on a false charge and banished to the Chateau d'If. The story of the count's escape and revenge gave Dumas celebrity status. It was the most popular book in the world.

But the tides of literary naturalism left him behind after 1850. He lived in Belgian exile from 1851 to 1854. He tried editing literary magazines and moving to modern story settings, but nothing seemed to work. He met Giuseppe Garibaldi (1807–1882) in Italy and took up the cudgel as a financial backer for the Italian cause. He also sent money to Abraham Lincoln to help support widows of abolitionists.

He fathered two illegitimate children, a son who became a noted writer and a daughter. As an older man, he continued to have scandalous flings but declined physically and mentally. He became enormously fat.

The drift of his thoughts might be indicated in the title of the last work he attempted: *Creation and Redemption*. It was never published. Toward the end of his life, he confessed to his son that he was "on a monument which is trembling, as if built on sand."[3]

----

1. A. Craig Bell, *Alexandre Dumas* (London: Cassell & Co., 1950), 137ff.
2. Ibid., 17. In *Mes Mémoires,* he remembers M. Collard and the Bible stories of his childhood and youth (263).
3. Ibid., 382. Interestingly, W. E. Henley, the English poet and skeptic, became an avid student of Dumas.

11.4.4 HUGO, MASTER OF MANY MODES

The day is not far distant when cannon will be exhibited in museums, just as instruments of torture are today. The day is not far distant when those two immense entities, the United States of America and the United States of Europe, shall be seen placed in the presence of each other, extending the hand of fellowship across the seas, exchanging their produce, their commerce, their industry, their arts, their genius, clearing the earth, peopling the deserts, improving creation under the eyes of the Creator, and uniting, for the good of these two infinite forces, the fraternity of men and the power of God.

—Victor-Marie Hugo
(address at the World Peace Congress, Paris, 1848)

Victor-Marie Hugo (1802–1885) remains larger than life as a writer since *Les Misérables* became an international musical favorite. Also, his perennially popular *The Hunchback of Notre Dame* was animated by the Disney organization in the mid-1990s. What he would have thought of a cartoon hunchback is unknown, but he would have been perturbed that the name of his novel, *Notre Dame de Paris,* had been changed. Victor-Marie Hugo displayed genius as a poet, dramatist, novelist, and literary critic. He evoked hysterical public adulation, lived on a grand scale, and defied every convention. At one time, he maintained three separate households for his endless succession of mistresses. He was a central figure in French political life for fifty years.[1] His funeral at the Arc de Triomphe in 1885 attracted more than 2 million people, exceeding the population of Paris at the time. He was buried in the Pantheon in Paris. He is to this day literally worshiped as the center of a cult in Vietnam, which has many temples.[2] His signature frock coat and pearl-gray vest and towering ego made him a distinctive and dashing figure in France and throughout Europe. His coat of arms featured the words "EGO HUGO."

He was born in Besançon, France, of old German stock from Lorraine. His father and his four brothers fought in the Revolution in 1789. His father became governor of Lorraine and one of Napoléon's generals. His mother hated men, but loved the writings of Voltaire. The home was deeply divided and disturbed. While growing up, he lived in Corsica, Italy, Spain, and Paris. Despised by other children as an "ugly little dwarf" as a child, he soon grew to more than full size and showed signs of ability to match his physical size. Hugo always was a very physical man and maintained a daily swimming and exercise regimen, though he ate prodigiously.

At fourteen, he translated Vergil and at seventeen, won the chief prize for poetry at Toulouse. In 1822 a book of his poems achieved literary stature. He pleased Louis XVIII and was given a pension. He was a liberal Roman Catholic, if he was anything. He married a childhood friend, Adele, who never understood his work and clung to her middle-class tastes. Adele became the center of a Hugo family calamity; Victor's brother had such a passion for her that he went mad on the day of the wedding.

They had five children, all of whom lived tragic lives. Even though he maintained Juliette Drouet as his chief mistress for over fifty years, he officially lived with Adele until her death, and they had something of a reconciliation on her deathbed.

He produced one hundred lines of poetry a day or twenty pages of prose. In 1831 he wrote *Notre Dame de Paris* in four months, with the beautifully grotesque character, Quasimodo; the priest Claude Frollo, who cares for the abandoned monster-child; and Esmeralda, the gypsy girl who gives the hunchback drinks of water. Hugo always prided himself on the accuracy of his historical novels (particularly as compared with Dumas). His Romanticism and skill brought him great public approbation and a peerage. He became a member of the French Academy in 1841 and was elected to the Assembly, where he spoke on behalf of the French people in deeply moving and eloquent terms.[3]

His influence was threatened when he was found guilty of flagrant adultery.

Ultimately his opposition to President Louis-Napoléon's coup sent him into a nineteen-year exile, first to Brussels but then to the channel islands of Jersey and Guernsey. For a time, he was attracted to spiritualist seances and allegedly was deluded into thinking that he spoke to his deceased children, along with Jesus Christ and the Holy Spirit.[4]

Though at no time did he attend church,[5] the Bible and the works of Shakespeare were primary influences on Hugo, notwithstanding his heterodox theology. His themes are frequently biblical, as in some of his best lyric poetry. In *Les Contemplations* (1856), he ponders the nature of God.[6] In his epic poem *La Légende des Siècles,* he begins with Genesis and Adam and Eve in the garden.[7]

Hugo had strikingly broad interests. He followed the cause of abolition toward war in the U.S. and was a fan of the freedom fighter Garibaldi in Italy. His masterpiece is, by almost any literary standard, one of the two or three greatest novels ever written. *Les Misérables* (1862) is about the dispossessed workers of the Industrial Revolution, but supremely the story is about one man and his relationship to God. Even in the musical rendition, one experiences elation in the depiction of redemption in Jean Valjean. When Valjean rescues a man pinned down by a cart, Inspector Javert recognizes that abnormal strength as belonging to fugitive convict 24601. This is, along with Sydney Carton in Dickens's *A Tale of Two Cities,* one of the greatest illustrations of vicarious love in fiction. This book will continue to inspire if read over and over again.[8]

In 1862 a banquet for two thousand honored Hugo in Brussels. When France was defeated by Germany at the Battle of Sedan, and Paris was besieged for four months (1869–70), Hugo returned home. He continued his prolific output, almost to the time of his death. *The Art of Being a Grandfather* (1877) was a bestseller. His *Le Pape* attacked the Roman Catholic Church; his play *Torquemada* confronted the anti-Semitism of the monarchists.

Nearing the end of his life, he exclaimed: "I believe in God." Unfortunately, he did not believe in the God of the Bible.[9] He could not accept Jesus as the Mediator, nor could he acknowledge the existence of original sin.[10] He believed there were two infinities—one without us (God) and one within us. In *Les Misérables,* which almost everyone acknowledges to be a deeply religious book, he shows a certain obsession with the cross. After 307 pages of dense text, we come to Valjean's spiritual rebirth.[11] But it is "salvation from below," with the barricades of the workers in Paris made into a modern Golgotha. He may use biblical terminology ("the last drop in the chalice"), but at the end, Hugo is a tragic lost soul.

Tapping into an old legend is the classic *The Wandering Jew*[12] written by Eugene Sue (1804–1857). Sue was a French naval physician who turned to writing after becoming heir to his father's wealthy estate. His sea stories are outstanding. He fled into exile when Louis-Napoléon declared himself Napoléon III (at about the same time as Victor-Marie Hugo left Paris in disguise). *The Wandering Jew* (1844–45) touches not only the plight of the Jew but also the arrogance of the Jesuits and other persecutors. This theme would become important in Western literature of the twentieth century, especially following the holocaust.

1. Samuel Edwards, *Victor Hugo: A Tumultuous Life* (New York: McKay, 1971), 4.
2. Graham Robb, *Victor Hugo* (New York: W. W. Norton, 1997). "Victor Hugo created an incredibly large Victor Hugo."
3. Edwards, *Victor Hugo,* 153. Hugo moved steadily toward democracy and a concern for freedom.
4. Ibid., 181, 183. Hugo's writings made him immensely wealthy. Hauteville House on Guernsey became a "Mecca."
5. Ibid., 62f. It should be stated that in the early 1830s, Hugo discovered his wife having an affair with his best friend.
6. Ibid., 191f. His mistress, Juliette, prepared his manuscripts for his publishers.
7. Ibid., 198. One of his many liaisons was with the famous Sarah Bernhardt. He was totally immoral but made a concerted effort at appearances for his family's sake and his own sake. His lifestyle was well known, however.
8. My own edition in two volumes is Victor Hugo, *Les Misérables* (New York: Thomas Crowell, 1887, 1915).
9. Edwards, *Victor Hugo,* 326. After Juliette Drouet died at seventy-seven, he never recovered and did no more writing.
10. Henri Peyre, "After 1852: God," in Harold Bloom, ed., *Victor Hugo* (New York: Chelsea House, 1988), 162f.
11. Victor Brombert, "*Les Misérables*: Salvation from Below," in ibid., 197. He spouted much but believed little.
12. New York: Modern Library. The original publication was 1844–45.

11.4.5 FLAUBERT, CURATOR OF CAREFUL COMPOSITION

What a miracle it would be if in one day I were to write two pages! Before this passage I had one of transition which contains eight lines and took me three days. There is not a superfluous word in it, nevertheless I have to cut it down still further because it drags.

—Gustave Flaubert

Born into the home of a surgeon and his wife in Rouen, Normandy, Gustave Flaubert (1821–1880) was a craftsman of the realistic novel, painfully sculpting an image of words. He was the novelist's novelist, yet he escaped the fate of having all style and no substance. From his youth, he loved to write stories and plays. A strange disorder debilitated him with spells of lights and aura and periods of unconsciousness. He had the first of these when he was studying the law in Paris and as a consequence isolated himself in his Normandy home. "I seldom leave my room," he reported to a friend.[1] He was much influenced toward skepticism by a friend who had read philosophy. He began speaking of "the comedy of religion and heresy" and "the farce of history."[2]

When both his father and sister died, he and his mother shared the responsibility of raising a niece. Still, he was free to write. He fed his mind with Emanuel Swedenborg (1688–1772), David Strauss (1808–1874), and

Teresa of Avila (1515–1582).[3] In 1848 he started writing about the temptation of Anthony and the ancient Alexandrian world. He took a two-year journey to the Middle East. There he was appalled by the bitter and endless controversies dividing Christians, but did concede: "One never stops thinking about the Bible for a moment!"[4] Even a decadent individual like Flaubert, who had a long affair with a married woman, cannot escape the grip of Scripture.

Depressed with the politics of the time, he wrote a novel of small-town Norman life. *Madame Bovary* (1856) was an instant success, although it caused outrage and societal scandal. Henry James called Flaubert morally shallow.

Emma Bovary is married to a colorless doctor, though she has a great capacity for love and life. A narcissist, she gorges herself on romances. "She lives in the present and is unable to resist the slightest impulse."[5] Desire for immediate self-gratification leads to infidelities and financial ruin. Madame Bovary seeks out a priest, but he shows himself to be "so stupid, flat, inept, that she goes away disgusted and quite cured of her piety."[6]

A kind of "mystic languor" hangs over the work. We marvel at Flaubert's description detail and ponder his use of symbolism. A significant example is the gradual destruction of an ecclesiastical statue, which parallels the disintegration of the Bovary marriage.[7]

He finally finished *The Temptation of St. Anthony* (1874) and wrote additional pieces, such as *Salammbô,* a novel of ancient Carthage. *Salammbô* shows the meticulously chiseled discipline we associate with Flaubert. But the other Flaubert hallmark is a cheerless pessimism, unbroken by any transcendent reality.

Like his stories, his life was sad and earthbound:

> He always declared that the discovery of human turpitude gave him more pleasure than any possible gift, and perhaps the most intense pleasure of this kind in his later years was caused by the discovery that the prosecuting attorney who had tried to imprison him for the alleged indecencies of Madame Bovary was himself the author of a book of pornographic poems which was circulating secretly in Paris.[8]

From the same era came Guy de Maupassant (1850–1893), a student of Flaubert. His uncle was Flaubert's best friend. He served in the Franco-Prussian War and then returned to the Seine Valley in Normandy to write such novels as *Pierre et Jean.* But it is mainly his great short stories that we remember. Read "The Necklace" and "The Umbrella." See also the biography *Guy de Maupassant.*[9] The fine introduction to this edition is by Francis Steegmuller. De Maupassant died of complications of syphilis after being confined for syphilitic insanity.

---

1. Francis Steegmuller, *Flaubert and Madame Bovary: A Double Portrait* (London: Collins, 1947), 18.
2. Ibid., 30. Even in unbelief, he said things like, "We are ordained by Providence" (36).
3. Ibid., 118. The combination of Strauss denying the existence of Jesus and St. Theresa shows he is at sea.

4. Ibid., 172. After his disillusioning experience at the Church of the Holy Sepulchre, he read from the Gospel of Matthew "a virginal swelling of the heart, easing the cold bitterness I had been feeling" (171).

5. Mical Peled Ginsburg, "Narrative Strategies in *Madame Bovary*," in *Madame Bovary*, ed. Harold Bloom (New York: Chelsea House, 1988), 137. This illuminating series does have many contributors who represent the more sterile structuralist and deconstructionist points-of-view. This volume is particularly laden with such baggage.

6. *Flaubert and Madame Bovary*, 270. Flaubert was so turned off by this dialogue that he wanted to vomit.

7. Victor Brombert, "The Tragedy of Dreams" in *Madame Bovary*, 13. The plaster statue of a priest breaks.

8. *Flaubert and Madame Bovary*, 312. This cynicism is so typically French and on the increase in our time. A contrast between *Madame Bovary* and *The Scarlet Letter* shows the tragedy of the French lack of the Puritan vision.

9. New York: Dell, 1959.

11.4.6 THIBAULT, KEEPER OF THE CUSTOMS

Today rhetoric is decried: in the Middle Ages it was called "Madam Rhetoric." I regret it: rhetoric teaches how to please, to instruct and to touch. Ideas pass; but rhetoric is eternal.

—Jacques-Anatole Thibault

Jacques-Anatole François Thibault (1844–1924) went by his pen name of Anatole France. Born in Paris, his father was a book dealer who hired his son to deal with libraries. Anatole abandoned the work when he decided he wanted to become a writer.[1] He was very close to his mother, who was a deeply religious person. While his father was "grandiloquent and bombastic," his mother was "simplicity itself" and a great storyteller. Although she was not well educated and read little beyond her cookbook and prayer book, she was a master of proverbs and her talk was like a garden.[2] "It was from her I got my style," France subsequently said.

In some ways this man who dominated French literature was the last of the classical writers. His was a conservative voice, calling for French literature to hang onto some of the old conventions. He himself wrote more than fifty books on various subjects and in different genres. He won the Nobel Prize in 1921.

He was educated in a religious school but had little interest in religion. He asked his young secretary M. Brousson:

Have you been liberated from religious beliefs? People are born churchy or unchurchy. Not all the preaching or all the proofs make any difference. Are there more unbelievers today than in the 15th century, for instance? I do not think so. But then people feigned devotion from fear of the stake. He who is born an unbeliever, remains one all his life, and vice versa. In relation to heaven he is a eunuch. I had that infirmity, or if you like, that advantage.[3]

He had a perverse streak, one time pretending he was having an epileptic sei-zure to escape punishment. He had strongly republican ideas politically but boasted, "I am a modernist." He knew the Bible and the Ten Commandments, but did not attend church.[4] He spoke about King Joash and about prayer, but they were not part of his life. French novelist Joris-Karl Huysmans (1848–1907), who converted to Roman Catholicism, said of France:

> He is a great writer, but he lacks the one necessary thing: faith. Yet he was brought up piously, I have heard, by Christian parents. But vanity, the thirst for applause, the love of paradox—in short, he is in a *parlous* state. Not for all his fame would I be in his place.[5]

He edited a famous literary magazine for many years and was a member of the French Academy. Had he been badly burned religiously? He observed sol-emnly: "There are no chaste people." He asked poignantly: "Why is virtue as a rule so ungracious?"[6] I have read several of his novels, and they pick up biblical themes in a graceful and somewhat detached manner. I would recommend *Thaïs,* which is an elegantly told story of an Egyptian courtesan who converts to Chris-tianity. Or I would suggest *The Crime of Sylvestre Bonnard,* about a sweet, old archaeologist who kidnaps the orphaned daughter of his former love when he learns how unhappy she is. One of his powerfully developed characters is Jerome Coignard, a rascal priest in *At the Sign of the Reine Pedauque.* He did think about hell but didn't really believe anyone was there. Perhaps it was wishful thinking, but he felt religion was passing away and leaving "the most ill-favored and ty-rannical of her daughters: the hideous sense of shame."[7]

There were those who were concerned about his soul. He was asked if he ever thought of his end and replied, "Never, madam, never." He thought death was comic, and he didn't care if he were with the sheep or the goats. Confession of his sins was a joke. Few have been so forthright about their unbelief.

A spectacular writer, both in his day and ours, is Jules Verne (1828–1905), who wrote the first science fiction. His greatest novels, *Around the World in Eighty Days* (with Phileas Fogg and Passepartout) and *20,000 Leagues Under the Sea,* are still widely read. Drifting from a staunch Catholic background, Verne projected a bleak prospect for the future. He was a keen stylist of words who wrote 103 volumes.[8]

---

1. Jean Jacques Brousson, *Anatole France Himself* (Philadelphia: J. B. Lippencott, 1925), 281.
2. Ibid., 166.
3. Ibid., 15. M. Brousson was himself a very deeply religious man and spoke mean-ingfully about true faith.
4. Ibid., 59, 232. He urged writers to say what they would about the Virgin or the Pope, but to have respect for Paul.
5. Ibid., 99.
6. Ibid., 86; cf. 351. It was likely for virtue's sake that he became passionately involved

in the defense of the Alfred Dreyfus affair, the Jewish military man falsely accused
of treason. Curiously, France sprinkled his own speech with anti-Semitic language.
7. Ibid., 349.
8. See Peter Costello, *Jules Verne: Inventor of Science Fiction* (New York: Scribner's,
1978); and idem, *Jules Verne: An Exploratory Biography* (New York: Martin's, 1996).

11.4.7 PROUST, BELLWETHER OF CHANGE

The past is hidden somewhere outside the realm, beyond the reach of
intellect in some material object (in the sensation which that material
object will give us) which we do not suspect, and as for that object, it
depends upon chance whether we come upon it or not before we ourselves die.

—Marcel Proust

There has always been a dark side to French literature, as represented in the
atheist pornographer, the Marquis de Sade (1740–1814), from whom comes the
word sadism;[1] the sensuous and perverse Charles Baudelaire (1821–1867); and
the viciously anti-Semitic Louis-Ferdinand Céline (pen name for Louis Fuch
Destouches, 1894–1961), who believed everything was insane.[2]

At the edge of this nihilistic urge is Marcel Proust (1871–1922), who wrote a
rambling multivolume fictional autobiography called *Remembrance of Things
Past*. This mammoth tome is still "the Mount Everest that French critics want to
conquer." The narrator of the novel is very much like Proust himself (and indeed
is once called "Marcel"). He wanders in and out of love and finally finds himself
in the writing of this novel. In preparing to write his masterpiece, Proust researched and wrote about memory. He recalled much from his childhood and
created the village of Combray to be central in his novel. Like G. Stanley Hall's
early research on memory, he found that a physical object associated by the mind
with long-past places or events could trigger a Niagara of memories.[3]

Proust was born in Paris and raised in a home not far off the Champs-Elysees.
His father was a prominent Roman Catholic physician; his mother was Jewish.
From age nine, he was virtually incapacitated by asthma. He was often taken to
the Channel shore to alleviate asthmatic symptoms. He recovered enough to serve
briefly in the army.

He also attended the Sorbonne, where he was enraptured by Henri-Louis
Bergson's philosophy of time. Bergson (1859–1941), who received the 1927
Nobel Prize, posited a theory of creative evolution. Time, he postulated, is "a
continuous flow in which past and present are inseparable from the memory and
the consciousness."[4] This philosophy drastically influences *Remembrance of
Things Past,* the title of which might be more accurately translated from the
French, *In Search of Lost Time*. Critic and writer John Ruskin's (1819–1900) love
of architecture and beauty also inspired him. Anatole France encouraged Proust
and wrote an introduction for an early work.

After his parents' deaths, Proust moved into a cork-lined apartment to ame-
liorate his symptoms. He had many, since he was known as a "world-class

hypochondriac" who was always in a chill, with a cough, runny nose, and itchy skin. He used twenty nonirritating towels each time he washed and seldom from this time got up out of bed.

How are we to understand the present surge of interest in Proust? His novel, quite frankly, is about nothing. Its final sections were published after his death and no one is exactly sure how much to include of the rambling manuscripts. Alaine de Botton's best-selling *How Proust Can Change Your Life* is really the self-help book developed to its highest form. Proust's father had been the guru of self-help in his day, and now de Botton offers nine chapters from the younger Proust on self-improvement.[5]

This "self-help" only goes so far; Proust does not get better, so he doesn't complete the victim-recovery cycle. His prescription is: Don't blame others. Seek silence. Solitude alone opens the door to the deep truth inside us, or that seems to be the experience of Charles Swann, the major figure in the novel. A nine-step program makes the book a "way of life."[6] Late-twentieth-century literary critic Shelby Foote confessed on C-SPAN's "Booknotes" program that he had read it through nine times. This reading is not easy but it is informative. Needless to say, Proust provided a heyday to analysts of all kinds.[7] Still we must face the fact: self-help and autosalvation are not enough. There has got to be more than "I have to be me." Significantly, he makes no allusion in six volumes of autobiography to his Jewish heritage. Nor does he refer to his deviant sexual preference.

A stalwart and unbending Roman Catholic writer is George Bernanos (1888–1948), whose *Diary of a Country Priest* is a treasure. He loved Pascal, Dostoevsky, and Charles Peguy. Unfortunately, he was an anti-Semite, a prejudice that was fatally common in France before and during World War II.[8]

1. John Attarian, "The Demonic Marquis: Why Sadism is the Philosophy of our Age," *Culture Wars,* July 1995, 10ff.

2. Thomas Molnar, "Celine and French Reactionary Modernism," *Chronicles of Culture*, August 1992, 16ff.

3. Phyllis Rose, *The Year of Reading Proust: A Memoir in Real Time* (New York: Scribner's, 1997).

4. William Rose Benet, *Benet's Reader's Encyclopedia,* 3d ed. (New York: Harper and Row, 1987), "Proust, Marcel"; cf. Bergson's religious ideas on "Henri Bergson," in Ibid.; and in Bergson's *The Two Sources of Morality and Religion* (New York: Doubleday, 1935). Henri Bergson was the son of Jewish-Polish immigrants who raised him in Paris.

5. Alaine de Botton, *How Proust Can Change Your Life: Not a Novel* (New York: Pantheon, 1997). This book's nine-step plan has been popular in the self-help market.

6. Reviewed in *The Chicago Tribune,* Book Section, 14 September 1997; also reviewed in *Tempo,* 5 November 1997.

7. Julia Kristeva, *Time and Sense: Proust and the Experience of Literature* (New York: Columbia Press, 1996).

8. See R. L. Bruckberger, *Bernanos Vivant* (Paris: Albin Michel, 1991).

11.4.8 GIDE, DEALER IN DECADENCE

I have never been able to give up anything.
                    —from a "loose leaf" in André Gide's Journal

André Gide (1869–1951) is not a writer I recommend without reservations, yet he cannot be ignored. He was born in Paris in a strict Protestant home. His father, who died when he was eleven, was a professor of law at the Sorbonne. An only child, he was educated privately at a Protestant secondary school. In a sense, his search for himself and for a new ethic became the paradigm of a whole movement that was exceedingly influential from 1890–1950. At least eighty monographs have been published about him, for he was a very complex person, and he fixated upon himself.[1] The narcissism we have traced through the French writers bears its logical fruit in Gide. He was inspired to keep a diary by the writings of Henri-Frédéric Amiel, the Swiss philosopher (1821–1881). This journal tended to be therapeutic and became the bridge to writing fiction.

The environment in which he was raised was that "atmosphere of minoritarian sensitivity that hangs over Calvinism in Catholic France."[2] His mother held up before him the Calvinistic ideals of "austerity, modesty and obedience." But evidently not much of the love and grace of God got through to him. He is called by some a cathartist because of his relentless theme of purity, but he never came to peace with the orthodox doctrine of evil. He declared war on the Epistles of Paul, trying to find "a way out of his discomfiture under the law."[3]

The war within was between Puritan morality and his Dionysian eroticism. His novels and poems were part of the Decadence and Symbolism Movement. In his first trip to North Africa in 1893, he openly broke with traditional morality but nonetheless married his cousin, Madeline, in 1895. After her death, he disclosed that they had never lived together as husband and wife. He accused her of leaning toward Catholicism.[4]

He became part of the French Romantic resurgence, although he was "held in check, barely, by his Protestantism." He was drinking deeply at the fountain of Goethe, Nietzsche, Henrik Ibsen (1828–1906), and August Strindberg (1849–1912). His unorthodox views and lifestyle were highly controversial but many young people found him to be a prophet. Sometimes he would pick up a biblical motif, as in his play *Saul* on the first king of Israel.[5] His running quarrel with Protestantism is most visible in the one piece I would recommend—*La Symphonie Pastorale (The Pastoral Symphony),* which he wrote in 1919, telling the story of a Swiss Protestant pastor who raises a girl who seems to be deaf and dumb. She learns to speak in this new environment, however, and the pastor becomes concerned that his son will fall in love with her; so he seduces her. The work is skillfully done (from the perspective of the pastor's diary). But it is bitter and sharp in exposing the hypocrisy that Gide saw everywhere in Protestantism.[6]

Having rejected Christian morality, he, like Nietzsche, desperately searches for a substitute. The entry on Gide in *Benet's Reader's Encyclopedia* makes a perceptive statement that Gide "was twice tempted to find self-development in commitment to something outside himself."[7] Clearly, he did not elect to take either road away from the comfort of his own psyche. So the tragedy of *La Symphonie Pastorale* was inevitable for Gide and Madeline.

■ **Émile Zola led the naturalist school** and was something of a Christian socialist. An example of his social awareness is his leadership of the effort is save Alfred Dreyfus, the falsely-accused Jewish military officer who was banished to Devil's Island off French Guiana. Zola (1840–1902) traces an unprincipled Parisian social–climber in *Nana* (1880) but shows no fulcrum by which we can transcend or transform the ugly.[8]

---

1. Thomas Cordle, *André Gide* (Boston: Twayne, 1969), 25.
2. Ibid., 28. French Protestantism over time generally surrendered all of its cultural connections to biblical authority, John Calvin's *Institutes of the Christian Religion,* and the supernatural. As a result, the main true evangelical presence at this writing is in mission churches planted from abroad.
3. Ibid., 29. Paul's teaching of "fulfilling the law" through Christ in us and death to self would be anathema to Gide.
4. Ibid., 59. For an understanding perspective of the Decadence and Symbolism Movement, see François Mauriac, *Memoires Intérieurs* (New York: Farrar, 1960), 165ff.
5. Ibid., 67. His rejection of conventional Christian morality was complete. Gide advocates a radical antinomianism.
6. André Gide, *La Symphonie Pastorale* (London: Penguin, 1963). Bound with his novella, *Isabelle.*
7. "André Gide," in *Benet's Reader's Encyclopedia.* For glimpses of Gide's and others' flirtations with communism, see Kenneth Murphy, *Retreat from Finland Station: Moral Odysseys in the Breakdown of Communism* (New York: Free Press, 1993). The study also touches on the lives of Arthur Koestler (1905–1983), Ignazio Silone (1900–1978), Milovan Djilas (1911–1995), and Aleksandr Solzhenitsyn (b. 1918).
8. For a thorough study of Zola, see Frederick Brown, *Zola* (New York: Farrar, 1995).

11.4.9 MAURIAC, GRAPPLER FOR GRACE

The gift of the novelist goes back precisely to the power of making evident the universality of this narrow world in which we have learned to love and to suffer. . . . Any writer who has maintained in the center of his work the human creature made in the image of the Father, redeemed by the Son, illumined by the Spirit, I cannot see in him a master of despair, however somber his painting may be.

—François Mauriac
(in accepting the 1952 Nobel Prize for Literature)

A refreshing figure amid the banality of the twentieth-century French literary landscape is the delightful François Mauriac (1885–1970), who is a writer of faith. He exposes the vain existence and pain in lives that are nonresponsive to the grace of God. Sin and redemption are his themes.[1] He wrote twenty novels, four full-length plays, two volumes of short stories, and much else.

He was born in beautiful Bordeaux in the southwest of France, the youngest of five children. He never knew his father, a lover of literature who had lost his faith. His mother was a pious Jansenist (see 5.2). His grandfather had not gone to church until he was carried there on his bed when mortally stricken.

Young Mauriac was deeply taken with what he saw—the old man put his hands together to pray and said, "We are saved by faith" before he died.[2] His grandmother was very rigid in her insistence, "Outside of the church there is no salvation." François often got into trouble, as when he tried to rub out a bad mark on a report card and rubbed a hole through the paper. Yet his home was a secure shelter in his childhood, and he wrote of all these things in his later works. He wanted in his writings to recover "the fragrant and sad world of childhood."[3]

A torn eyelid inclined him to feel ugly and inferior. He overcame his self-deprecation enough to study rhetoric with his beloved l'abbe Pequigot. When he went up to Paris in 1906, he began to write. He was almost immediately noticed and soon famous. He married Jeanne Lafont in 1913.

Several factors incubated a spiritual crisis in 1928. He had been devastated by Roman Catholic criticism of his work; he indulged an extramarital affair that left him guilt-laden; and he read in depth about Jean Racine (1639–1699; see 6.1.2) and his return to the Jansenism of his childhood. Confronting God's ultimatum, "I want all!" he responded. This was his conversion.[4]

Blaise Pascal (1623–1662) was a guide for his faith for sixty years. Mauriac departed from him only on predestination and his pessimism. At the same time, Mauriac developed cancer of the throat. X-ray treatments left him with a heavy hoarseness for the rest of his life, but he continued to have artistic success. He was elected to the French Academy (a literary society limited to forty members at any one time).

Beyond the influence of Pascal, Mauriac also revered Balzac and Dostoevsky. He met Proust twice but regretted the latter's lack of Christian faith.[5] He was often the antagonist in Gide's war against Christianity. Gide taunted him, mocking his conversion. He was arraigned by Jean-Paul Sartre (1905–1980) as not being a novelist at all.

The masterpieces of Mauriac show the human condition without grace. In *A Kiss for the Leper* (1922), we focus on an ugly young bridegroom; in *Genetrix* (1923), we meet a dominant mother and mother-in-law; in *The Desert of Love* (1925), a father and his son love the same woman; in *Theresa Desqueyroux* (1927), a woman attempts to poison her husband; in *The Knot of Vipers* (1932), the protagonist is a crusty and rich old lawyer; and in *Woman of the Pharisees* (1941), the plot revolves around a proud stepmother.

Mauriac carried on his crusade against French decadence in the 1930s and against Nazism in the 1940s. He had to hide when the Gestapo proclaimed him one of the leading enemies of the Third Reich.

Suffusing his whole life was the confidence: "I knew that nature could be imbued with grace, for I had lived with that knowledge long before I had had any idea of what 'grace' and 'nature' meant."[6] His answer to Gide was an extended essay, *God and Mammon*. God was alive and well for Mauriac.

▓ **For choice French novels of suspense,** no one can bypass Georges Simenon, creator of Chief Inspector Maigret. Simenon, who was actually born in Belgium but has written within the French experience, has written four hundred novels. There is a significant biography by Pierre Assouline.[7] Another writer in the same tradition is Nicholas Freeling, whose sleuth Henri Carstang ranges over France and the Low Countries. He is an appealing character.

---

1. *Benet's Reader's Encyclopedia,* 630. He shows the failure of having less than God.
2. Maxwell A. Smith, *François Mauriac* (Boston: Twayne, 1970), 17. With the male deaths, "women reigned."
3. Ibid., 15. Another put it, "He has taken [his roots in] Bordeaux with him" (25).
4. Ibid., 41. A recent convert brought him to a converted Jew, now a priest, who pointed him to the Savior.
5. Ibid., 145. Mauriac's characters are strongly presented; his character development techniques were studied by Graham Greene and others.
6 François Mauriac, *Memoires Intérieurs* (New York: Farrar, Strauss, 1960), 233ff. A remarkably revealing piece.
7. Pierre Assouline, *Simenon: A Biography* (New York: Knopf, 1997).

11.4.10 CAMUS, PIED PIPER OF EMPTINESS

> All those folks are saying: "It was plague. We've had the plague here."
> ... But what does that mean? "The plague"? Just life, no more than that.
> —Albert Camus
> an old patient to Dr. Rieux in *The Plague*

The roots of the modern "existentialist revolt" are really in Nietzsche and Søren Kierkegaard (1813–1855; see 5.14), but the climactic existential expression comes in Camus and Sartre, though they differed from one another in central ways. Albert Camus (1913–1960) was born in Mondovi, French Algeria. His father was a vineyard laborer from Alsace and his mother an illiterate Spanish woman, who was deaf and almost dumb. When Albert's father was killed early in World War I, his mother moved to a lower-class part of Algiers to work as a charwoman. The young boy was raised in poverty in a small apartment with his "sadistic grandmother" and a disagreeable uncle.[1]

A gifted teacher, Louis Germain, took an interest in him and recommended him for a scholarship. In his late teens, he went to Paris, where he studied and wrote, although he contracted tuberculosis and briefly was a member of the Communist Party.[2] He did not move permanently to Paris until 1942. By this time, he had been twice married, fought in the French Resistance, and wrote three acclaimed works: the novel *The Stranger;* the pivotal essay "The Myth of Sisyphus," which demonstrates the ceaseless futility of life; and the popular play *Caligula.*

Camus lived licentiously in elite literary and political circles.[3] Eventually, he broke with Sartre and Marxism and became enmeshed in the Algerian struggle.

He received the Nobel Prize for Literature in 1957. By then, his life was in serious decline, and he was broken in spirit by the time he was killed in a car crash at age forty-six. It had become harder and harder to roll the boulder up the hill.

Camus offers an exemplary and appealing passion for justice and freedom. He is still widely read and influential for more than his fatherhood of the beat generation. In *The Plague,* he tells the story of Dr. Bernard Rieux in the Algerian city of Oran, while the grim bubonic plague waylays the people. The devastation is so great that many give up, but not Dr. Rieux. He, like Camus, is a resolute atheist and has an ethical center more deeply thought out than that of the "Christians," like Father Paneloux, who want people to accept God's will. Paneloux's sermonic calls for self-surrender to God are rejected by Dr. Rieux.[4]

Camus renounced hope. He felt that, while other writers recognized life's absurdity, he alone carried the burden of absurdity.[5] He was utterly unable to accept Christianity. He was into the theatre of the absurd and the theatre of revolt. He condemned both Christianity and communism as "apologists for injustice."[6]

The Plague is not only a deeply moving story, but it is an articulation of the deep European depression and disillusionment following the two world wars. *The Plague* offers little in the way of remedy; having turned from God, Camus's saints exist without God. He wondered if Christians could be decent people. Even though he has rejected the idea of sin, in his deeply felt book *The Fall,* he tells us the story of Jean-Baptiste Clamence, who suffers guilt because he did not intervene when a young woman jumped into the Seine. Christian symbols abound, but there is no Christ the Savior.[7] Is there some nostalgia for God showing itself in these later writings of Camus? Humankind is not innocent, and we need a Savior.

The hedonism, flight from reason, and sexual permissiveness found in existentialism are epitomized by Jean-Paul Sartre (1905–1980). Sartre studied under Martin Heidegger (1889–1976) and in 1938 wrote his autobiography *Nausea.* "When I realized I existed, I got sick." In 1944 he wrote *No Exit,* a book whose title sums up its hopelessness well.[8] He won the Nobel Prize in 1964. "Hell is other people," he said. Paul Johnson shows Sartre's inability to be a giver of advice on morals or where to go in his hard–hitting *Intellectuals.*[9] Sartre also models the disastrous effect of putting ourselves in God's place.[10] (We now know that the illustrious Paul Johnson is also a hypocrite.)

1. Albert Camus, introduction to *The Plague* (New York: Time Reading Program, 1948), vi.
2. Olivier Todd, *Albert Camus: A Life* (New York: Knopf, 1996). A condensed version of the French original.
3. Roger Kaplan, "France's Most Reluctant Existentialist," *Insight,* 1 March 1998, 36. Kaplan witnessed an episode in which Camus prevented an inebriated Arthur Koestler from beating on a no-less-intoxicated Jean-Paul Sartre.
4. Phillip H. Rhein, *Albert Camus* (Boston: Twayne, 1969), 59. He blamed Jesus for the massacre of the innocents.
5. Ibid., 27. He had vociferous arguments on this issue with both the man of faith, Mauriac (100), and the atheist, Sartre (67).

6. Peter L. Berger, "Camus, Bonhoeffer and the World Come of Age," *The Christian Century,* 8 April 1959, 417.

7. William Mueller writes an incisive essay on *The Fall,* in *Pulpit Digest,* September 1959, 25ff.

8. See Vincent P. Miceli, *The Gods of Atheism* (Harrison, N.Y.: Roman Catholic Books, 1971).

9. New York: Harper, 1988, 225ff.

10. John T. Mullen, "Learning from Sartre," *First Things,* June/July 1994, 45ff.

11.5 ON THE ITALIAN INLET

Beautiful and scenic, Italy's countryside is dense with history. Though politically turbulent, it remains a tourist Mecca, gateway to Vatican City and *la Roma,* the city on seven hills.

We have noticed classical writers from this area, for example the comedians, Plautus (254–184 B.C.) and Terence (186–159 B.C.; see 2.6.2); the poets, Catullus (c. 84–c. 54 B.C.), Horace (65 B.C.–8 B.C.), and Ovid (43 B.C.–A.D. 17; see 2.6.3, 2.6.4, and 2.6.5); the historians, Livy (59 B.C.–A.D. 17), Pliny the Younger (A.D. 61–113), Tacitus (55–120), and Plutarch (46–120; see 2.7.1, 2.7.2, 2.7.3, and 2.7.4); the orators and philosophers, Cicero (106 B.C.–43 B.C.), Seneca (4 B.C.–A.D. 65), Epictetus (55–135), and Marcus Aurelius (121–180; see 2.8.1, 2.8.2, 2.8.3, and 2.8.5), and then Vergil, the greatest Roman of them all (70 B.C.–19 B.C.; 2.8.5).

From the collapse of the Roman Empire and the successor Dark Ages came Augustine of Hippo (354–430; see 3.1) and the immortal Dante (1265–1321; see 3.3). Think of the richness of the Italian Renaissance as represented in such figures as Petrarch (1304–1374; see 4.1), Boccaccio (1313–1375; see 4.2), and Machiavelli (1469–1527; see 4.3). Several modern writers merit mention.

11.5.1 LAMPEDUSA, TACKLING FREEDOM

> I belong to an unfortunate generation, swung between the old world and the new, and I find myself ill at ease in both.
>
> —Don Fabrizio
> nineteenth-century Sicilian Prince in *The Leopard*

The Oxford writer A. L. Rowse called *The Leopard* "the most remarkable, and the most significant literary sensation of our time."[1] The author, Giuseppe Tomasi, prince of Lampedusa (1896–1957), was from an old Sicilian noble family. He wrote several pieces, including this novel, as he neared the end of his life—all over the space of only a couple of months. He had talked about writing such a novel concerning the *Risorgimento* (movement for Italian unification) but did not do it until the very end of his life.

His hero, Don Fabrizio, is totally discombobulated by the fact and velocity of change. New upstarts are all around. He says of a boorish merchant who has gained influence: "His family, I am told, is an old one or soon will be." Don

Fabrizio is the Leopard, albeit a moth-eaten one. His nephew marries the daughter of the merchant, and Don Fabrizio is determined to be gracious and stylish despite his revulsion.[2] The chaplain, Father Pirrone, is rigid and a prude and not very helpful to the skeptical Don Fabrizio. This character reflects the author's wrestling with the collapse of European society. This is a rich study of the perennial problem of reaction to change.

1. A. L. Rowse, introduction to *The Leopard,* ed. Giuseppe di Lampedusa (New York: Pantheon, 1958), xv.
2. Di Lampedusa, editor's preface to *The Leopard,* xii. Another of Don Fabrizio's daughters, Concetto, turns to religious fanaticism.

11.5.2 SILONE, ON THE MARXIST ROAD

I do not believe in the lasting resignation of man.

—Ignazio Silone

A remarkably compassionate novel, *Bread and Wine,* has come to us through Ignazio Silone (1900–1978). Born into a poor family in Central Italy, he survived earthquakes that destroyed his village and killed his mother and all but one of his brothers. He commenced studies at a seminary, always believing that religion held the key to life. He became interested in communism and went into Swiss exile when Italy became a fascist state in the Axis Alliance.[1] In 1944 Silone returned to Italy disillusioned with socialism.

His great novel is about the return of an expatriate to Italy disguised as a priest to lead the underground partisans against fascism. The story revolves around Cristina, who becomes a convert, and Don Benedetto, the old priest, who dies from drinking poisoned communion wine. This a deeply moving and stirring study.

Silone also tells his story in one essay in *The God That Failed,* the volume edited by R. H. S. Crossman.[2]

Umberto Eco is at this writing a great success as author of one of the most accurate and well-crafted historical novels of the late twentieth century, *The Name of the Rose.* His next book was *Foucault's Pendulum,* which is a novel for those who want an in-depth look at medieval occultism.[3] Eco is professor of semiotics at the University of Bologna. Some have called this book "an erudite joke," and it will most appeal to scholars, but its excess of knowledge notwithstanding, it is a remarkable study of medieval occultism and the convulsives of Saint Medard and their mystical beverages.

1. Luigi Barzini, introduction to *Bread and Wine,* by Ignazio Silone (New York: Harper, 1937), xiv.
2. R. H. S. Crossman, *The God That Failed* (London: Hamilton, 1950). Various writers

from this era describe their disillusionment with Marxism, including André Gide, Arthur Koestler, Richard Wright, Louis Fisher, and Ignazio Silone.
3. Umberto Eco, *Foucault's Pendulum* (New York: Ballentine, 1990).

11.5.3 LEVI, TAKING ON THE FASCISTS

> But to this shadowy land, that knows neither sin nor redemption from sin, where evil is not moral but is only the pain residing forever in earthly things, Christ did not come. Christ stopped at Eboli.
>
> —Carlo Levi
> *Christ Stopped at Eboli*

Carlo Levi (1902–1978) was a doctor imprisoned by Benito Mussolini and banished for a year to a malaria-infested village in the desperately poor village of Gagliano. Survival, not fascism, was an issue in this destitute area. In writing *Christ Stopped at Eboli,* which is ostensibly factual, the author awakens awareness to the neglected and exploited area. The heavy pall of misery has begotten a "gloomy resignation, alleviated by no hope of paradise, that bows their shoulders under the scourges of nature."[1] This is an unforgettable album of portraits. "There's no grace of God in this village" murmurs the drunken priest, Don Giuseppe Trajella. Few have been baptized, bemoans the priest who had been a painter and teacher of theology.[2] Here is a more basic deprivation than fascism.

A most enjoyable description of modern Italy and Italian life, though not written by an Italian, is the novel of suspense by Ngaio Marsh, *When in Rome.*[3] Marsh is a native of New Zealand, and she takes her Scotland Yard hero, Roderick Alleyn, on a lively guided tour of the ancient and modern sites.

---

1. Carlo Levi, editor's introduction to *Christ Stopped at Eboli* (New York: Farrar, Strauss, 1947), viii.
2. Ibid., 39ff.
3. New York: Jove/Little, Brown, 1980.

11.6 OUT OF THE RUSSIAN RAGE

"Mother Russia" seems almost a womb for the world, vast geographically and historically. One thousand years of Russian Orthodoxy so indelibly marked this diverse peoples that neither czars nor communists could alter it.

Historically, Russia has been the most dangerous when she has appeared to be weak. The tyrannical rule of the czars—a century during which rebellion smoldered . . . the revolution . . . Stalinism . . . cold war . . . beginnings of democratization . . . broken-up empire. . . . We must understand the mass terror of the Russian Revolution in 1918 if we are to grasp subsequent events.[1] Who could have foreseen the turns of the 1990s?[2] What role will the Eastern Orthodox Church in Russia now play in the world and in relation to evangelical churches?[3]

1. W. Bruce Lincoln, *Red Victory: A History of the Russian Civil War* (New York: Simon and Schuster, 1989).

2. John B. Dunlop, *The Rise of Russia and the Fall of the Soviet Empire* (Princeton, N.J.: Princeton University Press, 1993); David Remnick, *Resurrection: The Struggle for a New Russia* (New York: Random House, 1997); Eleanor Randolph, *Waking the Tempests: Ordinary Life in the New Russia* (New York: Simon and Schuster, 1994). For a look at Russia as a predemocracy, see Daniel Yergin and Thane Gustafson, *Russia 2010* (New York: Random House, 1993).

3. Nathaniel Davis, *A Long Walk to Church: A Contemporary History of Russian Orthodoxy* (Boulder, Colo.: Westview, 1995). Peter Gillquist seeks to explain why some evangelicals have become orthodox; cf. "Evangelicals Turned Orthodox," *The Christian Century,* 4 March 1992, 242ff. Daniel B. Clendenin, who was one of the foremost observers of Orthodox happenings in the 1990s, offered a sensible response to the flight into the Eastern church in "Why I'm Not Orthodox," *Christianity Today,* 6 January 1997, 33. Among several serious flaws in Orthodox theology is the total lack of justification by faith alone apart from the works of the law (37). Clendenin has written several books on the new Russia, the new Russian church, and Orthodox theology in general.

11.6.1 DOSTOEVSKY, PROPHET OF FIRE

If anyone proved to me that Christ was outside the truth . . . then I would prefer to remain with Christ than with the truth.

—Fëdor Dostoevsky

Russian novels take two of the sparse slots for fiction in Great Books of the Western World. Reading some of these authors may be the best preparation one can make for visiting or understanding the complex people. Called by some "the prophet of the Russian Revolution," Fëdor Mikhailovich Dostoevsky (1821–1881) was born in Moscow, the son of a physician. After his mother's death in 1837, he was sent to St. Petersburg to the School of Military Engineers.

School was not to his liking, and he was characteristically seen with his nose in a (nonengineering) book. He wanted to write. He wrote a scathing rebuke to his father for neglect, but the latter was unable to reply. He had been murdered by his serfs in one of the century's numerous peasant revolts. According to family tradition and the comments of Sigmund Freud, it was upon hearing of the death of his father that Dostoevsky had his first epileptic seizure.[1]

His first novel, *Poor Folk,* was well received as striking in its psychological analysis of human suffering and anguish. In 1848 he was arrested for taking part in forbidden political activity and sentenced to death. Word was received that his sentence was commuted as he stood before the firing squad and the guns were cocked.[2] Banished to a Siberian camp, Dostoevsky received a New Testament from a devout woman as he boarded the train. He emerged from prison with a strong Christian testimony and identification with fellow human beings who were at the bottom in society. He wrote about them with skill and insight.

Upon his return, he married Marie, a widow, in what proved to be a loveless marriage. To compensate, he indulged in affairs (particularly with Polina Suslov, whose influence was largely negative) and fits of gambling and drinking. Despite his stressful poverty, he wrote to attack Russian nihilism, arguing that only Judeo-Christian morality could really stand against it. His own morality tended to be less than circumspect. He had a dalliance with Martha Panina and with Anna Korvin-Krukovsky, who later translated Karl Marx into Russian.[3]

"The usually gloomy and care-worn" Dostoevsky, with his trade-mark meager beard and dandyism, now wrote *The Gambler* (1866). In this book, he basically tells the story of his experiences with Polina Suslov at the tables in Weisbaden. He eventually settled into a stable marriage with the woman who had been his stenographer, Anna Grigorievna Snitkin.[4]

From a Christian viewpoint, Dostoevsky's greatest contribution was *Crime and Punishment* (1866), which tells the story of Raskolnikov, who feels he is liberated from the Christian ethic and murders an old woman. Sonya, a true Mary Magdalene, changes his life when she reads to him John 11 on the raising of Lazarus. This is an ideal place to start reading.

Dostoevsky was deeply moved by seeing Hans Holbein the Younger's (c. 1497–1543) "Christ Taken Down from the Cross" in Basel. That painting was the inspiration for *The Idiot* (1868), with its strong emphasis on his faith in Christ, the God-Man. He shares his vision of life in this novel, though it is artistically uneven. "The passion on the Cross shatters the mind," he exclaimed.[5]

The death of his little daughter Sofya at this time contributed to the portrait of the saintly Prince Myshkin, who was not good for anything but just good, as someone said. In this, his most original novel, he advances the idea of the interim Christian ethic between the incarnation of Christ and his imminent second coming.[6] This novel was not well received, but his reputation was restored by *The Eternal Husband,* "the most perfect and polished of the short works."

Out of envy of Tolstoy's immense scope and a desire to fully confess his faith in Christ, Dostoevsky set out to write an ambitious cycle of books called *The Life of a Great Sinner.* Only one of those stories was published, but it is arguably his best—*The Brothers Karamazov* (1880).

The book deals with the existence of God with a subtext about the problem of guilt in human experience. The vehicle for this consideration is a story of patricide, which recalls Dostoevky's own relationship with his father. This majestic, complex work is about old Karamazov's four sons: Dmitry, the passionate accused killer of the father; Ivan, the atheistic rationalist; Aloysha, the believing pilgrim and disciple who says to Ivan, "I do not know the answer to the problem of evil, but I do know love";[7] and Smerdyakov, the illegitimate son.

The clergy figure is Father Zosima, who has a real experience of the Word of God. Lenin may have asserted that "every idea of God is unutterable vileness," but Dostoevsky believes unswervingly that "the Bible is the ultimate of truth."[8] In "The Grand Inquisitor," a remarkable story within a story narrated by Ivan, Christ comes to Sevilla and is no more welcome than in the first century.

In other works, we meet the monk *Tihon,* who has been strongly influenced by German pietism, and then in *Death of a Poet,* we see the orthodox priest in controversy with an old believer. As he grew older, he loved and became more dependent on his wife. He was increasingly absorbed in his concern for "the moral and spiritual travails of the Russian spirit."

The Russian philosopher Nicholay Berdyayev (1874–1948) was shaken by Dostoevsky. He came to metaphysical idealism while studying under Windelband at Heidelberg and in 1907 to "faith in God." He was strongly opposed to Kantian septicism, for he recognized the impossibility that a consistent Kantian could believe in the resurrection of Christ. He is the most Christocentric of modern philosophers.

In the succession of Dostoevsky, Berdyayev wrote a statement at the time of World War I that seems very apropos today:

> An orgy of predatory instincts, of disgraceful greed, and speculation at the time of the great world war and of enormous trials for Russia, remains our greatest shame, a dark stain on our national life, an ulcer on Russia's body. The drive for enrichment has captivated too many sections of Russian society.[9]

Dostoevsky is among the preeminent Russian writers and one of the greatest novelists from any nation. J. I. Packer calls him, "the greatest Christian story teller."

---

1. Biographical note in Fëdor Dostoevsky, *The Brothers Karamazov* (Chicago: Great Books, 1952), v.

2. Joseph Frank, *Dostoevsky: The Miraculous Years, 1865–71* (Princeton: Princeton University Press, 1995), 10. This is the fourth of five volumes in an extraordinary series.

3. Hutterian Brethren, eds., *The Gospel in Dostoevsky* (Farmington, Pa.: Plough, 1988), 9ff.

4. Frank, *Dostoevsky: The Miraculous Years,* 221. For four years after their marriage they wandered much, and he struggled with guilt and depression.

5. Ibid., 265. The theme of immortality hovers throughout *The Idiot.* He argues, if there is no immortality, then do as you please. The future life is a necessity, not simply a consolation, 254.

6. Ibid., 313.

7. Philip Yancey, "Be Ye Perfect, More or Less: On Tolstoy and Dostoevsky," *Christianity Today,* 17 July 1995, 40.

8. Arthur Trace, *Furnace of Doubt: Dostoevski and* The Brothers Karamazov (Peru, Ill.: Sherward Sugden, 1992).

9. Vladimir Osherov, "Russia Repents?" *First Things,* December 1997, 46f. Invaluable analysis can be found in Nicholas Berdyaev, *Dostoevski* (New York: Meridian, 1957). See especially chap. 8, "Christ and Antichrist," 188ff. Eugene H. Peterson leans heavily on Dostoevsky in his *Under the Unpredictable Plant* (Grand Rapids: Eerdmans, 1992), 49ff.

11.6.2 TOLSTOY, PROPHET OF THE CYCLONIC WIND

> The test of observance of Christ's teaching is our consciousness of our failure to attain an ideal perfection. The degree to which we draw near this perfection cannot be seen; all we can see is the extent of our deviation. A man who professes an external law is like someone standing in the light of a lantern fixed to a post. It is light all round him, but there is nowhere further for him to walk. A man who professes the teaching of Christ is like a man carrying a lantern before him on a long, or not so long, pole: the light is in front of him, always lighting up fresh ground and always encouraging him to walk further.
>
> —Leo Tolstoy

Holy Russia, as Count Leo Tolstoy conceived of his native land, had a deep soul, and there are amazing mystical and spiritual overtones in many of her writers, not least Fëdor Dostoevsky and Tolstoy himself. Tolstoy (1828–1910) sees Christ as the preeminent teacher.[1] However, he rejects the deity of Christ and therefore has no Savior from sin, which leaves his approach languishing in moral defeat. Even evangelical devotee Philip Yancey's panegyric concedes:

> Tolstoy's religious writings in the main seem erratic and unstable. He saw "the extent of his deviation" and little else. As he stepped outside himself, looking inward to diagnose his own inner workings, he was filled with disgust. He saw moral failure and hypocrisy and faithlessness. Perhaps for this reason few people today read his spiritual musings. . . . If Tolstoy could hardly help himself, how could he be expected to help the rest of us?[2]

Tolstoy was born at Yasnaya Polyana, the family estate south of Moscow. His father was a veteran of the Napoléonic wars. His mother died when he was only two years of age. With the death of his father in 1837, Tolstoy and his four brothers were raised by their aunts. Young Tolstoy was largely self-educated and dropped out very quickly from the University of Kazan. He loved to read Rousseau, Goethe, and Dumas, and he was influenced by Russian folk stories and the Bible (especially the Joseph cycle) as a child.

He was in every way a child of the Enlightenment and began to translate such writers as the British novelist Laurence Sterne (1713–1768) into Russian. His diaries show that already as a young man he threw over his religious faith and became a libertine in lifestyle.[3] His trilogy, *Childhood* (1852), *Boyhood* (1854), and *Youth* (1857), show his efforts to manage the family estate seriously, but notwithstanding his great guilt, he gambled and caroused.

In 1851 he joined the army and fought in the Crimean War, memorializing his feelings in *Sevastopol Sketches*. He also traveled much in the West. In 1862 he married Sofya Behrs, the daughter of an army surgeon (she was eighteen, he thirty-four). His other great loves at the time were Homer (9th cent. B.C./8th cent. B.C.), William Makepeace Thackeray (1811–1863), and Dickens. He was particularly taken with Dickens's *David Copperfield*. He even named one of his dogs Dora, after Copperfield's first wife.

His marriage seemed to release a creative burst. For six years, he worked on his epochal and massive *War and Peace,* one of the great novels of all time and probably the greatest war novel ever written. In writing of Napoléon's invasion of Russia, he sifted through many sources and did some verbatim borrowing.[4] Though "congenitally hostile to dogma" and not "rationally satisfied with the liturgy and ritual" of the Russian Orthodox Church, he did worship during these years.

Tolstoy's gifts as a writer and thinker of depth are displayed in this complex work: his brilliant characterization of people and his sensitivity to the visual aspects of life; the architectonic craftsmanship with its "connections," although he is never "image-rich." He is not actually anti-French but is contemptuous of the Germans.[5] Commencing this work in 1863—the year of the American Civil War Battle of Gettysburg—Tolstoy agrees with Lincoln that human beings don't control and decide historical events. But, whereas Lincoln appealed to divine providence, Tolstoy goes no higher than "historical inevitability."[6] One of the main characters (of the hundreds firmly drawn) is Pierre, who searches out wisdom and even resorts to attempt a numerological analysis of Bonaparte's name and shaves off letters to make his calculation come out properly.[7]

Learning Greek in order to read the classics in the original, Tolstoy was urged by his wife and large family to write another book. *Anna Karenina* was the result. This is the story of a loveless marriage and a woman who leaves one inadequate man for another. Interestingly, Tolstoy shows disapproval of the character Anna's smoking and use of contraceptives.[8]

Matthew Arnold believed that this, and other Tolstoy books, were cluttered with characters, but this is the Tolstoyan carnival. This book has such a tragic ending, and we realize that Tolstoy is wrestling with serious metaphysical issues.

Indeed in the late 1870s, a time of depression and moodiness brought on a deep spiritual crisis. He professed conversion and turned to the Sermon on the Mount as the literal pattern for human life. He dressed as a peasant, made his own shoes, adopted a vegetarian diet, and abstained from the marital bed. He gave himself to an intensive study of the Gospels, translated them into Russian, and sought to harmonize them. His religion had two basic pillars: reason and love.[9] But there was no salvation and no resurrection. His wife and family were increasingly hostile to his thinking, especially when he divided up the estate and freed his serfs. He decided to forego all royalties, and this worked a great hardship on his family. He was first warned and then excommunicated by the Holy Synod. He believed that prayer was blasphemous and that Christ was in no sense God.

His third great novel, *Resurrection,* is the story of a rich young nobleman who seduces a young woman and then ultimately becomes her friend and deliverer. This book is not as well done but was very popular, and Tolstoy used the royalties to send the Dukhobor religious sect to Canada. The book does give us a magnificent description of Easter observance in Russia.

Tolstoy was wealthy (4,000 acres and 330 serfs), and he genuinely felt for the poor and disenfranchised of society. He was brilliant and accomplished and had "mesmeric power" as a writer.[10] His highly idealistic and self-centered religion, however, never altered his basic sexually indulgent lifestyle, except for the one time of abstinence. His wife said:

"There is so little genuine warmth about him; his kindness does not come from his heart, but merely from his principles. His biographies will tell of how he helped the laborers to carry buckets of water, but no one will ever know that he never gave his wife a rest and never—in all these thirty-two years—gave his child a drink of water or spent five minutes by his bedside to give me a chance to rest a little from all my labors."[11]

His analysis of the human predicament was so superficial as to allow him to prescribe education as the simple solution. His was self-adoration, and that shows how much he needed the cross of Christ.

Sadly, at age eighty-two, amid great acrimony and bitterness on the estate, he and his one loyal daughter, Alexandra, fled. His health broke, and he was removed from the train to die in the little station master's hut at Astropovo. He had hoped to reach a monastery, but his large public funeral was the first held in Russia without religious rites.[12] Thus ended the saga of a man whose novels must be read, but whose cupboard was bare.

> **If you would like to explore** earlier Russian literature, try Ivan Bunin (1870–1953). He was a Tolstoyan who left Russia for France in 1920. His *The Village* (1910) is a realistic portrayal of the Russian people. A friend of Tolstoy and Dostoevsky, Ivan Turgenev (1818–1883) wrote two strong novels, *Fathers and Sons* and *First Love*. Aleksandr Pushkin (1799–1837) is sometimes called "The Shakespeare of Russia." Unfortunately, his career was cut short when he was killed in a duel. His outstanding work is *The Queen of Spades* (1834), on which Tchaikovsky based a libretto for an opera. Not to be forgotten is the Ukraine author Nicolay Gogol (1809–1852). His *Dead Souls* (1842) is both a tragic and comic *tour-de-force*. He read Scripture and was virtually paralyzed by his fear of eternal damnation.

1. Leo Tolstoy, *What Men Live By and Where Love Is, There God Is Also* (Westwood, N.J.; Revell, n.d.).
2. Philip Yancey, "Be Ye Perfect, More or Less: Tolstoy, Dostoevsky and the Impossible Sermon on the Mount," *Christianity Today,* 17 July 1995, 39. One of the best biographies is that of A. N. Wilson, *Tolstoy* (London: Penguin, 1989). Wilson's style is lively and engaging.
3. R. F. Christian, *Tolstoy: A Critical Introduction* (Cambridge: Cambridge University Press, 1969), 17.
4. Ibid., 112. Despite shredding his faith, Tolstoy left the door open, 19.
5. Ibid., 116. There are symbolic overtones of Christ's passion in Tolstoy, but nothing more.
6. Mortimer J. Adler and Seymour Cain, *Imaginative Literature,* vol. 2 (Chicago: Great Books, 1962), 172. See also Harold Bloom, ed., *Leo Tolstoy's War and Peace* (New York: Chelsea, 1988). The 1956 film version is outstanding!
7. Stephen D. O'Leary, *Arguing the Apocalypse* (New York: Oxford, 1994), 82.

8. Christian, *Tolstoy,* 211. Tolstoy has not yet reached the "utopian anarchism" of later times (175).

9. G. H. Perris, *The Life and Teaching of Leo Tolstoy* (London: Grant Richards, 1901), 84.

10. Paul Johnson, "Tolstoy: 'God's Elder Brother,'" in *Intellectual* (New York: Harper, 1988), 112.

11. "Be Ye Perfect, More or Less," 39. Even discounting some simpering self-pity, one can only feel for his wife and family.

12. Biographical note in *War and Peace* (Chicago: Great Books, 1952), v.

11.6.3 PASTERNAK, PROPHET OF THE SOFTER SOUND

> The aim of creativity is self-giving
> And not sensations, not success.
> It's a disgrace, and signifies nothing
> To be the story of everyone's lips.
>
> —Boris Pasternak

Those of us living in 1958 will never forget the crashing impact of Pasternak's great novel, *Doctor Zhivago,* when it was made into a film. Especially moving was the haunting "Lara's Song." The manuscript had been smuggled out of Russia where Pasternak was in disfavor for his views and was first published in Italian. Boris Pasternak (1890–1960) was known in Russia primarily for his poetry.[1] Although he was not so flamboyant as Dostoevsky and Tolstoy, he too was a prophet, and his softer and quieter tones were masterfully focused.

Pasternak was born in Moscow, his father being a successful artist and his mother a pianist. He was early exposed to such great writers as Tolstoy and the German poet Rainer Rilke (1875–1926) and later spent a decade of life doing serious translation into Russian. At thirteen, he studied musical composition, but he pursued philosophy at the University of Moscow and at Marburg in Germany.[2] Poetry enthralled him as he sought "a second birth." A staunch moral element appears in his poetry. In fact, *Doctor Zhivago* concludes with a collection of some of Pasternak's finest poems (ascribed to the hero of the novel, Yurii Zhivago). Several of these have a radiant spiritual thrust, such as "Holy Week," which brings us right to Calvary and the resurrection.[3] "Star of the Nativity" brings us to the manger and is on a plane with John Milton's (1608–1674) "On the Morning of Christ's Nativity."[4]

Doctor Zhivago should be read. It traces its chief characters (above all Yurii Zhivago and his mistress, Lara) in the years leading up to World War I and the Revolution. Yurii is a young doctor who loves literature. The book tingles with love for Russia. It is, above all, a testament of freedom. Yurii's discussions with his uncle offer an ongoing critique of the Marxist state and obviously were objectionable to the Soviet censors. When given the Nobel Prize in 1958, Pasternak faced such an uproar that he declined the award.

The book is rich in imagery, and while the leading characters are not overtly religious, it celebrates the mystery of life in relation to which Yurii comes to an understanding and experience of Christ.[5] Edmund Wilson went so far as to argue that the theme of the novel is death and resurrection.

Pasternak alludes to the Bible and its great texts, as in his poem "Christ Entering upon His Passion."[6] Such open religiosity was intolerable to the Soviet regime. Yurii's father had disappeared, so the remembrance of his mother's funeral and how he and his uncle stayed in a monastery overnight after it are vivid. The thought is seriously advanced that "One must be true to Christ."[7] As in Orthodoxy, the resurrection is dominant, although the relevancy of faith is seen particularly in the cultural rites of passage. Neither Yurii's nor Lara's lifestyle (nor indeed Pasternak's lifestyle) encourage an in-depth application of the gospel. Is the religious expression chiefly cultural convention? Or does this reflect the virtual lack of any Puritanism or pietism in the equation? The kingdom of God, though mentioned, doesn't seem to provide an eschatological sanction for ethics.[8]

At last, winter comes in the lives of its characters. Was there to be a spring?

Other trails in Russian literature can be traversed in the works of Maxim Gorky (1868–1936), who was from Novgorod (which was renamed Gorky in his honor). Early a convinced Marxist, he turned against the destructiveness of the Soviet state and probably paid for this disloyalty with his life. His novel *The Artamonov Business* traces the serious decay of the business class in Russia. The greatest short-story writer of Russia (and possibly of this century) was the Odessa Jew, Isaak Babel (1894–1939), who disappeared after his arrest in one of the purges.[9] The Nabokov family, Russian liberals, fled to the West after the October Revolution. The son Vladimir (1899–1977) studied at Cambridge and taught at Stanford, Wellesley, and Cornell universities in the United States. The title I would recommend from the latter is *Bend Sinister* (1947), which is about mounting tensions in a one-party state featuring Professor Adam Krug and the dictator Paduk.

---

1. *Doctor Zhivago* has a poetic aspect in its lines and diction, which is not apparent in the English translation.
2. Edward J. Brown, *Major Soviet Writers: Essays in Criticism* (New York: Oxford, 1973), 102.
3. Boris Pasternak, *Doctor Zhivago* (New York: Pantheon, 1958), 524: "A god is being interred," his character says.
4. Ibid., 546. The imagery is closely attuned to the cattle stall: "His body was warmed by the lips of an ass and the nostrils of an ox."
5. Brown, *Major Soviet Writers,* 144. "I don't mean religion as a dogma or as a church, but as a vital feeling." This describes an existential emotional experience, not a true encounter with God.
6. *Doctor Zhivago,* 412–13. Mary Magdalene says: "Who can fathom the multitude of my sins or the depth of Thy mercy?" (415).
7. Ibid., 10.
8. Ibid., 123.
9. See A. N. Pirozhkova, *At His Side: The Last Years of Isaak Babel* (South Royalton, Vt.: Steerforth, 1996).

11.6.4 SOLZHENITSYN, PROPHET OF THE GREAT QUAKE

Men have forgotten God; that's why all this has happened.

All attempts to find a way out of the plight of today's world are fruitless unless we redirect our consciousness, in repentance, to the Creator of all.

It is time, in the West, to defend not so much human rights as human obligations.

—Aleksandr Solzhenitsyn

His long beard and his stentorian manner give him the aura of a prophet, and he indeed has been a respected spiritual guide for both the West and for Eastern Europe. Aleksandr Solzhenitsyn (b. 1918) is one of our greatest living writers. Such has been the impact of his books that David Remnick of *The New Yorker* says Solzhenitsyn has had more effect on the course of modern history than any other writer. Born in Kislovodsk in the Caucasus mountains, he was raised in southern Russia during the scorching early years of the Revolution, when everyone was "drowning in horror." It is estimated that more than 60 million died in the purges, the majority while Solzhenitsyn was growing up. As a dissident in 1951, he was among 10 million in "gulags," or prison camps.[1]

Solzhenitsyn's father died before he was born, and he was raised by women. He attended school in Rostov and was graduated from the Department of Physics and Mathematics at the University of Rostov in 1941. An army officer during the war, he became increasingly disillusioned with communism. In 1945 he was arrested for poking fun at Stalin and was sent into an eight-year exile. These years brought mounting strain to his marriage but also provided him a theme for his epochal account, *One Day in the Life of Ivan Denisovich,* the story of a prisoner in a gulag.[2] Curiously, Khruschev allowed this book to be published in the USSR.

Out of his incarceration came what should be considered his conversion experience, when he was discipled by a Jewish Christian.[3] Compelled by conscience, he wrote successive works exposing the oppressive system, such as *Gulag Archipelago, The First Circle,* and *Cancer Ward.* A large network of friends developed to copy, smuggle, hide, and place his works.[4] In 1970 he was awarded the Nobel Prize for his writing. Such a visible troublemaker with a world following caused the Soviet Union to expel him in 1974. He and his second wife and their sons moved to Switzerland for a brief stay and then to a Vermont farm and almost complete isolation in the United States. He did not officially marry Natalya Svetlova until 1973. By that time, the couple had two sons, causing discomfort among Christians about his lifestyle. During his eighteen years in the United States, he worked relentlessly on a massive World War I project, *The Red Wheel.* Always writing in the tradition of Dostoevsky and Tolstoy, Solzhenitsyn can be exceedingly tedious, as in this book.

He never escapes a grievous anti-Semitism in terms of which he argues for the superiority of the Gestapo over the KGB, a strange and grotesque blind spot.

Yet the theologian Alexander Schmeimann argues that Solzhenitsyn is a Christian writer who builds on the themes of creation, fall, and redemption through Christ.[5]

He ventured out of Vermont to give a much-discussed commencement address at Harvard University. In it, he blasted Western materialism and hedonism.[6] In a *National Review* article, "Men Have Forgotten God," he goes to the aorta of the contemporary dilemma.[7] His address to the National Arts Club on "The Relentless Cult of Novelty and How It Wrecked the Century" is especially provocative.[8]

In 1994 he and his family returned to the New Russia, where he has continued his indictment of the Enlightenment, particularly nuanced for the Russian dilemma. He prescribes for his countrymen the will to rebuild a moral Russia. As the prophet made a cross-country train trip upon reentry, large throngs came out to listen. But his message of repentance does not have many takers today. He is seen, according to a *Time* magazine analysis, as a pesky "revivalist preacher."[9] What a specter in our time—the voice crying in the wilderness again! Read *One Day in the Life of Ivan Denisovich* and then *The Gulag Archipelago*.

Side trips in Slavic literature are fascinating, such as the poetry of Czeslaw Milosz (b. 1911). The Lithuanian-born Pole won the 1980 Nobel Prize. His autobiographical novel *The Issa Valley* is fine, as is *The Seizure of Power*. For years, he translated the Bible into Polish. Also see the work of Václav Havel (b. 1936), a poet, playwright, and, for a time, president of the Czech Republic. Ivan Klima's novel, *The Ultimate Intimacy,* is about a Czech Protestant pastor, exiled to the Moravian highlands, who returns to Prague to pastor a church. He has an affair. The plot explores complex ethical ramifications.

---

1. The standard biography on Solzhenitsyn is Michael Scammel's work of 1984. Much happened after that publication. A later work that is superb is D. M. Thomas, *Alexander Solzhenitsyn: A Century in His Life* (New York: St. Martin's, 1998). Thomas observes: "The hardships and depression he endured somehow opened a way for his spirit to grow. . . . He would look back on his first cell as akin to first love."

2. Aleksandr Solzhenitsyn, *One Day in the Life of Ivan Denisovich* (New York: E. P. Button, 1963). Solzhenitsyn and his wife eventually were divorced after his release.

3. His conversion is described in *Gulag Archipelago II* (New York: Harper, 1974), 613–15. See also Charles Colson, *Loving God* (Grand Rapids: Zondervan, 1983), 25ff.

4. Aleksandr Solzhenitsyn, *Invisible Allies* (Washington: Counterpoint, 1995). He can now tell the story.

5. Edward E. Ericson Jr., "What Solzhenitsyn Has Done for us Lately," *Books and Culture,* July 1996, 7. See also, Edward E. Ericson Jr., *Solzhenitsyn and the Modern World* (Washington, D.C.: Regnery Gateway), 1994.

6. "Solzhenitsyn Asks: Why Is the Western World Joyful?" *Minneapolis Tribune,* 9 June 1978, 1A.

7. Aleksandr Solzhenitsyn, "Men Have Forgotten God," reprinted in *The Reader's Digest,* September 1986, 21ff.

8. Aleksandr Solzhenitsyn, "The Relentless Cult of Novelty and How It Wrecked the Century," *The New York Times Book Review,* 7 February 1993, 3ff. He charged that there was "a raucous, impatient 'avant guardism' at any cost."

9. "A Voice in the Wilderness," *Time,* 20 June 1994, 46ff. Includes a rare interview.

11.7 ON THE EASTERN TIDE

> When man no longer believes in God, he does not then believe in nothing,
> but in anything.
>   —G. K. Chesterton

Up to this point, this theological guide to great literature may well be accused of being "Eurocentric." The roots of Western culture, out of which this
survey is written, are largely the classics of Western Europe and North America.
In this territory, the postmodern dedication to the deconstruction of Christianity and all traditional values has been most pronounced. Stanford University
at this writing has discontinued its major course in Western Civilization.[1]
Georgetown University no longer requires English majors to read Shakespeare;
he is not politically correct. At Harvard, grade inflation is so rampant that 84
percent of one class was graduated with honors.[2] Multiculturalism threatens to
Balkanize America. Europe is being Islamized. Possibly some answers to these
tensions may come from a multicultural reading program. It is respectful and
fair to seek to understand others by seriously reading international classics. Here
we probe diversity.

---

1. Marvin Olasky, "True Deconstruction," *World,* 12 April 1997, 30.
2. Martin L. Gross, "At War with the New Establishment," *Insight,* 27 October 1997,
   20ff.

A. THE MIDDLE EAST

We shall have in chapter 12 an extended analysis of Israeli and Jewish literature. The reasons for the paucity of Arab and Muslim literature has been the subject of frustrated study. Unremitting hostilities and violence, an unwillingness to
make genuine peace with Israel, and radical Islamization are all factors.[1] Other
analysts consider the perpetuation of tribalism and traditional notions of honor
and shame as continuing to choke off significant literary and artistic growth and
development.[2]

---

1. Fouad Ajami, *The Dream Palace of the Arabs: A Generation's Odyssey* (New York:
   Pantheon, 1997).
2. David Pryce-Jones, *The Closed Circle: An Interpretation of the Arabs* (New York:
   Harper, 1989), 382–401.

11.7.1 MAHFOUZ, ENTRY TO EGYPT

> The new forms of literature like the novel are only 50 years old in our
> culture, so we are still developing.
>   —Naguib Mahfouz

Egypt, strapped between East and West astride the Nile River has remained in ferment throughout recent centuries. Artistically, ever since S. Y. Agnon received the Nobel Prize for Literature in 1966, Arab writers have longed for such recognition. In 1988 it came to an Egyptian writer, Naguib Mahfouz (b. 1911). Mahfouz was born and raised in Cairo (now a city of almost 20 million). His father was a low-ranking civil servant. His mother loved to show her son the pyramids and tombs and tell him Egyptian folktales.[1] While studying philosophy at the University of Cairo, he imbibed Darwin, Freud, Marx, and Nietzsche. Any Muslim rigidity was obliterated. He learned huge chunks of the Koran by heart, but remained a moderate. Early in his career, he did some translation, no small accomplishment since Arabic is notoriously difficult to render into English or any Romance language.[2] He ultimately turned from philosophy to writing and thoroughly immersed himself in Shakespeare, Balzac, Tolstoy, and Scott. Melville was tough going for him, but he loved Proust, Joyce, and Mann. Mahfouz definitely is not among Islamicists who have sanitized their thinking of Western influences.

He is more widely read among all classes than any other writer in the Arab-Muslim world.[3] His first novels were about Cairo's lower and middle classes. He is widely called "the Dickens of Cairo," but perhaps his style is more like that of Victor-Marie Hugo. His first novel was *Midaq Alley* (1947), but it was his Cairo Trilogy (1956–57) that brought him fame and fortune.

He is Egypt's favorite son of literature. Mahfouz has left Egypt only twice, on cultural missions to Yemen and Yugoslavia. While government censorship hangs as the sword of Damocles over all writers in this highly excitable environment, Mahfouz has written a weekly column for the large government newspaper. Every morning, the literati of Cairo meet in the Aly Baba Cafe where Mahfouz, like the sphinx, "silent but expressive," is honored in their midst.

In all, he has written more than forty volumes of prose and poetry. I would recommend starting with the volume that includes *Midaq Alley, The Thief and the Dogs,* and *Miramar*.[4] He makes the Midaq Valley come alive with the work of the marriage-maker, thieves, extortionists, shopkeepers, and an endless succession of real and lively characters.[5]

The Palace of Desire is a favorite title in the trilogy.[6] This book grabbed the Nobel committee's attention. It is so like any Mahfouz story, describing family tensions in a time of war, sexual tensions in a culture sharply dividing men and women, the oppression of women, and the stranglehold of tradition.[7] I own and treasure these two volumes. They are a trip into the *casbah* or *suq*.

While Turkey is not truly within the Arab sphere, and is a moderately Sunni Islamic nation with a secular constitution, my favorite Turkish writer is Yashar Kemal (b. 1922) whose *The Sea-Crossed Fisherman* is a superb piece. *Memed My Hawk* (1955) is antisocial and violently reactionary. The hero rises to power, not in any regard for justice, but because he is more ruthless than anyone else.

---

1. Naguib Mahfouz, *Echoes of an Autobiography* (New York: Doubleday, 1997). This biography is a good companion for better understanding of the novels.

2. Brad Kessler, "Laureate in the Land of the Pharaohs," *New York Times Magazine,* 3 June 1990, 62.
3. Ibid., 60. He has favored peace with Israel and brought great anger from militants who have threatened his life.
4. Naguib Mahfouz, *Midaq Valley, The Thief and the Dogs and Miramar* (New York: QPB, 1989).
5. "Laureate in the Land of the Pharaohs," 62. Mahfouz writes in classical Arabic, which is the equivalent of Shakespearean English today.
6. Naguib Mahfouz, *The Palace of Desire* (New York: Doubleday, 1957, 1991), Book-of-the-Month Club selection.
7. The more religious son Kamal observes: "Water can't wash away sins" (74). He argues: "Either the Qur'an is totally true, or it's not the Qur'an" (335). He is wrestling with the historicity of Adam against Darwinism.

B. THE SOUTH EAST

The deeper our foundations in the past, the more outstanding our participation in the present.

—Karl Jaspers

The masses of the Indian subcontinent, now almost a billion people—plus Pakistan, Bangladesh, and the large Indian diaspora elsewhere—constitute a huge chunk of the earth's population. The emergence of India after independence in 1947 and the collisions and interactions of culture there provide a historical backdrop for writers.[1] The tilt to Hindu nationalism poses special problems. We have noticed Kipling (7.4.8) and E. M. Forster (9.3.2). Paul Scott's *Raj Quartet,* about the India of 1942 to 1947, was made famous in the Public Broadcasting System production of *The Jewel in the Crown.* This fiction moves deep into the national psyche. Barbie Batchelor, the story's missionary teacher, is a worthy representative for the missions tradition that reaches back to William Carey (1761–1834).

---

1. Sunil Khilnani, *The Idea of India* (New York: Farrar, Strauss, 1997). This history recounts the amazing emergence of a powerful modern state.

11.7.2 NAIPAUL, MAN OF PERCEPTION

And year by year our memory fades
From all the circle of the hills. . . .
Till from the garden and the wild
A fresh association blow,
And year by year the landscape grow
Familiar to the stranger's child.

—Naipaul
inversion of a Tennyson poem

The most widely read Indian man of letters in the world, V. S. Naipaul (b. 1932) was born to Hindu parents in Trinidad. His grandfather had come from India. In 1950 he went to Oxford on a scholarship and began his outstanding career in writing fiction, history, and essays. He writes of England, where he lives in Wiltshire at this writing, and of Trinidad. In a "conflicted" way, he writes of India herself. His has been a struggle for identity within three cultures. His favorite writers have been Balzac, Flaubert, Proust, and the English diarist Samuel Pepys (1633–1703). One of his tributes to his ancestral land is a magisterial work, *India: A Wounded Civilization* (1977). His style is strikingly lucid, and he carries a burden of moral outrage in the face of oppression and human greed.[1]

Several of his novels are worth perusing. I recommend *The Enigma of Arrival,*[2] his frankly autobiographical novel about an expatriate in England. Using lavishly descriptive prose, Naipaul tells the story of a young Trinidadian who takes up residency in a cottage near Salisbury and Stonehenge. Although England is in many ways "savorless," compared with peasant India and colonial Trinidad, this émigré experienced "my second childhood of seeing and learning."[3]

His recollections of the Port of Spain on his home island are Dickensian. Krishna and Shiva only yield him "something like religion," as over against Bray, who was always talking about Christianity. He concedes that Bray's is not the religion of the "Victorian relics," which litter the landscape, but rather is very bibliocentric, with a strong emphasis on healing.[4] Yet we can but cringe that, for Naipaul and possibly some of his readers, Bray is the model Christian.

With all the movement of peoples in our time, this novel is an invaluable infusion of fresh perspective on what it is like to be an alien in a strange culture.

For fresh, unforgettable impressions of Bombay at the end of the twentieth century, H. R. F. Keating has many incomparable novels of suspense featuring Inspector Ghote. I have loved such fun stories as *Inspector Ghote Trusts the Heart* and *Inspector Ghote under a Monsoon Cloud.*

---

1. Mel Gussow, "V. S. Naipaul in Search of Himself: A Conversion," *The New York Times Book Review,* 24 April 1994, 3ff.
2. V. S. Naipaul, *The Enigma of Arrival* (New York: Knopf, 1987).
3. Ibid., 87. Naipaul shares his moving farewell celebration when he left for England and his six years of study.
4. Ibid., 302ff. The nominal Hindu's impressions of English churches and Mr. Bray particularly are invaluable.

11.7.3 NARAYAN, MAN OF THE PEOPLE

In a day when it is fashionable for novelists to be prophets or propagandists, he prefers a quieter way. Like Stendhal he is content to let his novels be a mirror on the roadway.

—*Time* magazine
from a biographical sketch on R. K. Narayan

After dozens of novels and many short stories about his imaginary Indian city of Malgudi (somewhere in the southern triangle of India), R. K. Narayan (b. 1906) speaks from the viewpoint of the people. His perspective is that of Faulkner and Trollope. Narayan is Hindu and was born in Madras, where he was largely raised by his grandmother. He attended the government school where his father was headmaster and then went on to Mysore University. He tried teaching to please his father, but gradually he turned totally to writing. Graham Greene (1904–1991) really discovered and promoted him.[1]

Narayan has written in English and was for a long time "the only writer in India who makes a living by writing imaginative literature."[2] His characters leap from his pages, bringing to life the smells and sights of the town. *The Financial Expert,* a good starting place for reading Narayan, is cleverly and realistically done. I have also loved *The Vendor of Sweets* and *The Painter of Signs.* This kind of background helps us understand something of India and Indians.

Not to be overlooked are the works of Shashi Tharoor, especially his *The Great Indian Novel,* in which he parodies an Englishman's way of describing India in "The Bungle Book." In *The Duet with the Crown,* he gives a similar critique of Indian writings, like "The Rigged Veda." With respect to Burma next door, we have already referred to George Orwell's (1903–1950) *Burmese Days* (9.3.4). Well worth reading is the French writer Pierre Boulle's World War II classic, *The Bridge on the River Kwai,* which also was made into a memorable film of the same name.

---

1. R. K. Narayan, editor's preface to *The Financial Expert* (Lansing, Mich.: Michigan State University Press, 1953), xi.
2. Ibid. His gentle humor cannot obscure for us his trenchant analysis of the complexity of Hinduism.

C. THE FAR EAST

In village churches up and down the country, in Britain as in the rest of Christendom, the most conspicuous decoration was a picture of the Last Judgment on the chancel arch facing the nave where the congregation assembled, portraying all humanity, past, present and future, being consigned to Heaven or Hell. Christians knew that in the sight of God a person's date of birth on the human scale was irrelevant, and that those not yet born would also be summoned to meet all other created humans and the Almighty.

—Peter Laslett and James Fishkin

We need to bear in mind that in the vastness of the East no such omega point in history or beyond history (such as the Last Judgment) has given sanction to ethics or thrust to hope and genuine accountability. We feel this with particular poignancy in relation to Japan.

It is intimidating to dip into Japanese literature. The best writer for introducing a Westerner to this body of works is Natsume Soseki (1867–1916), whose theme was invariably the Westernization of Japan. The Japanese have done a far better job of studying Western literature than Westerners have of Eastern books. Professor Kazuo Watanabe of the University of Tokyo was a foremost scholar on Rabelais, and Professor Hiromu Shimizu is an expert on Melville, Hawthorne, and Frost.

One other introductory view can be found in James Clavell's work on old Imperial Japan in *Shogun,* which was made into an impressive twelve-hour television adaptation. Clavell transports us magically into old Japan.

11.7.4 OE, THE DOOR AJAR IN JAPAN

> Without the surgery, Hikari wouldn't have survived; and yet this young father had hesitated some time before giving his consent. The fact was recorded there, in Dr. Moriyama's diary, reminding me yet again that if there is a god, some higher being who judges us, then when my time comes I will be unable to face this being with a clear conscience, condemned in advance by this one piece of evidence alone. . . . Still, the line in the diary contains more than my guilt, for it also reminds me that having decided, even after hesitating, ultimately I too was reborn along with Hikari.
>
> —Kenzaburo Oe

Opting for a Western "image system of grotesque realism," rather than the indirection and suggestion of Japanese literature, Kenzaburo Oe (b. 1935) has become the greatest postwar Japanese novelist. He was born on Shikoku Island in a heavily wooded area, opening his life's passion of long walks and botany. He is able to identify and classify most trees on earth.[1]

With the death of his father in 1944, he immersed himself in such works as *The Adventures of Huckleberry Finn.* He progressed to Dante in the original Italian, Confucius in Mandarin, Faulkner in English, and Rabelais and Sartre in French, the formalists in Russian, and *The Tale of Genji* in ancient Japanese.[2] His favorite European writer is William Butler Yeats (1865–1939).

Living his teenage years during the American occupation, Oe was not impressed with American trustworthiness, and he politically led those Japanese who opposed permanent security alliances with the United States. He spoke out of his own pain regarding nuclear proliferation in *Hiroshima Notes.*

Oe was troubled by a spiritual decline in Japan with the rise of consumerism. He also was deeply affected by the birth of his firstborn in 1963. The son, Hikari, suffered from cerebral hernia and required radical surgery to survive (see the introductory excerpt). Living with their disabled son is described in *A Personal Matter.*

His experiences led Oe toward his "nonreligious conversion." Hikari became his "metaphorical light for addressing victimhood everywhere." In *An Echo of Heaven* (1989) he tells the story of a mother whose accident-paralyzed son and severely-retarded son both take their own lives. The mother, Marie, seeks to make atonement (in the same fashion as does Flannery O'Connor) and tastes Catholicism, Filipino Guerrilla Theater, Swedenborgianism, and then Mexican peasant faith. Her search for redemption is a life process.[3] Though Oe remains an unbeliever, he speaks of "something akin to grace." As a humanist, there can be no supernatural dimension to deliverance and salvation.

A good place to start reading Oe is with his first novel, *Nip the Buds, Shoot the Kids*.[4] Obviously influenced by Camus, Samuel Clemens (1835–1910), and William Golding (1911–1993), Oe is an existentialist believer in deviancy. *Nip the Buds* is the story of fifteen delinquent outcasts during wartime. Some have wondered if acknowledgment of sin is ever possible within Oriental worldviews, but Oe, who won the 1994 Nobel Prize for Literature, shows the contradictions in the human heart. He simply does not take the next step to the answer in Christ.

Pearl S. Buck has already been flagged (10.2.6) as a major writer about China. Probably the most noted Chinese writer in modern times is Lin Yutang (1895–1976), who did his master's at Harvard and his doctoral work at Leipzig. He taught at Beijing. He wrote in many genre, expounded classic Confucianism, and wrote such novels as *Chinatown Family* (1948), *Red Peony* (1962), and *The Flight of the Innocents* (1965). With his old China and Western influence, he naturally had to leave China quickly after the communist ascendancy.

---

1. David Swain, "Something Akin to Grace: The Journey of Kenzaburo Oe," *The Christian Century,* 24 December 1997,1226. This is clear literary analysis of this writer.
2. Ibid., 1226. Reading Oe's novels gives incredible insight into these turbulent decades in Japan.
3. Ibid., 1228. Trauma can induce secular conversion. We see the phenomenon in Marxism, for example, Rosa Luxembourg.
4. Kenzaburo Oe, *Nip the Buds, Shoot the Kids* (London: Marian Boyars, 1995). His publisher says of this book: "He forms a disconcerting picture of the human predicament today." This is harsh realism.

11.7.5 CLAVELL, THE CHALLENGES OF THE CHINAS

When the 17th century Jesuits came to China they redrafted the Gospel to make it inoffensive to the Chinese literati, especially bleaching out the Cross of Christ. Characterizing what was left: " . . . an unobjectionable residue, with no divine power to win converts."

—Hugh Trevor-Roper,
Regius Professor of Modern History, Oxford[1]

Little of the significant impact of Christian missions founded by Robert Morrison (1782–1834), J. Hudson Taylor (1832–1905), and John Nevius (1829–1893) is reflected in the panoramas etched by James Clavell (1924–1994).[2] Clavell was born in England but became a United States citizen. We have referred to his major volume of Japanese history, *Shogun*. His first book, *King Rat*,[3] came out of his own imprisonment in a Japanese camp at Changi, near Singapore. There is no trace of Christian reality in this raw work of realism, such as in Ernest Gordon's testament in *Through the Valley of the Kwai*[4] or in the deeply moving film, *Paradise Road.* Critics fault the wordiness of Clavell novels, but he is always popular.[5] His two great novels on Hong Kong are as good as any that have been produced in the West. We feel the tensions between old and new Asia—East and West. In *Tai-Pan* (1966), Dirk Struan arrives in nineteenth-century Hong Kong determined to turn the desolate little island into a bastion of British military and economic power in the Orient. In the later and larger *Noble House* (1981), Hong Kong's people are entering their twentieth-century struggles for survival, identity, and hope.

Clavell's love for the Orient emerges in such descriptions as this:

> Dunross came out onto the Peak Road fast, heading for home, the traffic light and the engine sounding sweet. On a sudden impulse he changed direction and pulled up at the Peak lookout and stood at the rail, alone. Hong Kong was a sea of lights. Over in Kowloon another jet took off from the floodlit runway. A few stars came through the high clouds.[6]

For a scintillating suspense novel involving tourists to China and the exploits of Chief Inspector Wexford, try Ruth Rendell's *Speaker of Mandarin.* Her *Anna's Book* on a Danish family also is outstanding. The best on Chinese expatriate life in San Francisco is C. Y. Lee's works, such as *The Flower Drum Song.*

---

1. Taken from Jonathan D. Spence, *The Memory Palace of Matteo Ricci* (New York: Penguin Books, 1983). A remarkable study of the mixed success of missions to China.
2. Charles Horner, "China's Christian History," *First Things,* August/September 1997, 41ff. An excellent survey.
3. James Clavell, *King Rat* (New York: Dell, 1962).
4. Ernest Gordon, *Through the Valley of the Kwai* (New York: Harper, 1962). Human depravity is in evidence on every side, but so is the grace of God. Cf. Geoffrey T. Bull, *When Iron Gates Yield* (Chicago: Moody, 1955).
5. The largest of Clavell's works, *Whirlwind* (New York: Morrow, 1986), depicts Iran and the oil fields after the flight of the Shah. Clavell actually learned to fly helicopters in order to write this novel. It is huge and impressive but not a glimmer of Christianity—he ignores all issues.
6. James Clavell, *Noble House* (New York: Dell, 1981). Many are writing on the church in China today. I have been very fond of Leslie T. Lyall on the church in China and Fox Butterworth on the situation within China leading up to today.

11.8 LATIN AMERICA

Throughout the Third World and the former Communist bloc, a vibrant Protestant Christianity is radically remaking people's lives. Bureaucratic centralizers (and Cardinals) are, quite rightly, scared stiff.

—David Martin, author of *Tongues of Fire:*
The Explosion of Protestantism in Latin America

Our near neighbors, the people of Central and South America live atop great natural resources and amid extraordinarily beautiful settings and, in their great demographic and cultural diversity, are a very special people to us. Books and writings have always been important to them. Now in their rapid economic growth and social change there is a dynamic spiritual flood tide flowing almost everywhere.[1] We need to sample some of the good literature from "south of the border" to better understand those with whose lives we are becoming more and more deeply intertwined all the while.

---

1. Pedro C. Moreno, "Rapture and Renewal in Latin America," *First Things,* June/July 1997, 31ff. In *Tongues of Fire: The Explosion of Protestantism in Latin America* (Oxford: Basil Blackwell, 1990), David Martin shows that conservative Protestantism is a global movement, not cultural imperialism. He traces the indigenous paths of successive Puritan, Methodist, and Pietistic/Pentecostal waves.

11.8.1 ARIDJIS, LOOKING BACK

The year 1000 of the incarnation of the Lord was dawning when my brothers set out on the roads of this world. The nocturnal shadows had not yet withdrawn from the ground, and they were already descending the promontory where the monastery was situated. With their mules laden with crucifixes, statues of the enthroned Virgins, loaves of bread, cheeses, honey and water for the journey, they forded the swollen stream and took the first path they came upon on their left, eager to publish the signs of the Last Judgment throughout the villages of the kingdom. Some of their number, fleeing before the terrors of the millennium, fell prey to unknown terrors in the land of the Saracens and in the Murky Sea.

—Homero Aridjis
The Lord of the Last Days: Visions of the Year 1000

Beautiful Mexico—such warm people—such poverty—such progress through the twentieth century. The inglorious end to the Aztec and Mayan peoples at the bloody hands of Spanish conquistador Hernando Cortés (1485–1547) has been well chronicled.[1] One reason the Aztecs sacrificed humans was their fear of the end of the world. It came for them by a Spaniard from a warrior-class family, who chose brutal conquest over the priesthood. The pyramid versus the cathedral has remained the great tension in all Mexican history. James Michener in *Mexico* has done one of the more insightful explorations of this dichotomy.[2]

One American scholar of Latin American literature sees apocalypse as a dominant motif in this struggle.[3] This is certainly the case with the Mexican writer we have selected from among many to represent the flourishing literary scene there, Homero Aridjis (b. 1940). He was born in Mexico City to a Greek father and a Mexican mother. Trained as a journalist, his talent for writing classical poetry was recognized. He has, said one critic, "a keen eye for reality, a quick response to the physical world and an all-encompassing sensuality in both words and images."[4]

Aridjis has taught at Columbia, New York, and at Indiana universities. He also served as Mexican ambassador to the Netherlands and to Switzerland. He founded and serves as president of the Group of 100, an international environmentalist organization of writers, artists, and scientists.

His 1967 novel *Persephone* translates the Greek myth into modern Mexican life. Several impressive pieces have followed, but none match the quality of *The Lord of the Last Days: Visions of the Year 1000*. This dazzling work recreates medieval Spain in the year 1000. A Spanish monk, Alfonso de Leon, sees a bloody comet as the sign of the coming of the Antichrist and proof of the impending end of the age. Numerous allegedly supernatural signs intensify anticipation and Moors and Christians are about to do battle for the control of Spain. All is complete with the coming of a false messiah. The author dips into John's apocalyptic book of Revelation, but beyond picking up flavor and imagery, the author has little insight into the last book of the New Testament. Alfonso and his peers are ordered forth to preach the end of the world.[5] The message was that given by the Bishop of Leon, Don Froilland:

> The coming of Messiah is nigh. Let no one lead you into error, for first will come the Apostasy, and the man of iniquity, the son of perdition will rebel and set himself even in the temple of God, pretending to be God Himself.[6]

Highly impressionistic, the author has done a herculean job of researching the times and the topics. What H. H. Rowley described years ago as *The Relevance of the Apocalyptic* is seen in this realistic narrative.[7]

Another great Mexican novelist is Carlos Fuentes (b. 1928). While his background is wealth and privilege, his earlier work probes the fusion of Indian and Christian cultures in peasant communities. *The Old Gringo* (1985) fictionalizes the last days in Mexico of American journalist Ambrose G. Bierce, who disappeared in about 1914. Fuentes was greatly influenced by Stephen Crane (10.1.7). For a feel of Indian culture (north of the Rio Grande), no one has done better than Tony Hillerman in Navajo pieces such as *The Fallen Man*,[8] about Joe Leaphorn, Jim Chee, and their folk.

---

1. The standard work in this field was William H. Prescott's *History of the Conquest of Mexico* (1843), now supplemented and perhaps replaced by Hugh Thomas's *Conquest: Montezuma, Cortes and the Fall of Old Mexico* (New York: Simon and Schuster, 1994). This is heart-rending, but we must not romanticize the Aztecs in the "noble savage" myth. Among significant failings was a penchant for human sacrifice.

2. James Michener, *Mexico* (New York: Random House, 1992). Michener rambles, but his ably researched views of places enrich travel in these regions.

3. Lois Parkinson Zamora, *Writing the Apocalypse* (Cambridge: Cambridge University Press, 1989).

4. Emir Rodriguez Monegal, ed., *The Borzoi Anthology of Latin American Literature* (New York: Knopf, 1994), 855.

5. Homero Aridjis, *The Lord of the Last Days: Visions of the Year 1000* (New York: William Morrow, 1995), 3.
6. Ibid. Jürgen Moltmann maintains that "theology is eschatology." Biblical theology has an eschatological structure.
7. H. H. Rowley, *The Relevance of Apocalyptic* (New York: Harper and Row, 1946). Another fine story about the millennium is told in Irving Benig's *The Messiah Stones: A Novel of the Millennium* (New York: Villard, 1995).
8. New York: Harper/Collins, 1996.

11.8.2 BORGES, LOOKING ABOUT

> Borges had nostalgia for grand creations like "The Divine Comedy," but he believed, not without a touch of melancholy, that some works were impossible in the modern world. He felt the same way about intricate philosophical systems.
>
> —James Woodall

The twentieth century's best-known writer in Spanish prose was Jorge Luis Borges (1899–1986), a proud Argentinian. Argentina has large German and Italian populations and has a Euro-Latin American flavor. Borges was born to a lawyer/psychologist. His mother was English, a fervent Roman Catholic. He spent his childhood largely indoors and, at six or seven, was writing in imitation of the classics. His only sibling was a sister to whom he was close. Nearsighted as a child, he gradually went blind.

Erudite and broad in his reading, his favorite characters were Ralph Waldo Emerson (1803–1882); Jonathan Edwards (1703–1758), about whom he wrote a poem; and Spinoza. He published poetry and essays as early as twenty.

He early concluded that religion was for women and children.[1] He rejected any notion of a God who would punish wrong, for he was skeptical of any ultimate values.[2] Harold Bloom calls him a skeptical and naturalistic humanist.[3] Borges, like many Latin American literati, helped spread the values vacuum across American society. That vacuum was filled by competing faiths, notably Pentecostalism and evangelical Protestantism.

With no spiritual light, Borges found his favorite symbol in the labyrinth. He was greatly influenced by the Italian aesthete, Benedetto Croce (1866–1952), a theoretician largely shaped by German idealism. Borges dismissed Sigmund Freud (1856–1939) as irrelevant but was addicted to the psychoanalytical theories of Carl Jung (1875–1961).

Borges had a distinguished career as poet and essayist, teacher of literature around the world, editor, and librarian. He loved solitude and lived most of his years with his widowed mother. At the age of sixty-eight, he married his childhood sweetheart, but this marriage ended in divorce three years later. He then married a former student, his longtime secretary and traveling companion.[4]

When Juan Perón (1895–1974) came to power in 1946, Borges was dismissed from his prominent position in the library system and humiliated with an appointment to the job of poultry inspector. Still he continued his work in Old Norse, his lectures on the mystic Emmanuel Swedenborg (1688–1772), and his interest in things Jewish.[5]

Recognized and honored around the world, Borges is best known for his short stories. In his poetry and prose, he shows a rather impressive knowledge of things biblical, as in repeated references to Matthew 25:30 and the inescapable cross motif.[6] His characters are varied and remarkable. Juan Dahlmann, a descendent of German Protestant ministers and Argentinian war heroes, inhabits "The Gospel According to St. Mark," along with Nils Rundberg, a Swede so dissatisfied with the gospel account that he invents three versions of his own for the story of Judas. In "History of Eternity" and "The Theologians," there is a strong sense that Borges cannot totally dismiss the spiritual and biblical dimensions.[7]

In 1938, the year his father died and he narrowly survived an infected wound, his mother read to him from C. S. Lewis's *Out of the Silent Planet*. This exposure apparently did little more than reassure young Borges that he was not utterly irrational.[8] How sad that such a leader couldn't find his way out of the labyrinth.

---

1. Jorge Luis Borges, "Autobiographical Essay," in *"The Aleph" and Other Stories* (New York: Dutton, 1970), 207.
2. Richard Burgin, *Conversations with Jorge Luis Borges* (New York: Holt, Rinehart, 1968), 6, 29, 114. The philosopher Miguel de Unamuno was a friend, but Borges rejected his efforts to build upon a faith in God and immortality. He was also influenced by Kantian philosopher Jose Ortega y Gasset.
3. Harold Bloom, ed., introduction to *Jorge Luis Borges* (New York: Chelsea, 1986), 2.
4. James Woodall, *Borges: A Life* (New York: Basic, 1997). This is a helpful biography for understanding the writer and his context.
5. Borges, *"The Aleph."* "El Golem" is a masterful story of a rabbi, salted with humor. There is a large Jewish population in Argentina and much anti-Semitism. See Jacobo Timerman, *Prisoner Without a Name, Cell Without a Number* (New York: Vintage, 1982). Borges frequently lectured on Swedenborg.
6. Jorge Luis Borges, *A Personal Anthology* (New York: Castle, 1967), 33. This is a collection of short sketches.
7. Borges, *"The Aleph."* "Death and the Compass" (1942) is especially good. Short stories are so helpful for Christian communicators because their ideas are projected from such a confined light. This is a detective story in which Borges shows how to incorporate tragedy in a minor literary genre.
8. Borges, "Autobiographical Essay," in *A Personal Anthology,* 243. Bloom advances the curious notion that Browning was nihilistic (?), the precursor of Kafka, so Borges could never escape nihilism (Bloom, introduction to *Jorge Luis Borges,* vii).

11.8.3 COELHO, LOOKING OUTWARD

Magical novels of the human spirit.
> —*The New York Times Book Review*
> description of the novels of Paulo Coelho

Second only to Gabriel Garcia Marquez (see 11.8.4), Brazilian Paulo Coelho (b. 1949) was the Latin American author who was published around the world at the end of the 1990s. At the same time, he was dismissed by many critics as a purveyor of "snake oil." Perhaps the readers in this case sensed more than the critics about this gifted storyteller's ability to represent the people of vast, sprawling Brazil.

Comprising 20 percent of the land of Latin America, Portuguese-speaking Brazil was a sleeping giant that was stirring at the height of Coelho's career. Something of Coelho's optimism and adventurous spirit attached to this nation, notwithstanding the poverty of Sao Paulo's barrios. Masses remained in near starvation, the Amazonian rain forests were in crisis, yet a sophisticated and growing middle-class was arising, along with Pentecostal Protestantism, especially among the youth.

Coelho had given up his dream of becoming a professional writer and was rising rapidly in the growing radio and television music industry when he abruptly lost his job. He turned to writing again, particularly to grapple in his five novels with one fundamental issue:

> Whenever I thought myself the absolute master of a situation, something would happen to cast me down. I asked myself: why? Can it be that I'm condemned to always come close but never reach the finish line? Can God be so cruel that He would let me see the palm trees on the horizon only to have me die of thirst in the desert?[1]

In his first novel, *The Alchemist* (1993), Coelho takes us along a mystic path. Young Santiago, an Andalusian (Spain) shepherd boy, is preparing for the priesthood at seminary at age sixteen.

Suddenly he decides that he will not find God in the seminary, and that travel is more important than God anyway.[2] An old man convinces him that the greatest lie is that life is controlled by fate. The King of Salem (indeed an incarnation of Melchizedec of Genesis) advises him that people are capable of doing what they dream.[3]

Reading the omens and consulting the Urim and the Thummim, he goes to Tangiers in Africa and then on to Egypt to find the treasure. Amid the persistent symbolism of abandoned churches (Coelho has little truck for the institutional church), our young traveler finds that "everything is written in the Soul of the World," and there it "will stay forever."[4] This sounds like new age pantheism, and so Coelho has been read by many. His motto seems to be "Just try, and all will be well!"

In *The Fifth Mountain* (1998), Coelho builds on the biblical story of Elijah as a charger from which to joust with the question of God's goodness. It is significant that he reverts to the Bible and uses the biblical text Luke 4:24–26 as the frontispiece.

Overcoming tragedy and discovering one's own spirituality is Coelho's theme. Unfortunately, this isn't quite the biblical Elijah. Coelho's Elijah is a twenty-three-year-old carpenter who flees the Ahab-Jezebel chaos to Zarephath, where he has a romance with the young widow. He hears voices and has spoken with angels since his youth. Still, with the raising of the widow's son, the observation is made that "It seems that the God of Israel is keeping His Word."[5] A subplot involves the development of the alphabet at Byblos in Lebanon. In a war with Assyria, the widow is killed and the son who survives joins Elijah in collecting and piling up the dead.

We never come to the contest with the false Baals on the summit of Mount Carmel (1 Kings 18). There is a Day of Atonement and a long listing of sins,[6] and finally Elijah sets out for Israel as the widow's son becomes governor of the surrounding countryside in Lebanon. The action is updated to the New Testament references to Elijah, and then illogically the book ends with a prayer to Mary "who was conceived without sin."[7]

Anyone who would understand the attitudes of the modern Latin mind today should read Coelho. A residue of Catholicism remains, but it supplies little sustenance to life and no relevant God. In theology, Coelho is a Gnostic in the New Age tradition. He hungrily embarks on a spiritual quest, but only looks outward and inward, never upward. Writing with great feeling, such an author draws readers who long to share his optimistic wave. The "Soul of the World," after all, is good. He has sold more than 17 million copies in seventy-four countries and has been translated into thirty-four languages. It would seem that his belief system is shared by many.

From an entirely different viewpoint is the Brazilian novelist Moacyr Scliar's *The Strange Nation of Rafael Mendes*.[8] This is the story of Rafael, who discovers that he is the descendent of the prophet Jonah and therefore is a Jew. This information's impact on Rafael, his family, and particularly his daughter, who is a member of "the new Essenes" Christian sect, is well worth reading.

---

1. Author's note in *The Fifth Mountain* (New York: Harper Flamingo, 1998), viii.
2. Paulo Coelho, *The Alchemist: A Fable About Following Your Dream* (New York: Harper, 1903), 8.
3. Ibid., 24. "I am an adventurer—looking for treasure," says the main character (44). Thus Coelho picks up a more positive and appealing outlook in contrast with writers stuck in the philosophy of futility. Coelho does not share the hopelessness of many other Latin American writers, who stagger beneath the weight of a philosophical tradition that bypasses God's sovereignty for the more uncertain favors of saints. This theology does not provide the worldview for analyzing and dealing with Latin America's seemingly insuperable societal problems.
4. Ibid., 130. There is an interesting nuance in this book about conflict with Allah.
5. *The Fifth Mountain*, 40. The view of Elijah at Cherith being fed by the crow and the brook is great, 25.
6. Ibid., 217. The widow enigmatically comes back to him after her death.
7. Ibid., 245. We can only regret that, among its many threads, there is nothing of the mediatorial work of Jesus Christ.
8. New York: Harmony, 1988.

11.8.4 MARQUEZ, LOOKING UP

> The international success of *One Hundred Years of Solitude* has been so overwhelming that it has distorted any serious critical consideration of Garcia Marquez' work.
>
> —Emir Rodiguez Monegal[1]

Not translated into English until 1971, a number of years after its publication in Colombia, *One Hundred Years of Solitude* is the star burst of a Latin American renaissance of fiction. Gabriel Garcia Marquez is sometimes called the "Latin American William Faulkner." He was born in 1928 in the small Colombian town of Aracataca near the coast. Aracataca was to achieve fame as Maconda in *One Hundred Years of Solitude*. Gabriel's father, who was a telegrapher, left his family after a disastrous earthquake, and young Marquez was raised by his grandparents. His grandmother ceaselessly told stories. The grinding civil wars of his childhood and youth are the backdrop for much of his writing.

Gabriel was sent to a Jesuit private school near Bogota in 1946 and actually penned his first story in 1947. His studies in law did not captivate him, so he turned to professional writing. His first novel, *Leafstorm* (1955), mirrors both the fratricidal civil war and the banana harvest boom of the 1950s, the two "realities."[2] In all of his stories, the Roman Catholic Church is a dominating presence in society. But religion is not viewed as really important, beyond its effects on custom and convention.[3] He did early journalistic stints in Cartegena and Barranquilla and was in Italy in 1984 to cover the death of Pius XII.

Marquez was stranded abroad for some years because of turmoil in his home country and knew poverty in Paris for an extended time. In 1967 his fourth novel, *One Hundred Years of Solitude,* became "one of the most written about novels" of all time.[4] Mario Vargas Llosa calls it "the total novel." Buy it in paperback and read it several times, noting its overlay of biblical language. The little town of Maconda and its three hundred citizens are presented as a biblical type of paradise and its innocence, though the innocence is quickly shattered and the town shuttered.[5] The focus is on the Buendias family and the recurring appearance of a "pig's tail" among the offspring. He tells the story as his grandmother might tell it in his trademark "magic realism."

The work of Marquez is Faulkner plus Kafka. It has realism—giving many insights into Colombia's tortured history during the War of 1000 Days (1899–1902)—but it has an undercurrent of fantasy as well. A powerful eschatological impulse is discernible.[6] Rectilinear or straight lines of history are moving irrevocably toward cataclysm. Yet, as Harold Bloom says, "every page is rammed full of life."[7] But it is not a life from God. As gypsies read from Sanskrit parchments, and astrology and alchemy are revived in Maconda, the priest's sermons are from the Almanac weather forecasts instead of the Gospels.[8] The narrator, Melquiades, is like John on Patmos in Revelation 1:19. Maconda becomes the symbolic outline of the history of the world.[9]

In his marvelous short stories, we have more of the same, as in "A Very Old

Man with Enormous Wings" (1972). Father Gonzaga, at the behest of the Vatican, seeks to examine the creature with enormous wings. Is he angel or devil? Does he have a navel? "Father Watlerson's Fast" (1952), about a British vicar, should not be missed. In his novel *The Autumn of the Patriarch* (1975), Marquez portrays a South American dictator. His interest in detective stories is confirmed in his *Chronicle of a Death Foretold* (1981), in which he mentions his wife. Here we are aware of the "overwhelming presence of death." In *The Evil Hour,* Father Angel censors films based on the bell tolls. In another work, Father Antonio has seen the devil three times.[10] These also are apocalyptic motifs.

Such fecundity made the 1982 Nobel Prize for Literature almost a necessity. His *Love in the Time of Cholera* (1987) is a powerful telling of a love story in the context of the ravages of the cholera morbus. I must confess my partiality to his magnificent *Of Love and Other Demons* (1995). Get it on cassettes and listen to it on a long trip. The cast of characters is extraordinary and the reflection of the blend of "Spanish austerity, religious authority, classical humanism and African animism" is peerless. I am surprised that so few gringos have discovered Latin American literature of this caliber.

---

1. *Borzoi Anthology of Latin American Literature*, 886.
2. Raymond L. Williams, *Gabriel Garcia Marquez* (Boston: Twayne, 1984), 31.
3. Ibid., 78. Be on the lookout also for the recurring subtle humor in novels of Marquez.
4. Gabriel Garcia Maquez, *One Hundred Years of Solitude* (New York: Avon/Bard, 1970).
5. Williams, *Gabriel Garcia Marquez,* 75. His plot development is quite unique; it is "pieced together" skillfully.
6. *Writing the Apocalypse*, 26.
7. Harold Bloom, ed., *Gabriel Garcia Marquez* (New York: Chelsea House, 1989), 1.
8. *Writing the Apocalypse,* 11. Zamora argues that *100 Years* is like the book of Revelation in that it summarizes history.
9. Ibid., 63. Zamora depicts the eschatological pressure that drives novels of Marquez.
10. Williams, *Gabriel Garcia Marquez,* 139.

11.8.5 LLOSA, LOOKING FORWARD

Prophecies were beginning to come true. . . .
"These People are living in the grace of God," [said Father Joaquim].
—Mario Vargas Llosa
The War of the End of the World

Hailed as a great writer of the late twentieth century, and certainly known as a majestic story teller, Mario Vargas Llosa (b. 1936) expresses himself in many literary genres—as in life. He was a presidential aspirant in the 1990 Peruvian elections. He was born in middle-class circumstances, but his parents were divorced, and he lived with his mother and her parents. His grandfather was consul to Bolivia.

He started writing early and was graduated from the University in Lima at nineteen, almost immediately marrying a distant cousin. He lived abroad for a while, writing and teaching Spanish in Paris. He divorced and married another cousin. In 1974 he returned to Peru and moved away from his flirtation with Marxism. He was scorched by the brutality of state socialism and moved to the political right, a devotee of individual liberty and the free market.

Llosa's two-volume work, *Conversations in a Cathedral,* probes Peruvian politics in a somewhat scatological tone. Although he claimed to have lost his religious faith when he was fourteen or fifteen, he loved to use the biblical story of David and Goliath to portray the writer's struggle for justice.[1]

Highly respected in literary circles, Llosa is a writer's writer. He knows many quotations of Flaubert by heart and identifies closely with Camus. He loves to use humor and irony. He uses his stories to protest corruption and greed and could be characterized as moral, objective, and entertaining. He is skilled in developing structural parallels.[2] From 1979 to 1980, he was writer-in-residence in the Smithsonian Institution and gave himself to the production of an ambitious study of ideological fanaticism, *The War of the End of the World.*

Of his novels, this majestic and violent study of the impoverished backlands of northeastern Brazil merits close reading.[3] This is his seventh novel and his own favorite among his writings, despite the fact that it is historical rather than contemporary and about Brazil rather than Peru. It has been his most popular work.

Set in the closing years of the nineteenth century, *The War of the End of the World* is based on Llosa's reading of a radical republican history of four military invasions sent by the republican regime into northwest Bahia province. Euclides da Cunha wrote the facts, and Llosa told the story.[4] The monarchy, with all of its opulence at Rio and Petropolis, has tottered into its grave. Llosa shares the famous rebellion at Canudos inspired by Anthony the Counselor, an eccentric prophet who preached that in the new republicanism he saw "the devil wandering the earth."[5] The aura of "mystery, miracle and magic" hangs over this primitive socialistic experiment. Llosa shows us "the symbolic progression toward the apocalypse" and ultimate genocide.[6]

Coming after the great drought of 1877, the rebellion brought an amazing array of persons together in what can only be seen as a series of "conversions." In a veritable "Holy Land ambiance," the preacher is a Christ-figure who makes "evangelical prophecies" and shows that "religion may be more influential than politics."[7] The Counselor has "icy, obsessive eyes" and a "cavernous voice." He proclaims that the Antichrist is coming, and that the Last Judgment and resurrection are at hand. He calls for repentance and faith.[8] Appealing to those longing for "forgiveness, refuge, health and happiness," the Counselor supervises the building of a temple-cathedral and inveighs against gambling, tobacco, and alcohol.[9] His prophecies begin to come true and "the Kingdom of the Holy Spirit" is established (with definite overtones of Joachim of Fiore [c. 1135–1202], the medieval apocalypticist).[10]

Three expeditions sent to quash the rebellion fail disastrously. In all of this, these remarkable characters come to life—such as the Little Blessed One, the journalist known as the Scare Crow, the bearded lady, the idiot, the dwarf, Father Joaquim, and Colonel Moreira Cesar. The fourth expedition succeeds, and forty thousand perish, including the Counselor, of whom it is popularly reported: "Archangels took him up to heaven."[11]

Thoroughly researched, this novel is a classic study of two societies at a point in Brazilian history. "Literature is fire," Llosa has argued over the years. He is still allergic to dogma, but can only be seen to be an extraordinary figure in the increasingly bright constellation of Latin American writers of note and substance.[12]

A **significant sampling** from the beautiful islands of the Caribbean can be found in the writings of Jamaica Kincaid, whose autobiographical novel *Antigua* is stunning and whose ten short stories in *At the Bottom of the River* are most worthwhile. We feel the pain of appalling poverty very keenly in her work.

---

1. Dick Gerdes, *Mario Vargas Llosa* (Boston: Twayne, 1985), 3, 12. This biography provides good instruction on the narrative point of view.
2. Mario Vargas Llosa, *The Storyteller* (orig. *El Hablador*) (New York: Farrar, Strauss, Giroux, 1989), 6. He would seem to identify with El Hablador: "They were absolutely still. All the faces were turned, like radii of a circumference, toward the central point: the silhouette of a man at the heart of that circle . . . drawn to him as to a magnet, standing there and gesticulating . . . a storyteller."
3. Mario Vargas Llosa, *The War of the End of the World* (orig. *La guerra del fin del mundo*) (New York: Avon, 1981).
4. Mario Vargas Llosa, *A Writer's Reality* (Syracuse: Syracuse University Press, 1991), 128.
5. Gerdes, *Mario Vargas Llosa,* 168. The rebellion was ostensibly "pro-monarchy" but the lines are very confused.
6. Ibid., 168. Bahia's capitol is Salvador, a major African slave trade port.
7. Ibid., 184, 188. The devotees fervently believed in God and practiced Catholic religion.
8. Llosa, *The War of the End of the World,* 17.
9. Ibid., 51. Much admixture of superstition in Canudos is seen in the water diviners.
10. Marjorie Reeves, *Joachim of Fiore and the Prophetic Future* (New York: Harper Torchbooks, 1976).
11. Gerdes, *Mario Vargas Llosa,* 185. The characters of *The War of the End of the World* are memorable and well drawn.
12. Mario Vargas Llosa, *Making Waves* (New York: Farrar, Strauss and Giroux, 1997).

CHAPTER TWELVE

Exploring the Literature of and About the Jews and Israel

The absolute singularity of the Jewish people in the purpose of God is clear in the scriptural record and theological conviction of Christians and Jews. The Jews' election as God's sovereignly set-apart people, their survival through unparalleled vicissitudes, their miraculous resurrection and growth as a modern nation, and the bright prospects portrayed in Bible prophecy elicit joy and praise to God.[1]

The literature of and about this people is so extensive and artistically remarkable that it merits a section in this survey. Thomas Cahill has reminded us of the gifts of the Jews, "how a tribe of desert nomads changed the way everyone thinks and feels." The "intervening God" Himself has given through the Jews an integrated view of life that gets at the very center of life and human history. Prophetism and her sense of the interior journey have made this ancient people "the conscience of the west."[2] One scholar has argued that "the creation of the State of Israel and its survival is the outstanding event of the past two millennia."[3]

---

1. See David L. Larsen, "A Celebration of the Lord Our God's Role in the Future of Israel," in *Israel: The Land and the People,* ed. H. Wayne House (Grand Rapids: Kregel, 1998), 301–23. For a more extensive treatment of these themes, see David L. Larsen, *Jews, Gentiles and the Church: A New Perspective on History and Prophecy* (Grand Rapids: Discovery House, 1995).
2. Thomas Cahill, *The Gifts of the Jews* (New York: Doubleday, 1998). This long-awaited book makes some points, but it relies on higher critical notions that are dated and often disregards more recent scholarship.
3. Gerald Steinberg, "Remembering History and Making It," *The Jerusalem Post,* 18 April 1998, 13.

12.1 THE CORRIDOR OF HISTORY

The Hebrews have done more to civilize man than any other nation.
—U.S. President John Adams

The very idea of history as rectilinear rather than cyclical originated in the Bible. Walter Kaiser deals with this historiography and the devotion to God behind it in the magnificent *A History of Israel: From the Bronze Age through the Jewish Wars*.[1] For a splendid overview to modern times, no other work is comparable to Paul Johnson's *A History of the Jews*.[2]

---

1. Nashville: Broadman and Holman, 1998.
2. New York: Harper and Row, 1987. Johnson argues that "No people has ever insisted more firmly than the Jews that history has a purpose and humanity a destiny."

12.1.1 MICHENER, THE PANORAMA OF JEWISH HISTORY

Praise be to the LORD, the God of Israel, from everlasting to everlasting. Amen and Amen.
—Psalm 41:13

The ideal starting point for dipping into this massive literature is to read or reread the remarkable study of the Jewish experience over the centuries written by James Michener entitled *The Source*. Michener (b. 1907) was born in New York and educated at Swarthmore College. He was first a professor and then an editor, after which he served as a U.S. Navy lieutenant commander in the Pacific theater during World War II. We have already alluded to Michener's novel based on Central American history, *Mexico* (11.8.1). Michener has failings, not the least of which is his tendency to extend a work by hundreds of pages through his rambling. He also has a habit of filling in holes in historical knowledge with imagination. But his great contribution is to view the sweep of history and how it interrelates in a people.

The Source is Michener at his best, an amazing (if factually flawed) panorama of Jewish history.[1] Archeologists' experience in excavating the layers at Tell Makor (lit. "Source") is patterned on work done on the site of Roman Tiberias. As each level is revealed, Michener tells a story of that generation, who lived and died in this community on the Sea of Galilee. Beginning with very primitive life among the Bee-eaters in about 9831 B.C., we move to the ages of the patriarchs. In particular regarding Jacob, Michener recognizes a "carefully organized sexual behavior" that has been a part of this people from the beginning.[2]

In depicting 605 B.C., Michener shares a memorable description of what it meant for the Jews to gather for travel to Jerusalem for the feasts under the awesome sense of God's patient presence.[3] He shows the pressure of Greco-Roman culture on Old Testament spirituality. He is especially good in helping us see and feel Herod's slaughter of the innocents.[4] The book meanders through the rise of Islam, the coming of the Christian Crusaders and the survival of love for God and learning among the "saintly men of Safed." The story culminates in the twilight of the Ottoman Turk's influence, the British mandate and the establishment of the Jewish state in 1948. The history of any ethnic group bears special interest, but with the historical unfolding of Jewish history we see the interweaving strands of redemption history for a lost nation and human race. Much of this narrative is exceedingly painful and difficult.

---

1. James Michener, *The Source* (New York: Random House, 1965). Michener's title for the book carries meanings deeper than even he likely noticed.
2. Ibid., 148. Hebrew law and custom regulated young men staying together "lest there be abomination."
3. Ibid., 284, 308. Michener argues that God sent many punishments on the Jews to wean them from false gods.
4. Ibid., 365. Herod's cruelty and arbitrariness are clearly established. Over his reign he killed tens of thousands.

12.1.2 STEINBERG, THE PRESSURE WITHIN JEWISH HISTORY

The Jews are divinely preserved for a purpose worthy of God.

—Jerome

A novel on the ancient "culture wars" between Judaism and the Gentile world, is in Milton Steinberg's now-seldom-read *As a Leaf Driven*.[1] This is worth asking your library to order within the library system. Steinberg was rabbi of the Park Avenue Synagogue in New York City from 1933 until his death in 1950. He was brilliant, though allergic to dogma,[2] believing in the self-sufficiency of the individual. Sin was irrelevant. This is not a realistic philosophy, but the value of his novel, set in Jamnia early in the Christian era, puts the clash of cultures of Palestine into its historical context.

Young Elisha, son of Abuijah of Migdal, is ordained to the rabbinate and told "Thou hast expounded well." An unsatisfying marriage and the death of his twin children bring Elisha to a crisis of faith. His friends, Meir and Berviah, seek a new future through their faith. They want to rebuild the temple the Romans have destroyed over sixty years before.[3] Elisha cannot go along with their optimism, or with Rabbi Akiba and his emphasis on belief that is "beyond reason" (Akiba held that "we are all blind moles"). Elisha wants reason alone. Still, in his intellectual wandering, he is surprised that some philosophers quote and commend the Holy Scriptures.

In the Bar Kochba Revolt in A.D. 135, Elisha aids the Romans. Yet his quest for reason alone yields only a chasing after wind.[4] The Hellenistic/Judaic tension is paradigmatic here. A lively and pertinent piece.

1. Milton Steinberg, *As a Driven Leaf* (New York: Behrman House, 1939).
2. Arthur A. Cohen, ed., *Milton Steinberg's Anatomy of Faith* (New York: Harcourt Brace, 1960).
3. *As a Driven Leaf,* 180. The philosophic tension here is a product of the perennial face-off between Anselm and Hume.
4. Ibid., 471. Elisha was always seen as "an ass laden with his books."

12.1.3 ALEICHEM, THE PAIN OF JEWISH HISTORY

> Although we have been fleeing and running for hundreds of years, we have not lost our way.
>
> —Sholom Aleichem

The Jews of the *galut* (the Diaspora) scattered among the nations have frequently found themselves "with dread, never sure of their lives" (Deut. 28:66). Few have chronicled these woes more vividly than Solomon J. Rabinowitz (1859–1916) who wrote as Sholom Aleichem (the Hebrew greeting: "peace be with you"). He was a rabbi in the Ukraine but fled the bloody pogrom of 1905 to the United States. What he wrote of life in the shtetls (villages) of the Ukraine would obtain anywhere in the "pale of settlement," whether in White Russia, Galicia, or Lithuania. He began to write in Yiddish (a High-German language using Hebrew characters and written like Hebrew from right to left. It is still spoken by Jews in Russia and across central Europe).

Aleichem wrote three hundred short stories, five novels, and many plays. He was a master humorist, and his gallery of characters is compared to Mark Twain and Charles Dickens.[1] One of his dark novels is *The Bloody Hoax,* the story of a poor Jew and a wealthy Gentile in Russia who agree to trade identities for a year. The attacks on Jews described in this work inspired the 1920s Yiddish play, *Hard to Be a Jew*.[2]

A marvelous collection of the stories well-worth owning combines "The Old Country" and "Tevye's Daughters," about the irrepressible dairyman with seven daughters made so popular in *Fiddler on the Roof*. Here are the original stories. Tevye sees his seven beautiful daughters as the gift of God's grace, but he has neither luck nor money. Tevye and his wife, Golde, have their greatest sorrows in the marriages of their daughters. Tevye never takes advantage of an opportunity to go to Israel and in the pogroms of 1882 is driven from his land. Only his God and the Holy Word are left. He tells Aleichem at their final parting: "Our ancient God still lives."[3] Anyone who loves the Jewish people and who desires to understand their remarkable history would be well served to dig into these enjoyable pieces.

A marvelous companion in Jewish literature is Leo Rosten's *The Joy of Yiddish*.[4] Rosten not only indexes key Yiddish expressions but affords "serendipitous" excursions into Jewish humor, habits, history, and religious ceremonies. Great insights into life in the *shtetls*.

1. Sholom Aleichem, introduction to *Favorite Tales of Sholom Aleichem* (New York: Avenel, 1983), xi.
2. Shalom Aleichem, *The Bloody Hoax* (Bloomington, Ind.: Indiana University Press, 1991). Raises the specter of the Holocaust to come.
3. Aleichem, introduction to *Favorite Tales,* xviii. Although his stories are hilarious, Aleichem's Tevye is really a very tragic figure.
4. New York: Avon/Washington Square, 1968.

12.1.4 SINGER, THE PEOPLE OF JEWISH HISTORY

Twenty minutes later I was the same man with the same worries and troubles.

—Isaac Bashevis Singer,
on receiving the Nobel Prize

Jews from more than one hundred different nations have established a single national identity in Palestine. Isaac Bashevis Singer (1904–1991) tells the story of the Jews in one of those nations, Poland, where Jews have historically been consigned to ghettos and been severely restricted.[1] A fascinating mirror of Jewish life in Poland has been held up in the numerous and engaging works of a Warsaw native who emigrated to the United States in 1935. His father was in charge of the rabbinical court, the Beth Din, which traces its origins back to Jethro and his suggestion to his son-in-law Moses (Exodus 18). Isaac's mother was the daughter of generations of rabbis.

Singer wrote with astute insight and vast descriptive power of life on Krochmalna Street and the Hasidic miracle rabbis who wait for the imminent coming of the Messiah.[2] Through the shadow of World War I and its exigencies, Singer candidly shares his life. He writes of his brother Israel Joshua's questioning.[3] He introduces his country relatives, and we appreciate some of the strains on Jewish life.

Singer trained to be a rabbi, but he allows very little sense of personal faith to penetrate his words. This is, instead, journalism. Most of it first appeared in Yiddish newspapers in New York and Brooklyn. Faith had little influence on his life, either. He was a notorious womanizer and had little relationship with his own children. Glimpses of his own inner struggle break through in books like *Journey to My Father* (1994) and *A Little Boy in Search of God* (1976).

A persistent cynicism in Singer intertwines with Jewish cabalistic mysticism, about demons and magic.[4] His first book to appear in English was the story of a Polish-Jewish dynasty from the early 1900s to the beginning of World War II, *The Family Moskat* (1950). The ruin of the Moskats is metaphorical of the decline of Eastern Jewry.

His lilting *The Magician of Lublin* gives us a marvelous flavor of Jewish life and of Yasha Mazur, a man caught between God and Satan.[5] *Shosha* depicts the dilemma of a Polish Jew who must choose whether to flee from the impending Nazi invasion or stay and face an uncertain future with his childhood sweetheart.[6]

Singer also treats the experience of those who came to America, as he did. In *Meshugah* (lit. "Crazy"), he portrays a group of Holocaust survivors in Manhattan. Some of these characters ultimately go to Tel Aviv.[7] In his posthumously published *Shadows on the Hudson,* he again addresses the experiences of refugees from Hitler in the 1940s. The "aimless trajectory" of the central figure, Hertz David Grein, is typical. His male characters are libidinously in the wind.

He has been called anti-Promethean, and all of his writings reflect the influence of the pantheistic Jewish philosopher Benedict de Spinoza (1632–1677).[8] I strongly recommend that readers pick any of Singer's books off the full shelf you will likely find in the library. He will reinforce your identification with Paul's longing: "My heart's desire and prayer to God for the Isaelites is that they may be saved" (Rom. 10:1).

We have referred to Pearl S. Buck's great book, *Peony,* about Jews in China (10.2.6), but further study on this culturally-divergent mix would be enhanced by reading Michael Pollak's *Mandarins, Jews and Missionaries.*[9] The affairs of the Jewish community in Kaifeng, we learn, involved François-Marie Voltaire (1694–1778), Immanuel Kant (1724–1804), Gottfried W. von Leibniz (1646–1716), and Charles Dickens (1812–1870). A much more recent episode is traced in James R. Ross, *Escape to Shanghai.*[10]

1. The word *ghetto* was apparently coined in Venice of an area near the cannon factory where Jews lived (see *Jews, Gentiles and the Church,* 72). For a moving description of the indignities and insults endured by North African Jews, see Pierre van Paasen, *Days of Our Years* (New York: Hillman-Curl, 1939). Van Paasen also wrote *The Forgotten Ally,* about Jews in World War I.
2. Isaac Bashevis Singer, *In My Father's Court* (New York: Fawcett/Crest, 1962), 129.
3. Ibid., 197. His stories are about fascinating people, such as Moshe Blecher, the tinsmith, who was entranced by the prophecies of Daniel and finally went to Israel, only to return because conditions were so difficult, 81ff. He goes to Israel again.
4. William Rose Benet, *Benet's Reader's Encyclopedia,* 3d ed. (New York: Harper and Row, 1987), 903.
5. Isaac Bashevis Singer, *The Magician of Lublin* (New York: Fawcett/Crest, 1960).
6. Isaac Bashevis Singer, *Shosha* (New York: Fawcett/Crest, 1978). In *Scum* (1990), we see the underbelly of Krochmalna Street in Warsaw. Max Barabander takes "the road to Hedonism," like many of Singer's characters.
7. Isaac Bashevis Singer, *Meshugah* (New York: Farrar, Strauss, 1994).
8. Isaac Bashevis Singer, *Shadows on the Hudson* (New York: Farrar, Strauss, 1997). His brother I. J. Singer has written some very significant family novels, for example, *Yoshe Kalb* (1965), and *The Family Carnovsky* (1969). I have read these but have enjoyed most of all *The Brothers Ashkenazi* (1936). Also Chaim Grande's *Agunah* and *Yeshiva.*
9. Philadelphia: Jewish Publication Society, 1981.
10. New York: Free Press, 1994.

12.1.5 LEVIN, THE PROGRESS OF JEWISH HISTORY

> The people of all other nations but the Jewish seem to look backwards
> and also to exist for the present; but in the Jewish scheme everything is
> prospective and preparatory; nothing, however trifling, is done for itself
> alone, but all is typical of something yet to come.
>
> —Samuel Taylor Coleridge

The development of world Zionism and creation of the State of Israel in 1948
are fulfillments of Bible prophecies and promises awaited over the centuries by
Jews and Christians. To get historical perspective, several writers are of particular assistance. Among these is the journalist and novelist Meyer Levin (1905–
1981). He protested the sanitizing of *The Diary of Anne Frank.* The play and film
of this poignant story had been edited severely by Anne Frank's father. Ralph
Melnick in *The Stolen Legacy of Anne Frank* argues that the original play so
"avoids the particulars of the Jews' plight under Hitler that it almost becomes a
drama of people who were suffering through a housing shortage."[1] Levin's more
faithful adaptation was not deemed commercially viable, but his crusade bore
fruit in a later Broadway production that left a darker impression.

Levin's magnum opus is a two-volume epic that critics have called "the Jewish
War and Peace." In *The Settlers* and *The Harvest,* we follow the Chaimovitch family from their tenuous home in the Russia of the pogroms through the turbulence
of the last days of the czars. While most émigrés headed for the United States, a
small movement led by Socialist-Zionist zealots went to Israel, though the sultan
of Turkey had turned down Theodore Herzl's ambitious design for a Zionist state
in Palestine. The backdrop in all of this is world anti-Semitism, which is irrational
and transcends mere ethnic dislike. Indeed it arises out of Satan's revolt against
God's plan for history, which so conspicuously involves this ancient people.[2]

Yankel Chaimovitch and his wife, Feigel, come from the Ukraine, where he
was a poor Talmudic student and she a daughter of the wealthy Koslovsky family. They settle on the Jordan River near Tiberias. In *The Settlers,* we accompany
the little family as they drain swamps, face Arab hostility, and endure desperate
economic deprivation. In World War I, some fight for the Turks and the Germans
and others for the Allies through the Jewish Legion of the one-armed Captain
Trumpeldor from Russia. As we follow this heroic family, they come alive, and
the land becomes real. *The Harvest* begins with the youngest son, Mati, "the one
born in *Eretz,*" meaning "in the land." Mati goes to America to study at the University of Chicago. At every juncture, there is accurate and timely interaction
with the actual historical and political situation:

> Why trouble them over the well-meaning blunders of Lord Samuel, Mati
> reflected. What would they understand about his leaning over backward,
> giving the vast Beisan lands to some Bedouin goatherds, who proceeded
> to sell piece by piece to the Jews? Or worse, putting in Haj Amin el
> Husseini, the riot fomenter, as Mufti of Jerusalem! Responsibility would
> make him behave.[3]

The Harvest takes the story from 1927–1948, when the British withdraw and the United Nations decides for partition and the Jewish state. These two volumes must be read by those who want the historical panorama along with "the feel" of the birth of the modern nation of Israel, events which are so traumatic but at the same time so triumphant.

---

1. Richard Zoglin, "A Darker Anne Frank," *Time*, 15 December 1997, 110; see also Suzanne Fields, "Netanyahu, Arafat and the Diary of Anne Frank," *Insight*, 23 February 1998.
2. For a discussion and bibliography of anti-Semitism, see *Jews, Gentiles and the Church*, 79ff. One wonders how it is conceivable that any Christian be anti-Semitic.
3. Meyer Levin, *The Harvest* (New York: Simon and Schuster, 1978), 23. Each book runs to about 675 pages.

12.1.6 THOENE, THE PATHOS OF JEWISH HISTORY

For I, the LORD, do not change; therefore you, O sons of Jacob, are not consumed.
—Malachi 3:6 (NASB)

Not all great books about the Jews and Israel have been written by Jews. A great company of Christians delight in hearing how God fulfilled his promises in relation to the modern State of Israel. Those who have played a role have included such Britons as:

- General Charles George Gordon (b. 1833), heroic commander who died in the fall of Khartoum in 1885;
- Field Marshal Edmund Allenby (1861–1936), who wrested Jerusalem from Turkish control in 1917;
- Arthur James Balfour (1848–1930), the foreign secretary who led in developing the Balfour Declaration, a resolution declaring Britain's conditional support for establishment of a Jewish State;
- David Lloyd-George (1863–1945), the prime minister who was influenced by his Welsh boyhood training in the Old Testament;
- Orde Charles Wingate (1903–1944), an eccentric Scot who pioneered guerrilla warfare techniques and trained Jewish generals.

All of these, with the exception of Lloyd George, were evangelical Christians.

A more recent Gentile writer who has gained a wide audience for her very well-researched novels about the Jews and Israel is Bodie Thoene (b. 1951). She worked for John Wayne's Batjac Productions and ABC Circle Films as a writer and researcher. She and her husband do extensive interviewing and research for her novels.

In The Zion Covenant, four novels on European Jews during the devastating 1930s and 1940s, Thoene meticulously traces the tightening of the noose around

Europe as Adolph Hitler turned Germany toward war and the Holocaust. In *Vienna Prelude,* we meet a Jewish violinist for the Vienna Symphony Orchestra, Elisa Lindheim, who joins New York newspaperman John Murphy in an effort to save Jews from Hitler's tentacles.[1] In ensuing volumes, Elisa, John, and many other characters represent the providence-directed struggles of both Jews and Gentiles as Hitler seized Austria and advanced on Czechoslovakia.

In another series, The Zion Chronicles, the milieu is Israel war for Palestine:

> As early as January 14, 1948, Arab terrorists goaded on by British shut down the Jewish quarter of old Jerusalem. Arabs attacked settlements and wiped out the Haganah relief force. The secretary-general of the Arab League announced ominously: "This will be a war of extermination and a momentous massacre." At that time 650,000 Jews faced 1.3 million Arabs in Palestine, not including Arab-supporting states. The possibility of another Holocaust was real. On May 14, 1948, the British left Jerusalem for good, and the key to Zion Gate was handed over to Rabbi Mordecai Weingarten.[2]

Thoene's opening chronicle, *The Key to Zion,* is especially poignant.[3] Full-scale fighting breaks out before the declaration of statehood and the siege of Jerusalem begins. Palestinian refugees are caught in the middle. Moshe and his friends are seeking to supply food to the city. Thoene does not avoid tough issues, such as Jewish destruction of Deir Yassin.[4] The titanic struggle to preserve the Jewish state ceded by United Nations partition killed 1 percent of the Israeli population. The story of Latrun and their victory is a gripping drama, and Thoene's superb work reveals the picture and relives the pain of both Jew and Palestinian.[5]

The amazing career and strong Christian faith of Major-General Wingate in relation to the Israeli Defense Force are told in several books. Among them are Leonard Mosley, *Gideon Goes to War;*[6] Christopher Sykes, *Orde Wingate;*[7] and a later study was Trevor Royle, *Orde Wingate: Irregular Soldier.*[8] The story of Wingate is fascinating; he was frightfully odd but deeply devout.

---

1. Bodie Thoene, *Vienna Prelude* (Minneapolis: Bethany House, 1989).
2. *Jews, Gentiles and the Church*, 201.
3. Bodie Thoene, *The Key to Zion* (Grand Rapids: Bethany House, 1988).
4. Ibid., 86ff. That there were atrocities of terrorism and injustice committed on both sides of this conflict is not surprising, given what was at stake.
5. The best historical description of the battle for Jerusalem is Larry Collins and Dominique Lapierre, *O Jerusalem* (New York: Simon and Schuster, 1972). The best overall description of the 1948, early 1950s, 1968, and early 1970s conflicts is Chaim Herzog, *The Arab-Israeli Wars* (New York: Random House, 1982).
6. New York: Scribner's, 1955.
7. London: Collins, 1959.
8. London: Weidenfeld and Nicholson, 1996.

12.1.7 URIS, THE PERPLEXITY OF JEWISH HISTORY

The LORD said to Abram after Lot had departed from him, "Lift up your eyes from where you are and look north and south, east and west. All the land that you see I will give to you and your offspring forever."
—Genesis 13:14–15

By any criterion, Leon Uris's novel *Exodus* must stand as a classic on Israel's independence. Its powerful film adaptation extended its influence as a Jewish perspective of the death struggle in 1948. Uris was born in Baltimore in 1924 and left school at seventeen to join the United States Marines. His first novel was *Battle Cry* (1953), chronicling life in the Marines. He wrote about Ireland and a Muslim Haj (or pilgrimage to Mecca), but he is best known for his three novels on modern Jewish life: *Mila 18* (1961), about the Jewish revolt in the Warsaw Ghetto; *QB VII* (1970), about the trial of an alleged death camp doctor;[1] and *Exodus* (1958), about the return of European Jews to Palestine and establishment of the Jewish State.

Exodus unfolds in five sections, beginning in Cypress where the British have interred thousands of Jews, including hundreds of children. A quarter of a million Jews are desperate to enter Palestine.[2]

The novel begins with "Operation Gideon," which was dedicated to getting three hundred children to Israel on board a salvage tug renamed "The Exodus." Dramatic flashbacks illumine the fifty-nation approval of the Balfour Declaration in 1917 and the British White Paper of 1939 that repudiated the Declaration under Arab pressure. Uris describes the British decision to abandon their mandate, the story of the United Nations Special Commission on Palestine, and the Arab misjudgment of the situation that doomed their cause. Although the action runs down a bit, we are held by such stories as the siege of Safed in the north and airlifts from such places as Yemen. Certainly the return of so many Jews to their homeland, where they now total almost 5 million, is a miracle of prophetic fulfillment.[3]

---

1. For the true story of a German Christian who saved Jews, see Douglas K. Suneke, *The Moses of Rovno* (New York: Dodd, Mead, 1985). For a French doctor's heroism, see Albert Haas, *The Doctor and the Damned* (New York: St. Martin's, 1984).
2. Leon Uris, *Exodus* (Garden City: Doubleday, 1958), 118. Vignettes of tension with the British, development of the Warsaw Ghetto, and earlier intrigue to save Jews in Denmark are moving. One of the most accurate and chilling narratives coming out of the Warsaw Ghetto established by the Nazis is Martin Gray, *For Those I Love* (Boston: Little, Brown, 1972). The irony of *Exodus* is that many thousands of the death camp survivors end up interred in the Cypress refugee camps, which mainly exist to keep the people out of Palestine. See Abram L. Sachar, *The Redemption of the Unwanted: From the Liberation of the Death Camps to the Founding of Israel* (New York: St. Mark's, 1983).
3. Uris, *Exodus,* 435, 509. About the ups and downs of Leon Uris, see Pearl Sheffy Gefen, "From the Inside Out," *The Jerusalem Post,* 28 January 1995, 10f.

12.1.8 WOUK, THE PERSPECTIVE OF JEWISH HISTORY

> When the LORD brought back the captives to Zion, we were like men
> who dreamed. Our mouths were filled with laughter, our tongues with
> songs of joy.
>
> —Psalm 126:1–2a

One of America's foremost historical novelists, Herman Wouk is known for his incisive writings on modern war, such as his Pulitzer Prize-winning *The Caine Mutiny* (1951) and the sprawling *Winds of War* (1971); the former best known in its film adaptation and the latter popular as a television mini-series. *Marjorie Morningstar* (1955) tackled the issue of a Jewish girl and her principles and up-bringing in show business, and *Youngblood Hawke* (1962) looked at the climb of an impoverished young man.

Wouk was born in New York City in 1915 and has fervently supported Israel. His own Jewish faith is religious but not orthodox. He has written a best-selling work on the Jewish faith called *This Is My God*.

Wouk's books on modern Israel are expansive novels. The first volume, *The Hope,* demarcates Israel's founding in 1948 and the War for Independence to the 1956 Suez Campaign and the Six-Day War of 1967.[1] Wouk gives his story a some-what different feel from that of Meyer Levin, who concentrates on one family. Wouk works in depth about four Israeli army officers and their complex romances. Zev Barak is a refined Vienna-born army officer; Benny Luria is a fighter-pilot who has deep religious feelings; Sam Pasternak is employed by the Mossad, the Israeli intelligence and secret police; and Kishote (Quixote) is a dashing fighter who begins his military career as a refugee on a mule.

In *The Hope,* we see how critical it was in 1948 that the United States imme-diately recognize Israel, as President Truman did in opposition to the State De-partment and Secretary of State George Marshall. The sense in which the founding of the State took place behind the British shield in 1917 and then the American shield (1947–48) is explored.[2]

Wouk's sequel, *The Glory,* moves through the agonies of the Yom Kippur War, the rescue raid on Entebbe, Uganda, and the Camp David agreements. Wouk pays high tribute to such Bible believing Christians as Orde Wingate for steadfastly sharing in Israel's biblically-derived vision.[3] We get well-sketched profiles of the historical leaders at the time, as well as more on the four fictional military men. Barak is an attaché in Washington who loves an American woman; Luria and both of his sons are pilots; Pasternak is in love with Kishote's wife, Yael. Wouk is an excellent teller of stories, and this is a mosaic of scintillating yarns. Character Christian Cunningham shares in a memorandum to Barak what we might call a millennial vision:

> When these dry bones revive and stand again on Mount Zion (our Lord's
> people, the Jews, as a dry dead fossil of history), that will signal a new
> political time, an epochal if slow reconciliation, a digging down to the
> common bedrock, so as to defeat Marxist atheism and forestall the nuclear

devastation of the planet. The Second Coming may be a matter of my personal belief. But I predict that when the clouds of polemic and ancient prejudice clear, the New Politics of the Sacred Region will emerge, with a burst of peace and prosperity beyond all present imagining.[4]

The Standard Work on Zionism is still Walter Laqueur's *A History of Zionism*.[5] Beginning with Theodore Herzl and his antecedents, we trace the miraculous rise of this movement, which has been so central in the formation of the Jewish State.

---

1. Herman Wouk, *The Hope* (Boston: Little, Brown, 1993).
2. Ibid., 298. See also Shabtai Teveth, *Ben Gurion's Spy: The Story of the Political Scandal That Shaped Modern Israel* (New York: Columbia University Press, 1996). About the pivotal Lavon Affair, which opened the way for M. Begin.
3. Herman Wouk, *The Glory* (Boston: Little, Brown, 1994), 551.
4. Ibid., 641.
5. New York: Holt, Rinehart, 1972.

12.2 THE CALAMITY OF THE HOLOCAUST

In the days of her affliction and homelessness, Jerusalem remembers all her precious things that were from the days of old, when her people fell into the hand of the adversary, and no one helped her. The adversaries saw her, they mocked at her ruin.

—Lamentations 1:7 (NASB)

The horrors of the Holocaust are uniquely heinous in degree and kind; the 6 million victims were God's chosen people. Something diabolical attaches to this atrocity. That some crackpots persist in revisionist denials of the tragedy only confirms the depths of human depravity. Jacques Derrida's (b. 1930) deconstructionism, which denies any fixed meaning to text, opened the door to the Nazism of Yale University's Paul de Man and the anti-Semitism of philosopher Martin Heidegger (1889–1976).[1]

We must consider immediate victims and the circle of family tragedy as reflected in the suffering of surviving children.[2] The work of German philosopher Emil L. Fackenheim is worth perusing on this subject.[3]

Two Holocaust survivors are at the emotional heart of this immense body of literature, Elie Wiesel and Aharon Appelfeld.

---

1. One of the best overall surveys of the Holocaust as history is Leni Yahil, *The Holocaust: The Fate of European Jewry* (New York: Oxford, 1991). For an amazing book on the Holocaust written in Germany, read Jurek Becker, *Jacob the Liar* (New York: Arcade, 1969). On the movement to deny the historicity of the event, see David Lehman, *Signs of the Times: Deconstruction and the Fall of Paul de Man* (New York: Poseidon, 1990); and Deborah E. Lipstadt, *Denying the Holocaust:*

The Growing Assault on Truth and Memory (New York: Free Press, 1994). Lipstadt shows that "the modern-day attack of the Western rationalist tradition has fed Holocaust denial."

2. About a few who escaped, John Bierman, *Odyssey* (New York: Simon and Schuster, 1984). The general fate of the survivors is covered in Helen Epstein, *Children of the Holocaust: Conversations with Sons and Daughters of Survivors* (New York: Penguin, 1979). David Grossman's novel *See Under: Love* (New York: Farrar, Strauss, 1989) is about Momik Neuman, who is the only child of Holocaust survivors. Another excellent work by Grossman, *The Yellow Wind,* tells the story of the Palestinians.

3. Emil L. Fackenheim, *To Mend the World: Foundations of Post-Holocaust Jewish Thought* (New York: Shocken, 1982).

12.2.1 WIESEL, THE VICIOUSNESS OF THE HOLOCAUST

Upon your walls, O Jerusalem, I have set watchmen; all the day and all the night they shall never be silent. You who put the LORD in remembrance, take no rest, and give him no rest until he establishes Jerusalem and makes it a praise in the earth.

—Isaiah 62:6–7 (RSV)

Acquaintance with Elie Wiesel (b. 1928) is mandatory for Christians who would answer the relentless revisionists who minimize and trivialize the Holocaust.[1] Wiesel has become one of the most striking visible symbols of the Holocaust, along with such moving films as *Shoah* and *Schindler's List.* Wiesel was born in a village in Romania and was at Nazi death camps, including Auschwitz and Buchenwald, where his parents and sister perished. The French writer François Mauriac (11.4.9) urged him to write about his experience, and one product of this effort was his widely read book *Night* (1960).[2]

A veritable flood of material relating to the Holocaust and anti-Semitism in general has followed. He received the Nobel Peace Prize in 1986.[3] Wiesel has also penned some biblical studies. His *Five Biblical Portraits* is especially useful, touching Saul, Jonah, Jeremiah, Elijah, and Joshua.[4] His early writing was in French, but in recent years, he has lived in the United States and taught and lectured at various universities.

Among my favorites in his collection are *A Beggar in Jerusalem, The Oath,* and *Town Beyond the Wall.* Of particular interest is his fictional study of Elhanan Rosenbaum's desire to tell his son Malkiel about his experiences in his native Romania during the war as his memory begins to give way to disease.[5] The skills of the author are so apparent in this exploration of remembrance. One of the most deeply moving of his works is *The Gates of the Forest,* in which Gregor, a Hungarian Jew, hides in the forests and poses as a deaf-mute to escape the Nazis. It is in this work that we find Wiesel's famous quote, "God made man because he loves stories."[6] Inadvertently, Gregor becomes a betrayer, with complex consequences. No one who engages thinking people in significant communication in our time can ignore Elie Wiesel.

▓ **One of the most** heart-wrenching of the Holocaust survivor chronicles must be Avraham Tory's *Surviving the Holocaust: The Kovno Ghetto Diary*.[7] This was written in a situation of extreme danger in the Jewish ghetto of Kovno from June 1941 to January 1944. See also Yaffa Eliach, *Hasidic Tales of the Holocaust*.[8]

---

1. One of the most viciously anti-Semitic agencies is the Institute for Historical Review in Costa Mesa, California, which has published the like of Robert John's *Behind the Balfour Declaration* and other unsavory distortions.
2. Beyond the German Holocaust, we need to keep in mind that 100 million deaths have occurred in the Soviet Union, most under Joseph Stalin (1879–1953). This included millions of Jews, and millions more have suffered through an anti-Semitic atmosphere not far removed from the Germany of the 1930s. Curiously, Stalin planted a Yiddish-speaking colony five thousand miles east of Moscow to rid himself of Jews. See Robert Weinberg, *Stalin's Forgotten Zion* (New York: Oxford, 1997).
3. *Benet's Reader's Encyclopedia,* 1063.
4. Elie Wiesel, *Five Biblical Portraits* (Notre Dame, Ind.: Notre Dame University Press, 1981). Wiesel echoes quite a conventional Judaism but never gives us the feel of an Abraham Heschel, for instance. Edward K. Kaplan and Samuel H. Dresner, *Abraham Joshua Heschel: Prophetic Witness* (New Haven: Yale, 1998).
5. Elie Wiesel, *The Forgotten* (New York: Summit, 1992).
6. Elie Wiesel, *The Gates of the Forest* (New York: Schocken, 1982).
7. Cambridge: Harvard University, 1990.
8. New York: Avon, 1982.

12.2.2 APPELFELD, THE VILENESS OF THE HOLOCAUST

I see the modern Jew as being torn between two tendencies, or two worlds: the first is to escape from himself and his culture; the second is to return to his heritage. The first—the escaper—is much the stronger.
—Aharon Appelfeld

In Czernowitz, Bukovina, which at his birth in 1932 was part of the Austro-Hungarian empire, Aharon Appelfeld was an only child of wealthy parents. His grandparents spoke Yiddish and his parents German. His father made a fortune by motorizing mills in his country. His parents were thoroughly assimilated Jews who embarked on frequent forays to spas and resorts. In 1940 he saw the Nazis kill his mother, and at age eight, his father was taken off in a work detail. He ran away, trying to hide in the woods near villages. For some time, he lived in a prostitute's hut.[1] Accused of being a Jew, he fled again and this time took refuge with a horse thief. He was finally picked up by a Red Army unit.

Aharon reached Israel at age fourteen, "without roots, without my own world, without culture, possessions, luggage or language."[2] In *Bartfuss the Immortal,* he portrays a survivor much like himself, who finds that survival strategies needed in the past make communication difficult in nonthreatening situations. Aharon has written novels that are remarkably spare and lean in style and terse in dialogue.

His first was *Baddenheim* (1939), a portrayal of affluent, assimilated German Jews at an Austrian spa. Oblivious to the impending genocide, they do not realizing that the train they are waiting for will take them to the death camp.

In a later novel, *The Retreat* (1984), he returns to a crumbling resort in 1937 near Vienna. In *Unto the Soul* (1994), he depicts a brother and sister who maintain an ancient Jewish cemetery in their turn-of-the-century Eastern European village. These books are captivating and revealing. One of my favorites is *Tzili: The Story of a Life,* about a little girl who is mentally handicapped.

Philip Roth (b. 1933) championed Appelfeld's work and made him a character in his own novel, *Operation Shylock*, at a time when Appelfeld's reputation was waning. Eventually he married an Argentinean and became a practicing Jew in Israeli. He received the Israel Prize in 1983. Appelfeld teaches creative writing at Harvard University and at Ben-Gurion University in Beersheba (Amos Oz was one of his students; see 12.3.2).

In his 1991 novel, *The Iron Tracks,* a man bent on revenge tracks his parents' murderer on a train on the very tracks on which Jews went to the camps. His parents were leftist idealists, and after the war, Erwin tries communism and then makes a life by smuggling. As one reviewer put it: "With descriptions of such concision and such powerful reverberations, even a small book can carry an epic charge. Even if we never lived the Holocaust, even if we never rode endlessly in circles, we're all in here somewhere."[3]

Responses to the Holocaust are varied. Intellectual Jean Amery (1912–1978) took his own life.[4] Viktor E. Frankl survived the camps to give his life to the idea that a sense of "logos" (purpose) is the key to health. Because he touches the weaknesses and hesitations of the Jews, he has been accused of exonerating the Nazis. He does work hard on the angle that, despite the Holocaust, Jews cannot shrug off who they are as a religious people. Firsthand accounts and memories are important, such as Lawrence L. Langer's *Holocaust Testimonies: The Ruins of Memory,*[5] which are drawn from the huge collection of interviews at the Fortunoff Video Archives at Yale University. For a look at Jews who responded to the Holocaust by becoming extremists, see Yossi Klein Halevi, *Memoirs of a Jewish Extremist: An American Story.*[6]

---

1. Aloma Halter, "Appelfeld: The Man Who Helps the Words Escape," *Jerusalem Post,* 28 September 1991, 16.
2. Ibid., 16. *The Healer* is a story that epitomizes this author's subtlety and sensitivity.
3. Thomas Simpson, "Circle of Life," *Chicago Tribune,* 8 March 1998, 5. *The Iron Tracks* was translated from Hebrew by Jeffrey M. Green (New York: Shocken, 1997).
4. Jean Amery, *At the Mind's Limits: Contemplations by a Survivor on Auschwitz and Its Realities* (New York: Schoken, 1986). Amery was born in Vienna but joined the Belgian Resistance and was arrested by the Gestapo.
5. New Haven: Yale University Press, 1991.
6. Boston: Little, Brown, 1992.

12.3 THE COMPLEXITY OF THE PRESENT

> There's simply no logic in Jewish history. If there were, we would have
> disappeared a hundred times by now. We surely never would have had a
> state of our own.
>
> —Howard M. Sachar
> *Diaspora*

Tensions are always present between the Jews in the *yishuv* (in Israel) and those
in the *galut* (the world Diaspora). Jews in Israel have come from more than one
hundred nations. Because of my special interest in the Jews and God's plan for
them, I have scrounged through the bibliographies and endeavored to read both
fiction and nonfiction about Diaspora Jews, in Italy, for instance.[1] But several contemporary writers require attention for their interest in the Jews of the United States.[2]

---

1. Howard M. Sachar, *Diaspora: An Inquiry into the Contemporary Jewish World* (New
   York: Harper and Row, 1985).
2. Howard M. Sachar, *A History of the Jews in America* (New York: Knopf, 1992). He
   sees restiveness in U.S. Jewry.

12.3.1 MALAMUD, THE SNARL OF SECULARISM

> Of a young American Jew: "Even so, there is no equivocation in Adam
> Myer's tone, none whatever in the boy's choice of words. 'Israel is my
> home,' he replies. 'There I know where I am.' As he speaks, his father
> and grandfather listen thoughtfully, saying nothing."
>
> —Howard M. Sachar
> *A History of the Jews in America*

Most Jews in the West and in Israel are totally secular. Yet they feel the tug of
something older and deeper than Enlightenment values. Bernard Malamud (1914–
1986) embodies the conflict of Jews in the Diaspora. Born in Brooklyn, young
Bernard worked in his Russian-Jewish immigrant parents' grocery store. He pursued education at the City College of New York and at Columbia University. His
mother died when he was fifteen. The struggles and hardships of his parents are
reflected in many of his short stories and in his novel, *The Assistant* (1957), which
tells about "the travails of a merchant trapped between ancient habits and modern
marketing."[1] Malamud married and taught at Oregon State University before returning East to teach and write in Bennington, Vermont.

His first novel, oddly enough, was the story of a baseball player—*The Natural*
(1952). It was made into a movie starring Robert Redford. Showing some influence of Steven Hawthorne and much by Isaac Bashevis Singer, he like Philip Roth
and Saul Bellow echoed the realities of Jewish life in America.[2] His fifty-five short
stories are the kind that "sock in the belly."[3] He is excellent on "depression era
realities," and we see him applying his great quote: "All men are Jews," that is, the

Jews are the quintessential outsiders. He has "the skeptic's fascination with Hasidic mysteries." I have enjoyed *God's Grace* (1981) and *The Tenants* (1971), the latter about struggles between a Jewish and an African-American writer.

His best novel is his Pulitzer Prize winning *The Fixer* (1966), which also won the National Book Award. Malamud returns to the Russia of his parents in the powerfully visualized character of Yakov Bok. Yakov is a handy man or fixer, and he gets into all kinds of terrible trouble when he leaves the familiar surroundings of his provincial village to make his fortune in Kiev. Admonished by his father-in-law not to give up faith in God, he gravitates to reading rationalist Jewish philosopher Spinoza.[4] After giving a haven to an old Hasid, Yakov is arrested on the false charge of murdering a Gentile boy. His experiences in prison and his betrayal show raw anti-Semitism. Not a religious man, he does remember the psalms.[5] He puts on a prayer shawl but does not pray. He has feared to read the New Testament, but in prison he picks it up and is deeply moved by the crucifixion narrative:

> Jesus cried out for help to God but God gave no help. There was a man crying out in anguish in the dark, but God was on the other side of the mountain. . . . Christ died and they took him down. The fixer wiped his eyes. Afterwards he thought if that's how it happened and it's part of the Christian religion, and they believe it, how can they keep me in prison, knowing that I am innocent? Why don't they have pity and let me go?[6]

Malamud exemplifies the dilemmas of the Diaspora. He loved to say: "Jews are like other people only more so."

An illustrious, esteemed pillar of Israeli literature is S. Y. Agnon (1888–1970), the first writer in modern Hebrew to win the Nobel Prize. Born in the shtetl, he emigrated to Israel in 1907. *The Bridal Canopy* and later *Shira* are moving studies of the confrontation between old and new. Robert St. John's *The Tongues of the Prophets* relates how Eliezer Ben Yehuda led the development of modern Hebrew in Israel, rather than adopting German as the national language.

---

1. Paul Gray, "Transcending Denomination," *Time,* 31 March 1986, 73. Written on the occasion of Malamud's death. That same week also recorded the death of the British Arab nationalist, John Glubb Pasha, an evangelical English army officer who led the Arab Legion of Transjordan against the Vichy French in World War II and commanded the only effective Arab moves in 1948.
2. Saul Bellow's *To Jerusalem and Back: A Personal Account* (New York: Avon, 1976) shows the strains of two national loyalties. Bellow's *Herzog* and *Henderson the Rain King* are worth reading.
3. Bernard Malamud, *The Complete Stories* (New York: Farrar, Strauss, 1997), is a superb collection of all fifty-five short stories.
4. Bernard Malamud, *The Fixer* (New York: Farrar, Strauss, 1966), 17, 59–60. Malamud has a fine grasp of Spinoza.

5. Ibid., 208. This little fellow represents the innocent victim and shows himself to be a person of immense strength.

6. Ibid., 231. Malamud is adept at showing "the foibles of the little man," as well as the possibility of human change.

12.3.2 OZ, THE SCHISM IN THE JEWISH SOUL

> Jerusalem always makes one feel sad, but it's a different sadness at every moment of the day and at every time of year.
>
> —Amos Oz
> Michael in *My Michael*

> If I forget you, O Jerusalem, may my right hand forget its skill. May my tongue cling to the roof of my mouth if I do not remember you, if I do not consider Jerusalem my highest joy.
>
> —Psalm 137:5–6

Israel's best-selling author is a *sabra* (native Israeli). Amos Oz was born Amos Klausner in 1939 Jerusalem, but at age fourteen changed his name when he joined Kibbutz Hulda. There he remained as a teacher and writer. He has warned of the dangers of an aggressive Zionism and has been a leader in the Peace Now Movement. He has worked for reconciliation with Palestinians, but this has made his political views controversial.[1] He fought in several wars and, in a much discussed book, *In the Land of Israel*, records divergent views of various groups of Jews and Arabs.[2]

Oz is unequivocally a humanist who champions "spiritual pluralism." In a collection of short stories, *The Hill of Evil Counsel* (1976), he sets out his utopian ideals.[3] Each of his novels is a classic. I recommend *Elsewhere, Perhaps* (1976), and *A Perfect Peace* (1985).

But the giant of them all is his unforgettable *My Michael*. This story tells of the love of Michael Gonen, a geologist, and Hannah in the Jerusalem of 1950. The couple is a study in contrasts—he is a controlled and a kind person while she is vibrant, moody, and inquisitive. He has been brought up a Jewish socialist.[4] She has nightmares about the Arab twins who lived nearby when she was a little girl. Yet, they are married and have a son, Yair Zalman. *Benet's Reader's Encyclopedia* summarizes the book as a "painful examination of the gap between a comfortable husband and his despairing wife that is also a personification of the schizophrenic city of Jerusalem itself."[5]

Michael is patient and kind but plodding. Hannah rebels at "the dreary sameness" of their days. Her life drifts into the escape of fantasy, and their relationship deteriorates. And always around them is the city of Jerusalem, their fragile fortress.

The quest for unity by fragmented people in a fragmented society is a topic that Amos Oz constantly addresses but never finds a solution. *My Michael* evidently touched a chord in the Israeli heart. Its Hebrew edition sold fifty thousand copies in a country that at that time had under a million Hebrew readers.

1. Other Jewish commentators address these vexed issues with a sympathetic view of the Arabs. See Danny Rubenstein, *The People of Nowhere: The Palestinian Vision of Home* (New York: Times Books, 1991) and Michael Gorkin, *Days of Honey, Days of Onion* (Boston: Beacon, 1991).
2. Amos Oz, *In the Land of Israel* (New York: Harcourt Brace, Jovanovich, 1983). Little here is Bible-related.
3. Alan Lelchuk and Gershon Shaked, eds., *Great Hebrew Short Novels* (New York: Meridian, 1983), 269ff.
4. Amos Oz, *My Michael* (New York: Knopf, 1972), 10, 29.
5. William Rose Benet, *Benet's Reader's Encyclopedia,* 3d ed. (New York: Harper and Row, 1987), 728.

12.3.3 POTOK, THE CLASH OF CULTURES

From the rocky peaks I see them, from the heights I view them. I see a people who live apart and do not consider themselves one of the nations.
—Numbers 23:9

Whether it is his history of the Jews, *Wanderings* (1978), or any of his novels about Jewish America, Chaim Potok (b. 1929) is a brilliant author, and an important one to read. An ordained rabbi, he was raised a Hasidic Jew. In his education at Jewish Theological Seminary in New York, however, he identified with Conservative rather than Orthodox Judaism. He went on to obtain a Doctor of Philosophy from the University of Pennsylvania. Except for some writing about Korea, where he served as a military chaplain, the Potok books are inevitably about the clash of cultures. Robert K. Johnston compares Potok's view of the collision of cultures in contrast with Isaac Bashevis Singer's absorption with evil and Bellow's and Roth's depictions of the marginalized Jew.[1] All persons of faith and conviction have to grapple with their cultural stance—separation, isolation, or assimilation.[2]

But with Potok, it is not only Jewish versus Christian cultural conflict, it is orthodox and religious Jew versus secular; it is Orthodox versus Orthodox Hasidic; it is, as in *My Name Is Asher Lev* (1972) and *The Gift of Asher Lev* (1990), the tension between the religious and the aesthetic or artistic life. As a consummate storyteller, Potok explores and probes these sensitive and often painful strains. The more than 6 million Jews in the United States are by no means a monolith, and Potok is not content to look at their diversities casually or in any cavalier fashion.[3]

The place to begin reading Potok is with his earliest novels, *The Chosen* (1967) and *The Promise* (1969). The former is set in Brooklyn where Danny Sanders, the young son of a Russian Hasidic rabbi, and Reuven Malter, the son of an Orthodox scholar meet in a baseball competition toward the end of World War II. Mutual dislike dissolves into friendship. Danny is a genius with photographic memory in his Talmud studies, but he reads Hemingway and Darwin, books forbidden by the rabbis.[4]

In the stories of these boys, we see into the life of a yeshiva (training school).

Reuven attends the Hasidic synagogue and listens to his friend's father's sermon, which is met with "a chorus of loud and scattered amens."[5] Rabbi Sanders then publicly quizzes Danny and Reuven. Without blood sacrifice, these pious Jews depend on confession of sin for forgiveness.[6]

Danny drifts drastically from his roots, and learns German in order to read Freud's studies in the original texts. The book portrays tensions between orthodox faith and Darwinism, and Judaism's incompatibility with analytic psychology. Further fissures appear because of Zionist aspirations. The Hasidic rabbi is anti-Zionist, and Reuven's father is committed to the cause. Yet Reuven's father will not condemn the Hasids, because "their fanaticism kept us alive."[7] By war's end, the young men are in college together. We marvel at Reuven's extended recitation in Talmud class and Danny's criticism of Sigmund Freud (1856–1939).[8] The outcome is surprising.

Potok looks to the fusion of religions and cultures. "Only a theology of the middle will suffice," Johnston concludes in describing the approach. [9] This, of course, is not the conclusion drawn by truly orthodox Jews and certainly not by evangelical Christians (see Rom. 12:1–2).

A **less-well-known novelist** who should not be forgotten is Sholem Asch (1880–1957). Born in Poland, he immigrated to the U.S. and wrote some great historical novels in Yiddish. My favorites are *The Nazarene* (1939); *The Apostle* (1943); *Mary* (1949); and *Moses* (1951). He was remarkable as a Jew in that he saw Christianity as a continuation of Judaism.

---

1. Robert K. Johnston, "Pietism, Faith and Culture: The Fiction of Chaim Potok," *Covenant Quarterly,* May 1996, 4.
2. The classic study of this issue is in H. Richard Niebuhr, *Christ and Culture* (New York: Harper, 1951).
3. Ze'ev Chafets, *Members of the Tribe: On the Road in Jewish America* (New York: Bantam, 1988); also Barbara Meyerhoff, *Number Our Days: A Triumph of Continuity and Culture Among Jewish Old People in an Urban Ghetto* (New York: Simon and Schuster, 1978). America's kindness to the Jews is one reason for American strength.
4. Chaim Potok, *The Chosen* (Cutchogue, N.Y.: Buccaneer Books, 1967), 85. Made into an excellent film, also.
5. Ibid., 138. Anyone visiting Brooklyn on Sabbath is struck by the variety of Jewish groups. There were some 350 Brooklyn synagogues when I last obtained a count in the 1990s. Each "reb" and his disciples have a distinctive dress.
6. Ibid., 154. No wonder many Jews desperately want a temple, if they take seriously the ancient biblical teaching that "without the shedding of blood there is no remission of sins."
7. Ibid., 232. Both fathers are respectful, despite their sharp differences with each other.
8. Ibid., 258.
9. Johnston, "Pietism, Faith and Culture," 18. Johnston is a good example of vigorous literary analysis.

12.3.4 YEHOSHUA, THE ISSUE OF IDENTITY

> It takes a lot of imagination to identify with faraway times and places. I
> was trying to make the reader more involved.
>
> —A. B. Yehoshua
> describing Mr. Mani

A. B. Yehoshua is often linked with Appelfeld, Oz, and David Grossman as the
preeminent novelists of modern Israel. Yehoshua was born in Jerusalem in 1936, a
fifth-generation Israeli. He served in the army and lived four years in Paris before
returning to become professor of Hebrew and comparative literature at Haifa University. He is a vigorous political ideologue. He lives on beautiful Mount Carmel
overlooking the Mediterranean Sea.[1] Recipient of the Israel Prize for Literature in
1995, his novels, plays, and stories have been widely translated from Hebrew.[2]

His major novels are *The Lover* (1978), *A Late Divorce* (1984), and *Return to
India* (1990). In each novel and novella, he shows special interest and skill in interior monologue. The most recent book and the one that must be read in my view is
Mr. Mani (1992). This is a kaleidoscopic perspective on Jewish history through
the lens of one family. The author takes us back from 1982 through genealogical
layers to the middle of the eighteenth century through five speakers.[3] It is most
intriguing to watch a skilled craftsman use such a unique frame: (1) Hagar Shiloh
reflects on the dilemmas of younger Israelis; (2) a German soldier in Crete during
World War II writes his grandmother about Yosef Mani, a tour guide in the ancient
Minoan ruins; (3) British officer Ivor Horoawitz in 1918 pleads for the pardon of
Mani for passing secrets to the Turks; (4) Dr. Efrayim Shapiro in 1899 writes about
the Zionist Conference in Switzerland; (5) Avraham Mani, who was born in 1799
in Salonika and migrated to Turkey, is woven into the story.

So many of Yehoshua's themes, the Diaspora, the return, original sin, the
meaning of Zion, etc., are luminescent vehicles of truth.

For lighter moments, the suspense novels of Rabbi Harry Kemelman feature the
character Rabbi Small in such books as *The Day the Rabbi Left*.[4] Faye Kellerman, an
orthodox Jew, has given a series from the edge featuring Detective Peter Decker in Los
Angeles and his Jewish wife, Rina Lazarus. My favorite is *The Ritual Bath* (1986).
From Israel itself is Batya Gur. I am especially fond of her *Murder on a Kibbutz*.[5]

---

1. Allison Kaplan Sommer, "Prize Fighter," *Jerusalem Post,* 6 May 1995, 14.
2. A. B. Yehoshua, "A Poet's Continuing Silence," in *Great Hebrew Short Novels* (New
   York: Meridian, 1983), 357ff.
3. Yehoshua calls this novel, "intergenerational psychoanalysis," *The New York Times
   Book Review,* 1 March 1992, 3. It is interesting that so many psychoanalysts from
   the beginning have been Jewish. See Peter Gay, *A Godless Jew: Freud, Atheism and
   the Making of Psychoanalysis* (New Haven, Conn.: Yale University Press, 1987).
4. New York: Fawcett-Columbine, 1996.
5. San Francisco: Harper/Collins, 1991.

12.4 DELICACIES NOT TO BE OVERLOOKED

In a vast body of literature, I have seined out the bare minimum for reading in Judaica. I am reluctant to leave this significant category without touching on Joel Gross and Sylvia Tennenbaum. Gross is the Jewish-American author of *The Books of Rachel,*[1] which is the richly textured study of an old Jewish family whose lives intertwine with the growth of the diamond industry. This vital history touches Inquisition Spain, nineteenth-century Venice, and Palestine. In a later companion volume, *The Lives of Rachel,*[2] he goes back into the Middle Ages for the beginnings of this wonderful family.

Born in Frankfurt, Germany, but an immigrant to the United States in 1938, Sylvia Tennenbaum writes ably of an old Jewish family with roots in fifteenth-century Germany. The action in *Yesterday's Streets*[3] starts in 1903 with the Wertheims, who live in a grandeur equal to that of their neighbors the Rothschilds. What ultimately goes wrong is dramatically portrayed by one who knew the streets of Frankfurt. The fifteen major characters are exceedingly well drawn. This is Tennenbaum's best work.

---

1. New York: Seaview, 1979.
2. New York: New American, 1984.
3. New York: Random House, 1981.

CHAPTER THIRTEEN

Assessing the Literature of Drama and the Legitimate Stage

The play is done; the curtain drops,
Slow falling to the prompter's bell:
A moment yet the actor stops,
And looks around, to say farewell.
It is an irksome word and task;
And when he's laughed and said his say,
He shows, as he removes the mask,
A face that's anything but gay.
—William Makepeace Thackeray
"The End of the Play"

Drama is one of the oldest forms of artistic expression. We have noted Greek (2.3) and French dramatists (6.1.1), forerunners of William Shakespeare and the Globe Theater playwright himself (chap. 6). A play is an enacted story narrative. The dramatic monologue or first-person sermon is a dramatic soliloquy. Drama is no stranger to the church; the medieval miracle and morality plays come to mind. Many benefits accrue to the Christian communicator who gives attention to the representation of character and personality on stage. Reading plays aloud enhances oral interpretation.

The modern conception of the stage may be most directly owing to the Norwegian Henrik Ibsen and the Swedish August Strindberg, who moved beyond the sugary poetic idealism of Romanticism to realistic recreation of life in drama. Drama historian Maurice Valency argues that modern plays basically imitate the two Nordic bards in "a medium for the expression of the inmost subjectivity of the writer."[1] Valency says they and their successors, "the heroes of modern trag-edy, are ill with a disease of the soul which mirrors the illness of our culture. The adversary is not an external power. The adversary is within ourselves."[2]

This chapter will identify ten commanding writers in this art form.

---

1. Maurice Valency, *The Flower and the Castle: An Introduction to Modern Drama* (New York: Macmillan, 1964).
2. Quoted in a review of Valency's work by Norris Houghton in *Saturday Review of Literature*, 21 March 1964, 43.

13.1 THE PLAY MAKERS

13.1.1 CHEKHOV, THE DRAMA OF DECLINE

God preserve us from generalizations. There are a great many opinions in this world, and a good half of them are professed by people who have never been in trouble.

—Anton Chekhov

Still widely read, Anton Chekhov (1860–1904) was a multi-gifted Russian writer of short stories and plays. He was born in Taganrog in southern Russia, the third of six children. His grandfather was a liberated serf and his father a merchant. After local schooling, he studied in the School of Medicine at the University of Moscow in 1879, graduating in 1884. His famous quip is well-known: "Medicine is my lawful wife and literature is my mistress." Such of his plays as *The Seagull* and *Uncle Vanya* really established the Moscow Art Theater.

He first wrote stories to help with his family's finances, but his reputation spread. Struggling from his student days with tuberculosis, he was a kind, gen-erous, and unassuming man. He was tall, good-looking, witty and, according to the latest major biography, passionate.[1] His failing health necessitated his mov-ing to Yalta and an extended separation from his wife, actress Olga Knipper. He sought the baths in Germany and died there at the age of forty-four. While in Southern Russia, he wrote *The Three Sisters* and *The Cherry Orchard*.

The literary influences on Chekhov were certainly Leo Tolstoy (1828–1910), Arthur Schopenhauer (1788–1860), and Friedrich Nietzsche (1844–1900). There-fore, we can expect little from Chekhov with the perspective of faith in any form of a personal God. What he does give is sharp-eyed analysis of the decay of the gentry in Russia. The theme running through his greatest plays is "change and the tragedy of people who cannot adapt to it."[2] He knows his culture is in flux, and Chekhov vacillates between despair and hope. As Ibsen and Strindberg, his plays do not have complex plots or much dramatic action. We groan over the inability of his characters to understand each other, but then empathize with them in their existential loneliness and desolation.

It is always best to attend a play by the great dramatists and watch actors

514   THE COMPANY OF THE CREATIVE

interpret its dialogue. The next best alternative is to read the play aloud. An excellent Chekhov play to read still is often performed, *The Cherry Orchard*. The beautiful orchard represents the Russian aristocracy, which is old and venerable but threatened. Madame Ranevskaya has spent her family into insolvency. The orchard is finally auctioned off to avert penury and is purchased by a former serf, who commences to cut the cherry trees down to make way for houses. While the hapless family and servants prepare to leave, the sound of the axe is heard. Neither masters nor servants can come to terms with their reality. They flounder in futility.

The play ends with the old servant lying down helplessly (and permanently?). "A distant sound is heard coming from the sky as it were, the sound of a snapping string mournfully dying away. All is still again, and nothing is heard but the strokes of the ax against a tree far away in the orchard."[3]

Rejecting both Tolstoy's vain dreams of humanity's perfectibility and Fëdor Dostoevsky's (1821–1881) Christian truth, Chekhov is hard-pressed to present any solution to decadence. Leftist panaceas had little appeal. Is our resource then to grit our teeth stoically? Modern playwrights generally assist us in analyzing the problem. They are good at analyzing what is wrong. But without Christ and the Scriptures, they have little remedy to offer.

---

1. Donald Rayfield, *Anton Chekhov: A Life* (New York: Henry Holt, 1997). This study
   runs to 674 pages.
2. Essay on *The Cherry Orchard,* in *Gateway to the Great Books* (Chicago: Encyclopedia Britannica, 1963), 247.
3. Ibid., 294. Of course this and Chekhov's other plays are to be found in many anthologies and collections.

13.1.2 IBSEN, THE DRAMA OF DEFIANCE

I have made a great discovery. . . . It is this, let me tell you—that the strongest man in the world is he who stands most alone.

—Henrik Ibsen
Dr. Stockman to his family at the end of
An Enemy of the People

"The Colossus of the North," Henrik Ibsen (1828–1906), led with Strindberg to the modern theatre. He was born in Skien in Norway where his family had been sea captains for generations. However, his father was unsuccessful as a merchant and was bankrupt when Ibsen was eight years old. This hapless man is clearly seen in Old Ekdal in *The Wild Duck*.

Ibsen was apprenticed to a druggist in Grimstad, but he disliked the work so much that writing became an escape. In 1850 he trekked to the Norwegian capitol Oslo, then called Christiana, a city of fewer than twenty thousand inhabitants. He worked his way through the university and became involved in the theatre in Bergen until he was appointed director of the National Theater in Christiana. Ole Bull, the venerable man of Norwegian culture had taken Ibsen under his wing, but there was a bitter break in their relationship, after which Ibsen traveled abroad until 1891.[1]

While living in Germany and Italy, he wrote *Peer Gynt,* a brilliantly satirical folk tale (with music added by Edvard Grieg [1843–1907] as well as Brand). It is a symbolic tragedy.[2] From the beginning, Ibsen was seen as a leader of the revolt against all orthodoxy. He personifies the "new mood of anxiety and disquiet in society," which made him both resentful and repugnant.[3] He celebrates Julian the Apostate (331–363), the late Roman emperor who tried to undo the work of Constantine (c. 274–337), in his *Emperor and Galilean* (1873). His emphasis on "the supreme importance of the individual" for him expressed an unrestrained "selfism." He fathered at least one son out-of-wedlock, whom he never supported or cared for. He was not in touch with his father for forty years. He reveled in his creative selfishness, as he put it.[4]

His marriage was strange, and indeed in his plays (such as *A Doll's House*) he seems to loathe marriage. In *Ghosts,* he deals with venereal disease, and in his powerful *Hedda Gabler,* he portrays an acutely disturbed and destructive woman. His plays were controversial and disruptive, and this is not a negative as such except that his own character and lifestyle were so vain and inflamed by drink. His life was one row after another. He was a fearful man, and this is reflected in his output.

The play that must be read is the often performed *An Enemy of the People* (1882). Here he picks up the Emersonian dictum: "Whoso would be a man, must be a nonconformist." His critical principle of "self-reliance" destroys hope for community and spiritual interdependence. Dr. Stockman takes his stand against the "compact majority" of the town. He becomes the enemy of the people when he shows that the town's famous baths are contaminated and must be shut down. He mistakenly believes that he will be a hero for blowing the whistle at the "germ-infested baths." He seems to argue that the minority is always right. His idealism is out of touch, but Dr. Stockman does have a vision of loyalty and fidelity to truth, whatever it may cost.

---

1. Essay on *An Enemy of the People,* in *Gateway to the Great Books,* 162.
2. William Rose Benet, *Benet's Reader's Encyclopedia,* 3d ed. (New York: Harper and Row, 1987), s.v. "Ibsen, Henrik."
3. Paul Johnson, *Intellectuals* (New York: Harper and Row, 1988), 85.
4. Ibid., 101. Ibsen carried a mirror inside his hat and had a passion to wear medals and orders.

13.1.3 Strindberg, the Drama of Disintegration

In the midst of happiness grows a seed of unhappiness. Happiness consumes itself like a flame. It cannot burn forever, it must go out, and the presentiment of its end destroys it at its very peak.

—August Strindberg
A Dream Play

Although Ibsen and August Strindberg (1849–1912) had marked differences of taste, both nudged the modern theatre into naturalism. Strindberg, the great Swedish writer of novels, poetry, and plays, was born in Stockholm. His father was an insolvent nobleman and his mother a servant. His impoverished childhood was miserable.

Strindberg's plays frequently have religious themes, such as *Easter* (1901), in which the acts are named "Maundy Thursday," "Good Friday," and "Easter Eve." Strindberg repudiated his religious roots, but the influence remained.[1] As virtually all Scandinavians, he was raised a Lutheran. His family was Pietist, the strict wing among eighteenth- and nineteenth-century Lutherans.[2]

He worked as a journalist, a tutor, and an assistant at the Royal Library.[3] His writing in several literary genres marked him a leader of the move to realism. At one point, his writings were too avant-garde for his countrymen, and he was charged by the state Lutheran church with criminal blasphemy. He was acquitted, but the experience contributed to his complete breakdown in health in 1896. Three unhappy marriages contributed to the chaos in his personal life.

His plays *The Father* and *Miss Julie* portray a bitter duel between the sexes and disclose the author's almost pathological hatred of women. He became obsessed with both the physical sciences and occultism—particularly alchemy and mysticism—to the point of madness.[4]

Strindberg's historical plays *Gustavus Vasa* (1899) and *Queen Christina* (1903) have recently stimulated some revived interest, but his imaginative fantasy plays, which he called "expressionism," are the most intriguing. *The Ghost Sonata* (1907) shows the fleeting influence of theosophy and "the merciless exposure of life's most shameful secrets."[5] The themes are retribution and death, which ultimately seem to be inescapable. The influence of Nietzsche and Honoré de Balzac (1799–1850) are easily traceable here, as throughout his work.

The play I would most strenuously recommend is *A Dream Play,* which he wrote when he was fearful that he would lose his third wife, the young Norwegian actress Harriet Bosse, and their child.[6] By the time the play was presented in Stockholm, they were divorced, but she did have a leading role. The theme of the play is repeated many times and is very hard to translate: "Human beings are to be pitied," or "It's a shame about human beings."

One can only marvel at the fecundity of his production, the depth of many of his insights, and the profound unhappiness and sorrow of his life. Well ahead of his time, Strindberg tried to establish an experimental theatre in Copenhagen. Would Rosenius and his gospel way have been so bad?

------

1. August Strindberg, *Six Plays of Strindberg* (Garden City: Doubleday Anchor, 1955), 127.
2. Ibid. See the description of pietism and Carl Olof Rosenius in Sweden at this time in G. Everett Arden, *Four Northern Lights* (Minneapolis: Augsburg, 1964), 115. See also Rosenius, *A Faithful Guide to Peace with God* (Minneapolis: Augsburg, 1923). This is the theological food on which Strindberg was raised in the Fosterlands–stiftelsen.
3. *Benet's Reader's Encyclopedia,* 940.

4. Ibid., 941.
5. Strindberg, *Six Plays of Strindberg*, 265ff.
6. Ibid., 187ff.

13.1.4 SHAW, THE DRAMA OF DISSENT

> That Eliza is more sympathetic than Higgins is palpably true, but it remains his play. Shaw after all has no heroes, only heroines, partly because he is his own hero, as prophet of Corrective Evolution, servant only of God, who is the Life Force. Higgins is another Shawian self-parody, since Shaw's passion for himself was nobly unbounded.
>
> —Harold Bloom, on *Pygmalion*

A satirist without peer and arguably the most influential British playwright since Shakespeare, George Bernard Shaw or G. B. S. as he called himself (1856–1950), alternately amuses and angers.

Shaw was born in Dublin, the youngest child and only son of an unsuccessful alcoholic father and a refined and musical mother. From her, he learned about fine music. He attended the Wesleyan Connection School (later Wesley College) for a year. His exposure there to gospel truth made little noticeable impact.[1] This may in part explain certain recurring themes in his writing. The ongoing financial crisis in his family forced George to leave school at fifteen. But he did not like his work and in 1876 moved with his mother and sister to London.[2]

Here he started to write and became quite known as a literary, drama, and musical critic. His skill in writing was quickly apparent. In 1884 he became a Fabian socialist when he associated with radical thinkers who drank deeply from Karl Marx (1818–1883). He championed vegetarianism; he opposed vivisection, compulsory vaccination, and doctors. Shaw prided himself on his contempt for Shakespeare and Walter Scott. Rather, his roots were with James Joyce (1882–1941), Charles Darwin (1809–1882), Richard Wagner (1813–1883), and Ibsen (1828–1906). He wrote *The Quintessence of Ibsenism* in 1891. After writing five socialist novels for which he could find no publisher, he turned to drama, but initially failed there as well. His first major success, *Mrs. Warren's Profession,* was on the subject of white slavery. Its "advanced ideas" included hints of incest and a biting characterization of the clergy, all of which brought much criticism.[3] Shaw was delighted. He loved always to shock and scandalize.

He was part of the Celtic Renaissance and spoke unreservedly in favor of a united Ireland. The Irish cause received some vital public relations help when Shaw was given the Nobel Prize for Literature in 1925. He gave respectability to what had been perceived as a bloody band of revolutionaries. Shaw married Charlotte, a wealthy Irish woman in 1898, but this never inhibited him from partaking in notorious sexual affairs, including liaisons with leading actresses, such as Ellen Terry and Stella Campbell. Oscar Wilde said, "Shaw hasn't an enemy in the world, and none of his friends like him."[4]

This Niagara of creativity wrote more than fifty plays. Religiously, he was a Shelleyan atheist; that is, he did worship, after a fashion, Henri-Louis Bergson's

(1859–1941) homemade faith in Creative Evolution. At one time, he professed to use Puritan preacher John Bunyan as a life model, but he moved on to use Shaw the preacher, instead. His writing goal once was to emulate reformer essayist John Ruskin, but instead he became his own point-of-reference.

Some of his better known work includes *Arms and the Man* (1898), a rather low-voltage antiwar piece, and *The Man of Destiny* (1895) on Napoléon, in which it is evident that Napoléon is Shaw himself. He admired "supermen,"[5] and the work bulges with paradox, irony, and humor. In his *Three Plays for Puritans, Captain Brassbound's Conversion* is a fascinating story of reconciliation. He wrote this for Terry, with whom he sustained a relationship after he married Charlotte. He was pro-divorce and anti-marriage, as his play, *A Conversation,* indicates. Curiously, while writing a play denying romantic love, he married.[6]

Man and Superman (1901) is an important play, particularly act 3, subtitled *Don Juan in Hell,* which usually is performed as a separate work. This is outrageous parody, with a persistent underlying ache to the dialog that hints of a fear of hell. The significant work *Major Barbara* (1912) chronicles a young woman's break with the Salvation Army.[7]

In *A Fable Play* (1912), he takes on Christianity. His treatments of believers are bizarre. In *Joan of Arc* (1923), Joan is a Protestant. He says he likes Jesus as the practical man but "the miracles, Salvation, the Second Coming, Redemption and Atonement" are obstacles to the true ends of life. The cross has made Christianity into "crossianity," which he detests.[8] Still, biblical allusions recur, as in *Back to Methuselah* (1921), which expostulates on evolution.

The one play that should be read is *Pygmalion* (1912). Reviving the old myth in Ovid's *Metamorphoses* (2.6.5), in which the sculptor falls in love with his statue, brings her to life, and then marries her, Shaw very engagingly tells the story of Professor Higgins, who had "devoted his life to the regeneration of the human race."[9] Shaw tells how the professor sets out to reform the speech of the cockney flower girl, Eliza Doolittle. Higgins changes her speech, but not the essence of who she is, and he does not marry her. Shaw addressed the problematic end of the play with a series of revisions. He degrades Eliza more and more, and some critics say he humiliates his own paramour, Stella Campbell, in the process. There seemed be a "coarsening" of Shaw's taste and judgment. His personality turned toward sadism.[10] *Benet's Reader's Encyclopedia* reminds us that the adjective *Shawian* does not refer to a literary style derived from Shaw, but rather denotes "an iconoclastic way of life."[11]

1. Eldon C. Hill, *George Bernard Shaw* (Boston: Twayne, 1978), 20. The King James Version of the Bible had a deep influence on Shaw's style and themes (21).
2. Hill, *George Bernard Shaw,* 82. "My parents took no moral responsibility for me," he later testified.
3. Ibid., 47.
4. The many references of the friendship of T. E. Lawrence (of Arabia) can be checked in his authorized biography, Jeremy Wilson, *Lawrence* (New York: Athenaeum, 1990).

It appears to me that Charlotte was a kind of surrogate mother for Lawrence in a lonely and confused time for him. She was a remarkable woman.

5. Introductory essay to *The Man of Destiny,* in *Gateway to the Great Books* (Chicago: Britannica, 1963), 294.
6. Hill, *George Bernard Shaw,* 68.
7. Ibid., 91, 94.
8. Ibid., 117. Shaw always had an irrational hatred of the cross.
9. Louis Crompton, "Improving *Pygmalion,*" in Harold Bloom, ed., *Pygmalion* (New York: Chelsea, 1988), 51.
10. Arnold Silver, "The Playwright's Revenge," in *Pygmalion. My Fair Lady* adapts Shaw's story to the musical stage and film.
11. *Benet's Reader's Encyclopedia,* 3d ed., s.v. "Poetics."

13.1.5 Synge, the Drama of Daring

I was painfully timid, and while still very young the idea of Hell took a fearful hold on me. One night I thought I was irretrievably damned and cried myself to sleep in vain yet terrified efforts to form a conception of eternal pain. In the morning I renewed my lamentations and my mother was sent for. She comforted me with the assurance that the Holy Ghost was convicting me of sin and thus preparing me for ultimate salvation. This was a new idea, and I rather approved.

—J. M. Synge

Arguably the most brilliant playwright in the Irish Renaissance that centered in Dublin's Abbey Theater, John Millington Synge (1871–1909) was limited in output, but his work was creative and controversial. He was born near Dublin at Rathfarnham into a fervently Protestant family. His father, a lawyer, died the following year, leaving his widow to raise five children within the landed aristocracy and with a deep evangelical commitment. One brother, Samuel, was a missionary. Only the youngest, John, rebelled against Christianity.[1]

He read Darwin and renounced Christianity and thus "laid a chasm between my present and my past and between myself and my kindred and friends." He wrote in his notebook: "It seemed that I became in a moment the playfellow of Judas. Incest and parricide were but a consequence of the idea that possessed me."[2]

Synge substituted "a form of nature mysticism" for the Christian faith but never escaped the force of Christianity in his life. Synge graduated from Trinity College in Dublin and studied music in Germany. He settled in Paris where he met Yeats, who took an interest in him. In 1893 Yeats persuaded Synge to return to the Aran Islands in the west of Ireland and live with the primitive islanders to learn their ways and their stories. Out of this experience and exposure came his sketches *The Aran Islands* (1907) and his real voice in both poetry and drama. In 1897 he had surgery on a swollen gland, which turned out to be Hodgkins disease. Frail and failing health was to be a major battle for him until he was cut down in his thirty-eighth year.

He fell in love with numerous women, one of them Cherry Matheson, the daughter of a leading Plymouth Brethren luminary. She rejected him because of his atheism, and the experience spurred him to write his first collection of poems, which are despairing and desultory in tone.[3]

Synge stripped away the stereotype of the "stage Irishman" and showed us the real Irish. His first play, *When the Moon Is Set,* was started in Paris and rather ineptly reflects his agonies over Cherry Matheson's rejection. The uncle in the play is turned down matrimonially "because he did not believe in God."[4] The earlier play that should be read is *Riders to the Sea,* which gives us a good flavor of the psychology and colloquialisms of Irish country folk. The clash of cultures— the ancient pre-Christian versus the Christian "Almighty God" shows Synge's defection from any Christian credo.[5]

His most famous play is *The Playboy of the Western World* which, in its early presentations, fomented riots in both Dublin and New York because of its alleged indecency and criticism of Ireland. It would be considered tame by modern standards, but it made the Abbey Theater. This play took Synge seven years to write and saw ten complete drafts. Supposedly a comic drama, the play is about recessive Christy Mahon, who leaves home fearful that he has killed his father. His story makes him a hero and celebrity in the small remote Mayo town to which he goes, until his father reappears and they scuffle. This time the townspeople do not approve. How this scenario changes Christy, the townspeople, and Pegeen, the girl Christy loves (and another of Synge's very troubled women) is the stuff of the drama. How what is ostensibly comedy handles patricide and violence of this order is curious. Shawn, the official suitor of Pegeen is of course under the thumb of Father Reilly. We are not surprised by this swat at the clergy. Critics have always seen this play as "a masterpiece of terse statement."[6] Synge's style is rollicking. When Christy tries to finish what he had failed to complete, he is not accepted. In the last act, he is burned by the crowd, and Pegeen drops the noose about his neck and burns his leg. Indeed, Christy the narrator is more impressive than Christy the man of action.

Still, ironically, Synge is not able to banish his Christian foundations. Many have seen strong allusions to Christ in Christy being "bound and wounded." Interesting that Synge, no more than Melville or Hemingway, can escape the cross. Much Christian terminology is used in this part of the play. Some have gone so far as to argue that "*Playboy* presents a carefully developed analogue to the ministry and crucifixion of Jesus."[7] Everyone hears the New Testament echoes. If Pegeen is Judas, then Shawn and Father Reilly are the religious establishment, the Pharisees who call for the death of Jesus. The play also addresses the issue of whether the telling of a story can change the lives of those to whom it is told? The conclusion reached is that, yes, the story can affect a kind of alteration in the hearers, but only reality can produce and sustain the dynamic life changes that will endure.[8]

---

1. Robin Skelton, *J. M. Synge* (Lewisburg, Pa.: Bucknell University Press, 1972), 12–13.
2. Ibid., 20, 211. The ravages of Darwinism makes David N. Livingstone's *Darwin's Forgotten Defenders* (Grand Rapids: Eerdmans, 1987) utterly inexplicable, as if

evangelical opposition to Darwinism were ill-advised. For a popular-level critique devastating to Darwinist evolution, see Phillip E. Johnson, *Darwin on Trial* (Downers Grove, Ill.: InterVarsity, 1991). A convincing biochemical challenge to Darwin is found in Michael J. Behe's *Darwin's Black Box* (New York: Free Press, 1996).

3. Ibid., 21.
4. Ibid., 22. The first of the Irish plays was *In the Shadow of the Glen* (1903).
5. Introduction to *Riders to the Sea,* in Gateway to the Great Books (Chicago: Britannica, 1963), 342ff.
6. Patricia Meyer Spacks, "The Making of the *Playboy,*" in Harold Bloom, ed., *The Playboy of the Western World* (New York: Chelsea House, 1988), 14.
7. Donna Gerstenberger, "A Hard Birth," in *Playboy of the Western World,* 41; Skelton, *J. M. Synge,* 62. There appears to be a parody of the resurrection of Christ as well. See also Robin Skelton, "Character and Symbol," in *Playboy of the Western World,* 62.
8. Bruce M. Bigley, "The Playboy as Antidrama," in *Playboy of the Western World,* 97. The big issue in narrative theology.

13.1.6 Beckett, the Drama of Despair

I was brought up almost a Quaker—but I soon lost faith. I don't think I ever had it after leaving Trinity.

—Samuel Beckett

Probably one of the most erudite and well educated men of our time, Samuel Beckett (1906–1989) has been called "the last modernist" because he wrote without plot or climax, without beginning, middle, or end (Kenneth Tynan). We need to dip into his plays briefly because his own life epitomizes the predicament of modernism, and his work displays the total emptiness and absurdity of autonomous humankind.

Beckett was brought up in a very genteel Protestant suburb of Dublin. He remembered praying as a child and, as a college student, was abstemious in his habits, neither smoking nor drinking. His relatives weren't always the best molders of faith, as when his maternal grandmother told a granddaughter who loved chocolates, "You shouldn't love something to eat, my dear. You should only love God."[1] Nor was the early death of his father interpreted for him by family or clergy. His fragile faith foundered at Trinity College.

A lover of classical music and art, Beckett lost his faith but got a taste for Joyce and such French writers as Marcel Proust (1871–1922) at Trinity. He taught French at Trinity but abandoned teaching and entered psychoanalysis after the death of his father in 1933.

He fled Ireland and his mother after a fierce quarrel and traveled in Germany but settled in France. He wrote most of his works in French and then translated them into English. During World War II, he worked with the French Resistance and then the Irish Red Cross in France. Through it all, he was a desperately disturbed and lonely person. He was tortured by regrets and imaginary illnesses. His wife, Suzanne, tried to help him with his guilt in relation to his mother, but he found no reprieve. Not really finding his own "voice" until after World War II, Beckett's writings were shaped by his own troubles and above all by his morbid thoughts about the outrageousness of death.[2]

His first poetry was not published until he was twenty-three and, from the beginning, echoes his protest against realism and his "feeling of absence." He often belittled the English language and preferred the spare French because he was the consummate minimalist. As with Franz Kafka (1883–1924), there is something harsh about his writing. Often scatological, he secularizes salvation and damnation. In fact, the passion of Christ is the subject of witticism.[3]

Again we analyze a writer who cannot escape the "hound of heaven." In his early novel *Murphy* (1938), he touches Christ and the conversion of Mary Magdalene. In *Watt* (1944), we have "Christ-resonances."[4] His fiction is bizarre and rancorous and seems to easily slip from pantheism to solipsism's denial of the reality of the present moment. The fact that Beckett won the Nobel Prize for Literature in 1970 makes a statement in itself about the state of the arts at the dawn of the "postmodern" society.

In his astonishing fiction trilogy, *Molloy, Malone Dies,* and *The Unnamable,* we sense a flicker of self-consciousness left "in the biological blob." Poor Molloy, partially deaf and blind and severely handicapped, tries to get home to his mother across the forest but doesn't make it. Malone is confined to bed in an asylum and only wants "not to be hot or cold anymore," this against the rhythmic background, "They shall hunger no more, neither thirst anymore." *The Unnamable* is one of the most haunting novels ever written and is about an armless and legless "I" who lives in a large jar. This is reductionism with a vengeance and seems to climax in his thirty-two-second piece *Breath* (1971), in which all that is heard is a faint cry. Oddly enough, Beckett in these works speaks about "a veritable Calvary," and alludes to the Crucified One.[5]

After some false starts, Beckett ventured into drama. His single-set, five character play, *Waiting for Godot* (1953), is about two tramps, Didi and Gogo, who are waiting for Godot (presumably God) to come. A boy comes each day to tell them Godot will come tomorrow. But he never comes and the two tramps do nothing but interact with their appalling spastic tics and self-bruising. The critic Ruby Cohn speaks of "the Scriptural kernel of the play"[6] (i.e., the seed is Luke's account of the crucifixion with the two thieves). Certain refrains and repeated gestures along with the constant falling and stumbling of the principals underscore and reinforce the idea of unfulfilled promise. This is like Sartre and the theatre of the absurd.[7] It is necessary for us and our hearers to see the final end of man's revolt against God and His authority.

In the play *Endgame* (1956), which he wrote in the searing pain of the death of his mother and brother, he writes an anti-apocalypse depicting the death of the last human beings on earth. Again we marvel at his sporadic use of Scripture. The last couple, Nagg and Ham (obviously Noah and Ham from Genesis) give a final curse. The reference to "nearly finished" is another allusion to the cross of Christ.[8] Quite sadomasochistic, the play was banned in London for referring to the Deity as a bastard. The last pathetic lament in the work is: "There must be nothing out there."

Beckett reduces plot and dialogue until all that remains are mimes. The warning of Jesus was not heeded by this brilliant man: "What good is it for a man to gain the whole world, yet forfeit his soul?" (Mark 8:36). Beckett was a gifted writer who only had emptiness to peddle.

---

1. James Knowlson, *Damned to Fame: The Life of Samuel Beckett* (New York: Simon and Schuster, 1996). This fine biography is especially good on Beckett's childhood and youth. One of the best-read men of his time.
2. Anthony Cronin, *Samuel Beckett: The Last Modernist* (New York: Harper/Collins, 1997). He remained existentially a man in utter isolation.
3. Ruby Cohn, *Back to Beckett* (Princeton: Princeton University Press, 1973), 12, 20. He sees damnation as the erosion of the self; salvation as the recollection of the self.
4. Ibid., 53. Beckett sets theistic religion alongside astrology and spiritism as possible recourses in *Murphy*.
5. Ibid., 83. He speaks of "the shape of a pieta" and "like being crucified" (84).
6. Ibid., 127. The basic form comes from Augustine. The play concludes: "There's no lack of void."
7. On the theatre of the absurd, see Francis Schaeffer, *Escape from Reason* (Downers Grove, Ill.: InterVarsity, 1968), 68ff.
8. *Back to Beckett,* 144. While denying the resurrection in *Embers,* he can't shake loose from the cross.

13.1.7 WILDER, THE DRAMA OF DOMESTICITY

We all know that something is eternal. And it ain't houses and it ain't names, and it ain't earth, and it ain't even the stars—everybody knows in their bones that something is eternal, and that something has to do with human beings. All the greatest people ever lived have been telling us that for five thousand years and yet you'd be surprised how people are always letting go of that fact. There's something way down deep that's eternal about every human being.

—Thornton Wilder
Stage Manager, *Our Town*

Although his star dimmed somewhat after his death, Thornton Wilder (1897–1975) remains a major American playwright and novelist. His novels were all bestsellers; *The Bridge of San Luis Rey* won him the first of his three Pulitzer Prizes.[1] His *The Eighth Day* (1967), about the "earnest, self-righteous Bible-thumping itinerant textbook salesman, George Brush" is worth reading.[2] But this sketch will concentrate on the innovations in Wilder's plays.

Wilder was born in Madison, Wisconsin, where his father was editor of the *Wisconsin State Journal*. The family soon moved to China, where Mr. Wilder served as consul-general in Hong Kong and then Shanghai. After a childhood in China, Wilder returned to the United States to attend Oberlin College and then Yale University, the two separated by a brief stint in the army in World War I. He was graduated from Yale in 1920. Professor William Lyon Phelps of Yale said of him: "As an undergraduate he was unusually versatile, original and clever. He played and composed music, wrote much prose and verse, and stood well in the studies of the course."[3]

He served seven years as house master at a prep school and then obtained his M.A. at Princeton in 1925. He never married but lived with his sister in New Haven, drinking and smoking too much. His sister handled his business affairs. He had many acquaintances in the literary world, played the piano very creditably, and lectured on Joyce and Lope de Vega (1562–1635) at Harvard and the University of Chicago. In recalling him on the centennial of his birth, one writer observed: "He looked, Tyrone Guthrie said, like a piano tuner, owned only one suit at a time and spoke in a fidgety, accelerating, inexhaustible manner."[4] In the Second World War, he served as an intelligence analyst for the Air Force.

Thornton was of the conviction that something new was needed on the American stage. Comparing him with Beckett and others, we realize that he was not "one of the new dramatists," but in his own eyes "a rediscoverer of forgotten goods. . . . As I view the work of my contemporaries I seem to feel that I am exceptional in one thing—I give (don't I?) the impression of having enormously enjoyed it."[5] His two Pulitzer Prize-winning plays were *Our Town* (1938) and *The Skin of Our Teeth* (1942), the latter title coming from Job 19:20.

Our Town is the most performed play in the history of the American stage and is striking because it really has no scenery, few props, and little plot line. Yet its characterization of the people who live at Grover's Corner, New Hampshire, is deeply moving. Although Wilder has a kind of overarching optimism about the human situation, he has concerns about his country, but these do not appear to have any biblical or theological base. In act 1, Professor Willard of State University recalls concerning the use of alcohol that the drinkers will repent when the evangelist comes to town on his regular visit.[6] The Bible is a fixture in life, but not a force. The choir sings "Blest Be the Tie That Binds" and "Love Divine, All Loves Excelling," although the organist, Simon Stimson, is obviously an inebriate. The excerpts of the wedding homily are of interest,[7] and act 3 about funerals is lively and provocative. Questions about eternity are raised but not answered. Some sense of eschatological expectation is found strongly but altogether without biblical nuancing. Only Scripture can inform us of the afterlife.

In *The Skin of Our Teeth,* we are reminded that humankind staggers "from crisis to crisis." The Society for Affirming the End of the World is busy. References to the Bible and Bible characters suffuse the culture,[8] but how many will grasp the implications of the biblical referent, "They call me Cain"? Wilder very skillfully represents humankind horizontally, but he has nothing meaningful to say about the vertical reality of God in terms of which all meaning is derived.

---

1. Thornton Wilder, *The Bridge of San Luis Rey* (New York: Pocket Books, 1955). Brother Juniper investigates how five persons lost their lives in the collapse of a bridge in Peru 250 years ago.

2. J. D. McClatchey, "Wilder and the Marvels of the Heart," *The New York Times Book Review,* 15 April 1997, 35.

3. William Lyon Phelps, *Autobiography with Letters* (New York: Oxford University Press, 1939), 660–62. Phelps, the public orator at Yale, came to Christ through Robert Browning's works (207–10).

4. McClatchey, "Wilder and the Marvels," 35. Wilder's identical twin died at birth. He had no "sturdy last resource against the occasional conviction 'I don't belong'" (35). He was always driving "to allay an insatiable need."

5. Thornton Wilder, preface to *Three Plays* (New York: Harper and Row, 1985), xiv.

6. Ibid., 24. Wilder was "a compulsive traveler and socializer."

7. Ibid., 71. At the wedding as at the funeral, there is considerable groping for the meaning of it all.

8. After World War II, Protestant church attendance was at 49 percent. It is now 29 percent.

13.1.8 O'NEILL, THE DRAMA OF DESOLATION

None of us can help the things life has done to us. They're done before you realize it, and once they're done they make you do other things until at last everything comes between you and what you'd like to be, and you've lost your true self forever.

—Eugene O'Neill
Mary Tyrone in *Long Day's Journey into Night*

Generally acclaimed "America's greatest dramatist," Eugene O'Neill (1888–1953) embodies and expresses "a tragic attitude toward life" as much as any who ever wrote on the American scene. Born in a New York City hotel, O'Neill's parents brought him up in the loose living of the theatre. His father made a fortune playing in *The Count of Monte Cristo* for twenty years. His mother, although raised in a convent, was addicted to morphine. He was virtually homeless, without roots. O'Neill told the story of his family in the autobiographical drama "Long Day's Journey into Night" about the Tyrone family, a celebrated actor father, a mother, two sons and a servant girl. O'Neill's mother fit the personality of the continually intoxicated son. The audience watches as this family disintegrates. It is a tragedy in every sense of the term.

Matriculating briefly in both public and parochial schools, where he rebelled strongly against Catholicism, he was expelled from Princeton University after one year. His lifestyle is characterized by impregnating young women, heavy drinking, and near escapes from death.[1]

His life can be viewed in three parts. First (1888–1916) came O'Neill's rebellious and destructive phase. He went to sea as a sailor, prospected in Honduras; married the first time, went to Buenos Aires, returned to New York but not to his wife and child, attempted suicide, contracted tuberculosis, and was admitted to a sanitorium. Here he began to write; he was at this point "a bum."[2] Enamored with free love and anarchism, his friends included John Reed and Louise Bryant of *Ten Days That Shook the World*. They subsequently emigrated to Russia.

The second (1916–1932) was a philosophical reemergence and maturation in which O'Neill's influences were Strindberg, Friedrich Nietzsche (1844–1900), and Sigmund Freud (1856–1939). He developed the dramatic innovations for which he is especially noted. A second marriage fails. His play *Exorcism* (1916) is about his own attempted suicide; *The Straw* (1919) reflects his experience in the TB sanitorium; and *Welded* (1923) deals with the emotional problems in his two failed marriages. His trilogy *Mourning Becomes Electra* (1931) made a mark by retelling the classical Greek myth in an austere New England setting. In all of his plays, he seeks to probe inner thoughts and feelings.[3]

In the third phase (1932–1953), the author retreated into himself. He was the first American playwright to win the Nobel Prize (1936), but like Herman Melville (1819–1891), he did not produce much after middle age began. His last significant work came in 1939. That drama, *The Iceman Cometh*, may reflect the state of O'Neill's life. It is about derelicts who hang out at the End of the Line Cafe. O'Neill sat out the depression and World War II. Parkinson's disease wasted his creative gifts. His third marriage drained his resources to pay for estates in Bermuda, the South, and in Danville, California. His was not a happy retirement as he struggled but failed to regain his former eminence.

The play that I recommend is the half-length drama that made O'Neill famous, *The Emperor Jones*.[4] Produced in 1920, it is the least autobiographical of the O'Neill plays. On an island in the Caribbean, a former Pullman porter, Brutus Jones, has established himself as emperor. We feel the emotional primitivism of the situation. Tom-toms are beating throughout the last two-thirds of the action. The subjects rebel, and Jones must flee into the jungle. The tom-toms beat louder, and he is finally "cotched" and sadly dispatched. Paul Robeson made a name as an actor by playing the lead role in particularly excellent national productions. The beat of the drums represents Jones's guilt and fear. The play advances O'Neill's philosophy that "the terrible predicament of man is his struggle against unseen forces for his place in a universe that is essentially alien to him."[5] The real question here is: Are the demons internal or external to mankind? Frederic Carpenter is insightful when he says that O'Neill "never fully understood his own tragedy or transcended it."[6]

The essentially religious nature of all tragedy can be seen in *Anna Christie* (1920), which is about the regeneration of a fallen woman. The public rejected the manifest hypocrisy in some of his plays, as when the wealthy man in *More Stately Mansions* (1962) denounces American materialism. O'Neill was so obviously tangled up in what he supposedly rejected, that he was unsuccessful at raising the cultural social consciousness. In *Lazarus Laughed* (1925), he parodies Jesus who "wept" at the grave of Lazarus. The creation of paradise, along with the crucifixion of the lion and the representation of the resurrection, seem so out of place with this author.[7] In *Strange Interlude* (1928), which really was "banned in Boston," we hear his plaintive cry: "I want to believe in something!"[8]

O'Neill was a temperamental follower of nonrestrictive mores.[9] He melded Western and Eastern mysticism into an amorphous system that left him emotionally and intellectually bereft when his relationships collapsed. The "sickness of today" of hedonistic cultural malaise can be seen in both his life and writing.

1. Frederic I. Carpenter, *Eugene O'Neill* (Boston: Twayne, 1964), 29. His brother Jamie died from alcoholism related disease at age forty-five.

2. Ibid., 37. Loose morals brought O'Neill only troubles in the flesh, the mind, and the spirit.

3. O'Neill became fond of psychoanalyst Carl Gustav Jung (1875–1961). Jung was the son of a Swiss pastor and his book *Modern Man in Search of a Soul* seemed to leave the door open to religious concerns. He broke with his master, Freud, over the latter's pansexuality. See Stephen Goode, "Freud Is Losing Out to the Jung-at-Heart," *Insight,* 20 September 1993, 16ff. Jung was particularly influential in the 1990s. Unfortunately, however attractive his notions of "collective unconscious" may be to evangelicals, his Kantian epistemological presuppositions doom him to get no further toward the Ultimate than agnosticism.

4. Eugene O'Neill, *The Emperor Jones,* in *Gateway to the Great Books,* vol. 4 (Chicago: Britannica, 1963), 357.

5. O'Neill, introduction to *The Emperor Jones,* 354. All of his characters are "sensitive people in torment."

6. Carpenter, *Eugene O'Neill,* 92. Delusion and dream are contrasted in daylight reality and moonlight illusion.

7. Ibid., 120. This is a unique play. O'Neill was an extraordinarily gifted man, yet he had no hope.

8. Ibid., 125. The plot of *Strange Interlude* is the coming of age of a young woman, Nina Leeds, who can only become free as she throws over her moral upbringing as well as her possessive father.

9. Ibid., 173. O'Neill has a passion about his work, which brings him very close to his audience.

13.1.9 WILLIAMS, THE DRAMA OF DISSOLUTION

There are woven into his myth of the theatre, many figures drawn from Christian ritual. For Williams, like Shakespeare, is haunted with images of the suffering Christ. His works abound with symbols drawn from the passion plays: the Redemption of Mary Magdalene; Christ before Pilate; the Crucifixion; the Descent from the Cross; the Harrowing of Hell; and the Sorrowing Mother of God.

—Esther Merle Jackson on Tennessee Williams

Ralph Waldo Emerson's dictum was to: "Go beyond the great Defeat of the Crucifixion." Thomas Lanier "Tennessee" Williams (1911–1983) was heir to the great religious tradition of the American South. His moral conscience was informed by the English Reformed Episcopal and Scotch-Irish Presbyterian immigration, which set a Puritan stamp on the development of Southern culture. He tried to trade that heritage for a Nietzschean worldview (see 5.13), but as he got older, he was haunted by his past.[1]

The home in which he was raised was a shambles. His father was a rowdy and usually absent traveling shoe salesman. His mother was the "prim" daughter of a Southern Episcopal rector. Williams was actually born in the rectory in Columbia, Mississippi, and lived in the various rectories occupied by his grandparents. His play *Purification* is an obvious reaction against the value system within which he was raised.[2]

Williams knew great loneliness in his growing up years, and Signi Falk observes that there is more loneliness in his plays than in all the "lonely crowds" in the United States.[3] This loneliness and a severe bout with diphtheria when he was four led to marked introversion. This, in turn, led to an unhealthy reliance upon his sister Rose and a relationship between them that was too close to allow healthy self-development. The result was gender confusion in Williams and severe mental illness in Rose, who had one of the first prefrontal lobotomies performed in the United States. This left her "a mental vegetable."[4]

The family moved to St. Louis and then to Memphis, from which Thomas picked up the name *Tennessee*. Williams studied at the University of Missouri and Washington University, St. Louis, but was graduated from the University of Iowa. At age twenty-six, he began to write seriously.

From the beginning of his career, his "primitive violence" was shocking to critics and audiences. Here was a playwright who expressed creative modernism. He thought of himself first and foremost as a poet and experimented radically with language forms. He had what he called his "wandering years," from 1938 to 1940, when he scrounged through flop houses as a derelict. Coming out of this time were what critics call his "degrading stories."[5]

He shows animus against any clergy figure. He always sides with the societal "Cavaliers" against the strict-living "Puritans." Even in his story "The Yellow Bird," the bastard son of the fallen religious person builds a monument for his mother that includes a dolphin carrying a cross. Repression is treated with hatred on the one hand, but the cross is looked at wistfully on the other. The need for atonement is acute.

Christian readers will enjoy little of Williams. He is crass, and despite working in the inevitable "Pieta," he is fixated on depravity. His life and body of work demonstrate the axiom that "Everyone succumbs to depravity."[6] There was no lid on Williams's id. He frequently touches religious themes, but avoids personal interest or reference to revealed truth. His is a morbid preoccupation with the disease, without a hope of treatment. Even such well-known works as *A Streetcar Named Desire* is little more than a descent into insanity. *Cat on a Hot Tin Roof* has memorable characters, but its studied vulgarity is harsh and bitter.[7]

One play that should be read or watched is *The Glass Menagerie* (1945) because it is so autobiographical and searching.[8] In seven poignant scenes, the mother, Amanda, who speaks of herself and her two children as "Christian adults," twists history into a self-serving buttress of her own superior airs. The life of Laura, the handicapped daughter, revolves around her collection of glass animals. Tom, the son, who narrates the introduction and conclusion, voices the guilt Williams felt about his own sister.

At his mother's insistence, Tom gets his friend Jim O'Connor to come as "a gentleman caller" on Laura. Remarkable realities are symbolized in this encounter, during which Jim carelessly breaks the horn off the glass unicorn. By chance or the design of Williams, the unicorn developed in the late medieval era as a Christian symbol for purity.[9] This play was Williams' first commercial success and won him the first of many prizes.

Another play that picks up the usual family anxieties we expect in Williams, but gentler and more thoughtful, is the rarely seen *A Lovely Sunday for Creve Coeur* (1979). Set in St. Louis, the action is about women who are facing the passing of their opportunities. The characters are splendidly drawn, which is a main factor in drama.

Williams had a good heritage and actually understood so much. He is absorbed in the issues of guilt and atonement. He even sees the "sacrificial aspect of Christ as the scapegoat."[10] This is the heart of the gospel that Williams fled.

---

1. C. W. E. Bigsby, "Valedictory," in Harold Bloom, ed., *Tennessee Williams* (New York: Chelsea House, 1987), 137f. Williams conceded universal sin, "There is a passion for declivity in this world." Signi Lenea Falk, *Tennessee Williams* (New York: Twayne, 1961), 123.
2. Falk, *Tennessee Williams,* 152.
3. Ibid., 85.
4. R. B. Parker, "The Circle Closed," in Harold Bloom, ed., *The Glass Menagerie* (New York: Chelsea House, 1988), 127f. Both Rose and Tennessee came to sad ends. Williams died in 1983, choking on the plastic top to a container of barbiturates.
5. Falk, *Tennessee William,* 30. Falk describes Williams as having a "great affinity for lost souls." He was one himself, of course.
6. Ibid., 129. Williams stereotypes not only the church, but business, law, goodness, just about everything (117).
7. Ibid., 111.
8. *The Theater of Tennessee Williams,* I (New York: New Direction, 1971).
9. Gilbert Debusscher, "Tennessee Williams' Unicorn Broken Again," in Bloom, ed., *The Glass Menagerie,* 56.
10. Leonard Quirino, "Tennessee Williams' Persistent Battle of Angels," in Bloom, ed., *Tennessee Williams,* 48.

13.1.10 MILLER, THE DRAMA OF DECOMPOSITION

Oh, Ben, how do we get back to all the great times? Used to be so full of light, and comradeship, the sleigh-riding in winter, and the ruddiness on his cheeks. And always some kind of good news coming up, always something nice coming up ahead. And never even let me carry the valises in the house, and simonizing, simonizing that little red car! Why, why can't I give him something and not have him hate me?

—Arthur Miller
Willy Loman about his son Biff in *Death of a Salesman*

A craftsman of dialogue and shrewd analyst of character and culture, Arthur Miller is blind to anything transcendent. He was born in New York City in 1915 to middle-class Jewish parents. When his father lost everything in the Depression, Miller took jobs in an auto parts store, the Brooklyn Navy Yard, and a box factory. He worked his way through the University of Michigan, then returned to New York to write radio plays. Soon he was a preeminent playwright with finesse for exploring psychological and societal tangles.

Although considered "almost medieval" in his belief in conscience and personal responsibility, Miller was married three times, including his celebrated but unsuccessful nuptials with Marilyn Monroe.

He addresses many issues. *All My Sons* (1947) wrestles with accountability. *The Crucible* (1953) interprets Miller's battle with the Un-American Activities Committee of the House of Representatives through the Salem witchcraft trials of 1692. *The Crucible* is inaccurate history, but it raises pertinent questions about the human desire to oppress.[1]

To be fair to the other side in this issue, Miller and a few other idealistic writers definitely did have serious dalliances with the Soviets during the 1930s and 1940s. This could have posed a greater national danger than many have been willing to admit. Miller also has been accused of writing *The Misfits* (1961) as a vehicle for possibly exploiting Marilyn Monroe. In the positive column, he is most in his natural element in *Incident at Vichy* (1964).[2]

However, the classic work of Arthur Miller, the one to read, is *Death of a Salesman* (1949), one of the most popular plays in the history of the stage. Just about everything is going belly-up for aging salesman Willy Loman. Society and his family fall short of his expectations, but "it was no less his own doing."[3] The play is a window on post-World War II attitudes in America. The echoes of that culture persisted through the second half of the century in a generally superficial prosperity.

Willy, in his sixties, is becoming forgetful and feels beaten down and guilty. "Why am I always being contradicted?" he inquires with pain.[4] He has not been faithful to his wife, but he tries to clamp down on his two wastrel sons.[5] He does not want reality ("Don't give me a lecture about the facts!").[6]

Happy says of him "He had a good dream. It's the only dream you can have— to come out number-one man."[7] Biff says about his father: "He never knew who he was."[8] Happy is the unprincipled womanizer; Biff is the immature drunk who still cares for his father. Wife and mother Linda remains loyal to the man who doesn't deserve her. "The man is exhausted. He's only a little boat looking for a harbor," she pleads on his behalf.[9] In the final and fateful scene, Willy is out in his garden, trying to plant vegetables by flashlight. "How do we get back to the great days?" he puzzles.

Here is the pervasive emptiness depicted in Ecclesiastes.

■ **A notable 1990 English play** examines the church, politics, and the legal system. David Hare's *Racing Demons* is about an aging Anglican clergyman, Lionel Espy— a man of prayer and wisdom but politically inept. A young, ambitious and savvy man wants his position. As Tony Ferris seeks to topple the venerable saint, we see a quite accurate peak into the inner workings of church politics, which is too often a sordid and disillusioning reality. *Time* describes it as "politics in the vestry."

1. Marvin Olasky, "Witchhunts," in *World,* 11 January 1997, 30.
2. *Arthur Miller,* in Contemporary Authors, vol. 54 (Detroit: Gale, 1997), 315.
3. Arthur Miller, *Death of a Salesman* (New York: Viking, 1949).
4. Ibid., 17.
5. Ibid., 63.
6. Ibid., 107.
7. Ibid., 139. Loman is a selfish man who has always looked out for himself. While Linda was mending old stockings, Willy gave new ones to his mistress. Yet Linda is Willy's protector.
8. Ibid., 115.
9. Ibid., 76.

CHAPTER FOURTEEN

Searching Through the Vast World of the Imaginative and Informative Essay

We are all worms, but I do believe I am a glow worm.
—Winston Churchill

We have already noted that the French writer Michel Eyquem de Montaigne (1533–1592) was really the first to speak of the essay or rhetorical discourse as a literary form (4:4). The Englishman Francis Bacon (1561–1626) consciously used these tightly-structured compositions to set forth his ideas, as did such distinguished men of letters as Joseph Addison (1672–1719), Richard Steele (1672–1729), and Charles Lamb (1775–1834).

Christian communicators enjoy a special affinity for the essay because it is analogous in length and design to the sermon. Archbishop John Tillotson (1630–1694), a popular London preacher, developed the "essay sermon," which makes no pretense of wrestling with the text, but rather sets forth a nexus of ideas without rhetorical division.[1] This style of sermon has been quite acceptable in mainline denominations. It avoids making rhetorical transitions, and so is sophisticated and smooth in delivery. But it usually lacks scriptural substance.

The discipline of the essay is important in developing the ability to succinctly state ideas. Since "folly is still the dominant gene in the human race,"[2] the well-crafted and carefully-thought-out rhetoric of the essay can be helpful in reducing complexity; its insight can produce foresight.

1. David L. Larsen, *The Company of the Preachers* (Grand Rapids: Kregel, 1998), 6.2.7.
2. Michael J. O'Neill, *The Roar of the Crowd: How TV and People Power are Changing the World* (New York: Time Books, 1993). O'Neill grapples with how the stability of knowledge is upset and what that may imply for interpersonal communication.

14.1 THE GREAT ESSAYISTS

14.1.1 CARLYLE, CROTCHETY CRITIC

In books lies the soul of the Whole Past Time; the articulate, audible voice of the Past, when the body and material substance of it has altogether vanished like a dream.

—Thomas Carlyle
*On Heroes, Hero-Worship,
and the Heroic in History*

At one point, Thomas Carlyle (1795–1881) could wax eloquent about the power of history, then elsewhere dismiss history as "only a nightmare of mutability." Consistency was never a hallmark of logic for Carlyle. He was born the oldest of nine children to a poor but deeply devout Scottish Presbyterian stonemason and his wife in Ecclefechan, Dumfreisshire in Scotland. The father of Thomas was much like that described by Robert Burns (1759–1796), although Carlyle's was more severe.[1] His early schooling was spotty, but his father discerned his son's abilities and encouraged him to further study. At age fourteen, Carlyle walked ninety miles to study for the ministry at the University of Edinburgh. He studied German and read German writers voraciously.

His childhood faith became a casualty of Immanuel Kant and Johann Fichte and the Romantics Johann Wolfgang von Goethe and Johann Friedrich von Schiller. The Enlightenment notion that the universal categories are available to human reason, unaided by supernatural revelation, is appealing to human pride but devastating to faith.

Young Carlyle turned from the ministry to teach but drifted into a career writing magazine articles. He also translated his German icons and in 1826, he married the beautiful Jane Baillie Welsh, the young woman whom the gifted preacher and close friend of Carlyle, Edward Irving (1792–1834), also courted.[2] The Carlyles lived for a time on a farm in Scotland, but it became an impossible arrangement, both financially and because Carlyle suffered with dyspepsia or painful stomach ulcers. They moved to Cheyne Row in London, where Carlyle maintained residence after the passing of his wife until his own death. After her death, he was appalled to read her journals and learn how unhappy she had been with his irascible ways.

He and his friend Ralph Waldo Emerson (1803–1882) agreed on many things, but Carlyle was incensed that Emerson did not believe in a personal Devil. Carlyle asserted to Emerson that "Christ died on the tree; that built Dunscore kirk yonder; that brought you and me together."[3] Carlyle evidently did not notice how this confession clashed with his lack of christological affirmation. Carlyle thought Emerson was "close buttoned," and Emerson thought Carlyle was too much given to lament and whining. Carlyle wrote to Emerson that he did not care at all for the church, but he did warmly remember his "brave father's evening prayers at family worship."[4]

Another good friend was philosopher John Stuart Mill (1806–1873). Carlyle left his manuscript on the French Revolution for Mill to read, but Mill's maid used it for kindling a fire. Carlyle rewrote without his notes and without telling Mill of the loss.

Carlyle agreed with Denis Diderot (1713–1784) that "there is no proof for divinity," and yet in his greatest piece, *Sartor Resartus* (lit. "The Tailor Retailored"), he seems to have passing moments of spiritual conviction. This brilliant autobiographical satire faces doubt head-on. Using very little scriptural referent (although he does speak of "that Divine Book of Revelations"), Carlyle tells the story of Professor Diogenes Teufelsdrockh, a man who is wracked with doubt and takes refuge in the world-soul of transcendentalism.[5] Adam is dispossessed, and Christ is only a symbol.[6] His is "natural supernaturalism." The professor's defiant "everlasting no" leads to his rebirth, his "embodiment of the spirit of the universe."[7]

Carlyle went very little beyond *Sartor Resartus*. In his maturity, he did use more of the language of his childhood. Jesus is the supreme example, but not divine.[8] As one who held to "the great man theory of history," Carlyle could be moved to ecstatic utterance over the Napoléons and Goethes, the Oliver Cromwells and Frederick the Greats. He opposed democracy and despised nonwhite races. Majority government and the extension of the franchise were an aversion.[9]

Carlyle is a conundrum: He is often unclear or lacks civility. He seemed to be against everyone but himself. He had strong antipathy to the doctrine of Christ's vicarious sacrifice.[10] He played the skeptic, yet denounced atheism; he worshiped the great men of science, yet was doubtful that science could ultimately benefit humankind. He flagrantly dispensed with divine revelation and yet maintained its ethic.[11] He was optimistic that man could save himself and essentially banished the God of the Bible from activity in the universe.[12] He redefined heaven, earth, and hell.

Karl Marx (1818–1883) and Friedrich Engels (1820–1895) both benefited from Carlyle. He shared his love affair with the Middle Ages in the essay *Past and Present*.[13] A nostalgia for the medieval religious authority tempted him to convert to Roman Catholicism.

In essence, Carlyle anticipated Erich Fromm's *Escape from Freedom* and desired authoritarian life. Thomas Carlyle was one of many sowers of the apostasy that ravaged the Church of Scotland and Scottish Calvinism with Enlightenment skepticism. He admitted: "Men had at one time read it in their Bible" but these are "mean days that have no sacred word." Indeed he "envies the preacher his pulpit," because the only text is that of our own lives. The Bible is seen now as only history like the *Iliad*.[14]

Read Carlyle to learn from and appreciate his skill but not for hope.

1. Thomas Carlyle, *Essay on Burns* (New York: Macmillan, 1904), x. Carlyle always spoke with a heavy Scottish brogue.
2. *The Company of the Preachers*, 9.1.7.
3. Joseph Slater, ed., *The Correspondence of Emerson and Carlyle* (New York: Columbia, 1964), 13.
4. Ibid., 105. It is fascinating to read the letters between Emerson and Carlyle. These letters are almost essays in form themselves.
5. Thomas Carlyle, *Sartor Resartus* (New York: Oxford, 1987), 99.
6. Ibid., 169. He clung to Christian morality after jettisoning the belief system.
7. *English Literature from 1785* (New York: Harper/Collins, 1992), 114.
8. F. A. Lea, *Carlyle: Prophet of Today* (London: Routledge, 1943), 57. Christ was something of a "hero," a Ulysses. "Heroism is direct vision!" he held.
9. "The Hero as King," in *Doorways to the Great Books* (Chicago: Britannica, 1963), 110ff.
10. John Nichol, "Carlyle," *English Men of Letters* (London: Macmillan, 1894), 215.
11. Ibid., 223. Nichol finds him "bewilderingly inconsistent" and "vague" (214).
12. Eloise M. Behnken, *Thomas Carlyle: Calvinist Without the Theology* (Columbia: Missouri, 1978), 35.
13. Thomas Carlyle, *Past and Present* (London: Chapman and Hall, n.d.). He sees England dying of the loss of moral and intellectual vigor.
14. John Holloway, "The Life of Carlyle's Language," in *Thomas Carlyle*, ed. Harold Bloom (New York: Chelsea, 1986), 17. The Bible was compared to Homer in his *Latter-Day Pamphlets*.

14.1.2 RUSKIN, CRUSADING COLLECTOR

Anything which elevates the mind is sublime, and elevation of the mind is produced by the contemplation of greatness of any kind, whether of matter, space, power, beauty or virtue.

—John Ruskin

Although he is not read so much anymore, John Ruskin (1819–1900) is worth discovery because of his skillful essays and his rare interest in aesthetic philosophy, the consideration of beauty and the arts. Ruskin's works on architecture or paintings are rich for the communicator, because preaching is art as well as science (technique).

Ruskin was the only child of a wealthy Scottish wine merchant who lived in Croydon, London. His parents doted on him, and he was not permitted to mix with other children. He was not allowed toys other than a box of bricks and a set of keys. Until he was ten, only his mother taught him, reading the Bible through again and again. On his third birthday, he was able to repeat the 176 verses of the 119th Psalm. At age eleven, he wrote a two-thousand-line poem. By sixteen, he knew the *Iliad* and the *Odyssey* as well as the Apocalypse of John by heart.[1] From age six, he traveled with his parents throughout Europe and was taught how to draw and sketch the churches and cathedrals.

Critics speak of his mother as a "grim evangelical," who made sure her family was regular in attendance at the Beresford Chapel, Walworth. His "life was bounded by a hedge of prohibitions," and he was severely disciplined for infractions.[2]

Everyone regarded young John as an "incipient bishop."[3] At Christ Church, Oxford, he won a prize for his long poem. However, Darwinian ideas were eroding his faith. Illness and travel as well as meeting artists such as English painters Joseph Turner (1775–1851), John Millais (1825–1896), and Holman Hunt (1827–1910) filled his days. He knew the evangelical preacher F. W. Robertson, who liked him.[4] He decided not to enter the ministry, saying that "I am not fit to be a clergyman." It did not help his mental and spiritual stability that Ruskin unhappily married fellow Scot Euphemia Gray. While he was laid up with a sprained knee, his wife took up with Millais, whom she ultimately married.[5]

He began to write the masterpieces for which he became widely known: *The Poetry of Architecture, Modern Painters,* and *The Stones of Venice.* He would live his life as a writer/philosopher and Oxford don. He held the Slade Professorship, which gave him the most satisfaction of anything in his later life.

In the downdraft of the trauma over his wife's unfaithfulness, Ruskin came under the influence of F. D. Maurice (1805–1872), who was to the left both theologically and politically. Charles Darwin (1809–1882), John William Colenso (1813–1883), and Maurice turned him against the concept of any sort of eternal punishment. That led to doubts about eternal salvation. At one point, he visited Charles Spurgeon (1834–1892).[6] He now repudiated the evangelical doctrine that eternal salvation depends on faith in Christ. He was "unconverted from his evangelical faith." The dullness and "languid prayers" of a small Waldensian Church in Turin did not help him.[7]

He became more like Carlyle in his aristocratic and elitist views and found it in no way incongruous to be a socialist who justified slavery. In some ways, he never advanced beyond the theology in a sermon he preached when he was only five years old. The first words were "People, be good." There is no evidence he ever returned to faith in Christ. Rather, he resorted to spiritualism and had bouts of very deep depression. He continued to hate the doctrine of justification by faith alone.[8]

His loss of faith and turn to humanism plunged his old parents into sorrow and contributed to his own unhappiness. For years, he tried to marry a woman named Rose, but her parents opposed the union because Ruskin was not a believer. The young woman and her family had come to Christ under the ministry of Spurgeon.[9] Resentful as he was with "Rose's inconvenient piety," he continually pursued her, pouring out his heart to his confidante, the novelist George MacDonald (1824–1905; see 9.2.10). Rose saw the self-justification and incoherence of his philosophy, telling him: "I do not wonder that your faith is shipwrecked."[10] Rose suffered a physical collapse and died while still a young woman.

Kenneth Clark, director of the National Gallery and Slade Professor of Fine Arts at Oxford, attributes the swing against Ruskin to the general perception that he was a "popular moralist and preacher." Poor Ruskin, according to Clark, had been raised "A Bible Christian," and although he sloughed off most of this, he had remaining assumptions and cadences that turned people off.[11]

1. Paul Johnson, *The Birth of the Modern: World Society 1815–1830* (New York: Harper/Collins, 1991), 725. Johnson is helpful in analyzing and reflecting on the arts, particularly painters and painting.

2. Derrick Leon, *Ruskin: The Great Victorian* (London: Archon Books, 1969), 10. Leon's analysis of Ruskin's childhood is perhaps discolored by his hostility to Christianity. When his aged mother died, he testified, "I never loved my Mother" (ibid., 471). Ruskin's life became a harvest of long-planted bitterness toward others. With the passing of his father, he became an extremely wealthy man, but he didn't use his money wisely.

3. Ibid., 16.

4. Ibid., 83. For a sketch of Robertson, see *Company of the Preachers*, 9.3.5.

5. *The Great Victorian*, 162.

6. Ibid., 292. It does appear that he returned much later to some form of belief in the immortality of the soul (507). He also had problems with "the darkness of Revelation" (159), unwilling to see that he accepted mysteries elsewhere in life and nature.

7. Kenneth Clark, *Ruskin Today* (London: Penguin, 1964), 51. Clark provides the best selection of Ruskin's writings.

8. *The Great Victorian*, 488.

9. Ibid., 363. This is an interesting example of Spurgeon's influence.

10. Ibid., 565. Though he fulminated against "unworthy believers," he did not see himself as a sinner.

11. Clark, *Ruskin Today*, xiii. Clark likes him because he was a poet, had a quality mind, and was complex.

14.1.3 MACAULAY, CAGEY CHRONOLOGER

A Christian of the fifth century with a Bible, was neither better nor worse situated than a Christian of the nineteenth century with a Bible—candour and natural acuteness being of course supposed equal. It matters not at all that the compass, printing, gunpowder, steam, gas, vaccination and a thousand other discoveries and inventions, which were unknown in the fifth century, are familiar to the nineteenth. None of these discoveries and inventions have the smallest bearing on the question whether man is justified by faith alone, or whether the invocation of the saints is an orthodox practice. It seems to us, therefore, that we have no security for the future against the prevalence of any theological error that has prevailed in time past among Christian men.

—T. B. Macaulay *(History of the Popes)*

More people read Thomas Babington Macaulay (1800–1859) than any other essayist of his time. The oldest of nine children born to a father of Scottish Presbyterian descent, his line included several ministers; his mother was of Quaker extraction. The family lived for a while at Clapham and were thus exposed to William Wilberforce (1759–1833) and the Clapham Saints (5.8). His father, Zachary (1768–1838), was a national leader in the movement to abolish slavery and edited *The Christian Observer*. School was painful for young Macaulay because he preferred to stay at home and read. Evangelical faith was deeply grounded into his life from childhood. A strong leader of the Clapham Sect and good friend of Samuel Johnson (1709–1784) was Hannah More, his mother's teacher. She read some hymns by Thomas and found them "quite extraordinary for such a baby."[1] Macaulay was precocious and had a photographic memory. For example, he demonstrated total recall of *Paradise Lost* and *Paradise Regained*. From age three, he was a prodigious reader in a course of study guided by his mother.

As an adult, his writing was vivid, colorful, and interesting, if somewhat pontifical. His poems in *Lays of Ancient Rome*, about classical heroes, were popular. He learned several languages by studying different Bible translations as his texts.[2] He did considerable writing for his father's paper, and hooked many, including the great preacher Robert Hall (1764–1831), with his extended essays on Dante and Milton. He wrote many articles for Britannica.

Although he had tensions with his father's rigidity in a number of respects, he picked up all of Zachary's debts when his business failed in 1823. William Gladstone (1809–1898) opined that, except for William Pitt the Younger (1759–1806), and George Gordon, Lord Byron (1788–1824), no one won higher honors at such a young age than did T. B. Macaulay. He was graduated from Trinity College, Cambridge, and went on to study for the law, which he did not care to practice.

In 1830 he entered Parliament and was distinguished there on many accounts but particularly for his eloquent advocacy of the Reform Bill, which was credited to him. He also served as a high administrator for India and Secretary of War. He could use the sledgehammer of invective as few before or after him. He wrote of Archbishop William Laud (1573–1645): "We are tempted to forget the vices of Laud's heart in the imbecility of his intellect."[3] Lord Melbourne reportedly said: "I wish I were as sure of one thing as Macaulay is of everything."

A great walker who would think nothing of taking a sixteen-mile walk from Clapham, he did much meditating and reading on his walks. His great publishing feat was his two thousand-page *History of England* from the accession of James II (1685). Some 140,000 copies of this work were purchased in England, and it was read widely in the United States and around the world. The work is amazingly lively, but its coverage extends only to the death of his hero William III in 1702.[4] Macaulay writes in an almost fictional style. In describing the visit of a Russian diplomatic mission, he rather graphically portrays their personal hygiene. The ambassador and the grandees who accompanied him were so gorgeous that all London crowded to stare at them and so filthy that nobody dared to touch them. "They came to the court balls dripping pearls and vermin."[5]

Certainly one of the best storytellers, Macaulay disdained Kant and the German rationalists and asserted what Ruskin called "a penetrative imagination." He did not have strong passions and was never known to be romantically in love. Always prudent, he exemplified what psychologists now call overcontrol. J. Cotter Morison observed that "he never made us feel 'what shadows we are and what shadows we pursue.'"[6] He did not have much prescience for the future.[7]

A good starting point to catch the flavor of Macaulay's essays is *Essay on Lord Clive*. Well qualified to write about the great British figure in Indian history, Macaulay draws aside the curtain in a singularly masterful way.[8] In a classic section, Macaulay tells how Clive was accused of benefiting materially from his Indian contacts. He denied this categorically, pleading "eminent disinterestedness." Macaulay shows Clive in vaults piled high with gold and jewels "thrown open to him alone," and frames a vehement statement for Clive: "Mr. Chairman, at this moment I stand astonished at my own moderation."

Although he preferred seclusion, Macaulay was solicitous for his siblings and generous to the poor. On the day of his death, he dictated a letter to an underpaid clergyman enclosing twenty-five pounds. He was struck down by heart disease and asthma in 1852 and died in 1859; he was buried in Poets' Corner in Westminster. His style is an example of a communicator who preferred the definite, the positive, and the concrete. His prose brings the picture into vivid focus masterfully using comparison for clarification.[9]

He also kept his orthodox faith clarified and in focus.

---

1. J. Cotter Morison, "Macaulay," in *English Men of Letters,* X (London: Macmillan, 1885), 2. For good insight on Hannah More (1745–1833), see David Lyle Jeffrey, ed., *A Burning and Shining Light* (Grand Rapids: Eerdmans, 1987), 480. Influenced by William Law and John Newton, Hannah More became a champion of female education after her conversion.
2. J. W. Pierce, ed., *Macaulay's Essay on Lord Clive* (New York: Macmillan, 1907), xiii.
3. William Henry Chamberlain, "The Magnificent Middlebrow," *Saturday Review,* 9 October 1965, 28.
4. Ibid., 29. While attacking Robert Peel in the House: "How white poor Peel looked while I was speaking."
5. Ibid., 29f. His descriptions of Peter the Great of Russia are just as humorous.
6. Morison, "Macaulay," 56.
7. In Albert Barnes's classic apologetic discussion, Macaulay's prophecy on the Roman Catholic Church is cited as inane: "She may still exist in undiminished vigor when some traveler from New Zealand shall, in the midst of a vast solitude, take his stand on a broken arch of London Bridge to sketch the ruins of St. Paul's." See John Gerstner, *Reasons for Faith* (Grand Rapids: Baker, 1967), 107.
8. Pierce, *Macaulay's Essay on Lord Clive,* 1.
9. Ibid., 133. Thackeray said of Macaulay: "He reads 20 books to write a sentence; travels 100 miles to write a description." Chamberlain speaks of him as "a buoyant personality and a brilliant writer."

14.1.4 CHESTERTON, COMMANDING COMMUNICATOR

For a landlady considering a lodger, it is important to know his income, but still more important to know his philosophy.

—G. K. Chesterton

Gilbert Keith Chesterton (1874–1936) has been the object of a striking up-surge of interest, even devotion. He is unquestionably one of the most original and forceful writers of the twentieth century and probably the premier essayist in the English language at the time of his death. Often polemical and always cru-sading for his adopted Roman Catholicism and social conservatism, he wrote in many literary genres—novels, poems, essays, plays, and biographies. He boasted: "I never discuss anything but politics and religion. There is nothing else to dis-cuss."[1] His style has been described as "sparkling energy, immensely readable, very quotable."[2] He was a staunch defender of religious dogma, things medieval and "traditional" Christianity. His targets were the modernist theologies of R. J. Campbell (1867–1956) and others, Darwinian evolution's notion of inevitable progress, determinism, eugenics, and the concept of a developing "superman."[3] Yet he may be best known for his delightful Father Brown Mysteries (the proto-type for which was his good friend Father John O'Connor). Whenever he needed money, he wrote another mystery.[4] His philosophical/literary nemeses were H. G. Wells (1866–1946) and George Bernard Shaw (1856–1950).

Chesterton was born in London into a middle-class family of well-known real estate brokers. So successful was the enterprise that G. K.'s father could virtu-ally cease working on the pretext of weak health and live comfortably the rest of his life. His parents were Spencerian liberals, molded by Unitarianism, although his maternal grandfather was a Methodist lay preacher and a strong teetotaler.[5] When his sister Beatrice died at age eight, he was inconsolable. His rather Pickwickian father led the family into a pattern of repression about the tragedy, but both parents encouraged Gilbert and his younger brother Cecil to join in all family discussion.

With the Scottish on his mother's side, he devoured Walter Scott (1771–1832) and Robert Louis Stevenson (1850–1894). He was something of a dunce at St. Paul's School, but he began to write early. His poem on "Frances Xavier" won the Milton Prize. Because of his own struggles and temptations, he began to be-lieve in sin and a real devil, contrary to his Unitarian upbringing.[6] While study-ing art at the Slade School of Art at the University of London, he "became a Christian unawares."[7] While editing book manuscripts, he met Frances Blogg, whose theological family background was Huguenot. They were well matched intellectually, and after they were married, she gradually convinced him of the "intellectual rightness of Orthodox Christian faith."[8]

Chesterton's father financed publication of several novels that sold poorly. He was more successful writing book reviews for the *London Daily News*. He was now recognized as a "comer" among Fleet Street journalists. His successful biog-raphy of Robert Browning (1812–1889) in the English Men of Letters series was a great boost. There followed books of essays: the philosophical presuppositional studies in *Heretics* and the autobiographical *Orthodoxy,* in which he makes his case for traditional Christianity against modernist theologies. The curious fact is that, traditional as he was, neither he nor his wife was active in a local parish.[9]

Chesterton was never afraid to espouse an unpopular cause. He was pro-Boer in the South African war, inveighed against the Fabian Socialists, and wrote in opposition to the philosophy of pacifism. Unfortunately, he also was a virulent anti-Semite. He illustrated books for his good friend Hilaire Belloc and wrote hymns, several of which are found in modern collections. Chesterton's faith kept his life in balance during hard times, as in the tragic suicide of his wife's brother. Chesterton did go through a long physical and emotional collapse after the death of his brother as a casualty of World War I. Ironically, both his brother and brother-in-law had converted to Roman Catholicism shortly before their deaths, and his brother had married before going to war. After his father died, and in view of the ascendancy of modernism in the Church of England, he joined the Roman Catholic Church in 1922. Frances followed in 1926. The man called "the Prince of Paradox" died in 1936 at the age of sixty-two.

It was his "paradoxical" eccentricities of thought and appearance that made him popular. Many saw him as a lovable buffoon, and he played and looked the part. Such overarching titles as *What's Wrong with the World?* were immensely popular. Young Malcolm Muggeridge could not take his eyes off Chesterton when he first saw his immense hulk, "his great stomach and plump hands, the pince-nez on its black ribbon almost lost in the expanse of his face and the inevitable cape."[10] He was a totally disorganized person, as when he sent a telegram to his wife: "Am at Market Harborough. Where ought I to be?" The answer came: "Home."[11]

Captivated by Lawrence of Arabia, he and Frances traveled to Jerusalem (though this did not modify his hatred of the Jews) and made several well received lecture tours of America. He was not an impressive speaker. He was disorganized in his presentation, used long literary quotes, and had a high-pitched voice.[12] He was better at the one-on-one debate. He was debating Clarence Darrow in New York City when the microphone failed. He yelled out to the audience: "This shows that science is not infallible!"[13]

The Chesterton Society and *The Chesterton Review* advanced his reputation long after his death. He is one of the most frequently quoted of authors by persons as diverse as heads of state and stirring preachers. He was particularly a favorite source for U.S. President Ronald Reagan. His collected quotations are well worth the investment for anyone who speaks or writes; they abound with notable and memorable sentiments.[14]

His literary output was vast, sixteen hundred essays of two thousand words each for the *Illustrated London News* over thirty-one years was one of his projects. For a time, he edited his own newspaper and continued to write significant volumes, such as *Charles Dickens* (one of his favorite authors), *The Outline of Sanity,* and *Robert Lewis Stevenson.* He urged readers to return to the great novels of the past. The modern novel, he said, is driven by the description in great detail of aimless appetites. Such volumes have little to offer those who want to think about substantive things. "The old literature, great and trivial, was built on the idea there is a purpose in life, (but) modern philosophy has taken the life out of modern fiction . . . (which) is dissolving into formlessness . . . and deserves the modern reproach of being 'sloppy.'"[15]

The beginner in Chesterton ought to pick up his two short treatments on Francis of Assisi[16] and Thomas Aquinas.[17] Here is an author with whom we can find ourselves identifying more often than not.

1. Lawrence J. Clipper, ed., *G. K. Chesterton: Collected Words,* XXVII (San Francisco: Ignatius, 1986), 25.
2. Alzina Stone Dale, *The Outline of Sanity: A Life of G. K. Chesterton* (Grand Rapids: Eerdmans, 1982), 142.
3. Clipper, *Chesterton: Collected Words,* 29. I recommend spending time with any of the volumes of the collected works.
4. *The Outline of Sanity,* 271.
5. Ibid., 6. The family lived for many years in the accessible Kensington area.
6. Ibid., 33. The family attended Bedford Chapel with the Irish preacher Stopford Brooke (1832–1916), who became a Unitarian.
7. Ibid., 39. Though he never completed a university program, he did attend some classes in literature at University College and took others by correspondence.
8. Ibid., 55. His brother Cecil became an Anglo-Catholic when Newman and the Tractarians were on the march.
9. Ibid., 120. Chesterton pointed out that "heresy" used to be considered to be what was wrong and "orthodoxy" what was right. Modern society had switched the poles.
10. Ibid., 195. He and Shaw carried on a long-running series of successful debates. They disagreed but not disagreeably.
11. Ibid., 133.
12. Ibid., 279.
13. Ibid., 281. Like Roman Catholics, he averred: "My faith is not in eschatology but in history" (293).
14. George J. Marlin, Richard P. Rabatin, John L. Swan, *The Quotable Chesterton* (San Francisco: Ignatius, 1986).
15. *The Outline of Sanity,* 284f. There is a difference between a man reading a book and a man who wants a book to read, he argued. To read a Charles Dickens novel is to wish it would never end.
16. G. K. Chesterton, *Saint Francis Assisi* (New York: Doubleday, 1924). An excellent conservative treatment of Chesterton is found in Michael Coren, *Gilbert: The Man Who Was G. K. Chesterton* (New York: Paragon, 1990).
17. G. K. Chesterton, *Saint Thomas Aquinas: "The Dumb Ox"* (Garden City: Image, 1933).

14.1.5 BELLOC, CAUSTIC CATHOLIC

> My religion is of course of greater moment to me by far than my politics, or than any other interest could be, and if I had to choose between two policies, one of which would certainly injure my religion and the other as certainly advance it, I would not for a moment hesitate between the two.
>   —Hilaire Belloc

When his friend Chesterton converted to Roman Catholicism, Hilaire Belloc (1870–1953) was sure he didn't really mean it. Belloc lacked the sense of humor of his friend, though he was deeply infected with the same anti-Semitism that seemed endemic in Western society. Still, he wrote more than 150 books of essays, history, fiction, poetry, and plays. He was also known as the author of such lively children's poetry as *The Bad Child's Book of Beasts* (1896). Though often a bit raspish and lemon-soaked in his disposition, he was a master of the essay form.

Belloc was born in La Celle St. Cloud near Paris in 1870. His father was a lawyer who had become an invalid, and his mother an English woman. When his father died in 1871, his mother was disconsolate, so that in truth he lost both parents.[1] Although he spent summers in France, he was raised in a house on Wimpole Street in London where his mother read the Bible and *The Pilgrim's Progress* to him. He was not much taken with the Old Testament. Raised a staunch Roman Catholic, his Wesleyan nurse nonetheless taught him Moody-Sankey hymns.[2] Although his mother lost their funds through the betrayal of a confidante, Belloc did attend the Oratory in Birmingham, which John Henry Newman (1801–1890) founded. He loved acting and did some study at College Stanislas in Paris before serving in the French army. After discharge, he went to England to study at Balliol College, Oxford, where he became known as an effective speaker, especially for his "fierce invective against the supporters of privilege."[3]

He became president of the Oxford Union, but after receiving first class honors, he was turned down for a fellowship at All Souls. His offense was probably his stubborn zeal for his faith. When Belloc took his examination, for example, he placed a statue of the Virgin Mary on the table. This zeal was more exterior than interior, however. During his school years, he drifted from his faith and began drinking heavily. His rejection at All Souls and five years' separation from the love of his heart, Elodie, of Napa, California, both contributed to a serious bout with mental illness. He now wrote his first book of poems and his first book of children's comic humor. He also found time and finances to travel to America and marry Elodie in 1896.

He emerged from this vexed time with new resolve for his Catholicism. He became even more militant and vociferous. At this time, Dean William Inge of St. Paul's (1860–1954)[4] accused him of being the only Englishman alive who believed Alfred Dreyfus to be guilty.[5] He did some lecturing on French and other literary topics but was advised not to even apply for an opening at the University of Glasgow because of his religion. He was by conviction a republican, an advocate of dissolving Britain's monarchy. This was an unusual position for a Catholic. He also avoided association with the most prominent Catholic literary figure of the day, historian John Emerich, Lord Acton (1834–1902), who led the liberal Catholic movement and denounced the development of papal as infallibility.

During this period, he seems more of a religious propagandist than a gifted writer. Belloc's mind-set was to put the church first and above all else. When asked how he could believe in the doctrine of transubstantiation, he replied: "I would believe the elements changed into an elephant if the church told me to do so."[6] He regularly pounced on H. G. Wells and George Bernard Shaw. He lamented the lack of religious fervor and the dearth of enthusiasm.[7]

A person of immense and undeniable erudition, Belloc was known for his "formidable controversial power," although his ability was diminished by a melancholy that deepened as the years went by.[8] He read little contemporary literature.

His artistic tastes ran to Wolfgang Amadeus Mozart (1756–1791) and the paint-ings of Albrecht Dürer (1471–1528).

A steady succession of splendid books, including *Danton and Robespierre,* his work on the French Revolution, and *The Path to Rome* confirmed him as a writer of stature in the literary establishment. He tended to be less popular with the average reader because he leaned on Latin-derived words and avoided what he regarded as more common (Anglo-Saxon-derived) expression. His style had descriptive and creative power. His prose extended far beyond pretty descrip-tions of a sunset; the reader could "feel" the sunset.[9]

Belloc's expressive ability stood him well in the early 1900s, when he plunged into Britain's rough-and-tumble political scene and served in Parliament from 1906 to 1910. Beyond his speaking ability, he had a striking appearance, some-thing like Chesterton along the lines of a walrus.

In 1914 his beloved wife died. He wore black and wrote on paper with a black edge thereafter. A son died in World War I. In later life, his major project was a four-volume *History of England.* Out of this massive output, I would recommend reading "The Mowing of a Field," a sparkling essay.[10] "Narbonne" and "Hattin" are examples of his travel essays. This is a popular and important subgenre of essay.[11]

---

1. Robert Speaight, *The Life of Hilaire Belloc* (New York: Farrar, Strauss, 1957), 9.
2. Ibid., 14. His mother had some Puritanism in her background and the nurse, Sarah Mew, also represented this.
3. Ibid., 86. Edward Caird the Hegelian philosopher from Glasgow succeeded Jowett; J. A. Froude also taught there.
4. Ibid., 121. Inge, called "the gloomy dean," was no mean essayist himself, cf. his *Lay Thoughts of a Dean* (Garden City: Doubleday, 1926). The first essay on "John Colet" is worth the price of the book. Inge's Bampton Lectures for 1899 on *Chris-tian Mysticism* (London: Methuen, 1899) are important.
5. Ibid., 153. Alfred Dreyfus (1859–1935) was a French army officer arrested in 1895 and convicted of treason in a controversial 1898 trial. His case became a popular cause, especially in the literary community, among those who believed Dreyfus had been framed because he was a Jew. The case was reopened in 1899, and it was dis-covered that the evidence against him was forged. He was restored to his rank in 1906. Freemasons and the Jews were favorite targets for Belloc's pen.
6. Ibid., 376.
7. Msgr. Ronald Knox had a great influence, but his convert's zeal in attacking pietists vitiated *Enthusiasm: A Chapter in the History of Religion* (Oxford: Oxford Univer-sity Press, 1950). Still, this volume is worth reading.
8. Ibid., 163. During times of deep depression, he wrote as slowly as three pages in six days.
9. His historical essays are considered some of his best. A good example is a study of statesman and cardinal Armand de Richelieu (1585–1642).
10. W. N. Roughhead, ed., *Hilaire Belloc* (London: Mercury, 1962), 83ff.
11. Ibid., 240, 273. Roughhead's anthology gives a rich sampling of the broad range of Belloc's work.

14.1.6 *MUGGERIDGE, ICONOCLAST CONVERT*

Contrary to what might be expected, I look back on experiences that at that time seemed especially desolating and painful. I now look back upon them with particular satisfaction. Indeed, I can say with complete truthfulness that everything I have learned in my seventy-five years in this world, everything that has truly enhanced and enlightened my existence, has been through affliction and not through happiness whether pursued or attained. In other words, I say this, if it were to be possible to eliminate affliction from our earthly existence by means of some drug or other medical mumbo-jumbo, the result would not be to make life more delectable, but to make it too banal and trivial to be endurable. This, of course, is what the cross signifies, and it is the cross, more than anything else, that has called me inexorably to Christ.
——Malcolm Muggeridge *(A Twentieth Century Testimony)*

When it was becoming painfully apparent that Enlightenment modernism was leading toward the demonization of the human race and the annihilation of the family, many did not know where to go. Malcolm Muggeridge (1903–1990) was reared in "this Sargasso Sea of fantasy and fraud." He had minimal exposure to "the Christian proposition," having been raised in a socialist setting in Croydon, London. One of five sons, Malcolm later saw "the vague Marxism" that threaded his earlier circumstances. His Dickensonian father gave his son a much-thumbed copy of *The Pilgrim's Progress,* and reading that classic made an impression on him.[1] A leftist activist, his mother was suspicious of societal standards of morality. On the other hand, the boy had a strong Christian teacher, Miss Lidiard, at the Tolstoyan colony school where he had early education. "When young Malcolm disparaged the Prophet Daniel, Miss Lidiard responded: 'If Daniel isn't true, nothing is.'"[2] While his atheistic father came from Quaker stock, his mother descended from a family tree filled with ministers. Through their modernism, the family had lost its faith or settled for the platitude that each person's purpose is to make the world a better place.[3]

As he relates in the first of two remarkable autobiographical pieces titled *Chronicles of Wasted Time,* Ruskin's socialism and Fabianism were his sacred texts, and he chose Darwin over Bunyan. When he went up to Cambridge, he had to be baptized and confirmed in the Church of England and pass an examination on William Paley's (1743–1805) *View of the Evidences of Christianity.* Here began his friendship with Alec Vidler, the Anglo-Catholic, and he was attracted to the New Testament.[4] It appeared to him that Jesus was God or nothing.

Muggeridge went to India to teach at Union Christian College in Travancore and here met the Mar Thomas Christians.[5] He met many evangelical missionaries in this adventure and actually heard Mohandas Gandhi (1869–1948) lead his favorite hymn, Newman's "Lead, Kindly Light."

He married Kitty Potter, daughter of a genial Irish Protestant and his wife, the sister of Fabian socialist Beatrice Webb.[6] Another sister was the mother of Richard Stafford Cripps (1889–1952), English statesman and air warfare minister through much of the Battle for Britain. This sister was a devotee of pyramidology.

Writing now a novel and a play, Muggeridge found a job with the *Manchester Guardian* and was assigned as Moscow correspondent. In Moscow, he became acquainted with the celebrated American journalist Alexander Woollcott (1887–1943).

In 1933 he spent some time working for the International Labor Organization in Geneva, Switzerland, but after that he hit bottom in his restless wanderings. He returned to Calcutta for a year where his infidelities and Kitty's almost destroyed their marriage. Kitty at this time had a child by another man.[7] Their strong conviction against abortion meant that they raised the child. During the war, Muggeridge served with the Ministry of Information in Lisbon, South Africa, and in other places. In Angola, he talked about Scripture with Plymouth Brethren missionaries,[8] but he was bereft. He had "no God to turn to, no Saviour to take my hand."[9]

At one point, the despairing Muggeridge determined to take his own life by drowning, but he found himself swimming to shore. After the war, he was correspondent of the *Daily Telegraph* in the States, editor of *Punch,* and a major force in the development of television programing for the British Broadcasting Company (BBC).

Not until the mid-1960s, when Malcolm and Kitty became grandparents, did Christ mean everything to Muggeridge.[10] Vidler and he traced the journeys of the apostle Paul in Asia Minor. The resulting book, *Paul, Envoy Extraordinary* (1972), was an important link in his commitment to Christ. He participated in the Festival of Light "antipornography campaign" in 1971. His *Jesus, the Man Who Lives* (1975) is a beautiful statement of his faith.[11] He had written a book and produced a film on Mother Teresa called *Something Beautiful for God,* and in 1972, she led him to seek admission to the Roman Catholic Church. He was elected Rector of the University of Edinburgh, but he resigned in 1973 because he was unwilling to back the liberal distribution of "pot and pills."

Read anything by Muggeridge, but especially his lectures at the University of Waterloo in Canada in 1978 called *The End of Christendom, but Not of Christ.*[12] In the throes of confusion and disillusion, Muggeridge wondered if there were another way. He found it, or rather, it found him.

----

1. Malcolm Muggeridge, *Chronicles of Wasted Time: The Green Stick,* I (New York: William Morrow, 1973), 31. Muggeridge's middle name is Thomas. His father named him after Thomas Carlyle.

2. Ibid., 41. Muggeridge describes his life during these years as "a part in search of a play."

3. Ibid., 55. He cites as a tame clergyman William Temple's statement often repeated: "Christianity is the most materialist of religions, and how the socialists loved it." He rather commends William Blake's response to those who made his New Jerusalem into a welfare state: "Dante made the same mistakes as Swedenborg in believing that 'in this world is the ultimate of heaven.' This is the most damnable falsehood of Satan and his Anti-Christ" (56).

4. Ibid., 82. Another very close friend in this time was the Rev. Wilfred Knox, brother of Ronald and son of the bishop.

5. Ibid., 107. He later filmed a provocative piece entitled *The Twilight of Empire.*

6. Beatrice Potter Webb (1858–1943) and her husband, Sidney James Webb (1859–1947),

were both economists and writers on social issues who provided an intellectual voice for English socialism. Many of their ideas were adopted by Britain over the course of the twentieth century.

7. Malcolm Muggeridge, *Chronicles of Wasted Time: The Infernal Grove*, II (New York: William Morrow, 1974), 36.

8. The Plymouth Brethren missionary enterprise in Angola is immortalized in T. Ernest Wilson's *Angola Beloved* (Neptune, N.J.: Loizeaux, 1965). See also, T. Ernest Wilson, *Mystery Doctrines of the New Testament: God's Sacred Secrets* (Neptune, N.J.: Loizeaux, 1975) for a feel of what those conversations must have included.

9. Muggeridge, *The Infernal Grove*, 182. He desperately needed a refuge at this time, and the "incestuous world of British socialism" ultimately had nothing to offer to give solace or sustain him. This is something his recent biographer, Richard Ingrams, *Muggeridge: The Biography* (San Francisco: Harper's, 1996) does not understand. Ingrams totally misreads the character of Muggeridge.

10. Malcolm Muggeridge, *Jesus: Rediscovered* (New York: Doubleday, 1969); see also Hugh T. Kerr and John M. Mulder, eds., *Conversions* (Grand Rapids: Eerdmans, 1983), 251ff.

11. New York: Harper, 1975.

12. Grand Rapids: Eerdmans, 1980. Muggeridge's style is rich and polished.

14.1.7 ADAMS, CULTIVATED COMMENTATOR

> I regard the universe as a preposterous fraud and human beings as fit only for feeding swine; but, when this preliminary understanding is once fully conceded, I see nothing in particular to prevent one from taking a kindly view of one's surroundings.
>
> —Henry Adams to one of his brothers

Henry Adams (1838–1918) is a fascinating and important figure with a basic pessimism and cynicism and an essential pragmatism. He was a fourth generation in that remarkable New England Adams dynasty that began with his great-grandfather, the second president, John Adams (1735–1826). Henry's grandfather was John Quincy Adams (1767–1848), the sixth president; and his father was the distinguished diplomat and statesman Charles Francis Adams (1807–1886).

Born in Boston and a graduate of Harvard, Adams traveled widely. Entries in various family diaries show that even his father, with all of his outward facade of respectability, had lived with a mistress.[1] He was private secretary to his father, U.S. ambassador to Britain during the American Civil War.

Henry Adams was not drawn to the family tradition of politics, but rather to teaching and to writing.[2] His two volume *The Education of Henry Adams* is a classic. Seemingly autobiographical, although written in the third person, it is high political and social commentary. His prose style is elegant and clear. Indeed, historian Arthur Schlesinger includes it in his list of the thirteen most important works that should be read by anyone who wants to understand the United States.

He edited the *North American Review* and taught history at Harvard. He wrote a nine-volume *History of the United States* on the administrations of Thomas

Jefferson and James Madison. He also wrote a charming study called *Mont-Saint-Michel and Chartres* about twelfth-century France. He probably chose this era to describe the kind of world in which he would have been better suited to live.[3]

His writings about himself often seem simpering and self-pitying, yet "the Adams iron" does appear. He was "often restless, deeply unhappy, and generally at odds with the world." He gives vent to these feelings in the two novels he wrote, *Democracy* and *Esther.* His immoral lifestyle became troubling to his family, but his liaisons seem symptomatic of what Henry James (1843–1916) called his friend's "melancholy outpourings" and "unmitigated blackness."[4] He had no spiritual heritage upon which to draw.

In 1872 he married Marian "Clover" Hooper, who quickly became estranged from the Adams family and showed symptoms of mental illness. Henry found her dead from a drug overdose.[5] The couple had no children. In *Education,* he makes no reference to this great sadness. Rather, he picks up the thread of his narrative after twenty years.[6]

The Adamses were New England Unitarians. John Quincy, whose hymn "Send Forth, O God, Thy Truth and Light" is still found in many of our hymnals, wrote to his son from St. Petersburg, Russia, about the importance of reading the Bible daily. He testified that he did so for an hour every day.[7] But of course, he had a low opinion of Jesus. A leading Unitarian minister in Boston, Theodore Parker (1810–1860), at about this time had caved in to German higher criticism. Parker's deistic transcendentalism argued that Christianity was in no sense dependent on the existence of Jesus Christ.[8] Young Henry was ten years old when he heard his grandfather's Christian virtues lauded at his funeral.[9]

Henry Adams himself was taught that "education is divine and man needed only a correct knowledge of facts to reach perfection." The clergy that the Adamses heard preach taught that, and they controlled society and Harvard. "They proclaimed as their merit that they insisted on no doctrine, but taught or tried to teach, the means of leading a virtuous, useful, unselfish life, which they held to be sufficient for salvation."[10] Young Henry was puzzled that this family was so quick to throw over their religion in later generations. In *Education,* he says: "The boy went to church twice every Sunday; he was taught to read his Bible, and he learned religious poetry by heart; he believed in a mild deism; he prayed; he went through all the forms; but neither to him nor to his brothers and sisters was religion real."[11]

The only family member with anything approaching a living faith seems to have been his grandmother, Louisa Catherine Adams. She found Christian faith the key to resolving the family tension between "futility and ambition."[12] She gave considerable attention to her skeptic grandson and sent him *The Vicar of Wakefield.*

In crisis, he did pray and sometimes wrote that he felt close to God. Yet he spoke of himself as a (theological) liberal.[13]

Contrast this spiritual descendent of Emersonian gnosticism with David Brainerd (1718–1747), who labored among the Native Indians: "I never got away from Jesus and Him crucified and I found that when my people were gripped by this great evangelical doctrine of Christ and Him crucified I had no need of giving them instructions about morality. I found that one followed as the sure and inevitable fruit of the other."

The Education of Henry Adams is a must for a modern Christian's education, if only for the evidence it shows that ego-centrism like that of the Unitarians never can replace pardon and forgiveness through the blood of the Lamb.

---

1. Aida Donald and David Donald, eds., *Diary of Charles Francis Adams,* II (Cambridge: Harvard, 1964). See the entry for April 24, 1827. At least he decided to conclude his "licentious intrigues" when he was about to marry.
2. Paul C. Nagel, *Descent from Glory: Four Generations of the Adams Family* (New York: Oxford, 1983). Great!
3. Granville Hicks, "A Man Against His Times," *Saturday Review,* 21 November 1964, 27.
4. Henry Adams, *The Education of Henry Adams,* II (Boston: Houghton Mifflin, 1918), 88.
5. Nagel, *Descent from Glory,* 280. Clover had a strong family history of depression.
6. Hicks, "A Man Against His Times," 28.
7. Quoted in "America's Christian Heritage," *Sword of the Lord,* 30 May 1997, 6.
8. John Fea, "Theodore Parker and the Nineteenth-Century Assault on Biblical Authority," *Michigan Theological Journal* 3 (1992): 65–80. The article also shows the dominance among Christians of the doctrine of the infallibility of Scripture at this time.
9. Edward Chalfant, *A Biography of Henry Adams,* 3 vols. (New York: Archon, 1982), 1.27–28.
10. Adams, *The Education of Henry Adams,* I, 35. The tidal wave from declining New England Congregationalism was to Unitarianism.
11. Ibid., 35.
12. Nagel, *Descent from Glory,* 341.
13. Chalfant, *A Biography of Henry Adams,* 108, 171, 402. Thus the spiritual declension of one generation has grievous consequences for those to come.

14.1.8 WHITE: CULTURAL COSMOPOLITE

You have been my friend. . . . That in itself is a tremendous thing. I wove my webs for you because I liked you. After all, what's a life, anyway? We're born, we live a little while, we die. A spider's life can't help being something of a mess, with all this trapping and catching flies. By helping you, perhaps I was trying to lift up my life a trifle. Heaven knows anyone's life can stand a little of that.

—E. B. White
Charlotte the spider to Wilbur the pig in *Charlotte's Web*

Columbia University philosopher and writer Irwin Edman (1896–1954) called him "the finest essayist in the United States." Elwyn Brooks White (1899–1985) was born in Mount Vernon, New York. He was the youngest child born to Samuel and Jessie White, who had lived most of their lives in Brooklyn. Samuel's success in the piano business allowed the move to Westchester County, though he had the ongoing worry of litigation by the company founder, who alleged that he had been cheated out of the business.[1] Samuel White was a teetotaler and an avid follower of the theologically liberal Henry Ward Beecher (1813–1887). For young White, the light of the gospel was the Enlightenment, which frees from superstition. With his parents, he attended church faithfully, and his father "prayed well out loud," but his father's conception of faith is clear when he writes to his son, "You have been born a Christian."[2]

But even as a child he "could feel heaven slipping." After much vacillation between Congregational and Baptist churches, his father stopped attending and spent his last years "in a miasma of melancholy doubt and died outside the church, groping and forlorn."[3]

Generally a fearful child, Andy, as his grandfather called him, enjoyed the family's August holidays in Maine more than he cared for school, although a poem on a mouse won his first literary prize in 1909. At an early age, he decided to keep a journal. He attended Cornell University, where the celebrated Dr. Andrew Dickson White's *A History of the Warfare of Science with Theology in Christendom* had ostensibly made mincemeat of biblical faith.

While at Cornell, E. B. White was editor in chief of the daily college newspaper. The student developed close relationships with English professor William Strunk and a Professor Adams, who encouraged him to try a career in journalism. Later White revised and enlarged Strunk's *The Elements of Style,* and it has been a standard reference for writers ever since.[4] His own added essay on "An Approach to Style" underscores the pristine clarity and conciseness of White's prose. Every serious communicator should read White for an appreciation of his insights into grammar and language.

Disinclined to teach, he restlessly floated about for some years, including a stint on the *Seattle Times.* He made a visit to Alaska. He visited Seattle's evangelical First Presbyterian Church but greatly disliked Mark Matthews, the dynamic Bible preacher.[5] He began his association with *The New Yorker* magazine, where he started writing "newsbreaks" or funny fillers. He wrote more than thirty thousand. His "Notes and Comments" under "Talk of the Town" became famous, and his association with the humorist writer and artist James Thurber (1894–1961) gave him access to the ideal illustrator for a book such as *Is Sex Necessary?*

This book, along with a long affair with a married staff member at the magazine, deeply troubled his parents. White then married Mrs. Katherine Angell, and they had one son. When the marriage developed problems, White prayed and even wrote about prayer to "the God I half believe in."[6] William Soskin called him "the perfect modern skeptic." On the Sunday Britain and France declared war on Germany in September 1939, a solemn E. B. White did a most unusual thing—he took his family to church.[7] Other than to attribute to his deceased dachshund a "massive dose of original sin,"[8] he takes sin no more seriously than does Henry David Thoreau. In 1943 he had another "nervous crack-up" and reflected in all of his writing his conclusion that "life is essentially inconsequential."[9]

He often felt uneasy about the unceasing levity of *The New Yorker* and the management's indisposition to interact with serious topics during the depths of the depression. Because of his frustration, he moved the family up to a farm in Maine. He also began to write for *Harper's* magazine. Over the war years, he would be more and more taken with the necessity of world government. In his first children's book, *Chicken Little,* Stuart argues for a King of the World as the answer to the human predicament of war.

White's children's fables are virtually peerless, and *Charlotte's Web* is especially remarkable. In the spider Charlotte's endeavor to save the pig Wilbur, we have "a fabric of memories" etched by White into the action. Clearly death and the fear of death are very serious subjects for him at this stage.[10] *The Trumpet of the Swan* is intensely autobiographical.

After he was recognized as one of the century's most gifted writers, White saw many books and essays to publication. His *The Second Tree from the Corner* and *Essays* collect his best.[11] Many have commented that White was "a prime noticer." His stepson remarked in an introduction to a new edition of some earlier pieces that White had written that White was a very private person and left out more than he included in a piece.[12] The prose of such a keen observer is refreshing to read.

Yet when Katherine died in 1977, there was no funeral as such, and he did not attend the graveside service. The sad fact about E. B. White and his brilliant accomplishments is that they are totally horizontal in perspective. He had long since dismissed any vertical dimension.

---

1. Samuel White gained control of Horace Waters and Co. through "an illegal but not fraudulent act." Finally the piano manufacturing business failed, which deepened an already existing depression in Samuel White.
2. Scott Elledge, *E. B. White: A Biography* (New York: W. W. Norton, 1984), 10.
3. Ibid., 5, 11.
4. William Strunk Jr., and E. B. White, *The Elements of Style* (New York: Macmillan, 1979), 66ff.
5. E. B. White, *Essays* (New York: Harper, 1977), 170. After reading a report of one of Matthews's sermons in the newspaper, White went the next Sunday but was turned off by "the smugness of his doctrine."
6. Elledge, *E. B. White,* 158. Katherine at one point lived in a separate house with her children.
7. Ibid., 222. The minister preached on "the meek shall inherit the earth," and they sang "Am I a Soldier of the Cross?"
8. Ibid., 260.
9. Ibid., 277. As an educated and alert observer, White knew the theological categories.
10. Ibid., 305. White's children's stories influenced the way all writers in the genre approach their craft. See Vigen Guroian, "Friends and Mentors: The Message of Children's Stories," *The Christian Century,* 3–10 June 1998, 574ff.
11. E. B. White, *The Second Tree from the Corner* (New York: Harper, 1935). This is a good anthology of shorter pieces. E. B. White, *Essays* (New York: Harper's, 1977).
12. Roger Angell, introduction to *One Man's Meat,* by E. B. White (Gardiner, Maine: Tilbury House, 1996).

14.1.9 ROGERS, COMMONER COMIC

A comedian is not supposed to be serious nor to know much. As long as
he is silly enough to get laughs, why, people let it go at that. But I claim
you have to have a serious streak in you, or you can't see the funny side
in the other fellow. Last Sunday night a young girl who had made a big
hit in the Salvation Army preaching on the Street in New York, decided
to go out and give religious lectures of her own. So on her first appearance I was asked by her to introduce her. She said she would rather have
me than a Preacher, or a Politician, or any one else. Well, I could understand being picked in preference to a politician, as that is one class us
comedians have it on for public respect, but to be chosen in preference
to a preacher was something new and novel.

—Will Rogers

It would not be an exaggeration to describe Will Rogers (1879–1935) as "the
most beloved person in his time" in the United States. Will was the youngest of
seven children on a ranch near Oologah in the Indian territory that was to become Oklahoma. His parents both had a Cherokee heritage. His father taught
him the lariat. His mother died when he was very young, and when his sisters
married and his father remarried and moved away, young Will was quite alone.

His father sent him to Scarritt Collegiate Institute, but he was asked to leave.
The same happened at Kemper Military Academy and even at a Presbyterian
mission school, even though he won several medals in elocution along the way.
He preferred ranching to school.

After working in the Texas Panhandle, he wandered into show business with
his roping routine, touring Argentina and South Africa. Back in the U.S., he became part of Texas Jack's Wild West Circus. After a trip to Australia, he appeared
for a summer with the Wild West Show at the St. Louis World's Fair (1904). He
appeared with the Apache chief Geronimo (1829–1909).[1]

Soon he was on the vaudeville circuit telling understated jokes as he twirled
his rope and did tricks. In 1909 he married Betty Blake, who was a stabilizing
influence in his restless life. He traveled constantly and joined the Zeigfeld Follies in 1915. Rogers remarked that among the Zeigfeld dancers he "often appeared
as a grinning puritan in a sea of pulchritude."[2] Next he tackled the movies, where
he had little success, and began writing books, where he did very well. His first
included such titles as *The Cowboy Philosopher on the Peace Conference* and
The Cowboy Philosopher on Prohibition. This was contagious humor mixed with
some rather serious social commentary.

Will Rogers was a skillful writer, and his weekly column was carried in 350
papers. He traveled Europe as Calvin Coolidge's "ambassador of good will."[3]
He paid high tribute to Coolidge (1872–1933), was close to Herbert Hoover
(1874–1964), and then developed a genuine friendship with Franklin Delano
Roosevelt (1882–1945). He loved politics and actually ran for the presidency
in 1928. Probably it was Theodore Roosevelt (1858–1919) who launched him
into political humor, but F. D. R. actually adopted some of Rogers's ideas as

part of his plan for America.[4] He traveled through Mexico with Charles Lindbergh (1902–1974).

Whether in his autobiography, which was essentially a compilation of his best columns, or in such books as *The Illiterate Digest* (1924) or *Letters of a Self-Made Diplomat to His President* (1927), we see how a man used good humor to great advantage. Rogers also knew how to incorporate serious communication into the situation of the moment.

Shortly before his untimely death in a plane crash with Wiley Post in Alaska, he remarked: "A fellow can't afford to die now with all this excitement going on."[5] It did seem Rogers had more to contribute, but it was a call he could not make. Historian Will Durant (1885–1981) asked him to participate with a raft of notables in articles that responded to the question: "What is your philosophy of life?" Durant was probing: "Where do you find your consolation and your happiness? Where is the last resort your treasure lies?"[6] His reply is sad:

So I cant tell this doggone Durant anything. What all of us know put together dont mean anything. Nothing dont mean anything. We are just here a spell and pass on. . . . There aint nothing to life but satisfaction. . . . Each one lives in spite of the previous one and not because of it. And dont have an ideal to work here. Thats like riding towards a Mirage of a lake. And when you get there it aint there. Believe in something for another World, but dont be too sure on what it is, and then you wont start out that life with a disappointment.[7]

Clearly there's a pretty good-sized vacuum here that fairly heavy alcohol consumption didn't fill. In general, he was very critical of firm religious beliefs; he conceded:

I was raised predominately a Methodist, but I have traveled so much, mixed with so many people in all parts of the world, I dont know now just what I am. I know I have never been a non-believer. But I can honestly tell you that I don't think that any one religion is the religion. . . . I am broadminded . . . which way you serve your God will never get one word of argument or condemnation out of me.[8]

He makes passing but slighting reference to the cross and to Easter. This is the American religion of congeniality, Emersonian religion without doctrines, pleasantness without a way to find pardon. Richard Ketchum admits that Rogers seldom attended church but argues that "he was a deeply religious man on his own terms."[9] He loved to take a drive Sunday morning thinking that "Folks are just as good as they ever were, and they mean well, but no minister can move 'em like a second-hand car."[10] This is gallows humor.

Given the importance of humor in communication, I also recommend Robert Benchley (1889–1945). Billy Altman's recent study, *The Life of Robert Benchley: Laughter's Gentle Soul*,[11] traces the life of this Worcester, Massachusetts, spoofer who was raised in the church but reacted to a Sunday school environment in which "lemon drops 'round us are falling." At Harvard, he wrote "My Defense of Heaven and Hell" and was a total abstainer from alcohol as a young man. Later drinking and womanizing were his undoing. Books such as *From Bed to Worse* (1934) and *Chips off the Old Benchley* (1949) are classic studies in humor. Those who preach might pick up insights on Benchley and others in John W. Drakeford, *Humor in Preaching.*[12]

1. Richard M. Ketchum, *Will Rogers: His Life and Times* (New York: American Heritage, 1973), 87ff.
2. Ibid., 146. His comments while swinging the lasso seemed inane but were really shrewdly designed for each audience.
3. Donald Day, ed., *The Autobiography of Will Rogers* (Boston: Houghton Mifflin, 1949), 200.
4. A newer work, which is superb in this area, is Ben Yagoda, *Will Rogers* (New York: Knopf, 1993).
5. Day, *The Autobiography of Will Rogers,* 387. He was an early enthusiast for aviation. Very well worthwhile is some reading and research into the lives of the Wright Brothers whose father was a United Brethren bishop.
6. Ibid., 247. The book Durant projected was published with telling contributions from many interesting people.
7. Ibid., 248. At the bottom line, Rogers was totally a pragmatist; he didn't have much of a worldview.
8. Ibid., 309.
9. Ketchum, *Will Rogers,* 313.
10. Ibid., 314.
11. New York: Norton, 1997.
12. Grand Rapids: Zondervan, 1986.

14.1.10 KIRK, CAREFUL CONSERVATIVE

> In the United States at this time liberalism is not only the dominant but even the sole intellectual tradition.
> —Lionel Trilling *(The Liberal Imagination)*

> If Christianity goes, the whole of our culture goes.
> —T. S. Eliot

In some circles, it did seem that post-World War II Christianity deserved the scorn that Lionel Trilling and others heaped upon it. Providentially, there arose after the war a large company of conservative writers who chose to speak to modern humankind's "disenchantment with disenchantment." At one end of the spectrum were such pagans as Mencken. Although he had cleverness, the meanness of his harangue against Jews, Christians, and blacks offered nothing to the increasingly deranged and dysfunctional culture. It is an interesting intellectual exercise to compare Mencken's three-volume autobiography, *The Days of H. L. L. Mencken* (1947),[1] with the charming autobiographical volume by Russell Kirk (1918–1994), *The Sword of Imagination* (1995).[2] Prolific, vigorous, incisive in thinking, broad in his reading, critical but not carping, Kirk proposed making "a radical revaluation of the entire Enlightenment project"[3] and drew around him an amazing band of compatriots.

The son of a railroad engineer, Kirk was born in Plymouth, Michigan. The Bible and *Pilgrim's Progress* were read in the home, but the family did not attend church often. The family background had tended toward Swedenborgianism and spiritualism. This persisted in Russell's claim to be "more mystical than metaphysical" and in his experience in the occult.[4] He claimed to have derived most of his religion from the nihilistic *Mysterious Stranger* by Mark Twain, which is more about Satan than anything else.[5]

Kirk attended Michigan State University from 1936 to 1940 and received his master's degree in history from Duke University. His thesis on John Randolph (1773–1833) ultimately became an important work on the early 1800s.[6] He spent time in the armed service on assignment in both Utah and Florida. During this time, his mother died, and he turned for comfort to the stoic philosophers.[7] After teaching for a time, he went to St. Andrews University in Scotland and was awarded the D.Litt. His dissertation was on Edmund Burke (1729–1797). His doctoral work eventuated in the best-selling *The Conservative Mind* (1953).[8]

He took a teaching position at Michigan State, where he and his ideas were not popular. He was passed over for a permanent academic appointment. He then began the frenetic set of occupations that would characterize his life. He lectured widely and was popular on the circuit as a master of repartee and debate. He edited periodicals and wrote a steady stream of political and philosophic critiques as well as several Gothic novels. At the same time, he was producing a widely syndicated newspaper column that became a conservative watchcry.

Six principles were the moorings that made Russell Kirk a spokesman for conservatism:

1. Kirk was "suspicion of the gospel of progress." Whatever his personal religion, he took sin seriously and poked holes in the particularly American "bootstrap" perfectionism and its Pelagian self-justification.
2. Dedicated to "the doctrine of the soul" and "permanent things," he fought to recover societal "norms" that transcended culture.
3. He believed ethical standards must be prescriptive, rather than merely describing the majority behavior. He took a strong stand against abortion.
4. He saw the absolute necessity for human beings to have reference to something that transcended the material universe.
5. His personal goal was to live a life of "decent independence" and to raise a healthy family within a monogamous union.
6. He maintained "a cheerful countenance" even in the heat of the "culture wars."

He was forty-six years old in 1964 when he married beautiful Annette who was half his age. They had a happy marriage and four daughters. He was baptized a Roman Catholic before his wedding, but this was not a mere expedient to clear the way for matrimony. He had begun struggling with theological issues and taking instruction in 1953.

Piety Hill, Russell's Mecosta County Michigan home, became a "Mecca" for such conservatives as William F. Buckley Jr.,[9] Malcolm and Kitty Muggeridge, and Richard Weaver.[10] Close friends included T. S. Eliot, Wyndham Lewis, Flannery O'Connor, R. A. Nisbet, and Crane Brinton of Harvard.

Blessed with almost perfect recall, he moved audiences around the world and engaged the best minds in his seminars on Piety Hill. A good sampling of some of his best lectures is found in *The Wise Men Know What Wicked Things Are Written on the Sky*.[11] As a Roman Catholic, Kirk remained true to his convictions, championing the conservative wing in its struggle against the new political and theological radicalism.[12] He spoke at the International Congress on the Family in Rome in 1983. He edited *The University Bookman* and continued to supply conservatives with stimulating and provocative literature. The range of his interest extended to the science fiction literature of Ray Bradbury.[13]

Evangelicals must realize that philosophic affinity with a social conservative (or social liberal) does not mean a fit. At his most enlightened, it isn't always possible to tell whether Kirk sees Christianity as anything more than a "religion." Ralph C. Wood, who penned a biographical essay and critique of Kirk's conservatism, shudders at Kirk's adulation of Spanish dictator Francisco Franco's (1892–1975) Valley of the Fallen.[14] Still, Russell Kirk and company are refreshing. What is at stake has been chillingly described by University of London philosopher C. E. M. Joad, who points out the characteristics of a decadent society: "luxury, skepticism, weariness, superstition, preoccupation with the self and its experience—a society promoted by and promoting the subjectivistic analysis of moral, aesthetic, metaphysical and theological judgments."[15]

---

1. A less verbose work is Mencken's *My Life as Author and Editor* (New York: Knopf, 1992). He was a truly "Nietzschean character."

2. Russell Kirk, *The Sword of Imagination: Memoirs of a Half-Century of Literary Conflict* (Grand Rapids: Eerdmans, 1995). The book is written in the third-person, which handles a kind of awkwardness (as was Henry Adam).

3. Ralph C. Wood, "Russell Kirk, Knight of Cheerful Conservatism," in *The Christian Century,* 23 October 1996, 1016.

4. Kirk, *The Sword of Imagination,* 15. Kirk was involved with Tarot reading for a while (267).

5. Ibid., 27. This is Twain at his dyspeptic worst, mocking morals and shaking a fist at heaven.

6. Russell Kirk, *John Randolph of Roanoke: A Study in American Politics* (Indianapolis: Liberty, 1951).

7. *The Sword of Imagination,* 69. He acknowledged that he did not have "a religious mind." He oddly affirmed the importance of the "fear of the Lord" (232).

8. Ibid., 109; Russell Kirk, *The Conservative Mind from Burke to Eliot* (Washington: Regnery, 1953).

9. William F. Buckley Jr.'s *God and Man at Yale* (Washington, D.C.: Regnery, 1951, 1986) is a classic Christian response to the late Enlightenment.

10. See Richard Weaver's *Ideas Have Consequences* (Chicago: University of Chicago, 1948) and his *The Ethics of Rhetoric*.

11. Washington: Regnery, 1987.

12. E. Michael Jones, *John Cardinal Kroll and the Cultural Revolution* (South Bend, Ind.: Fidelity, 1995).

13. Ray Bradbury used science fiction and fantasy writing techniques to probe social and human issues. He is best known for *The Martian Chronicles* (New York: Time Reading Program, 1946, 1963).

14. Wood, "Russell Kirk, Knight of Cheerful Conservatism," 1,020. Was Kirk blind to evil in the life of a fellow Catholic? See also *Enemies of the Permanent Things* (New Rochelle, N.Y.: Arlington, 1969); *Confessions of a Bohemian Tory* (New York: Fleet, 1963); *Edmund Burke: A Genius Reconsidered* (Peru, Ill.: Sugen, 1967, 1988). The Valley of the Fallen, west of Madrid, is a massive memorial to the Civil War dead. It is Franco's burial place.

15. Kirk, *The Sword of Imagination*, 471. Cf. *Eliot and His Age* (Peru, Ill.: Sugen, 1984).

CHAPTER FIFTEEN

Selecting the Best in the Daunting Array of Biography and Autobiography

Read no history, nothing but biography, for that is life without theory.
—Benjamin Disraeli

Although his statement is too sweeping, when the British prime minister and statesman Benjamin Disraeli (1804–1881) advises us to read biography rather than historical studies, he makes a point. Thomas Carlyle (1795–1881) posited a "great man" theory of history—not that the world's historical events are of lesser import, but rather that the truly relevant story of history is the story of its leaders and the people. One need not subscribe to that theory to appreciate the contributions of biographical studies to our understanding of the human experience. We should supplement good history with well-researched biography or autobiography (although the latter is sometimes better classified as fiction). As a preacher, I have looked to the biographical genre as a rich source of illustration.[1]

The difficulty with this kind of reading is that the choices are vast, and the good is not always easy to identify. I target one epoch to learn about each year, perhaps the American Civil War or England's Puritan Revolution. Then I read general surveys, supplemented by key biographies. This views the forest and the trees. We need the interpretive and structural outline to grasp what is transpiring and why.

Not all reading should be of the grand figures, lest we draw our impressions only from the elite. This chapter is more about examples than truly an overview of the genre, which would itself require a book-length treatment. This chapter will suggest starting points and good biographers. Because so many biographies will be covered, and not all are of equal merit, only select citations will be given. Most of the biographies are readily available in libraries or bookstores specializing in history.

---

1. As an example, I cite William Manchester's superb biography, *American Caesar: Douglas MacArthur* (New York: Dell, 1978). Manchester speaks to the puzzle of MacArthur's passivity after the attack on Pearl Harbor. He had expected the attack on the Philippines, and in the acute tension after the attack, MacArthur seemed unable to act. Manchester likens this to "computer overload" and sees parallels in Napoléon's "catatonic" state at Waterloo, or George Washington at Brandywine, or Stonewall Jackson at the Battle of White Oak Swamp (231). This phenomenon is possibly a form of "global amnesia."

15.1 LIVES WORTH READING ABOUT

15.1.1 SAINT-EXUPÉRY, AVIATOR

Lindbergh Flies Alone.—Alone? Is he alone at whose right side rides Courage, with Skill within the cockpit and Faith upon his left? Does solitude surround the brave when Adventure leads the way and Ambition reads the dials? Is there no company with him for whom the air is cleft by Daring and darkness is made light by Emprise? True, the fragile bodies of his weaker fellows do not weight down his plane; true, the fretful minds of weaker men are lacking from his cabin; but as his airship keeps her course he holds communion with those rarer spirits that inspire to intrepidity and by their sustaining potency give strength to arm, resource to mind, content to soul. Alone? With what other companions would that man fly to whom the choice is given?
—Editorial in the *New York Sun*

I begin with an almost unheard-of figure. Pioneering in creating a literature of aviation has not made Antoine de Saint-Exupéry (1900–1944) a household name. The more recent quality biography of this interesting man opens a number of doors for us.[1] He was born in Lyons, France, into a family of impoverished nobility. When his father died of a stroke, "Little Tonio" was but four years of age, and his mother had to depend on her in-laws. There was conflict between the boy and his strict grandfather.

From an early age, he was fascinated with airplanes. He invented what he called "the flying bicycle." When Wilbur Wright (1867–1912) made a series of demonstration flights in Europe, his shop at Le Mans beckoned to Antoine when he and his mother arrived there in 1909. He took his first plane ride at twelve in a plane designed and built by the Polish version of the Wright brothers, the

Wroblewski brothers, who were sons of the pioneering physicist of gases, Zygmunt Wroblewski (1845–1888). A mediocre student, he spent his student years in Paris in galleries and literary salons. At age fifteen, he was writing epic poems and at twenty-one entered the military. Serving in Morocco, he fell in love with the desert and earned his pilot's license.

His first marriage ended in divorce and despair. His wayward ex-wife later was mistress to André Malraux (1901–1976), the French man of letters. He wandered listlessly over France, working as a truck salesman and driver (most unsuccessfully) and doing some writing for *Le Navaire d'Argent*.

He flew mail planes, establishing mail routes over Northwest Africa and South America. Out of this experience came his novels *Southern Mail* (1933) and *Night Flight* (1932), about the pilot Riviere's exploits over the Andes. His memoir, *Wind, Sand and Stars* (1939) is a classic on exploration. It was voted the best nonfiction book in 1939 by the American Booksellers Association.[2] In 1940 Saint-Exupéry took his unhappy second wife and children to New York City for two years. There he wrote *Le Petit Prince (The Little Prince)*, which became a popular book of fantasy for children, but with a serious underlying message about life values. It has been translated into eighty languages, more than any other book in French history. It still sells 125,000 copies a year in the U.S. alone.[3]

When he could stay on the sidelines no longer after his country was overrun, he joined the Free French forces as a pilot. He was fearless and had already crashed once in Libya. When his unit was transferred to Corsica, the generals decided to ground him in 1944 because he was so absentminded. He pled for one more flight and took off on one more reconnaissance flight in his P-38. Armed only with his camera, he took off over the mountains of Corsica and across the sea toward occupied France. He was tracked over the French border, then disappeared forever.[4] His death has stimulated theories similar to those revolving around Amelia Earhart's South Pacific disappearance in 1937.

I recommend the biography and autobiographical *Wind, Sand and Stars*.

---

1. Stacy Schiff, *Saint-Exupéry* (New York: Knopf, 1994).
2. Antoine de Saint-Exupéry, *Wind, Sand and Stars* (New York: Harcourt Brace, 1939). He argues that "To be a man is to be responsible." I gleaned a favorite illustration from these passages. He tells of bringing some Bedouins from the Sahara to a waterfall in Switzerland and how they stood endlessly waiting for it to stop (96).
3. Helle Bering-Jensen, "Vive Antoine, le Petit Prince," *Insight,* 6 February 1995, 27. Children's stories do have a point and some carry a load of political and emotional baggage. The Grimm Brothers fairy tales are flagrantly anti-Semitic. Hans Christian Andersen's beautiful stories are replete with oblique references to his hang-ups.
4. Pierre Clostermann, introduction to *Wind, Sand and Stars,* xxii.

15.1.2 *CHURCHILL: LISPING STATESMAN-ORATOR*

Before he can inspire them with any emotion [a speaker] must be swayed by it himself. . . . Before he can move their tears, his own must flow. To convince them he must believe. . . . He who enjoys [an understanding of these things] wields a power more durable than that of a great king. He is an independent force in the world. Abandoned by his party, betrayed by his friends, stripped of his offices, whoever can command this power is still formidable.

—Winston Churchill (unpublished 1897 essay, written when he was a young cavalry officer in India)[1]

Indubitably the towering national and world leader of this century has been Winston Leonard Spencer Churchill (1874–1965). His stature as the greatest orator of modern times also commends him. Many readers of biography concentrate on an era such as World War II or even confine themselves quite narrowly as to the German general staff. Certain figures are so commanding as to merit study by anyone, regardless of their interest.[2] A huge body of literature has grown around Churchill, but the best overall is William Manchester's trilogy.[3]

Not all of the treatments are positive, such as John Charmley's *Churchill: The End of Glory,* which makes Neville Chamberlain, his sniveling predecessor, the real hero. Norman Rose's *Churchill: The Unruly Giant* faults "Winnie" for his ambition and inward assurance, a quality many leaders in the modern age have been embarrassed to own. Charmley feels Churchill should have negotiated a peace with Hitler in 1940 to save the British Empire. Others accuse him of racism and of being too generous to the Jews or of "declinology."[4] One scholar has argued that because of his fanatical hatred of Russia, Hitler sent Rudolf Hess (or someone people believed was Hess) to England to propose that British blood could be saved (and the Blitz ended) at the cost of Russian blood. In return, it is alleged, Hitler promised Churchill that Britain could have an opening in the Middle East. It is an interesting theory.[5]

Churchill was born to nobility in Blenheim Palace. His father, Randolph (1849–1895), was a Tory political leader and an incurable syphilitic; his mother, Jennie, was a beautiful American socialite. Winston spent a lonely childhood and then attended Harrow. He was not a good student, and his father thought him limited in intelligence. At Harrow, however, his great love for the English language began to flourish. As he later described it, "the essential structure of the English sentence" got into his bones. He graduated from the Royal War College at Sandhurst and went to Cuba as a journalist observer with the Spanish. He was a soldier in India and then fought in the Sudan. He covered the Boer War for a London newspaper, was captured, and escaped by scaling a wall and traveling three hundred miles to safety. He returned to England as a hero.

Churchill made up for his lack of a university education as a voracious reader. His speaking style and thought were particularly influenced by Edward Gibbon (1737–1794) and above all by T. B. Macaulay (1800–1859), the English writer and politician. A more painful influence throughout his life was a serious bipolar disorder. The "black dog" that he spoke of as his continual companion was a depression that ran through his family's history. This great orator also had a slight lisp that was most noticeable when he formed the letters "r" and "s."[6]

He was elected to Parliament when he was twenty-six years old. In 1904 he

bolted from the Tories to the Liberals. He had a seemingly insatiable lust for power,
even as he served as a junior minister in the Campbell-Bannerman government. In
1908 he married Clementine Hosier, who had been raised in France. They had a
very positive marriage, and she managed some of his adventurous impulses. Sadly,
three of their four children committed suicide, victims of the family illness.

As first lord of the admiralty, he gambled with fate in the naval bombardment
and subsequent bloody invasion in the Battle of Gallipoli (1915–16) in the
Dardanelles. When Britain finally had to evacuate their hard-won beachhead,
Churchill was dismissed in disgrace. One lesson from Churchill's life is that he
failed again and again, but he always came back resolutely. As minister of muni-
tions and then as colonial secretary, he was the vortex of Britain's mobilization
after the war and the protectorate policy in the Middle East. This policy had long-
lasting ramifications, such as the creation of the Transjordanian state.

In 1931 he was still regarded as "a brilliant failure," so his warnings of the danger of German belligerence were dismissed. In view of Edward's pro-German sympathies, it was fortunate that Churchill lost his battle to keep Edward VIII
(1894–1972) from abdicating. Because of his fear of Germany's intentions, Chamberlain (1869–1940), "the grim and the graceless," did not want Churchill in the
cabinet. Finally in the crisis of 1939, Chamberlain's hand was forced. Churchill
regained his seat as first lord of the admiralty, and in 1940, at sixty-six years of
age, he became Britain's prime minister.

Churchill's own literary output as a memoir writer and historian warrants attention. He was in a unique position to understand many of the events he covered. He produced a history of World War I and an extraordinary four-volume *A
History of the English-Speaking Peoples*. His six-volume history of World War
II, The Second World War, provides one of the great repositories of knowledge
on those years. To get the greatest advantage from these six volumes, one needs
to read them *ad seriatum*, starting with *The Gathering Storm*.[7] He received the
Nobel Prize for this achievement in 1953.

Churchill's defeat after the war, when he was seventy-one, understandably
brought on one of his worst bouts of depression, but he returned to power in 1951.
A series of strokes and illnesses were kept from the English people. He had a
massive stroke after the coronation of Elizabeth II and was forced to retire from
office in 1955. He withdrew from the House of Commons in 1964. His last speech,
shortly before his death, was the commencement address at Harrow. He could
scarcely rise to speak and then said: "Never, never, never give up." Then he sat
down. It was an amazing moment in the history of eloquent oratory. At his funeral, after the traditional "Taps," the bugler sounded the wake-up call "Reveille."
The moment was characteristically Churchillian.

He was always the agnostic, notwithstanding an unusually frank conversation with Billy Graham. He was frequently "hungover."

One study deals with Churchill's use of the bully pulpit. His speaking skills
have been well analyzed by James C. Hume. Here is a man who early on lisped
and stuttered and fainted out of fear in his first speaking opportunity. Axiomatic
to this master was the conviction that "people don't care how much you know
unless they know how much you care."[8]

1. Quoted in William Manchester, *Churchill, the Last Lion: Alone 1932–40,* 3 vols. (Boston: Little, Brown, 1988), 2.210.
2. One of my seminary professors, Dr. Wilbur M. Smith, challenged us to choose one New Testament book and one doctrine as special areas of concentration for our lifetime ministries. Then, he assured us, when we are fifty we might have something worthwhile to say. I chose Romans and Christ's atonement. I have benefited from this good advice.
3. The original edition was by Little, Brown. In 1989, Dell published *The Last Lion: Visions of Glory, 1874–1932; Alone, 1932–40* as Laurel trade paperbacks.
4. Andrew Roberts, *Eminent Churchillians* (New York: Simon and Schuster, 1995). The British philosopher, Isaiah Berlin, was closer to the mark when he paid tribute to Churchill who "saved our lives, and he alone."
5. Louis C. Kilzer, *Churchill's Deception: The Dark Secret That Destroyed Nazi Germany* (New York: Simon and Schuster, 1994). The evidence is striking. For twenty-eight years the family of Rudolf Hess (1894–1987) was not allowed to see him. It would appear that the man who died in Spandau Prison was not Hess.
6. John Pearson, *The Private Lives of Winston Churchill* (New York: Simon and Schuster, 1991).
7. Winston S. Churchill, *The Gathering Storm* (Boston: Houghton Mifflin, 1948). Subsequent volumes in The Second World War are: *Their Finest Hour, The Grand Alliance, The Hinge of Fate, Closing the Ring,* and *Triumph and Tragedy.*
8. James C. Hume, *The Sir Winston Method: Speaking the Language of Leadership* (New York: William Morrow, 1991).

15.1.3 DE GAULLE, LEADER AGAINST ODDS

History advances masked.

—Charles de Gaulle

He talks of Europe but means France.

—Harold MacMillan of de Gaulle

The feast of biography is endless. Avoid modern psycho-biography, with its flawed premises, as well as much "Christian biography," which glosses over truth in its hagiography. A model for what Christians should do as they write with candor about historical people from a historical viewpoint can be found in Elizabeth Elliot's *Who Shall Ascend?* on Kenneth Strachen.[1]

One of the most engrossing objects of biographers was a giant in height (six feet, four inches) and in leadership through conditions that few leaders could endure. His principles and high values stand in sharp contrast with the management style that usually passes for leadership. Charles-André Marie Joseph de Gaulle (1890–1970), like Churchill, is bigger than life. His two best biographers are Charles Williams for a one-volume work,[2] and Jean La Couture for a scintillating two-volume study.[3]

Known as "the man of the storms" or "the man of heavy weather," de Gaulle

wrote poetry, had a prodigious memory, and kept notebooks of quotes and apho-
risms. He was a master of the works of Victo Hugo (1802–1885). His motto
was: "Concise in style; precise in thought; decisive in life." He devoured the
works of the French Catholic theologian-philosopher Reguey and Henri-Louis
Bergson (1859–1941). He believed that his beloved France had an exceptional
and unique mission among the nations and saw his life in relation to that mission. He had a strong sense of objective in a time when many leaders floun-
dered in expediency.

De Gaulle was born in Lille, on the Belgian border. His father, Henri, a teacher,
was a veteran of the Franco-Prussian War. His mother's family traced its lineage
to the French knights defeated by the English in the Battle of Agincourt in 1415.
Lille was very Roman Catholic, very nationalistic, and very provincial. He was
raised in modest means with a sister and three brothers. His parents had two goals
for him: (1) to be a soldier and (2) to be a religious Roman Catholic.[4] He immersed himself in French military history as a boy and always took the side of
France when playing soldiers with his friends. His parents were devotees of Catholic monarchianism[5] and his father a strong supporter of Alfred Dreyfus.[6]

He studied with the Jesuits and served in the infantry.[7] He graduated from the
French Military Academy at St. Cyr. He was wounded four times in World War I,
was captured at Verdun, escaped, and was captured again. After the war, he served
in Poland with the French Army, taught at the École de Guerre in St. Cyr, and in
1920, married Yvonne Vendroux of Calais, with whom he would have a son and
two daughters. One daughter, to whom he was very close, Anne, was retarded
and died at the age of twenty in 1948.

France's grand old man, Marshal Philippe Pétain (1856–1951), considered him
his protégé and penman. Unfortunately, Pétain sank increasingly into wishful thinking about Europe's problems, until he ended his career treasonously as head of the
Nazi Vichy government.[8] De Gaulle was not an advocate of the fixed defense or
Maginot strategy. He pressed for heavy armor in his book *The Army of the Future*
(1934). He broke with Pétain over this issue.

Good biographers stress two very strong sides to de Gaulle's personality. On
the positive side, he was a man of authority who had expansive insight and vision. He was absolutely fearless as a risk taker. But even the very few who enjoyed close relationships with him conceded that, on the negative side, he was
arrogant, aloof, stubborn, shy, lonely, and proud.[9]

France waited too long to listen to his calls for upgrading the army's armored
divisions. When Hitler's panzer tanks and aircraft invaded in 1940, France was
virtually defenseless. He served in this doomed cause as a brigadier general and
was under-secretary of state for war. He left Bordeaux for England rather than
be party to the surrender. In England, he was considered a Don Quixote without
portfolio, but against all odds, he built the Free French Army.[10] He waged a one-
man defense of France: "I have only one aim: to set France free!" he exclaimed
in his abrupt but flowing eloquence.[11] The Americans never accepted de Gaulle
and constantly snubbed him, stupidly backing instead the Vichy sympathizer Henri
Giraud (1879–1949), who was organizing a French colonial force in North Africa.
De Gaulle succeeded as he continually "played every stroke with his medium or

long-range goals in view."[12] Dwight Eisenhower (1890–1969) was one key friend. His lapidary statements, great rhetoric echoing great Christian orators, were stirring![13]

He became the ruler of France in 1944 but left office after nineteen months to protest the trends toward socialism and petty politics. Twelve years later, he came back to lead, at sixty-seven years of age, a France on the very verge of civil war. He was elected in 1958 and again in 1965 as president. He faced the Algerian crisis, France's struggle to find a place in the nuclear age and in modern Europe. He remained a stout supporter of Israel until the 1967 "Six Day War," when it seemed the better decision for France was to cultivate relationships with the Arabs. His vision for France as a unique people—"sure of themselves and dominating"—was never obscured. When visiting French-speaking Quebec, he shouted *"Vive Québec libre"* ("Long-live free Quebec"). Such a politically charged statement sent out shock waves, for many *Québecois* were then demanding that Canada be partitioned to allow them their own national government. But it never seemed to trouble him. His health started failing in 1965, sapping his energy and effectiveness. He faced assassination attempts, the onslaughts of the left, and abandonment by his old Resistance cohorts.

He quit in 1968. His memoirs in three volumes, *The Call to Honor, Unity,* and *Salvation* are a significant legacy of his superb literary style.[14]

_____

1. New York: Harpers, 1968.
2. Charles Williams, *The Last Great Frenchman: A Life of General de Gaulle* (New York: John Wiley, 1994).
3. Jean La Couture, *De Gaulle: The Rebel, 1890–1944* (New York: Norton, 1990); and *De Gaulle: The Ruler, 1945–1970* (New York: Norton, 1991).
4. When early in his long career he renounced all for France, he held up his crucifix to his uncle: "Here is my Legion of Honor."
5. Monarchianism arose in the third century as an attempt to explain how God can be Father, Son, and Holy Spirit. Monarchian-type theologies teach either that God ceased being the Father when he became the Son and ceased being the Son when he became the Holy Spirit (modalism) or that Jesus was only a human being who was adopted to become the Son of God (adoptionism). Adoptionism has been a ubiquitous element of modernistic theologies and some modern Roman Catholic reasonings.
6. For details of the Dreyfus Affair, see 11.4.8, 14.5n.
7. Ernest John Knapton, *World Book Encyclopedia,* s.v., de Gaulle, Charles.
8. Herbert R. Lottman, *Pétain: Hero or Traitor* (New York: William Morrow, 1985).
9. La Couture, *De Gaulle: The Rebel,* 242. His self-assessment was that "I had to reach the heights and never come down."
10. Ibid., 267. Some referred to him as "Charles-all-alone," but leadership is lonely.
11. Ibid., 436. He studied language even during the war. When he visited the U.S. in July of 1944, he spoke English. He had a virtuosity with public relations.
12. Ibid., 449. He utterly refused to accept defeat. He is great to read on the lessons and hazards of history. Cf. Lottman, *Pétain: Hero or Traitor,* 282. Marshal Pétain admitted that he had "no firm determination to resist."

13. La Couture, *De Gaulle: The Rebel,* 434ff.
14. The De Gaulle memoirs are published in a one-volume translation, *The Memoirs of Charles de Gaulle* (New York: Simon and Schuster, 1964).

15.1.4 DISRAELI, PRIME MINISTER

Life is too short to be little.

—Benjamin Disraeli

Because of my interest in the Victorian pulpit, I have done some concentrated reading in the lives and experience of those who were roughly contemporary to Charles Spurgeon (1834–1892), H. P. Liddon (1829–1890), Joseph Parker (1830–1902), and Alexander Maclaren (1826–1910). Of course Queen Victoria (1819–1901) was a mover of the age, as was the devout William E. Gladstone (1809–1898), who was prime minister four times in the nineteenth century.[1] But equally important was Benjamin Disraeli (1804–1881), the Tory Party counterpart to Gladstone among the Liberals.

Disraeli was born in London the son of Sephardic Jews whose original roots were in Spain and then Venice, where the word *ghetto* was coined to identify the Jewish quarter. His father, Isaac, was an author with an immense library. Isaac had problems at the Spanish and Portuguese synagogue, largely because of his Voltairean ideas. In 1817 Isaac and his family departed the synagogue. A few months later, Benjamin was baptized into the Church of England. His parents never followed him in this step. His "conversion" was a matter of expediency, not faith. A friend persuaded Isaac that most opportunities in Britain were closed to those without Christian baptism.[2]

Young Benjamin was not physically sturdy, and like Churchill, he was prone to mood cycles. He attended a Unitarian school, where he had to learn to fight in order to defend himself. Because of these persecutions, he never went to the university. His father warned him: "Beware of endeavoring to become a great man in a hurry, my boy."[3] He tried business and the law, and wrote rakish novels in the hope of getting rich. The books were read, but Disraeli was thoroughly depressed. As a writer, Disraeli became a close friend of the novelist Edward Bulwer-Lytton (1803–1873).

He turned to politics and, after several attempts, was elected to Parliament in 1837. His beginning as an M.P. were less than auspicious. He overdressed and sat down embarrassed after his maiden speech. Disraeli became the orator of the Tory Party. He alone in his party spoke for the "Jew Bill" of 1848, which would have allowed Jews the right to be seated in Parliament, even if they had not been baptized as he had. An advocate of high tariffs, Disraeli served as Chancellor of the Exchequer four times.

Sadly, anti-Semitism was always lurking. One historian described him as "the loathsome Jew," and German's Chancellor Bismarck wrote of *"der alte Jude."* Henry James dismissed him as "the tawdry old Jew," and Lytton Strachey shunned him as that "absurd Jew boy." He visited Palestine and experienced a rebirth of identification with his Jewishness to the extent that he favored the establishment of a Jewish homeland in Palestine. Consistently in his novels (such as *Tancred*), he echoes the Jewish longing for their land, their temple, their "holy creed," and their simple manners and "ancient customs." Young Henry Stanley (1841–1904) remembered Disraeli's "great earnestness about restoring the Jews to their own land."[4] Perhaps his desire to give people a place influenced him to give great assistance to Judah Benjamin, the distinguished Jewish financier of the Confederate States in the American Civil War.

Always a lady's man, in 1839 Disraeli married Catherine Lewis, the wealthy widow of a fellow member of Parliament. Before she died of cancer in 1872, she wrote: "Dizzy married me for my money, but if he had the chance again he would marry me for love." On their wedding day, they read the Bible together, and he declared, "This daily practice, I trust, will last as long as our joint lives."[5] Although the Disraeli marriage was very happy, it never had the spiritual roots in which the Gladstones thrived.

Disraeli was Queen Victoria's darling "Dizzy," and she much preferred him to the unctuous Gladstone. She said that when Gladstone spoke to her it was as if he were addressing the House of Commons. This partiality was important to Disraeli in the frequent times when he was beaten down politically by his nemesis Gladstone. He advised a young preacher who was to speak before the Queen: If you preach thirty minutes she will be bored; if you preach fifteen minutes she will be pleased; if you preach ten minutes she will be delighted. The young preacher asked what he could say in only ten minutes. Disraeli responded: "That will be a matter of indifference to her Majesty."[6]

He led the first comprehensive social reform act in Britain to victory in 1867. Championing the poor at home, Disraeli was pointman for the Empire abroad, obtaining British control for the Suez Canal and the title "Empress of India" for his Queen. Gladstone was to have the last word. Disraeli chose not to be buried in Westminster but beside his dear wife in the little churchyard. The inscription on the marble reads:

> To the dear and honored memory of Benjamin Earl of Beaconsfield.
> This memorial is placed by his grateful sovereign and friend, Victoria, R. I.
> "Kings love him that speaketh right." Proverbs XVI. 13

1. Roy Jenkins, *Gladstone: A Biography* (New York: Random House, 1996); see also David W. Bebbington, *William Ewart Gladstone: Faith and Politics in Victorian Britain* (Grand Rapids: Eerdmans, 1993).
2. André Maurois, *Disraeli* (New York: D. Appleton, 1928), 14f. Maurois was a French Jew who wrote many books. He was born Émile Herzog in 1885 and, like Disraeli, was baptized into the National Church.
3. Ibid., 23.
4. Stanley Weintraub, *Disraeli* (New York: Truman Tally/Dutton, 1993), 112, 301. Regarding the Zionism that was developing at mid-century, see David L. Larsen, *Jews, Gentiles*

and the Church (Grand Rapids: Discovery House, 1995), 69, 334. Benjamin Jowett wrote to Florence Nightingale: "The nation is being run by a wandering Jew." Though there was strong interest in a Jewish homeland, the Ottoman Turks resisted it. Disraeli said: "A race that persists in celebrating their vintage, although they have no fruits to gather, will regain their vineyards" (Weintraub, *Disraeli,* 266). Weintraub's is a 1990s biography and so more in tune to research into Disraeli's context. Maurois, however, remains the insightful and elegant biographer who is more in tune with the man.

5. Maurois, *Disraeli,* xx, 138.

6. Ibid., 246.

15.1.5 MONTGOMERY, PLANNER

Uninformed criticism is valueless. Although information may be lacking or incomplete, the Commander must still make a plan and begin early to force his will on the enemy. . . . If he has no plan he will find that he is being made to conform gradually to the enemies' plan.

—Bernard Law Montgomery

Because the Christian life is a battle, warfare analogies to military engagement are especially useful to a preacher. I have tended to concentrate on generals in the American Civil War on both sides. But having lived through World War II, I also am intrigued by the Allied and Axis commanders. Head and shoulders above any other British military figure in his time was Field Marshal Viscount Bernard Law Montgomery (1887–1976), the hero of El Alamein. Called by some "the people's general" and recognized as one of the great military orators of all time, he is a strange and often bewildering complex of conflicting passions.

Bernard was born in London into an old Ulster family. His father was a minister in the Church of England and later Bishop of Tasmania. Henry Montgomery was totally immersed in his calling and isolated from his large family. Nigel Hamilton's superb two-volume biography analyzes in depth his mother, Maud, who was the daughter of the distinguished Victorian preacher F. W. Farrar, Rector of St. Margaret's, Westminster.[1] Farrar's influence helps explain the spirituality that was the foundation for Montgomery's life. She was a hard woman, who had stormy relationships with her children, including "Monty," her fourth.[2] Bernard was never close to his father, but he honored him and came to be much like him.

Bernard was an awkward youth and not a good student. In 1908 he went to India to serve with the forces and fought with honor in World War I. Nigel Hamilton, in his volume on Monty's pre-World War II years, said that, serving in Ireland after the war, there was "evidence of a distinct leap in Bernard Montgomery's stature and sagacity."[3] He began to think clearly on tactical and strategic issues. He had a good friendship with the eminent military historian Basil Liddell Hart (1895–1970). He became an instructor at the War College and eventually married a widow with two teenage children when he was forty years old. His marriage to Betty Carver was immensely satisfying, and they had a son, David.

A fascinating aspect for Christians is the journey of faith in the life of Montgomery. He had an agnostic phase, rejecting the faith of his parents and the very idea of the church. In the jubilation of marriage and parenthood and assignments in Palestine, Egypt, and India, Montgomery returned to the faith with vigor in his forties. This spiritual dimension was a great asset in the hard war years. He assumed that "proper religious truth" was essential to strong leadership.[4] He was a morale-builder. He visited his units. He was a man of character, who could be counted on. He openly confessed his beliefs.[5]

Betty's tragic death in 1937 shattered him, but it did not shake his faith. As a single parent, Montgomery became almost destructively possessive of David, the child of his marriage. He had a physical collapse while he was on duty in the Middle East, but he walked off "fit-as-a-fiddle" in what seemed to doctors a miraculous recovery. He never touched alcohol or tobacco again.[6]

As war loomed, military planners recognized Montgomery's genius—but they wondered if he was also mad. His answer came in managing what seemed an impossible withdrawal from Dunkirk that saved Britain from destruction. He took charge of preparing Southeast England for impending invasion. He lived in considerable tension with his staff and superiors, but Churchill took a liking to him. He was flexible to meet changing conditions, he was uncanny at choosing the right staff, and he radiated confidence. This Churchill wanted for North Africa, where the brilliant German field marshal Erwin Rommel (1891–1944) threatened Alexandria and Cairo.[7]

When Montgomery took command in the desert in 1942, his impact was "electric" among the troops. He inspired his force for the great battle against a superior force. He was called "the Oracle" by his men because he seemed to know every person by his name.[8] He stirred his men with an address he gave to his units at every opportunity. Its main point was simple: NO RETREAT!

Churchill pressed for immediate action, but Monty determined to prepare thoroughly. When the critical Allied offensive began, Rommel cracked, "The swine is attacking." But he didn't realize that the 8th Army Corps had been transformed. When he did see what was happening, Rommel hastily returned from Germany to take command, but it was too late. The Allied victory at the Battle of El Alamein was the turning point in the war. Monty went on to the invasion of France and helped forge the multinational coalition that drove toward Berlin.[9]

After the war, he commanded the British occupation zone and went on to lead in the European Union and North Atlantic Treaty Organization (NATO). An intricate interweave of personal and public issues in the life of a spiritual man overcame opposition and personal odds to make a difference.

---

1. David L. Larsen, *The Company of the Preachers* (Grand Rapids: Kregel, 1998), 10.6.8.
2. Nigel Hamilton, *Monty: The Making of a General, 1887–1942* (New York: McGraw-Hill, 1981), 37.
3. Ibid., 176. He became known by his colleagues for his "uncompromising iron character," but he learned to choose with care the issues on which compromise was necessary.
4. Ibid., 245. Nigel Hamilton, *Monty: The Making of a General II* (New York: McGraw-Hill, 1981), 570, 618.

5. In a written testimony, Montgomery affords significant insights. He read *When It Was Dark* by Guy Thorne. This centered his thought on the divinity of Jesus. He confessed the resurrection and ascension. He shared his new conviction with his wife, and they bowed their knees in prayer each night. See Field Marshal, Lord Montgomery, "A Personal Testimony" *Prophetic Witness,* November 1983, 11.

6. Hamilton, *Monty: The Making of a General,* 341. What was diagnosed as tuberculosis suddenly disappeared and never recurred.

7. Hamilton, *Monty,* vol. 2, 649. Rommel lost the initiative in North Africa and the result was disastrous. My favorite book on Rommel is David Irving's *The Trail of the Fox* (New York: Avon, 1977). Irving is prejudiced against Montgomery, as have been most Americans. See also David Fraser, *A Knight's Cross: A Life of Field Marshal Erwin Rommel* (New York: Harper/Collins, 1993). General Rommel was not a spiritual man, but his son, Manfred, for many years mayor of Stuttgart, was a confessing Christian.

8. Hamilton, *Monty,* vol. 2, 791. His motto was "Strength through concentration and mobility."

9. Alistair Horne with David Montgomery, *Monty: The Lonely Leader 1944–45* (New York: Harper Collins, 1994). Horne shows how Montgomery "achieved victory with inexperienced American forces, exhausted British ones and flawed armor."

15.1.6 WILSON, DREAMER

> I cannot refrain from saying it: I am not one of those who have the least anxiety about the triumph of the principles I have stood for. I have seen fools resist Providence before and I have seen their destruction, as will come upon these again—utter destruction and contempt. That we shall prevail is as sure as that God reigns.
>
> —Woodrow Wilson in his last public address

An exercise is to read a solid biography of every major leader of your nation. For those in the United States, of course, that covers a great many American presidents, and I have tried to read at least one major biography on each. One of my favorites was the twenty-eighth, Thomas Woodrow Wilson (1856–1924). Wilson was one of the most gifted, insightful, and able men who ever held that office.

Like James Madison (1751–1836) he was associated with Princeton University and Seminary. Unfortunately, the Princeton of Wilson's day was a far different institution than it is today, as it is increasingly infected with modernism. Wilson was naive about theological nuances, so he lent his allegiance as an influential layman and administrator to those who were pulling the churches from their moorings.[1]

Wilson was born in Staunton, Virginia, the son, grandson, and nephew of Presbyterian ministers. His mother was the daughter of a Scottish immigrant pastor. His father served as pastor in Augusta, Georgia, and as a professor at Columbia Theological Seminary until he was dismissed from his position as Professor of Theology and Rhetoric because of his Darwinian inclination. Young

Wilson professed conversion in 1873 and, throughout his life, read his Bible daily and prayed. He retained an aversion to working on Sunday.

With Professor Arthur Link's volumes in the Princeton Wilson project, we have an incredible resource for understanding Wilson, although the studies tend to be hagiographic. The single best volume on Wilson, in my view, is August Hechscher's splendid study, which is particularly rich on the early life of Wilson.[2] He describes vividly Wilson's first year of study at Davidson College in the south and then on to Princeton and graduation under the spell of Dr. James McCosh, who was much like the Parliamentary paragons in England whom Wilson admired like Edmund Burke (1729–1797), John Bright the Quaker (1811–1889), and William Pitt (1708–1778).

Wilson's great hero was Gladstone. He studied law at the University of Virginia and practiced briefly but turned aside from it.[3] Now his goal was the Ph.D. at Johns Hopkins University, where his dissertation was his book *Congressional Government: A Study in American Politics*. This book published in 1885 is considered the best of the many Wilson wrote. He had a massive intellect and strong Presbyterian faith, although it was somewhat tinctured with Ralph Waldo Emerson (1803–1882). He taught history at Bryn Mar, then taught and successfully coached football at Connecticut Wesleyan. He was married to Ellen Louise Axson, the daughter of a Presbyterian minister in 1885. They had three daughters.

In 1890 Wilson went to Princeton as Professor of Jurisprudence and Political Economy and ultimately became a reform-minded Princeton president in 1902. This intense visionary suffered a stroke in 1896 that left his right hand impaired. Wilson lost the vision in his left eye because of hypertension.

Biographers describe a "complex dualism" (Hechscher) in Wilson. He was "the Presbyterian priest," with ideals and a lofty morality. Yet he had affairs, as with the socialite Mary Hulbert Peck. He was called "Peck's bad boy" in Washington society circles.[4] Wilson was defeated in his aspirations for Princeton. He was too far ahead of the pack. He went on to become governor of New Jersey and then quite unexpectedly was elected President of the United States when William Jennings Bryan stepped back in the Democrat Party and Theodore Roosevelt and William Howard Taft split the Republican vote.

His two terms embraced America up to, during, and after the war. He had an ambitious agenda both domestically and internationally, which was to a great degree shaped by romantic idealism. His Fourteen Points for the world grew from two centuries of Western belief in evolutionary social progress.[5] French prime minister Georges Clemenceau cracked that God had required only ten commandments.

Wilson was the first American president to leave the country (for the signing of the Armistice ending the war). His vision involved him in many significant bits of history. On March 2, 1919, he met with a delegation of Zionists led by Rabbi Stephen S. Wise, then issued a statement affirming the Balfour Declaration and giving formal U.S. support to the idea that "in Palestine shall be laid the foundations of a Jewish Commonwealth."[6]

Wilson's last years saw the increasing physical debility. His last great crusade—for U.S. participation in the League of Nations—foundered. He had a penchant for irritating the Congress and, like many exceedingly brilliant people, probably lost touch with the common man.[7] He collapsed on a Western trip, and his wife helped him sign documents, and his cabinet met without him from that point on. In 1920 he received the Nobel Peace Prize.

Although beleaguered and battered, he never gave up his optimistic outlook. Something of his childhood faith continued to resonate and gave him calm and composure in the face of huge disappointments. Biographers past and present will find in Wilson a window into the foundations of the twentieth century.

With all of the perils and pitfalls of autobiography, one can obtain remarkable insights from what a writer chooses to cover or omit. I recommend, for instance, Nelson Mandela's *Long Walk to Freedom: Nelson Mandela*[8] as an important statement. Mandela (b. 1918) relates how his mother became a Christian and how he was baptized into the Methodist or Wesleyan faith. He speaks positively about the mission schools and how he himself taught Bible classes. His colleague Albert Luthuli was the son of a Seventh-Day Adventist missionary. He and his first wife sent their children to an Adventist School. When Mandela's first wife, Evelyn, became a Jehovah's Witness, they were divorced, and he married Winnie (1958). The story of his detention and twenty-seven-year imprisonment are gripping. P. W. Botha also read the Bible, he is amazed to relate. Many well-known Christian names are mentioned from Mandela's fascinating perspective.

---

1. William Lee Miller, *James Madison: The Business of May Next and the Founding* (Charlottesville: University of Virginia Press, 1992). Shows how Madison derived his political ideas from New Light Presbyterians at Princeton. The New Light controversy split American Calvinists in the era of the First Awakening. That division mostly was healed by 1790, but its implications were horrendous. Most Old Lights drifted into the rationalism of deism, Unitarianism, and Hegelianism, setting the stage for Continental higher criticism. A "conventional American Protestant," Wilson had little interest in theology, and so was used by others. John Milton Cooper Jr., *The Warrior and the Priest: Woodrow Wilson and Theodore Roosevelt* (Cambridge: Belknap, 1983), 19.
2. August Hechscher, *Woodrow Wilson* (New York: Charles Scribner's, 1991). The author is the president of the Woodrow Wilson Foundation. He does not indulge in psychobiography. His is not as gripping a description of Wilson's presidency as are some other biographies.
3. Cooper, *The Warrior and the Priest,* 45. This dual biography technique is rarely used well. This example is quite good.
4. Ibid., 57.
5. John Morton Blum, *Woodrow Wilson and the Politics of Morality* (Boston: Little, Brown, 1956), 7. Jan Willem Schulte Nordholt, *Woodrow Wilson: A Life for World Peace* (Berkeley: University of California, 1991).
6. Hechscher, 540. These sentiments were expressed in a letter from Wilson to Rabbi Wise.
7. Gene Smith, *When the Cheering Stopped: The Last Years of Woodrow Wilson* (New York: William Morrow, 1964).
8. Boston: Little, Brown, 1994.

15.1.7 John Paul II, Conservator

> I prefer to speak ungrammatically and be understood by the people, rather than appear learned and not to be understood.
>
> —Augustine

With 900 million adherents, the Catholic Church was no longer a megalith at the end of the twentieth century; its institutions and theological streams still were in ferment from Vatican Council II. The steadying hand who guided the Catholics through these seas was a Polish churchman, Karol Wojtyla, who took the name John Paul II at his election in 1978. He was a scholar, a gifted communicator, and conservative to the extent of stirring controversy. The pontificate of John Paul II was an extension of the man's Polish heritage.

An excellent study by Tad Szulc shows how this gifted archbishop of Kracow won admirers through his prayerful and charming ways. His steadfast convictions also baited critics.[1] Szulc well presents the man and his background. David Willey is stronger in interpreting the years of John Paul's pontificate and his unmatched record for itineration.[2]

Wojtyla is a biographer's dream. Not only a world-class leader who greatly extended the prestige of the Roman Church after the hard days of activistic clergy and widely divergent theologies, Wojtyla was a man of intellectual and moral stature and even heroism.

A bent toward mysticism was shown in his doctoral dissertation on John of the Cross (1542–1591). He was professor of ethics at the University of Lublin and lived under both Nazi and Marxist regimes. The KGB attempted to assassinate him in 1981 to keep his political activism from infecting Eastern Bloc Catholics. John Paul played a role in the Solidarity Movement, the labor movement that changed Poland and spread through Eastern Europe.

Once an organizer of classes and lectures and study groups and ski and hiking trips, John Paul was sensitive to social change and the economic morass in the third world. He took a strong prolife stance and was unmoved by tremendous pressure to allow the ordination of women priests. He saw the peril of liberation theology, which Paul VI had encouraged.[3] He guided advances in Africa and Asia and even such unlikely lands as Sweden and Iceland. He expressed concern about the environment and the HIV crisis. His ethnicism also placed him among conservatives who practice devotions to Mary. He had an almost fanatical loyalty to the Black Virgin in Poland and believed the Virgin had saved him at Fatima.

Such a strong and theologically conservative personality was critical to the Catholic Church in the face of declining numbers of clergy and doctrinal erosion in the orders (particularly the Society of Jesus).[4] The West was on a slippery-slope decline in spirituality, paralleled by a decline in confessions and the proliferation of "cafeteria Catholics," who believed however much they liked.

Some have described him as intransigent because of the early loss of his mother, brother, and father, and his grueling labor as a young man. Reading of key biographies affords us invaluable insights into the doctrinal trails and travesties of significant persons like John Paul II.

1. Tad Szulc, *Pope John Paul II: The Biography* (New York: Scribner's, 1995). John Paul also was an actor as a young man.
2. David Willey, *God's Politician: Pope John Paul II, the Catholic Church and the New World Order* (New York: St. Martin's, 1992). John Paul was Pope long enough to appoint a new generation of orthodox conservatives to episcopal office.
3. Michael Novak, *Will It Liberate? Questions About Liberation Theology* (New York: Paulist, 1986). One of the best descriptions of liberation theology from a Roman Catholic perspective.
4. Malachi Martin, *The Jesuits: The Society of Jesus and the Betrayal of the Roman Catholic Church* (New York: Simon and Schuster, 1987). Martin goes right at "the new unbelief" and the repudiation of doctrine and preaching. He shows the apostasy John Paul faced and what he attempted to do about it.

15.1.8 MERTON, WANDERER

And now for the first time in my life I began to find something of Who this Person was that men called Christ. It was obscure, but it was a true knowledge of Him, in some sense truer than I knew and truer than I would admit. It was in Rome that my conception of Christ was formed. It was there I first saw Him, whom I now serve as my God and my King and Who owns and rules my life. . . . It is the Christ of the Apocalypse, the Christ of the Martyrs, the Christ of the Fathers. It is the Christ of St. John, and of St. Paul, and of St. Augustine and St. Jerome and all the Fathers— and of the Desert Fathers. It is Christ God, Christ King.

—Thomas Merton

If such writers as Fëdor Dostoevsky, Graham Greene, and Walker Percy have been suspected of harboring multiple personality disorder, no modern was ever a likelier candidate than Thomas Merton (1915–1968), the brillian Bohemian.[1] Of his several dozen books and the 3,500 large pages of his journal now being published, his 1948 autobiographical *Seven Story Mountain* is the book to read. Its publication stirred virtually a cult following for Merton. Anne Carr calls him "the quintessentially restless American" who was interested in spirituality but not religion, contemplation and mysticism but not the organized church.[2] His writing style is clear and thought provoking. At the end of the twentieth century this volume was still in print and widely read by Catholics and Protestants.

Merton was born in France, one of two boys born to expatriate artists. His father was from New Zealand from a staunch Church of England background.[3] His mother was a sometime attendee at a Quaker meeting and was American Baptist in upbringing, but she lacked interest in spirituality. Her mother's solace had become the Christian Science of Mary Baker Glover Patterson Eddy (1821–1910).

After the death of his mother from cancer in 1921, Thomas traveled to the U.S. and other countries with his father. The works of poet and fiction writer John Masefield (1878–1967) were shared in the family on these trips; their religion was basically the movies. The outlook boiled down to human beings lifting themselves up to God.[4] Merton attended Cambridge University, where he was exposed to the Unitarianism of Dr. Hering, a professor of theology.

Profoundly confused, he wanted to find out who Christ indeed is and had what he called a "semi-conversion" to Christianity. While he did not believe in hell, he continued to read the Bible.[5] Gerard Manley Hopkins (1844–1889) and Dante (1265–1321) were of great interest. He moved to New York and there became a convert to communism. The easy religion of getting rid of capitalism as the solution to the earth's problems was his cup of tea. At Columbia University, imbibing Daniel Defoe (1660–1731), Jonathan Swift (1667–1745), and T. S. Eliot (1888–1965), he "indulged his appetites in the world." He drank and smoked heavily and led a sexually loose lifestyle. In one of his several affairs, he fathered a child, an element of his life the Roman Catholic censor would not allow him to chronicle in his autobiography.[6]

When his grandfather died, he turned to prayer and divine grace (although this grace was strangely lacking in the cross).[7] He became interested in medieval philosophy, particularly the writings of John of the Cross.[8] The Episcopalian minister didn't really believe much and wanted to talk about literature and politics, not theology and God.[9] He was enamored with Julian Huxley's (1887–1975) mystical evolutionary vision. His master's thesis at Columbia was on the artist mystic William Blake (1757–1827). He was drawn more and more to the Roman Church. "I wanted to know about doctrine, about what to believe."[10]

After converting, he struggled with vocation but finally entered the Trappist Abbey of Gethsemane in rural Kentucky. His writings drew hundreds into this Cistercian order, but he fought with the abbot, Dom James Fox. In the 1960s, he almost came to disaster when he was hospitalized for back surgery and fell in love with a young student nurse.[11]

As a Trappist, he wrote poetry and novels and cultivated such friends as the Nicaraguan leftist Ernesto Cardenal. He came increasingly to feel that the United States and the Soviet Union were morally equivalent. He wrote many best-selling books but more and more became controlled by unresolved anger. He applauded such radicals as the socialist philosopher Herbert Marcuse (1898–1979). He drifted into a fascination with Eastern religion, particularly Zen Buddhism.[12] While on a Southeast Asian trip related to this interest, he died in a freak accident when he was electrocuted by an electric fan.

The extraordinary influence of Merton's writings is at least partly because he personifies the pluralism so valued in the late twentieth century. Some go so far as to call him "the symbol of the century" for the Roman Catholic Church. If so, that would mean the church in Rome has become truly sick. If only Merton had known Scripture as did his spiritual idol, John of the Cross, he might have found his way to the cross.

---

1. For analysis of this split thinking in Merton, see Robert Royal, "The Seven-Storied Thomas Merton," *First Things*, February 1997, 34.

2. Anne Carr, "Prose into Prayer: Merton in His Journals," *The Christian Century*, 22–29 May 1996, 570.

3. Thomas Merton, *The Seven Story Mountain* (New York: Dell, 1948), 14. Merton's New Zealand grandmother taught him to pray.

4. Ibid., 42. His father worked for awhile at Grosset and Dunlap Publishers.

5. Ibid., 115, 118. The authority of Scripture was never foremost in his epistemology. It is the reasoning of his mind first and then the church.

6. Ibid., 165. He never makes any reference to his child in any of his writings.

7. Ibid., 167. His view of salvation is confused, reducing basically to: "We depend on one another for our salvation" (176).

8. Many have been touched by John of the Cross. See *St. John of the Cross: Selected Writings,* The Classics of Western Spirituality series (New York: Paulist, 1987), 28. John, who was called "the Mystical Doctor," has a strong view of Scripture, but as in the case of other pioneering theologians, not all of his readers have shared his grasp of balance and nuance.

9. *The Seven Story Mountain,* 171. Mark Van Doren, his English professor at Columbia University, and Dan Walsh, advisor to Catholic students at the university, influenced him greatly.

10. Michael Mott, *The Seven Mountains of Thomas Merton* (Boston: Houghton/Mifflin, 1990), 111. This is the best biography of Merton.

11. "The Seven-Storied Thomas Merton," 37. He broke his vows on numerous occasions. In this case, one wonders what became of the young woman under such a misguiding spiritual influence.

12. An example of his output is *No Man Is an Island* (New York: Dell, 1955). There are some glimmers of soundness in this work but some dangerous trails that evidently led to Zen.

15.1.9 TOYNBEE, THINKER

Man and dog can have great fellowship—but on a dog's level.
—Arnold J. Toynbee

Among the most widely quoted writers of the twentieth century—and one of the least understood—is Arnold Joseph Toynbee (1889–1975). More than a historian, he can be regarded as "a poet, mythologist and metaphysician than empirical historian."[1] It is hard to avoid caricaturing this thinker. His massive twelve-volume *A Study of History* (what he called his "nonsense book") or its two-volume abbreviated form must be tackled eventually. I would recommend starting with his fine biography by the historian and classicist William H. McNeill.[2]

Toynbee was born in London and received a splendid classical education on scholarship at Winchester and Balliol College, Oxford. He spent a year walking through Greece and returned to teach ancient history at Oxford.[3] But this was too restrictive for his high-voltage personality. He was exempted from military service in World War I because of dysentery suffered in Greece.

Employed to draft military intelligence policy during the war, he won the chair of Byzantine history at the University of London, then lost his position by alienating his benefactors when he criticized Greece in its war with Turkey in 1921. He became director of the Institute of International Affairs (Chatham House), which gave vent to his broad interests, and at the same time became Professor of International Studies at the University of London.

Although Toynbee married Rosalind Murray, the daughter of the famous Oxford classicist Gilbert Murray, he was never close to his family. The Murray money more than sustained the Toynbees and their children, but he suffered personal tragedies. His father had to be institutionalized following a mental breakdown, and his oldest son committed suicide in 1939. Three years later, his wife left him. Toynbee's very survival can be credited to his dedicated assistant and devoted friend, Veronica Boulter. Her contribution to the "Survey" was vast. Contrary to her Christian principles, she married him in 1946 when it became clear that his wife would never come back to him, despite his pleas.

Time magazine gave him a cover story in 1947, in which he opined that "Our civilization is not inexorably doomed."

Toynbee traced the rise and fall of twenty-six great civilizations. He had been early on influenced by Oswald Spengler's *The Decline of the West* (1918–22), in which Spengler advances the thesis that civilizations rise and fall in cycles, and that the West was then in its natural cycle of decay and decomposition.

Toynbee was committed to seeing history as a world phenomenon, and he was one of the first historians to reach out broadly to include India, China, and the Islamic world as part of the whole picture. He saw these civilizations as different from, but analogous to, Western civilization.[4] On the basis of his wide range of interest and amazing grasp of facts, his critics asserted that he had no depth, that he saw the forest but not the trees. His books sold well and he traveled widely, on one North American lecture tour delivering forty-three lectures and three talks in six weeks. His fees were large. Even though his basic thesis was pessimistic and his health was never good, Toynbee kept bobbing up, even serving as member of the British Delegation to the Paris Peace Conferences following both world wars.

Although pessimistic like Spengler, he had a hope. Since the chief function of a civilization was to create a religion, he advocated the formation of a world government and a world religion.[5] Western civilization could only be saved by a religion comprising of fragments from Christianity, animism, Buddhism, and other major faiths. These fragments were joined in a religion of love. *Time* called him "An Anglican with a yen for syncretism."

Nowhere do we see the issues more clearly than in his 1952–1953 Gifford Lectures at Edinburgh: "An Historian's Approach to Religion." Toynbee takes original sin seriously and argues that history and our experience show that transcending "self-centeredness is not really possible."[6] Although some elements of nature worship are embedded in the higher religions, he feels nature worship and man-worship are a mistake. In the "Epiphany of the Higher Religions," he sees the effort to transcend our innate self-fixation.

Using many Scriptures, he laments the diversions that lead away from the otherwise emerging new world religion. Chief among these stumbling blocks are theologies of the incarnation and uniqueness of Jesus Christ and the Christian missionary impulse. The Absolute Reality (his notion of God) "is a mystery to which there is more than one approach."[7]

In seeking a consensus among the five great living religions, he advocates disengaging the essence from the nonessentials. He believes that all religions are carriers of the true light that lights every man (John 1:9). The chaff must be winnowed away, and theology and its exclusives must be sacrificed.[8] One Toynbee scholar sees a dilemma in the historian's Hegelian rationalism—what room is there for a "chosen people" or a unique incarnation in a system that synthesizes one pair of historical streams, then synthesizes the synthesis with another stream, and then another, *ad infinitum* (see 5.12)?[9]

Joel Carpenter, in his recent history of fundamentalism, sees Toynbee's grand-scale survey of the history of thought to be the model for much evangelical cultural analysis, for example Carl F. H. Henry's *Remaking the Modern Mind.*[10]

Both Toynbee and Will Durant (1885–1981) marvel at the survival of Israel in contravention of their general schema of civilization cycles.[11] But Toynbee can scarcely conceal his disdain as he snarls about "Semitic fossils." The fact is that he just cannot process anything unique or transcendent within his system. He stands in succession to Leonardo da Vinci (1452–1519), who exclaimed, "Anyone who conducts an argument by appealing to Authority is not using his brain." The clear fact is that it is not a question of using an authority (for even Leonardo did that intuitively) but which authority has primacy. How can God have fellowship with human beings on a human level, unless there was a radical once-for-all divine intervention into humanity?

---

1. William Rose Benet, *Benet's Reader's Encyclopedia,* 3d ed. (New York: Harper and Row, 1987), s.v. "Toynbee, Arnold Joseph."
2. William H. McNeill, *Arnold J. Toynbee: A Life* (New York: Oxford, 1989). McNeill is from the University of Chicago.
3. Arnold J. Toynbee, *Greek Civilization and Character* (New York: Mentor, 1953). Especially good on Greece.
4. Mary Lefkowitz, "The Historian Kept His Cool," *New York Times Book Review,* 28 May 1989, 12.
5. Billy Graham, *Approaching Hoofbeats: The Four Horsemen of the Apocalypse* (Waco, Tex.: Word, 1983). Graham quotes Toynbee: "Only a world government can save mankind from annihilation by nuclear weapons" (227).
6. Arnold J. Toynbee, *An Historian's Approach to Religion* (New York: Oxford University Press, 1956), 10.
7. Ibid., 259. Toynbee's problems of belief concerned Christ's deity, the revealed Word of God, and the sovereignty of God in choosing his people, 132, 134, 138.
8. Ibid., 284. He disparages what he calls "the sinful claim to uniqueness" (144).
9. M. Whitcomb Hess, "The Toynbee Dilemma," *The Christian Century,* 1 January 1964, 8ff.; and developed from Edward Whiting Fox, "The Divine Dilemma of A. J. Toynbee," *Virginia Quarterly Review,* winter 1963.
10. Joel A. Carpenter, *Revive Us Again: The Reawakening of American Fundamentalism* (New York: Oxford, 1997), 200.
11. Arnold J. Toynbee, *A Study of History* (New York: Oxford University Press, 1957), 194.

15.1.10 HEIDEGGER, PHILOSOPHER

> Poets are the shepherds of words.
> Language is the house of Being. In its home man dwells.
>
> —Martin Heidegger

Looming large in existential philosophy and hermeneutic theory in the twentieth century was Martin Heidegger (1889–1976). Though he denied his Nazi ties and was at least a philosophical coconspirator in all that happened to the Jews, he has been the guru for Jean-Paul Sartre (1905–1980) and Hans-Georg Gadamer, the father of the "new hermeneutics." I recommend as a point of entry into his very abstruse philosophy the biography of Rudiger Safranski, who concedes that Heidegger was "a resentful, ungenerous, disloyal and deceitful man," yet unquestionably brilliant and influential beyond our understanding.[1]

This biography is very Germanic and heavy, but it gives a well-balanced account of a philosopher. In general, biographers know and have mastered the thought of their subject, so a biography is often the best introduction to the thought and writings of the subject, especially one who is prone to be misunderstood. This approach is especially valuable if the biographer is steeped in the thought and is a fervent apologist for it. Whether you agree with the thought, a defender can be easier to learn from than a critic.

Heidegger was born in the Black Forest area of Swabia, Germany, in the town of Messkirch where his father was a sexton. He was raised a devout Catholic and was a novice Jesuit headed toward the priesthood, until the Jesuits and the local bishop rejected him. After the First World War, he threw over his Catholicism, became a Protestant, and then repudiated all religion and became a follower of the "phenomenology" of German philosopher Edmund Husserl (1859–1938) at the University of Freiburg. Deeply indebted to the psychologist Franz Brentano and his doctrine of "intention," Husserl wanted to make philosophy a science of "the essences."[2] Heidegger followed his master in emphasizing "being" and dedicated his earthshaking *Being and Time* to Husserl.

In his collected works of more than one hundred volumes, Heidegger emphasizes not only theoretical insight but also practical application. This has contributed to his popularity among Western existentialists.[3] He was by his own light being true to his thought when he joined the German National Socialist Party and supported Adolf Hitler's rise. As a result, Heidegger was appointed rector of the University of Freiburg, where he had succeeded Husserl in 1929 as chair of Philosophy. Heidegger never recanted for his support of the Third Reich.

A frenetic critic of rationalism, Heidegger attempted to fuse Friedrich Nietzsche (1844–1900) and Søren Kierkegaard (1813–1855) with Leo Tolstoy (1828–1910) and Fëdor Dostoevsky (1821–1881) to build an overarching philosophical system. This synthesis influenced such thinkers as Emil Brunner (1889–1966), Rudolf Bultmann (1844–1976), Paul Tillich (1886–1965), and the death-of-God theologians, as well as Richard Rorty in the late twentieth century.

There are significant redefinitions and new hermeneutic ideas that turn meaning on its head in Heidegger's thought. For example, *original sin* means ceasing to be the persons we are. Lurking in the background is always atheism. Death can never be overcome. Any philosophical or ethical tenet borrowed from Christianity is automatically rejected. Some have wondered if he had any ethic at all, but if he did, it can only be seen in terms of self-actualization.[4] Many familiar strains of the late 1900s are first heard in Heidegger, and to really understand them, one must understand what he said about them. Only through such understanding can we understand Gadamer's "fusion of horizons" and the "reader-response" school of textual interpretation. Only in Heidegger and his school can we see how textual meaning can be obliterated by existential subjectivity.[5]

His immanentalism made any meaningful search for truth in religion or life impossible. "Truth is always in the way," he said.[6] He would only speak of God as "the one before whom David sang and danced," a God with no reality or significance. His "spiritual asphyxiation" parallels his conviction (1933) that "the Führer and he alone is the present and the future."[7]

For Heidegger, there was no Jewish question. He was incontrovertibly anti-Semitic and refused to think about the Holocaust or its ethical implications.[8] When his contemporaries were forced to look at what was happening or had happened, Heidegger only referred on rare occasions to the Jews or "Jewification" and then only in a derogatory sense.[9] He had a part in the expulsion of Jews from Freiburg, and he of course broke with his Jewish mentor, Husserl, personally signing the document dismissing him. He opposed an appointment for his student Baumgarten because of his close ties with the Jew Viktor Frankl.[10] Ironically, he had a long affair with the Jewish philosopher Hannah Arendt. He destroyed careers or blocked the promotions of even friends who expressed anti-Nazi sentiments, such as Karl Jaspers (who had a Jewish wife) and Max Müller.

After the war, when Heidegger was banned from teaching or publishing for five years, Arendt believed his statements of innocence; Jaspers did not.[11] Something of the horrific tragedy of German nationalism and Heidegger's view of German privilege strikes us forcefully. This nationalism nurtured vicious anti-Semitism and gave birth to the Holocaust. Heidegger is inextricably linked to the tragedy.

Students of communication and propaganda will want to dig into the unsavory story of Goebbels by Ralf Georg Reuth.[12] Joseph Goebbels (1897–1945) came from a poor Roman Catholic background but stopped going to church during World War I. Much taken with Nietzsche, he received his Ph.D. degree and took an interest in Eastern philosophy, particularly that in India. For him, love of the fatherland was the worship of God; salvation was through self-sacrifice. He started to turn against the Jews as early as 1922. In 1931 he married Magda Quandt in a Protestant Church festooned with swastika banners. He was a brilliant campaign strategist. He argued that Paul the Jew falsified Christ's teaching (222). He took complete control of the film industry, a critical move in the plan for Nazi dominance. He gave himself to the pursuit of "masterpieces of rhetorical skill" (315). Always involved in some sexual affair, he and his large family died in the Berlin bunker.

1. Rudiger Safranski, *Martin Heidegger: Between Good and Evil* (Cambridge, Mass.: Harvard University Press, 1998).

2. Kurt F. Reinhardt, *The Existentialist Revolt: The Main Themes and Phases of Existentialism* (Milwaukee: Bruce, 1952), 121. Reinhardt was a student of both Husserl and Heidegger and helps us understand the truly radical nature of their ideas.

3. Stephen Goode, "The Unequivocal Heaviness of Being," *Insight,* 9 March 1992, 12ff.

4. J. M. Spier, *Christianity and Existentialism* (Philadelphia: Presbyterian and Reformed, 1953), 27ff.

5. David E. Cooper, *Heidegger* (London: Claridge, 1996). Cooper is especially good on Husserl's influence. See Grant R. Osborne, *The Hermeneutical Spiral* (Downers Grove, Ill., InterVarsity, 1991), 369, 370, 384, 392, 402, 433.

6. Thomas Molnar, "Selling Heidegger Short," *Chronicles of Culture,* June 1988, 34ff. For an evangelical critique, see Anthony Thiselton, *The Two Horizons: New Testament Hermeneutics and Philosophical Descriptions* (Grand Rapids: Eerdmans, 1980). On the other hand, John Macquarrie in *Heidegger and Christianity* (New York: Continuum, 1995) is a defensive and unconvincing apology for the man. Clearly Heidegger's God is "an ersatz divine principle" and not more.

7. Berel Lang, *Heidegger's Silence* (Ithaca, N.Y.: Cornell University Press, 1996), 15, 24. For a fine analysis of his worship of Hitler, see Vincent P. Miceli, *The Gods of Atheism* (Harrison, N.Y.: Roman Catholic Books, 1971), 273ff.

8. Lang, *Heidegger's Silence,* 15. He affirmed "the inner truth and greatness of the movement [of National Socialism]." Therefore, he need not confront what the Party said was not truth.

9. Ibid., 36. He used much nationalist rhetoric and believed that only the *Volk* ("people") would lead to truth.

10. Ibid., 70. Lang argues there is systematic entailment between his philosophy and his Nazism.

11. Elzbieta Ettinger, *Hannah Arendt, Martin Heidegger* (New Haven, Conn.: Yale University, 1997). After 1950 he wanted his wife, Elfride, and Hannah to shake hands and call each other "du," the German form for "you" that expresses affection. Arendt's compromising relationship and whitewashing of Heidegger continued as he worked on the Commission on Jewish Cultural Reconstruction and she wrote her book *Origins of Totalitarianism.*

12. New York: Harcourt Brace, 1993.

Reading and Its Future

Probably the worst mistake a minister can make in his reading is to limit himself to strictly contemporary productions. Old books now available have survived the sifting process of human experience. The vast majority of books published today are absolutely worthless. The wonderful effect of immersing one's mind in really great writers, rather than trashy ones, is that something of their character wears off on the reader.

—D. Elton Trueblood[1]

More new books are being published and at a faster rate—the number of new titles published each year increased 42 percent from 1991 to 1996.[2] People are buying more books and reading more via the internet. Technology is changing drastically what is read and in what forms. At this writing, just before the year 2000, some educators predict that the textbook will be extinct in five years, as reading material is delivered to students in new and cheaper ways. Will the library of the future simply be a cyberspace network with text file downloads? These are questions you who read this volume some years hence may be in a better position to answer.

In the midst of this new wave of literacy, emphasis on the classics has been receding. Most students can get a bachelor's degree in a technical field and come away from college ignorant of world literature. Even literature majors may miss great writers in a "politically-correct" educational environment.

All is not bad news. The classics are making something of a comeback because of new scanning and typesetting technologies that allow publishers to return out-of-print volumes to the marketplace for a fraction of the cost. New series of the great books are finding ready acceptance as film and television producers return to them because of the dearth of good new stories.[3] The movie *The English Patient* stimulated a 450 percent increase in the sales of the history of the ancient Greek Herodotus (fifth century B.C.). Recent revivals in reading Jane Austen and Henry James have paralleled the issuance of films or movies made for television. Even animated versions of the classics are becoming popular fare.

But all that is only a baby step toward true intellectual development for Christians in general and their shepherds in particular. For those who would truly interact with their culture, I recommend a few publications that discuss this problem of Christian cultural and philosophical illiteracy and its solution via books.

- "Why Read" is the title of an engaging article by Holly Halverson who makes a case for an omnivorous consumption of good books.[4] A broad sampling of Christian and non-Christian books affords us the best chance for understanding ourselves and our culture.
- Frank Gaebelein considers evangelical interaction with the broader cultural currents to be strategically critical.[5]
- While Alister McGrath is generally serene about the evangelical future, a stubborn anti-intellectualism among us worries him.[6] McGrath says we must not abdicate the high ground of insisting that biblical supernaturalism can satisfy both the mind and the heart.
- David Wells has struck the same note, especially with reference to theology, in *No Place for Truth* (Grand Rapids: Eerdmans, 1993); *God in the Wasteland* (Grand Rapids: Eerdmans, 1994); and *Losing Our Virtue* (Grand Rapids: Eerdmans, 1998).
- Os Guiness speaks persuasively about "the crisis of cultural authority."[7] In a later volume, he characterizes the inertia and apathy of evangelicals as well as the societal pressures and demons that assault Christian truth.[8]
- Mark Noll has stabbed us awake with critiques of evangelical culture.[9]

Just to look at one of these volumes, it is interesting to look at one of the more acidic commentators on the mental failings of modern evangelicals. In his widely acclaimed *The Scandal of the Evangelical Mind,* Noll overstates his case that there is no such thing as a truly "evangelical" mind. I would suggest that Noll's fine volumes on church history and culture demonstrate that mind of which he denies the existence. The evangelical worldview is at least partly defined intellectually by such thinkers as Francis Schaeffer (whom Noll does not mention), J. Oliver Buswell, and Carl F. H. Henry.

Noll believes evangelicals in the second half of the twentieth century spent all of their time on biblical exegesis and hermeneutics to defend the faith against liberalism. As a result, they abandoned "the whole spectrum of modern learning."[10] Noll certainly makes a point about "the disaster of Fundamentalism," but his criticism seems not quite fair with respect to those who laid their lives on the line for the defense of historic Christianity. He labeled as anti-intellectual all dispensationalists, Pentecostals, Keswick Convention followers, creationists, revivalists, and prophetic futurists. At the same time, he strangely overlooks the neglect of the inner life, the incursions of worldliness and materialism, and the drift from the Word of God in the pulpit and in the homes. I mention these things because I feel it necessary to make some corrections and caveats about what is otherwise a sharp-sighted look at the kind of no-mind anti-intellectualism that has plagued our house. Noll, I think, would also commend a balanced reading agenda, along with a daily experience directly in Scripture as part of the antidote for what ails us.

Anna Zuindlen, the Pulitzer Prize-winning contemporary writer, has celebrated the influence of books in her life. Seduced by literature when she was young, she shows how books have been the means by which she found a home and sustenance. Zuindlen quotes Thoreau that "many a man has dated a new era in his life from the reading of a book." Her soul-sister is Elizabeth Barret-Browning, who in "Aurora Leigh" exclaims: "Books, books, books!" and finds them always nibbling and "beating under the pillow in the morning's dark."[11]

The door is open for us to enter if we long to move from mere entertainment to that which has substance.

1. D. Elton Trueblood, *The Teacher* (Nashville: Broadman, 1980), 25f. I am indebted to my good fiend, Dr. Warren Benson, for calling this question to my attention.
2. "The More the Books, the Fewer the Editors," *The New York Times,* 29 June 1998, B1.
3. "Classics Make a Kind of Comeback," *Insight,* 21 July 1998, 36f.
4. Holly Halverson, "Why Read," *Aspire,* February–March 1997, 52ff.
5. Frank E. Gaebelein, *The Christian, the Arts and the Truth: Regaining the Vision of Greatness* (Portland, Ore.: Multnomah, 1985).
6. Alister McGrath, *Evangelicalism and the Future of Christianity* (Downers Grove, Ill.: InterVarsity, 1995).
7. Os Guiness, *The American Hour: A Time of Reckoning and the Once and Future Role of Faith* (New York: Free Press, 1993). Guiness shows that the beliefs and ideals which once held us have lost their binding address.
8. Os Guiness, *Fat Bodies, Fat Minds: Why Evangelicals Don't Think and What to Do About It* (Grand Rapids: Baker, 1995). He calls for Christians to indulge in good antithetical thinking.
9. Mark Noll, *The Scandal of the Evangelical Mind* (Grand Rapids: Eerdmans, 1994).
10. For an interesting panel, which seizes the opportunity to whack evangelicals, see *First Things,* March 1995. Mainline church members and especially leaders tend to see only the acculturation in evangelicalism. I find it difficult to see B. B. Warfield's (1851–1921) doctrine of an inerrant, God-breathed revelation that comes to us in Scripture as one of evangelicalism's problems. The apologists of Warfield's day directly launched such "evangelical minds" as J. Gresham Machen (1881–1937) and Harold J. Ockenga (1905–1985). Still, Noll has a point to make and we must not miss his voice.
11. Anna Zuindlen, *How Reading Changed My Life* (New York: Ballentine, 1998), 8.

APPENDIX 1

Suggestions for Further Reading

Christianity and Literature

Alexander, Pat, ed. *Eerdmans Book of Christian Poetry*. Grand Rapids: Eerdmans, 1981.

Dillenberger, Jane. *Style and Content in Christian Art*. New York: Crossroad, 1986.

Edwards, Michael. *Toward a Christian Poetics*. Grand Rapids: Eerdmans, 1984.

Gaebelein, Frank E. *The Christian, the Arts and the Truth: Regaining the Vision of Greatness*. Portland, Ore.: Multnomah, 1985.

Larsen, David L. *The Company of the Preachers: A History of Biblical Preaching from the Old Testament to the Modern Era*. Grand Rapids: Kregel, 1998.

Niebuhr, H. Richard. *Christ and Culture*. New York: Harper Torchbooks, 1951.

Strong, Augustus Hopkins. *American Poets and Their Theology*. Philadelphia: Griffith and Rowland, 1916.

Strong, Augustus Hopkins. *The Great Poets and Their Theology*. Philadelphia: American Baptist, 1897.

Literature Study and Theory

Adler, Mortimer. *How to Read a Book*. New York: Simon and Schuster, 1972.

Alter, Robert. *The Pleasures of Reading: In an Ideological Age*. New York: Simon and Schuster, 1996.

Anatomy of Literature, The. New York: Harcourt Brace, 1972.

Benet, William Rose. *Benet's Reader's Encyclopedia*, 3d ed. New York: Harper & Row, 1987.

Boorstin, Daniel J. *The Creators: A History of Heroes of the Imagination*. New York: Random House, 1992.

Burn, Christopher, ed. *Seashell Anthology of Great Poetry*. New York: Park Lane, 1996.

Denby, David. *Great Books: My Adventures with Homer, Rousseau, Woolf and Other Indestructible Writers of the Western World*. New York: Simon and Schuster, 1996.

Gateway to the Great Books. Chicago: Britannica, 1963.

Giants of World Literature Series. New York: American Heritage, 1968.

Great Ideas Program, The. Chicago: Britannica, 1963.

Loeb Classical Library. London: Heinemann, 1952.

Manguel, Alberto. *A History of Reading*. New York: Viking, 1996.

McCrum, Robert; William Cran; and Robert MacNeil. *The Story of English*. New York: Penguin, 1986.

Norton Anthology of Poetry, The. New York: W. W. Norton, 1983.

Raine, Kathleen. *The Inner Journey of the Poet*. New York: George Braziller, 1982.

History of Literature

Greek and Roman

Adler, Mortimer J. *Aristotle for Everybody*. New York: Macmillan, 1978.

Bloom, Harold, ed. *The Odyssey*. New York: Chelsea House, 1988.

Bullfinch's Mythology. New York: Modern Library, 1863.

Bury, J. B. *A History of Greece to the Death of Alexander the Great*. New York: Modern Library, 1937.

Calasso, Roberto. *The Marriage of Cadmus and Harmony*. New York: Knopf, 1993.

Ferguson, John. *The Heritage of Hellenism*. New York: Science History, 1973.

Grant, Michael. *The Rise of the Greeks*. New York: Scribner's, 1987.

Hadas, Moses. *A History of Latin Literature*. New York: Columbia University Press, 1952.

Hamilton, Edith. *Mythology*. New York: Mentor, 1953.

_____. *The Greek Way to Western Civilization*. New York: Mentor, 1948.

Kennedy, George. *Classical Rhetoric and Its Christian and Secular Tradition from Ancient to Modern Times*. Chapel Hill, N.C.: University of North Carolina Press, 1980.

Kerenyi, C. *The Gods of the Greeks*. London: Thames and Hudson, 1951.

Kinney, E. J., ed. *The Cambridge History of Classical Literature*. Cambridge: Cambridge University Press, 1982.

Kitto, H. D. F. *The Greeks*. London: Penguin, 1951.

Macrone, Michael. *It's Greek to Me!* New York: Calder, 1991.

May, James M. *Trials of Character: The Eloquence of Ciceronian Ethos*. Chapel Hill, N.C.: University of North Carolina Press, 1989.

Prentice, William Kelly. *The Ancient Dramas Called Tragedies*. Princeton, N.J.: Princeton University Press, 1942.

Stob, Ralph. *Christianity and Classical Civilization*. Grand Rapids: Eerdmans, 1950.

Taylor, A. E. *Socrates: The Man and His Thought*. New York: Doubleday Anchor, 1952.

Thackeray, H. St. John. *Josephus: The Man and the Historian*. New York: Ktav, 1967.

Wechsler, Herman J. *Gods and Goddesses in Art and Legend*. New York: Pocket Books, 1950.

Yamauchi, Edwin. *Greece and Babylon: Early Contacts Between the Aegean and the Near East*. Grand Rapids: Baker, 1967.

Medieval

Augustine. *Augustine: Earlier Writings*. Philadelphia: Westminster, 1953.

Bark, William Carroll. *Origins of the Medieval World*. Stanford, Calif.: Stanford University Press, 1958.

Burleigh, John H. S. *The City of God: A Study of St. Augustine's Philosophy*. London: Nisbet, 1949.

Cahill, Thomas. *How the Irish Saved Civilization*. New York: Doubleday, 1995.

Cannon, Christopher. *The Making of Chaucer's Language: A Study of Words*. Cambridge: Cambridge University Press, 1998.

Chesterton, G. K. *Saint Thomas Aquinas: "The Dumb Ox."* Garden City, N.Y.: Doubleday Image, 1956.

_____. *Saint Francis of Assisi*. New York: Doubleday Image, 1989.

Dante Alighieri. *The Inferno*. John Ciardi, translations: New York: Modern Library, 1996; Robert Pinsky, London: Dent, 1994.

_____. *The Paradiso*. John Ciardi, trans. Repr. ed. New York: Modern Library, 1996.

Eco, Umberto. *Art and Beauty in the Middle Ages*. New Haven, Conn.: Yale University Press, 1986.

Geisler, Norman L. *Thomas Aquinas: An Evangelical Appraisal*. Grand Rapids: Baker, 1991.

Houston, James M., ed. *St. Teresa of Avila, A Life of Prayer*. Portland, Ore.: Multnomah, 1983.

Howard, Donald R. *Chaucer: His Life, His Works, His World*. New York: Dutton, 1987.

Lightfoot, J. B., gen. ed. *The Apostolic Fathers,* rev. ed. Grand Rapids: Baker, 1980.

McGinn, Bernard. *Visions of the End: Apocalyptic Traditions in the Middle Ages*. New York: Columbia University Press, 1979.

Merchant, Elizabeth Lodor, ed. *King Arthur and His Knights*. Philadelphia: John C. Winston, 1957.

Ottley, R. L. *Studies in the Confessions of St. Augustine*. London: Robert Scott, 1919.

Payne, Robert. *Fathers of the Western Church*. New York: Viking, 1951.

Reeves, Marjorie. *The Influence of Prophecy in the Later Middle Ages*. Oxford: Oxford University Press, 1969.

Van Oort, Johannes. *Jerusalem and Babylon*. Leiden: E. J. Brill, 1991.

Warfield, B. B. *Calvin and Augustine*. Philadelphia: Presbyterian and Reformed, 1956.

White, T. H. *The Sword in the Stone*. New York: Putnam, 1939.

Renaissance and Reformation

Bishop, Morris. *Petrarch and His World*. Bloomington, Ind.: Indiana University Press, 1963.

Brown, Huntington. *Rabelais in English Literature*. New York: Octagon, 1967.

Evans, J. M. Paradise Lost *and the Genesis Tradition*. Oxford: Clarendon, 1968.

Fish, Stanley. *Surprised by Sin: The Reader in* Paradise Lost. London: Macmillan, 1967.

Gardner, Helen. *A Reading of* Paradise Lost. Oxford: Clarendon, 1965.

Hale, John. *The Civilization of Europe in the Renaissance*. New York: Athenaeum, 1994.

Kantor, Norman F. *The Civilization of the Middle Ages*. New York: Harper/Collins, 1993.

Lewis, C. S. *A Preface to* Paradise Lost. Oxford: Oxford University Press, 1942.

Manchester, William. *A World Lit Only by Fire: The Medieval Mind and the Renaissance*. Boston: Little, Brown, 1992.

McGrath, Alister E. *A Life of John Calvin*. Oxford: Basil Blackwell, 1990.

Oberman, Heiko A. *Luther: Man Between God and the Devil*. New Haven, Conn.: Yale University Press, 1982.

Rivers, Isabel. *Classical and Christian Ideas in English Renaissance Poetry*. London: Allen and Unwin, 1979.

_____. *Luther's Theology of the Cross*. Oxford: Basil Blackwell, 1985.

Shaw, Robert B. *The Call of God: The Theme of Vocation in the Poetry of Donne and Herbert*. Athens, Ohio: Ohio University Press, 1965.

Enlightenment

Calliet, Émile. *Pascal: The Emergence of Genius*. New York: Harper Torchbooks, 1961.

Gay, Peter. *The Party of Harmony: Essays in the French Enlightenment*. New York: Norton, 1954.

Guiness, Os. *The Mind on Fire: An Anthology of the Writings of Blaise Pascal*. Portland, Ore.: Multnomah, 1987.

Harris, R. W. *Reason and Nature in the Eighteenth Century*. New York: Barnes and Noble, 1969.

Johnson, Paul. *Intellectuals*. New York: Harper, 1988.

Kirk, Russell. *Edmund Burke: A Genius Reconsidered*. Peru, Ill.: Sherwood Sugen, 1967.

Lloyd-Jones, D. M. *The Puritans: Their Origins and Successors*. Edinburgh: Banner of Truth, 1987.

Packer, J. I. *A Quest for Godliness: The Puritan Vision of the Christian Life*. Wheaton, Ill.: Crossway, 1990.

Stout, Harry S. *The Divine Dramatist: George Whitefield and the Rise of Modern Evangelicalism*. Grand Rapids: Eerdmans, 1991.

Vyverberg, Henry. *Historical Pessimism in the French Enlightenment*. Cambridge: Harvard, 1958.

Wain, John. *Samuel Johnson*. New York: Viking, 1974.

Wakefield, Gordon. *Bunyan the Christian*. New York: Harper, 1992.

Ward, W. R. *The Protestant Evangelical Awakening*. Cambridge: Cambridge University Press, 1992.

Nineteenth/Twentieth Centuries

apRoberts, Ruth. *Arnold and God*. Los Angeles: University of California, 1983.

Bradbury, Malcolm, and David Palmer, eds. *Metaphysical Poetry*. Bloomington, Ind.: Indiana University Press, 1970.

DeJean, Joan. *Ancients Against Moderns: Culture Wars and the Making of a Fin de Siecle*. Chicago: University of Chicago Press, 1996.

Gill, Stephen. *William Wordsworth: A Life*. Oxford: Clarendon, 1989.

Johnson, Paul. *The Birth of the Modern: World Society 1815–1830*. New York: Harper/Collins, 1991.

McConnell, Francis John. *Evangelicals, Revolutionists and Idealists*. Nashville: Abingdon-Cokesbury, 1942.

Miller, J. Hillis. *The Disappearance of God: Five Nineteenth Century Writers*. Cambridge: Belknap, 1963.

Modern Drama

Batson, E. Beatrice, ed. *Shakespeare and the Christian Tradition*. Lewiston, N.Y.: Edwin Mellen, 1994.

Battenhouse, Roy W. *Shakespeare's Christian Dimension*. Bloomington, Ind.: Indiana University Press, 1993.

Boas, Frederick A. *An Introduction to Eighteenth-Century Drama*. Oxford: Clarendon, 1953.

Boas, Frederick S. *Christopher Marlowe: A Biographical and Critical Study*. Oxford: Clarendon, 1940, 1953.

Brown, Ivor. *Shakespeare*. 1949; repr. ed., New York: Time Reading Program, 1962.

Chute, Marchette. *Shakespeare of London*. New York: E. P. Dutton, 1949.

Fernandez, Ramon. *Molière: The Man Seen Through the Plays*. New York: Hill and Wang, 1958.

Knoll, Robert E. *Ben Jonson's Plays: An Introduction*. Lincoln, Neb.: University of Nebraska Press, 1964.

Leithart, Peter J. *Brightest Heaven of Invention: A Christian Guide to Six Shakespearean Plays*. Moscow, Idaho: Canon, 1996.

Milward, Peter. *Shakespeare's Religious Background*. Chicago: Loyola University Press, 1973.

Nicoll, Allardyce. *English Drama: A Modern Viewpoint*. New York: Barnes and Noble, 1968.

Philosophy, Religion, and Culture

Auerbach, Erich. *Mimesis: The Representation of Reality in Western Literature*. Princeton, N.J.: Princeton University Press, 1946.

Birkerts, Sven. *The Gutenberg Elegies: The Fate of Reading in an Electronic Age*. New York: Faber and Faber, 1994.

Brinton, Crane. *The Shaping of the Modern Mind*. New York: Mentor, 1953.

Burke, Edmund. *A Philosophical Inquiry into the Origin of Our Ideas of the Sublime and Beautiful*. Notre Dame, Ind.: University of Notre Dame Press, 1958.

Burtt, E. A. *The Metaphysical Foundations of Modern Science*. New York: Doubleday Anchor, 1954.

Burtt, Edwin A. *Types of Religious Philosophy*. New York: Harper, 1951.

Clark, Gordon H. *The Philosophy of Science and Belief in God*. Nutley, N.J.: Craig, 1964.

Conley, Kieran. *A Theology of Wisdom*. Dubuque, Iowa: Priory, 1963.

Durant, Will. *The Story of Philosophy*. New York: Simon and Schuster, 1926.

Gilson, Etienne. *Reason and Revelation in the Middle Ages*. New York: Charles Scribner's, 1938.

Goethals, Gregor T. *The Electronic Golden Calf: Images, Religion, and the Making of Meaning*. New York: Cowley, 1991.

Grenz, Stanley J. *A Primer on Postmodernism*. Grand Rapids: Eerdmans, 1997.

Heilbroner, Robert L. *The Worldly Philosophers: The Lives, Times and Ideas of the Great Economic Thinkers*. New York: Simon and Schuster, 1953, 1961.

Henry, Carl F. H. *Remaking the Modern Mind*. Grand Rapids: Eerdmans, 1946.

Henry, Carl F. H. *The Drift of Western Thought*. Grand Rapids: Eerdmans, 1951.

Kingwell, Mark. *Dreams of Millennium: Report from a Culture on the Brink*. Toronto: Viking, 1996.

Popkin, Richard. *The History of Skepticism from Erasmus to Descartes*. Berkeley, Calif.: University of California Press, 1979.

Postman, Neil. *Amusing Ourselves to Death: Public Discourse in the Age of Show Business*. New York: Penguin, 1985.

Randall, John Herman Jr. *The Role of Knowledge in Western Religion*. Boston: Beacon, 1965.

Thiselton, Anthony.8 *The Two Horizons*. Grand Rapids: Eerdmans, 1980.

Windelband, Wilhelm. *A History of Philosophy*. New York: Harper Torchbooks, 1958.

Sussman, Henry. *The Hegelian Aftermath*. Baltimore: Johns Hopkins, 1982.

Anderson, Deland S. *Hegel's Speculative Good Friday: The Death of God in Philosophical Perspective*. Atlanta: Scholars, 1996.

Brinton, Crane. *Nietzsche*. New York: Harper Torchbooks, 1941, 1965.

Greek and Roman Mythology

Three Dynasties

Chaos
Uranus — Gaea
Sky   Earth

↓

The Titans
Chronos — Rhea

↓

Twelve Olympians
Poseidon – Zeus – Hera – Pluto
Vesta – Ares – Athena – Apollo
Aphrodite – Hermes – Artemis – Hephaestus

The Pantheon

Greek Name	Roman Name	Roles	Symbols/Data
Zeus	Jupiter	Ruler of sky and weather; king of gods and men	Thunderbolt, staff, eagle
Hera	Juno	Zeus's sister, consort, and queen; patroness of women	Crown, scepter, peacock
Athena	Minerva	Goddess: wisdom; defender of citadel	Helmet, shield, owl, snake
Apollo	Phoebus	Prophecy, music, poetry; medicine and the bow	Tripod, bow/quiver, raven, crow
Artemis	Diana	Goddess: hunting, wildlife; childbirth	Cypress; wild animals; deer
Poseidon	Neptune	Waters; earthquakes; horses	Trident; horse; bull; dolphin
Dionysius	Liber	Wine; promoter of civilization, peace	Also called Bacchus
Hermes	Mercury	Messenger of gods; rode on Pegasus	Winged sandals, lyre
Aphrodite	Venus	Beauty, love, fertility; mother of Eros	Mirror, apple, dove
Ares	Mars	War; violent, brutal, cowardly	Spear, breastplate
Hephaestus	Vulcan	Fire; smithy of gods; lame	Hammer, anvil, forge
Demeter	Ceres	Goddess: grain, nature, vegetation	Grain, vineyard
Helius	——	Sun; drives chariot across the sky	Archer, sees everything
Hestia	Vesta	Goddess: hearth; her fire by Vestal virgins	Home
Hades	Pluto	Underworld; presides at River Styx	Three-headed dog Cerberus
Prometheus	——	Gave fire to humankind; punished by gods	Celebrated by Byron, Shelley
Eros	Cupid	Love; lover of Psyche	Bow/quiver of golden arrows
Heracles	Hercules	Extraordinary strength and fierce temper	Echoes of Samson
Callisto	——	Nymph; changed by Hera into bear	Zeus put her into constellation
Pygmalion	——	Artist; fell love with own handiwork	Venus brought artwork to life
Narcissus	——	Fell in love with own reflection in pool	Loved only himself
——	Daphne	Huntress; Apollo's first love	Changed into laurel tree
Persephone	Proserpine	Goddess: underworld; wife of Pluto	Each year descended to underground
Pan	——	Goat herds; Hermes's son; part animal	Reed pipes; most bestial of Gods
——	Saturn	Roman protector of sowers, seeds	Winter Saturnalia feast
Ganymede	——	Cupbearer to gods on Olympus	Rumored to be child used sexually
Castor & Pollux	——	Twin offspring of Leda and the swan	Managed horses, boxed
Asklepios Soter	——	Healing arts; son of Apollo	Dedicated to healing centers
Orpheus	——	Musician; son of Apollo	Given lyre by father
Aristaeus	——	Beekeeper; son of water-nymph Cyrene	Celebrated by Cowper, Milton
Aurora	——	Goddess: dawn; loved a mortal	——
Cadmus	——	Son of King Agenor; married Harmony	Founder of Thebes
Daedalus	——	Builder of Labyrinth; escaped by thread	Changed into a partridge
Phaëthon	——	Insisted on driving sun chariot; son of Apollo	Fell as a shooting star
Perseus	——	Slew Medusa; son of Danaë	Used Mercury's sword; wed Andromeda

Select Name Index

Note: Names of significant fictional characters as well as real individuals are included in this section. Fictional names have been compiled according to most common identification.

592

Select Title Index

Prose and Theatrical Works

Subject Index

Timeline Index

Printed in the United States
57974LVS00005B/3